LIVE & WORK IN

AUSTRALIA
AND
NEW ZEALAND

Deborah Pen...
Susan Kel...

Distributed in the USA by
The Globe Pequot Press, Guilford, Connecticut

Published by Vacation Work, 9 Park End Street, Oxford
www.vacationwork.co.uk

LIVE AND WORK IN AUSTRALIA & NEW ZEALAND
First Edition 1995, Fiona McGregor & Charlotte Denny
Second Edition 1999, Elisabeth Roberts & Susan McIntosh
Third Edition 2002, Dan Boothby & Susan Kelly
Fourth Edition 2005, Deborah Penrith & Susan Kelly

Copyright © Vacation Work 2005

ISBN 1-85458-330-1

Cover design by mccdesign

Title page illustration by Mick Siddens

Text design and typesetting by Brendan Cole

Cover photograph; sheep rancher leaning against his pickup

Printed and bound in Italy by Legoprint SpA, Trento

Contents

AUSTRALIA

– SECTION 1 –
LIVING IN AUSTRALIA

– SECTION II –
WORKING IN AUSTRALIA

NEW ZEALAND

– SECTION 1 –
LIVING IN NEW ZEALAND

– SECTION II –
WORKING IN NEW ZEALAND

STARTING A BUSINESS

APPENDIX I

APPENDIX II

MAPS

FOREWORD

This fourth edition of *Live and Work in Australia and New Zealand* has been revised throughout to help anyone planning a prolonged trip to the lands down under in order to experience a way of life so different in culture, diversity of landscapes, and weather you'll probably end up asking yourself why you didn't emigrate years ago. *Live & Work in Australia and New Zealand* provides information on all aspects of making the move to the Antipodes: from the first step of making an application and being granted the right visa to suit your needs, to arranging accommodation and work once (and even before) you have arrived in either Australia or New Zealand. This book contains many useful addresses and websites of companies that can smooth your way, and gives details of work and business opportunities in the various regions of Australia and New Zealand.

Australia has vast areas of desert and bushland that give way to tropical rainforests, high-tech cities and beautiful coastlines; New Zealand has a hint of Victorian Englishness about it combined with the strongly felt influences of Polynesia and the Maori culture. The film epic *Lord of the Rings*, made on location in New Zealand in 2001, has helped to introduce millions more people to the beauty of the country and the next tourist seasons are looking to become the most successful yet.

Migration continues to shape Australia and the country is on the threshold of demographic change – in 40 years a quarter of Australians will be 65 and over – therefore employment prospects for migrants is at an all time high. Industry after industry warns of the problems they face with labour shortages, not only skilled, but semi-skilled and unskilled people alike.

There is scope for embarking on a successful new life in both countries, with many business opportunities available to the entrepreneur and jobseeker. Funding and tax incentives are also often offered to those wishing to invest in new or existing businesses. With the current low exchange rate on the Australian and New Zealand dollar many visitors to the region find that they are better off than they were back home. Australia has long been a country where long-term 'career' expats, who may have spent much of their working lives living in rather more austere countries, have decided to finally settle down and start a small business. New Zealand, although quieter than Australia, and definitely more remote, nevertheless can be the right place for many people looking for a high quality, outdoor, less stressful lifestyle.

Australia remains part of the Commonwealth and although located in the Asia-Pacific region, it has strong ties with Europe and North America. The European Union is its largest economic partner, while links with the United States are seen as vital for national security and prosperity. Having won a fourth-term in office, the prime minister highlighted the approval of a free trade agreement with the US in 2004 as being one of his government's key achievements.

Australia is recognised as a leading growth economy in the world, underpinned by low interest rates and high levels of consumer and business confidence;New Zealand is a modern, stable, and strong democracy with a forward-looking and environmentally-conscious government. New Zealand and Australian immigration departments continue to favour young, educated and/or skilled migrants, while still allowing family-linked and a small amount of humanitarian immigration to take place. Working Holiday visas for both countries remain very popular and give those aged 18-30 a year's grace to live, work and holiday, and perhaps to discover whether they would like to commit themselves for longer and take the bigger step of emigrating.

The popularity of the earlier editions of *Live & Work in Australia and New Zealand* has proved that both Australia and New Zealand exert a strong pull on those who wish to escape the dreary winters of northern Europe, find a sunnier climate and make a new start in life.

Deborah Penrith
Susan Kelly
February 2005

ACKNOWLEDGEMENTS

This is the fourth edition of *Live and Work in Australia and New Zealand*. The first was written by Fiona McGregor and Charlotte Denny, the second edition by Elisabeth Roberts and Susan McIntosh, the third by Dan Boothby and Susan Kelly. This edition has been fully revised and up-dated by Deborah Penrith and Susan Kelly. The book owes its origins to all of these people who have over the years contributed to the content.

The authors and publishers would like to thank the many other people who provided information and assistance in compiling this book. In particular, thanks are due to Linden Hall, Reference Librarian, Research & Information Centre, Department of Industry and Resources, Perth; Mark Tranthim-Fryer, Senior Project Officer, *education.au.ltd*; Leigh McAdam, Manager, Communication Media and Marketing, Centrelink; Jane Trethewey, Partner, Blake Dawson Waldron, Melbourne; Clare Hartley, Managing Editor and Associate Publisher, Fairfax Business Media, Melbourne; and Geraint Davies of Montfort International for his contributions. Debts of gratitude are also due to Megan Kelly, Statistics New Zealand, for her assistance with research; Dale Dudman, for providing research material; Nigel Worsley, Tony Mullen, John and Linda Kelly, Kim Cullen and James Pennicott for their contributions; Kate Mitchell, Department of Labour, New Zealand; the staff at New Zealand House, London; and Ron Mair, Information Analyst at Statistics New Zealand. Special thanks are owed to Helen Cunningham and Kevin James for their support, patience, advice and encouragement.

TELEPHONE NUMBERS

Please note that the telephone numbers in this book are written as needed to call that number from inside the same country. To call these numbers from outside the country you will need to know the relevant international access code; these are currently 00 from the UK and France and 011 from the USA

To call Australia: dial the international access code +61 and the number given in this book minus the first 0.

To call New Zealand: dial the international access code +64 and the number in this book minus the first 0.

To call the UK: international access code +44 then the number given in this book minus the first 0.

To call the USA: international access code +1 then the complete number as given in this book.

Australia

SECTION 1

LIVING IN AUSTRALIA

GENERAL INTRODUCTION

RESIDENCE AND ENTRY REGULATIONS

SETTING UP HOME

DAILY LIFE

RETIREMENT

GENERAL INTRODUCTION

CHAPTER SUMMARY

o **Beginnings.** The first convicts to be transported to Australia landed at Jackson Harbour (now Sydney) in 1788.

  o The first free settlers arrived in 1793, lured by promises of unlimited land and free convict labour.

o **Economy.** Australia has an average annual growth rate of 3.8% with an inflation rate of 2.8%.

  o The countries of the Pacific Rim are Australia's biggest export market.

o **Republic or Monarchy?** Despite growing republicanism, 55% of the Australian electorate voted in a 1999 referendum to remain a constitutional monarchy.

o **Sheep and Cattle.** Australia leads the world in wool production.

  o 120 million sheep and 26 million cattle graze the plains of Australia.

  o Livestock farms are known as stations and the largest is the size of Belgium, or Maryland.

o **Minerals.** Over 60 different kinds of metals and minerals are mined in Australia.

o **Aboriginals.** Three years after the arrival of Europeans, two-thirds of aboriginals had been wiped out by European diseases and a deliberate policy of annihilation.

  o Today, about 1% of Australians have aboriginal blood and of these 10,000 are pure blooded aboriginals.

o **Creatures that Bite.** Australia is notorious for its deadly insects, life-threatening snakes and many species of sharks.

  o Don't bathe at dawn or dusk as these are the usual shark feeding times.

o **Sun Warning.** Australians have the highest rate of skin cancer in the world.

o Children in Australia wear total body, zip-up swimsuits against the sun.

Destination Australia

For several generations, Australia has been one of the world's most popular migration destinations. The promises of eternal sunshine and prosperity, and of freedom from the class-bound traditions of the Old World have proved a magnet both for young, independent travellers and for families seeking a new life. In some cases, they have been disappointed. Australia is not a utopia and, although it is fiercely loved and defended by its citizens, it would not claim to be. Like any other country in the industrialised world, it experiences its share of contemporary social malaise: recession, unemployment, crime and public corruption have all made their mark in recent decades. Nonetheless, the attractions of good weather (but not *every* day!) and a high standard of living remain as strong as ever, and there has been no decline in the numbers of people seeking to emigrate from Europe and, increasingly, from South east Asia and other regions.

The days of the 'ten pound pom', though, are long gone. Australia no longer needs to offer inducements to build up its population and skill base, and immigration quotas are now strictly regulated. The application procedure is lengthy, complex and expensive, with an emphasis on the net gain to Australian society. While the country actively pursues a programme of humanitarian immigration most applicants will need to be able to demonstrate financial security and significant professional experience.

The Pacific Rim is Australia's biggest export market and for more than a decade the country has pursued a policy of 'asianisation', forging close political, cultural, and economic ties with its near neighbours. Although the Australian dollar is relatively weak (good news for 'poms' who currently get about $2.45 to the £1) the Australian economy is in its best shape in 30 years, enjoying a sustained convergence of steady growth, low inflation, low interest rates, and a falling external deficit. During the 1990s Australia recorded an average annual economic growth rate of nearly 4% a year in the 1990s, the second-fastest rate in the developed world (behind Ireland) and Australia looks set to remain 'comfortably off' well into the 21st century.

Australia's greatest attractions remain unchanged whatever the state of her economy. The expansive landscape with its infinite variety, the oceans and waterways which are at the heart of the Australian way of life, and the spacious and attractive cities are all valued and enjoyed. Australian society is refreshingly open and vigorous, the people are friendly, and the ethical cornerstones of equality and freedom are championed in a kind of congenital anti-authoritarianism. Whether you are considering a short holiday or a lifetime's move, you will find that Australians will always be prepared to give you a 'fair go'.

Pros and Cons of Moving to Australia

Australia's climate has always been a motivating factor in the decision of many European migrants to leave their home shores. The warm, sunny weather in most coastal regions allows people to enjoy an outdoor lifestyle with an emphasis on leisure. Even hardship seems better when the sun shines; there are acknowledged health and psychological benefits to living in a favourable climate.

Fruit and vegetables are abundant, fresh, and almost invariably locally grown. There is a huge variety available, including many tropical and exotic fruits rarely seen in Europe, and prices are significantly lower. Meat is particularly cheap and of

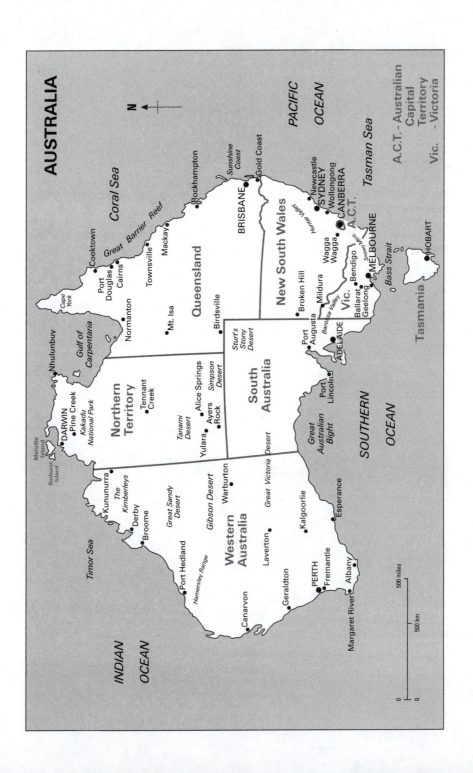

AUSTRALIA

N

PACIFIC

OCEAN

Tasman Sea

A.C.T. - Australian
Capital
Territory
Vic. - Victoria

Coral Sea

Great Barrier Reef

Rockhampton

Sunshine
Coast

Gold Coast

BRISBANE

Cooktown

Cairns
Port
Douglas

Cape
York

Townsville

Mackay

Queensland

New South Wales

Newcastle
SYDNEY
Wollongong
CANBERRA
A.C.T.

Hunter Valley

Broken Hill

Mildura
Wagga
Wagga

Bendigo

MELBOURNE

Snowy Mtns

Gulf of
Carpentaria

Normanton

Mt. Isa

Birdsville

Sturt's
Stony
Desert

Port
Augusta

Barossa Valley

Ballarat
Geelong

Vic.

Bass Strait

Nhulunbuy

DARWIN
Pine Creek
Kakadu
National Park

Northern
Territory

Tennant
Creek

Alice Springs
Ayers
Rock
Yulara

Tanami
Desert

Simpson
Desert

South
Australia

ADELAIDE

Port
Lincoln

Great
Australian
Bight

SOUTHERN

OCEAN

Tasmania

HOBART

Melville
Island

Bathurst
Island

Kununurra
The
Kimberleys

Derby

Broome

Port Hedland

Great Sandy
Desert

Gibson Desert

Warburton

Great Victoria Desert

Laverton

Kalgoorlie

Esperance

Western
Australia

Hamersley Range

Timor Sea

Geraldton

Canarvon

PERTH
Fremantle

Albany

Margaret River

INDIAN

OCEAN

500 miles

500 km

0

0

excellent quality, and there is no risk of BSE infection in Australian beef.

Most Australians live in large, modern cities, which compete successfully in the global economy. Australian scientific and technical research lead the world in many areas, and technology, engineering, commerce and banking are now as important to the economy as its agricultural and mining industries. Salaries are not as high as in the UK when converted dollar-to-pound, but with a much lower cost of living an average wage goes much further. Real estate is very much cheaper and most Australians own their own home, which will be large by European standards. Sydney and Melbourne are the most expensive cities in which to purchase property, and although these cities have a higher population density than others in Australia, residents retain the expectation of a large, detached house with a garden and garage, even in central city areas. Relatively few people live in flats.

In spite of these and other advantages, many immigrants do find certain aspects of Australian life difficult at first. In particular, new arrivals are sometimes painfully aware of their geographical isolation in Australia. Homesickness and the prohibitive cost of international air travel occasionally promote a sense of exile. Many are overwhelmed and it is not uncommon for immigrants to return permanently to their home country within a couple of years.

Although the cost of living is, in general, low, imported goods carry a substantial luxury tax, which may place familiar or favourite brands and items outside financial reach. Local alternatives are always available, but there are those migrants for whom no amount of sun, sea and sand can compensate for an over-priced tin of mushy peas.

CREEPY CRAWLIES AND WORSE

Australia is also notorious for its unpleasant insects, life-threatening snakes and its many species of shark. With the warm weather come flies – swarms of them – and if you live near freshwater, probably mosquitoes too. It is wise to assume that any spider you encounter is probably venomous until you learn to recognise those which pose an actual danger. Red-back, funnel web, and trapdoor spiders are all potentially fatal to adults as well as children, and Australians learn from an early age where these are likely to lurk. Even local bushland parks may harbour snakes such as dugites, whose bite will be lethal unless treated immediately. Most Australians know how to apply a tourniquet and suck out venom from a snakebite (though most *never* need to use this knowledge), and it may be reassuring to take a first aid course when you arrive, especially if you have a young family. Sharks live in Australia's coastal waters and most beaches have an aerial shark patrol, as well as lifesavers on duty. Shark attacks are extremely rare and their possibility does not discourage Australians from beachlife. Once again, however, it is important to be alert and born-and-bred Australians do not swim at dawn or dusk, which is known to be the sharks' feeding time.

In spite of these disadvantages, Australia has a cultural vitality and diversity which is invigorating. The population is very cosmopolitan and this is reflected in the enormous choice of restaurants, and the range of entertainment available in every city. From the European perspective, the main pros and cons of living in Australia can be summarised as follows:

Pros
Warm, sunny climate
High standard of living, including better pay
Better work conditions
Low cost of real estate
First class educational standards and facilities
Excellent medical facilities
Multicultural diversity
Low cost of living and high quality produce

Cons
Geographical isolation
Expensive national and international travel
High cost of imported goods
Annoying and dangerous insects and animals

Nathan Males found Australia superior to England in many ways

I can put my hand on my heart and say that the standard of living you can achieve for the same money is far, far higher in Hobart than in England. Rent and housing is inexpensive, cars and fuel are cheaper. Life is outdoors and the best things are free.

There is something about the values system and attitudes here that make life simpler and rather more enjoyable. It is acceptable to drive a shabby car, nearly everyone does, and the dirt roads make new cars into shabby ones quickly anyway. The sense of sprinting to keep up with the Joneses just isn't so strong here and it gives you time to relax, go to barbecues and play cricket with the lads in the paddock.

For me, the exciting thing about Australia is the sense of extremes. Rural and outback Australia has a heady sense of frontier. The land is harsh, dry and hot and there is a sense of being out there, humans against the elements. In the outback people wear big hats and drive pick-ups. I've seen men on horseback driving huge herds of cattle along wide dusty roads, a cloud of red dust kicked up by the hooves. In stark contrast, the big cities, especially Sydney, are ultra-modern.

POLITICAL AND ECONOMIC STRUCTURE

Australia is divided into six states – New South Wales (NSW), Victoria (VIC), Queensland (QLD), South Australia (SA), Western Australia (WA), and Tasmania (TAS) – and two territories, the Northern Territory (NT), and the Australian Capital Territory (ACT). The states and territories of Australia each have their own parliaments, capital city, flag, and emblems depicting regional flora and fauna. Australian mapmakers, atlases, and educationalists use cartographic projections which show Australia and the Southeast Asian region at the centre of the world map, with Europe to the extreme left and the American continents to the right.

Historical Background

Although archaeological and historical evidence suggests that Australia was first settled over 50,000 years ago by Aborigines, and later mapped by Dutch and Portuguese galleons in the 16th century, Australia's founding myths centre on the 'discovery' of the east coast by Captain James Cook in 1770. It was Cook who claimed the 'Great South Land' for the Crown. Eighteen years later, in response to a crisis in English jails and a shortage of natural resources following the American Declaration of Independence, the First Fleet arrived in Port Jackson (now known as Sydney Harbour) with 11 ships, 736 convicts and a contingent of guards. The majority of convicts came from the cities of London, Manchester, Liverpool, Dublin and Glasgow and were transported for what now seem petty offences. A total of 160,000 convicts were brought to Australia over the next 70 years, and many of those who survived their sentences, chose to stay on in the country as farmers.

Free Settlement. The first free settlers, lured by the promise of cheap land and convict labour, began to arrive in 1793, while explorers gradually opened up new country, discovering rich grazing land to the west. Wool soon became one of Australia's most important industries and remains so to the present. The discovery of gold in the 1850s brought a fresh influx of immigrants from Europe, China and America, and rich gold seams were found at Ballarat, north of Melbourne, and in central Western Australia, at Kalgoorlie. Large copper deposits were found in the York Peninsula in South Australia. Settlements were established in Hobart, Tasmania in 1803; on the Brisbane River, Queensland, in 1824; on the Swan River, in Western Australia in 1829; on Port Phillip Bay, Victoria in 1835; and on Gulf St Vincent, South Australia in 1836. The capital cities of each state have grown from these sites. In 1900 the colonies, which were previously independent entities, united in order to encourage economic expansion, regulate the postal system and build a military defence force. The constitution was presented to the House of Commons in London in 1900 and was signed by Queen Victoria. Australia became the Commonwealth of Australia on 1 January 1901, and this date is known as Federation Day. Australia Day is celebrated on 26 January every year and commemorates the arrival of the First Fleet at Port Jackson.

Government

Australia is governed by three levels of elected government – local, state, and federal – and has been called the most over-governed country in the world. Local government operates through city and shire councils who have responsibility for local amenities, town planning, parks and pet and vermin control. State governments fund and administer roads, vehicle licensing, the police force, education and health care (among many other departments) while the Government of Australia (the Federal or Commonwealth government) takes care of international trade, foreign affairs and the national treasury. State governments are located in the capital city of each state and the national parliament is in Canberra, the administrative capital of Australia. Although there are both state and federal taxes, income earners fill out only one tax return per year, remitted to the Australian Taxation Office, which then distributes revenue to the various states to fund their public services.

State and federal governments are run according to the British Westminster system, with two key differences. Firstly, unlike Britain, Australia has a written constitution, inspired by the constitution of the United States; and secondly, Australia's upper house, the Senate (equivalent in function to the British House of Lords) is a democratically elected body. The lower house is known as the House of Representatives, and its parliamentarians as Members of the House of Representatives (MHR). The legislative power of the Commonwealth of Australia is vested in the Parliament of the Commonwealth. Queen Elizabeth II is Australia's Head of State (under the Australian *Royal Styles and Titles Act* of 1973 her title is 'Queen of Australia and Her Other Realms and Territories, Head of the Commonwealth') and her representative in Australia is the Governor-General, who has the powers to prorogue Parliament and to dissolve the House of Representatives, and to assent in the Queen's name to any proposed law passed by both the Houses of the Parliament. The Governor-General is Commander-in-Chief of the Australian Defence Forces. In practice, the Governor-General's role is largely ceremonial and there has been only one occasion in recent memory where he has interfered in the democratic government of the nation. This incident, widely considered by Australians to have been an insupportable intrusion of monarchical power in Australian affairs, occurred in 1975 when the then Governor-General, Sir John Kerr, dismissed the democratically elected Prime Minister, Gough Whitlam, after backroom manoeuvring by opposition parties. Australia's real political power is held by the Prime Minister, currently John Howard, and the elected representatives of the upper and lower houses. Howard is head of the Liberal party and governs in coalition with the conservative National party and has been prime minister since 1996. He was re-elected in 1998, 2001, and in 2004 won a fourth term, making him the second longest serving leader in Australia's history. This recent victory means that the Liberal and National party coalition now control the Senate, previously controlled by the opposition Labor party and minor parties. The House of Representatives formulates and debates proposed legislation which is then passed on to the Senate for further reading and eventual ratification. A cabinet of ministers with responsibilities for various portfolios, such as trade and foreign affairs, is appointed by the Prime Minister on election, and is subject to frequent reshuffles during the lifetime of a parliament.

State Governments. State governments are constituted under the same bicameral system as the federal parliament, except in Queensland, which abolished its Upper House in 1992. The lower house of the state parliaments of New South Wales, Victoria and Western Australia is known as the Legislative Assembly, and in South Australia and Tasmania as the House of Assembly. The governments of Queensland, the Northern Territory and the Australian Capital Territory are known as the Legislative Assembly. In each state a Governor acts as the representative of the Queen, exercising prerogative powers conferred by Letters Patent issued under the Great Seal of the United Kingdom, as well as various statutory functions defined by the state constitution and by the Commonwealth *Australia Act 1986*. A Governor of a State assents in the Queen's name to bills passed by the Parliament of the State but acts on the advice of state cabinet ministers.

Suffrage. Australia has universal adult suffrage, and electoral registration and voting in both state and federal elections is compulsory for all eligible persons. In order to qualify to vote, you must be either an Australian citizen (or a British subject who was on the Commonwealth Roll on 25 January 1984), over 18 years of age, and resident in Australia. People who fail to vote in an election may be charged and fined (currently $50 for a first offence).

Political Parties

There are six mainstream political parties in Australia: the Australian Labor Party (ALP), the Liberal Party (LP), the Country Labor Party (CLP), the National Party of Australia (NPA), the Australian Democrats (AD), and the Australian Greens. The ALP is traditionally a left-wing party but has become increasingly centrist so that it now embraces such previously right-wing policies as privatisation. The Liberal Party is conservative in orientation and is currently the party of government. The Country Party and National Party are also conservative organisations whose power base lies in rural areas, and although they are never likely to hold power in their own right, they inevitably enter into a coalition with the Liberal Party when that party is in government. In many cases, including the current parliament, the Liberal Party holds power only by the consent and co-operation of the NCP. The Greens are active in environmental issues, particularly in states such as Tasmania where development threatens natural wildernesses, and they, together with the Australian Democrats, are usually successful in gaining seats in the Senate rather than in the House of Representatives.

A recent ugly development in Australian politics is the foundation and expansion of the One Nation Party, which espouses overtly racist policies. Sadly, the platform of this party appeals to redneck communities in highly conservative outback areas, particularly in Queensland. It is, however, reviled by the majority of Australians, and its leader, Pauline Hanson, is generally considered an embarrassment to the country. The antics of the One Nation Party have caused several diplomatic incidents between Australia and its Southeast Asian neighbours, and the government is at pains to stifle its sphere of influence as far as democratically possible. At the time of writing One Nation has a Senator, as well as local government councillors. In January 2002, Pauline Hanson resigned from the National Executive as National President of One Nation. She remains a member of the Party and continues to play an active role in it.

Republicanism

Support for a republican Australia has been growing steadily since the 1970s, taking centre stage in national debate in the 1990s. In 1993, the Prime Minister of the day, Paul Keating, established a Republican Advisory Committee, which founded its enquiries on the premise of 'when and how' rather than 'if', enraging pro-monarchy factions. Although traditionally the conservative Liberal Party has opposed the formation of a republic (in the 1960s, Liberal PM Sir Robert Menzies was an arch-monarchist), the Liberal government, under John Howard, has been forced to bow to the public clamour for independence, and a referendum was held in 1999. In February 1998, a Constitutional Convention, comprising democratically nominated delegates from all areas of Australian society, was held in Canberra to consider firstly, whether or not Australia should become a republic and secondly, which republican model of government should be adopted. The Convention found in favour of the formation of a republic under the 'Bipartisan Appointment of President' model, and subject to a successful referendum outcome in 1999, it had been likely that the new republic would come into effect on 1 January 2001. However, although public support for a republic was high, on 6 November 1999 the majority of Australians – around 55% – voted to keep the Constitutional Monarchy. The only state to return a vote of 'yes' to a Republic was

Victoria, and that by the narrowest of margins – 49.6% for a republic and 49.4% against.

If, and when Australia does become a republic (and it is very likely that this will occur at some point in the future), it may be initiated by Australia, or by Britain itself. A new flag without the Union Jack inset will have to be invented. It is likely that it will be designed, probably by public competition, and will be placed before the voters in a referendum before being formally adopted. The Australian national anthem, 'Advance Australia Fair', which replaced 'God Save the Queen' in 1984, will be retained.

The Economy

Australia has a free-market economy, which is subject to extensive regulation and tariff controls. Government policy, however, currently favours privatisation and deregulation, and has embarked on the process of reducing the role of government in the national economy over the long term. Many of Australia's industries have already been deregulated and government monopolies in domestic airlines, banking and telecommunications have been opened up to private competition.

Australia's major trading partners are the USA, Japan, the EU, ASEAN (the Association of Southeast Asian Nations), New Zealand, Hong Kong, China, Taiwan and Korea. It is one of the world's largest suppliers of coal, iron ore, bauxite, alumina, petroleum, natural gas, gold, wool, beef, cotton and sugar. However, traditional trading patterns are changing, with manufactured goods now accounting for 47% of all exports. Around 53% of Australian exports have gone to East Asian countries in recent years. Exports of goods and services account for around 19% of Australia's national income. Manufactures make up the largest sector of merchandise imports, especially capital goods, transport equipment and consumer goods.

Manufacturing industry accounts for around 13% of Australia's GDP, and has developed behind high tariff walls. Protection is now being reduced to make Australian industry more competitive and export-orientated. Approximately 98% of all manufacturing firms are small businesses. The main industries are chemicals, aerospace engineering, food processing, motor vehicles, iron and steel, paper, wood-chipping and forestry.

Australia's enormous natural resource base has allowed it to develop an efficient and competitive agricultural industry, which contributes around 3.4% to the GDP. Australia leads the world in wool production and is a major supplier of cereals, dairy produce, meat, sugar and fruit. More than 120 million sheep and over 26.7 million cattle are grazed on the nations plains and farms (known as stations), which are of a size undreamed of in Europe. The world's largest cattle station, Strangeray Springs in South Australia, comprises 11,594 square miles (30,029 square km) – about the same size as Belgium or Maryland! The export market for Australian wines has grown exponentially in recent years and fisheries products, especially crustaceans, are exported in large number to East Asia and the USA.

Australia is also a major producer and exporter of energy resources, and is one of the world's biggest producers of minerals and metals. More than 60 different minerals are mined, including bauxite, mineral sands, diamonds, and black and brown coal. Mineral ores containing gold, silver, lead, zinc, iron, copper, nickel, tin, manganese and uranium are also mined in various locations all around Australia. Australia imports its heavy crude oil but exports light crude and liquefied natural gas. It is also an important producer of precious and semi-precious stones, most notably diamonds, sapphires, opals and pearls. Most electricity is produced using coal-fired power stations and Australia's large coal deposits allow it to produce its electricity at relatively low cost. Hydroelectricity is another important source of power and is generated in the Snowy Mountains and in Tasmania. The Australian government has become very environmentally-conscious in recent decades, and strict regulations govern the disposal of industrial waste. Flouting these regulations can result in the forced closure of a business as well as heavily punitive fines. Major mining companies, such as ALCOA, have for many years replanted and landscaped exhausted bauxite mining sites to a level where they are, in many instances, indistinguishable from native wilderness.

Australian science and technology has effected many advances in manufacturing, mining and agricultural industries, and private sector research and development has achieved an increasingly high profile in the last decade. The government has sought to discourage the traditional view of Australia as the 'Lucky Country', replacing it with a new ethos – the 'Clever Country'. The CSIRO (Commonwealth Scientific and Industrial Research Organisation) is Australia's main scientific body, and its work focuses on industry, the natural environment, minerals, energy and construction industries. Australia has bilateral agreements on technical co-operation with India, Russia, Germany, China, Japan, Mexico, France, the European Union and Indonesia.

Trade unionism in Australia is declining rapidly as new information-led industries arise to replace traditional blue-collar ones. Only around 30% of the Australian workforce belongs to a union, and in recent years many unions have amalgamated into coalitions in order to remain viable.

GEOGRAPHICAL INFORMATION

Geography and Topographical Features

Australia is one of the world's biggest islands, which is referred to by some as a continent. It has a landmass of 2,966,136 square miles (7,682,300 square km), and is the sixth largest country in the world after Russia, Canada, China, the USA and Brazil, and is 31 times larger than the United Kingdom. The coastline, which stretches over 22,826 miles (36,735 km), encompasses a wide variety of coastal seascapes from the wild surf and dramatic cliffs of the Australian Bight, to the tranquil bays of the Southwest. It is bounded by the Pacific Ocean to the east, the Indian Ocean to the west, the Arafura Sea to the north, and the Southern Ocean to the south. The Great Barrier Reef, the largest natural reef in the world, runs almost parallel to the Great Dividing Range from the northernmost tip of Queensland at Cape York down to Fraser Island, approximately 124 miles (200 km) north of Brisbane. Australia's marine conservation reserves cover more than 146,718 square miles (380,000 square km).

Australia is characterised by the flatness of its topography and much of central Australia is a giant plateau; its highest mountain, Mount Kosiusko (7,309ft/2,228m), is only half as high as the tallest peak on any other continent. The coastal strip is fertile, but it is insignificant in size compared to the vast inland deserts at the dry heart of the continent. This inland region, known as the Outback, is broken by salt lakes, starkly beautiful mountain ranges such as the MacDonnell Ranges near Alice Springs and the Kimberly Ranges in WA, and by mysterious rock formations such as Uluru (Ayers Rock) and Mount Olga (Kata Tjuta). Deserts such as the Great Sandy

Desert, the Gibson Desert and the Great Victoria Desert are barren, unpopulated wastes of red dust, low scrub and spinifex (hardy tufts of spiny grass) and are extremely hot by day, freezing by night. The harshness of this land is sometimes reflected in the names given to geographical features, such as Lake Disappointment in Western Australia.

> **It took Nathan Males a while to fully appreciate his new surroundings**
> *The one thing that took me a long time to appreciate was the bushland. Most forest and woodland here is eucalyptus trees. They are dry-looking scraggy things with long ribbons of loose bark hanging down and a dusty, grey appearance. For a few years I would look at it and think, 'what a mess'. I remember the day when I first looked at a bit of bush and thought, 'that is beautiful'. Now I love it.*

The Murray River and the Darling River are the main internal waterways of Australia and form the Murray-Darling River Basin. This drainage basin comprises the major part of the interior lowlands of Australia, and covers more than one million square kilometres (around 14% of the country). The headwaters of the Darling, Australia's longest river, are found in the Great Dividing Range between Queensland and NSW, and finally reach the coast southwest of Adelaide some 2,094 miles (3,370 km) later. Australia's three largest lakes, Eyre, Torrens and Gairdner, are located in the interior lowlands of South Australia and are fed by the rare run-off of heavy rains in the desert. Lake Eyre was filled only three times during the 20th century, and Lake Torrens only once.

Around 202,316 square miles (524,000 square km) of public land in Australia has been designated as nature conservation reserves, and a further 424,710 square miles (1.1 million square km) is preserved as aboriginal and Torres Strait Islander land.

Other Territories

Australia is responsible for administering seven external territories: Norfolk Island, Cocos (Keeling) Island, Christmas Island, Ashmore and Cartier Island Territories, the Territory of Heard Island, Coral Sea Islands Territory, the sub-Antarctic McDonald Islands, and the Australian Antarctic Territories.

Neighbouring Countries

Australia's nearest neighbour is Papua New Guinea, which lies less than 124 miles (200 km) across the Torres Strait to the north of Cape York. To the north west of Australia lies the Indonesian archipelago and further away to the north east are the Solomon Islands, the French Island of New Caledonia, Fiji, Western Samoa and Tonga. Australia's nearest neighbour in a cultural sense is New Zealand, lying approximately 1,056 miles (1,700 km) east of Sydney. Beyond Tasmania to the south, there is nothing but ocean until Antarctica, and to the west beyond Perth nothing before the islands of the Seychelles, Mauritius and Madagascar, near the African coast.

Population

The population of Australia is currently around 20.2 million. Most of this population is concentrated in cities situated in coastal areas, and although population density figures are as low as two people per square kilometre, this figure averages population over the vast inland areas of Australia and does not reflect Australia's urban environment. Population growth is in excess of 1% per annum, and the projected population for the year 2021 lies in the region of 24 million. The ageing of Australia's population leads to the number of deaths exceeding births. It is possible that in the 2030s immigration may be the only source of growth in population. Around 92% of Australia's population are of Caucasian descent, a further 7% are Asian, and a mere one per cent are of Aboriginal extraction. Approximately 76% of Australians are Christians (mainly Roman Catholic and Anglican). Australia's official language is English and 100% of Australians are functionally literate.

Australia prides itself on its multicultural composition. Its multicultural policies enshrine the right to individual cultural identity and to social justice regardless of race, ethnicity, culture, religion, language, birthplace or gender. All Australians, whatever their background, are expected to have an overriding commitment to Australia and its interests and to accept the basic structures and principles of Australian society. Australia's multicultural policies have gone through three main phases over the decades. Until the 1960s, a policy of assimilation was in place, which drew its rationale from the long-discredited and disbanded 'White Australia Policy'. This policy effectively excluded non-European immigration but was weakened by attitudinal changes after the Second World War and is now regarded with shame by younger generations of Australians. From the mid-1960s through to 1972, the government adopted a policy of integration, recognising that large numbers of migrants, especially those whose first language was not English, required direct assistance and intervention to help them become integrated into Australian society. Finally, multiculturalism became established as government policy in 1973, and today minority groups are assisted in promoting the survival of their language and heritage within mainstream institutions.

In 1978 a comprehensive review of immigration in Australia led to the adoption of new policies and programmes as a framework for Australia's population development. Three-year rolling programmes were implemented to replace annual immigration targets, as well as developing a more consistent and structured approach to migrant selection, emphasising the need for skilled people who would represent a positive gain to the nation. Today, nearly one in four of Australia's population were born overseas, and in 2001-2002 (latest available figures from Australian Immigration), the number of new settlers totalled 88,900. Of these, 17.6% came from New Zealand, 9.8% from the UK, 7.5% from China, 6.4% from South Africa, 5.7% from India, and 4.7% from Indonesia. There are around one million British-born permanent residents and citizens in Australia, more than in any other country except the UK.

The Aboriginal People and Reconciliation

The native Australian and Torres Strait Islander people are the custodians of one of the world's oldest cultural traditions. This tradition is an oral one, in which legal, social and religious structures and customs are transmitted through story, dance and song. Art plays a central functional, rather than solely aesthetic role, in aboriginal culture; mapping out the Dreamtime (or creational mythology), explaining tribal law and describing ceremonies and events or historical happenings. Aborigines have traditionally subsisted as hunters and gatherers in small, tribally based communities and their unique relationship with the land has enabled them to survive for millennia in one of the harshest environments on earth.

The arrival of British settlers in Australia presaged the beginning of the end for traditional aboriginal culture and today their population, which was never huge, has been decimated. In the early years of settlement, the British sanctioned the deliberate destruction of the Aboriginal population; and a policy of genocide in Tasmania was effective in murdering every last indigenous inhabitant. Systematic campaigns of extermination, in the form of 'hunting parties', pursued their human quarry in every early settlement and within a mere three years of the arrival of the First Fleet in Sydney the Aboriginal population was reduced by two-thirds through imported diseases, accidents and violent death. Aborigines were considered by British settlers to be a sub-human species and were treated as animals, scientific specimens, or the subjects of social experimentation. Such attitudes prevailed, to some extent, into the 1970s and it was not until then that Aborigines were released from curfew restrictions or entitled to the rights of citizenship. The Aboriginal people now suffer from high rates of alcohol dependency, infant mortality, suicide, death in custody and criminal involvement. Their life expectancy is shorter than other Australians and they are four times as likely to suffer unemployment. There are very few pureblood Aboriginal people in Australia today, and aboriginality is defined by ancestry and identification, rather than racial purity. The population of pureblood Aborigines stands at approximately 10,000 – reduced from an estimated 100,000 at the time of the arrival of the first settlers. Although those who remain are now struggling to regain their cultural and historical heritage, many feel a sense of fragmentation, isolation, displacement, as well as a deep bitterness towards the successive governments responsible for their near-destruction.

Today, Aborigines have found a new voice and are actively defending and reinstating their rights within society and on their traditional lands. Reconciliation is now the cornerstone of public policy and seeks to foster co-existence, respecting the different rights of people in the same land. In May 1998, a National Sorry Day was held to allow all Australians, regardless of racial origin, to express their regret for the tragic past treatment of the nation's indigenous people. In particular, National Sorry Day sought to raise awareness of the distressing truths behind the forced removal of aboriginal children from their families well into the 1970s. It highlighted the consequences of this policy in terms of broken families, physical and mental abuse and the loss of language, culture and connection to traditional lands.

Land Rights. In 1992 the High Court of Australia handed down the Mabo Decision, which recognised that under Australian law indigenous people had land rights. This right was called 'native title', and reversed the long-standing legal fiction that the continent of Australia was *terra nullius*, land belonging to no one, at the time of British settlement. As a result of the Mabo Decision, in 1993 the Commonwealth Government passed the Native Title Act after extensive consultation between the Australian government and indigenous Australians. Past grants of land away from indigenous ownership (for example, to pastoralists) were made valid, in return for the reinstatement of the common law rights of indigenous people according to their traditions, laws and customs. In particular, Aboriginal and Torres Strait Islander people sought the right to contribute to, if not control, future planning and development on native title land. Native title rights still exist on much Crown land and in national parks, where the traditional owners have maintained their cultural and religious connections. In 1997 the Wik Decision, which was handed down by the High Court following a case brought by the Wik people of Northern Queensland, enlarged native title rights by permitting the right of access to land held under pastoral leases for ceremonial and traditional activities. Mining companies wishing to operate on land held under a pastoral lease were also obliged to negotiate directly with the native titleholders. Although the rights of indigenous people under native title are still limited (native title is extinguished on land held under freehold or ordinary leases), the issue has become a controversial one in Australia, and is generally clouded by fear and misinformation.

CLIMATE

Australia's size means that it encompasses several climatic zones. The more southerly regions have a temperate, Mediterranean climate with hot, dry summers and mild, wet winters while areas nearer the equator are sub-tropical. Northern Queensland and parts of the Northern Territory experience heavy rainfall between January and March ('the wet').

> **Nathan Males realised that he was fortunate in the climate of his chosen new home**
> *I acclimatised to Hobart instantly. The climate is something like the best of English weather most of the time. I imagine it would be different if I had moved to tropical or arid Australia. Australia has a whole range of climatic conditions and it is impossible to generalise.*

The seasons in the southern hemisphere are inverted: the summer months are from December to February, autumn is from March to May, winter from June to August, and spring from September to November.

Sun Protection

Australians these days are highly aware of the dangers of their climate. The hole in the ozone layer, which is concentrated over the southern hemisphere, means that more and more ultra-violet rays are penetrating the atmosphere, with an increased risk of skin cancer. The greatest damage is done in childhood, and today everyone is prepared to cover up to an extent undreamed of by British holidaymakers. Factor 15-plus sunscreen should be worn at all times, and many people choose to wear the impenetrable zinc cream on their faces (often in fluorescent colours). Most adults and all children wear hats every time they step outside, and clothing often comes with a protection rating, depending on sleeve length, colour and fabric. Sunglasses are not a fashion accessory but an essential item, and you should choose a pair with high quality lenses, such as Raybans. All sunglasses are sold with a removable sticker on the lens indicating the level of ultra-violent rays against which they offer protection, and you should only buy those which screen 100% of these dangerous rays. Sunglasses are available for all ages, from babies upwards; baby glasses come with colourful elasticated straps to keep them in place. All of the above points apply in winter as well as summer. On the beach, throw away those ideas of a mini bikini and a great tan. Today, tanning is out, and no one wears bikinis.

Young women generally choose a one-piece swimsuit, and both men and women cover up with t-shirts and hats. Children *all*, without exception, wear swimsuits reminiscent of the Victorian era neck-to-knee bathing costume. These sunsuits are made of UV-resistant lycra and come in fluorescent colours. They have wrist or elbow length sleeves, cover the whole body, and extend to the knees or even the ankles, zipping up at the front like a diver's wetsuit. They are quick drying, designed for speed in the water and are generally thought 'cool' by children. Should you let your children on the beach in a European-style swimming costume the under-the-breath tut-tutting all around you will probably drown out the sound of the waves. Australian-style children's swimsuits are available in all surf shops and department stores as well as, and more cheaply, from Cancer Foundation Shops in most cities.

WEATHER CHART

Average temperature (Celcius), rainfall (mm), sunshine in hours per day

	Jan	Feb	Mar	Apr	May	Jun	Jul	Aug	Sep	Oct	Nov	Dec
Adelaide												
Max	29	29	26	22	19	16	15	16	19	22	25	27
Min	17	17	15	12	10	8	7	8	9	11	14	15
Rainfall	21	11	25	38	58	79	82	69	62	43	29	29
Rainydays	4	4	6	8	12	15	17	17	14	10	8	7
Sunshine	10	10	9	7	5	4	5	6	7	8	9	9
Brisbane												
Max	29	29	28	26	23	21	21	22	24	26	27	29
Min	21	21	20	17	14	11	9	10	12	16	18	20
Rainfall	160	173	140	89	98	70	62	41	33	93	96	126
Rainy days	13	14	14	11	10	7	7	6	7	10	10	11
Sunshine	8	8	8	7	6	7	8	8	9	9	9	9
Canberra												
Max	28	27	24	20	15	12	11	13	16	29	22	26
Min	13	13	11	7	3	1	0	1	3	6	9	11
Rainfall	62	55	53	50	49	39	42	46	51	66	64	53
Rainy days	8	7	7	8	8	9	10	11	10	11	10	8
Sunshine	9	9	8	7	6	5	6	7	7	9	9	9
Darwin												
Max	32	31	32	33	32	31	30	31	32	33	33	33
Min	25	25	24	24	20	19	21	23	25	25	25	25
Rainfall	431	344	316	98	22	1	1	6	16	72	141	234
Rainy days	21	20	19	9	2	1	0	1	2	6	12	16
Sunshine	6	6	7	9	10	10	10	10	10	9	8	7
Hobart												
Max	22	22	21	18	15	13	12	13	15	17	19	20

Min	12	12	11	9	6	4	4	5	6	7	9	11
Rainfall	42	36	37	46	37	29	47	49	41	49	45	58
Rainy days	9	8	10	11	12	11	14	14	14	14	14	12
Sunshine	8	8	7	6	5	4	5	5	6	7	7	8
Melbourne												
Max	26	26	24	20	17	14	13	15	17	19	22	24
Min	14	14	13	11	9	7	6	7	8	9	11	13
Rainfall	49	47	52	58	57	50	48	51	59	68	60	60
Rainy days	8	7	9	12	14	14	15	16	15	14	12	11
Sunshine	9	8	7	6	4	4	4	5	6	7	7	8
Perth												
Max	32	32	29	25	21	19	18	18	20	22	25	29
Min	17	17	16	13	10	9	8	8	9	10	13	15
Rainfall	7	16	15	42	106	174	163	118	70	47	27	12
Rainy days	2	3	4	8	13	17	18	16	13	10	7	4
Sunshine	12	11	9	8	7	6	6	7	8	9	10	12
Sydney												
Max	26	26	25	22	19	17	16	18	20	22	24	25
Min	19	19	17	15	11	9	8	9	11	13	16	17
Rainfall	7	16	15	42	106	174	163	118	70	47	27	12
Rainy days	2	3	4	8	13	17	18	16	13	10	7	4
Sunshine	12	11	9	8	7	6	6	7	8	9	10	12

A GUIDE TO THE STATES AND TERRITORIES

Information Facilities

Tourism is one of Australia's most important industries and enjoys an increasingly high profile in the domestic economy. Every capital city has a large and well-supplied Tourist Bureau, and most regional towns have a smaller Tourist Information Office providing specialist and local information. Isolated regions and national parks which are not served by an office will usually have a tourist information point with maps, general information and points of interest displayed for reference. Most railway and bus stations also have counters where you can obtain information on your journey as well as advice on accommodation, facilities and attractions in the area you are visiting.

Tourism Australia has an office in London (open Monday to Friday from 9am-5.30pm) which will answer your travel queries and assist with itineraries. They also stock an extensive range of pamphlets, maps and guides, and will forward free literature to you on request. Tourism Australia has an excellent website at www. australia.com. The Australia Centre at the Australian High Commission in London provides information supplied by all the states except Queensland (which maintains its own office at Queensland House in the Strand, London), including an extensive range of booklets. This office also has a reading room where you can consult up-to-date newspapers from each capital city, including the classifieds pages.

There are many guidebooks available covering every region of Australia, for every type of traveller. The specialist travel bookshop, *Stanfords* (12-14 Long Acre, London, WC2E 9LP; ☎020-7836 1321; fax 020-7836 0189; www.stanfords. co.uk) has a particularly extensive range, and publishes an Australian and New Zealand Book List on its website.

Useful Addresses

Tourism Australia (UK), 1st Floor, Gemini House, 10-18 Putney Hill, London
   SW15 6AA; ☎020-8780 2229; fax 020-8780 1496; www.australia.com.
Tourism Australia (USA), 6100 Center Drive, Suite 1150, Los Angeles, CA 90045;
   ☎310-695 3200; fax 310-695 3201; www.australia.com.
Tourism Australia, GPO Box 2721, Sydney, NSW 2001; ☎02-9360 1111; fax 02-
   9361 1388; www.australia.com.
Queensland Tourism, Queensland House, 392-393 Strand, London WC2R 0LZ;
   ☎020-7836 1333; fax 020-7420 8770; www.qld.gov.au.

WESTERN AUSTRALIA (WA)

Capital: Perth.
Area: 1,515,300 square miles (2,525,500 square km) = over 10 times the size of the UK.
Total area of Australia: 32.87%.
Coastline: 7,813 miles (12,500 km).
Climate: Average Perth daily maximum temperature in January (Summer) 81°F (27°C); in July (Winter) 59°F (15°C). Note that there is significant variation in temperatures throughout the state from the temperate South to the tropical North.

Western Australia's huge size (the whole of Western Europe can easily fit into Western Australia and still leave room for more) encompasses the whole range of climatic and geographical zones. From the endless white sands and crystal waters the tropical north to the arid zones of the Nullarbor Plain, through to the vineyards of the southwest, WA is the Australian landscape encapsulated. Its features include the spectacular Ningaloo Reef, a marine reserve less well-known than the Great Barrier Reef but equally impressive, majestic Karri forests, ancient and massive gorges, and geological formations such as Wave Rock and the Pinnacles (an ancient fossilised forest now standing in a desert landscape). The Stirling and Porongorup Ranges very occasionally see snow in winter.

The State is rich in a wide variety of natural resources and is a leading producer of iron ore, gold, industrial diamonds, alumina, mineral sands, wool, wheat, salt and forest products. While wheat and wool account for around two-thirds of the state's income from primary industry, Western Australia is also developing more unusual primary industries; farming cashmere and angora goats, emu and deer. Western Australia's fishing industry produces rock lobster, prawns, shrimp and scampi, which are mainly exported to the USA and Japan. Mineral and petroleum production adds a further $8 billion per annum to the State's economy, and comprises 84% of the value of the State's overseas exports and about 50% of Australia's total mineral and energy exports. The minerals and petroleum industry in WA contribute about 30% of the Gross State Product.

Since the 1960s, the Western Australian economy has grown faster than that of any other State, with an average real Gross State Product growth of 4.9%. The state's economy is export-based and its overseas trade surplus is more than double that of the rest of Australia. Its major export markets are Japan and the Southeast Asian nations as well as the USA and the EU. It has the second lowest levels of unemployment in the country. Western Australia is second to New South Wales as the most popular destination for business migrants. More than a quarter of Western Australia's population was born overseas, and it consequently enjoys a broad and cosmopolitan lifestyle. It also has a young population, second only to the Northern Territory, with an average age of 30.4 years. Western Australian medical and health services are considered among the best in the world. At a doctor-patient ration of 1:288, the state now ranks with Norway, Sweden, Finland, Denmark, France and the Netherlands, and is considerably ahead of the USA, UK and Japan. The average life expectancy in Western Australia is high, and currently stands at 76 years for men and 82 for women.

Western Australian education is of a very high standard, both in the public and private sector. With five universities and over a thousand schools and colleges throughout the State, Western Australia has world-class education facilities, and is a world-leader in certain areas of research, such as wave technology.

Real estate costs are among the lowest in the country, and Western Australians enjoy a high rate of home ownership with more than two-thirds of all residences being privately owned.

Perth: Perth is the most geographically isolated capital city in the world and has a population of 1.41 million people (WA has a total population of 1.9 million). The city is stunning, situated along the banks of the Swan River, and has a relaxed and friendly atmosphere and easy-going lifestyle. The most popular residential areas are built along the river and coastal strip, with suburban sprawl extending inland to the edge of the escarpment of the coastal plateau. Perth summers are very hot, and although the average temperature is only 80°F (27°C), the mercury frequently hovers around 104°F (40°C) for days at a time. The heat is very dry and as it is not sticky or cloying can easily be dealt with by staying in the shade. In the afternoons, the sea breeze comes in off the Indian Ocean and by sunset the weather is usually extremely pleasant. This breeze is known affectionately as 'The Fremantle Doctor', for its remedying effect on the wilting population. Perth is, in fact, Australia's windiest city, and the third windiest city in the world. It enjoys more sunshine and clear days than any other Australian capital and while it also has one of the wettest winters, rains are usually short and sharp, interspersed with cool, sunny periods.

The centre of Perth is dominated by King's Park, which consists of approximately 1,000 acres (404,686 ha) of natural bushland, wildflowers and landscaped gardens. This park is a focus for family life and its various cycle tracks, nature walks, adventure playgrounds and water features are popular with all sections of the community. King's Park is the home of the state botanical gardens, which features the full array of native flora, and hosts the Wildflower Festival in September.

Perth has an active cultural scene, with a permanent symphony orchestra, ballet company and opera company performing year-round at the city's two main arts venues: the Perth Concert Hall and His Majesty's Theatre. The enormous Entertainment Centre hosts large-scale popular events and commercial productions such as the Moscow Circus and ice shows. The Festival of Perth is held every year and is centred on the venues of the University of Western Australia. Major national and international performing artists in the fields of music, dance and theatre are brought in for the four week event, so that every year, the world's best can be seen on the local stages. In addition, the Festival Fringe offers cutting-edge comedy and experimental theatre and music, and the concurrent film festival screens art movies from around the world. Musica Viva operates a national and international chamber music touring scheme, the largest of its kind in the world.

Perth has an efficient public transport system made up of ferries, electric trains and buses, all run by Transperth. In Perth, travel on the Central Area Transport (CAT) system is free throughout the central business district. City planners are actively seeking to improve public transport to alleviate congestion in the city centre. Long distance commuting is rare in Perth, and most people live within about 20 minutes of their place of work.

The beaches and the Swan River provide a perfect water-playground for Perth's population, and the swimming, water-skiing, windsurfing, surfing and sailing are the cornerstone of Perth leisure activities. There are more boats per capita in Perth than in any other Australian city. The other major sports played in Perth include cricket (the Western Australian Cricket Association, affectionately known as the WACA, often hosts One-Day International and Test matches), various codes of football (Aussie rules, soccer, rugby), horseracing, tennis, hockey, lawn bowls and golf. Basketball and baseball are also increasingly popular.

Western Australia's healthy economy, its growing population, developing industries and technology, outdoor lifestyle, cheap real estate and prime facilities contribute to a general feeling of well-being, which occasionally borders on smugness, and most locals consider themselves lucky to live there.

Useful Addresses

Online WA. Portal website for the Government of Western Australia: www.wa.gov. au.

Real Estate Institute of Western Australia, REIWA House, 215 Hay Street, Subiaco, WA 6008; ☎08-9380 8222; fax 08-9381 9260; e-mail admin@reiwa.com.au; www.reiwa.com.au. REIWA produces an illustrated weekly property guide, 'The Homebuyer', available free every Friday from REIWA and local REIWA Agents.

Department of Education and Training of Western Australia, 151 Royal Street, East Perth, WA 6004; ☎08-9264 4111; fax 08-9264 5005; www.eddept.wa.edu. au.

Department of Industry and Resources, Mineral House, 100 Plain Street, East Perth, WA 6004; ☎08-9222 8333; fax 08-9222 3862; www.doir.wa.gov.au. The DoIR produces a quarterly economic briefing on Western Australian economy.

Business Assistance. The DoIR site for business help at www.doir.wa.gov. au/BusinessAssistance.

NORTHERN TERRITORY (NT)

Capital: Darwin.
Area: 807,720 square miles (1,346,200 square km) = 5.5 times the size of the UK.
Total area of Australia: 17.52%.
Coastline: 3,720 miles (6,200 km).
Climate: Average daily maximum temperature in January 87°F (31°C); in July 87°F (31°C). In Alice Springs temperatures vary more widely, as the town lies in the semi-arid central region rather than the tropics. The average daily maximum summer and winter temperatures for Alice Springs are 95°F (35.2°C) and 68°F (20.5°C).

The Northern Territory (also known as 'The Top End') is situated in central northern Australia, to the east of Western Australia. It is bordered by South Australia in the south and Queensland to the east. The Northern Territory's history of development is closely linked with that of South Australia, as in 1863 the British Government handed over control of the Northern Territory to the Colony of South Australia. Within a year, the first sale of land in the Territory was held in Adelaide. In 1869 an expedition led by the Surveyor-General George Goyder resulted in the establishment of a permanent settlement, now known as Darwin. South Australia's control was relinquished in 1901 after Federation, and control over the Northern Territory was held by the Commonwealth Government until 1 July 1978, when the Territory was granted self-government. The powers of government differ from those of other states in the title only. Its assembly consists of a single lower house, and its leader is known as the Chief Minister. For inter-governmental financial purposes the Northern Territory has been regarded as a State by the Commonwealth since July 1988.

The remoteness and harshness of the Northern Territory has made it unique in many ways, not the least of which is its relatively tiny population. Its 199,900 residents (June 2004) comprise 0.75% of Australia's population and it has a population density of only one person per nine square km. The population of Darwin is around 107,000 and of Alice Springs, 24,640. The annual population growth rate in 2004 was 0.7%. This rate has slowed recently due to changing patterns of interstate migration, but the Northern Territory continues to have the youngest population in Australia, with an average age of 29 years, compared with the Australian average of 34.7 years. Almost 28% of the population are Aboriginal, although overall Aboriginal and Torres Straits account for only 1.5% of the Australian population. More than 50 different ethnic groups are represented in Darwin, and 24% of people speak a language other than English.

Although the Territory is hampered by its distance from major Australian economic and political centres, and by restricted transport and communication links, its economy has experienced a growth rate in Gross Domestic Product (GDP) which has generally exceeded that of Australia as a whole. Its rapid growth can be attributed mainly to developments in mining, to tourism, and especially to oil. The abundance of natural resources such as alumina, manganese, gold, bauxite and uranium, as well as oil and gas, has enabled the Northern Territory to participate substantially in the international market, and the value of exports for the Northern Territory per capita is almost double the national figure.

There are three main interstate highway links in the Northern Territory: the

Stuart Highway from Darwin to the South Australian border, the Barkly Highway from Tennant Creek to the Queensland border, and the Victoria Highway from Katherine to the Western Australian border. Although there are roadhouses along these highways, there are stretches of road which are not serviced for more than 174 miles (280 km). It is always advisable to notify the Automobile Association of the Northern Territory before embarking on an unfamiliar road (especially in the wet season), or before undertaking long journeys over unsealed or unserviced roads. You should ensure that you take supplies of petrol, water and food, and if possible a CB radio. In the case of breakdown or emergency, stay with your vehicle at all times.

The cost of housing varies widely within the Northern Territory. Rented accommodation in Darwin is among the most expensive of all Australian capital cities, and suitable properties may be scarce.

Education has been the responsibility of the Northern Territory government since 1979, and in recent years it has modified its schools' curriculum to reflect the multicultural nature of its classrooms, promoting intercultural understanding and literacy. There are also correspondence schools, known as 'Schools of the Air', which use two-way radio, video and computers, to bring the classroom to isolated students. The Northern Territory Secondary Correspondence School offers an excellent range of secondary courses up to university entrance level for those who do not have access to normal school facilities. Tertiary education in the Northern Territory is usually undertaken through either the Northern Territory University or the University's Institute of Technical and Further Education which specialises in trade and technical courses. In 1985, the postgraduate research institution, the Menzies School of Health Research, was established at the Royal Darwin Hospital and it is currently enjoying a reputation as a centre of scientific excellence in its field. One of its primary objectives is to assist in improving the health of people in tropical and central Australia. The School has an academic link with the Northern Territory University and its students may qualify for the higher degrees of that university.

The Northern Territory Health Services are remarkable, considering the distance and difficult terrain that must be covered. There are modern, well-equipped hospitals in Darwin, Alice Springs, Katherine, Tennant Creek and Nhulunbuy. All hospitals provide general in- and out-patient, accident and emergency services. The Royal Darwin and Alice Springs Hospitals offer a wide range of specialist services and are both special teaching hospitals affiliated with the University of Sydney. A private hospital is also available in Darwin. Mobile services are also provided in remote areas and the Northern Territory government subsidises missions and Aboriginal organisations in the provision of health services. While there are health centres in all major towns and settlements, in extremely remote regions the Royal Flying Doctor Service (RFDS) and the Aerial Medical Service operate in cases of serious injury or illness. The Patient Assisted Travel Scheme (PATS) provides financial assistance to people from isolated areas that have had to travel for specialist consultation and treatment. The Northern Territory government also provides mental health care, blood banks, services for the aged, caring for family, youth and children, services for the disabled and women's information services as well as women's refuges and shelters, alcohol and other drug programmes, a Sexual Assault Reference Centre, and the Ruby Gaea Darwin Centre Against Rape which provides counselling, support services and emergency accommodation.

The Northern Territory lies within the torrid zone of the Tropic of Capricorn and much of its area is semi-arid. Although its landscape contains Australia's great 'dead heart' of claypan desert, which covers an area 500 miles (805 km) long and 200 miles

(322 km) wide, the tropical northern part of the Territory is luxuriantly verdant. These two climatic regions result in a diversity of vegetation within the Territory, ranging from mangrove and freshwater swamps and billabongs (pool or backwater), rainforest, eucalyptus and mulga woodlands, to spinifex grasslands, gibber plains and sandy deserts. There are no major rivers in the Northern Territory's interior, and rivers and creeks flow only after rains in the wet season (October-April). The Todd River, on which Alice Springs is located, is usually dry. 'The wet' is a period of high humidity, and torrential rain and thunderstorms occur in the transition from 'the dry' to the wet season. These rains often cause flooding, and transport and communications in the Northern Territory can be difficult or even disrupted at times. All of the Territory's major rivers are on the coastal fringe. The Roper River which flows into the Gulf of Carpentaria, is the Territory's largest. Among other smaller rivers are the Daly, Victoria, Adelaide, Mary, South and North Alligator rivers. The Northern Territory is prone to cylones or hurricanes, the most famous of which, Cyclone Tracy, destroyed Darwin on 24 December 1974. The city has subsequently been rebuilt and is now a modern showcase of urban planning. Houses are constructed to withstand cyclone conditions, and government authorities maintain crisis plans against future disasters.

Although the Northern Territory is best known to non-Territorians as one of the world's great wilderness, the capital, Darwin, is a modern city which provides the services and lifestyle expected of any Australian city. Like any other Australian state, the Northern Territory offers a huge range of outdoor activities, including a wide variety of sports, as well as diverse cultural events, including theatre and festivals. In general, the towns are small, sparsely populated, have a relaxed atmosphere and a strong sense of community.

Useful Addresses

The Territory. Portal website for the Northern Territory Government: www.nt.gov.au
Department of Business, Industry and Resource Development, 2nd Floor, Development House, 76 Esplanade, Darwin, NT 0800; ☎08-8982 1700; fax 08-8982 1725; e-mail info.dbird@nt.gov.au; www.dbird.nt.gov.au.

SOUTH AUSTRALIA (SA)

Capital: Adelaide.
Area: 380,070 square miles (984,377 square km) = four times the size of the UK.
Total area of Australia: 12.81%.
Coastline: 2,300 miles (3,700 km).
Climate: Average daily maximum temperature in January 84°F (29°C); in July 59°F (15°C).

South Australia is situated in the middle of the southern coast of Australia along the Great Australian Bight. It is bordered by Western Australia to the west, the Northern Territory to the north and Victoria to the east. It has a Mediterranean climate, ideally suited to the production of wine, and vineyards established by early European settlers are prolific throughout the Barossa Valley. South Australia produces more wines that any other state or territory in the country and has a population of 1.5 million, or around 8.5% of the total population of Australia. Most of South

Australia's population lives in Adelaide, the capital, which has a population of 1.1 million. Adelaide is situated on the River Torrens, between the waters of the gulf and a range of low hills on the coastal plateau and the city stretches 56 miles (90 km) from its southernmost to northernmost suburbs. The rest of the state's population is scattered throughout the major regional centres of Whyalla, Mount Gambier, Port Augusta, Murray Bridge, Port Pirie and Port Lincoln.

Adelaide. Adelaide's transport system is a well-oiled machine that rarely experiences breakdown or congestion. This is largely due to the city's first planner, Colonel William Light, who planned Adelaide with such geometric symmetry that all major city roads are straight and wide. Adelaide enjoys a unique bus service called the *O-Bahn*, which is a right-of-way guided transport system on which commuters are shuttled to and from the city at speeds of up to 62 miles/h (100 km/h).

Most of the housing follows the pattern of single-storey houses on spacious blocks, ensuring off-street parking and a private back garden. The standard of homes in South Australia is among the highest in the country, and rented accommodation is cheaper than most other states. Industrial property rental is on average 35% cheaper than in other Australian capitals.

South Australia is an important industrial and scientific centre, and is home to a rapidly expanding electronics industry. The Advanced Engineering, Electronic Research and Electronic Surveillance laboratories at the Defence Science Technology Centre are world-leaders in laser research, and the academic centres of the Adelaide and Flinders Universities support this research, as well as enjoying a fine reputation in many other disciplines. The University of Adelaide is one of Australia's premier universities, and consistently ranks high among the top universities in the Asia-Pacific region in winning research funds. Australia's first planned centre for high-technology development and manufacture, Technology Park Adelaide, is integrated with the campus of the University of South Australia. South Australia's industrial base is supported by vast mineral resources in the form of oil, gas and other hydrocarbons which are tapped in the Cooper Basin area. Brown coal is mined at Leigh Creek, and copper, uranium and gold are extracted at Roxby Downs. Australia's biggest opal fields are at Andamooka.

South Australia has a warm, friendly ambience, and Adelaide is a rapidly developing city. The capital has the highest ratio of health professionals per capita in Australia and has 173 public and private hospitals. It has excellent sporting and entertainment facilities and a highly regarded education system. The city has a permanent symphony orchestra, ballet, and opera company, and hosts the world-famous Adelaide Festival every summer. Adelaide offers a very attractive environment with some fine architectural features and is known as the 'City of Churches'. The cost of living and real estate is generally low in South Australia, making it an appealing place in which to live.

Useful Addresses

South Australia Central. Portal website for the Government of South Australia: www.sa.gov.au.

Department of Trade and Economic Development, Level 10, Terrace Towers, 178 North Terrace, Adelaide, SA 5000; ☎08-8303 2400; fax 08-8303 2410; www.southaustralia.biz.

Department of Immigration and Multicultural and Indigenous Affairs, Level 4, 55

Currie Street, Adelaide, SA 5000; ☎131 881; fax 08-8237 6699; www.immi.
gov.au.
Immigration South Australia, PO Box 2343, Adelaide, SA 5001; ☎08-8204 9250;
fax 08-8204 9244; www.immigration.sa.gov.au.

TASMANIA (TAS)

Capital: Hobart.
Area: 26,375 square miles (68,331 square km) = 0.22 times the size of the UK.
Total area of Australia: 0.88%.
Coastline: 1,920 miles (3,200 km).
Climate: January 71°F (22°C); July 51°F (11°C).

Tasmania is Australia's smallest state. It is an island separated from the south
east corner of the mainland by the Bass Strait, a shallow body of water with
an average width of 149 miles (240 km). Tasmania's coastline is bounded by the
Southern Ocean to the south and west, and the Tasman Sea to the east. Tasmania
spans 184 miles (296 km) from north to south and 196 miles (315 km) from east
to west. Despite the fact that it is Australia's smallest state it is, nonetheless, still
twice the size of Wales. Tasmania is the only Australian state, which does not have
a desert region and it is fertile throughout. It is the most mountainous state and
one of the almost completely mountainous islands in the world. It has the largest
rural population in relation to its size of all the Australian states, and is one of the
world's most richly mineralised areas. Tasmania is the leading Australian state in
terms of the production of minerals in point of value of output per capita, and
almost all of Australia's tungsten is extracted from King Island, situated in the
Bass Strait.

Orchard and berry fruits are grown in the south of the state and due to its high
production of apples and because of its shape, Tasmania is often referred to as
the Apple Isle. Industries in the southern region include the Cadbury Schweppes
cocoa and confectionery factory, the Electrolytic Zinc Company, the Australian
Newsprint Mills, Stanley Works (manufacturers of hand tools such as the Stanley
knife), Sheridan Textiles, International Catamarans and the Cascade Brewery, which
was established in 1824 and is the oldest brewery still in operation in Australia.

Fishing is the major industry on the east coast of Tasmania and is based in the
ports of St. Helens and Bicheno. Catches include crayfish and abalone. Tasmania
has a rapidly developing fisheries industry and now farms salmon and oysters for
the international market.

In the north east of the state, the fertile soil provides ideal farming land. Beef
and dairy cattle, wool sheep and prime lambs are all farmed in this region. Market
gardening is also important, as it is in the northwest of the state, where vegetable
and dairy farming predominate. Other types of farming in the northwest include
pig, sheep and also poppy farming (to provide oil for pharmaceutical preparations).
Manufacturing here is dominated by forest-based industries, whereas in the central
northern region of the state industries include the knitting yarn producers Coats
Patons, the automotive parts manufacturers ACL Bearing Company, and the
aluminium smelter and refinery Comalco. Central and northern Tasmania has
developed a viticulture industry, and is the home of the Ben Lomond Ski Fields.

The west of the state is a region of dense forests and mountain ranges, raging rivers and rugged hills, and has a treacherous coastline and wild, inaccessible beaches. Mining is the predominant industry in the west, and metal ores such as copper, zinc, tin and iron are extracted here. Much of the southwest region is inaccessible and uninhabited, containing some of the most spectacular scenery in the world. The southwest wilderness area has been listed by the World Heritage Commission and consists of dense rain forests, scrub, wild rivers, rapids, ravines and harsh mountains, which can only be tackled by experienced bush-walkers.

Approximately 20% of Tasmania is World Heritage Area, and there are extensive cave systems, many of which are Ice Age aboriginal cave art sites.

The central lakes area is dominated by the hydroelectric schemes which produce the state's electricity. Trout-fishing is also popular. In the flatter midland area sheep farming, particularly for wool, and beef cattle grazing are also popular.

Many parts of Tasmania are reminiscent of the green but windswept landscapes of some parts of Scotland, and over the decades a large number of British and other European immigrants have settled on the island. The resident population of Tasmania is currently 482,100, of which two-fifths were born outside Australia, mostly in England, Scotland and Germany and approximately 23% of whom are under the age of 15. Tasmania's climate and farming conditions are most comparable to those of northern European countries such as France and the UK, which also helps new British settlers feel more 'at home' than they might in the harsh dry regions of the Northern Territory or the tropical areas of Queensland.

Hobart. Hobart is Tasmania's capital city. It was founded in 1804 and is situated in the southwest of the state, 12 miles (20 km) from the mouth of the Derwent River. It is Australia's second oldest city, with a population of around 180,000, and extends over both sides of the river. To the west of the city lies Mount Wellington (4,163 ft/1,269 m), which is usually snow-capped in winter. The city was founded as a penal colony and was reputed to be one of the harshest prison settlements. Transportation to Van Diemen's Land (as Tasmania was originally called) was as good as a death sentence, and many convicts did not survive. Despite its ruthless beginnings, the city flourished in the mid-nineteenth century thanks to its shipbuilding, whaling and port facilities. Today, Hobart is more likely to make the shipping news during the famous Sydney-Hobart yacht race held every year commencing on Boxing Day.

In 1869 Tasmania became the first colony in the British Empire to make education compulsory and in 1898 school attendance was made obligatory between the ages of seven and 13, expanding to between six and 14 years in 1912. In 1946 Tasmania became the only Australian state to make attendance up to the age of 16 compulsory. It has its own university, the University of Tasmania, as well as numerous colleges of advanced education and conservatorium of music. Tasmania's main employment sectors are retailing and manufacturing, however, employment is depressed and the outlook for young people is considered poor. Unemployment continues to rise in Tasmania, and it currently has the highest unemployment rate of all states.

Tasmania is becoming increasingly popular as a migration destination. The high standard of education, modern health facilities and cheap housing are all strong attractions. However, the cost of living can be slightly higher than in other states due to freight costs. Although some love the small-community feel of the state, others feel that the sense of isolation that almost inevitably affects new settlers is exacerbated by Tasmania's separation from mainland Australia.

Tasmania's geographical isolation has meant that the state has developed a unique flora and fauna. Tasmania has 10 species of mammal not found elsewhere, including the Tasmanian Devil (a carnivorous, nocturnal marsupial) and the 'Tasmanian Tiger', generally believed to be extinct although occasional sightings are claimed, fourteen indigenous species of birds and two species of indigenous reptiles. The duck-billed platypus is more common in Tasmania than elsewhere and the Tasmanian mountain shrimp which is only known outside Tasmania as a fossil has remained obstinately unaltered and very much alive.

In terms of natural environment, Tasmania is breathtaking, and perhaps feels a little more familiar to the European settler than the harsh, sandy, sun baked land of mainland Australia.

Useful Addresses

Tasmania Online. Portal website for the Government of Tasmania: www.tas.gov.au
Department of Economic Development, 22 Elizabeth Street, Hobart, TAS 7000;
☎03-6233 5888; fax 03-6233 5800; e-mail info@development.tas.gov.au;
www.dsd.tas.gov.au

VICTORIA (VIC)

Capital: Melbourne.
Area: 136,560 square miles (227,600 square km) = 0.93 times the size of the UK.
Total area of Australia: 2.96%.
Coastline: 1,080 miles (1,800 km).
Climate: January 77°F (25.1°C); July 57°F (14°C), but the weather in Victoria, particularly in Melbourne, is notoriously unpredictable. Victoria's exposure to frequent cold fronts and southerly winds results in changeable weather patterns, popularly known as the 'Four Seasons in One Day' phenomenon.

Victoria is situated in the south-eastern corner of Australia, bordered by South Australia to the west and New South Wales to the north. Even though Victoria is the smallest of all Australian States, it still offers a wide geographical diversity ranging from the Victorian Alps, which lie on the shared border with New South Wales, fertile wine-growing regions in the Murray and Yarra River Valleys, rainforest in the Gippsland region in the southeast corner of Victoria on the Errinundra Plateau, and desert beauty in the northwest inland Mallee region. Victoria has the world's third largest volcanic plain, situated in the Western District. The Great Dividing Range, which forms a spine down the inland 'back' of Victoria and New South Wales, is known as the 'High Country'.

The land on which Melbourne was built was purchased in 1835 from Aborigines of the local Dutigalla clan. The Aborigines had no concept of land as a commodity at that time, and in exchange for their ancestral home they received articles of clothing, 50 pounds of flour, handkerchiefs, knives, tomahawks, looking glasses and blankets.

> The driving force behind the founding of Melbourne was John Pascoe Fawkner, the son of a convict. A self-educated bush lawyer who also established several newspapers, Fawkner sat on the Legislative Council of Victoria for 15 years, where he was an energetic campaigner for the rights of small settlers and convicts,

and instrumental in ending the transportation of convicts from Great Britain to Australia. His energy was drawn from his own personal experience of the harsh penal code – he received 500 lashes when he was 22 for assisting seven convicts to escape and he bore the scars for the rest of his life.

The population of Victoria (the most densely populated state in Australia) is 4.9 million, and consists of immigrants from the UK and EU as well as the Middle East and Southeast Asia. There are approximately 12,000 Aborigines in Victoria. All of these different ethnic groups give the state a real cultural diversity and have a positive influence on Victorian culture. Melbourne has a population of around 3.5 million, and other major regional centres include Geelong, Bendigo, Ballarat, Horsham, Mildura, Warrnambool, Castlemaine and Shepparton.

Victoria's economy has suffered in the past from industrial unrest and from poor economic government. In an attempt to boost the State's economy, the Victorian Government sponsors successful overseas entrepreneurs and senior executives intending to live permanently in Victoria through the Australian Government's State/Territory Nominated Independent Scheme Migration Category. Victoria is the site of research and development in the areas of food, paper, chemicals and petroleum, transport equipment, electrical equipment and biotechnology.

The standard of tertiary education in Victoria is particularly high. There are eight universities in the State, three of which specialise in technology, as well as numerous technical and further education institutions. The Commonwealth Scientific and Industrial Research Organisation is based in Victoria.

Melbourne. In 1990 the Population Crisis Committee, based in Washington DC, rated Melbourne the world's most liveable city in terms of safety, health, and air quality. Melbourne's location on the coastal plain between the Pacific Ocean and the beautiful Dandenong hills provides a superb living environment, and its cultural and sporting facilities are unequalled elsewhere in Australia.

Melbourne flourished during the great gold rush of the 1850s and as a consequence it became the Australian centre of business and commerce. Today, 16 of Australia's top 50 innovative companies have their headquarters in Melbourne. In the 1880s Melbourne was known as 'The Paris of the Antipodes', and it was the capital of Australia from 1901 (Federation) until 1927, when the capital was moved to Canberra (to avoid in-fighting between Melbourne and Sydney).

Melbourne is one of Australia's leading exporters of computers, engines and pharmaceuticals, and it is the location of eight major medical research institutes, including the Walter and Eliza Hall Institute, the home of modern immunology and one of the world's best known medical research centres. Australia's main telecommunications research and development facilities are based in Melbourne, and Victoria accounts for more than 30% of Australia's information and telecommunications technology turnover. Melbourne is a popular destination in the Asian region for conventions, meetings and exhibitions.

The 3.4 million population of Melbourne is a cosmopolitan one and, with nearly 200 different nationalities represented, it is one of the most multicultural cities in the world. It has the world's third largest Greek community, behind Athens and Thessalonia.

Melbourne is widely considered to be the cultural capital of Australia, and it enjoys the facilities of a world-standard Arts Centre. The Australian Ballet Company is based in the city. Melbourne is also the home of the Australian film industry and of much of Australian television output (including *Neighbours* and *Home and Away*). The city is Australia's premier shopping location, with an unlimited selection of designer shops and other stores. Melbourne also hosts the Melbourne Cup, the nation's richest horse race, the Australian Rules Football Grand Final, and the Australian Open at the impressive Koorong Tennis Centre. Melbourne will play host to the Commonwealth Games in 2006.

Useful Addresses

Victoria Online, www.vic.gov.au.

Business Victoria, Level 5, 55 Collins Street, Melbourne, VIC 3000; ☎132 215 (local) or 03 9651 9387 (International); fax 03-9651 9725; e-mail enquiries@iird. vic.gov.au; www.business.vic.gov.au.

Department of Innovation, Industry and Regional Development, Level 46, 55 Collins Street, Melbourne, VIC 3000; ☎03-9651 9999; fax 03-9651 9907; www.dsrd. vic.gov.au.

AUSTRALIAN CAPITAL TERRITORY (ACT)

Capital: Canberra.
Area: 1,440 square miles (2,400 square km) = 0.01 times the size of the UK.
Total area of Australia: 0.0003%.
Coastline: 0 (except 21 miles/35 km in Jervis Bay Territory).
Climate: January 82°F (28°C); July 51°C (11°C).

Canberra was established in 1901 (at Federation) to provide a 'neutral' headquarters for the new seat of government. Sydney had threatened to refuse to join the Federation unless the capital was in New South Wales; Melbourne, for its part, considered it had the greater claim. As a compromise, the Australian Capital Territory was established mid-way between the two states in a move which was, as it was said, 'acceptable to everyone, but satisfactory to nobody'. The American architect, Walter Burley Griffin, won the international competition to design the new capital city, resulting in a completely planned city where even the sites of trees have been carefully selected. The effect can appear sterile, and this sterility is reinforced by the fact that 60% of Canberra's residents are civil servants. The weekend sees an evacuation of politicians back to their state of origin, giving Canberra the reputation for city without a soul. During the week, however, Capital Hill, through which the artificial Lake Burley Griffin cuts, is the hub of the nation's political activity. Canberra is a derivative of an Aboriginal word *kamberra* which means 'meeting place'. The city is home to the Australian National University, the Australian Institute of Sport, the Australian National Gallery and the Australian War Memorial and Museum. Canberra does not have a commercial centre and its big shopping centres are all located in suburban areas. Instead, the city has many parks and recreational areas, and traffic congestion is virtually unknown.

Canberra, with a population of 309,800, is an attractive city, although it is much derided by most Australians who find its planned and highly ordered environment less than easy to appreciate. Nonetheless, it has a friendly atmosphere, and is not inferior to other Australian cities, merely different.

Useful Addresses

Australian Capital Territory, www.act.gov.au.
Business ACT, Nara Centre, 1 Constitution Avenue, Canberra, ACT 2600;
☎1800-244 650; fax 02-6207 0033; www.business.gateway.act.gov.au.

NEW SOUTH WALES (NSW)

Capital: Sydney.
Area: 309,572 square miles (802,000 square km) = 3.25 times the size of the UK.
Total area of Australia: 10%.
Climate: The mean January temperatures along the coast are usually between 46°F (8°C) and 69°F (21°C), but 71°F (22°C) at Sydney. The plateaux are about 39°F (4°C) cooler and the temperatures in the plains increase in direct relation to the distance from the sea. Temperatures at the Queensland border are about 80°F (27°C) to 87°F (31°C). The maximum temperature in July is 62°F (17°C) and the minimum is 46°F (8°C).

New South Wales is probably the Australian state most visited by tourists and business people, and is the state which receives most international publicity. This is largely due to its spectacular capital city, Sydney, which played host to the Olympic Games in 2000. There is, however, so much more to New South Wales than Sydney, and it is well worth venturing beyond the city limits to explore its diverse regions.

New South Wales is bordered to the north by Queensland, to the east by South Australia and to the south by Victoria. The Australian Capital Territory lies wholly contained in the southeast corner of New South Wales. From Sydney, it is 719 miles (1,157 km) west to Broken Hill, almost on the South Australian border, 564 miles (908 km) north to Tweed Heads which borders Queensland, and 309 miles (498 km) south to Eden, the last sizeable town before Victoria. Within these extremes lie mountain ranges, beaches, fertile farmland, rainforests and arid desert.

The Blue Mountains, 62 miles (100 km) west of Sydney, is a national park containing some of the most breathtaking scenery in the world. Standing at one of the numerous lookouts it is possible to survey hundreds of miles of unbroken, uninhabited bush and to view the immense unusual rock formations at Echo Point known as 'The Three Sisters'. The area was home to Aboriginal people at least 14,000 years ago and they have left their mark in the numerous rock carvings and cave paintings. The rugged 617,762-acre (250,000 ha) park is composed mainly of sandstone which has been eroded over the ages by rivers and creeks, to form dramatic valleys and sheer escarpments.

Approximately 93 miles (150 km) north of Sydney lies the main wine producing region of New South Wales, Hunter Valley. The Valley is divided into two distinct regions, the Lower and the Upper Hunter areas. Cessnock, 113 miles (183 km) from Sydney, is the centre of the Lower Hunter region and was originally founded on the coal-mining industry. The area produces some of the state's best wines and famous wineries include McWilliams, Mount Pleasant, Lindemans, Hungerford Hill, Tyrells and Brokenwood. One hundred kilometres further to the northwest is the smaller and less well-known Lower Hunter, home of the renowned Rosemount Estate.

Muswellbrook is the centre of this region and is known for its coal and agriculture.

To the southeast of the state lie the Snowy Mountains, less than a three-hour drive from Canberra in the ACT. Thredbo is a popular ski resort which has hosted various World Cup Ski events, and it is possible to take a chair lift to the top of Crackenback and then hike up Australia's highest mountain, Mount Kosciusko which, at 7,328 feet (2,241 metres), is less than half the height of Mont Blanc in France. On the northern side of Mt. Kosciusko, in Perisher Valley, lie two of the most popular ski resorts, Perisher and Smiggins Holes. This is Australia's 'alpine country' that, surprisingly, contains more snow-covered area than Switzerland. Instead of pine trees and alpine scenes be prepared for ghostly eucalypts silhouetted against the snow. The Australian ski season runs from June to October and the snow is usually best between late July and mid-September. Mount Kosciusko is located at the heart of the Kosckiusko National Park, which contains 1,554,290 acres (629,000 ha) of rugged moorland, glacial lakes, caves and the source of the Murray River, Australia's largest waterway. There are more than 200 species of birds here, and an abundance of wildlife including kangaroos, possums and wombats. The Snowy Mountains support seven hydroelectric stations which supply a large proportion of the state's power grid.

The Murray River rises in the Great Dividing Range and flows for more than 1,553 miles (2,500 km), forming the border between Victoria and New South Wales. From Wentworth, in the far west of New South Wales, the Murray continues through South Australia and veers south, flowing into Lake Alexandrina and to the ocean. The river is used extensively for irrigation and is crucial to the region's agricultural industries. One of the state's most important agricultural districts is the Riverina which lies along the northern borderlands of the Murray River. Crops as diverse as rice, vegetables and citrus fruits are grown here, and cattle and merino sheep are also important. Albury is at the heart of this fertile region and its population is approximately 42,000. It is a National Growth Centre, the aim of which has been to encourage the decentralisation of industry from major state capitals. Wentworth is important as the heart of the region's irrigation scheme and both the citrus and avocado growing areas.

Broken Hill is one of the state's most easterly settlements, lying almost on the border with South Australia. It is isolated and remote, but nearly 25,000 people live here and it is famous for its silver mines and the Royal Flying Doctor Services. The mining industry has survived, and silver, lead and zinc are still mined in significant quantities. In the northern desert region of the state, along the border with Queensland, lies the town of Lightning Ridge, famous for its opal mines. Over 1,000 people from 30 different nations are based at Lightning Ridge, and manage to survive the extreme weather conditions and limited water supply (artesian bore water is the only kind available here) to mine the fields for the highly prized black opals. Visitors are allowed to tour various mines and to *fossick* (prospect) for the gems.

New South Wales' north coastal region is one of the state's favourite holiday destinations, and the region contains spectacular surf beaches, lakes, rivers, small coastal towns and beautiful inland scenery. Byron Bay, Australia's most easterly point, is considered to be the unspoilt gem of the New South Wales coast. Cape Byron is home to many people who prefer an alternative lifestyle away from the rat-race of the busy cities. Coffs Harbour, closer to Sydney, is a popular harbour and port town, with many top-class tourist resorts. There is plenty of good surf, and it is also a famous yachting centre. Bananas are grown in this semi-tropical area and the nearby Dorrigo National Park contains rainforest, waterfalls and lush vegetation.

Inland from Coffs is the Nymboida River, a popular spot for white-water rafting. Grafton is situated in this area, some 40 miles (65 km) inland, and is at the centre of a region which specialises in both dairy and sugarcane industries.

New South Wales also controls Lord Howe Island and originally owned Norfolk Island, although this is now a Territory of Australia. Lord Howe Island is a tiny island, 6 miles (11 km) long and 1.7 miles (2.8 km) at its widest point, some 435 miles (700 km) northeast of Sydney. It has a population of around 300 and was listed as a World Heritage area in 1982 because of its soaring volcanic peaks, the world's most southerly coral reef, exceptional bird life and scenic beauty. Lord Howe Island was first sighted in 1788 and was named after the first Lord of the Admiralty. The numbers of visitors to the island is strictly controlled to protect it from becoming overrun by crowds, and the island's 23 miles (37 km) coastline provides plenty of opportunity for fishing, coral reef viewing and relaxation. Norfolk Island is a much larger and more isolated island, 994 miles (1,600 km) to the east of Sydney. It was first discovered by Captain Cook in 1774 and later became a penal settlement for the colony of New South Wales between 1788 and 1855. Norfolk Island was the home of the Pitcairn Islanders who included descendants of the *Bounty* mutineers. There are still many Pitcairn descendants on the island who speak 'Norfolk', a curious mixture of Tahitian and English. The island has a population of about 2,000, most of whom are involved in either tourism or agriculture.

Sydney. Sydney has a population of nearly 4.1 million people, around 60% of the state's total population of 6.6 million. The second largest city in New South Wales is Newcastle, on the northern coast 105 miles (170 km) from Sydney, with a population of 350,000, and Wollongong, some 51 miles (82 km) south of Sydney, is the third urban area. The city of Sydney is open and spacious, surrounded on three sides by national parks and on the fourth by 37 miles (60 km) of beautiful and quite spectacular coastline. Sydney Harbour, on which the city is built, has 149 miles (240 km) of foreshore, much of which remains as it was when the First Fleet made its initial investigative journey up the waterway in 1788. Sydney has been described as 'the best address on earth', and although Sydney has its share of the problems associated with big cities, such as pollution, ugly industrial areas, traffic congestion, homelessness, unemployment, drugs and crime, one still cannot help but feel that Sydney is perhaps even more beautiful now than it was over 100 years ago. The Sydney Harbour Bridge and the Opera House, which are the most dramatic features of the Harbour, were opened in 1932 and 1973 respectively.

Sydney is one of Australia's most historical cities, as it was into Botany Bay, just south of Sydney, that Captain Cook sailed in the *Endeavour* in 1770. In May 1787, the First Fleet of 1,044 people, including 759 convicts (191 of whom were women) set sail from Portsmouth and arrived in Australia eight months later. Unimpressed with Botany Bay's windswept barrenness, the Fleet moved north in search of a more suitable site and six days later the ships arrived at what became Port Jackson, described by Captain Phillip as 'the finest harbour in the world'. Even though Port Jackson was superior to Botany Bay, the first years of the colony were harsh, as crops failed and the anticipated supply ships failed to arrive. However, the colony managed to survive and slowly, began to grow. Captain Phillip was replaced by Governor Macquarie, known as the 'Father of Australia', in 1810 and over the next 11 years streets were laid down and fine new buildings erected. Convict transportation to New South Wales continued until 1840, but free settlers began to arrive from 1819. From 1831 to 1850 more than 200,000 government-assisted migrants streamed into the colony to begin a new life as far away as possible from the urban nightmare of Victorian Britain. During the 1850s, a gold rush brought a new influx of settlers which continued until the end of the 19th century, and by 1925 the area around Sydney had a population in excess of one million.

Sydney today boasts Australia's most influential Central Business District (CBD) and most national and international businesses choose to have their major Australian offices in Sydney. Darling Harbour houses the Sydney Aquarium, Chinese Gardens, Powerhouse Museum and the National Maritime Museum, and is linked to the CBD by monorail. The Rocks is Sydney's most historic area, and much of it has been restored to its former glory. Doyle's Restaurant at the foot of the Rocks is a haven for the seafood connoisseur, with fresh fish a house speciality. There are many beaches around the Sydney area, the most famous of which are, perhaps, Bondi (grossly overrated) and Manly (slightly overrated). The most beautiful, unspoilt and uncrowded beaches lie further north and south of the city. The northern coastal suburbs are particularly beautiful as the coastline is made up of rugged headlands interspersed with long sandy beaches. Most beaches have seawater swimming pools naturally carved out of the rocky headland, which provide safe, sheltered swimming areas. The beaches of Dee Why, Long Reef, Collaroy, Narrabeen, Newport, Avalon, Whale Beach and Palm Beach are among the most beautiful Sydney beaches.

Sydney is a cultural centre and is home to the Australian Opera and the Sydney Symphony Orchestra, both based at the Opera House. Standing tickets for the opera can be bought for as little as $25, and many agents sell last-minute tickets at half price. Sydney is also home to the Museum of Contemporary Art and the Sydney Observatory. The city's Gay and Lesbian Mardi Gras is an international crowd-puller, as the country's gay, bisexual and transvestite population take to the streets in bizarre and outlandish costumes. The Queen Victoria Building houses many chic boutiques and plenty of bargain shops, but better bargains can be found at Paddy's Markets in Paddington.

In 1988 a re-enactment of the First Fleet entering Sydney Harbour was staged as part of the bicentennial celebrations and the view included a bank-to-bank flotilla of small pleasure boats, the old 'Coathanger' and Centrepoint Tower in the background, in front of which stood the Sydney Opera House, the sun gleaming off the millions of highly polished white tiles that make up its shell. Mark Twain described the harbour as 'the darling of Sydney and the wonder of the world.' There is no doubt that Sydney Harbour is stunning and the city is an exciting place in which to live. Some Australians do, however, tire of the bright lights and relatively fast pace and prefer to move to quieter, calmer and perhaps safer cities.

New South Wales has many special events during the calendar year. The Festival of Sydney usually takes place in January, as does the New South Wales Tennis Open and the Country Music Festival. The Sydney Royal Easter Show usually occurs between March and April, and the Sydney Film Festival takes place in June, as does the Darling Harbour Jazz Festival. The Rugby League Grand Final is held in Sydney in September. Other major state sporting events include the Tooheys 1000 Bathurst Touring Car Race at Bathurst in October, and the Sydney to Hobart yacht race which commences on Boxing Day every year.

Sydney is one of the most expensive areas in Australia in which to live, but many of the outer suburbs and regional areas are less expensive. Rent in Sydney is very high by Australian standards, but is still markedly lower than current rental rates in London or New York for comparable properties. The state's unemployment rate is the lowest in Australia. Major employment sectors in the city are commerce (banking, insurance and finance), retail, manufacturing, hospitality and tourism. Agriculture and tourism are the biggest employment sectors in regional areas.

Education and health services are exceptionally good in New South Wales, which is home to many large and excellent tertiary educational institutions. New South Wales currently attracts more new settlers than any other state/territory.

Useful Addresses

New South Wales Government, www.nsw.gov.au.

Department of State and Regional Development, Level 44, Grosvenor Place, 225 George Street, PO Box N818, Sydney, NSW 1220; ☎02-9228 3111; fax 02-9228 3626; www.business.nsw.gov.au.

New South Wales Government Trade and Investment Office, The Australia Centre, Strand, London WC2 B4LG; ☎020-7887 5871; fax 020-7887 5246; e-mail invest@nswq.co.uk.

QUEENSLAND (QLD)

Capital: Brisbane.
Area: 1,035,000 square miles (1,725,000 square km) = seven times the size of the UK.
Total area of Australia: 22.48%.
Coastline: 4,440 miles (7,400 km).
Climate: In Brisbane, the average daily maximum in January is 84°F (29°C) and in June is 69°F (21°C). In Cairns, the average daily maximums for the same months are 87°F (31°C) and 78° (26°C).

Queensland is Australia's second largest state, but has the largest habitable area defined by rainfall. Queensland's habitable area is a staggering 599,999 square miles (1,554,000 square km). By contrast, a mere 57% of Western Australia is considered habitable (555,984 square miles/1,440,000 square km). Queensland is situated in the north-eastern corner of Australia and it is bounded by the Northern Territory to the west, South Australia to the southwest and New South Wales to the south. It stretches from the temperate and densely populated southeast to the tropical and sparsely populated Cape York Peninsula in the north.

Queensland epitomises the marketed image of Australia overseas. With the Great Barrier Reef, the Whitsunday Islands, World Heritage areas such as the Daintree Rainforest and Fraser Island, and a beautiful climate, it is not surprising that Queensland is one of the most popular tourist destinations in Australia. Queensland is known as the 'Sunshine State' and Queenslanders are affectionately called 'banana-benders'. They are also considered to be the rednecks of Australia, and as such are renowned for their very conservative political outlook.

Like most of Australia, Queensland is rich in natural resources. Its four major products are sugar, meat, grains and wool, and the growing areas are spread throughout the state. Australia is the world's second largest exporter of raw cane sugar, and 95% of Australia's production comes from Queensland. The State also contains vast mineral deposits, including coal, bauxite, gold, copper, lead, zinc, silver and magnesite. Besides agricultural and mining industries, Queensland's biggest industries are manufacturing and tourism. Queensland's economic growth is significantly higher than the national average, and tourism accounts for 10% of Gross State Product.

For more than 20 years, Queensland has experienced a consistently higher rate of population growth than the national average. Queensland's population growth can be attributed to overseas immigration, natural increase, and most importantly, to interstate migration. Queensland, it seems, is the place where most Australians want to live, and more Australians are moving to Queensland than to any other state or territory. Popular opinion has it that more and more Australians are moving to Queensland to retire. Census figures from the Australian Bureau of Statistics show that 31% of Queensland's population lies in the 25-44 year age range, however, it is predicted that by 2021 at least 43% of the population will be over 45.

Queensland's population is much more decentralised than that of any other state. The population of around 3.7 million is scattered over major regional centres such as the Gold Coast, Bundaberg, Toowoomba, Rockhampton, Longreach, Townsville, Cairns and Mount Isa, as well as Brisbane, which is home to 1.6 million people.

The Queensland Government has for many years had a reputation for ultra-conservativism. For most of those years the state was under the leadership of the Premier, Sir Joh Bjelke-Peterson, and became notorious for its repressive and racist attitudes. Vestiges of this xenophobia remain, and Queensland is the seedbed of the racist One Nation Party, until recently led by Pauline Hanson. Antipathy is particularly directed towards the Japanese who have invested large sums in Queensland property, however, most Queenslanders recognise that Japanese investments are tourists play a significant part in promoting Queensland's healthy economy. The Queensland Government has suffered from allegations of corruption at the highest levels. When the Labour Party was elected in September 1992, its leader, the Hon. W K Goss, became the first Labour Premier in Queensland since 1957. The new government represented the desire of Queenslanders to end the corruption and hypocritical moralising of the old government, and stood for a fresh start.

Queensland's health and education services are broadly comparable with the national standard. Brisbane is home to the University of Queensland and to Australia's first private university, Bond University, established by entrepreneur Alan Bond. The multi-millionaire Western Australian, after whom it is named, served a three-year prison sentence for illegal business ventures and was released in March 2000; however, the university that bears his name is none the less regarded as a centre of excellence.

Most Queensland residents own their own home, and the high standard of living combined with an extraordinary natural environment makes Queensland a popular choice for settlement.

Useful Addresses

Queensland Government, www.qld.gov.au.
State Development and Innovation, Floor 21, 111 George Street, Brisbane, QLD 4000; ☎07-3225 1915; fax 07-3224 8661; www.sd.qld.gov.au.
Queensland Government Trade and Investment Office (Europe), Queensland House, 392 Strand, London WC2R OLZ; ☎020-7836 1333; fax 020-7420 8770.

GETTING THERE

These days, if you want to get to Australia, you have to fly. Qantas is Australia's national carrier, and is legendary for its outstanding safety record, although its reputation for quality and service allows it to charge premium fares. More than 30 international airlines fly direct to Australia, usually to Perth or Sydney from destinations all round the world. The flight time from Europe to Australia, depending on your route, point of departure, and destination, is likely to be between 19 and 26 hours. From the United States' west coast the flight to Australia takes around 14 hours.

Fares to Australia vary dramatically according to the seasons, and are also affected by special events, such as Christmas. Prices skyrocket in early December, for example, but drop dramatically on the 26th of December, so delaying your departure by a few days may save you the cost of a couple of internal flights once you arrive in Australia. The cheapest time to fly to Australia is during the Low Season, from March to June (precise dates differ from airline to airline). Mid Season (or Shoulder), from July to November, and during February, is somewhat more expensive; and Peak Season, from December to January, is really best avoided from a financial point of view, unless you can only travel at that time. Once you have decided when to travel, you should try and book as early as possible – seats fill up very fast, and flights during the Australian summer may be fully booked as early as July.

Scheduled flights by various national carriers will usually offer the possibility of a stopover in their home country, which allows a welcome break in the arduous journey at the same time as providing a cheap exotic holiday. If flying with Malaysian Airlines, for example, you may be offered a stopover in Kuala Lumpur as well as a free internal flight, so that if you choose, you can fly to the resorts of Penang or Langkawi for a few days. Return fares are usually valid for 12 months, and travel agents are required to request proof of residency if you wish to purchase a one-way ticket. An open-jaw return ticket will allow you to enter Australia via one port and leave from another, however, this type of ticket is likely to be more expensive.

Charter flights, operated by tour companies rather than airlines, are usually the cheapest way to travel to Australia. They won't get you there in much style, but they are ideal for travellers on a budget. There are a number of websites (www. cheapflights.com; www.deckchair.com; www.expedia.com to name just a few) that provide details on last minute and budget flight deals from locations worldwide. In the UK bargains can also be found on teletext.

Currently, you can expect to pay around £500+ for a London to Sydney return flight; and from US$800 for a return flight from Los Angeles and from US$900 if you are starting your journey in New York. The disadvantage of charter flights is that they generally operate on a short-term return basis, so that you are likely to have to return two weeks after arrival. Flights book out very early, and stopovers are not permitted. Many airlines also offer savings on Australian internal flights once you have booked with them.

Insurance

Working travellers and those on speculative job finding trips to Australia are strongly advised to take out comprehensive travel insurance. Insurers offering reasonable and flexible premiums include:

Atlas Insurance, 37 King's Exchange, Tileyard Road, London N7 9AH; ☎020-7609 5000; fax 020-7209 5011; www.atlasdirect.net.

Columbus Direct Travel Insurance, 17 Devonshire Square, London EC2M 4SQ; ☎020-7422 5505; fax 020-7375 0274; www.columbusdirect.net.

The Travel Insurance Agency, Suite 2, Percy Mews, 755B High Road, North Finchley, London N12 8JY; ☎020-8446 5414; fax 020-8446 5417; e-mail info@travelinsurers.com; www.travelinsurers.com.

Worldwide Travel Insurance Services Ltd, The Business Centre, 1-7 Commercial Road, Paddock Wood, Tonbridge, Kent TN12 6YT; ☎01892-833338; fax 01892-837744; e-mail sales@worldwideinsure.com; www.worldwideinsure.com

Discount Fare Specialists for Australia & New Zealand

STA Travel, 6 Wrights Lane, London SW8 6TA; ☎0870-160 6070; www.sta-travel.co.uk. Specialises in student and youth travel with more than 450 branches worldwide. Offer budget to luxury accommodation, adventure tours, round the world flights, package holidays, city breaks, and insurance.

Austravel, 152 Brompton Road, Knightsbridge London, SW3 1HX; ☎0870-166 2140; e-mail knightsbridge@austravel.com; www.austravel.net. Austravel also has offices in Manchester, Leeds, Edinburgh, Bristol, Bournemouth and Birmingham, and produces a fares guide which gives price comparisons between all the major airlines.

Bridge the World, 45-47 Chalk Farm Road, Camden Town, London NW1 8AT; ☎0870-814 4400; e-mail info@bridgetheworld.com; www.bridgetheworld.com.

Cresta World Travel, Cresta House, 32 Victoria Street, Altrincham, Cheshire WA14 1ET; ☎0870-013 0303; fax 0161-929 7951; www.crestaworldtravel.co.uk.

Platinum Travel Centre, 40 Earls Court Road, Kensington, London W8 6EJ; ☎020-7937 5122.

Travelbag plc., 3-5 High Street, Alton, Hampshire, GU34 1TL; ☎0870-814 4440; fax 01420-82133; www.travelbag.co.uk; and 373-375 Strand, London WC2R OJE; ☎0870-814 4444; fax 020-7497 2923. Travelbag also has offices in other parts of the UK including Nottingham, Cheshire and Solihull.

The Australian Youth Hostels Association, Level 3, 10 Mallett Street, Camperdown, NSW 2050; ☎02-9565 1699; fax 02-9565 1325; e-mail yha@yha.org.au; www.yha.com.au. Offers complete travel packages including accommodation and 12 months coach travel. Offices in Sydney, Darwin, Brisbane, Adelaide, Hobart, Melbourne, and Northbridge.

RESIDENCE AND
ENTRY REGULATIONS

CHAPTER SUMMARY

○ **Immigration Programme.** Australia's immigration programme is managed with quotas and categories regularly changed to adapt to the needs of the nation.

- ○ In 2003-2004, there were 40,600 Family Stream places and 63,300 in the Skilled Stream migration programme; 12,000 entered Australia under the Humanitarian programme.

- ○ Immigration has been reduced considerably since the 1980s when the yearly total was 140,000.

- ○ In 2004-2005, there are likely to be 120,000 places compared to 114,362 selections in 2003-2004 in the immigration programme.

- ○ Applying to live in Australia can be a time-consuming and expensive exercise.

- ○ It is possible to use a migration consultancy to help you through the procedures.

○ **Tourist Visa.** Three- six- and 12-month visas cost $65.

- ○ You can apply for a Visitor's visa on the Internet or at some travel agents.

- ○ Aged parents and relatives of Australian residents may be eligible for permanent entry into Australia under certain conditions.

The Current Position

Immigration has recently become a contentious policy area in Australia with many people reacting to economic stringencies by calling for an end to Australia's migration programmes. The rationale for this position (that 'foreigners take our jobs') has been proved to be completely erroneous. This has not prevented anti-migration activists, generally operating from a distinctly racist platform, from continuing to dominate debate on the issue in the media. In response, the government has stressed its commitment to Australia as a 'deeply tolerant, fair-minded and generous society' and outlined the benefits of immigration in a recent booklet, *Dispelling the myths about immigration* (available from the Department of Immigration and Multicultural and Indigenous Affairs, or in electronic form at www.immi.gov. au/kits/the_facts/booklet.htm). The current government recognises that migrants have made, and continue to make, an enormous contribution to Australian society, bringing new ideas, technologies and skills to the nation's economy and skill base. In the context of the globalisation of Australia's economy, migrants' awareness of the nuances of international cultures provides an important asset for its international and domestic competitiveness. Migration to Australia is dependent on your ability to meet the migration criteria of the day and Australia's interest and needs. The migration programme is carefully managed, with annual quotas imposed on each area of temporary and permanent residency category after extensive assessment of the current economic circumstances. Migrants are chosen from two broad categories – Family Stream and Skill Stream – while the Humanitarian Program caters for refugees in need of resettlement. In 2003-2004, there were 40,600 Family Stream places, 63,300 Skill Stream, and 12,000 available in the Humanitarian Program, which offers entry to refugees of civil war and human rights abuse. The government's intention is that migration should become more focused on the intake of skilled migrants, although it retains a commitment to bona fide immediate family migrants. During 2002-2003, at least 58% of new migrants came from the Skill Stream category.

Although racist polemics in the popular press would suggest otherwise, Australia operates an entirely non-discriminatory immigration programme. It is selective on the basis of skills, age and language ability, but is open to anyone in any part of the world, regardless of their country of birth, ethnic origin, race, sex or religion. Figures from the Australian Bureau of Statistics show that from June 2001 to June 2002, the number of settlers arriving in Australia, by country of birth, were UK 9.8%, China 7.5%, South Africa 6.4%, and North America 1.9%. Between 1965 and 1970, 47% of settler arrivals to Australia were born in the United Kingdom and Ireland; however, in the five years to June 2000, the United Kingdom and Ireland contributed 12% of settlers to Australia. Applying to live in Australia can be a time-consuming and expensive exercise, and a number of migration consultancies offer services which can help prospective applicants with the procedures. The Australian consular service advises prospective visa applicants that although such consultancies cannot 'get round the system' and guarantee success, a reputable firm may ease the pressure and provide valuable advice to those unfamiliar with the migration application process. Migrants, either permanent or temporary, must undergo comprehensive health examinations and provide evidence of good character.

Useful Address

The Emigration Group Ltd., 7 Heritage Court, Lower Bridge Street, Chester, Cheshire CH1 1RD; offices also in London and Manchester; ☎0845-2302526; fax 01244-342288; e-mail info@TEGltd.co.uk; www.emigration.uk.com. Provides full assistance with applications for residence in all categories (general skilled, family, retirement and business categories) and/or work visas.

All migration agents and consultants charge for their services.

Useful Publication

Australian Outlook, published monthly by Consyl Publishing Ltd. (3 Buckhurst Road, Bexhill-on-Sea, East Sussex TN40 1QF; ☎01424-223111; fax 01424-224992; www.consylpublishing.co.uk). Aimed specifically at migrants, this publication is a useful way of keeping up with Australian migration policy and entry regulations. In the UK six issues cost £12.00 and 12 issues £16.50; in Europe six issues cost £15.00 and 12 issues £21.20; elsewhere six issues cost £18.00 and 12 cost £29.90.

Entry for Australian Citizens

Travellers holding an Australian passport, a New Zealand passport, or a British passport with Australian permanent residency are exempted from the requirement to obtain a visa prior to entry into Australia. All other travellers, whether making a short-term visit as a tourist or for business purposes, or anticipating a longer stay on a working holiday or as a migrant, must obtain the appropriate visa from their nearest Australian mission before leaving their home country. Visitors who arrive in Australia without a visa are immediately deported and are held responsible for any costs arising from their deportation. If you are in doubt over whether you are an Australian or New Zealand citizen, or whether you have an entitlement to permanent residency, the Australian High Commission, which is responsible for all visa and migration queries, will be able to advise you. In general, if you wish to visit Australia as a tourist you will need a Visitor's Visa; if you are planning to go on a working holiday or to retire, you will need a Temporary Residence Visa in the appropriate category; and if you are hoping to settle permanently in Australia, you will need to be accepted as an immigrant and be granted permanent residence.

Visitor's Visa

To visit Australia as a tourist, you will require a Visitor's visa obtainable from the Australian High Commission and many travel agents. This form can also now be downloaded as a pdf.file from the Internet at www.immi.gov.au/allforms/index.htm. Visitors' visas are classed as either 'short-stay' (three months) or 'long-stay' (up to one year), are multiple entry visas and are valid for 12 months from the date of issue. The application fee for the short- and long-stay visitor's visas is a non-refundable $65 if lodged outside Australia. Travellers visiting Australia to conduct business of a short-term nature which is deemed not to disadvantage local residents, should also apply for a Visitor's visa. Retired parents of Australian residents are entitled to a Visitor's visa valid for a period of 12 months. In order to be eligible for this extended visa, you need to provide proof of funds sufficient to support yourself during the entire period of the visit. If you intend staying with family or friends for any or all of this time, the level of funds required will be assessed at a lower level than that for a tourist.

The three-month Visitor visa can be applied for by post, with a processing time of approximately three weeks. Enclose a large, stamped, self-addressed envelope for the return of your documents. Applications can be made in person at the Australian High Commission in London, the Australian Embassy in Washington and from Australian Government offices elsewhere. The Australian High Commission in London can be very busy, especially from September to February, and you should expect a long wait; Mondays to Wednesdays are generally the busiest days.

It is possible to extend a three-month visitor's visa to one of six months duration while in Australia, however, if you wish to stay longer in Australia, it is most important to extend the visa before it expires. The Department of Immigration and Multicultural and Indigenous Affairs will deport immediately any applicant who holds an expired visa. You must leave the country on a valid visa and renew it overseas before returning, although some travellers following this procedure have been refused re-entry into Australia despite leaving Australia on a valid visa and renewing their visas in New Zealand or Singapore.

Electronic Travel Authority. The Visitor's visa has now been pretty much superseded by Australia's state-of-the-art 'Electronic Travel Authority' (ETA) system, which is currently available to passport holders from 34 countries and locations including British and US citizens, and most citizens of EU countries. The ETA system was introduced in 1996 and is an 'invisible', electronically-stored authority for short-term travel to Australia which can be issued in less than 10 seconds at the time of making travel bookings. It is claimed that the ETA is currently the most advanced and streamlined travel authorisation system in the world, permitting visitors to be processed in seconds on arrival at their destination. At this end, the advantages include an end to form-filling, queues and embassy visits: the whole process is completed on the spot. The ETA system can be accessed by 300,000 travel agents worldwide, and more than 75 airlines. A worldwide trial of Internet access to the ETA system was announced in May 2001 which enables tourists and business travellers intending to visit Australia for three months or less to apply on-line at www.eta.immi.gov.au at a cost of $20 (payable by credit card only). More than 17 million travellers have chosen to visit Australia on ETAs, which now account for around 85% of all tourist and short-term business visas issued worldwide. There are three different types of ETA and travellers should make sure that they obtain the one appropriate to their needs: tourists and those visiting family or friends for a period of three months or less need a Short Validity Tourist ETA, while business visitors need a Long Validity Business ETA, or a Short Validity Business ETA. It has recently been reported that some British travel agents are charging their clients to issue an ETA. The amount of work involved in supplying this visa can in no way justify this charge, and travellers should be alert to this potential rip-off.

TEMPORARY RESIDENCE

Visitors intending to enter Australia temporarily for the purpose of work or otherwise need to obtain a temporary residence visa. There are currently 21 different temporary residence sub-classes which are issued according to the type of activity the applicant will undertake in Australia. The temporary residence programme is designed to allow people from overseas to come to Australia for specific purposes, which are expected to provide some benefit to Australia. The programme consists of three streams: economic, social and cultural, and international relations. During 2002-2003, more than 170,392 temporary resident visas were issued – 47,382 skilled visas (economic), 19,312 social and cultural, and 103,698 international relations.

The categories for temporary residence visas are as follows:

ECONOMIC STREAM

Business Entry. Allows employers to recruit skilled personnel from overseas for a stay of up to four years.

Educational. Allows entry of staff to fill academic, teaching and research positions in Australian educational institutions, which cannot be filled from within the Australian labour market. A letter of appointment is required.

Temporary Medical Practitioner. Allows entry of suitably qualified medical practitioners, sponsored by Government, community bodies, or prospective employers, which satisfy labour market requirements. There is a strong focus on providing service to rural and remote communities.

SOCIAL AND CULTURAL STREAM

Entertainment. Allows entry of actors, entertainers, models and their associated personnel for specific engagements or events in Australia. Visa assessment will take into account the need to protect the employment of Australians in the industry.

Media and Film Staff. Allows entry of foreign correspondents to represent overseas news media organisations in Australia, and television or film crew members or photographers, including actors and support staff, involved in the production of films, documentaries or advertising commercials in Australia which are not being produced for the Australian market.

Sport. Allows entry of amateur and professional sportspeople, including officials and their support staff, to engage in competition with Australian residents and to improve general sporting standards through high calibre competition and training.

Religious Worker. Allows entry of religious workers, including ministers, priests and spiritual leaders to serve the spiritual needs of people of their faith in Australia.

Family Relationship. Allows secondary school-age children to have an extended holiday with relatives or close family friends who are Australian citizens or residents.

Retirement. Allows for people over 55 an extended temporary stay in Australia. Individuals can work for up to twenty hours per week.

Public Lecturer. Allows entry of specialists and recognised experts to deliver public lectures in Australia.

Visiting Academic. Allows entry of people as Visiting Academics at Australian educational and research institutions, with the intention that their presence will contribute to the sharing of research knowledge. A letter of invitation is required and you may not receive a salary from the host institution.

INTERNATIONAL RELATIONS STREAM

Working Holiday. Aims to promote international understanding by giving young people the opportunity to holiday in Australia, while working to supplement their funds. The Working Holiday visa has numerous conditions attached which are explained in the section **Working Holiday** below.

Foreign Government Agency Staff. Intended for foreign government officials conducting business or teaching duties on behalf of their government, where that government has no diplomatic or official status in Australia.

Exchange. Allows visitors to come to Australia to broaden their work experience and skills under reciprocal arrangements by which Australian residents are granted similar opportunities abroad. Includes people seeking entry under certain bilateral exchange agreements. A letter of invitation is required from the organisation offering the position.

Special Program. Intended for people visiting under approved programmes for the purpose of broadening their experience and skills. It is generally used for youth exchanges and programmes such as the Churchill Fellowship. A letter of support is required from the organisation.

Diplomatic. For temporary entry of people wanting to travel to Australia in a diplomatic or official capacity. Those who are eligible should apply for this visa regardless of their intended period of stay.

Domestic Worker (Diplomatic/Consular). Allows entry of private domestic staff for work in the households of diplomatic and consular staff posted to Australia where Australian Department of Foreign Affairs and Trade (DFAT) supports the entry.

Domestic Worker (Overseas Executive). Allows the entry of domestic staff of certain holders of visas in class 457 long-stay temporary business entry. A visa of this category will only be granted where it can be shown that the entry of such staff is necessary for the proper discharge of representational duties.

Occupational Trainees. Allows entry of persons for occupational training appropriate to their background and/or employment history, for the acquisition or up-grading of skills useful to their home country. A nomination must be provided unless the training is to be given by the Commonwealth of Australia.

Supported Dependent. Allows a temporary stay of dependents of either an Australian citizen or a holder of a permanent residence visa who is usually resident outside Australia and intends to remain temporarily in Australia. A letter of support is required from the Australian citizen/permanent residence visa holder.

Expatriate. Allows a temporary stay of certain spouses or dependents of persons employed by international companies in remote locations near Australia, such as Southeast Asia, the South Pacific or Papua New Guinea.

Professional Development. For temporary entry of groups of professionals, manager and government officials from overseas who are seeking to enhance their professional/managerial skills by taking part in tailored training programmes designed by an Australian sponsoring organisation.

Health and Character Check. People who wish to enter Australia on the temporary residence visas listed above must meet the normal health and character requirements for entry. Some applicants may be asked to have a medical examination before a visa will be granted. In most cases, if you have your application for temporary residence approved, you will then be granted a multiple entry visa for the period of the approved stay.

Re-entry Visa. If you need a further re-entry visa, you will need to apply to an office of the Department of Immigration and Multicultural and Indigenous Affairs (DIMIA). Fees for temporary residence visas are currently £170. Temporary residence visa processing times are currently around three to six weeks.

Students

Australia's student visa programme provides for the entry of overseas students who wish to undertake full-time study in registered courses in Australia. In 2003-2004, visas granted to overseas students totalled 171,616, a 5.6% increase on the previous year. Of these 10,723 were granted to students from the USA, a 2% increase and second only to China as the major source of student visa grants. Students have the right to work up to 20 hours per week while their course is in session, however, the intention is that income derived from working in Australia should be a supplement to the main source of funding, and applicants will need to produce evidence of their financial resources when applying for a visa. There are seven subclasses of student visa:

Independent ELICOS. For overseas students undertaking an ELICOS (English Language Intensive Courses for Overseas Students) as a stand-alone course, and not as a prerequisite to commencing another course (for example, a degree course).

Schools. For overseas students undertaking a course of study at a primary school or a secondary school. This subclass is also for overseas school students participating in a formal registered secondary exchange programme. The period of exchange may vary from one month to one year.

Vocational Education and Training-VET. Covers certificate I, II, III and IV, Diploma, Advanced diploma and Advanced certificate.

Higher Education. Covers a Bachelor degree, Associate degree, Graduate certificate, and Graduate diploma.

Postgraduate Research. Covers a Masters degree by coursework or by research, and a Doctoral degree.

Non-award Foundation Studies/Other. Covers foundation, bridging or other courses that do not lead to the award of a degree, diploma or other formal award.

AusAID or Defence. Covers full-time study undertaken by AusAID- or Defence-sponsored students for the whole or part of an education or training course offered by an Australian education provider.

Student visas do not automatically provide for the holder to be granted permission to work in Australia. Students and their dependents are only able to apply for work rights once they arrive in Australia and the student has commenced their course of study. There is a charge of $50 made for this. Students may work full-time during holiday periods. Note that student visas are subject to cancellation if a student works in excess of his or her entitlements. Currently student visas take four weeks to process and cost $410. For more information see form 157A or 157E, available from DIMIA. The government now offers eVisa, a convenient electronic visa application as an alternative. You can lodge an application 24 hours a day and no more than four months before your course commences. As from November 2004, a new facility allows accompanying family members to be included in a student eVisa application lodged outside Australia.

Working Holiday

The Working Holiday programme aims to promote international understanding by giving young people the opportunity to experience the culture of another country. It allows working holiday-makers to enjoy an extended holiday by supplementing their travel funds through incidental employment, thus experiencing closer contact with local communities. Australia has reciprocal working holiday arrangements with Belgium, Canada, Cyprus, Denmark, Estonia, France, Germany, Hong Kong Special Administrative Region of the People's Republic of China, Finland, Ireland, Italy, Japan, Republic of Korea, Malta, the Netherlands, Norway, Sweden, Taiwan, and the United Kingdom. Although there are specific arrangements with these countries, the Australian working holiday scheme is applied globally, and applicants from other countries are considered where there might be a benefit both to the applicant and to Australia.

The Working Holiday visa is available to applicants between the ages of 18 and 30. Applicants may be either single or married, but must not have any dependent children. You must not have previously entered Australia on a Working Holiday visa and you will also need to meet health and character requirements and be outside Australia at the time of the visa being granted. The visa is valid for 12 months from the day of issue, and allows a stay of 12 months from date of entry into Australia.

When you apply for a Working Holiday visa, you must demonstrate that your main purpose in visiting Australia is to holiday, and that any work you expect to undertake will be solely to assist in supporting you while on vacation. You must have a good chance of finding temporary work, and may study or train for up to three months. You must also have a return ticket or sufficient funds for a return airfare, in addition to being able to demonstrate $5,000 in funds for your travels (or a parental guarantee for the same amount). A Working Holiday visa usually allows for multiple entry, which means that you may leave and re-enter the country as many times as you like (within the time restriction of your visa). When the visa is granted, ensure that it has been stamped 'multiple entry'. You cannot get an extension on a Working Holiday visa under any circumstances (though you can apply to change your visa status if you meet requirements), and must leave the country on or before the expiry date of your visa.

A limit (reviewed annually) may be imposed on the number of Australian Working Holiday visas granted. A number of factors influence the volume of applications for Working Holiday visas, such as the strength of various economies around the world, and the popularity of certain kinds of tourism. Some prospective working holiday-makers have suffered under the new 'capping' rules, and have had their application for a visa refused after paying for their travel. Travel agents who specialise in Australian travel suggest that one way of avoiding this is to plan to commence the working holiday shortly after the beginning of July, which is the beginning of the annual visa allocation period. Applications made at this time have a good chance of succeeding. In the period 2003-2004, 93,760 working holiday visas were granted. Of these 35,061 were granted to British citizens, 12,260 to Irish citizens, and 6,517 to Canadians.

Once in Australia, surveys show that most working holiday-makers find temporary or casual employment in farming, clerical and hospitality industries. Fruit picking, bartending, secretarial and clerical work obtained through temp agencies, and labouring are all popular options for travellers, and this work tends to be widely available on a seasonal basis. Most travellers, on average, experience three or four different jobs over the period of their visit, holding each for six to eight weeks at a time. The Working Holiday Maker scheme permits you to work for a maximum of three months for any one employer. If you are found to be working beyond the approved time limit you may have your visa cancelled. At present, Working Holiday visas cost $170 and processing takes about four to five weeks. Form 990i available from DIMIA contains additional information on the scheme. It is also now possible to apply directly through DIMIA's website for an electronic visa. Processing priority will be given to applications lodged in this way, while those lodged at an Australian mission abroad may take considerably longer.

Retirement

Retiring to Australia is a popular option for many people, particularly those with family connections there. Initially you must apply for the Temporary Residence Retirement visa (subclass 410). This visa does not officially entitle the applicant to permanent residence but in effect does allow you to stay indefinitely. If your visa is approved it will initially be granted for a period of four years, which may then be extended in two-year increments while in Australia. You will not have to demonstrate that you meet health and financial prerequisites on your subsequent applications for extension.

The Retirement visa is available both to single applicants, and to couples in a married or *de facto* relationship. One partner must be at least 55 years of age, be of good health and character and have comprehensive health insurance, realise that you will not be covered by Medicare or entitled to Australian security benefits, and have no dependents other than your spouse. Regulations now allow visa holders to undertake 20 hours of work each week. You must also be able to meet 'Funds transfer requirements' on the day you lodge your application. This means that you should have sufficient funds to maintain yourself (and your spouse/partner, if applicable) in Australia. You need to prove that you have capital for transfer of at least $870,000, or $800,000 if you have a non-dependent child permanently in Australia; or that you have a combination of capital for transfer of at least $350,000 and a pension or income, or further capital providing an income of at least $52,000 per annum, or $315,000 and a pension or other capital for investment to provide an income of more than $50,000, if you have a non-dependent child living permanently in Australia. If you need to sell a house to meet the funds transfer requirements, the Immigration Department requires that the sale be completed within 12 months of the date of your application. Approval of the visa takes approximately three to six months and costs $170.

Aged parents and relatives of Australian residents may also be eligible for entry under the Family Stream of Australia's migration programme. For more detailed coverage of visa and other issues relating to retirement in Australia, see the section on **Retirement** later in this book.

PERMANENT RESIDENCE (MIGRATION)

Most applications for permanent residency in Australia are dealt with under three categories: Family Stream Migration, which entails sponsorship by a relative resident in Australia; Skilled Stream Migration, requiring skills or outstanding abilities that will contribute to Australia's economy; and migration under the Humanitarian Program. Generally, a successful applicant for migration to Australia must meet the personal and occupational requirements of the category for which he or she is applying, be able to settle in Australia without undue cost or difficulty to the Australian community, and be of good health and character. In addition, successful applicants will need enough money to travel to and settle in Australia. In 2003-2004, 114,362 migrants were selected in the Migration Program. In 2004-2005, the likely outcome will be 120,000.

Family Stream Migration

Approximately 37% of the migrants entering Australia each year do so under the Family Stream of the Migration Programme. In 2003-2004, this amounted to 42,229 successful applications for entry, all of whom were sponsored by a close family member or fiancée with the right of permanent residence in Australia. Family Stream migrants are selected on the basis of their family relationship with their sponsor in Australia, and there is no test for skills or language ability as there is for Skilled Stream migrants; they are still required, however, to meet the requirements of health and character which are applied to all migrants. Family Stream applicants can be sponsored for migration (permanent residence) under four main categories: Partner, Child, Parent and Other Family:

PARTNER
Spouse. Issued to a husband, wife or *de facto* partner of the Australian sponsor. Since May 1997, it has been required that a *de facto* or interdependent partner of an Australian citizen or permanent resident must be able to demonstrate one year of co-habitation with the sponsor. The co-habitation requirement also applies to gay and lesbian partners of Australian sponsors, who should apply for an interdependency visa, but who otherwise are assessed in the same way as those applying for a spouse visa. In compelling cases, such as where a child of the relationship exists, the co-habitation requirement may be waived.

Prospective Marriage. Fiancées overseas must apply for a 'prospective marriage' visa which is valid for nine months from the date of issue. They must travel to Australia, marry their sponsor, and apply to remain permanently during that period. It is a requirement that the parties to a prospective marriage have met and be known to each other in person. If all requirements are met, applicants will be granted a temporary visa, followed by a permanent visa if the relationship is still continuing at the end of two years.

Interdependent Partner. Interdependency visas are for people who have an interdependent relationship with an Australian citizen or permanent resident which demonstrates a genuine, continuing and mutual commitment to a shared life together. The application process is the same as for the spouse visa.

CHILD
Dependent Child. Parents are able to sponsor for migration their natural child, adopted, or stepchild of the Australian spouse. The granting of a dependent child visa must not prejudice the rights and interests of any person who has custody or guardianship or access to the child.

Adopted Child. A child adopted overseas and is under 18 years of age.

Orphan Relative. This visa permits the migration of orphans (as defined in the Migration Regulations), who are under 18 years old, unmarried and a relative of the sponsor.

PARENT
Parent. Applicants must be the parent of a person who is a settled Australian citizen or an Australian permanent resident.

Contributory parent. Applicants must be a parent of a child who is a settled Australian citizen or an Australian permanent resident. There are more visa places available in this category, however, the visa application charge is substantially higher. The parent must be an aged parent (pensioner) if normally resident in Australia.

OTHER FAMILY
Carer. To apply for a carer visa you must be willing and able to give substantial, continuing assistance to an Australian relative (or a member of their family) who has a medical condition that is causing physical, intellectual or sensory impairment of their ability to attend to the practical aspects of daily life. The need for assistance must be likely to continue for at least two years. You must be sponsored or nominated by the relative requiring care in Australia, who must be an Australian citizen, Australian permanent resident or eligible New Zealand citizen.

Aged Dependent Relative. To apply for an aged dependent relative visa you must be old enough to be granted an Australian age pension (for males 65, for females the qualifying age is gradually being increased from 60 to 65), be single, having never married, or is widowed, divorced or formally separated from your spouse and have been dependent, and remain dependent, on your Australian relative for a reasonable period (normally three years).

Remaining Relative. This visa allows for entry of the last remaining brother, sister or non-dependent child outside Australia. You or your spouse must not have a parent, sibling or non-dependent child or step-relative (within the same degree of relationship) living outside Australia, and again your sponsor must have lived in Australia for at least two years prior to the sponsorship being lodged.

The Australian Government has established processing priorities for applicants under the Family Stream scheme. Priority is given to dependent children (including adopted and interdependent families). Lower priority is given to all other Family Stream categories.

Some Family Stream applicants are subjected to a mandatory Assurance of Support (AoS) which is a legal commitment to repay the Commonwealth of Australia any recoverable social security benefits paid by Centrelink to those covered by the assurance. Other applicants may be subject to a discretionary AoS if they are at risk of becoming a burden on the Australian social welfare system. An AoS is also a commitment to provide financial support to applicants so that they will not have to rely on any government forms of support. There are also limitations on the number of sponsorships any sponsor can make and the timeframe in which they may be made. A number of visa classes, such as Prospective Marriage and Interdependency, can be subject to 'capping.' This means that once the number of visas for a visa class in a particular programme has been reached, no further visas can be granted in that class for that year.

Skilled Stream Migration

The skilled stream of Australia's migration programme is especially designed to target migrants who have skills or outstanding abilities which will contribute to the Australian economy, have a high level of English, and are under 45 years of age. Current government policy is committed to increasing migration in the skilled stream, and seeks to address specific skill shortages in the Australian labour market, as well as to enhance the size and skill-level of the Australian labour force. There are five main categories of skilled migration:

Independent. Independent migrants are people selected on the basis of their education, skills and work experience, who are likely to contribute to the Australian economy. They are not sponsored by an employer or relative in Australia. This group is the largest sector of the skilled migration programme. In November 1997, a new component of the Independent migrant category was announced, known as the State/Territory Nominated Independent Scheme (STNI). This scheme enables State and Territory Governments to sponsor skilled migrants and their families on the condition that the selected migrants live and work in nominated regional areas. Regions and skills are identified through a skill-matching scheme, providing a resource for potential employers who are considering nominating overseas workers to fill their requirements. In 2002-2003, the number of Independent visas totalled 38,120, representing 57.7% of the Skilled Stream. Applicants must meet the pass mark which changes from time to time.

With effect from July 2004 there is also the Skilled Independent Regional (Provisional) Visa for individuals who cannot meet the Skilled Independent Pass Mark and are not eligible for the STNI scheme. The visa is a temporary one providing three years residence in a regional area of Australia and the visa holder and family can apply for permanent residence on completion of two years' residence including at least one year's employment.

Employer Nomination. Employers may nominate personnel from overseas for migration through the Employer Nomination Scheme (ENS), the Regional Sponsorship Scheme (RSMS), and a Labour Agreement. These options are available only when the position cannot be filled from the Australian labour market. They may also sponsor skilled workers under a Labour Agreement, which was negotiated to allow the recruitment of an agreed number of personnel subject to various conditions. Labour Agreements provide for the permanent entry of workers with skills in demand in certain industries.

Distinguished Talent. This small category permits distinguished individuals with special or unique talents to enter Australia, and is generally reserved for outstanding sportspeople, musicians, artists and designers who are internationally recognised in their field. It is open to very few applicants.

General Skilled Migration. Migrants in this category are selected on the basis of skills, age, English language ability, and family relationship. Chances of success in this category are improved if the candidate is sponsored by a relative already living in Australia or intends to live in a designated area of Australia. A points test provides the criterion for selection under this programme. Applicants must meet the pass mark which changes from time to time. There are three categories of visas: Offshore General Skilled, Onshore General Skilled, and Onshore New Zealand citizen, within which there are four visa classes: Skilled-Independent, Skill-Matching, Skilled-Australian Sponsored, and Skilled-Designated Area Sponsored.

Business Skills Migration. The Business Skills programme is designed to encourage successful entrepreneurs and other business people to settle in Australia and develop new businesses of benefit to the Australian economy. The current government has a strong commitment to increasing the entry of high quality business migrants, with numbers of visas granted almost doubling every year since 1994. Australia is actively encouraging Business Skills entrants to set up businesses in regional, rural, or low growth areas. Applicants may seek sponsorship from a state or territory government. The Business Skills programme is divided into four categories: Business Owner, Senior Executive, Investor, and Business Talent. You may be eligible for a Business Skills visa if you have a reasonable ownership share in a business in your own country, have significant business and personal assets, and have achieved significant annual turnover; if you are a senior executive employed in top tier management of a major business; or if you make a significant investment in a government approved Designated Investment for four years. The expectation is that a business migrant will establish a new business or become an owner or part owner of an existing business in Australia, and participate in the management of that business. The progress of business migrants is monitored after arrival in Australia, and where no significant steps are taken towards these goals within three years, the visa may be revoked. In 2003-2004, the top 10 source countries of citizenship for Business Skills visas were China, UK, Malaysia, South Africa, Singapore, Taiwan, Zimbabwe, South Korea, Hong Kong, and Indonesia.

The Points Test

The Department of Immigration and Multicultural and Indigenous Affairs operates a 'points system' for international immigration applications under the Skilled Migration programme. Applicants must meet certain criteria, based on their skills, experience, age, language ability, occupation in demand, Australian qualifications, regional Australia, and spouse skills and relationship. Points are awarded for each criterion, and applicants must gain sufficient point to reach the Pass Mark. The Pass Mark currently stands at 120 points, but changes from time to time. Applicants who score close to the Pass Mark are held in a reserve Pool for up to two years following assessment, however, if you do hit the pool mark your chances of making it to Australia as a migrant are considered to be slim. There are a number of consultancies, advertised in *Australian Outlook*, which provide assistance in preparing for the points test by advising applicants on how to maximise the number of points they can accrue.

Generally, the baseline requirements for success in the points test are that you must be under 45 years old at the time your application is lodged, you must reach either the pool or pass mark in force at the time of assessment of your application (which may not necessarily be the same as the marks at the time your application was lodged), and you must be proficient in English. Points for skill are awarded on the basis of your usual occupation, which is determined by the migration officer. Normally, you will have worked in this occupation continuously for at least twelve of the last eighteen months or two of the last three years. If you have held more than one job which fits this description, you will be assessed against both of your usual occupations, and will be allocated the one which provides you with the best score. The Australian authorities will also assess your qualifications and experience, and the resulting 'skill level' of your occupation will affect how many points you can score.

The occupation that you nominate as fitting your skills and qualifications must be on the 'Skilled Occupations List' at the time of assessment. You receive points allocated for your nominated occupation; for most occupations where training is specific to the occupation you will earn 60 points; for more general professional occupations 50 points, and for other general skilled occupations you will earn 40 points. Points are awarded for the amount of time you have worked in your nominated occupation and also if that occupation is in demand in Australia. Further points can be earned if you have gained an Australian qualification from an Australian educational institutional, studied for at least one academic year in Australia, or have Australian work experience (you must have legally worked in Australia in any occupation on the Skilled Occupations List for at least six months in the four years before you apply). You may also be eligible to claim points for having lived and studied for a minimum of two years in regional Australia or low population growth metropolitan areas. You may earn extra points depending on the skills of your spouse; if you have capital investment in Australia (a minimum of $100,000) or fluency in one of Australia's Community Languages (other than English). For Skilled – Australian Sponsored applicants you may receive points if you have or your spouse has a relative who is an Australian citizen or permanent resident and willing to sponsor you. The costs of applying to migrate to Australia are as follows:

TABLE 1 MIGRATION APPLICATION PACKAGES AND CHARGES	
Application for Migration to Australia Booklets	$20
Application for Long-Stay Visitor's Visa (up to one year)	$65
Application for Temporary Residence Visa (most categories)	$170
Application for Student Visa	$410
Application for Working Holiday Visa	$170
Application for Temporary Business Short-Stay	$65

Application for Temporary Business Long-Stay	$170
Application for Partner Migration	$1,245
Application for Prospective Marriage Visa	$1,245
Employer Sponsored Migration (1st instalment)	$1,245
Application for General Skilled Migration (1st instalment)	$1,845
Application for Business Skills Migration (1st instalment)	$2,450
Application for Sponsored Business Visa	$65
Application for Special Migration	$1,245

A second instalment of charges for permanent residency is payable only after the application has been accepted. Religious workers are fee-exempt in the Employer Nominated category. These costs are quoted in Australian dollars and will vary according to the exchange rate. The Australian High Commission will be able to advise of the current cost in local currency. Applicants for permanent residency should also allow for the cost of a medical examination by an approved practitioner, which will include screening for tuberculosis (chest X-ray), HIV and hepatitis.

Visa processing times vary according to the type of visa, and according to current demand. As a general guide, a spouse visa will take around six months, while family and skill stream migration visas can take up to 20 months. DIMIA has decided that priority is to be given to applications sponsored by Australian citizens; those sponsored by non-citizens will now go to the back of the queue, and it is expected that waiting time on such applications will become even longer. Visitor's visas can be issued the same day, or instantly if applying for an ETA.

Becoming an Australian Citizen

Many migrants, once they have completed all the requirements of permanent residency and feel settled in their new home, decide to show a commitment to Australia by becoming a citizen. Approximately 62% of migrants take up citizenship within five years of arrival and 76.7% do so after 15 years of residence. In recent years the Australian government has strongly encouraged immigrants to take up citizenship, and now offers various incentives for them to do so. There are, of course, various rights that come with Australian citizenship: you will have the right to vote; the right to apply for any public office; the right to apply for an Australian passport and to leave and re-enter the country without a resident return visa; the right to seek assistance from Australian diplomatic representatives while abroad; the right to enlist in the Australian armed forces as well as the right to apply for government jobs; and the right to register your child as an Australian Citizen by descent.

Many public sector jobs, especially in areas of national security, are now also open only to Australian citizens. A booklet, *What it Means to be an Australian Citizen* is available from the Department of Immigration and Multicultural and Indigenous Affairs and there is a dedicated Australian Citizenship website at www.citizenship.gov.au.

As a migrant, you will become eligible for Australian citizenship when you have lived in Australia as a permanent resident for a total of two out of the previous five years. You must be over the age of 18 to apply, though children may be included on their parents' application, and must expect to live permanently in Australia or maintain a close and continuing link with it. There is a fee of $120 to apply for the grant of citizenship, which is reduced to $20 for those on certain social security benefits.

Useful Addresses

UK Passport Service (UKPS): London Passport Office, Globe House, 89 Eccleston Square, London SW1V 1PN; ☎0870-521 0410 (*UKPS* Adviceline); www.ukpa. gov.uk. There are also offices in Belfast, Glasgow, Liverpool, Newport, Durham and Peterborough.

Australian High Commission: Australia House, The Strand, London WC2B 4LA; ☎020-7379 4334; fax (DIMIA) 020-7465 8218; Recorded Information Line (24 hours) 09001-600 333; www.australia.org.uk. Open: Monday to Friday 9am-5pm (Office hours); 9am to 11am Monday to Friday (Migration/Visas); telephone service hours 2pm-4pm Monday to Friday.

Australian Consulate: First Floor, Century House, 11 St Peter's Square, Manchester M2 3DN; ☎0161-237-9440; fax 0161-237 9135; www.australia.org.uk. Passport interviews only. Open: Monday to Friday 1pm-3pm.

Australian Embassy: 7th Floor, Fitzwilton House, Wilton Terrace, Dublin 2, Ireland; ☎01-664 5800; fax 01-678 5185; www.australianembassy.ie. Open: Monday to Friday 8.30am4.30pm. There is no visa office at the Embassy. Visa services for those living in Ireland can be obtained from the Australian High Commission in London only.

Australian Embassy: 1601 Massachusetts Avenue, NW, Washington DC 2006; ☎202-797 3000; fax 202-797 3168; www.austemb.org.

Department of Immigration and Multicultural and Indigenous Affairs: DIMIA North Building, Chan Street, Belcommen Street, ACT; ☎02-6264 1111; fax 02-6264 4466; www.immi.gov.au. For all immigration and visa information.

SETTING UP HOME

CHAPTER SUMMARY

○ It is a legal requirement for a house to have a laundry room separate from the kitchen in Australia.

○ **Home Ownership.** 67% of householders are owner-occupiers

○ By 2016 childless households will be in the majority.

○ **Hazards.** Apart from the climate, bushfires, the greatest threat to buildings with structural timbers is white ants (termites).

   ○ All homes have fly-screens over the doors and windows for fresh air without insect access.

○ **Prices.** Property prices generally are much lower than in the UK or USA.

○ **Mortgages.** Almost half the home loans in Australia are arranged through a broker.

○ **Project Homes.** Very popular are 'off-the-peg' architectural designs which can be customised to suit individual tastes and built on the purchaser's own land or the developer's.

○ **Home Open.** This is the preferred method of selling property. The owner agrees a regular time slot where the estate agent can show prospective buyers around while the owners are out.

   ○ Estate agents give far fewer details, dimensions and descriptions than British ones which is why the Home Open system is vital.

○ **Auctions.** Buying at auction can lead to a high price if it's a competitive sale, or a bargain if it's a distress sale.

The Australian Way of Life

The demography of Australia is rapidly changing, in line with trends in other industrialised nations. The traditional family unit no longer dominates Australian society, and the Australian Bureau of Statistics expects the number of households of childless couples to outstrip the number of couples with children and will be the most common family type by 2016. One parent families are also on the increase and are expected to increase by 30% to 66% over the next 20 years. The 'greying' of the population is well documented; as Australia's baby-boomers move into late middle age and their own children abstain longer and longer from establishing families of their own. The northern NSW/Queensland coastline is the premier 'grey spot' of Australia with dozens of retirement communities although statistically South Australia has the oldest population of all the states. Areas with a high proportion of children are generally located outside major towns and cities, especially in outback Queensland and the Northern Territory.

Australia has one of the highest levels of home-ownership in the world, with more than 67% of Australian households either mortgaged or owner-occupied and 28% rented on the private market. Most Australians live in single-storey houses with a garden at both the front and the back of the house. Gardens are usually designed to take advantage of the weather and will generally have at least one shaded patio to create an external living area. Most will have a semi-detached lockable garage, or at the very least, a 'car-port' (covered hard-standing). A basic family home is expected to comprise three bedrooms, an open-plan living and dining area, fitted kitchen, at least one bathroom, and a separate laundry (including a large sink known as a trough, and fitted plumbing for a washing machine). Every home without exception (indeed, by law) will have a laundry, and it is unheard of to install a washing machine in a kitchen. Four-bedroom houses are also very common, but there are very few, if any, recently built two-bedroom houses. Most houses are likely to have a family room (informal living area) in addition to the usual two reception rooms and will generally have two bathrooms, one of which is usually en suite. The focus of the bathroom is always the shower, which is *never* located over the bath. Australian showers come on hot and strong from the mains, and electric showers and booster pumps are not required; bathrooms are always tiled, thus a carpeted bathroom is a source of amusement to Australians visiting Britain. Kitchens always include a cooker (known as a stove) and fitted cupboards, which in modern houses will include a large pantry cupboard. Carpets, curtains and light fittings are always included in the price unless stated otherwise.

A very large number of homes in Australia have a swimming pool and these must be secured with childproof fences and gates. Local councils inspect swimming pools annually to ensure that they comply with legal requirements in terms of safety and security, and regulations are strictly enforced: fences must be unclimb-able and more than 5 ft (1.5m) in height, and pool gates must be locked and on a self-closing spring.

Pool cleaning equipment (vacuum, hoses, and leaf rake) should be included among the house fixtures and fittings. Most home pools are chlorinated, which means that you will need to add chemicals daily, however, increasingly people are choosing either to install salt-water pools or to convert existing pools to saltwater technology. If you are lucky enough to have a salt-water pool you will only need to add salt once a year, and then leave the converter to do the rest. Salt-water pools also maintain a higher water temperature than chlorinated pools.

Australian houses are usually built either of double brick or of brick veneer (an external brick 'skin' over a timber-framed dwelling). Building regulations in Western Australia require double brick construction, however, in the eastern states, where the topography is more inclined towards earth movement, brick veneer is more structurally sound. Roofs are generally tiled with terracotta or, in cheaper construction, (indistinguishable) coloured cement tiles, but colour bonded steel sheeting is currently fashionable, mimicking the traditional Australian tin-roof. Most Australian homes are fitted with insulation in the roof space and, often, the walls. This insulation, made from fibreglass or wool fibre compacted to the size of a hay bale, helps to keep the house cool in summer and warm in winter. All homes are fitted with fly-screens over the doors and windows, so that doors and windows can be left open without admitting insects.

Buying a Home or Land

Properties and vacant land are advertised for sale in the Real Estate supplements of all capital city newspapers, often on Wednesdays and Saturdays. Most local papers, including weekly freesheets, also carry extensive advertisements and are a good place to start if you have decided on a particular area. Government or 'Crown' land is also occasionally advertised for sale, especially in outer suburban areas undergoing new development. If you are interested in building a new home at an economical cost (that is, *not* by subcontracting your own architect and builder), you should look at the newspaper section headed 'Display Homes' or 'Project Homes'. A project home is an off-the-peg architectural design offered by a builder and built especially for you, either on your own land, or on land supplied by the builder and offered as part of a package. Once you have selected a suitable design, you are free to customise it to a certain extent, choosing internal finishes, bricks, tiles, and landscaping. Many people choose to have the ceiling heights raised in project homes (they are usually designed to the legal minimum of eight courses of brickwork), and this will add a few thousand dollars per course to the cost of the design. Project homes are an extremely popular choice in Australia, and rather than simply buying a new home in a development, most people prefer this more individual option. A project home package for a home comprising four bedrooms, two bathrooms, and two or three reception rooms, including plans, building and land, in an outer suburban area of Perth can cost as little as $90,000. If you choose to build on your own land, your new home can be built for around $60,000. Examples of builders' project homes, known as 'display homes', can be viewed at various 'display villages', the locations of which are advertised alongside the relevant floor plans.

A guide to the sort of price you can expect to pay for an average family home around Australia is given below. For the price listed, you are likely to get a three-bedroom, two-bathroom residence on about a third of an acre of land in a low/mid-range suburban area.

TABLE 2   PROPERTY PRICES IN THE PROVINCIAL CAPITALS

Property Values by Capital City ($'000)

	Sydney	Melbourne	Brisbane	Adelaide	Perth	Hobart	Canberra
House	520.0	357.0	180.0	250.0	242.8	120.0	203.0
Townhouse/ terrace/duplex	233.3	205.2	139.2	116.7	128.2	99.2	119.8
Flat	420.0	148.3	166.6	115.4	128.5	N/A	252.6

If you are moving to the ACT, you should note that there is no freehold land available in Canberra. Instead, the Commonwealth Government grants 99-year leases on blocks of land for residential purposes, and these are released for sale to keep pace with demand. All residential land is sold at public auction, and unsold sites are available after auction at the Land Sales Office. Reserve prices are set at 80% of the assessed market value. Leaseholders are obliged to commence construction within 12 months and to complete construction in 24 months. All land released for sale under this system is within 19 miles (30 km) of the city centre, and all sites are fully serviced, with social amenities added as the suburb develops.

Rent or Buy?

In the late 1980s Australia witnessed a massive property boom. Prices escalated by 60% to100% within two years. Home loan rates were at around 18%. It's no wonder that this market was unsustainable. The early 1990s saw a slump and prices remained low until about 1994. The prospect of the Olympic Games coming to Sydney in 2000 led to a fall in interest rates and the rise of the property market. Prices have increased steadily, especially in beachside and inner city suburbs, since the late 1990s. The Australian property market has seen controlled, sustainable growth and home loan rates are the lowest they've been for 40 years. However, the events of September 11, a faltering US economy and the Australian government's introduction of the Goods and Services Tax (GST) in July 2000 went some way to upsetting the boom. To compensate for the potential negative effect of the GST on the property market (it was feared that the new GST to add another 10% on to the price of property), the Government introduced the *First Home Owner Grant* of $7,000 Grant (later increased to $14,000). Interest rates have continued to drop, Australia's economy has remained buoyant and because of the low rate of exchange on the Australian dollar expats continue to buy property as an investment.

So the cost of property in Australia remains at an affordable level; interest rates are low, banking is highly competitive, and prices are relatively stable. Financial experts agree that buying your own home is the best step that you can take towards financial security, offering both the peace of mind of a secure roof over your head as well as significant tax benefits on your investment. It is currently very easy to obtain mortgage finance, and with low interest rates, paying off a property is likely to cost you less than renting one of an equivalent standard. Initial establishment costs can be high, however (see below), and it is likely to take several years before you can offset these against any gain on your investment. Residential property prices are affected by a number of variables, including migration, interest rates, government policy, consumer confidence and general economic conditions. There is an observable cycle in the property market, and if you arrive at the peak of a particular cycle, you may be well advised to rent and invest your money elsewhere until a downturn occurs. *The Real Estate Institute of Australia* monitors property cycles, and publishes bulletins and statistics which can help you assess where the market currently stands. Market analysts currently forecast an 11.8% per annum increase in property values in all Australian capitals, except Hobart, which should remain static, and Sydney, where demand is expected to fuel a property boom.

FINANCE

The home loan market in Australia has been highly competitive in recent years with a number of new players entering the fray and a myriad of options available. Having negotiated the maze, however, borrowers can currently enjoy exceptional value for money in their choice of investment. Non-bank lenders are now offering more flexible features, including the option to redraw on extra payments, and loans are being offered at competitive rates by established banks, credit unions, building societies, and new-style mortgage originators. Lenders will consider loans of up to 95% of the property value, and mortgage eligibility is calculated on a formula based on the income level of the applicant, or of the applicant and partner in combination (usually three times one salary or 2.5 times both salaries). There are an increasing number of lenders offering no-deposit home loan packages to encourage potential buyers into the market, including builders who will supply no-deposit finance for buyers to purchase their project homes. Usually such offers will have hidden (or not-so-hidden) costs – such as higher interest rates.

Application or establishment fees are charged by both banks and other lenders to cover the cost of setting up a loan agreement, including legal and valuation fees, and disbursements such as mortgage registration and stamp duty. The amount of these initial fees varies widely between lenders: some simply pass on their costs, others absorb them (a no-fees mortgage), while some of the bigger players, who have less to fear from competition, may charge as much as $800.

Lending terms and conditions can vary considerably between lenders, but in late-2004 the interest rate stood at around 5.38% per annum for standard variable home loans. The maximum term for a standard home loan is 25 years, with a few lenders offering 30-year terms, depending on the age of the applicant. Fixed loans are popular as they provide security against interest rate rises, and such loans are now more flexible than they have been with lenders offering the facility of extra repayments without penalty.

Australia's four largest banks are the Commonwealth, the ANZ, Westpac, and the National Australia Bank. All offer mortgage products and applications for a home loan can be lodged at any branch. Increasingly, suburban branches operate as little more than shop-fronts, with management and lending decisions taken at head office, so you need not necessarily approach your own branch for information. The Commonwealth Bank and the ANZ both have excellent websites, which describe their full range of products, and by entering your details online, you can receive an instant assessment of your eligibility for a mortgage. You can access the Commonwealth from the UK on www.migrantbanking.co.uk or from Australia on www.commbank.com.au and the ANZ on www.anz.com.au.

Non-bank lenders are playing an increasingly important role in the mortgage market and are known as mortgage originators or mortgage managers. Such lenders, who include insurance companies and credit unions, act as intermediaries between borrowers and larger institutions. These big institutions are the real lenders behind mortgage originator loans, and are usually organisations which do not wish to participate in the market directly. Other funds are obtained from securitisers, who raise funds on the financial markets and then redistribute them to originators. Industry standards require that independent trustees oversee originators and the loan monies that they collect to protect the interests of the borrower. Aussie Home Loans (www.eaussie.com.au) is the most aggressive of the mortgage originators and advertises extensively on radio and in newspapers. Other major originators include Macquarie Mortgages (www.macquarie.com.au), Aussie Mortgage Masters (www. beatthebanks.com.au), and AMP Home Loans (www.amp.com.au).

In such a complex environment, borrowers are increasingly seeking the services of mortgage brokers, who are able to source the most suitable and cheapest loan for your needs. A good broker will be able to find you the best loan, explain it in detail, help complete the loan documents, and guide the application through to acceptance. Brokers make their money on commission from the lender, and there are no fees charged to the borrower. Almost half the home loans in Western Australia are now written by brokers and the trend is steadily increasing in the eastern states. Mortgage brokers advertise widely in the press and yellow pages, and some of the franchise real estate chains, such as Ray White Real Estate (www.raywhite.com.au) and LJ Hooker (www.ljhooker.com.au) also offer broking services. 1st Australian Mortgage (www.1stam.com.au) is an independent mortgage broker, associated with a national network of mortgage lenders and claim to be able to provide you with the finance that suits best depending on your needs.

Useful Addresses

Australian and New Zealand Bank (ANZ), Minerva House, Montague Close, London SE1 9DH; ☎020-7378 2121; fax 020-7378 2378; www.anz.com.

Commonwealth Bank of Australia, Financial & Migrant Information Service, Senator House, 85 Queen Victoria Street, London EC4V 4HA; ☎020-7710 3999; fax 020-7710 3939; www.migrantbanking.co.uk.

Westpac Banking Corporation, 2nd Floor, 63 St Mary's Axe, London EC3A 8LE; ☎020-7621 7000; fax 020-7623 9428; www.westpac.com.au.

PURCHASING & CONVEYANCING PROCEDURES

Every state in Australia has its own laws pertaining to real estate transactions, and its own licensing laws for real estate agents. In general, you should expect your real estate agent to hold certification from the appropriate state government authority, and preferably, that they or their agency should be a member of the Real Estate Institute of Australia (or state-affiliated branch). If your agent is a member of the REIA or its affiliates, such as REIWA (the Real Estate Institute of Western Australia), you will be protected in the case of any malpractice. Estate agents who are the Principals (proprietors) of an agency must be certified at a higher level, and any agent intending to conduct a sale by auction must hold a separate licence to do so.

There are five types of fees for which you must budget when purchasing a property in Australia:

○ **Solicitors'/Settlement Agents' Professional Fees**. These are fees charged by a solicitor or settlement agent for conducting the legal business of the purchase on your behalf.

○ **Search Fees and Outlays**. These fees cover the cost of the searches undertaken to ensure that the property is free from encumbrances.

○ **Stamp Duty**. Stamp duty is a state government tax on the purchase price of the property. It is calculated as a percentage of the value of the transaction, and is affected by the area of land purchased and whether the purchasers intend to reside in the property. Concessions apply in some states (for example, Queensland) to first time buyers who will reside in the property. Stamp duty varies considerably and is calculated on *ad valorem*, nominal or concessional rates of duty depending on the state or territory.

○ **Registration Fees**. Fees are charged by the state department of land management or natural resources to effect the registration of transfer of ownership and related mortgage documents.

○ **Lender Fees**. It is common practice for lenders to charge administration fees for setting up a mortgage. As the home loan market becomes increasingly competitive, however, such fees (which can be as high as $800) have become more negotiable, and can be avoided completely if you shop around.

Settlement

The process of exchanging contracts to complete a property transaction is known in Australia as 'settlement'. Settlement is a far easier process in Australia than the UK and the concept of the 'chain' does not exist. Once a vendor agrees to an offer on a property, a contract is signed stipulating a date for settlement, which will usually be 30 days from the date of offer. During this period, the purchaser arranges finance and completes all the legal formalities. Settlement MUST take place on the nominated date, and if it cannot, the party at fault becomes liable for the payment of penalty interest.

Conveyancing

The conveyancing market has been deregulated in recent years and is no longer the exclusive province of solicitors. Most people now turn to specialist 'settlement agents' instead, who are trained in conveyancing and property law, but who are not lawyers. Settlement agents' fees are almost always much lower than those charged by solicitors for an identical service, and are generally in the region of $400-$1,000, depending on the value of the property and the state in which you reside. In South Australia the legal legwork on most property transactions is handled by a land broker. It is possible to do your own conveyancing, but it is not recommended: the risk of steep penalty interest payments in the case of delay through error or lack of expertise can outweigh the saving of a few hundred dollars.

Buying Without Residency Status

If you have not been granted permanent residency in Australia, any residential property purchase will require the prior approval of the Foreign Investment Review Board. Generally speaking, the Board will *not* approve the purchase of second-hand residential real estate by non-residents; however, if you are a temporary resident wanting to acquire a home for your stay in Australia, you may be granted foreign investment approval, subject to you meeting certain conditions. If you are an overseas investor hoping to buy a holiday home or invest in residential real estate in Australia, you should seek advice from the *Foreign Investment Review Board*, The Executive Member, Department of the Treasury, Langton Crescent, Canberra, ACT 2600; ☎ 02-6263 3795; fax 02-6263 2940; e-mail firb@treasury. gov.au; www.firb.gov.au). Additionally you could obtain advice from a solicitor specialising in Australian property law.

Real Estate Agencies

Most people buy and sell their property with the services of a local real estate agent, and few owners market their own properties. Agents act on behalf of the vendor and not the purchaser, and their responsibilities include advertising and contract negotiation to obtain the best possible price for their client (who, you should always bear in mind when you are buying, is *not* you). Homes for sale will be advertised in the local press, and the larger state-wide newspapers will generally publish a property section at the weekend (often on Saturday). In addition, most agents will have extensive photo displays in their office window. The distribution of detailed description sheets giving measurements of each room, location of power points and other features is not an Australian practice, although top-of-the-range homes are often marketed through glossy, descriptive brochures. Instead, when you approach an agent regarding a property, you can expect to be told only the price (or, increasingly, an acceptable price range), the number and types of rooms and any other facilities, swimming pool, reticulation, and air conditioning. If the property is still of interest, the agent will arrange to accompany you on a private inspection, or you may be asked to attend the next 'Home Open'. The Home Open is a standard property marketing tool in Australia and involves opening the property to all-comers at a specified, advertised time, usually for an hour or two every weekend. During this time the agent is in attendance and the owners are absent. Prospective purchasers, who are most likely to have seen the property advertised in that morning's paper, are free to walk around the house and garden and examine its suitability in privacy. The agent will take your name and address, and will chat a little to determine your bona fides. The Home Open is generally considered to be a convenient and low-key way of finding a property, and if you are house hunting it is an easy way of lining up four or five likely places to view in one morning.

LISTING A PROPERTY WITH AN ESTATE AGENT

There are three different methods of listing a property with an estate agent, and you will often see one of the following terms somewhere in an advertisement:

Sole/Exclusive Agency. This means that the property is being offered by one agent only, and can be viewed only by contacting the specified office. Advertisements for sole agency properties will carry the name of the particular agent (for example, Mike Jones of Smith White Realty) who has obtained the listing. All contact and requests for information must be directed to the named agent.

Open Listing. Under an 'open listing', any number of agencies can offer the property to buyers. This method is common in some states (Queensland) and unusual in others, or in some states (e.g. Western Australia), common for more down-market properties or areas, and unusual at the middle and upper end of the market. It is not generally considered to be an effective way to sell, as there is no single agent with a keen incentive to make the sale.

Multilisting. Multilisting is very similar to the American 'Multiple Listing Service' (MLS), and means that a property is listed by a number of specified agencies. Multilisting is the least common method of marketing a property.

If you are looking for a property to buy, you can approach an agent to act on your behalf in the search. The agent will then obtain lists of all the properties for sale in your price range and desired area, and will arrange for you to view them. There is no fee to the purchaser for this service; it can be a good way for a newcomer to find a suitable property, as the agent will have detailed local knowledge about shops, schools and amenities, which you may lack. Your agent makes his or her money, once you decide on a property, by negotiating a *conjunctional sale*: the vendor's agent splits the sale commission 50/50 with the introducing agent. Conjunctional sales apply to properties marketed under sole agency as well as by other methods, and there are very few agents who will refuse to conjunct.

Buying at Auction

Many Australian properties at every level of the market are sold by auction. Auctions, and attitudes to sale by auction, vary from state to state. Some franchise groups push vendors to sell by auction, but they are not universally popular: some agents consider them to be most suitable for distress sales (in which case, they can result in bargains), while others use them only in a competitive, rising market (in which case, you can end up paying too much). Vendors who sell by auction are responsible for the advertising costs of the agent.

Buying at auction can be an intimidating experience, and it is advisable to attend a few as a kind of 'dry run', to get the feel for what you will be up against. In Western Australia, auctions are conducted in the front garden of the property for sale, so it is easy to wander up and listen. In other states they are usually held in auction rooms.

Success at auction depends on doing your homework: first, know your financial limits by visiting your bank manager beforehand, and *never* bid above that limit, no matter how persuasive the auctioneer's patter; secondly, know the market, so that you have a clear idea of the true worth of the property; shop around, comparing prices of similar houses. Once you have identified the house you want, spend several weeks before the auction date visiting other auctions in the area to evaluate the level of bidding; thirdly, make prior enquiries about the contract, establishing what the property includes, and making sure it is free from any important defects. Examine the building report and pest certificates, and ascertain the level of deposit which will be required in cash on the fall of the hammer (it is likely to be 10%).

On auction day, you should check the contracts again, to ensure that no changes have been made. Arrive early, and have a last look around if possible. At this point you should introduce yourself to the auctioneer and let them know that you are interested in buying. Sit in easy view of the auctioneer, preferably near the front or at the sides, where you can observe competing bidders. The auctioneer will then commence the patter and ask if there are any questions: bidders who play tough like to take this opportunity to unsettle the opposition by fielding queries about six-lane highways or high-rise tower blocks. Try and ignore such strategies and bid with confidence; bid low and bid often is the approach recommended by experienced agents. When bidding is slow, a common tactic of the auctioneer is to pull out 'phantom bids' or bids on behalf of the vendor, but if you suspect this, you are within your rights to stop the auction and demand to know against whom you are bidding. Properties are always auctioned with an undisclosed reserve price, and if it is eventually passed in, you will be able to try and negotiate privately after the auction.

Finally, some agents advise that if you really want the house, you could try making an offer in advance: the vendor may be as nervous as you are, and only too glad to tie it up without going through with the whole ordeal.

Contracts

Most property sales are concluded through the exchange of a simple standard contract issued by the state Real Estate Institute. This contract will specify the sale price and deposit (notionally 10%, but in practice, highly negotiable), the date of settlement, and the fixtures and fittings to be included in the sale. You should note that it is expected that fixtures and fittings will be included in a sale and, if you are selling, you will be in breach of contract if you so much as remove a light bulb without specifying your intentions. Cookers and dishwashers are considered fixtures and must remain in the property. The contract will also require that all appliances are in good working order, and this includes external plant such as swimming pool filters, air conditioning, and ducted vacuum systems. At the time of making an offer, certain conditions are usually appended to the standard contract, and the failure of either party to meet the stated conditions will invalidate the sale. Usually a contract is signed subject to two main conditions: firstly, that the purchaser provide proof of mortgage finance or cash resources within 48 hours; and secondly, that the vendor provide a current white ant certificate within one week. White ants are a type of termite, which can cause havoc with a building's structural timbers; they are a serious concern and their control is monitored by law. A white ant inspection certificate ensures that your property is free from infestation or, if white ants have been found, that they have been destroyed by chemical treatment. Evidence of previous, treated white ant infestation is not an impediment to the sale of a property. A white ant inspection certificate costs around $200 and this cost is born by the vendor. If these conditions and any others particular to your property are met, the contract becomes binding. Should you change your mind for any reason, you will forfeit your deposit. Similarly, should the vendor break the contract, your deposit will be refunded plus the same amount again as a penalty payment.

Useful Addresses

Foreign Investment Review Board, The Executive Member, Department of the Treasury, Langton Crescent, Canberra, ACT 2600; ☎02-6263 3795; fax 02-6263 2940; e-mail firb@treasury.gov.au; www.firb.gov.au.

L.J. Hooker is one of Australia's largest real estate groups with offices throughout the country. Their customer service centre (freephone 1800 621 212) will be able to recommend an office in your intended area as well as provide local information. They also have an excellent website at www.ljhooker.com.au, which provides useful advice on all aspects of buying and selling, and on-line property information.

Realestate.com.au, Level 3, 678 Victoria Street, Richmond, VIC 3121; ☎03-9897 1121 (freephone 1300 134 174); fax 03-9890 5322; e-mail propertycustomers@realestate.com.au; www.realestate.com.au. Realestate.com.au, exclusively endorsed by the Real Estate Institute of New South Wales (REINSW) and the Real Estate Institute of Tasmania (REIT), provides a medium for real estate agents to advertise their listings and for potential buyers to search for properties.

Useful Publications

Consyl Publishing Ltd., 3 Buckhurst Road, Bexhill-on-Sea, East Sussex TN40 1QF; ☎01424-223111; www.consylpublishing.co.uk, distributes the Australian magazines, *Real Estate Weekly* and *The Homebuyer*, which contain illustrated for-sale advertisements for property around Australia.

RENTING PROPERTY

Australians have a strong home-owning ethos. Most people prefer not to rent if at all possible and those who do rent in general occupy their rented property for less than a year. Rented housing in Australia is very much less expensive than in Europe, and both tenant and landlord rights are well protected. Among other things, tenancies are always covered by leases and there is no indefinite security of tenure. Renting out a property is not a risky venture for a landlord, who can easily have unsuitable tenants evicted so people are very willing to place their investment properties and homes on the rental market. Changes in taxation law have meant that it is no longer as financially advantageous as it once was to buy property for the purposes of renting it out, and as a result the amount of property available to rent has declined, with a concomitant rise in rentals. Nonetheless, the average weekly rental for a three bedroom house in Melbourne, which is generally considered an expensive city in terms of property prices, is $195, clearly far less than in most major European cities.

Rents are not subject to state control in Australia, but are set by the lease agreement signed by both tenant and landlord. Usually, such an agreement will set the rent for a six-month period, with a reassessment at the end of the lease period. In some states residential rents may be controlled, but only on properties which were tenanted prior to changes in the law. The Federal Discrimination Act prohibits discrimination by landlords against prospective tenants, and it is illegal to refuse a tenant on the grounds of sex or marital status, pregnancy, or ethnic origin. If you suspect that a landlord or agent has made an illegal refusal of your application to rent his or her property, you should contact the nearest Office of Consumer Affairs, which will be able to advise you further. In general, however, landlords are interested in having their property occupied by rent-paying tenants, and you are unlikely to have your application for tenancy turned down if you can provide good references and evidence of sufficient financial means.

Properties for rent are advertised in the 'To Let' section of the property pages in city and state newspapers and in weekly, free community newspapers. Real estate agents also usually have a specialist property management division, which will also have listings of available properties, and you can approach agents directly in the areas in which you hope to find accommodation.

Tenancy Agreements

Very short-term rented accommodation can be difficult to find in Australia as most property owners will only accept tenants prepared to sign a tenancy agreement valid for six months. It is occasionally possible to find an owner who is prepared to make a short-term lease available, and in such cases the lease may later be extended by private agreement, allowing you to remain on a weekly or monthly basis after the expiry of the lease. Although this can be convenient for travellers, it does not give much security to longer-term visitors, and you will need to be willing to move at short notice should the owner decide to make other arrangements. In general, a first lease is given for six months and can be extended, provided that you and the owner both agree to any change of conditions, including a rent rise (most landlords do *not* automatically raise the rent every six months). Properties are almost invariably let unfurnished, but will include a cooker and, often, a fridge. Lease agreements in Australia usually conform to a standard format, and the contract can be purchased for a couple of dollars at any newsagent. They are simple to understand and offer fair and equal protection to both landlord and tenant. The underlying assumption in Australian rent law, however, is that the property belongs to the landlord, who has greater rights in terms of protecting and enjoying the benefits of his or her investment. There is, therefore, no concept of the 'sitting tenant' or of 'squatting', and unruly, destructive or non-paying tenants can be swiftly and effectively evicted.

Letting agents or property owners generally require tenants to pay a bond or deposit of four weeks rental, in addition to a month's rent in advance. The bond can sometimes be as much as six weeks rent, and owners may occasionally ask for up to two months rent in advance. You should, therefore, allow several thousand dollars to establish yourself in a rented property. The bond can be entirely or partly forfeited if the tenant defaults on payment or conditions of the lease. If you leave the premises and any provided furniture and fittings in a good condition, allowing for reasonable wear and tear, your landlord will refund your bond at the end of your tenancy. Most landlords will provide an inventory of the property, particularly if it is let furnished, and this will detail the condition of the house at the start of the lease (it might list, for example, existing scuff marks or cigarette burns). You should read and assess this inventory before you sign your lease, as signing will imply your agreement with its contents. The property will be inspected at the end of your lease, and may be inspected at any time during the period of the tenancy, providing the owner or agent gives 48 hours notice of their intention to enter. They must, however, by law, have good cause to effect entry, for example, if neighbours report obvious signs of neglect; and you have the right to be present during any inspection. End-of-lease inspections are usually very thorough indeed: expect to have extractor fan covers removed and inspected for dirt and grease, pictures moved, and carpets lifted. You will need to seek permission under the terms of a standard lease to effect any change to the fabric of the property, even if it is just to put up a picture hook.

The owner of a rented property is responsible for all council and water rates, as well as strata and management fees, but the tenant pays costs for all utilities such as electricity, gas and telephone.

Rental Costs

In Australia there is very little 'social housing' of the type provided by councils and district authorities in Europe. Traditionally, the 'Great Australian Dream' has meant that even in the lowest socio-economic groups there has been a high expectation of home ownership, and concomitantly, that to be housed by the state 'Housing Commission' has been an object of shame. In addition, rent laws, as outlined above, have kept the private rental sector competitive and stable, so that few people have needed to fall back on the state to provide them with accommodation. Most commonly, state housing is available to socially marginalised groups, such as Aborigines and refugees. The criterion for eligibility is that the applicant must demonstrate an inability to secure decent accommodation in the private sector at a rent, which is within their capacity to pay. However, given that rent assistance for private tenants, whether unemployed or on a low income, is available from Centrelink (the government agency responsible for social security payments), there are very few people to whom this might apply.

Danny Jones found that accommodation can be difficult to find in major cities

...Especially when you're from overseas, as it's not so easy for agents to check your history. Leases are normally for one year so choosing the right area is important. However, the standard of living is higher than in the UK, and you get paid more while being taxed less. And houses, fuel and food are all far cheaper – although the gap does seem to be narrowing.

In the private sector, there is almost always a good variety of properties available to rent, although it is usually easier to find flats (known as 'units') than houses. A rough guide to current weekly rental values for unfurnished property around Australia is given below:

TABLE 3 RENTAL VALUES BY CAPITAL CITY($/WEEK)

	Sydney	Melbourne	Brisbane	Adelaide	Perth	Canberra	Hobart	Darwin
3-bedroom houses	270	195	190	185	165	230	160	240
Townhouses/ 2-bedroom flats/units	265	185	175	180	133	195	125	180

TABLE 4 PROPERTY GLOSSARY

Duplex/Triplex. Property development in which two or three compact, single-storey houses in a unified architectural style are built on a large suburban block.

Freehold. Most Australian houses and land are held on a freehold title.

House. In Australia, a house is usually of the 'bungalow' type, i.e., it is likely to be single-storeyed, unless stated otherwise.

Strata Title. Flats, townhouses, villas, duplexes and triplexes are usually held on a strata title. Under this system a property owner owns absolutely all the space enclosed by the exterior walls of the property, as well as a pro-rata percentage share of all the communal space of the development in its entirety. Strata fees are payable quarterly to a 'body corporate', which is a democratically-constituted management authority, and cover the maintenance of the fabric of the structure and communal garden areas.

Terrace. A terraced house, with party walls on both sides. This type of housing is only found in old, inner-city areas and is often sought after for its 'character and charm'.

Town House. A compact house of two or more stories in a small development. It will usually share one or more party walls with neighbouring townhouses.

Unit. A term in common use to describe a flat or apartment. A unit can be located either in a high- or low-rise development.

Villa. A compact bungalow-style house in a small, unified development, usually with one or more party walls and a shared driveway.

RELOCATION

Relocation Companies

Although there are many relocation service companies offering assistance with intra-European and transatlantic moves, the antipodean sector of the market is poorly served. Relocators can assist corporate and domestic migrants with establishing the basis for life in a new home abroad, including finding accommodation, schools and employment. However, many of those that operate between Europe and Australia concentrate almost entirely on the corporate market. The cost of using such services can be prohibitive for the individual, and in many cases removal companies may be more helpful for people undertaking a domestic move. Many of the larger removal companies offer more than a shipping service, and may be able to advise and assist in many other aspects of your relocation. There are a number of relocation companies in Australia, and these will usually be better able to act on your behalf in organising the essentials for your arrival.

Useful Addresses

Expat International Pty Ltd, Level 2, 423 Bourke Street, Melbourne, VIC 3000; ☎03-9670 7555; fax 03-9670 7799; e-mail info@expat.com.au; www.expat. com.au, offer expatriate HR consultancy to corporations worldwide, visa documentation, international and interstate relocations, and cultural awareness programmes. They are affiliated with the Migration Institute of Australia and the Employee Relocation Council (USA) and have offices worldwide: check the white pages telephone directory of your capital city.

Four Winds International Movers, 32 Londor Close Hemmant, Brisbane, QLD 4174; ☎07-3890 6800; fax 07-3890 6888; e-mail sales@fourwindsmovers. com; www.fourwindsmovers.com.

Nuss Removals, 708 Mowbray Road West, Lane Cove, Sydney, NSW 2066; ☎02-9425 4600; fax 02-9427 2956; e-mail sydney@nuss.com.au; www.nuss.com.au, and 29 Edward Street, Oakleigh, Melbourne, VIC 3166; ☎03-9569 6277; fax 03-9569 6377. Nuss belongs to the Federation Internationale des Demenageurs Internationaux, the British Association of Removers, the Household Goods and Forwarders Association of America, Omni, and is an accredited IATA (International Air Transport Association) agent.

Weichert Relocation Resources International, 1st Floor, 56 Buckingham Gate, London SW1E 6AE; ☎020-7802 2500; www.wrri.com. One of the largest relocation firms in the world.

Assistance from Religious Organisations

Many people find that the common bond of faith is an excellent opening to new friendships, and that their co-parishioners are a useful source of assistance in settling in to a new environment. The Council of Christian Unity forms part of the World Division of the Archbishops' Council of the Church of England and helps those looking to explore ways of working with other Christian churches. For further details, contact the Assistant Secretary, *Council of Christian Unity,* Church House, Great Smith Street, Westminster, London SW1P 3NZ; ☎020-7898 1000; www.cofe.anglican.org/info/ccu/.

The World Council of Churches is an ecumenical organisation promoting Christian unity in faith, witness, and service to the world. The General Secretary of the *World Council of Churches* can be contacted at 150 Route de Ferney, 1211 Geneva, Switzerland; ☎+41 22-791 6111; fax +41 22-791 0361; www.wcc-coe.org. While in Australia, the General Secretary of the *Anglican Church of Australia* can be contacted at PO Box Q190, QVB Post Office, Sydney, NSW 1230; ☎02-9265 1525; fax 02-9264 6552; e-mail qsoffice@anglican.org.au; www.anglican.org.au.

Other Denominations. Members of other denominations or religions should contact the organisational headquarters of their religious group in their present country in order to obtain a list of religious contacts in Australia. The *National Council of Churches* in Australia is a council of 15 member churches and further information can be obtained from their office at Level 6, 379 Kent Street, Sydney, NSW 2001; ☎02-9299 2215; fax 02-9262 4514; e-mail gensec@ncca.org.au; www.ncca.org.au.

INSURANCE AND WILLS

Home Insurance

An increasingly competitive insurance market in Australia has meant that in recent years both the number of policies available to the consumer, and their variety, is widening all the time. Buying the right insurance for your particular needs can be confusing, and many Australians now use brokers to help them negotiate the maze of options. Noel Pettersen, executive director of the National Insurance Brokers Association, advises that selective purchasing is the key to proper coverage, rather than purchasing new insurance every time a new need arises. Buildings and contents policies are very long and involved, and when shopping around you should ensure that you obtain a copy of any contract you are seriously considering and assess it before you sign. The most important section is found under 'Exclusions', that is, what is *not* covered. This list can be long, and should be thoroughly checked against your own requirements. In particular, note which *fixtures* are covered: hot water systems, air conditioners, carports, pergolas, fences, and outside blinds may or may not be included. Bushfires, landslides and riot damage may also be excluded, and should be weighed up against your likely need. Anyone living in a well-timbered bushland suburb *must* ensure that they have bushfire cover. Most policies cover damage by fire and explosion, but not flood; once again, assess this according to your proximity to water sources or the climate and topography. Note, however, that some policies may include bushfire or flood damage cover, but the small print may specifically exclude homes situated in high-risk areas. You should also consider whether the sum insured includes cover for demolition costs, clean-up, temporary accommodation, and architect's fees, in the case of major damage to the fabric of your home.

Home insurance premiums, like car insurance, vary according to assessable risk factors. The insurers will take into account factors such as the age of the house, the type of construction (brick, brick veneer, or weatherboard), the value of the house, its size and location. Home insurance is usually payable on a yearly or half-yearly basis (although for a small credit charge, some companies will even allow monthly payments); a typical four bedroom, two bathroom Australian family home in a suburban location is likely to cost around $400-$500 per year to insure. Excess levels vary markedly from company to company, and generally by electing a higher excess level of, say $500, the premium can be significantly reduced. The Insurance Council of Australia considers under-insurance to be the biggest trap in the insurance industry, with at least 40% of homes under-insured.

Under-insurance is the biggest cause of dispute between insurance companies and their clients, and you must be aware that if you are under-insured by a certain amount, any claim you make will be reduced by a pro-rata percentage by the insurance assessor. This could have serious consequences in the case of the destruction of a family home, and may mean that you are unable to rebuild in spite of being insured. You should make sure that your level of insurance keeps pace with inflation in the building industry.

Contents Insurance. Home contents insurance provides cover for personal effects kept in and around the home. Most contents insurance is of the 'new for old' replacement type; there are very few indemnity policies (which pay out only the current second-hand value of the insured items) available. Replacement policies should be read closely for restrictions. The best policies will replace new for old unconditionally, however, others will impose an age limit on items so covered (generally 10 to 12 years), and some exclude soft furnishings. To discourage fraudulent claims, many insurers offer a voucher system for replacement in the case of theft or destruction; instead of receiving a cheque for the sum involved, you will be sent a voucher for the amount which must be 'spent' at an appropriate shop (for example, an electrical retailer, if your television has been stolen). Such a policy can be irksome, as you, the customer, are not given any choice of retailer, and so may be limited in your choice of replacement item.

The level of premium payable varies quite widely from company to company, and depends to a large extent on the amount of cover that you require. Good home security will attract lower premiums, and before you start shopping around you can take a few simple steps by fitting deadlocks to external doors, keyed locks to windows, and becoming part of your Neighbourhood Watch Scheme. A replacement policy on contents valued at $30,000 is likely to cost around $350 per annum, however, if you take out a contents policy in conjunction with buildings insurance through the same company, you will generally receive a discount of between five and ten per cent on both policies. If you are aged over 55, you make fire or safety improvements to your home, you don't make a claim for a certain period or you take out multiple policies with an insurance company you may also be entitled to discounts.

Life Insurance

Personal, or life, insurance, is also available through all major insurance companies, as well as through many smaller specialist insurers. There are an ever-increasing number of different types of life insurance policies available, and most people turn to a financial advisor to choose a suitable one for their own particular needs and level of income. Combined savings/insurance policies are popular, providing for both life cover and medium term investment. Basic life insurance policies, in general, attract lower premiums, but are less financially advantageous during the lifetime of the policyholder. Most insurers will offer free (though not necessarily unbiased) consultation services. In addition, you should note that if you are employed and therefore paying into a superannuation fund, you are likely to have automatic life insurance (death benefits) which will be paid to your nominated beneficiary in the event of your accidental or natural death.

If you already hold life/personal insurance before you enter Australia, you must consult your insurers regarding your relocation. You should also discuss your policy with a tax accountant experienced in overseas investments, as any capital growth and income derived from your policy is likely to be taxed at the maximum rate in Australia. It is often possible to have your policy and funds transferred to an Australian company without incurring any costs or sacrificing any bonuses, and this may be financially advantageous in the long term.

Wills

If you die without having made a will, your estate will be distributed to your next of kin according to the various statutes of the state which provide for intestacy. These statutes vary from state to state, and distribution of the estate will vary according to the number and relationship of any immediate kin; in cases where there is no traceable family, the estate usually passes to the State Treasury. Clearly, it is preferable to make a will, especially if you have a *de facto* partner: the state of Victoria, for example, does not recognise the automatic right of inheritance of *de facto* spouses. Estate duties and State death duties have been abolished in Australia, and under the present law no such taxes are payable on any deceased estate, regardless of its size.

Proper estate planning can be complex, especially where large assets are involved, and in many cases can be complicated by the usefulness of family trusts. Professional assistance is highly recommended in order to maximise an estate's freedom from capital gains tax for the beneficiaries. A will must also fulfil certain formal and legal requirements in order to be valid and thus it is advisable to seek professional legal advice. Solicitors' costs for this service are likely to be high (around $150 per hour), although some solicitors now offer will making 'kits' which guide clients through the process for a much reduced fee. There are a number of kits available, and you can now even access these online, however, you should make sure that a kit satisfactory covers all aspects of will making, including family provision and capital gains tax. The 'Legal Kits of Victoria Will Kit' is recommended for its coverage of all such essential matters. Lawyers are permitted to advertise in Australia, and testamentary services are frequently advertised in newspapers. Most Australian states have, in recent years, relaxed many of will-making formalities in an attempt to protect the true intentions of testators, but there are still important obligations which must be followed to ensure the validity of your will. A will must be in writing and must be signed by the testator in the presence of two witnesses. If a witness is a beneficiary, or married to a beneficiary of that will, the gift to that beneficiary will fail (although the whole will may not necessarily fail). It is of the utmost importance that beneficiaries are not requested to witness the will. Wills may be revoked by the testator at any time after execution, by destruction, by a later will, or by marriage. Divorce, however, does not automatically revoke a will.

A will made overseas which is valid according to the law of the country where it was made, will be accepted for probate in Australia (a probate is an order or grant by the Supreme Court in favour of the executor authorising him/her to collect the assets of the deceased and deal with those assets according to the terms of the will), even though that will may not be valid according to the law of the particular state in which the deceased lived. A testator who has already made a valid will overseas can deal with assets acquired in Australia by means of a separate ancillary will.

Useful information on will making and other financial planning matters can be found on the 'Money Manager' website at www.moneymanager.com.au.

UTILITIES

Electricity, gas and water supplies are controlled throughout Australia by regional state authorities and costs vary to some extent between states, and between urban and rural areas. Remote outback areas may attract particularly high charges, especially for water.

Electricity and Gas

Most new homes in Australia are connected to both gas and electricity supplies. Australia's plentiful supplies of Natural Gas mean that this energy source is relatively cheap, and savings are passed on to domestic consumers; most people thus choose to use gas in preference to electricity wherever possible. Many older homes, however, are not connected to the gas supply, and although this can easily be arranged by contacting the local state gas authority, it is likely to cost several hundred dollars for the service to be installed. Some remote areas do not have a natural gas supply, and in these regions, LPG (liquid petroleum gas) is commonly used, obtained in bottled form, usually from the local garage.

Electricity is the most important source of domestic energy, but is considerably more expensive than gas. In an effort to make electricity more competitive, state authorities such as Western Power (www.westernpower.com.au), in Western Australia, have introduced 'SmartPower'. SmartPower is a demand management system which relates the price paid for electricity to the cost of producing it, which is greater at times of peak demand. In order to take advantage of this system, a SmartPower Meter must be installed (at a cost, currently, of $199 to be installed into a new home and $329 to be installed into an existing home). The SmartMeter records the amount of electricity used in your home during different charging periods, enabling you to monitor your appliance usage and thus shift the times you run your appliances (washing machines and swimming pool filters, for example) in order to lower your electricity costs. In general, a family with a swimming pool will recoup the cost of the SmartMeter within a short time, and will make ongoing savings of at least 30% on their previous power bills.

The voltage in Australia is 240/250V and the current is alternating at 50 Hz. The power points take three-pin plugs which have two diagonally slanting pins above one straight pin. Appliances brought from the UK will work throughout Australia, after changing the plugs, but those brought from the USA will not.

Solar Power. Australia is a world leader in solar technology, and Australian homes first began using solar power back in 1953. Today, many homes in areas with enough sunshine (most areas!) use solar power to heat water. A solar hot water heater provides around 95% of hot water energy needs (for washing and home heating) free from the sun, resulting in enormous savings on traditional energy costs. The capital cost of a solar hot water heater is high, but once installed, they are maintenance-free and have a very long lifetime, so that the initial high cost is soon outweighed by the benefits. A solar hot water system looks like a large, flat, black rectangle, with a cylinder at the top; it is installed on the roof, usually on the western side of the house where it will receive the most sun, and is aesthetically unobtrusive. Solahart, Australia's largest supplier of solar hot water systems, has an informative website at www.solahart.com.au.

Domestic Climate Control

Australian homes are very seldom centrally heated, except in those few areas where the climate is sufficiently cold to require it. Instead, most homes are heated on a fairly *ad hoc* basis, usually by a combination of portable electric fan heaters or radiators, reverse-cycle air conditioning, and slow combustion stoves. Pot-belly stoves or other solid fuel enclosed fires are becoming increasingly popular as a means of heating the main living areas of the home, and can even be installed so that they heat the water supply as well. Coal fires are banned by law, and coal-substitute fires are extremely unusual; open fires and slow combustion stoves are wood-fuelled, though in Adelaide mallee roots (very dense knots of gnarled wood which do not need chopping), which can be bought by the tonne, dominate the fuel market. Wood suppliers (who are often farmers clearing their fields) advertise in the classifieds columns of local newspapers. Only about 50% of residents using firewood for heating actually buy their wood and thousands of Australians (the majority of them in metropolitan areas) collect their wood from roadsides, stock routes, private property and reserves. Of the six million tonnes of wood consumed in Australia each year, two thirds is used for domestic heating.

Home cooling rather than heating is the focus of most Australian climate control, and almost every home will have some method of lowering the internal temperature. Electric ceiling fans are popular and very effective, as well as being cheap to run and to install. There are several different types of air-conditioning in common use: the evaporative type is the cheapest and is generally portable, but requires an open window to work effectively; reverse-cycle is more effective, and can also be used to heat the room in winter. The unit for reverse-cycle air-conditioning is installed in an external wall. Homes in the upper end of the market will often have ducted air-conditioning, which is run from a central plant in the roof or garage, distributing cold air through vents to every room. Air conditioning is essential in the northern regions of Australia, both in the home and the car, and all offices and shops throughout Australia are air-conditioned.

Keeping Cool on the Cheap. Australian architects are very aware of the need to design for the climate and new houses will, for example, have few or very small windows on the hot, western side. Large windows and patio doors will always be shaded by a pergola, often covered with UV resistant plastic. Solar films, which allow in light but not heat, can be applied to windows, and are a cost effective way of keeping homes cool. Climate management in Australia is second nature to locals, but methods may surprise those brought up in a cooler climate. The British response to the sun is to throw open all the windows and enjoy; in Australia, this would be considered eccentric, if not completely mad. If you want to keep your home cooling costs down, you should do as the locals do:

- ○ At sunrise, get up and close every single window in the house. Pull down all blinds and close all curtains; if there are awnings or shutters on outside windows, pull them into place. Close any vent that allows the entry of external air.
- ○ When entering and leaving your home during the day, make sure that any door is open for as brief a time as possible. The aim at all times should be to prevent the hot external air from coming inside.
- ○ When the exterior temperature drops below the interior temperature (usually at sunset), it is time to open up. Throw open everything that has been closed; windows and doors will have lockable screens which will allow you to do this in safety. Leave everything open all night, to allow the house to cool down before the next day's onslaught.
- ○ On really extreme days, try 'hosing down' (but not if there are water restrictions in operation). This method involves soaking the exterior walls and patio areas

> with water from the garden hose, and should be done after dark to avoid instant
> evaporation.

Water

Water is a scarce and valuable commodity in Australia, and is treated with respect
by most people. All urban areas are well served by high quality, clean water
supplies from reservoirs, but extreme summer conditions and drought can mean
the frequent imposition of water restrictions on non-essential water use. Public
education campaigns encourage water-saving measures, such as shorter showers
and water recycling (using washing-up water on the garden, for example). Garden
watering is generally done after dusk to avoid evaporation.

Water is supplied to homes and businesses by state authorities who build and
maintain reservoirs, and ensure the safety and management of the water supply.
Water provision charges are imposed to fund these services and are paid annually
or quarterly by consumers. Water and Sewerage Service Charges apply to every
connected residential property, along with a metered Water Usage Charge currently
68 cents per kilolitre (1,000 litres) in Melbourne, and 93 cents per kilolitre in
Sydney. A Sewerage Disposal Charge is also levied, and takes into account seasonal
factors affecting water usage. Other charges may be applied depending on the state
water authority, for example, in Melbourne a Parks Charge and a Water Drainage
Charge is levied on all rateable properties. Depending on your circumstances rebates
and concessions on water charges may be available and families suffering financial
hardship can apply to make payments under pre-payment budget schemes.

High water charges mean that it is expensive to keep domestic gardens green
during the summer months using mains water. Many Australian homes, therefore,
have irrigation/sprinkler systems, known as 'reticulation', which water the garden
automatically from a private artesian bore. Homeowners frequently pay to have a
bore sunk in their garden, sometimes to a depth of up to 492 feet (150 metres), to
tap into the water table. The cost of the bore can be very high (around $4,000) and
is determined by its depth and the geographical structure of the land, however, in the
long term, a bore enables enormous savings on water bills. Bore water can *only* be used
for gardening, as it is unsuitable for drinking and its high mineral content means that
it will stain swimming pool surfaces. During periods of water restriction, bore owners
are the only people who are able to water their gardens sufficiently to maintain them.
All mains garden watering must be done before dawn or after dusk to reduce wastage
due to evaporation (and, in fact, even homes with bore reticulation usually follow
this method to avoid scorching leaves and grass). Most newer Australian gardens have
moved away from the traditional British garden towards gardens in which native
Australian plants predominate. Native plants have adapted to dry conditions over the
millennia and require very little water to stay alive; their cultivation also encourages
native bird life. Wood chips and extensive patio areas are also popular, reducing the
area of garden devoted to lawn, which is expensive and time consuming to maintain
in Australia.

In rural areas, domestic rainwater tanks are frequently used to collect precipitation
for drinking, washing, and gardening. If your home or holiday cottage has a
rainwater tank, make sure that it has a cover to prevent rodents and native marsupials
drowning in it and contaminating the water.

Australian mains water is completely safe, and the taste is generally good. In most areas the supply is fluoridated to promote dental health. Unlike the water supply in most British areas, Australian water is 'soft', that is, it does not contain lime-scale. This means that soaps lather easily, tap fittings and appliances do not require the same maintenance, and dishwashers do not need the addition of salt. During the summer months, however, garden hoses and domestic swimming pools can be the site of the bacteria which cause amoebic meningitis, and it is extremely important to maintain chemical levels in pools, and to let the water run for a while before allowing children to play with or drink from garden hoses.

Residential Rates and Other Charges

Council rates are levied annually and are the responsibility of the property owner. They are a tax on property and not on the individual. Tenants do not have to meet any council rates charges, which include a Refuse Charge for the collection of domestic rubbish, and charges for amenities provided by the council. Council rates are determined by the location and size of the property, and are calculated by the Valuer-General on its gross rental value. Property valuations are made approximately every two years. Rates will be higher if you buy a house in a high demand area with excellent services and amenities. On an average, middle-class Australian suburban family home, you can expect a general rates charge of around $600 as well as an additional levy for refuse collection.

Rates and charges are payable to the local or shire council can be paid in two instalments, in which case an instalment surcharge applies. A discount is sometimes given for prompt payment, but more often prompt payers are rewarded by entry into a council draw which will offer a substantial prize, such as an international holiday or free rates for a year. Details of the council raffle will be published in the local newspaper in addition to being supplied with the rates notice.

Telecommunications

Until the late 1980s, Australia's telecommunications were controlled by a state monopoly, Telecom Australia. Since then, the market has gradually been deregulated, allowing at first just a single competitor, Optus. In 1997, however, full deregulation was achieved, and there are now a host of options in the telecommunications market, resulting in vastly reduced costs and, in general, a much more competitive service. Telstra (formerly known as Telecom Australia and 51% government owned) still dominates the local and domestic market, although Optus has a significant share of the interstate and international long-distance market. Today, there are more than 100 telecommunication providers. Telephone lines are mostly land-based and reach about 96% of all households. There are about eight million mobile phone subscribers (42% of the population and one of the highest user rates in the world) and over seven million Internet users in Australia. International telecommunications links are provided by the Overseas Telecommunication Commission (OTC). Since deregulation, ISDN suppliers have multiplied exponentially, and it is now possible to call abroad very cheaply by subscribing to one of these services, such as Primus or DigiPlus. Services and special offers are advertised in daily newspapers, and after subscribing, you simply prefix a special call-code to the number you want to dial. You will receive a separate bill from your supplier, and the service can be run concurrently with your Telstra or Optus account. International call rates are falling almost daily due to competition among phone companies. Calls to the UK and the USA are currently around $0.21 per minute – compared to a charge of around $1.60 per minute 10 years ago.

All Australian homes are fitted with a telephone line, and a second line with a different number can be installed for $190 from Telstra, but there are special deals and packages available from all suppliers and it is a good idea to shop around. Telephone bills are issued quarterly by each of the suppliers whose services you use. Telstra and Optus bills include local metered calls, STD (interstate/long distance national) calls, and IDD (international) calls, as well as service fees, equipment and any other charges. Service charges are around $20 a month, and customers can choose either to buy their own telephone handsets (in which case there are no equipment charges), or to rent handsets from Telstra or Optus for around $5 per quarter per phone. Fax machines operate via the standard phone line, and their use is charged in the same way as a phone call. Mobile phone services are run by various cellnet providers, such as Vodaphone, and offer much the same range of contract options as available in the UK and USA; once again, they are billed separately from the main phone number.

In Australia, local calls are charged at a *flat rate* of 25 cents from a domestic phone (on a payphone, 40 cents), regardless of the length of the call. Whether you are on the phone for three seconds or three hours, the cost of the call is always the same, and you never need to worry about running up your phone bill or calling during economy periods if you are phoning within the suburban boundaries of your city or town. Flat rate local calling is of particular significance in the electronic communications sector and is one reason why Australia leads the world in domestic internet access: for the cost of a 25 cent call to your internet service provider, you can surf the net for as long as you wish without incurring any further calling charges. Long distance national and international calls are, however, charged according to the distance and the length of the call, as well as by time zone: Day rate (8am-6pm) is the most expensive, Economy rate (7am-9am, 6pm-9pm) is somewhat cheaper, and Night rate (9pm-7am and all weekend) the most economical for national calls.

THE CODES FOR DIALLING AUSTRALIA DIRECT FROM ABROAD ARE:	
Adelaide	00-61 8
Brisbane	00-61 7
Canberra	00-61 6
Darwin	00-61 8
Hobart	00-61 3
Perth	00-61 8
Melbourne	00-61 3
Sydney	00-61 2

The code should prefix the local number, which will be 8 digits long in most capital cities, and six digits long in more rural areas. If you are dialling a number within Australia you must place a zero before the area prefix above before dialling. International directory assistance (from the UK, call 118505) can advise on changes should you have any out-of-date contact numbers. To dial overseas from Australia, prefix the number you require firstly with your international call supplier over-ride number, then add the international dialling code 0011. International faxes are sent using the code 0015. Other phone companies include AAPT (www.aapt.com.au), Go*talk* Australia (www.gotalk.com.au), Omniplus (www.omniplus.com.au), and Primus Telecommunications (www.primus.com.au). Ensure that your preferred company provides a service in your area.

REMOVALS

Most people making a long-term or permanent move abroad will want to arrange to take some or all of their personal effects with them. The costs involved in doing so can be high, but a carefully planned move will save you money by minimising setting-up expenses on arrival. Household items vary widely in replacement value from country to country; so a little research will pay off in deciding what to take and what to leave behind. In making your calculations you should consider the second-hand sale value of your effects in your home country against both the cost of shipping and insurance, and the cost of replacement. Car boot sales are an excellent way to dispose of the accumulated junk that you will inevitably uncover when you start going through your cupboards with a major international move in mind, but don't underestimate the sentimental value of items: there are some things that will simply have to go with you, no matter how worthless or unlikely.

Household Goods

There are many removal companies specialising in international shipping. The large national firms advertise in the regional Yellow Pages telephone directories, along with smaller local firms, and any reputable firm will be able to outline their costs (charged per cubic meter) over the telephone. The quality of the service provided is an important consideration when undertaking an international move and you should make sure that the remover offers 'export-quality packing' and deals with every aspect of the customs and shipping process. Once you have established a short-list of remover, you should request a formal quote (which will be free of charge). An estimator will visit your home and examine the contents of every room to assess the cubic meterage to be packed and shipped. Antiques and other items of special value may be assessed at a different rate. Most removers also broker their own insurance packages, which are generally charged at around three per cent of the value of the consignment, and although this can amount to a considerable sum on an average family's effects, it is an indispensable expense. Your valued possessions will spend around three months going from store to ship to customs warehouse before finally being unpacked in your new home, and it is very rare for a consignment to arrive completely undamaged.

Professional removers are remarkably efficient and can pack an average family house in one or two days. For a move to Australia, they will use export-quality packing, which is much more time-consuming than packing for a local removal. The removals men will wrap all furniture items in paper blankets, dismantling them where possible, and will also individually wrap every item of kitchenware and any other small items. Everything else will be packed in specially designed heavy-duty cardboard cartons (such as book boxes, linen boxes and picture boxes). International shipping is costed by volume not weight, and a good remover will pack lightweight items, such as linen, inside empty furniture (for example, chests-of-drawers) to reduce volume. You should bear this in mind when considering what to take: it may mean that if you plan to take certain furniture items, you will in effect be able to take linen or children's stuffed toys for 'free'. It is possible to self-pack for an international move, but the small cost saving it permits is cancelled out by the higher insurance premiums you must then pay.

Extensive list making will probably play a large part in your daily life when organising a move on this scale, and it is important to consider carefully which items to take with you to Australia. The *British Association of Removers* (address below) provides a useful list which may help in planning. As a general rule, it is much cheaper and easier to ship furniture than to replace it with new items at your destination, with some exceptions. Beds do not travel well, as a mattress which is packed vertically for three months will generally arrive with sagging springs; pianos do not benefit from the sudden climate change, may warp in the moist sea air, and frequently cannot be properly retuned; and vinyl seating is inappropriate for hot-weather countries. All Australian homes, whether rented or bought, come with a cooker installed (which is never taken with you when you move) and it is therefore redundant to ship your own. You would also be well advised to buy a new refrigerator on arrival, as Australian fridges are much larger and have extra fan assistance to cope with the climate, as well as a new television and video. Televisions from home can be converted to work in Australia, but it is expensive and often less than successful. Fax machines and telephones cannot be imported unless they conform to the Australian telecommunications standards. Most modern Australian homes also have built-in wardrobes, and so you may also decide to leave these behind, especially as their large volume makes freestanding wardrobes expensive to ship.

Taking your Car

Most removal companies also offer the option of shipping your motor vehicle and will supply all the necessary information including lists of customs and port charges, as well as providing a quote for shipping a private motorcar to Australia. The services provided by the shipper should include full preparation for containerisation, for example, covering the interior with floor mats and seat covers, and inserting silica desiccant bags or pillows to help avoid the possibility of condensation damage in the car. The car will be packed into a 'sole use' twenty foot ISO Reefer Container and secured in accordance with manufacturers' recommendations at the removers' warehouse. The quote should include return haulage of the container to the export loading berth, all port and handling charges, all export and customs documentation, provision of Bills of Loading to a nominated address on arrival, and all freight charges through to the destination port. Insurance is calculated at around 1.5% of the car's insured value, and Australian unpacking and quarantine inspection charges are payable on arrival. Shipping to Australia takes between four and eight weeks, depending on the final destination. In addition to meeting the costs involved in transporting your vehicle to Australia, you will also be liable on arrival for the cost of ensuring that your vehicle meets Australian safety standards under the Motor Vehicle Standards Act of 1989. This process, known as 'compliance', can be very expensive, and your car will not be able to receive temporary registration (and thus be driven) until it has been completed. The total amount of money involved in shipping a car to Australia including freight, taxes, insurance, compliance, and re-registration, means that unless your vehicle is a very special, rare or luxurious, it is very rarely worthwhile. For those who decide to proceed, further information is given below in the section on Australian Customs.

Taking Pets

Moving your pets to Australia is as complicated and expensive a process as moving yourself and your family. Australian quarantine rules are extremely strict in order to protect the disease-free status of Australian livestock afforded by the country's geographical isolation. Most commonly, new arrivals choose to import their family pets, generally cats or dogs, and for this an Import Permit must be obtained from Australian Quarantine and Inspection Service (AQIS) in the State or Territory into which you plan to bring your animal. Stringent health and certification requirements must be met, which include identifying your pet with a microchip number, vaccinating the animal against an extensive list of diseases as well as testing for the absence of certain viruses 21 days prior to export. All cats and dogs must be treated for internal parasites 14 days before export and must pass a clinical examination 48 hours before shipment. Each animal must be accompanied by a certificate of inspection issued by an Official Veterinarian of the country of export. The types of containers in which animals may be exported are also strictly specified by Australian law and an animal will not be permitted to enter the country if it arrives in a non-IATA approved container. Both dogs and cats are required to undergo a period of quarantine on arrival in Australia at one of three centres (in Victoria, New South Wales and Western Australia). If you are moving to another state, you will incur additional costs in freighting your animal to your new home after it completes its period of quarantine. Dogs and cats from approved rabies-free countries, which meet all the vaccination and certification requirements for import, are currently quarantined for a period of 30 days on arrival in Australia.

Costs for importing pets are high: the cost of transportation depends on the size rather than the weight of the object shipped, so taking your cat to Australia with you will be far cheaper than shipping a dog the size of a labrador. The cost of the extensive veterinary treatment and testing required for import needs to be taken into account, and you must also allow for the quarantine costs payable in advance in Australia. Currently the cost of quarantine for a cat is $12 a day and for a dog $16 a day. If you add to this additional charges incurred during the quarantine and inspection process, transporting a pet will add at least another $1,000 to your moving costs.

Information on exporting pets from the UK is dealt with by local Animal Health Divisional Offices. A full list of these offices and contact details is available at http://www.defra.gov.uk/corporate/contacts/ahdo.htm

Useful Addresses

Air Pets Oceanic, Willowslea Farm Kennels, Spout Lane North, Stanwell Moor, Staines, Middlesex TW19 6BW; ☎01753-685571; fax 01753-681655; e-mail info@airpets.com; www.airpets.com.

Allied Pickfords, Heritage House, 345 Southbury Road, Enfield, Middlesex, EN1 1UP; ☎020-8219 8000 (freephone 0800-289 229); fax 020-8219 8001; www.alliedpickfords.co.uk.

Anglo Pacific International Plc, Units 1 and 2, Bush Industrial Estate, Standard

Road, London NW10 6DF; ☎020-8838 8434; e-mail info@anglopacific. co.uk; www.anglopacific.co.uk.

British Association of Removers, 3 Churchill Court, 58 Station Road, North Harrow, Middlesex HA2 7SA; ☎020-8861 3331; fax 020-8861 3332; e-mail info@bar. co.uk; www.removers.org.uk.

Crown Worldwide Group, Security House, Abbey Wharf Industrial Estate, Kingsbridge Road, Barking, Essex IG11 OBD; ☎020-8591 3388; fax 020-8594 4571; www.crownworldwide.com.

Karman Shipping, Timber Lodge, Plantation Road, Leighton Buzzard, Bedfordshire LU7 3JB; ☎01525-851545; fax 01525-850996; e-mail info@karmanshipping. com; www.karmanshipping.co.uk. Motor vehicle shipping specialists.

Ladyhaye, Hare Lane, Blindley Heath, Lingfield, Surrey RH7 0HJ; ☎01342-832161; fax 01342 834778; e-mail info@ladyhaye.co.uk; www.ladyhaye.co.uk. International pet travel agent.

Worldwide Animal Travel, 43 London Road, Brentwood, Essex CM14 4NN; ☎01277-231611.

The *Australian Quarantine Information Service (AQIS)*, Australian Government, Department of Agriculture, Fisheries, and Forestry, Edmund Barton Building, Broughton Street, Barton, Canberra, ACT 2601; ☎02-6272 3933; www.aqis. gov.au, provides quarantine inspection services for the arrival of animals into Australia and inspection and certification of animals exported from Australia.

Australian Customs Regulations

The Australian Customs Service is extremely stringent in order to protect Australian flora and fauna from the many diseases affecting plants and animals, such as rabies, foot-and-mouth disease, and BSE, found elsewhere in the world. Any wood or wooden artefacts, including furniture, must be declared to Customs on arrival in the country, so that it can first be quarantined and fumigated. This provision extends to items such as straw hats and wooden kitchen utensils. Garden equipment, lawnmowers, and outdoor furniture will be specially inspected, fumigated and cleaned (at your expense). Products made from protected wildlife species, non-approved cordless phones, live animals and weapons and firearms (which are either prohibited or require a permit and safety testing) are also prohibited imports. You must also declare all goods of animal and plant origin, including all fresh, frozen or tinned food, fruit, vegetables and flowers. Penalties of $50,000 to $100,000 and jail terms of five to10 years may be levied on people who contravene customs regulations, so it is important to take some care when filling out your customs declarations forms before shipping your personal effects, and when arriving in the country.

> International flights are fumigated before passengers are allowed to disembark to ensure that no diseases enter the country on your person, your clothing or luggage. Although the spray used can be slightly irritating (it is recommended that you cover your nose and mouth, although the chemicals have been declared perfectly safe), it is an important part of the process of *making* sure Australia stays disease-free.

Like most countries in the world today, illicit drugs, including marijuana, are strictly prohibited and Australian Customs are very efficient in policing the entry of drugs into Australia. Flights arriving from Asia are often very slow to clear customs as officials will be especially rigorous with checking passengers travelling from or through this region. Under *no* circumstances should you agree to carry illicit drugs or any other package for anyone else, as you will bear the responsibility for any prohibited substance found in your possession.

Personal effects shipped into Australia for your own use, and owned and used by you previously, do not attract duties or other taxes on arrival in port. If you are thinking about taking your vehicle with you to Australia you should take into account the costs (and hassle) involved in the process - freight costs, customs duties and entry processing charges, the cost of steam cleaning the vehicle for quarantine purposes, wharf and transport charges and costs involved in having the vehicle meet state or territory registration requirements. Tourists and temporary residents can take a motor vehicle or motorcycle into Australia for a period of up to 12 months without paying duty provided that the vehicles are re-exported from Australia at the end of that period. For this concession to apply, you will need a *Carnet de Passages en Douanes* issued by an overseas organisation which has a reciprocal arrangement with the Australian Automobile Association, as well as a cash or bank security equal to the amount of duty and GST otherwise payable.

Since 1 July 2000, a 10% tax on goods and services (GST) has replaced the old sales tax which applied to the purchase of goods. The current duty-free allowance for travellers includes 1125 ml of alcohol, 250 cigarettes or 250 grams of cigars or tobacco products other than cigarettes and up to $400 of duty-free goods. It is your responsibility to declare anything else that may be liable for GST. Duty-free shops at Australian airports are often cheaper than those at home, and there are shops prior to Customs in the arrivals hall of most international airports, which means it may be better not to 'buy before you fly'.

The Australian Customs Service provides full information on all aspects of its operations atwww.customs.gov.au.

BUYING A CAR IN AUSTRALIA

Australian cars are right-hand-drive, as in the UK, and since 1989 the importation of left-hand-drive vehicles has been prohibited. Although there remain a small number of left-hand-drive cars imported before 1989, in general, these cars are not well suited to Australian driving conditions, and parts and servicing are expensive. For the UK immigrant, driving conditions and road regulations will be reassuringly familiar, although you will notice that cars tend to be larger than in Europe. Cheaper petrol, wider roads and easier parking all contribute to a preference for more spacious and powerful family vehicles. Australia has a well-established motor industry with Ford and General Motors Holden building a large proportion of cars on the road. Japanese cars also have a much stronger presence than in Europe, and Mitsubishi, Toyota and Nissan all produce cars in Australia to Japanese levels of quality control. The practice of 'rebadging' means that many models will be familiar in their appearance to visitors and new arrivals, although they are likely to have different names. European cars of any model are very expensive in Australia because of high importation costs, which now includes a prohibitive 'luxury car tax'. This tax applies not only to obviously up-market luxury vehicles, such as Mercedes, but also to cheaper makes such as Peugeot, Fiat and VW; as a result there is a certain prestige value in driving such vehicles, although in many cases home-grown versions are superior in finish and performance. The luxury tax also applies to imported parts which can make servicing a car of European origin very expensive. As a general rule, you should expect to pay considerably more for a vehicle in Australia than you would back home, especially if you are considering a second-hand car.

The registration and taxing of vehicles is the responsibility of State Departments of Transport, and while some states (for example, NSW) have a system equivalent to the British MOT, others do not. As a result of this, and because of the high cost of new cars, there tend to be many more older cars on the road than you will find at home and people tend to hang on to their cars for a number of years before deciding to upgrade. It is important, especially if you buy an older vehicle, that you keep your car's registration (equivalent to a tax disk) current, as, once lapsed, renewal cannot be effected until the car has undergone an extremely thorough safety check at the police vehicle registration centre. Once headed for the pits because of expired registration, it is usually difficult and expensive to get the car back on the road. Police also have the power to stop any vehicle in an obvious state of disrepair, and will frequently issue a 'Yellow Sticker' which identifies the car as unroadworthy. The car must not be driven until it has been repaired and inspected by the vehicle licensing authority. Emissions control is also taken very seriously and other drivers may, and often do, report vehicles with dirty exhaust emissions; the driver of such a car will receive a letter requiring that the problem be remedied, and this may be followed up by an inspection.

Most newer Australian cars have automatic transmission in preference to manual, and many have air conditioning and tinted windows to reduce problems of heat and glare. Sunroofs are unusual, as extreme temperature conditions makes them impractical – Australians aim to keep heat out, not bask in it. All modern cars run on unleaded petrol, and for older cars a 'lead replacement petrol' is sold. Many larger cars, particularly of the popular off-road variety, run on diesel, which is significantly cheaper than petrol.

New Cars

Buying a new car in Australia is little different from doing so in the UK, USA or elsewhere. Manufacturers market their vehicles through licensed dealers who advertise in the daily press and in the local Yellow Pages. The new car market is currently very competitive and it is important to shop around widely. There is always room for negotiation on price or on bonus extras such as air-conditioning, stereo, and additional safety features. Traditionally, new car prices are discounted significantly at the end of the Australian financial year which falls in late June, when dealers particularly aim to attract the business and fleet buying markets. Car models which are about to be superseded are also often very much reduced in price to enable dealers to clear their stock and can be excellent buys; look out, too, for ex-demonstration vehicles which may have no more than a few hundred kilometres on the clock. The daily newspapers in each capital city generally allocate one day of the week to a motoring section or motoring advertising (on Wednesday and Saturday in *The West Australian*, for example), and scouring these pages will generally reveal the best buys and allow you to compare dealer prices. A number of car buyers' guides and magazines are widely available in newsagents, providing detailed technical information and assessments of every car currently on the market. Note that there are a number of abbreviations in common use in car advertisements, including abs (anti-lock braking system), ac (air conditioning), at (automatic transmission), cc (cruise control), cl (central locking), ps (power steering), pw (power windows), srs (supplementary restraint system), and mags (alloy wheels).

A very high proportion of new cars bought in Australia are registered in company names and if you expect to use your car for business purposes, most dealers will have specially tailored schemes to maximise the tax benefits for your company. Popular manufacturers like Ford, Holden, Toyota and Mitsubishi also provide business versions of their mainstream models. Leasing, rather than buying, is frequently advantageous to the business car user and offers both tax efficiency and ease of replacement. Other schemes offer a guaranteed replacement value (if the car is bought with dealer finance and serviced by them throughout the period of the contract), allowing an upgrade to a new model after a designated number of years.

Used Cars

New cars tend to depreciate dramatically in value once in use, and given the high price of a new car in Australia, many people prefer to buy second hand models. These are available from both specialist second-hand dealers and through the used car division of licensed new car dealers, as well as by private sale. Cars offered for sale privately are usually advertised in the classifieds section of the main state and local newspapers, and in auto classifieds magazines. Many dealers of new cars also sell used cars obtained by them through part-exchange (known in Australia as a 'trade-in'); such cars are likely to be more expensive than an equivalent vehicle sold privately, but will usually have the advantage of a dealer's warranty. By law, used cars offered for sale above a certain benchmark price (which varies from state to state) may not be offered for sale by a dealer without the provision of a warranty, the minimum terms of which are also laid down by the state government.

Travellers and temporary residents may find it more convenient to purchase a vehicle under a guaranteed buy-back arrangement. A number of firms specialise in selling cars by this method, ensuring that the vehicle is legal and roadworthy at the time of purchase and guaranteeing to repurchase it at the end of the stay.

Car theft is prevalent in many cities in Australia, so if you choose to buy a car privately you should ensure that the vehicle is neither a stolen one nor otherwise financially encumbered; if you buy a car on which the vendor still owes money the vehicle can be repossessed if they default on any payment. Remember that the loan company has first call on its security, and you could lose a considerable amount of money. Vehicle registrations may be checked free of charge against the government registers of financially encumbered vehicles, listed below:

NSW/ACT/NT: Register of Encumbered Vehicles (REVS), Level 5, 1 Fitzwilliam Street, Parramatta, NSW 2150; ☎ 02-9633 6333; fax 02-9891 5135; www.revs. nsw.gov.au.

QLD: Motor Vehicles Securities Register, Office of Fair Trading, Level 21, State Law Building, 45 Ann Street, Brisbane, QLD 4001, ☎ 07-3246 1500; www.fairtrading. qld.gov.au.

SA: Vehicle Securities Register, Ground Floor, EDS Centre, 108 North Terrace, Adelaide, SA 5000; ☎ 131 084; fax 08-8204 8308; www.transport.sa.gov.au.

TAS: Transport Division, Department of Infrastructure, Energy and Resources, GPO Box 936, Hobart, TAS 7001; ☎ 1300-135 513; fax 03-6233 3441; www.transport.

tas.gov.au/regstat/.

VIC: Vicroads, Vehicle Securities Register, 60 Denmark Street, Kew, VIC 3101; ☎ 131 171; www.vicroads.vic.gov.au. There are also maxi kiosks situated at various locations across Victoria.

WA: Register of Encumbered Vehicles (REVS), 219 St. George's Terrace, Perth, WA 6000; ☎ 1300·304 024.

When buying a used car, it is usual to pay an authorised, qualified mechanic from one of the automobile associations to make a thorough mechanical examination. The cost of such an examination (between $100 and $150) could well save you thousands of dollars by warning you off a potential lemon. It is not necessary to be a member of an automobile association to use such a service, although members will receive a discounted rate. Federal regulations govern safety standards including seat belts, emissions, tyres and engine noise; and state governments may have additional legislation. A vehicle that fails to conform to safety standards will not be registered until modifications have been made.

Once you have found and purchased your new used car, you will need to fill out a form to transfer ownership into your name. These forms are available from the local vehicle-licensing centre, and it is usually the vendor's responsibility to supply them at the time of purchase, signing the appropriate sections. The value of the vehicle must be declared on the form, and from this a transfer tax or stamp duty is calculated, the amount ranging from tens to hundreds of dollars, and must be paid within 30 days to affect the transfer of ownership.

Motor Insurance

In Australia the vehicle, rather than the driver, is covered by any insurance. Thus, anyone who has your permission to do so may drive your car (providing that they have a full Australian or equivalent licence and the car is privately owned) and will be fully covered by your existing insurance. Motor vehicle insurance tends to be slightly cheaper in Australia than at home, but is subject to the same kinds of variables. Around 80% of Australian car owners choose to take out extra private insurance. Factors affecting insurance costs include the make and model of the car, the location of your residence, and the age and experience of the usual driver. Sports cars and high performance cars attract higher premiums, as do 'modified' vehicles; and drivers resident in non-metropolitan areas are likely to pay less for their insurance, although this varies widely and may mean significant differences in quotes if you shop around. Young drivers under the age of 25 will invariably be charged more, however, most companies now offer scaled premiums for those over 25, as well as discounted policies for the over-55s. Drivers who borrow to finance the purchase of their vehicle will usually also pay more in premiums. Insurers are increasingly offering policyholders a choice of excess, ranging from $50 to $500: a lower excess will generally mean a higher premium, although this can be offset by your no-claims record. Drivers with a motor vehicle insurance history gained overseas are usually able to 'import' their no-claims bonus, up to its full value. It is important to bring a letter from your previous insurer confirming your no-claims status so that it can be immediately applied to your new policy.

A new development in Australian car insurance has been the introduction of 'agreed value' sum-insured options. In the past, most policies paid on the basis of the 'market value' of your car at the time of the claim, however, the agreed value type of policy enables you to agree a fixed value for the term of your policy. An agreed value policy is generally a little more expensive, but may be worthwhile especially for older vehicles. Some policies also offer added extras such as travel and medical insurance. Covering the cost of car hire and accommodation in case of accident may also be useful, as may be the use of a courtesy car while repairs are made, while some policies offer brand-new replacement vehicles for damaged cars less than one year old.

Compulsory Third Party Insurance. Third Party Insurance (CTP Greenslip) is compulsory in Australia and the cost of this insurance is included in the vehicle registration charge paid to the State or Territory government. Third Party Insurance covers the driver for injuries to any other person caused in the course of driving, however, insurance against third party property damage must be taken out separately, and is the responsibility of the car owner. Expect to pay upwards of $230.

Third Party Property Insurance. Third Party Property Insurance (TPPI) covers the cost of any damage done *by* your vehicle in the course of an accident, but does *not* cover the damage done *to* your own car. TPPI is a very economical insurance option, rarely exceeding $200, and is popular with owners of old cars with little resale value.

Comprehensive Insurance. Comprehensive cover costs considerably more than TTPI and ranges between $275-$600, with discounts of up to 60% available to holders of a full no-claims bonus. Comprehensive insurance covers your car for accidental damage, theft and fire and gives liability cover for damage you may cause to someone else's car or property. Insurance companies assess their premiums by the following criteria:

- Accident Record: Do you have one?
- Age: Of both you and your vehicle (if you are less 25 years old, you will pay more).
- Business or Private Use: Insurance premiums are higher for business vehicles.
- Experience: How long have you been driving?
- Finance: Unfinanced vehicles are cheaper to insure.
- Make and Model: Some models pose a higher risk of theft or are more expensive to repair.
- Residence: Do you live in a high risk area?
- Sex: In certain age groups females have fewer accident claims than males.
- Trailer/Caravan: You are likely to need a separate policy for these vehicles to cover against damage caused by side-swiping.
- Value: Of the vehicle.

The cost of comprehensive motor vehicle insurance varies widely according to the above criteria and other factors. The best policy is to shop around – through the Yellow Pages, or by using an insurance broker. Forty per cent of policies are now placed through brokers, who have immediate access to a huge range of policies and are thus able to obtain the cheapest one for your needs with a minimum of difficulty. A broker is legally bound to operate in the interests of the policy buyer and not of the companies whose policies he represents. Nonetheless, it is important to ensure that a broker is reputable, and so you should check that the firm is registered with the NIBA (National Insurance Brokers Association). Brokers are paid either by commission from insurance companies, or by fees charged for their advice to the consumer. Most brokers, however, will not charge a fee when arranging simple domestic and motor vehicle insurance. If a broker does charge a fee it must be fully declared at the beginning of the transaction.

Insurance companies, automobile associations offering insurance, and insurance brokers can all be found in the Yellow Pages. In addition, some companies now allow customers to take out insurance over the Internet meaning that transactions can be undertaken 24 hours a day with the whole quote-confirmation-payment process conducted online in a secure environment. Australia's biggest and most reputable insurance companies include AMP, Allianz, AAMI, SGIC, GIO, and RAC.

Useful Contacts

Australia Associated Motor Insurers (AAMI), PO Box 14180, Melbourne City Mail Centre, VIC 8062; ☎132 244; e-mail aami@aami.com.au; www.aami.com.au. Branches in NSW, Queensland, Tasmania, and ACT.

Allianz Australia Ltd, GPO Box 4049, Sydney, NSW 2001; ☎132 664 (local call); www.allianz.com.au.

AMP, to find the location of the nearest AMP insurance adviser ☎133 888 (within Australia); www.amp.com.au.

SGIC General Insurance Limited, South Australian Main Office, 211 Victoria Square, Adelaide, SA 5000; ☎133 233; fax 08-8233 1086; www.sgic.com.au.

GIO Insurance, GIO branch ☎131 010; www.gio.com.au.

National Insurance Brokers Association of Australia, (*NIRA*) Level 18, 111 Pacific Highway, North Sydney, NSW 2060; ☎02-9964 9400, or 1800-252 558; fax 02-9964 9332; e-mail niba@niba.com.au; www.niba.com.au.

National Roads and Motorists' Association Limited (NRMA), Podium Level 3, Bankstown Square, North Terrace, Bankstown, NSW 2200; ☎132 132; www.nrma.com.au.

Royal Automobile Club of Australia, 89 Macquarie Street, Sydney, NSW 2000; ☎02-8273 2300; fax 02-8273 2301; e-mail raca@raca.com.au; www.raca.com.au.

DAILY LIFE

CHAPTER SUMMARY

○ **Population.** Nearly 90% of the Australian population lives in coastal cities.

○ The beach is the cornerstone of Australian life.

○ **Children and Education.** Distance education is vital for outback children of all ages living miles from anywhere.

   ○ Distance lessons are given by radio and Internet.

   ○ Factor 15 sunscreen is provided free to all primary school students.

○ **Motoring.** It is legal to overtake on the inside on a dual carriageway and is known as 'undertaking.'

   ○ On a three-lane highway you can overtake in any lane.

   ○ Hitch-hiking is illegal in Victoria.

   ○ Drink-driving is considered a serious issue and motorists can be stopped and tested at random.

○ **Railways**. Rail travel is expensive and is done for the experience, not convenience.

   ○ One of the great railway trips of the world is between Perth and Sydney.

○ **Banking.** Even those with bad credit records can open accounts easily, provided that they meet the criteria for proving identity and place of abode.

○ **Tax.** The Australian tax year runs from July 1st to June 30th.

○ **Health.** The perceived healthy lifestyle of the Australians is gainsaid by the fact that 56% of adults are overweight and cholesterol busting drugs cost the health service more than half a million dollars annually.

One of the great attractions of Australia for many immigrants and other new arrivals is the quality of life it offers. Cosmopolitan cities border a landscape of sometimes awe-inspiring beauty, and most people enjoy circumstances in which work and play combine to provide the sort of relaxed and comfortable lifestyle available only to the very wealthy in Europe. Public facilities of all types are generally good, and standards in health care and education are very high, relative to other industrialised nations. Housing is also generally more spacious and affordable than in the UK and other European countries although more expensive than in the USA, and most homes have gardens and outdoor living areas designed to take advantage of the climate, and opportunities for family and other entertaining. Australia is one of the world's most urbanised societies, and nearly 90% of the population live in coastal cities consisting of sprawling suburbs with a high-rise city centre or CBD (central business district). All of Australia's state capitals are built on or very near the water – even the inland city of Canberra has been designed around a giant artificial lake, allowing residents to partake in the water-based activities which are part of the Australian lifestyle. In the shadow of the cities' skyscrapers, labyrinths of interconnecting courtyards and arcades offer shopping, cafés and restaurants, and the country has in recent years become world-famous for its restaurant culture and cuisine. Leisure is important to Australians, and the weekend has become a sacred institution devoted to pottering in the garden, preparing the family barbecue, or sports. Parks and ovals are taken over with children playing cricket, football, or riding their bicycles; some families head for the bush, others for the beach, and national parks are busy with picnickers. There is still significant resistance to Sunday trading but changes to trading regulations mean that shops which previously closed at 1pm on Saturday are now open all day, and in the more touristy areas of Australia Sunday trading is permitted. Larger shops in the larger cities will generally open for at least a part of Sunday and more and more working people are using the weekend to catch up on their shopping. In the summer, beachlife rules. Called the 'great leveller', the beach is accessible to all ages and social classes and is the cornerstone of Australian life.

EDUCATION

Australian education is internationally regarded as being of a high standard, particularly in tertiary institutions. An Australian honours degree holds a higher status than a UK honours degree in the UK university system, and holders of such degrees on scholarships to premier universities, such as Oxford and Cambridge, are exempted from one year of study at postgraduate level. International surveys of educational standards recognise Australia scoring up at the top of the list, with Germany and Japan, in terms of science education. Early education practice in Australia is significantly different to that of the UK or USA and many experts attribute later academic success to the different emphasis in teaching methods of young children where emphasis is put on self discipline, on learning by finding out, by questioning and by encouraging a child's interest and enthusiasm for learning.

Education is the responsibility of state governments, and is compulsory between the ages of five and 15. Upper secondary schooling begins at 12 or 13 years old and continues on to age 17 or 18; these extra years are mandatory for students considering further education and school retention rates are very high, averaging around 70%. Around 70% of Australian children attend free, public state-funded schools, which are mostly co-educational and non-religious. A parallel fee-paying, private sector also exists, and most such schools are run by various religious institutions and are single sex institutions. Children who need to attend boarding school in their secondary school years because of rural isolation will usually attend schools of this type, and their boarding costs are subsidised by the government. In the primary years, children in the outback are educated by the 'School of the Air' which provides distance learning by radio and correspondence. There are now a number of schools offering the International Baccalaureate programme to those in their final years of schooling. For children of parents who might be on short-term work contracts in Australia, the International Baccalaureate programme allows them to gain entry into universities in their home country, and into some universities in the USA.

Two magazines for emigrants to Victoria and New South Wales, *Choosing a School for your Child in Victoria* and *Choosing a School for your Child in NSW*, are available by subscription from Consyl Publishing, details of which are given below. These publications give useful information regarding the kinds of schools available in these states and answer many of the questions which arise when choosing a new school in an unfamiliar country. The New South Wales version of the magazine also covers boarding schools in NSW, Victoria, Queensland and Canberra.

Australia's academic year of three or four terms, depending on the state, follows the calendar year, running from January to December, so that the long summer holidays of around seven weeks coincide with the Christmas period.

The Structure of the Education System

The educational system is uniform in Australia and both the private and state sectors operate on the same patterns and curricula. Primary education in Australia takes six or seven years, depending on the state, and secondary education either five or six years, depending on the state. Wherever you live in Australia, the combined length of primary and secondary education is 12 years, and school years are numbered Years 1 to 12.

Pre-School. Pre-schooling is available for children aged four and five years old, and provides educational programmes in which young children are encouraged to develop their abilities, skills and knowledge of the world. Preschool centres operate in association with local primary schools, and, where possible, are located in the same grounds. In Western Australia and some of the eastern states, there is an early learning continuum, which covers children aged three to eight years (K-3). The principles of this system recognise the distinctive learning patterns of young children, the nature of children's growth and development, and the value of home and community in learning. Children are encouraged to learn through play, experimentation, and interaction with other children and adults, learning to explore, manipulate objects, materials and technologies. Early reading is neither required nor pushed, and most children enter school in the year they turn six without any reading skills. Current research suggests that this is in fact more effective in encouraging later literacy than enforced early reading in the nursery years, and Australian results bear this out. Instead, preschools focus heavily on creativity and thinking skills, which can be applied later to more academic purposes. Children attend preschool mornings only in their first year, and from

9am to 3pm in their second year.

Primary School Education. Children enter primary school in the year they turn six, and there is no concept of 'rising fives' or term-by-term age-group entry. There is very little multi-age teaching in primary classrooms, except where numbers and resources require combined classes (in some rural areas, and in suburbs with falling rolls). Classes in state schools have a maximum of 30 students and many are smaller, depending on area. State primary schools are almost invariably co-educational, however, many private schools offer single-sex education at this level. Each state sets its own curriculum, but all have common elements, emphasising English language, mathematics, social studies, health education, and physical education. Many primary schools offer foreign languages from year three and there is a much greater focus on languages of the region, for example, Mandarin Chinese, Japanese and Indonesian. It is less common for children to study French or German, and Latin is not a commonly taught subject. Philosophy and thinking skills are now taught in most schools from year five, and there is a strong emphasis on creative work from the earliest years. Oral communication skills are developed early, and children as young as five will be expected to speak to the class regularly on topics of interest. Sports are an important part of the school day, and in summer all children will have daily swimming lessons. School assemblies provide an opportunity for classes to make drama presentations and are largely the responsibility of the students. Parents are encouraged to attend these weekly occasions. The school day usually runs from 8.50am to 3.15pm, but this will vary slightly from state to state.

Secondary Education. After finishing either year six or seven, depending on the state, children progress on to secondary school, which is known as 'high school'. In the state sector these are usually of the comprehensive variety, although some states still run a streamed, grammar school system, and other offer special programmes to children gifted in certain fields. These specialist programmes in music, theatre studies, art or sport offer scholarships to talented students from all over the state or territory, and entry is highly competitive. High school students enjoy modern facilities, and are taught a variety of subjects, which include the core studies of English, maths, science and social studies (history and geography), as well as art, home economics and languages. In many high schools, students in the first year must take the whole range of subjects available despite personal preferences in order to try and help them develop wider interests or recognise previously undiscovered talents. This means that regardless of gender, all students will have to study cooking, sewing, woodwork, metalwork, art, music, drama and sport, as required by the school. As students progress through the high school system, they are allowed to specialise in subjects of their own choosing, until they reach the final two years of school, where subject choices will be determined by future career preferences.

Special Needs Children. Special schools are provided for physically and mentally disabled children. Within the state system, children with learning disabilities are provided with special tuition inside the regular primary or high school structure. Individualised programmes are delivered by specialist teachers or a team of special educators. Provision is made for children with dyslexia and dyspraxia in most schools.

Gifted and Talented Children. State education departments recognise the needs of gifted and talented children, and provide special programmes for them. All schools are responsible for the ongoing identification of gifted and talented children, and monitor their progress carefully. Such children are offered a 'differentiated curriculum', the guiding principles of which are: a stimulating and interactive environment, an acceptance of individual differences and potential, a willingness to provide appropriate teaching methods and materials to match those differences, and flexibility. Teachers must, by law, provide for gifted and talented children at all times.

Technology in Schools. The various state education systems place a high priority on educating students to take advantage of new technologies. The present government has promised $130 million over four years to government schools for the purposes of achieving better scientific and technological literacy, to develop school based innovation and build supportive school environments. It has also promised $34.1 million over five years towards the development of online curriculum resources, services and applications. Schools are well equipped with information technology facilities and offer teaching in this field to even the youngest students. Most schools are also on the Internet and provide every class or student with an email address. In many private schools students are provided with their own laptop.

Vocational Education. There has been significant change in post-compulsory schooling in recent years, with an increasing emphasis on work-based learning. Work experience has been an important part of school programmes for many years, and this has now been expanded into structured work-based learning programmes which combine school and industry-based learning. A number of initiatives have been introduced including VET (Vocational Education and Training in Schools Programme), school-based new apprenticeships, vocational programmes, fast track programmes, and several others. Approval and certification arrangements provide a means of recognising students' achievements in work-based programmes.

Distance Education. Australia's vast size means that many students in rural areas are hundreds of miles from the nearest schools. Every state, therefore, runs an active distance education programme, which caters not only for students who are unable to attend school by reason of their location, but also for ill or otherwise isolated children. State governments provide professional staff, resources, and support, as well as radio broadcasts and internet services, to children of all ages.

Post-Compulsory Education. The compulsory years of secondary education finish at the end of year 10 (age 16). Secondary Education Authorities in each state issue School Leaving Certificates of achievement, based on coursework and exams and roughly equivalent to the British GCSEs, to students leaving school at this stage. Students who leave after year 10 tend to be less academically inclined and will generally seek an apprenticeship or some other form of vocational training. Retention rates for years 11 and 12 are high, with between 70% and 90% of students staying on, depending on the state and prevailing economic conditions. Students who hope to enter tertiary education take public examinations at the end of year 12. These go by different names in each state (in WA, it is the TEE, or Tertiary Entrance Examination; in NSW and Victoria, the HSC, or Higher School Certificate). Students study between five and seven subjects at this level, and these grades are combined to form a tertiary entrance aggregate, which is the sole criterion for entry to university. If your children are likely to be transferring to an Australian University course at this crucial stage, it may be worth them considering the International Baccalaureate as a post high school qualification as this is accepted internationally as an appropriate level for entry by most universities.

The Academic Year. Most schools begin their academic year at either the end of January or the beginning of February, and the year ends before Christmas in December. The year is divided into four ten-week terms, with holidays of approximately two weeks interspersing the middle terms. There are no mid-term breaks or 'half-terms'. Public and religious holidays are observed – students and teachers are given the day off along with the rest of the workforce.

Uniforms. State school education is free from kindergarten to year 12. Parents do have to pay the costs of books and uniforms for state schools, but these are kept at a very low level. Uniform may or may not be compulsory, but is generally favoured by both pupils and parents. Schools try to keep it simple: in summer, shorts and a polo shirt for boys, a cotton dress for girls; in winter, a tracksuit in school colours with a crest on the sweat shirt is most common. Hats, usually of the legionnaire type, are compulsory in years one, two and four, and this policy is strictly enforced. The motto learnt by all small children is 'no hat, no play', and anyone who comes to school without a hat will be kept indoors. Uniform shops are run by most school Parents and Friends' Associations, and the cost of a complete uniform shouldn't break the bank. Trainers are usually worn with winter uniform, and sandals with summer uniform. Flip-flops (known in Australia as thongs) are forbidden. Secondary school students tend to prefer the Australian Akubra-style hats (wide-brimmed and made of felt) or straw hats. Factor 15+ sunscreen is provided free to all primary school students, and you should make sure your child goes to school with some on. It will be re-applied during the day by teachers.

Independent and Private Education. Australia's 900-odd independent, or private, schools account for more than 300,000 pupils, approximately 10% of enrolments in Australia. Around two thirds of overseas students in Australian schools are enrolled in private schools. Such schools are becoming an increasingly popular choice, despite the often considerable expenses involved. Private school fees usually begin at around $4,000 per year per child, but may go up to as much as $15,000. Independent schools are usually associated with the various Christian denominations, especially the Catholic Church and the Church of England, and these Christian and Catholic schools tend to charge lower fees than the big independent schools. There are also a number of schools in each state associated with the Baptist Church and non-denominational churches, as well as Jewish and Islamic Schools. Australian Bureau of Statistics surveys have shown that in 2003 there were 3,318,620 full-time school students, 67.9% of whom attended government schools. Over the period 1993 to 2003, the number of full-time students attending government schools grew by 1.2%, while the number attending non-government schools increased by 22.3%. Many parents believe that their children will receive an enhanced education at private school, as the teacher-student ratio is usually lower. Class sizes in Australian schools average 30 students, but may be higher or lower than this, depending on the state budget and resources.

Upper-school classes also tend to be much smaller, and in private schools the upper-school class sizes are often as low as 15-20 students, while in state schools the size is more often around 18-25. There are, however, some outstanding state schools which consistently achieve standards of excellence in academic, sporting and creative fields. Information about special programmes is available from the local Education Authority, via the Department of Education, Science and Training in your state or territory, and rankings of academic excellence are published annually in the press.

Extra Curricular Activities. Australian students generally participate in a number of extra curricular school activities, which typically include camps, excursions, environmental groups and sports. Most schools have a concert band or orchestra, a choir, a dance troupe and drama society, which rehearse and perform throughout the year. Government schools provide free music tuition to certain children who have been recognised as talented after testing in years three, four, and six. Once selected, children receive tuition and an instrument through to year 12, as well as specialist ensemble opportunities.

Entry of New Arrivals. If you have children currently enrolled in the education system at home, you should bring with you recent school reports, including a reference from their teacher or head teacher. Samples of their work will also help the school assess the appropriate grade for your child. Ordinarily, children are placed in a year commensurate with the age of their peer group. Children who are significantly in advance of or behind the level of work being done by other children of the same age may be placed according to their ability. It is rare for a child to be placed with children more than a year older or younger. The difference in the commencement of the academic year can create problems in choosing the right level – the Australian academic year beginning in January/February.

Parents' and Citizens' Committees in Schools. Parents can expect to be more involved in their children's education than they may have been previously. Every Australian school has its own Parents' & Citizens' Committee (P&C), sometimes known as Parents' and Friends', which consists of parents, teachers and student representatives. These committees raise funds for school excursions or tours, school equipment, and assist in the administration of some aspects of school life, such as the canteen. The Australian school canteen is quite different to the school canteen system in the UK, as hot lunches are rarely supplied. Australians do not eat a large meal in the middle of the day due to the heat. Instead, school canteens are more like subsidised sandwich shops, and sell sandwiches, rolls, salads, pies, some sweet items, and drinks. Many P&C committees have designed healthy, economical and tasty lunch menus which have seen chips and crisps banned in favour of less fattening alternatives. P&C committees also decide on issues such as school uniform, homework policies and behaviour management policies.

Student Councils. Most schools no longer operate a prefect system in which certain children are appointed to school office by the teachers or head. Instead, in primary schools, all year sevens are given special responsibilities, and heads of sporting houses are elected by the student body. In secondary school, there will usually be a school council, consisting of representatives elected by each year group at the end of the previous year, who meet and advise school staff of student needs and problems, and who carry designated responsibilities. In general, schools try and operate an open and democratic process in the appointment of student officers, who in turn take their responsibilities seriously.

Further Education

Universities. The university academic year follows the calendar year, and teaching usually takes place between March and November. The university year is 'semesterised', and both semesters are divided into two halves by a one-week 'study break'. Enrolments usually take place in December of the year prior to commencement, but application must be made through the student's school to the state tertiary admissions centre by the August before final public examinations are undertaken. Australia's tertiary education sector has been undergoing a process of overhaul during the last decade, mainly for budgetary reasons. The most significant change has been that institutions which were established as technical colleges or colleges of further education have now acquired university status. This has created a divided system, with a group of six universities – the universities of Sydney, Melbourne, Adelaide, Western Australia, Queensland and Tasmania – acquiring a kind of 'Ivy League' status; a prestigious second level of long-established polytechnic-type universities, such as the University of NSW, Curtin and RMIT; thirdly, a group of respectable but lesser institutions such as Murdoch University and the University of New England; and lastly, the ex-technical colleges, like Edith Cowan University. There is a constant scrabble among the various institutions for research funding, and rankings are very important. Although officially all on a par, there is no doubt that in the perception of the public, employers, and overseas institutions considering students for postgraduate research, there remain clear differences in the levels of academic excellence attained by these institutions and competition for entry to the top two levels is always intense. Australian universities offer a wide choice of subjects and qualifications. Currently, for a population of 20.2 million, there are 45 universities. The vast majority of tertiary institutions are funded by a combination of state and federal grants, however, public investment in university teaching and learning on a per student basis, with the exception of a period in the early 1990's has been declining since 1983. Nevertheless, in spite of changes in the funding system, Australian tertiary education remains financially accessible to all.

A report by the Organisation for Economic Co-operation and Development (OECD) has ranked Australia fourth behind the USA, Finland and Japan for entry into full-time tertiary education and also fourth, behind Canada, Norway and the USA, in the percentage of graduates produced. The report also found that of all degrees awarded, engineering accounts for approximately 5.3% of degrees conferred by Australian institutions compared with 22.8% in Japan, 18.9% in Germany and 7.1% in the USA (the OECD average is 12.1%). In natural sciences, however, Australia is a world leader with 14.1% compared with 9.1% in Germany, 4.7% in the USA and 2.9% in Japan.

Fees and Other Costs. Until 1989, tertiary education for was absolutely free for all students regardless of means. By 1990, however, budgetary constraints had forced a rethink on this sacred cow of education policy, and the system was changed so that students became liable for fees under the Higher Education Contributions Scheme (HECS). Under HECS, students paid *part* of the cost of their further education, with the Commonwealth meeting the balance. In 2002, the Australian Government conducted a review of Australia's higher education system. The Government's response to the review was announced in the policy statement, *Our Universities: Backing Australia's Future*. The majority of reforms emanating from the review commenced in 2005. The fundamental principle of HECS, whereby the Australian Government sets the contribution amount for subsidised places, has not changed. The Australian Government has also maintained the principle that eligible students should not be prevented from participating in higher education because of an inability to pay their student contribution upfront. The deferred payment arrangements and discount for upfront payments that were available under HECS are now grouped together as HECS-HELP assistance.

HECS places are now Commonwealth supported places. From 2005, higher education providers are able to determine student contribution amounts for Commonwealth supported places within ranges from $0 up to a maximum set by the Australian Government. Student contributions are paid either upfront or deferred and paid later through the tax system. The options available for paying the student contribution depend on students' citizenship or residency status. If a student defers their student contribution, the Australian Government pays the contribution to the higher education provider on behalf of the student. The debt must eventually be repaid once the student's income reaches the minimum repayment threshold. The Australian Government has increased the minimum repayment threshold for compulsory repayment of a HECS debt from $25,348 in 2003-2004 to $35,000 in 2004-2005, and $36,184 in 2005-2006 for a HELP debt. This means you will not be required to start repaying your debt until your income is above $35,000. Payments are deducted in the form of a tax levy of between 4% and 8%. Compulsory repayments increase as the income increases. There is no interest charged on HELP debts, but the debts are indexed annually to bring it in line with the cost of living. The adjustment is made on the first of June each year and applies to the portion of debt which remains unpaid. Further details on Commonwealth supported places and HELP assistance is available at www.goingtouni.gov.au.

Compulsory repayments increase as the income increases, and the debt is usually painlessly paid off within a few years. Students who opt to complete an additional honours year on top of pass degree may be eligible for HECS exemption for that year, which is known as a HECS scholarship. There is no interest charged on HECS debts, but the debt is indexed annually to bring it in line with the cost of living. The adjustment is made on the first of June each year and applies to the portion of debt which remains unpaid.

In addition to tuition fees, students must meet the costs of their own textbooks, which may be between $200 and $1,000 per year depending on the course, however, most institutions have good second-hand bookshops where texts may be purchased more cheaply. Students are also charged fees to join their student organisations, known as unions, associations or guilds. These organisations provide and are involved in the administration of a large number of benefits, including sporting facilities, discounts, the issuing of student identification cards, insurance cover, photocopying, bookshops, catering, social functions such as balls, and student newspapers. Membership costs range from $65-$300 per annum. Until recently, membership of a university's student union was compulsory (except for conscientious objectors, who could choose to have their dues paid to a charity instead); however, in 1995, government legislation, aimed at weakening a united student voice in the light of controversial changes in the higher education sector, made it illegal to require compulsory membership. As a result, student unions now battle to attract new members, and are able to provide fewer benefits to students because of their diminished income.

Choosing a University. Selecting a university can be difficult, and most capital cities have a number of different institutions from which to choose. Every institution and department publishes a prospectus, and university libraries will usually hold a number of these from a range of universities across the country, and careful consideration of these will give a good idea of what is on offer. Most universities have an officer who deals with enquiries from prospective students, and schools will always offer careful guidance on appropriate institutions and courses. The Australian Department of Education, Science and Training runs a website (www. goingtouni.gov.au) outlining all course and university options available in the country while the publication *The Good Universities Guide* (www.thegoodguides. com.au) covers all 45 universities in Australia, giving a brief summary of each, including breadth of course offerings, depth, flexibility of admissions policy, mature-age opportunities, student-staff ratios, gender balance, research track record, affluence, graduate salaries, employment prospects, library quality, popularity with fee paying students and tuition fees. Details of various courses run by the different institutions, the entry marks required for each course, and entry procedures for the various courses are also given as well as a rating of Australia's top 10 universities and details of comparative graduate employment rates and starting salaries. Annual rankings of the nation's university are published in *The Australian*, as well as most city newspapers. Year after year, the top performing institutions include the Universities of Melbourne, Sydney, Western Australia, and NSW, Monash and Macquarie Universities, RMIT, and ANU (the Australian National University in Canberra).

Student Funding and Loans. Australian university students usually survive financially on scholarships, part-time jobs, their parents (about 50% of all university students still live with their parents throughout their academic careers), the Youth Allowance, or a combination of all of these. Until July 1998, eligible students were funded by a national educational grant system known as Austudy. Only about 33% of students received Austudy, which was designed as an income support scheme rather than a full living allowance. Many students were not eligible for any Austudy allowance whatsoever on the basis of their parents' income, and relatively few were eligible for the full Austudy allowance. Austudy for students aged between 18 and 24 years has now been replaced by the Youth Allowance, a single payment made to all eligible young people and replacing not only Austudy but also the dole and other social security benefits. The Allowance is still subject to parental means test, but offers some advantages to students over the old system, insofar as they are now also eligible for rent assistance (up to the value of $90.60 per fortnight for a single adult with no dependents). An interest-free loan of $500 is also available.

A pared-down version of Austudy remains in force for students over the age of 25. Eligibility for Austudy, and the amount which a mature or independent student can receive under the scheme depends upon enrolment in an approved full-time course (almost all university courses are approved), and on the applicant's income and assets, and, if applicable, those of his or her spouse. If you receive Austudy, you are also allowed to earn an income of up to $6,136 per annum without affecting your allowance. If you earn above this amount, your Austudy payments will be reduced proportionately. The Austudy supplement provides further funding through a government-sponsored personal loan, the Student Financial Assistance Scheme. Note that while Austudy is a *grant*, the Austudy Supplement is a *loan*, and although it can help students in need, many choose not to take it up as repayment conditions are onerous.

TAFE. Tertiary education is also available at Technical and Further Education Centres (TAFEs) which offer vocationally orientated qualifications. There are approximately 250 TAFE institutions in Australia, but many of these have additional affiliated campuses, training centres and ancillary teaching centres. Every state and territory has a large number of TAFE colleges and centres, in both capital cities and major regional areas. More than a million students are enrolled in TAFE courses, though many of these are part-time students. Many school leavers who want to upgrade their skills or adults who wish to retrain or re-enter the workforce study at TAFEs either on a full-time or part-time basis. TAFEs specialise in training and pre-apprenticeships in a diverse range of trades, including building, the vehicle, metal, electrical and automotive trades, electronics, plumbing, printing, catering, gardening, dairy farming, hairdressing, textiles, jewellery and watch-making, and secretarial and business studies. Both evening and day classes are usually available for most courses. School Certificate and Higher School Certificate subjects are also available for mature students who may be aiming for university entrance. TAFEs also offer literacy and numeracy classes, as well as English as a Foreign Language for migrants and other new arrivals. There are also a number of short-term, part-time courses available in subjects like bar service, typing, commercial floristry and woolclassing. In a recent survey conducted by the National Centre for Vocational Education, nearly 85% of TAFE graduates rated their general level of satisfaction with the quality of training, very highly.

The cost of attending a TAFE is significantly lower than university. Fee-exemptions are given to students in receipt of Youth Allowance or Austudy, and there are concession rates for low-income earners. TAFE students do not pay HECS. Usually TAFE colleges will allow you to pay fees in instalments.

Overseas Students at Australian Universities

Australian universities rely increasingly on overseas students for a proportion of their funding. Southeast Asian students make up a significant proportion of enrolments, and are concentrated in faculties offering business, commerce and economics, with some entering medicine and law. The latest figures from Australian Government Department of Education and Training, show that in 2004 there were 186,432 overseas students studying in Australia. Around half of these were studying at a secondary level, attending short intensive English language courses (ELICOS) in public or private institutions, enrolled on TAFE courses, or preparing for university on special bridging courses. The remainder were attending university courses. The number of overseas students studying at Australian universities has grown incredibly over the years, and some universities now hold graduation ceremonies in Singapore and Kuala Lumpur to cater for their Southeast Asian alumni. The Australian government requires all institutions which accept overseas students to register with state authorities to assure continuing high standards of management and education.

If you wish to enter Australia to study, you will need to apply for a Student

Visa, and this cannot be issued until you can provide evidence that you have been accepted for a course of study and have paid half the first year's annual fee for your course. It is important to note that you cannot change from Visitor status to Student status while you are in Australia, and that application for a Student Visa can only be made in your own country of residence. In order to retain your visa, you must have a satisfactory record of attendance at your institution, and achieve satisfactory academic results. On completion of your course, you must leave Australia before your Student Visa expires, and the Australian Government offers no leniency in this area.

Overseas students do not receive the privileges of government-funded education as offered to Australian citizens and permanent residents. Universities vary considerably in the fees that they charge overseas students, and costs are determined by the demand for the course, the location of the institution, and its level of prestige. The government sets a minimum fee structure for each course, but institutions are free to charge above this level, and frequently do. Fees vary considerably between disciplines and are subject to regular revision: as a general rule, you should expect a humanities degree to cost in the region of $14,000 per annum, a science degree to cost around $18,000, and professional courses like medicine and engineering, anything up to $40,000 a year. Various grants and scholarships may be available depending on your qualifications and circumstances. Individual institutions will have information about these.

Most universities have student accommodation associated with the campus, and overseas students will receive help in finding housing and settling in generally. Establishment costs have been estimated by the University of Sydney to be around $900, and annual living costs for a single student to be around $16,000 taking in rent, food, travel expenses and 'entertainment' costs. Australian universities are committed to equity policies, and seek to provide an environment of equal opportunity, free from discrimination, for all students and staff. They will make special arrangements for students with disabilities, and usually provide good childcare facilities for students with children.

Overseas Student Societies. Most universities have student-run societies which cater for overseas students from specific countries and regions. These associations organise camps, social functions, speakers and orientation programmes, and will also offer assistance if you contact them before you arrive at the institution. Your university will supply you with contact names for appropriate on-campus student organisations. Universities in Australia are completely free from religious discrimination, and those with large overseas student populations, like the University of Western Australia, provide worship facilities for most major religious groups.

Useful Addresses

Australian Education International, International Education Network, Department of Education, Science and Training, GPO Box 9880, Canberra City, ACT 2601; www.studyinaustralia.gov.au. Advice on study in Australia for international students.

EdNA Online, 178 Fullarton Road, Dulwich, SA 5065; ☎08-8334 3210; fax 08-8334 3211; www.edna.edu.au. Funded by the Australian federal and state governments, it provides information about education and training in Australia and a database of Internet resources and free online tools useful for teaching and learning.

National Centre for Vocational Education, Level 11, 33 King William Street, Adelaide, SA 5000; ☎08-8230 8400; fax 08-8212 3436; e-mail ncver@ncver.edu.au; www.ncver.edu.au.

Studylink, www.studylink.com.au. An Internet based directory exploring higher and vocational educational courses in Australia.

The Commonwealth Department of Education, Science and Training, 16-18 Mort Street, Canberra, ACT 2600; ☎02-6240 8111; www.dest.gov.au.

State Tertiary Admissions Centres:

NSW & ACT. Universities Admissions Centre (UAC) Pty Ltd, Quad 2, Australia Centre, 8 Parkview Drive, Homebush Bay, NSW; Postal address: UAC, Locked Bag 112, Silverwater, NSW 2128; ☎02-9752 0200; www.uac.edu.au.

NT. Students must apply direct to Charles Darwin University, Uni Info Shop, Ellengowan Drive, Casuarina, Darwin, NT 0909; ☎08-8946 7766 or 1800-061 963 (Toll Free); fax 08-8946 6642; e-mail uni-info@cdu.edu.au; www.ntu.edu.au .

QLD. Queensland Tertiary Admissions Centre, Level 2, 33 Park Road, Milton QLD 4064; Postal address: PO Box 1331, Milton, QLD 4064; ☎07-3368 1166; www.qtac.edu.au.

SA. South Australian Tertiary Admissions Centre (SATAC), Ground Floor, 104 Frome Street, Adelaide, SA 5000; ☎08-8224 4000; fax 08-8224 4091; www.satac.edu.au.

TAS. Students must apply directly to The Admissions Office, University of Tasmania, GPO Box 252-45, Hobart, TAS 7001; ☎03-6226 7151 or 1800- 030 955 (Toll Free); www.utas.edu.au.

VIC. Victorian Tertiary Admissions Centre (VTAC), 40 Park Street, South Melbourne, VIC 3205; ☎03-9954 3220 or 1300-364 133; www.vtac.edu.au.

WA. Tertiary Institutions Service Centre (TISC), 100 Royal Street, East Perth, WA 6004; ☎08-9318 8000; fax 08-9225 7050; e-mail info@tisc.edu.au; www.tisc.edu.au.

TAFE:

NSW. TAFE Information Centre, 47 York Street, Sydney NSW 2000; ☎02-8234 2777 or 131 601; www.tafensw.edu.au

QLD/NT. There are no central information centres, but information can be obtained directly from your nearest college. College contact numbers are found in the government section at the beginning of the telephone directory.

SA. TAFE Information Centre, Da Costa Arcade, Shop 4, GHD Building, 68 Grenfell Street, Adelaide, SA 5001; Postal Address: PO Box 320, Adelaide, SA 5001; ☎1800 882 661; e-mail tafe.info@saugov.sa.gov.au; www.tafe.sa.gov.au

TAS. Institute of TAFE Tasmania, PO Box 2015, Hobart, TAS 7001; ☎03-6233 7019 or 1300 655 307; fax 03-6233 7830; www.tafe.tas.edu.au.

VIC. The TAFE Virtual Campus, PO Box 266D, Melbourne, VIC 3001; ☎1800-896 122; www.tafevc.com.au.

WA. Training Info Centre, 2nd Floor, City Central Building, 166 Murray Street, Perth, WA 6000; ☎08-9421 1344 or 1800 999 167; www.training.waa.gov.au/tic.

Youth Allowance and Austudy: Telephone the enquires line on freecall 132 490 for information.

International Schools

International Baccalaureate Schools (headquarters in Geneva, Switzerland) are becoming increasingly common in Australia, and most capitals have at least one. A regional list of the schools offering the IB is given below. A complete list of such schools (71 in Australia) can be found on the International Baccalaureate Organization's website (www.ibo.org).

ACT
Narrabundah College, Jerrabomberra Avenue, Kingston, ACT 2604; ☎02-6205 6999; fax 02-6205 6969; www.narrabundahc.act.edu.au.

NSW
S.C.E.C.G.S Redlands, 272 Military Road, Cremorne, NSW 2090; ☎02-9908 6479; fax 02-9909 3228; www.redlands.nsw.edu.au.

NT
Kormilda College, PO Box 241, Berrimah, NT 0828; ☎08-8922 1611; fax 08-8947 0792.

QLD
Mountain Creek State High School, PO Box 827, Mooloolaba, QLD 4557; ☎07-5477 8555; fax 07-5477 8500; www.mtncreekshs.qld.edu.au.

SA
Glenunga International High School, L'Estrange Street, Gelnunga, SA 5064; ☎08-8379 5629; fax 08-8338 2518; www.gihs.sa.edu.au.
Mercedes College, 540 Fullarton Road, Springfield, SA 5062; ☎08-8372 3200; fax 08-8379 9540; www.mercedes.adl.catholic.edu.au.
Pembroke School, 18 Holden Street, Kensington Park, SA 5068; ☎08-8366 6245; fax 08-8366 6863; www.pembroke.sa.edu.au.

TAS
The Friends' School, PO Box 42, North Hobart, TAS 7002; ☎03-6210 2288; fax 03-6234 8209; www.friends.tas.edu.au.
Launceston College, 107-119 Paterson Street, Launceston, TAS 7250; ☎03-6332 7777; fax 03-6332 7800; www.launc.tased.edu.au.

VIC
Lauriston Girls' School, 38 Huntingtower Road, Armadale, VIC 3143; ☎03-9864 7555; fax 03-9822 7950; www.lauriston.vic.edu.au.
Wesley College, 620 High Street Road, Glen Waverley, Melbourne, VIC 3150; ☎03-9881 5394; fax 03-9886 3276; www.wesleycollege.net.
Presbyterian Ladies' College, 141 Burwood Highway, Burwood, VIC 3125; ☎03-9808 5811; fax 03-9808 5998; www.plc.vic.edu.au.
St. Leonard's College, 163 South Road, Brighton East, VIC 3187; ☎03-9592 2266; fax 03-9592 3439; www.stleonards.vic.edu.au.
Tintern Anglican Girls' Grammar School, 90 Alexandra Road, Ringwood East, VIC 3135; ☎03-9845 7820; fax 03-9845 7713; www.tintern.vic.edu.au.

WA

Montessori School, PO. Box 194, Landsdale, WA 6065; ☎08-9409 9151; fax 08-9409 1682; www.themontessorischool.wa.edu.au.

Useful Publication

Choosing a School (New South Wales, Victoria, or Queensland's Private Schools) magazines are available from the Subscription Department, Consyl Publishing, 3 Buckhurst Road, Bexhill-on-Sea, East Sussex TN40 1QF; ☎01424-223111; www.consylpublishing.co.uk.

MEDIA AND COMMUNICATIONS

The Australian media provide much the same type of services as in the UK, Europe and the USA. Its film, television and radio output is highly regarded internationally and much of it is distributed overseas (including children's television and art films, along with *Neighbours, Home and Away* and *Mad Max*). Each state has a range of local and regional newspapers, as well as access to the national press. Editorial content is considered to be mostly fair and unbiased, although media monopolies are under constant surveillance to maintain standards and to prevent the exercise of undue political influence. Australians are news-hungry, and newspaper and magazine readership per capita is one of the highest in the world. Most news providers offer a good balance of domestic and international news. In the communications sector, the monopoly of the state-owned Australian Telecom has now given way to a more open market with several providers competing to supply both domestic and business users. The government agency, Australia Post, provides mail and ancillary services to the whole country. Australia has one of the highest proportions of personal computer and mobile telephone ownership in the world and the Internet take-up rate is second only to the USA (consider: population of the USA 286.6 million people; population of Australia 20.2 million people). As a result, Australian communications are heavily geared to the electronic environment – noticeably more so than in Europe – and most government agencies, schools, television channels, newspapers, and community services have websites on which they post constantly updated information. Even the telephone directories are online and at the touch of a button you can access and search Telstra's telephone databases for both business and residential numbers.

Newspapers

Australian newspapers are largely state, or indeed, capital city-based. There is one national daily newspaper, *The Australian*, owned by Rupert Murdoch's *News Corp*, and sometimes referred to as 'Murdoch's Australian charity'. This broadsheet newspaper is of a calibre equivalent to, say, *The Times* or *The Guardian* in Britain, but like most broadsheet newspapers, it fights a continuing battle for profitability. *The Australian*'s weekend sister publication, *The Weekend Australian*, is similar in style and, as with broadsheet weekend papers, comes groaning with additional arts, lifestyle, sports and business sections. Apart from the omnipresent Rupert Murdoch, the other big player in Australia's newspaper industry is Fairfax Holdings.

This group publishes respected major titles including *The Sydney Morning Herald*, *The Age* (both broadsheets, from Sydney and Melbourne respectively), *The Sun-Herald, Business Review Weekly,* and *The Australian Financial Review*, the Australian equivalent of *The Financial Times*. Currently, Sydney, Melbourne and Brisbane all have at least three major daily newspapers, and other capitals and major regional centres have at least two. In addition, almost every area has a local community newspaper (usually weekly, and often of very high quality).

Expats can keep up with news from home which may not make the international new pages of the Australian press by subscribing to weekly news digests from home or by logging on to home newspaper websites. *The International Express*, sold throughout Australia and New Zealand, is the international sister paper of the *Express* and *Express on Sunday* and has the same tabloid format and human-interest focus. It is printed in Sydney, Melbourne and Perth, and is available in Australia from local newsagents. A six-month subscription costs $90 and is available by writing to: International Publishing Group, PO Box 107, Sydney, NSW 2001; e-mail subscriptions@theinternationalexpress.com; www.theinternationalexpress.com. The *Guardian Weekly* is also widely available and offers a selection of higher-brow articles and features in English derived from the previous week's *Guardian*, *Washington Post* and *Le Monde*. Subscriptions are available from *Guardian Weekly*, 164 Deansgate, Manchester M3 3GG; ☎0870-066 0510; fax 0161-876 5362; e-mail gwsubs@guardian.co.uk; www.guardianweekly.com; and PO Box 2515, Champlain, New York 12919-2515; ☎1-888 834 1106 (toll free); fax 514-697 3490; e-mail gwsubs@guardianweekly.com. In Australia subscriptions to the *Guardian Weekly* can be taken out by writing to PO Box 70, Sydney, NSW 2001; ☎02-9543 7616; fax 02-9543 8842; e-mail australia@guardianweekly.com.

Addresses of the major Australian newspapers are given below:

NSW

Sydney Morning Herald, 201 Sussex Street, Sydney, NSW 2000; ☎02-9282 2833; www.smh.com.au .

The Australian, 2 Holt Street, Surry Hills, NSW 2010; Postal address: GPO Box 4245 Sydney, NSW 2001; ☎02-9288-3000; fax 02-9288-2250; www.theaustralian.news.com.au.

The Australian Financial Review, 201 Sussex Street, NSW 2007; ☎02-9282 2833; www.afr.com.au .

The Daily Telegraph, 2 Holt Street, Surry Hills, NSW 2010; ☎02-9288 3000; fax 02-9288 2300; www.dailytelegraph.news.com.au.

QLD

The Courier Mail, 41 Campbell Street, Bowen Hills, QLD 4006; ☎07-3666 8000; fax 07-3666 6696; www.couriermail.news.com.au

VIC

The Age, 250 Spencer Street, Melbourne, VIC 3000; ☎03-9600 4211; www.theage.com.au

Herald Sun, HWT Tower, 40 City Road, Southbank, Melbourne, VIC 3000; ☎03-9292 2000; fax 03-9292 2002; www.heraldsun.news.com.au

The Weekly Times, Level 9, 40 City Road, Southbank, VIC 3000; ☎03-9292 2000; fax 03-9292 2002; www.theweeklytimes.com.au

WA

Sunday Times, 34 Stirling Street, Perth, WA 6000; ☎08-9326 8326; www.sundaytimes.news.com.au

The West Australian, Newspaper House, 50 Hasler Road, Osborne Park, WA 6017; ☎08-9482 3111; fax 08-9482 9080; www.thewest.com.au

Australian Magazines

ACP Magazine, 54-58 Park Street, Sydney, NSW 2000; ☎02-9288 9600; fax 02-9283 4849; www.acp.com.au; and 53 Chandos Place, Covent Garden, London WC2N 4HS. Produces Australian magazines such as *The Australian Women's Weekly, Street Machine,* and more than 50 other titles.

Magazines

Australian editions of *Woman's Day, New Idea, Vogue, Cosmopolitan* and *Marie Claire* are available in all newsagents and most supermarkets, and there are innumerable special interest publications, such as *Australian Gourmet Traveller* and *House and Garden,* which are also of very high quality.

> *The Australian Woman's Weekly* is the most popular Australian women's magazine. Don't be misled by the name; this is a *monthly* magazine. When this longstanding publication underwent a makeover, including name change, a couple of decades ago, they decided against 'The Australian Woman's Monthly' as a title – for obvious reasons! The quality of this magazine is unmatched and its readership and circulation make it the most widely read magazine in the history of Australian publishing. It is particularly famous for its outstanding cooking sections, and Australian Consolidated Press publish a continually updated range of cookbooks developed by the magazine staff. It is said that you can never go wrong with a *Woman's Weekly* recipe. The cover price of the *Woman's Weekly* is $5.70.

The *Business Review Weekly* is probably the most important financial magazine, roughly equivalent to the *Economist* (which is available in good newsagents), and the main domestic current affairs magazine is *The Bulletin,* which incorporates the American publication, *Newsweek. The Bulletin* is an old and prestigious publication, particularly well regarded for its efforts to foster new writing, especially poetry. Most international magazines with any significant level of circulation, such as *Time* and *National Geographic* are widely available, although their cover price may reflect import costs where special Australian editions are not printed.

Books and Bookshops

Books in Australia used to be expensive but are now pretty much equivalent in price to those in Britain and the USA. All major publishers distribute in Australia, although if you are looking for something unusual you may have to order. Scholarly publications and new hardcover releases tend, however, to be expensive in Australia. There is also a significant Australian publishing industry, and much highly regarded fiction is currently being written there, and meeting with international success. Peter Carey, for instance, has won the Booker Prize twice for *Oscar and Lucinda* (1988) and *True History of the Kelly Gang* (2001) and Thomas

Keneally won the Booker Prize in 1982 for *Schindler's Ark*, which was later filmed as *Schindler's List*. Large bookshops are found in all Australian cities, including a number of chains, such as Dymocks, and Angus & Robertson; there are also many smaller independent booksellers. The 'book café' has recently arrived in Australia and proved a popular innovation. Book cafés, as the name suggests, incorporate a small, high quality café in among the books, where people can meet for coffee, or just enjoy a break while they browse.

Book clubs and reading groups are hugely popular, and most cities will have hundreds of these small, informal groups which meet monthly for friendship and literary discussion: book cafes provide both a venue for meetings, as well as a selection of new texts for the next get-together. Some specialist bookstores are listed below:

All Arts Bookshop, 43 Queen Street, Woollahra, NSW 2025; ☎ 02-9328 6744; fax 02-9328 9822; e-mail books@allarts.com.au; www.allarts.com.au. Collectors' reference books on antiques, Australian, Asian and tribal art. Phone and mail order.

Angus & Robertson Bookworld, 195 Murray Street, Perth, WA 6000; ☎ 08-9325 5622; www.angusrobertson.com.au. Stores Australia-wide.

Boffins Bookshop, 806 Hay Street, Perth, WA 6000; ☎ 08-9321 5755; fax 08-9321 5744; www.boffinsbookshop.com.au. Range of technical, practical, and specialist books. Local and overseas special orders.

Dymocks Booksellers, 424 George Street, Sydney, NSW 2000; ☎ 02-9235 0155; fax 02-9233 8793; and 705-707 Hay Street Mall, Perth, WA 6000; ☎ 08-9321 3969; fax 08-9481 1964; www.dymocks.com.au. Stores Australia-wide with comprehensive range of general, technical and education books. Computer access to more than 100,000 titles. Will obtain any book in print.

Television

Many television watchers are probably as familiar with Australian television productions as Australians themselves. Series such as *Burke's Backyard, Neighbours, Home and Away, A Country Practice* and the *Flying Doctors* are all regularly broadcast in the UK, and indeed, the popular soaps *Neighbours* and *Home and Away* have a much higher profile in Britain than in their country of origin, so that Australians visiting the UK are often bemused by fervent requests for updates on the latest from down-under. Other famous TV exports include Clive James and Dame Edna Everage, and the majority of children will tell you about *Bananas in Pyjamas* or *The Ferals*.

There are four main channels broadcasting nationwide. The Australian Broadcasting Commission (ABC) operates Channel Two, and is equivalent to the BBC. The ABC is funded by the federal government and provides commercial-free television and radio throughout the country. Advertisements for forthcoming features are screened only at the end of programmes. The three other channels, Seven, Nine and Ten, are commercially owned and operated networks which broadcast around Australia and like commercial television elsewhere in the world they are funded by advertising, the airing of which tends to be fairly frequent.

Although the channels are operated by national networks both advertising and news output tends to be state-specific. In very remote areas, it may only be possible to receive Channel Two and perhaps one other commercial channel specifically aimed at country viewers such as, in Western Australia, GWN (Golden West

Network).

The Special Broadcasting Service (SBS) provides multi-lingual and multicultural broadcasting (both television and radio) across the country. It is specifically designed for viewers of ethnic origins and regularly broadcasts foreign language films. SBS is an optional channel for which you will require a special receiver or antennae. The SBS antennae can usually be installed cheaply enough but these days most houses will already have one fitted. Many people consider that the SBS news is the best available on Australian television, with a high international news content and in-depth analysis. SBS also broadcasts minority and international domestic sports coverage, and is a good way to keep up with your favourite teams back home. Weather forecasts on Australian television in general are more detailed and meteorologically sophisticated than those in the UK.

The best British and American television productions all come to Australian television, and you will not have to miss out on *Friends, The X-Files, Sex and the City* or any other favourites. Australian television is ratings-dominated, and during ratings periods the television programming is outstanding, with the best films and series from around the world competing for your attention and the advertising dollar. At other less crucial times, programming may be more mundane but sports coverage tends, in general, to be very good. The government requires a certain percentage of Australian-produced output (which must *not* be cheap-to-make games shows and the like), so that there is always a good flow of new and interesting local productions.

Cable and satellite television are available in Australia, with cable far more widespread than satellite. The channels available are exactly the same as in the UK or the USA: Nickelodeon, the Disney Channel, MTV, CNN, UK Gold, the Movie Channel, and so on. Cable networks are operated by Foxtel (another Murdoch venture), and Optus Vision. Subscription rates are around $50 (basic) to $98 (platinum) per month. There are also satellite stations available by subscription, which once again broadcast much the same international fare as the cable channels. The majority of Australians do not yet subscribe to pay channels but the takeup rate is growing all the time. Most do, however, own a video, and increasingly a DVD player, and video rental shops are found in every high street. Videos and DVDs are cheap to hire and many stores offer special rental deals. A new release video will cost approximately $7 to hire for 24 hours, and older movies can be rented for up to a week from as little as $3.

Television programmes are advertised daily in local newspapers, and a weekly lift-out programme guide, usually in magazine format, is available in the weekend papers. There is a TV listings guide, *TV Week*, which is produced in different editions for the different states (due to the time zones across Australia programme schedules differ throughout the country).

Probably the most important difference between Australian and British television is that there is no television licensing system. Naturally, you must pay for your own television sets and antennae, but you may have as many televisions in your home or business as you like and you do not have to pay for the privilege of watching them. The Australian Broadcasting Commission is funded from taxation revenue and no further charge is made for broadcasting services.

Radio

The Australian Broadcasting Commission owns and runs four national radio networks which can be received Australia-wide and one international radio service. They are renowned for their excellent news coverage. Radio National is the ABC's general current affairs and talk station, and is middle to highbrow in its orientation. It produces programmes such as *The Science Show, The Law Report,* and *The Book Programme,* as well as daily drama, book readings, interviews. It also has a classical music station, and supports an orchestra in each state. The Australian airwaves have been deregulated for decades and across Australia there are more than 100 commercial stations on the AM band, more than 50 commercial FM stations, 200 community radio stations, run by universities, ethnic groups, and Aborigine-run radio stations which service the outback regions. Radio stations are often advertised on car bumper stickers, on television and in the newspapers, so it is easy to find something to your taste and tune in. Australians own nearly 30 million radio receivers and most households own four or more radios.

Film Industry

The Australian film industry has been thriving for the last 30 years, and is one of Australia's major cultural exports. The Australian Film Commission assists in the growth of this industry by aiding project development through script, pre-production assistance grant giving, and international promotion. The government is keen to support a vigorous and diverse cultural environment, and this is reflected in Australian films, which find a big audience both at home and abroad. Recent hits have included Baz Luhrmann's *Moulin Rouge, Muriel's Wedding, The Castle* and *Shine* and Australian actors are a big feature of Hollywood these days. All the big international releases find their way to Australian cinemas, generally about six months before they hit the screens in Britain. Film-going is a popular pastime, and tickets cost about $10. In some cities, certain weeknights are 'concession nights', with all tickets costing under $6, and this has greatly boosted mid-week sales. In the summer months, the Festival of Perth hosts the *Lotteries Film Season* which shows art-house movies at the two outdoor venues of the Somerville Auditorium in Crawley and the Joondalup Pines Picture Garden at Edith Cowan University. It is one of the great pleasures of life in Perth to take a picnic to the Somerville at dusk and sit in a deck chair under the pine trees by the banks of the Swan River, sharing a bottle of wine and watching a movie.

Post

The Australia postal service is owned and run by the Australian Government, and in general provides excellent services. Post offices and PostShops are open from 9am to 5pm Monday to Friday, and 9am to 11am on Saturdays, but are closed on Sundays and public holidays. Letters between Australia and the UK and the USA take between three to 10 days to arrive, and parcels take between seven and 10 days. The cost of postage for a letter to Britain or the USA is $1.50, and an aerogramme costs $1. Sea mail and Surface Air Lifted (SAL) mail services are also available at a significantly cheaper cost, but are, naturally, much slower services. Most people send parcels SAL or Sea mail, particularly Christmas parcels, and Australia Post issues a list of send-by dates for guaranteed pre-Christmas delivery all over the world. To send parcels back home in time for Christmas, the send-by date is usually at the beginning of October. Australia Post also offers a cheaper rate for Christmas cards, which should be in unsealed envelopes marked 'card only', and there is a different send-by date for international cards, usually four weeks before Christmas. There is no division between first and second-class services for local letters, but only one standard service and cost. Local letters cost 50 cents and it usually takes one working day to deliver letters posted within the same metropolitan area, or two working days if the letter is from outside the metropolitan region or from interstate. Mail is usually delivered once a day from Monday to Friday in metropolitan regions, but in remote and/or rural regions the mail may only be delivered once a week and can also often be delayed by adverse conditions such as flooding, torrential rain or even snow. There is no Saturday delivery. Mailboxes are located at the front of properties, and mail is never delivered through a slot in the front door. In the case of blocks of flats, there is usually a structure containing one letterbox for every flat, at the front entrance to the property. In some urban areas, it can be wise to lock your mailbox with a small padlock if it is in a communal block, as your mail is not otherwise secure.

Australia Post deals with around 5.3 billion letters per year and seeks to maintain a uniform standard letter service at a uniform price. It has a 'community service obligation' to fulfil this mandate. As well as letter services, Australia Post offers a telephone bill paying service. It has a website at www.auspost.com.au where you can assess your postage costs, locate postcode numbers, find out about services and special offers, and check the location of your nearest office or agency.

If you intend to travel extensively through Australia during your stay, it is possible to have letters and parcels sent to you at any office of Australia Post using the international postal convention of Poste Restante. Providing it is clearly addressed with your name and the words *Poste Restante*, followed by the name and address of the post office, the letter/parcel will be held for up to a month during which time you may, on producing proof of your identity, collect it. If the letter or parcel is not claimed within a month, it will be returned to the sender. For travellers, there are also private mail holding and forwarding services available, which can be useful if you have no permanent address. These services work on a membership basis, so that after paying a joining fee you are then able to call the service from anywhere in Australia to check if there is any mail or messages for you. The service will then forward your mail/messages to your present address.

Useful Addresses

A privately owned travellers' mail service is operated by the *Travellers' Contact Point*, Level 7, Dymocks Building, 428 George Street, Sydney, NSW 2000; ☎02-9221 8744; fax 02-9221 3746; e-mail info@travellers.com.au; www.travellers.com.au. Open Monday to Friday 9am to 6pm; Saturday 10am to 4pm. Also at 2-6 Inverness Terrace, Bayswater, London W2 3HX; ☎020-7243 7884; fax 020-7243 7888; e-mail enquiries@travellersuk.com. Open Monday to Friday 9am to 5.30pm; Saturday 10am to 4pm. The main Australian post offices (known as GPOs) are at:

ACT	King George Terrace, Canberra, ACT 2600
NSW	1 Martin Place, Sydney, NSW 2000
NT	31-33 Hartley Street, Alice Springs, NT 0870

	48 Cavenagh Street, Darwin, NT 0800
QLD	Shop 6A, 366-370 Shute Harbour Road, Airlie Beach, QLD 4802
	261 Queen Street, Brisbane, QLD 4000
	13 Grafton Street, Cairns, QLD 4870
	Paradise Centre Shop 165, 2-10 Cavill Avenue, Surfers Paradise, QLD 4217
	Post Office Plaza Shop, Sturt Street, Townsville, QLD 4810
SA	141 King William Street, Adelaide, SA 5000
TAS	9 Elizabeth Street, Hobart, TAS 7000
	3/25 Wellington Street, Launceston, TAS 7250
VIC	250 Elizabeth Street, Melbourne, VIC 3000
WA	Ground Floor, 3-7 Forrest Place, Perth, WA 6000

Telephones

The Australian telecommunications sector was deregulated in 1997 and the monopoly of Australian Telecom has now given way to a new era of competition. The national government-owned provider has been 'rebranded' as Telstra, and its major competitor is Optus. To have a telephone line connected to your new residence, you should contact either of these two providers, who will supply you with your new phone number. If you connect with Optus, you can still receive and make calls to Telstra numbers, and vice versa. New customers are not usually required to pay a deposit (unless they have a bad credit rating), and fully itemised bills are sent quarterly. There is a constant battle to provide the cheapest international calling rates, and if you expect to make a lot of overseas calls, it is worth watching the newspapers for special offers, such as Telstra's '0018 Easy Half Hours' package where customers pay for the first half hour block of a call and the next half hour block is free. Using this service, calls to the USA or the UK will cost you $5.25 for an hour's chat. In addition, there is an ever-increasing number of international call providers, who offer exceptionally low rates, and these also advertise extensively in newspapers. If you see a special deal with, say, Telstra, and you are an Optus customer, you can still take advantage of it by prefixing your call with a special dialling code (which will be clearly stated in the advertisement). You will then receive a separate bill from the service you have been using at the end of each quarter.

Local calls in Australia are not charged on a timed basis – a single connection charge of around 25 cents on a domestic phone allows you to talk all day if you want to; similarly, phone calls made for the purpose of connecting to the internet are also charged on a connection-only basis, making web-time much more economical in Australia than in many other countries where you are charged for time spent online.

Telstra's most popular value-added products (and Optus offers very similar inducements), are call forwarding, call waiting and faxstream (multi-recipient fax sending), the Telstra telecard, which allows you to automatically charge calls made overseas to your home number, and messageBank, an answering service. The PhoneAway card is a prepaid international and domestic telephone card.

Public Telephones. Public telephones in Australia are very similar to those found in Europe. Local calls cost 40 cents, and STD and international calls are charged according to the rate (determined by the time of day at which you call), distance covered and the length of the call. The telephones accept 10 cent, 20 cent, 50 cent and $1 coins. Many telephones have the facility to accept major credit cards or automatic teller cards from the bigger Australian national banks. Phone cards are also available from newsagents and vending machines in denominations of $5, $10, $20 and $50. STD public telephones are available throughout metropolitan suburbs, outside post offices and in shopping centres. These phones accept all Australian coins, as well as Telstra's Telecard, allow uses to switch from coin to card in mid-phone call if necessary, and have an easy-to-read display providing instructions in four languages. They also feature an adjustable volume level and hearing aid coupler in the handset. The booths are accessible by wheelchair. Most public telephones will be equipped to send text (SMS) messages in 2005.

If you are British and resident in Australia temporarily or short-term, it may be useful for you to apply to British Telecom for a BT Chargecard. This card is free and means that all calls you make from Australia are charged to your own British account. Contact BT on 0800-345 144 or check the website at www.payphones.bt.com for an application form and further details.

To call the UK from Australia, you will need to dial 0011-44 and then the number, deleting the first 0 from the area code. To send faxes from Australia, the process is the same, except the international prefix is 0015 followed by the country code, area code (minus the 0) and the number. For example, to send a fax to Oxford, the code necessary would be 0015-44 1865 + number. To call Australia from the UK, dial 00-61 followed by the area code (omitting the initial 0 of the area code) and then the number. To call the USA from Australia, dial 0011-1, then the area code (example 212 for Manhattan) plus the local number. The procedure for sending a fax to Australia is exactly the same as telephoning. The area codes for major Australian cities are given in the previous section (*Setting Up Home, Utilities*).

Australia's mobile network operates on the 900 and 1800 bands for the European GSM and 800 for the American CDMA technology. Vodafone, Optus, and Telstra are the main networks. CDMA is the biggest network and offers greater coverage in rural and remote areas. Customers can swap networks and keep the same number and text messages can be sent between networks. Competition is fierce and you can buy a pre-paid mobile for as little as $50.

The emergency number throughout Australia is 000.

CARS AND MOTORING

The wide roads in Australia and the low risk of hazards such as fog and snow make driving in Australian conditions reasonably easy. City traffic in Australia, as all over the world, is subject to the problems of congestion and tortuous one-way systems, but the suburban and country roads are usually excellent. In more remote areas the roads are often rough dirt or gravel surfaces best suited to rugged four-wheel drive vehicles. These are also the only vehicles suited to the tough conditions of the outback. Even in comparatively populated rural areas, apart from main roads and highways, most roads will be unmetalled. Generally, it is a good idea to keep your speed down on such roads as vehicles do not respond as quickly as they do on bitumen roads, and are likely to slide around a bit. On city and suburban roads, highways and freeways, driving is straightforward, and with many of the major interstate and intercity highways hugging the coast, you can often enjoy some outstanding scenery on your travels.

Fuel. Leaded petrol has been phased out in environmentally-friendly Australia, and the owners of old cars now use a 'lead replacement petrol' instead. Fuel costs vary from one area to another, and even within the metropolitan area, prices may vary considerably from suburb to suburb. Petrol tends to be more expensive in rural and remote areas due to freight costs. Petrol has seen continued increases due mainly to record high oil prices (in excess of US$50 a barrel) and in 2004 prices increased from 95 cents to $1.19 per litre. Regular (91 octane) and premium (96 octane) grades of unleaded petrol, and Diesel are readily available at petrol stations (often the cheapest petrol can be bought at supermarket garages), and two-stroke petrol is available for lawnmowers, boat engines. Most garages also sell LPG (liquefied petroleum gas) for taxis (many now run on LPG rather than petrol) and for topping up the boat and barbie.

Driving Regulations

Australians drive on the left of the road, as in Britain. There are, however, significant differences in speed limits, overtaking and other rules. Some of the basic differences between Australian and European driving are therefore worth noting.

Speed Limits. Speed is restricted to 37 miles/h (60km/h) in built-up areas (defined as those with kerbs and street lighting) and to 62 (100) or 68 miles/h (110km/h) on freeways or in country areas.

Overtaking. It is legal to overtake in the left (or inside) lane of a dual carriageway/ freeway (this is known as undertaking).

> On a three or more lane freeway (motorway), it is legal to overtake in any lane. The extreme right lane is not established exclusively as a fast lane, but it is courteous to keep to the left. It is not, however, obligatory to do so, so the British custom of driving up behind a car in the right lane, sitting on its tail and flashing your lights until it moves over to let you pass, is completely inappropriate. This kind of driving is likely to be interpreted as aggressive and may be met by an angry response from Australian drivers.

Road Etiquette. It is imperative that you give way to your right when entering a freeway or dual carriageway from a slip road. It would be considered bad driving to come onto a freeway and expect cars in the left lane to move over to the right in order to let you enter the flow of traffic. Courteous drivers may do this, but it is not common practice, and drivers who do not change lanes to let you onto the freeway or dual carriageway are not considered rude.

The practice of flashing your lights also carries a different meaning in Australia. In Britain you may flash your lights to indicate to another car that it may enter your lane, that you wish to overtake them, or to warn another driver that their headlights are not on. In Australia, you may also flash your headlights to indicate to another driver that their headlights are not on, but most commonly drivers will flash their lights in order to warn oncoming drivers that there is a police speed trap ahead. It is, in some states, illegal to warn other cars that they are approaching a speed trap, but the tradition of Australian anti-authoritarianism lives on and most drivers derive satisfaction from helping others avoid a speeding fine.

Highway Code. You can check the rules of the road by obtaining a copy of the Highway Code from your local police station or traffic-licensing centre. The Highway Code varies in its details from state to state, often on minor points, but there are a number of differences on such crucial points as priority at intersections. If you wish to drive interstate, it would also be helpful to obtain the Highway Code relevant to your destination as each State/Territory writes its own road laws. It is compulsory to wear seat-belts, both in the front and back, and the practices of both hitch-hiking and picking up hitch-hikers is actively discouraged, and in Victoria, illegal.

Licence Penalty Points. For minor driving offences, most States have a system of penalty points. Every driver has 12 points, and a certain number of points are deducted according to the gravity of the traffic offence. Details of the points allocated to a particular offence are outlined in the Highway Code. If a driver loses all 12 points within a certain period of time, the driver loses his/her licence for a minimum of three months; this, however, can be much longer if there is serious damage to property or persons involved. Serious traffic offences may be punishable by a jail term.

Drinking and Driving. Penalties for drinking and driving in Australia are very severe, and may result in a criminal record. One Australian commentator has described the obsessive drives by the State and Territory governments to eradicate drink-driving as surpassed only by the similar fanatical endeavours of the Scandinavian governments. Random Breath Testing (RBT) is now legal and means that a driver can be pulled over at any time by the police, who will ask you to blow into a breathalyser in order to check the alcohol level of the blood. RBT vehicles are popularly known as Booze Buses and are found at all times of the day and night, on both major and suburban roads. The permitted blood alcohol level in Australia is currently 0.05%. You will reach 0.05% after only one or two glasses of wine or beer depending on the individual. For learners, provisional licence holders there is a zero blood alcohol limit, and for drivers of commercial vehicles, many States also have a zero limit. Australian drivers take the risk of being caught extremely seriously. Do not drink and drive in Australia. You are almost certain to get caught, may get a criminal record, will definitely get a very large fine, and will definitely lose your licence for at least three months. These days, very few people, even the young and foolish, take the risk. The positive side of this draconian policy is that statistics now show that the RBT system is successful and the number of alcohol-related road deaths has fallen considerably. In Victoria, random roadside drug tests are in operation on a trial basis until laws are introduced in 2005. A drug-affected driver faces a $600 fine and a three-month licence cancellation. Those who have used amphetamines in the previous eight hours or cannabis in the past three hours are expected to fail.

Breakdowns and Accidents

Automobile Associations. There are a number of accident and breakdown services in Australia, but the biggest is the NRMA (National Roads and Motorists' Organisation). All companies offer varying levels of cover, but home-start is part of basic cover rather than an optional extra. Policies change and prices fluctuate, so you will need to contact the companies directly to obtain current details. On the whole, accident and breakdown cover is much cheaper than in Europe, and it is the car, not the driver, which is covered. In general, you can expect to pay around $50-$100 for a year's breakdown cover. If you need a breakdown service and you are not a member, you can join at the roadside, however, a premium is charged for this service. The bigger companies also offer national and international accident and/or breakdown cover free, or at a minimal rate, and will cover the cost of towing a car from remote areas, or, in the event of a fatality, the cost of flying a body home. The standard of cover is excellent and membership is well worth the fee, particularly if your car is over five years old. Up to 75% of Australian motorists are members of an automobile association, twice the European rate of membership. As on European motorways, there are telephones every kilometre on Australian freeways for the purpose of calling for roadside assistance. Automobile associations also offer other benefits such as tourist information, including hotel guides and maps, as well as the facility to have one of their qualified mechanics check over a used car that a member may wish to buy.

Accidents. If you are involved in a motor vehicle accident in Australia, whether as a passenger, pedestrian or driver, it is essential that you record the details of the other parties involved, including their full names, addresses, phone numbers, driver's licence numbers, the name of the insurance company of the other party or parties, the names, addresses and phone numbers of any witnesses, and a list of damage to the vehicles involved. This inventory should be made at the scene of the accident if at all possible. If the total cost of damage caused by the accident is thought to exceed $500-$1,000 (depending on the state/territory you are in) you must call the police, and in this case, it is helpful to record the name of any attending officers. If you sustain any physical injury, no matter how minor, you should attend your GP and describe how your injuries were caused, and their extent, in detail. Medical records will often affect any amount awarded as compensation in any personal injury claim.

Driving in the Outback. It is very important to never underestimate the danger that is ever present for wanderers in the outback. If you intend to drive in the outback, or undertake long distance trips, Tourism Australia can provide information detailing city-to-city links, motoring clubs, information on vehicle rental and accommodation, as well as essential rules for outback motoring.

Drivers are advised to prepare thoroughly for a trip through the outback, to notify friends and relatives of expected times of arrival, and to inform them on arrival, to check intended routes carefully, to refuel at every opportunity and to keep an additional week's supply of food, water and fuel in case of a breakdown in remote areas. Many people have died of exposure and dehydration after breaking down in the outback. You are advised *always* to remain with your car if it breaks down in the outback, as the vehicle will provide shelter from the sun and serves as an obvious point of reference for rescue teams. _

The Royal Flying Doctor Service of Australia (RFDS) offers a service for outback travellers which includes advice on touring and emergency procedures, as well as hire of transceiver sets with emergency call buttons. It is advisable to contact the RFDS for information before embarking on a trip into the outback.

Useful Addresses

Australian Council of the Royal Flying Doctor Service, Level 5, 15 Young Street, Sydney, NSW 2000; ☎02-9241 2411; fax 02-9247 3351; e-mail enquiries@rfdsno.com; www.flyingdoctor.net. Contact this office for a list of RFDS bases Australia-wide.

Australian Automobile Association (AAA), 216 Northbourne Avenue, Braddon, Canberra, ACT 2612; ☎02-6247 7311; fax 02-6257 5320; e-mail aaa@aaa. asn.au; www.aaa.asn.au.

Automobile Association of the Northern Territory (AANT), 78-81 Smith Street, Darwin, NT 0800; ☎08-8981 3837; e-mail information@aant.com.au; www. aant.com.au.

National Roads and Motorists' Association (NRMA), Podium Level 3, Bankstown Square, North Terrace, NSW 2000; ☎02-9848 5201; www.nrma.com.au.

Royal Automobile Club of Australia, 89 Macquarie Street, Sydney, NSW 2000; ☎02-8273 2300; fax 02-8273 2301; e-mail raca@raca.com.au; www.raca.com. au.

Royal Automobile Association of South Australia Inc., 55 Hindmarsh Square, Adelaide, SA 5000; ☎08-8202 4600; www.raa.net.

Royal Automobile Club of Queensland (RACQ), 300 St Pauls Terrace, Fortitude Valley, QLD 4006, ☎07-3872 8456 or 131 905; www.racq.com.au.

Royal Automobile Club of Tasmania (RACT), Cnr Patrick and Murray Streets, Hobart, TAS 7001; ☎03-6232 6300; or 132 722; e-mail info@ract.com.au; www.ract.com.au.

Royal Automobile Club of Victoria (RACV), 550 Princes Highway, Noble Park, VIC 3174; ☎131 955; fax 03-9790 2843; www.racv.com.au.

Royal Automobile Club of Western Australia Inc., 228 Adelaide Terrace, Perth, WA 6000; ☎08-9421 4444; www.rac.com.au.

Driving Licences

Each of the states and territories has a separate authority responsible for the issuing of driving licences. The minimum age for holding a licence is either 17 or 18 years, depending on the State or Territory. A Learner's Permit may be obtained by a potential new driver three months before they reach driving age (at either 16 years 9 months or 17 years 9 months of age depending on state/territory), after first passing a written test on the Highway Code. A learner driver may only be accompanied or instructed by someone who has a clean driving licence and who has been driving for at least seven years. Learners are not permitted to drive on freeways or in the dark, and must always display 'L' plates attached to the car. Although in practice most learners get at least some driving experience in the presence of a suitably qualified friend or member of the family, it is nonetheless compulsory to have lessons with a qualified instructor before attempting the driving test. Once a learner feels confident with the basic driving skills, the driving instructor will make an appointment for the driving test with a police examiner. On passing the test, which is usually at the second attempt (unless you are very lucky or proficient), a driver is granted a 'probationary' licence and is required to display 'P' plates on the car every time they drive, for their first year as a licence holder. Probationary drivers are subject to restrictions on speed and blood alcohol limits, and face severe penalties if caught exceeding these limits. After one year, the probationary driver is considered to be sufficiently experienced to be awarded a full driving licence. Driving licences are not issued for an indefinite period (or until your 70th birthday) and must be renewed periodically, generally every five years.

If you arrive in Australia with a driving licence issued overseas, different regulations apply. If you are considered to be a visiting driver (you are temporarily in Australia and usually reside outside Australia), you may drive any vehicle, including a locally registered one, provided you hold a current full driving licence or International Driving Permit (issued in your home country) for the class of vehicle to be driven. In Britain, an International Driving Permit can be obtained from the AA, even if you are not a member, and from most main post offices.

Obtaining an Australian Driving Licence. If you intend to become a permanent resident of Australia, you must obtain a driving licence issued by the relevant state or territory authority. Although you may be given a period of grace, which varies from state to state but is usually three months, you will be required to obtain a driving licence as soon as you take up permanent residence. New settlers holding a current valid British driving licence must take a written test based on knowledge of the State/Territory Motor Traffic Handbook (also known as the *Highway Code*) as well as a practical driving test. In addition, it is necessary in most states to undergo an eyesight test. A driver's licence issued in one particular Australian State or Territory is valid Australia-wide.

Car Registration

Registration fees are payable according to the type of vehicle and the expected wear and tear that vehicle will inflict on the State's or Territory's roads over the course of a year. In most states or territories, temporary residents and visitors are exempt from registration fees as long as the registration of the vehicle continues to be valid in the country of origin. A vehicle imported from abroad must be inspected on arrival by the nearest registration authority to ensure it is roadworthy immediately after its arrival in Australia. In addition, you will need to provide the following documents: a *Carnet de Passage* or other evidence that security has been lodged with Australian Customs, evidence that it is covered by Third Party Insurance in Australia, a current registration certificate from the country or origin, and a valid driver's licence from country of origin. Registration payments include Third Party Injury Insurance (CTP), and costs vary between States. The combined cost of registration and CTP of a popular six-cylinder family sedan ranges from $400-$600. Fees differ depending on whether the vehicle is intended for business or commercial use (for which standard fees apply) or solely for family or personal purposes (for which family vehicle fees apply). A family vehicle will receive a discount of around $50 on the annual registration fee.

To register your vehicle, contact your local traffic authority (listed below). In New South Wales you must get an endorsed Compulsory Third Party Certificate (The Green Slip) from an insurance company in order to be able to register your vehicle. Payment of the combined vehicle registration and CTP can be made at any metropolitan Post Office or at the office of the relevant authority, although payment procedures are subject to change and you should check with the proper registration authority. In Western Australia, payment of vehicle registration can only be done by cheque or via the metropolitan Post Office branches, and not at the Police Department. Once registered the vehicle will be fitted with Australian number (registration) plates.

Useful Addresses

ACT. *Road User Services*, Technical Standards Section, 13-15 Challis Street, Dickson, ACT 2602; PO Box 582, Dickson, ACT 2602; ☎02-6207 7000; e-mail roaduserservices@act.gov.au; www.transport.act.gov.au

NSW. *Roads and Traffic Authority*, Centennial Plaza, 260 Elizabeth Street, Surry Hills, NSW 2010; PO Box K198, Haymarket, NSW 1238; ☎02-9218 6888; fax 02-9218 6286; www.rta.nsw.gov.au

NT. *Motor Vehicle Registry*, Department of Infrastructure, Planning, and Environment, PO Box 530, Darwin, NT 0800; ☎08-8999 3111; fax 08-8999 3103; www.nt.gov.au

QLD. *Queensland Transport,* Customer Service Centre, 229 Elizabeth Street, Brisbane, QLD 4006; ☎132 380; fax 07-3305 8350; www.transport.qld.gov.au. Service Centres are located throughout Queensland.

SA. *Transport SA*, Registration and Licensing Office, EDS Centre, 108 North Terrace, Adelaide, SA 5000; ☎131 084; e-mail enquiries@transport.sa.gov. au; www.transport.sa.gov.au. Transport SA has 15 Customer Service Centres throughout South Australia which deliver Registration and Licensing services.

TAS. *Registrar of Motor Vehicles*, PO Box 1002, Hobart, TAS 7001; ☎1300 851 225; e-mail info@dier.tas.gov.au; www.transport.tas.gov.au

VIC. *Vic Roads*, Vehicle Registration, PO Box 1644N, Melbourne, VIC 3001; ☎03-9854 2666; www.vicroads.vic.gov.au

WA. *Licensing Services*, ☎08-9427 6404 or 131 156; fax 08-9427 81191; e-mail call.centre@dpi.wa.gov.au; www.dpi.wa.gov.au/licensing/. Licensing centres are located throughout WA.

TRANSPORT

Although Australia is a vast country, transport networks are very good and it is relatively easy to explore it by air, rail and coach. Around 567,310 miles (913,000 km) of roads and 5,877 miles (9,458 km) of rail networks span the continent, and several major airlines offer a choice to travellers. Qantas was one of the world's first commercial airlines and has an unrivalled safety record. Virgin Blue, Australia's only low-fare carrier, currently serves 20 destinations throughout the country. Scheduled domestic flights carry more than 18 million passengers a year. Trains operate in all states except Tasmania, and there are interstate lines travelling deep into the outback and along the lush coastline of the eastern seaboard. Rail Australia provides a nation-wide service linking the major tourist orientated passenger rail operators Queensland Rail, Countrylink, and the Great Southern Railway. In addition, Australia has about 70 ports of commercial significance, used mainly for trade, although cruise ships are enjoying a prolonged popularity and regularly call at the ports of Sydney and Fremantle.

Air

Domestic air travel in Australia isn't particularly cheap, due in part to the huge distances which separate major cities, but also because of lack of competition among the airlines. Tourists will find it is often cheaper to book internal flights from their home country through a travel agent than arrange them in Australia, although clearly this option is not available to anyone who has already taken up residence in Australia. Many international airlines offer free or discounted internal flights with their tickets, and there are also a number of air passes available which offer more economical travel within Australia. If you fly to Australia with Qantas (www.qantas.com.au), you can choose between four fare types – Super Saver, Flexi Saver, Fully Flexible or Business Class - to explore Australia. A return economy class ticket from Sydney to Melbourne will cost £110.70. Offers are constantly changing, but there are regular specials available for overseas visitors. Check with your travel agent for the latest information.

Rail

Australia has an extensive rail network, although it is impossible to travel the whole country by train. The remote outback of both the Northern Territory and Western Australia is not served by railway lines at all (the intense heat can cause track to buckle), and Tasmania, being both small and sea bound, has never developed a rail system. The eastern coast of Australia, however, is well served by trains, and one of the great railway lines of the world, *The Indian Pacific* runs between Perth and Sydney and operates weekly. This transcontinental journey is 2,704 miles (4,352 km) long, takes 65 hours, and travels through two time zones. After watching the sun rise over the Pacific Ocean in Sydney, you can enjoy the Perth sunset over the Indian Ocean. Other legendary train journeys include *The Ghan* (from Adelaide via Alice Springs to Darwin), and *The Overland* (from Melbourne to Adelaide). Coastal destinations, including the Great Barrier Reef and Whitsunday Islands, are reached aboard *The Sunlander* or on Australia's most modern train, the Tilt Train. More than 360 NSW regional and interstate destinations, including Brisbane, Canberra, and Melbourne, are serviced by the CountryLink network. Interstate rail travel is expensive, and most travellers will choose to undertake it for the experience rather than for the convenience.

There are several Rail Passes available for rail travel within Australia, which can be booked before departure. All passes are valid for travel in Economy/Kangaroo seating. Further details of these passes can be obtained through local travel agents, Rail Australia (PO Box 445, Marleston Business Centre, Marleston, SA 5033; ☎08-8213 4592; fax 08-8213 4490; e-mail reservations@railaustralia.com.au; www.railaustralia.com.au; or its appointed specialist in the UK, International Rail (Chase House, Gilbert Street, Ropley, Hants SO24 0BY; ☎0870-751 5000; fax 0870-751 5005; e-mail info@international-rail.com; www.international-rail.com. In the USA, bookings can be made through Down Under Answers, 400 108th Avenue NE 700, Bellevue, WA 98004; ☎1-800 788 6685. As some long distance rail services operate on a weekly basis, you are well advised to book ahead, particularly if you have a limited travelling time or are travelling in peak season. Tickets may be booked up to six months in advance and there are often discounts on those tickets purchased in advance. Single tickets are valid for two months and return tickets must be used within six months of using the outbound section of the ticket.

Bus

Travelling by coach around Australia, while time consuming, is actually one of the best ways to see the country, as well as one of the cheapest. Nearly 80% of independent travellers use coach services to get around Australia. There are a number of independent bus companies, and daily services travel to almost anywhere in the country from every major city. Prices are competitive and the standards are very high. Long-distance coaches are usually fitted with video and stereo facilities, and the bus drivers often consider themselves to be part of the entertainment, maintaining humour levels should they begin to flag in the middle of a long trip. Every bus is fitted with air conditioning, a toilet and drinking water fountains, and there are frequent stops at roadhouses for food, drinks, toilets and even showers. All coaches are strictly non-smoking.

Bus Companies. Greyhound Australia is Australia's national coach operator providing services to more than 1,100 destinations throughout the country. Greyhound has booking agents in the UK and these can be contacted for further details or you can log onto www.greyhound.com.au. In Tasmania, the state bus company is Redline Coaches (www.tasredline.com).

For Greyhound Australia, contact Visit Australia (21 Norman Road, St Leonards-on-Sea, East Sussex, TN37 6NH; ☎01424-722152; fax 01424-722 304).

Bus and Combined Bus/Rail Passes. There is a range of bus passes available for travellers in Australia and information can be obtained from travel agents in the UK, USA, or Australia. For example the *Aussie Kilometre Pass* allows you to travel a certain amount of kilometres over a period of 12 months from the first day of travel in Australia, with the freedom and flexibility to hop on and off the coach as well as changing direction as often as you like. A 1,242-mile (2,000-km) pass costs $295 while a 6,213-mile (10,000-km) pass will cost $1,133. The *Aussie Explorer Pass* lets you choose a pre-set travel route and you can stop off as often as you like, travelling in one direction. Selected passes include free tours and transfers to destinations like Kakadu National Park and Ayers Rock. There are 23 pre-set routes and passes are valid for one to 12 months from the first date of travel depending on the pass. All passes are cheaper to buy outside of Australia by 10% and you will be able to exchange Aussie Passes on the trans-Nullarbor services (Perth-Adelaide, or vice versa) for Red Kangaroos Day/Night seats on the Indian Pacific train.

Urban Transport

Most Australian cities are well served by public transport. Within the city centre, there are frequent and economical buses; trains also service the central business district. In Melbourne, the city transport system also includes trams, which have become a feature and an attraction of the city, and which are now considered to point the way forward in public transport planning strategies. Trams on certain city routes are free. Sydney has an underground rail system (commonly referred to as the City Circle), and in Adelaide commuters use the O-Bahn, the world's longest and fastest guided busway. In Perth, the city council provides free bus services within a restricted area of the city. The Central Area Transit System (CATs for short) is a bus service which operates in the City Centre and also in Fremantle.

Routes are colour-coded and you can catch one of the service buses at any point along its route and stay on as long as you like, without paying a cent. In both Perth and Melbourne, these free transport services are provided to encourage city workers to leave their cars at home thus reducing city traffic congestion, however, many tourists and shoppers also take advantage of the excellent services.

In common with many European city transport systems in many Australian cities public transport tickets are valid for a certain length of time rather than for a single or return journey. If, for example, you buy a ticket (which is priced according to how many zones you need to cover), that ticket will be valid for a specific length of time, and will remain valid regardless of how many times you get on and off any buses or trains within that time period, and within the specified zones. Zones are set in concentric circles, so it is possible to travel out again from the city centre to the other side of the city without purchasing extra zones. In addition, in Perth it is possible to use bus and train tickets interchangeably, so you can catch the bus into Perth and then use the same ticket to catch a train to another destination, or vice versa, within the zonal distance. You usually pay the driver for your ticket as you board, and at stations there are automatic ticket vending machines. Australian cities are very sprawling and there are often long distances to be crossed between various areas. In consequence, the public transport is perhaps not as frequent or as well established as in European cities. There is, however, considerable new investment in rail services, especially in Perth, which is constantly increasing its track miles. Most Australians still like to drive to work, although there are an increasing number of 'Park & Ride' schemes by which you drive to a convenient bus/rail depot and travel into the city centre by public transport.

BANKS AND FINANCE

Banking in Australia is straightforward and the tellers (cashiers) are generally courteous and helpful. All banks are open the same hours nation-wide: from 9.30am to 4.00pm Monday to Thursday, and from 9.30pm to 5.00pm on Fridays. Building societies and some banks may open on Saturday mornings from 9.00am to noon, but regional and remote branches may have more restricted opening hours. Australian banking has all the usual electronic facilities that a customer will expect, plus a few extras. ATM machine cards can be used in all supermarkets, and Electronic Funds Transfer at Point of Sale (EFTPOS) facilities are available in most stores, petrol stations, grocery stores and boutiques, with the larger outlets also allowing cash withdrawals. Australians are big on the idea of a cashless society. The four largest national banks (known as 'the big four') are Westpac, the National Australia Bank, the Commonwealth Bank of Australia, and the ANZ (which also has branches in New Zealand). Many building societies, including the St. George, have gone through the same demutualisation process as those in the UK and now operate as banks.

Bank Accounts

If you are going to Australia for more than six months, or to work, it is worth opening a bank account either before you leave your home country, or immediately on arrival in Australia. It is much easier to open an account with an Australian bank when you are actually in Australia, but accounts can also be arranged through bank offices in the UK. The Commonwealth, ANZ and Westpac all have branches in London which offer services particularly geared to new arrivals and migrants. Their advisors are extremely helpful, and will guide you in choosing the best accounts to meet your requirements, as well as providing general advice about services. The Commonwealth Bank, for example, will establish a bank account for you with a convenient branch in Australia and transfer your funds prior to your departure so that when you arrive in Australia you have immediate and full access to their range of banking facilities (including automatic telling machines throughout the country). The Commonwealth Bank can only establish an account for you prior to your arrival if you intend to work in Australia, if you are migrating, or if you are a resident returning home after an extended period abroad. To qualify for their services in the UK branch you will need to be able to show them evidence that you have been given the relevant visa. Contact the Commonwealth Bank of Australia's Migrant Banking Services (details listed below) for further details or to speak with one of their consultants, 9am to 5pm Monday to Friday.

The One Hundred Points System

Banking is relatively open and available in Australia and there are very few people who will be excluded from having an account, even with a bad credit record. References or proof of income are not required, however, proper identification is crucial and all banks must by law operate the '100 points system' of identification. Under this system you must conclusively demonstrate your identity and place of residence by providing various forms of identification, which are scored by the level of their official authority. A passport, for example, will provide you with 70 points, which you might back up with a Visa or Mastercard (25 points), a birth certificate (70 points), or a driver's licence (50 points). When you go to the bank to open an account, be sure to take a selection of appropriate documents with you, as you will be sent away empty-handed if you cannot comply with this government requirement. Note, however, that if you apply for a bank account within six weeks of arrival in Australia you will only need to show your passport as proof of identification.

International & Internal Money Transfers

If you wish to send an international money transfer to Australia, it will cost you a flat fee regardless of the amount of money sent and the transfer may only be sent through a bank, using the 'Swift' service. The Commonwealth Bank offers customers a superior foreign exchange service and highly competitive exchange rates. For further information contact the Commonwealth Bank 020-7710 3999 or www.migrantbanking.co.uk. You can also send money through American Express and Western Union offices but these services, although quick, are expensive. In Australia, international money transfers are made either by bank draft, or electronically. Within the country, travellers without a cheque (current) account may send money within the country by bank cheque (costing approximately $5, although the charge varies from bank to bank), or by Australia Post Money Orders, which can be bought to a maximum value of $1,000 for a cost of around $2.50. Express Money Orders can be bought to a maximum value of $10,000 and cost around $20. Money Orders are generally the cheapest way to send money and can be cashed at any of Australia Post's 3900 post offices Australia-wide.

Making use of a specialist currency broker can help you to obtain the best rate of exchange. One such is *HIFXplc,* Morgan House, Madeira Walk, Windsor SL4 1EP; ☎01753-859170; fax 01753-859169; e-mail migration@hifx.co.uk; www. hifx.co.uk; 909 Montgomery Street, Suite 105, San Francisco, California 94133; ☎415-678 2770; fax 415-773 1822; e-mail info@hifx.com; www.hifx.com; and Level 7, 35 Clarence Street, Sydney, NSW 2000; ☎02-9279 1123; fax 02-9279 1272; e-mail info@hifx.com.au; www.hifx.com.au.

Other Banking Services

Credit Cards. All Australian banks offer a credit card facility, and all the usual international credit cards, including Mastercard, Visa, Diners Club and American Express, are available via your local bank branch. If you intend to stay in Australia for less than 12 months, you may prefer to apply for a credit card in your home country before you leave and then establish a standing order to pay off your monthly credit card bill. It is a good idea to deposit any savings in a high interest account whilst you are away, allowing the interest from this account to cover the approximate charge of 2% on cash advances made against your credit card in Australia.

Direct Debits. Australian banks offer direct debit facilities, known as standing orders for the payment of regular bills, and many now also offer telephone and Internet banking facilities which enable you to authorise and conduct transactions by telephone and online from your home or office.

Cheque Accounts. The chequebook facility only applies to specific accounts, and it is important to check whether the account you are considering offers this service. There is no cheque card system in Australia, so there is also no limit as to the amount of the cheque you are able to write. In order, however, to write a cheque, you will need to have your driver's licence or other acceptable form of identification showing your full name and address, with you, and this information will be noted on the reverse of the cheque. Not all shops will accept cheques as payment if not guaranteed, so with smaller shops, ask first if they are prepared to accept one. Almost every shop now prefers the cashless transaction, and even the smallest corner deli will accept your ATM card. Very few Australian bank accounts offer free cheques and as a result, Australians use cheques sparingly, prefer to use cash or credit cards. Cheques take three working days to clear, but foreign cheques may take up to four weeks and you are likely to be charged a commission on the exchange of cheques made out in a foreign currency.

Investment Advice. Many expatriates tend to seek advice on money related matters such as employee benefits, retirement income funding, personal investments and savings. Companies specialising in providing worldwide financial services include *Brewin Dolphin Securities* of 5 Giltspur Street, London EC1A 9BD; ☎020-7247 4400; fax 020-7236 2034; e-mail info@brewin.co.uk; www.brewindolphin.co.uk; and *Aon Consulting* of 15 Minories, London EC3N 1NJ; ☎020-7767 2000; fax 020-7767 2001; www.aon.com/uk/en/.

Money

Australia has had a decimal currency for more than 40 years, abandoning the archaic

Heading to NZ or OZ? Move your money before moving yourself.

Moving to a new country is exciting. Worrying about your finances isn't. So it's good to know that the Commonwealth Bank of Australia and ASB Bank in New Zealand can give you a head start.

That's because we can set up your bank accounts and transfer funds at a competitive commercial foreign exchange rate – before you even leave.

From basic transaction accounts to business finance solutions and managing foreign exchange risk, you can trust a local bank to make sure you've got everything covered. In fact, we are the only banks in the region with a dedicated migrant banking office in London.

Ask us about how we can help before you even step foot in the country. As established banks, with branches all around Australia and New Zealand, you'll be glad you did.

Call **+44 (0)20 7710 3990** or email **londonmbs@cba.com.au**

ASB BANK

CommonwealthBank

www.migrantbanking.co.uk

imperial pounds, shillings and pence system in 1965. The basic unit of currency is the Australian dollar, which is worth 100 cents. In 1993, 'coppers', or one and two cent pieces, were withdrawn from circulation, having become virtually worthless and more of a nuisance than an item of value. Their withdrawal has provided a certain complicating factor into Australian shopping, which will confuse the new arrival. Although coppers are no longer available to be given as small change, goods for sale are still marked up in terms of single cents (for example, $2.98). Your shopping will be rung up in these hypothetical numbers and the final total will be rounded off – always, by law, in favour of the customer. Thus, if your supermarket till total comes to $47.68, it will be rounded down to $47.65. Items paid for by cheque or cashcard, however, will cost the precise amount as stated, and not rounded off. This system sounds complicated but has been quickly accepted by Australians, and few people are nostalgic for the bad old days of a wallet full of dirty little coins. Australian coinage consists of the silver-coloured, cupronickel 5, 10, 20 and 50 cent pieces, and of gold-coloured $1 and $2 coins, which replaced notes of the same value in 1994. The 5 cent coin is very similar in size to an old sixpence, the 20 cent coin is easily confused with a UK 10 pence, and the 50 cent coin has the same hexagonal shape as its UK equivalent. The $1 coin is about the same size as the 20 cent piece, and has irregular milling which allows it to be easily distinguished by blind people. The $2 coin is smaller and thicker, and is much like a UK £1 in dimension. Australian notes are in denominations of $5, $10, $20, $50 and $100. In recent years, the Australian currency has been gradually redesigned to make it both counterfeit-proof and longer lasting. New $5, $10, $20, $50 and $100 notes have now been released, and are made of a kind of plastic, which mimics paper but cannot be torn. It is considered virtually indestructible. The plastic notes bear a forgery-proof transparent seal in the corner (you can see right through the note), and a hologram in the centre of the seal. All notes and coins bear the head of Queen Elizabeth II on the reverse side. Old paper notes have been quickly withdrawn from circulation and destroyed. Paper money is still legal tender, but will be returned to the mint for destruction on receipt.

The Australian mint also coins gold bullion and coin, known as Australian Nuggets. Each coin has a set purchase price (from $15-$100), but the actual value is determined by the daily-fluctuating price of gold, and the demand for the coins. The Australian Nugget can be bought Australia-wide at banks as individual coins or as full sets. They are popular as souvenirs for wealthier visitors.

Visitors are permitted to import and export an unlimited amount of foreign currency into Australia, but if you intend to import or export more than $10,000 you need to contact customs or the *Australian Transaction Reports and Analysis Centre* (PO Box 5516, West Chatswood, NSW 1515; ☎02-9950 0055; fax 02-9950 0054; www. austrac.gov.au), Australia's anti-money laundering regulator and specialist financial intelligence unit. Should you be lucky enough to clean up at that illegal Australian coin game, 'Two-up', you might have to leave your winnings behind or, if you've been really lucky, invest it in Australian business or property. Banks are also legally obliged to report deposits of more than $10,000 in cash made into Australian bank accounts, primarily to safeguard against money laundering activities.

Useful Addresses

Australian and New Zealand Bank (ANZ), Minerva House, Montague Close, London SE1 9DH; ☎020-7378 2121; fax 020-7378 2378; www.anz.com

National Australia Bank Ltd, 88 Wood Street, London EC2V 7QQ; ☎020-7710 2100; www.national.com.au

Reserve Bank of Australia, Basildon House, 7 Moorgate, London EC2R 6AQ; ☎020-7600 2244; fax 020-7710 3500; www.rba.gov.au; and 46th Floor, 1 Liberty Plaza, New York, NY 10006-1404; ☎212-566 8466; fax 212-566 8501.

Commonwealth Bank of Australia, Financial & Migrant Information Service, Senator House, 85 Queen Victoria Street, London EC4V 4HA; ☎020-7710 3999; fax 020-7710 3939; www.migrantbanking.co.uk.

Westpac Banking Corporation, 2nd Floor, 63 St Mary's Axe, London EC3A 8LE, ☎020-7621 7000; www.westpac.com.au

TAXATION

Income Tax

Australia revised its taxation laws a few years ago and on 1 July 2000 a new tax system was introduced, bringing in new measures such as the Goods and Services Tax (GST), Pay-As-You-Go (PAYG) taxation and some business tax reform measures. Australia's government structure means that each tier imposes its own taxes: The Commonwealth Government administers general taxes such as income tax, GST, customs and excise, fringe benefits tax, superannuation guarantee charge, and taxes on natural resources projects; State and Territory governments administer taxes such as payroll and workers' compensation taxes, stamp duties, bank account taxes and land tax, and the Municipal governments levy rates and charges on the owners of real estate.

Income Tax in Australia can be quite a complicated business and the completion and lodgement of a tax return is the responsibility of the individual. To help to demystify the taxation procedures Tax Packs containing forms and an information magazine, produced by the Australian Taxation Office, are available free from newsagents and Taxation Offices Australia-wide. The Tax Pack is reviewed annually, in an effort to make completing a tax return less difficult, but even so, the Tax Pack is a formidable publication with detailed information and instructions. Both format and terminology are quite daunting and for this reason, fewer and fewer Australians are choosing to complete their own taxation returns and are turning to chartered accountants or licensed tax agents to complete the forms for them.

The Australian financial year begins on 1 July and ends on 30 June, and tax returns must usually be lodged by the end of October. Even if you think you are not liable to pay any tax, you are generally required to lodge a tax return in Australia if you are normally resident there, or if you are a non-resident who has derived an income in Australia. Every taxpayer requires a Tax File Number (TFN). To apply for a TFN you will need to contact the Australian Tax Office on arrival in Australia.

Although taxation rules and regulations are subject to continual re-assessment and change, clearly most Australian adults will fall somewhere within these categories and are therefore required to complete and lodge an annual taxation return.

Completing a Tax Return

In order to complete a tax return, you need to attach official statements of the amount of tax you have paid over the year. These statements are known as PAYG Payment Summaries and are issued automatically by employers at the end of the financial year. If you do not receive a Payment Summary from your employer you must request one.

If either you or you employer have lost your PAYG Payment Summary, or they have gone missing in the post, you are usually able to get a copy from your employer. If your employer is unable to provide you with a copy, then he/she can give you a letter showing all the details of the original documents. In the unlikely event that you are not able to obtain a letter from your employer, you can fill in a Statutory Declaration of lost or missing Payment Summaries (available from your local Tax Office). If any information on your Payment Summary is wrong, your employer must provide a letter showing your correct income and tax details.

Self-Assessment. If you choose to complete your own tax return, the tax office will work out your refund or tax bill based on the information you have provided. The tax office assumes the information you have provided is true and correct but you should note that after they have calculated your rebate or bill and informed you of their calculations in your Notice of Assessment, their computers continue to check for missing or incorrect information. Your tax return may also be subject to an audit and, should the original assessment be judged incorrect, the tax office will change it and send you an amended assessment. In addition to extra tax, you may be liable for a penalty if you fail to show reasonable care in the preparation of your return. Knowing this, it is understandable why many Australians simply don't want to take the risk and so pay a professional to shoulder the responsibility.

Professional Assistance. If you would like assistance filling out your own taxation return, you will be able to find chartered accountants or other professional taxation assistance services in the Yellow Pages phone book. It is advisable to phone around as the cost of the service can vary greatly. The Tax Office recommends that if you get someone (other than them) to help you complete your return, you should ensure that that person is a registered tax agent. Some agents offer a free initial assessment, and discounts to pensioners. Tax return fees charged by a registered tax agent are tax deductible against your *next* annual tax return. The company *Destini Global Financial Services* (address below) specialises in helping those emigrating to Australia with their tax and financial matters.

Tax help is available for seniors, people from non-English speaking backgrounds, the disabled and those on low incomes who cannot afford assistance with completing their tax returns. Tax help centres are run by community volunteers, and you should contact your local tax office for details of your nearest one.

It is obligatory to lodge a tax return at the end of the financial year if any of the following are applicable:

- O You had tax deducted from your pay or other income (including Australian Government pensions, allowances or benefits);
- O You had tax deducted from interest, dividends or unit trust distributions (applicable only to residents) because you did not quote your TFN or Australian Business Number (ABN) to the investment body;
- O You were required to lodge an activity statement under the PAYG system and pay an instalment amount during the year;
- O Your taxable income for the previous year was more than $6,000 (residents) or $1 or more (non-residents);
- O You incurred a net taxable loss, or are entitled to a deduction for a

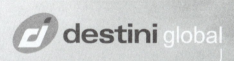

prior year loss;

- O You were entitled to a distribution from a trust, or you had an interest in a partnership and the trust or partnership carried on a business of primary production;
- O You were an Australian resident for tax purposes and you had exempt overseas employment income and $1 or more of other income;
- O You are a special professional covered by income averaging provisions;
- O You received income from dividends or distributions exceeding $6,000 and you had imputation credits or amounts withheld because you did not quote your TFN or ABN to the investment body;
- O You conducted business in Australia;
- O You paid provisional tax on your previous year's assessment;
- O You were under 18 years of age as at 30 June and your total income was not from a salary or wages, and was more than $643;
- O You are the liable parent under a child support assessment;
- O You have a reportable fringe benefits amount on your PAYG payment summary;
- O You are entitled to a tax offset;
- O You received a pension, allowance or benefits and your assessable income was more than: $15,970 if you were single, widowed or separated at any time during the year; $15,164 if you had a spouse but either of you lived in a nursing home or you had to live apart due to illness; $13,305 if you lived with your spouse for the whole income year.

There is also a Translating and Interpreting Service (TIS) available specifically to help non English-speaking people with their tax returns. The TIS offers joint meetings with interpreters and tax officers, and you simply call the TIS to make an appointment. TIS phone numbers are found in the community information pages of your phone directory.

The postal addresses and phone numbers of the various state and regional Tax Offices are listed at the back of Tax Packs and in the government section of the telephone book.

Useful Address
Destini Global Financial Services, 29 Ely Place, London EC1N 6TD; ☎020-7611 4777; fax 020-7611 4701; e-mail global@destinifs.co.uk; www.destiniglobal.co.uk, specialise in offering specialist tax and financial advice and transferring UK pensions to Australia.

E-Tax. During October 1998, the Australian Taxation Office (ATO) trialed a new electronic tax preparation and lodgement software package, *e-tax*, which was based on the hard-copy *TaxPack*. Following trials, the *e-tax* facility is now available to the public and in 2003, 800,000 Australians lodged a tax return through the *e-tax* service. The ATO has developed high levels of security to ensure that personal income tax information is secure. When you complete your return online, you sign it electronically using the in-built public key technology, and the *e-tax* software will encrypt your tax return file for transmission over the Internet using a secure link.

The Australian Taxation Office has a very comprehensive and informative website at www.ato.gov.au.

Claiming Back Tax on Expenses. Deductions are generally available for work-related expenses of a non-private or domestic nature, as well as certain other expenses (such as gifts to organisations that are endorsed as deductible gift recipients. If audited, you will have to substantiate your work expenses claims, for example motor vehicle, travel, clothing, tertiary studies, tools of trade, reference books and other expenses. It is therefore necessary to keep records of any work-related expenses in order to avoid additional tax and a possible penalty.

If you are an employee and the total of your claims is $300 or less, you must keep a record of how you worked out each of your claims. If the total of your claims is more than $300, you must keep records of receipts, invoices and similar documentary evidence supported by or on behalf of the supplier of the goods or services. Cheque stubs are not considered acceptable as evidence. The receipt, invoice or documentary evidence must be in English or the language of the country where the expense was incurred, have the date on which the expense was incurred, name the person who (or business which) supplied the goods or services, show the amount of the expense in the currency in which the expense was incurred, give details of the nature of the goods or services, and show the date the document was made out.

A diary may be used to prove your claims for expenses that are no more than $10 each and which add up to no more than $200, or for which it was unreasonable to expect to get a receipt. The diary should contain all the details that would be required on a receipt or invoice. In addition, you must sign each entry in the diary.

The information outlined above should be kept for a period of five years after lodging your tax return. Records of other business-related expenses incurred by self-employed persons should also be retained for five years after lodging their tax return. If you appeal against an assessment, you must retain your records until the dispute has been finalised if that period exceeds the given record retention period.

You can claim for the cost of using your car for work or business purposes; for example travelling directly from one place of work to another, or from one job to another. You cannot, however, generally claim for the cost of travelling from home to work.

If you are to be audited, you will usually receive written notification at the beginning of the audit and you should follow the instructions contained in the letter.

Table of Income Tax

The following table shows personal income tax rates for those resident in Australia for the financial year 2005-2006. There is currently a tax threshold of $6,000 in Australia which means that the first $6,000 earned is tax-free. The tax rate applicable on earning over this amount is described below:

TABLE 5	INCOME TAX RATES
Taxable Income	**Tax rate %**
$0-$6,000	Nil
$6,001-$21,600	17
$21,601-$63,000	30
$63,001-$80,000	42
$80,00 and over	47

If you become a resident of Australia during the financial year you are entitled to a pro rata amount of the $6,000 tax threshold. For the tax year, you calculate this amount by adding up the number of months from when you became a resident of Australia up to the 30 June. This amount is then divided by 12 to give you the proportion of the year spent in Australia, then multiplied by $6,000 to give you your tax-free threshold. If, for example, you have only been resident in Australia for two months, your tax threshold is assessed as 2/12 x $6,000 = $1,000, but if you have been resident for 11 months, your tax threshold is 11/12 x $6,000 = $5,500. Your assessment can take up to eight weeks after lodging your tax return. If you are required to pay tax, you will be given 30 days notice. Tax can be paid by cheque or postal money orders made payable to the Deputy Commissioner of Taxation, in cash or cheque at any Post Office (you must take your Notice of Assessment with you), by mail (cheque or postal order only), at Tax Offices (take your Notice of Assessment), or by direct debit/refund. This last service is available from tax agents who lodge tax returns electronically.

If you cannot pay your tax by the due date, you may be given extra time to pay depending on your circumstances. You will have to provide details of your financial position including assets, liabilities, income and expenditure, and the steps you have taken to obtain funds to pay your debt. If granted additional time, you will have to pay a general interest charge (GIC). The GIC is a commercially linked interest rate that compounds daily and varies every quarter with changes in the money market.

Rebates

There are numerous tax offsets (formerly called tax rebates) which may be available to you, and it is certainly worth being aware of them even if you are not currently eligible. If your tax offsets are greater than the tax on your taxable income, they can only reduce the amount of tax you pay in that year to zero. There are three exceptions to this rule: the 30% private health insurance rebate, where any excess is refunded to you; the landcare and water facility tax offset, where any excess is refunded to you; and the franking tax offset, where any excess imputation credits on dividends paid to you on or after 1 July of the tax year are refunded to you. Generally, tax offsets do you reduce your Medicare levy. Where you have excess refundable tax offsets available, these can be applied to reduce your tax, including the Medicare levy. Being eligible to claim a tax offset depends on things like maintaining a dependant, or living in a remote area, or on how much taxable income you earned. A brief summary of some of the tax offsets available is given below:

SOME TAX OFFSETS
○ You were involved with heritage conservation work.
○ You were earning interest from government securities.
○ You were earning interest from the land transport facilities tax offset scheme or infrastructure borrowings scheme.
○ You were entitled to the landcare and water facility.
○ You were living in a remote or isolated area of Australia.
○ You were responsible for the maintenance of your parent, spouse's

> parent or invalid relative.
> - Your net medical expenses were more than $1,250 in the tax year.
> - You were serving overseas as a member of the Defence Force or a United Nations armed force.
> - You were responsible for superannuation contributions on behalf of your spouse.
> - Low income tax payers · if you were an Australian resident for tax purposes and your taxable income was less than $24,450.
> - You claimed family tax benefit.
> - You are a low income, aged person.

Other Taxes

Capital Gains Tax

Australia has had a Capital Gains Tax (CGT) since 1985. You will be liable for this tax if you make capital gains from selling or otherwise disposing of any CGT assets or if you receive certain other capital amounts in a financial year, unless a relevant CGT exemption replies. Examples of capital amounts include a forfeited deposit, premium received for granting a lease, or a capital gain distributed to a beneficiary of a trust. Net capital gains (after offsetting any capital losses you may have) are included in your assessable income and taxed at your applicable income tax rate, subject to the CGT 'discount' rules. Under the CGT discount rules, if you have held the CGT asset for at least 12 months, only one half of the next capital gain is taxable, unless you choose to apply indexation. For assets acquired before 21 September 1999, you may choose to apply indexation to the cost base of the asset (with the cost base being increased by reference to movements in the Consumer Price Index from the quarter in which you acquired the asset up to the quarter ending 30 September 1999) instead of the CGT discount. Any assets you may have acquired before 20 September 1985 are not subject to capital gains tax. CGT assets fall into three categories: collectables, personal use assets, and other assets:

Collectables. Include items that are used or kept mainly for personal use including paintings: sculptures, drawings, engravings or photographs; reproductions of these items or property of a similar description or use, jewellery, antiques, coins or medallions, rare folios, manuscripts or books, and postage stamps or first day covers. A collectable can also be an interest in, a debt that arises from, or an option or right to acquire any of the above items. Any capital gain or capital loss you make from a collectable acquired for $500 or less is disregarded. A capital gain or capital loss you make from an interest in a collectable is disregarded if the market value of the collectable when you acquired the interest was $500 or less. However, if you acquired the interest for $500 or less before 16 December 1995, a capital gain or capital loss is disregarded. If you dispose of collectables individually that you would usually dispose of as a set, you are exempt from paying capital gains tax only if you acquired the set for $500 or less. This does not apply to collectables you acquired before 16 December 1995.

Personal Use Asset. Deemed to be a CGT asset, other than a collectable, that is used or kept mainly for personal use including: an option or a right to acquire a CGT asset of this type, a debt resulting from a CGT event involving a CGT asset kept mainly for your personal use and enjoyment, or a debt resulting from you doing something other than gaining or producing your assessable income or carrying on a business. Personal use assets also include such items as boats, furniture, electrical goods and household items. Land and buildings are not personal use assets. Any capital loss you make from a personal use asset is disregarded. If a CGT event happened to a personal use asset during or after the 1998-99 income year, any capital gain you make from the asset or part of the asset is disregarded if you acquired the asset for $10,000 or less. If you dispose of personal use assets individually that would usually be sold as a set, you obtain the exemption only if you acquired the set for $10,000 or less.

Assets that are not collectables or personal use assets include: land and buildings, shares in a company, rights and options, leases, units in a unit trust, instalment receipts, goodwill, licences, convertible notes, your home (although there is a CGT exemption for your main residence), contractual rights, foreign currency, and any major capital improvement (above the improvement threshold) made to certain land or pre-CGT assets.

A full explanation of Capital Gains Tax with all its separate clauses can be had from the Australian Taxation Office at www.ato.gov.au.

Fringe Benefits Tax. The Fringe Benefits Tax (FBT) was introduced in July 1986 by the government in an effort to control the amount of non-cash (and therefore often non-taxable) benefits offered by employers as part of a job package. FBT is payable (at the rate of 48.5%) by the employer on the 'grossed up' taxable value of all non-exempt fringe benefits provided by the employer during the FBT year (which runs from 1 April to 31 March). Fringe benefits are not taxable in the hands of the employee. Companies also cannot claim expenses such as business lunches and entertainment costs on behalf of the company. Taxable fringe benefits include company cars, free or low-interest loans, free or subsidised accommodation or board, goods and services sold at a reduced rate or provided free, and expenses paid on behalf of an employee.

Cars are probably the most common fringe benefit, and Fringe Benefits Tax is normally paid by an employer when a car is owned or leased by a company and made available to an employee (or family member) for private use. Fringe Benefits Tax on cars does not normally apply to self-employed people or to a partnership if the vehicle is used wholly and exclusively for business. It does not apply to cars owned or leased by an employee, even when the cost of operating the car for business use is claimed as an expense against the taxable income. When Fringe Benefits Tax is chargeable, it applies to all passenger cars, wagons, minibuses, panel vans and utilities designed to carry less than one tonne or a bus with fewer than nine seats. There are many variations and exemptions to the Fringe Benefits Tax and probably the safest way of working out whether you are liable or not is to get a professional to do it for you.

Goods and Services Tax. The GST was introduced on 1 July 2000. Bearing some similarity to the system of VAT in the UK, the GST is a broad-based tax of 10% on the supply of most goods, services and anything else consumed in Australia. You must register for GST if the annual turnover of your business is $50,000 or more ($100,000 or more for non-profit organisations). You may choose to register if the annual turnover of your business is less than $50,000 (less than $100,000 for non-profit organisations). GST is charged on imported goods, but not on wages or salaries. The amount of GST payable on a taxable supply is 10% of its value. To work out how much GST is included in the price of a taxable supply, you need to divide the price of the goods by 11. Some supplies are not taxable and are called GST-free supplies. These include most food, some exports, most health and childcare services, educational supplies, and cars for use by disabled people. The GST has not been greeted too warmly by Australians.

Higher Education Contributions Scheme. HECS regulations are described in detail in the Higher Education section of this book. The rate of HECS tax varies from 3% to 6% of your taxable income. In addition, since 1994, the Australian government has instructed employers to deduct additional taxation instalments to cover any possible Higher Education Contributions Assessment Debt in future years. These deductions will only be made if you earn more than $441 per week. For further details on HECS and taxation, you should request a copy of the booklet *HECS; Your Questions Answered,* available from your educational institution, or any Tax Office or at www.goingtouni.gov.au.

Death Duties. Currently, there are no Death Duties in Australia, although Capital Gains Tax is widely considered to be death duty by another name and widely resented as such (although capital gains arising when an asset passes to the deceased's estate and then to the beneficiaries are generally disregarded, although pre-CGT status or an exemption, such as for a main residence may be lost). If you are making a will, you should seek tax advice on the most effective method of disposal of assets.

HEALTH INSURANCE AND HOSPITALS

A report published in 1998 by the Australian Institute of Health and Welfare reveals that Australians born in the 1990s are expected to live 15 years longer than those born in the 1920s; boys born in 1994 can expect to live to an age of 75 while girls will live to an age of 80.9. In 1999, Australia's mortality rate was around 5.87 per 1,000 people per year, although Aboriginal people continued to have a mortality rate far higher than the national average. Interestingly, the report also compared the mortality rates of migrants and Australian-born residents and found that most migrant groups had death rates significantly lower than the Australian average. Greeks, Italians, Central and South Americans, Vietnamese and Yugoslavs had the lowest rate. In addition, among Australians aged 25-64, the death rate was 15% higher for men living in rural regions, and 9% higher for women in rural areas.

The report also noted an increase in the rate of multiple births with improving technology in the field of artificial conception, such as IVF treatment, and that dental health has improved dramatically over recent years to an extent where few people under 35 years of age have lost all their teeth. Despite the large number of people on hospital waiting lists, the report also indicated that trends showed a continued decline in basic and supplementary private hospital insurance, and government measures have been put in place to offset this decline, by offering incentives to insure privately.

The report also showed that the nation's health was dogged by a rising suicide rate, with more Australians dying by their own hands than in traffic accidents.

For the most part, victims were males between 15 and 24 years old, but women of the same age were also at risk. The survey indicated strong links between suicide and the socially disadvantaged and the unemployed, particularly in the Aboriginal population. The number of Aboriginal deaths in custody in the 1990s, which were statistically disproportionate when compared to the average rate of suicides in prison were so alarming that the government ordered a Royal Commission to investigate. Despite the Royal Commission's findings (released in May 1991) and its 339 recommendations, indigenous people are still 14 times more likely to be imprisoned than non-Indigenous Australians; in the Northern Territory for instance, 72.8% of the prison population is indigenous.

High cholesterol levels are a major contributor to health problems in Australia, affecting nearly three million people nationwide and killing 50,000 each year. Public health concern over this issue is reflected in the amount spent on drugs. Between 1998 and 2000 the cost of the cholesterol lowering drug subsidy paid by the Federal Government rose by more than $110 million. The number of prescriptions for these drugs increased by nearly two million and now tops the Pharmaceutical Benefit Scheme (PBS) in cost, amounting to over half a billion dollars in 2000 and rising by around 25% each year.

Cancer rates also appear to be on the increase, currently accounting for more than 30% of male deaths and 25% female deaths each year. Breast, lung and skin cancers are the most common killers. As a result of increased public awareness of these health risks, most Australian buildings, including restaurants, are now completely smoke-free. Australians are highly educated about the risk of skin cancer and the dangers of the sun, and now almost universally take thorough protective measures when outdoors.

The perception that Australians have apparently healthy lifestyles has also been challenged by the 1995 National Nutrition Survey which showed that some 56% of the adult population (18 years and over) were overweight, with 19% of these classified as obese.

Six priority areas of concern have been endorsed by Australian Health Ministers. These are: cardiovascular health; cancer control; injury prevention and control; mental health; diabetes mellitus and asthma. A range of program initiatives has been established, aimed at improving health in these areas, which together account for approximately 70% of the burden of disease and cost in Australia – a high demand on the nation's health services.

The Health Care System

Using the General Practitioner. The first point of contact in obtaining health care in Australia is the local GP, whom you are free to choose yourself. While most people will have a preferred doctor, it is not necessary to register with a doctor, and you are able to go to a different practice at every visit, should you so wish. Depending on the doctor, you will either be billed for the consultation, for which you will be reimbursed by Medicare, the Australian national health system, or the doctor will 'bulk-bill' which means they will claim reimbursement directly from Medicare. Doctors who practise in low-income areas generally bulk-bill in order to avoid asking their patients for payment, however, this is largely a gesture of goodwill on behalf of the GP. The benefits that you get from Medicare are based on a Schedule of fees (index linked) set by the Commonwealth Government. Medicare pays either 85% of the Schedule fee for outpatient services or 75% of the Schedule fee for inpatient services, or the Schedule fee less an amount of up to $52.50, whichever is greater. If the charge is less than 85% of the Schedule fee, Medicare will only pay the amount equal to the charge. GPs are able to charge fees they consider suitable for the services they provide, however, any extra amount about the Schedule fee with not be included in the calculation of Medicare benefits and the patient is liable for any amount in excess, which is known as the 'gap'.

Should you wish to have a second medical opinion, you simply make an appointment with another doctor. Generally, appointments are made over the telephone, and you can usually see your GP within two days of your call.

If a GP refers you to a consultant or specialist, you will be given a letter and required to make the necessary arrangements yourself. Even specialists seeing public patients consult in their own rooms, and there is no system of attendance at hospital outpatients' clinics. There may be a waiting period before you are seen, although it is usually not long, and once again you will be billed and reimbursed through Medicare. You may choose to see a consultant on a private basis, without referral, for which you will be unable to obtain a refund either from Medicare or from your private insurer.

There are an increasing number of clinics and medical centres opening in suburban areas. Most large practices will provide a Well-Woman Clinic, minor surgery, and other services. There may also be a pharmacy housed within the centre, from which you can purchase your prescriptions immediately.

Prescription charges are subsidised under the Pharmaceutical Benefits Scheme (PBS). Patients pay the full cost of medication up to the value of approximately $22.40, and the PBS meets the balance up to the list price; patients on benefits of any kind pay only $3.60. Contraception is not free in Australia, but is covered by the PBS.

Using Hospitals. Patients who require hospital attention or surgery can also choose to be treated either publicly or privately. If you opt for private treatment, you can choose both your attending consultant and the hospital, but will pay a considerable amount for this privilege. On the other hand, you can expect a great deal of luxury for your money, including five-star food chosen from a daily menu, as well as immediate treatment. If you choose to be treated under Medicare, you do not have a choice of hospital or doctor (although you will have had some say in choosing your specialist during discussions with your GP in the early stages), and you may face a long wait for a bed; on the other hand, your treatment will be completely free. In the event of an emergency, all patients will be taken directly to a public hospital, and may be transferred if they wish once their condition has stabilised. Ambulance transport is not free, and many people choose to pay a small insurance premium annually to the St. John's Ambulance Brigade to cover themselves in case they or their family need to call on this service.

Health Insurance Contributions

Every Australian is covered by Medicare, which is financed through progressive income tax and an income-related Medicare levy. There is no additional charge equivalent to National Insurance in the UK. The Medicare levy is paid at a rate of 1.5% of taxable income above an earning threshold of around $13,807, or $23,299 for couples. In the 1996-97 budget the Federal Government announced that a 1% Medicare levy surcharge, in addition to the 1.5% levy, would be introduced for higher income earners ($50,000 per year for single earners, $100,000 per year for couples) who do not have private patient hospital cover through private health insurance. This surcharge is part of a package of measures designed to encourage people to retain or take up private health insurance. People receiving state benefits fall below the earning threshold of the Medicare levy, and payments are made on their behalf by the government. If you choose to be privately insured, you are not exempt from the Medicare levy.

THE AUSTRALIAN NATIONAL HEALTH SYSTEM

Australia's national health system, Medicare, is outstandingly good but its services are becoming increasingly oversubscribed with the increasing population of Australia and the fact that the population is a 'greying' one. Many Australians, however, do choose to take out additional private medical cover. There has been a recent surge in so-called 'medical tourism', whereby people in need of major treatment, such as a hip replacement or heart surgery, visit Australia specifically to take advantage of the good facilities, medical expertise and reasonable costs. Medicare is funded by the Australian Government, and administered by the Health Insurance Commission (134 Reed Street North, Greenway, ACT 2900; ☎ 02-6124 6333; fax 02-6124 6222; e-mail hic.info@hic.gov.au; www.hic.gov. au). Hospitals and other facilities are built and run by the various state health departments who are responsible by law for maintaining a uniform minimum standard of care.

In order to be eligible for Medicare, you must first register by completing an application form obtainable from a Medicare regional office (call 132 011 to find your nearest office). You need not necessarily have registered with Medicare before you receive any medical treatment, but will be required to do so before you can make any claim. After you have registered, you will be sent a Medicare card, which looks like a credit card, and this should be carried with you at all times. You will need to present this card on arriving at a hospital for treatment. Any children under 15 years old will be listed on the card of one or other of their parents. When you lodge a claim for a Medicare rebate, you will be required to quote your number or present your card; rebates can be made in cash over the counter, and the process is straightforward. You can also lodge claims by post, which takes considerably longer, and forms are available in chemists, doctors' surgeries and post offices.

All immigrants are covered by Medicare, provided they pay the Medicare levy (included in general taxes), and temporary residents who stay in the country longer than six months may be covered by Medicare without having to pay the levy. Medicare covers in-patient and outpatient treatment at public hospitals, as well as hospital accommodation costs in public hospitals. If you need regular, expensive treatment, Medicare will cover all of the scheduled fees incurred over the rest of the year once the gap has reached a total of $302.30 for any financial year. Most medicines available on prescription are subsidised under the Pharmaceutical Benefits Scheme (PBS). Most PBS-listed medicines cost the consumer a maximum of $22.40, or $3.60 for relevant concession cardholders. If you have a record of spending $716.10 on PBS medicines for yourself and your family in a calendar year you will be entitled to any further PBS medicines for only $3.60 for each item for the rest of the calendar year.

Medicare does not cover physiotherapy, chiropractic or dental treatment, although some orthodontic treatment is refundable, particularly if surgery is involved. Neither medical repatriation nor funeral costs are covered, and ambulance costs (including transport and treatment) cannot be refunded through Medicare.

Reciprocal Agreements

Visitors to Australia from the UK, Malta, Italy, Finland, Norway, Sweden and the Netherlands are also covered by Medicare under reciprocal arrangements, and can receive limited subsidised health services for immediately necessary trreatment If you are from the UK, Finland, the Netherlands, Norway or Sweden you are covered for the duration of your approved visit to Australia. As a resident of Italy or Malta you are covered for six xmonths from the date of your arrival. You are not, however, entitled to claim health benefits for a medical condition which existed before your arrival in Australia, including any illness caught on your journey to Australia, or for any on-going medication. Travellers from the countries listed above should enrol at a Medicare office, presenting a passport containing an appropriate visa, and proof that you are enrolled in the national healthcare scheme of your home country. If you are a short-term visitor and you do not come from a country which has reciprocal health agreements with Australia, it is advisable to take out private medical insurance, which is usually available through your travel agent and is likely to be included in any travel insurance policy. Students are not covered by Medicare and you should therefore take out your own health insurance cover.

Medicare Exclusions. There are two categories of new settler which are exempt from eligibility for Medicare. These are people entering Australia to retire, and those who have been granted permanent residence in the family stream migration category, who are the parents of their sponsor and are more than 55 years old (men) or 50 years old (women). Retirees need to take out travel insurance and private medical insurance (either in their country of origin or in Australia), as they are liable for all expenses incurred in the case of medical and hospital treatment, including the cost of hospital accommodation. In the case of migrants on a parent visa application, any medical or hospital expenses be incurred by the migrant parent (over the stipulated age limit) will be the responsibility of the sponsor, unless the migrant has private insurance. If only one of the sponsor's parents is over the age limit, then the sponsor is only responsible for the medical expenses incurred by that parent. In addition, if you enter Australia as a foreign diplomat or as a member of a foreign diplomat's family, you are not covered by Medicare. It is advisable to take out private medical insurance either before you leave your home country or take out a policy in Australia immediately upon your arrival.

Private Medical Insurance

Private health insurance is widespread in Australia, with around 70% of the population choosing to take out additional cover. Private health cover is much cheaper in Australia than in Britain, and premiums are not indexed for age or gender. Most people enjoy the security of knowing that they have the right to choose both the hospital where they will be treated and their specialist who will treat them. In addition, private cover offers refunds for medical services not covered by Medicare, such as physiotherapy, prescription glasses and sunglasses, and dental work. Different levels of cover are available, from basic table (shared-room) through to a fully comprehensive, deluxe table. Costs vary from around one dollar a week, up to around five dollars per week for the ultimate in hospital care. Premiums are usually payable in monthly, quarterly or annual instalments and discounts are sometimes given for prompt payment or for payments made annually. Children and dependants are normally covered by their parents' private medical insurance.

The Private Health Insurance Incentives Scheme, developed to make private insurance a more attractive proposition, especially to the young and healthy, was replaced by the Federal Government 30% Rebate on 1 January 1999. The 30% Rebate means that for every dollar you contribute to your private health insurance premium, the Government will give you back 30 cents. All those who are eligible for Medicare and who are members of a registered health fund are eligible for the Rebate-no matter what their level of cover, income or type of membership. Further information on the Federal Government 30% Rebate can be obtained by calling the Private Health Insurance Information Line (☎ 1800 676 296) or by visiting the Department of Health and Ageing at PO Box 9848, Canberra, ACT 2601; ☎ 02-6289 1555; fax 02-6281 6946; www.health.gov.au.

When choosing a health fund, points to consider should include whether there are any exemptions for previously known illness or for AIDS, what the waiting period is before you can make a claim, and what the benefit limits are for each service covered. Private health insurance companies advertise widely in the local newspapers and on radio and television, with some of the largest and best-known being Medibank Private (www.medibank.com.au), the Hospital Benefits Fund (www.hbf.com.au), and the Medical Benefits Fund (www.mbf.com.au). Some smaller funds now offer rebates for alternative medical treatments, such as homeopathy and acupuncture, so if you use these services, it will be worth shopping around quite carefully.

Useful Addresses

BUPA International, Russell Mews, Brighton BN1 2NR; ☎ 01273-208181; fax 01273-866 583; www.bupa-intl.com.

Columbus Travel Insurance, 17 Devonshire Square, London EC2M 4SQ; ☎ 020-7375 0011; www.columbusdirect.net.

Department for Work and Pensions, Overseas Branch, Tyneview Park, Whitley Road, Benton, Newcastle-Upon-Tyne NE98 1BA; ☎ 0191-218 7777.

The Travel Insurance Agency, Suite 2, Percy Mews, 755B High Road, North Finchley, London N12 8JY; ☎ 020-8446 5414; fax 020-8446 5417; e-mail info@travelinsurers.com; www.travelinsurers.com.

CRIME AND POLICE

Australia has many of the crime problems associated with developed nations and urban life, but on the whole, residents and visitors report feeling relatively safe. In particular, compared with other western countries, Australia's homicide statistics are very low, and, in spite of popular opinion, which seems to indicate an escalation, they have remained fairly static over the last decade. The Australian Bureau of Statistics recently found that the most frequently reported crime is unlawful entry with intent, with motor vehicle theft the next most common crime, followed by robbery and sexual assault. The defining feature of Australian crime is the rarity with which firearms are employed. Australia has very stringent gun laws (which have become even more so since the tragic Port Arthur massacre), and only 20% to 25% of homicides in Australia involved the use of a gun, compared to around 70% in the USA.

Crime patterns differ throughout the states and territories: the Northern Territory, for example, has the highest per capita rate for homicide and sexual assaults, but the lowest for armed robberies. Western Australia has the highest number of motor vehicle thefts and burglaries, but its rate of murder and attempted murder are at or below the national average. New South Wales had the highest rate of armed robbery, which is attributed to the fact that it has the largest heroin-dependent population in Australia. Canberra had the highest rate of kidnapping, attributed to acrimonious marital disputes over custody of children, and South Australia has the highest incidence of robbery and blackmail. The International Crime Victims Survey has noted that urban dwellers in Australia are four times more likely to install security devices than their rural cousins, and 62% more likely to feel the need for special locks on exterior doors and windows. These levels are exactly comparable to similar communities in other western industrial nations. Australian crime figures are, in general, much more closely in line with European ones, than with US figures, and Australian rates of motor vehicle theft are very low compared with those in the UK.

Police forces are the responsibility of state/territory governments, and are headed in each state by a Commissioner for Police. Regulations for each force vary, and some may carry guns on duty, depending on the state. There is also a Federal Police Force. This is Australia's international law enforcement and policing representative, and the chief source of advice to the Australian Government on policing issues. It enforces Commonwealth criminal law, and protects Commonwealth and national interests from crime in Australia and overseas. In recent years, allegations of police corruption in several Australian states have resulted in purges and high public accountability. In general, the police enjoy a good public profile and maintain open communications with the community.

LOCAL GOVERNMENT

Below the level of State government, the administration of local areas is undertaken by an elected town or shire council. This body is responsible for the provision and maintenance of public facilities and amenities, such as leisure centres, libraries, and rubbish collections. Payments for all housing rates, and even dog licensing, are made to the local government. Planning permission for new buildings, demolitions and extensions are also the responsibility of the local government, and vocal public meetings are frequently held to hear public discussion over topical local issues such as town planning and new developments. The local government level is the only one at which voting is not compulsory and, in general, most Australians are somewhat apathetic and avoid close involvement in local government decisions. Addresses and telephone numbers of local governments are available under the 'Local Government' section at the front of state telephone directories.

SOCIAL LIFE

Australians are generally friendly and outgoing people. They find the British extremely reserved and often find it difficult to establish relationships with them because of this cultural barrier. Most Australians will quickly invite you into their home, often on introduction, and a barbecue is the most likely first point of association for both neighbours and colleagues. Nothing, however, will repel this friendly approach more than polite formality. First names rule in Australia, from top to bottom, and people are likely to be insulted by any other form of address. So, how can you break the ice, meet the locals and both accept and be accepted by them? This section tries to give you a little insight into Australian social life and the kinds of people and attitudes you are most likely to meet.

Manners and Customs

On the whole, Australians are a lot more casual than their British or European cousins. You will find that people, while friendly and courteous, will be far more direct in asking questions or in telling you what they think. You are much less likely to experience the occasionally chilling British reserve, and are more likely to know exactly where you stand. When you meet an Australian for the first time at a social gathering you may find that you are asked a lot of questions which you may think 'forward' or even intrusive. This directness is the normal form of social discourse, and a similar directness of response will be expected. It is generally considered to be a time-saver, enabling friendships to develop to a deeper and more interesting level more quickly. Titles are rarely used, and most people regardless of their position will expect to be addressed in first name terms. It would be quite normal, for example, for an undergraduate student to be comfortable calling the Vice-Chancellor of their university, say, 'Fay' or 'Derek'; and the corollary of this is that it would be extremely insulting for a person of senior position to address someone of lower status as Mr or Mrs. Far from being respectful, it would be considered patronising. Australian women will expect others to use the title Ms on occasions when a title is required, and eyebrows will be raised if a woman chooses to indicate her marital status by the use of Miss or Mrs.

One Australian custom which cuts across all social barriers is the use of 'mate' as a form of address. The concept of mateship is a peculiarly Australian phenomenon and has been much studied anthropologically. Mateship generally refers to a specifically male bond, and constitutes a somewhat macho, but nonetheless powerful, kind of friendship. Many Australian men consider their mates to be as important, or even more important, than their female partner; and this bond often lasts to the grave. To be described as someone's life-long mate is the highest of compliments. Conversely, however, Australians also often use the term 'mate' ironically, or as an aggressive indicator in potentially explosive situations. The tone of voice will clearly indicate the level of use. Australian men, regardless of ethnic origin, will almost invariably use this form of expression.

Nathan Males is full of praise of the Australian way of life
The Australian social life is fantastic. There is a great outdoor culture and a great tradition of a couple of cold beers after work. A regular social event in Hobart is an outdoor band that plays Latin jazz in a courtyard every Friday after work. People

> *pour out of their offices and come along. There is a total cross section of society ranging from suits to scruffy-types, all drinking and dancing together. There is much less snobbery here. It still exists but it doesn't pervade society.*

Australians have a great respect for people who get out there and try something new or difficult. They love to support the underdog, and newcomers who really 'give it a go' will readily win the admiration and friendship of their new acquaintances and colleagues.

There are a number of associations of migrant communities in Australia, and all major cities will have branches of the Chung-Wah Chinese Association, and Greek, Italian, Yugoslav, and Irish Clubs. The United Kingdom Settlers' Association (First Floor, 146 Toorak Road West, South Yarra, VIC 3141; ☎03-9787 3112; fax 03-9866 1799) is specifically intended to provide assistance and a point of contact for new migrants from Britain and publishes a journal, 'Endeavour' every second month. Other clubs may be found in the Yellow Pages or your telephone directory, or by contacting the Department of Multicultural Affairs in your state. About 53,688 USA-born people live in Australia, mostly in NSW, followed by Victoria. The Australian American Association (see Retirement), based in Sydney and Melbourne, is a good place to start for support and information.

Sport

Sport is popularly considered to be the Australian national pastime, and is central to the social life of many Australians. Most Australian children are encouraged to play at least one sport from a very early age. Little Athletics, an athletics training programme for children from the age of five upwards, is held on Saturday mornings around the country, and is very popular. Regional and national competitions are attended by club scouts on the lookout for new talent. Similarly, cricket and football (Australian Rules) are enormously popular at every age and skill level, and most Australian boys play at some time or another for their local club. Cricket is becoming increasingly popular with girls, but usually not until secondary school age or even later. Sporting centres all over the country also offer volleyball, netball and five-a-side soccer, and single-sex or mixed teams often have their own leagues. Many young working Australians will play in one such team at least one night per week as a way of keeping fit and meeting their friends.

Australian Rules Football. Australian football is the most popular winter game, and is a predominantly male sport. Aussie Rules football is a national institution, and the AFL Grand Final is comparable to the FA Cup Final in the UK in the level of interest it excites around the country. Every state has its own team or teams which play in the national league, with the West Coast Eagles, the Sydney Swans, Carlton, the Geelong Cats, and the Essendon Bombers among the big names. Aussie Rules is a fast and athletic game, with much handling of the ball and some impressive jumping and mid-air collisions. The game is played by two teams of 18 players who try to score goals against each other. The goal posts consist of four tall, evenly spaced poles, the two outer ones slightly shorter than the inner ones, and there is a goal at each end of the oval. The oval-shaped football field is about three times the size of a soccer pitch. If a player touches the ball over the line between the two middle posts, he has scored a goal, the team gains six points, and the goal umpire (always dressed in a white coat) will gesture and energetically wave two white flags. If the player touches the ball over the line between a middle and an outer pole, he will have only scored a single point, and the goal umpire will gesture with one of his index fingers, waving just one of the flags. The game consists of four quarters, each quarter lasting 45 minutes. Running with the ball is allowed, as long as it is bounced every three seconds; failure to do this means being 'caught with the ball'. Bouncing the ball while on the run is in fact not easy as the ball is oval-shaped, like a rugby ball. Although some of the players at the interstate level have started to wear head protection and gloves (to give them a better grip on the ball), Aussie Rules players pride themselves on their toughness and fitness. The game is gruelling and extremely hard on the players. It is long and very physical, but can also be intense and exciting. The best way to see a game is to go to an important interstate match, and catch the enthusiasm of the crowd.

Rugby and Football. In the eastern states, rugby (both league and union) is also known as football, and Queenslanders in particular take the game very seriously. Western Australia, the Northern Territory and Tasmania do not share the enthusiasm of the other states for rugby, but the nation as a whole is proud of its top-level international rugby team, the Wallabies. Football of the kind played in the UK is always known as soccer and has a small but enthusiastic following, particularly among European ethnic communities who often field their own teams in state soccer competitions.

Hockey. Hockey is very popular with men, women and children, and Western Australia prides itself on its exceptional facilities at Curtin University, and on its track record of providing most of the players in the national team. The Australian Institute of Sport trains its specially selected hockey stars of the future at these facilities. The Australian men's and women's hockey teams are respected and feared worldwide and they both compete at the very top of the international circuit.

Basketball and Tennis. These are widely played throughout the country, and Australia has produced many Wimbledon champions. Basketball is played at regional and interstate levels, and the national league is extremely well supported and avidly watched on television. Australian players have gone on to positions in America's NBL teams, and there is considerable interchange between the two countries. Obtaining a ticket for an interstate match can prove to be very difficult as they are snapped up as soon as they become available. Baseball is an even newer sport to Australia, but there is also a national league which is becoming increasingly popular.

Netball and Softball. Netball and softball also enjoy almost universal participation among young girls. Around 90% of Australian schoolgirls play in non-school netball teams during winter, and there are also summer competitive leagues, playing on weekday evenings, which are very popular. Most schoolgirls play softball in the summer.

Sport and Schools. The Australian school curriculum incorporates sport into the normal school day, and each school, whether private or state, usually participates in both an interschool swimming carnival and an interschool athletics carnival every year. In addition, there are interschool cricket, netball, football, and softball leagues with games scheduled during school time or immediately after school.

Many private schools, however, hold their interschool sporting matches on Saturdays. In fact, Saturday mornings and afternoons are unofficially dedicated to sport around the country, and parents should resign themselves to the inevitability that for at least five years they will have to get out of bed early on a Saturday morning to deliver their offspring to the relevant sporting venue.

Modified Rules for Children. An important difference in Australian sport for children is the widespread use of 'modified rules' in almost every game. Under modified rules sports, even quite young children are able to compete in complete safety, while learning the basic skills of the sport. Primary schools will undertake careful coaching in every sport played, and there is a strong emphasis on skill development. Modified rules sports are known by names which differentiate them from their big brother sports: junior hockey is called minkey, a game based on baseball and softball for kids is called tee ball and is currently wildly popular, junior Aussie rules is touch football, and junior tennis, short tennis.

Water Sports. Above all, though, water sports are the cornerstone of Australian social and sporting life. Water-skiing, windsurfing, surfing, boating and diving are all common leisure activities, as well as highly competitive sports. Many Australians own their own pleasure boat, whether a yacht, power boat, or launch. Swimming is an essential part of every school's sporting curriculum at both primary and secondary levels, and in summer students will swim in either the school or local pool at least two or three times a week, if not every day. Pupils are divided into classes according to their age and swimming ability, and are rigorously coached by qualified instructors. Students are expected to attain swimming qualifications to a high level, and from the age of 13 are coached towards attainment of life-saving qualifications. Most students will leave high school with the Royal Life Saving Society's Bronze Medallion and Instructors Certificate. Every public swimming pool is home to a competitive swimming club, and many young Australians join these at an early age, often eventually swimming at a state or even national level. Almost every Australian child is a safe swimmer by the age of six, and school classes are focused on the development of refined technique and stamina. If you are moving to Australia with children, it would be advisable to have swimming coaching before you leave, so that they are not left high and dry at school. Once in Australia, do not allow your children to swim 'widths' in public swimming pools: this is considered highly anti-social and derisory, and even three year olds will be expected to tackle the length or keep to the baby pool. The Australian swimming, diving and water polo teams are amongst the world's best, and proved the point during the 2000 Olympic Games in Sydney.

Arts

Although Australians are famous for their love of sport, they are also enthusiastic supporters of the arts. Their expenditure on arts products ranks among the highest in developed countries, and research shows that they read more newspapers per head than any other nation. Australian cultural achievements are now well known internationally, through the awards gained by its many arts exports. The movie *Strictly Ballroom* won the Prix de la Jeunesse at Cannes in 1992, and *The Piano*, the Palme d'Or in 1993. Australian actors such as Russell Crowe (originally from New Zealand), Nicole Kidman, Mel Gibson, Cate Blanchett and Geoffrey Rush are now big players in Hollywood. Thomas Kenneally and Peter Carey have both won the Booker Prize for Literature in Britain, and the Australian Ballet was described by the New York Times during one of its world tours as 'world class'. The Australian Youth Orchestra is widely regarded as one of the best in the world, and is the training ground for the country's finest musicians.

Government support has been an important factor in developing the arts, and funding currently totals about $3.5 billion per annum. Funding for the development of Australia's cultural heritage comes from all three levels (Federal, State/Territory and local) of government. The Arts are also heavily supported by corporate and business sponsorship. The Australian Broadcasting Commission supports orchestras in each capital city, and the Sydney and Melbourne orchestras are flagship ensembles which frequently tour internationally. There are two major organisations involved in ballet and opera on a national basis, the Australian Ballet, and the Australian Opera, and most states also have state opera and ballet companies of a high standard. Musica Viva, established in 1945 to promote chamber music in Australia, now co-ordinates one of the largest ensemble music concert networks in the worlds. It also organises overseas tours for Australian chamber music groups and commissions works by Australian composers. Youth Music Australia, formed in 1948, has helped the careers of thousands of young musicians, and the Australian Chamber Orchestra is at the cutting edge of early music performance.

Aboriginal Arts. Aboriginal art, indigenous dance and music have recently begun to be introduced to national and international audiences. Companies like Bangarra and the Tjapukai Dance Theatre now take their performances around Australia and around the world. Aboriginal art, once confined to the ethnographic sections of local museums, now takes its place in contemporary art galleries internationally. Aboriginal writers, such as Sally Morgan and Jack Davis, and the late Kevin Gilbert and Oodgeroo Nunuccal, are well known throughout Australia. Sally Morgan's *My Place* is a moving account of the discovery of her Aboriginal heritage, and provides a keen insight into some regrettable episodes in Australia's history.

SOME ANNUAL FESTIVALS AND OTHER IMPORTANT CULTURAL EVENTS

Artrage: The Festival of Perth Fringe
Moomba Festival (Melbourne)
Sydney Festival
Sydney Gay and Lesbian Mardi Gras
The Festival of Adelaide
The Festival of Perth
Wangaratta Jazz Festival (Victoria)

Every state has excellent library services both at the local and state level, and the National Library of Australia provides research facilities for scholars from all around the country. It is also home to the national archives. There are good art galleries in every state, and a strong commitment to bringing international touring exhibitions to Australia.

SHOPS AND SHOPPING

Shopping in Australia's metropolitan centres is generally excellent. In suburban areas, large shopping centres offer speciality shops for clothing and goods, as well as supermarkets. Bigger shopping centres often also have a 'food hall', offering a wide variety of economical cuisines from around the world. Many also have cinema complexes. Most of the older suburbs will have a 'high street' (although it will never be known by this name) very similar to a British high street, with smaller retailers, chain stores, and service outlets. Newer suburbs tend to be planned around a US-style shopping mall, and do not usually have the convenience of a 'corner shop' – known in Australia as a 'deli'. In areas with large immigrant populations, delis often stock a wide range of exotic foods in addition to essential items. Shops are generally open from 8.30am to 5.30pm, Monday to Friday; 8.30am to 4.40pm on Saturdays; with 'late night trading' until 9pm one night a week (usually a Thursday). Many shops now open on a Sunday, especially in tourist and city centre areas, but Sunday trading is frowned upon in some states. Delis are usually open from 8am to 8pm and every city will have a number of chemists which are open 24 hours a day, 365 days a year. There are an increasing number of 24-hour shops in Australia, of the 7-ll type, and most cities have a handful of these scattered throughout the suburbs.

The quality of Australian produce and goods is generally good. Items bearing a green and gold kangaroo trade mark symbol have been manufactured in Australia, and these are generally more expensive than equivalent goods manufactured in Southeast Asia, due to the higher cost of Australian labour. The high quality of Australian-made products is also reflected in their higher prices. In general, however, Japanese, Taiwanese and Korean products, particularly vehicles and electrical goods, conform to Australia's strict quality standards and are usually very competitively priced. Australia is constantly seeking to improve its balance of trade by encouraging consumers to buy Australian, and in many cases appeals to loyalty and patriotism to counteract the imperative of the hip pocket.

Shopping in Australia can be an enjoyable experience, with a wide range of products available in modern, well-equipped shopping centres, as well as ample car parking. In the rural and more remote areas, however, the situation can be very different. Choice is much more likely to be limited as shopping centres service much smaller populations, and prices may be significantly higher because of freight costs. Most country dwellers prefer to wait until a trip to the city before shopping for electrical goods or clothing.

Supermarkets. All supermarkets use the barcode shopping system, and groceries are electronically scanned at the tills. Under the ruling of voluntary Code of Practice for Computerised Checkout Systems in Supermarkets, if an incorrect price registers on the supermarket scanner – and you are on-the-ball enough to spot the mistake – the price of the item is voided from your receipt and by law you are given the item for free. Supermarkets thus have a keen incentive to keep their barcodes accurate.

Loyalty cards have not been introduced in Australian supermarkets on a wholesale basis yet (although some small boutiques and restaurants operate similar schemes), however, many of the larger supermarkets, such as Coles and Woolworths, print vouchers on the back of their itemised receipts offering free meal deals (on a buy one, get one free basis) at local restaurants and chains, and discounts on anything from carpet cleaning to photo processing.

Edge-of-town superstores are rare, and most people shop in either a large supermarket located in a shopping mall, or in one of the many smaller franchised supermarkets, such as *Supa-Valu* or *Foodland*, in the local high street. Supermarkets large and small advertise pages of weekly 'specials' in the local papers, and prices are very competitive.

The vast majority of shops accept cheques and major credit and debit (EFTPOS) cards with adequate proof of identification.

Bottle Shops. By law, alcohol may not be sold in Australian supermarkets. Alcoholic drinks can only be bought from licensed liquor stores, also known as 'bottle shops'.

> Drive-in bottle shops are very common and provide the convenience of allowing you to drive up to a shop, roll down the car window and give your order and money to an attendant in exchange for cartons of beer or casks of wine. If availing yourself of a drive-in bottle shop, remember that in Australia you cannot drink and drive!

Bottle shops are usually open from 10am to 10pm, Monday to Saturday, and until 8pm on Sunday. They generally stock an extensive range of quality wines, as well as the usual beers and spirits. Most will have a giant walk-in coolroom, where all white wines are kept chilled so you need *never* visit a bottle shop in summer and come home with a warm bottle of white wine. Australians visiting the UK are incredulous at the lack of refrigeration in off-licences. Larger alcohol-retailing chains, such as Vintage Cellars, hold regular wine tastings, wine discussion evenings for regular customers, and publish monthly newsletters analysing the latest releases and the grape harvests. If you are having a party, most shops will accept the return of unopened bottles purchased from them in a bulk order (as long as labels and seals are not water-damaged from immersion in ice).

Clothes. Many European immigrants to Australia are of the opinion that the quality of clothing in Australian department stores is not as high as that found in equivalent stores in the EU. European clothes are usually made from better quality materials and to higher standards than the same kind of clothing in Australian stores, which are largely imported from Southeast Asia. Having said this, the cost of clothing from a budget-priced Australian store such as KMart or Target, as well as from other mid-range chain boutiques, is, depending on the current exchange rate, as much as 50% less than clothing from UK stores of a comparable standard. Classic Aussie 'clobber' such as moleskins, Driza-Bone coats, RM Williams boots, and Akubra hats are all going to be cheaper if bought in Australia. European designer label fashions can be bought in all the capital cities, but at a price, and Australia has some very highly regarded designers of its own. You will find, however, that the dress code, both at the office and at most social occasions, is informal by European standards, especially in summer. Leather goods, especially shoes and bags, tend to be expensive in Australia, to the extent that it may be worth investing in a few good quality items before you leave home; for women, the same applies to Marks and Spencers lingerie, which is always gleefully acquired by the bagful by Australians travelling through the UK.

FOOD AND WINE

Food

Australian food and eating habits have changed enormously in recent decades. The practically cuisine-less country has become one of the trendy food meccas of the world. As recently as the 1980s, Australian cooking was known only for its meat pies, slabs of steak, lamingtons, pavlovas, and pumpkin scones. In the post-war years, however, the gradual influx of waves of immigrants from Italy, Greece, Yugoslavia, Turkey, Lebanon, India, Thailand, China, Malaysia, Indonesia and Vietnam, meant the enrichment of the longer-standing Anglo-Irish eating style. The sunny climate and outstanding fresh produce and seafood provided the perfect seedbed for the cuisines of the Mediterranean and Southeast Asia, so that now chefs are renowned for their 'fusion food', mixing traditions from around the world.

Meat still plays an important part in the Australian diet, and the choice and quality is impressive by European standards. It is also largely inexpensive. Beef, lamb, pork and poultry of all cuts and types are available, as are more unusual 'bushmeat' options, such as kangaroo, emu and crocodile. These latter items are speciality fare, but are beginning to be farmed for both the export and domestic markets. In recent years 'bush tucker' has become popular, at least as a concept, and in each state there are a number of restaurants offering native aboriginal foods elevated from the campfire to the table. If you have a strong stomach, you may like to try witchetty grubs, usually served, tongue-in-cheek, poking out of a bush apple. More appetisingly, Australia has a superb range of delicious seafood, including prawns, lobsters, crayfish, octopus, oysters, mussels, mudcrabs and Balmain bugs (a type of crustacean). A huge variety of fresh fish, mostly unfamiliar to European visitors, is available: try dhufish in Western Australia, for example. If you buy fish from a fish and chip shop you are most likely to be served either shark or snapper; don't be put off by the idea of shark, as it is considered to be a good quality eating fish. The menu of the average fish and chip shop will also offer crab, prawns, squid (calamari), oysters or mussels, as well as a choice of homemade marinated pickles. Fruit and vegetables are all grown locally, and include many tropical varieties, such as lychees, avocados, and papayas.

Barbecues continue to be an integral part of Australian social life, but the menu has broadened. A respectable barbecue will be laden with tiger prawns, marinated rump steak and chicken fillets, or perhaps a whole fish garnished with ginger and spring onions. Even without the spectacular beaches, Finlays Fresh Fish BBQ in Kalbarri, Western Australia, makes the six-hour drive north from Perth worthwhile. This little shack in the sand will cook you up unbelievable prawns fresh out of the water, as well as fish and enormous steaks, barbecued for you by Mr Finlay himself. Finlay's mum takes your cash (about $12-$14 depending on what you are having) and prepares a range of about six salads, and as many sauces, for your meal, from which you help yourself as you sit on the benches with a drink and watch the sun set the vast sky, your prawns sizzling next to you on the barbecue.

Whether you have a barbie prepared by professionals like the Finlays, or one in your own back yard, or you grill-up on coin-operated gas barbecues provided by the local council, the food is likely to be great and the company congenial.

Restaurants

Australian food is distinguished by the outstanding quality and freshness of the produce. You can expect to eat at a cheap-and-cheerful restaurant for between $15-$20 for a two course evening meal and coffee, excluding wine. Portions are usually generous. In cities with big multicultural populations (most of the capitals, and many larger regional towns), you will usually find family-run restaurants which offer great food at incredible prices: in Sydney, 'No Names' used to be famous for serving up giant plates of spaghetti with a hunk of ciabatta and olive oil for just $2, and in Perth, 'The Roma', run by the same Italian family for 30 years, still has queues outside on a Friday night for a plate of mama's pasta. You can eat at The Roma, and dozens of places like it, for a few dollars a head. The decor is basic, but the service is good, and children are welcomed. In Northbridge, there are very similar restaurants run by Vietnamese families, serving up dozens of hot and spicy specialties. The variety of restaurants available in all major Australian cities is enormous, and is at least as varied as in London or New York. Greek, Vietnamese, Mongolian, ethnic Chinese and Indian, Mexican, Lebanese, Portuguese, Italian, Russian, Thai and Polish are all available Australia-wide. Japanese food is very popular, and *ramen* shops and sushi bars are found in most suburban areas. Street markets, like shopping centres, will often have a food hall (in Perth, try Subiaco Markets), where you can buy a good Japanese, Thai, or Italian meal for as little as $8. Australians are generally very accommodating towards families who bring their children to eat in restaurants, probably because of the influence of child-loving Eastern European and Chinese immigrants, and you will be treated with consideration and respect if you choose to introduce your offspring to fine dining at an early age.

At the top end of the market, there are innumerable first-class restaurants, offering the finest food and wines. Modern Australian cuisine emphasises the quality of the ingredients rather than fanciful techniques, and there is a horror of 'over-worked' food. Service is discreet, and there will usually be a qualified *sommelier* to advise on appropriate wines (which will be predominantly Australian). Expect to pay up to $150 a head in the best restaurants, but it will be worth it, especially if, as many do, the restaurant comes with spectacular views over a river, harbour or ocean.

Café culture is firmly established in Australia. You can be sure of a really good cup of coffee in most establishments. The *Dome*, a national franchise of coffee vendors, takes its coffee very seriously indeed, and even casual staff spend a week in training, learning how to make cappucino, macchiato, and espresso as they are made in Italy. If your preferred cuppa is of the type known as a *latte*, you should ask for a 'flat white' (or with low-fat milk, a 'skinny flat white'). Any decent café will sell all its various coffees in decaffeinated style as well.

Tipping is discretionary in Australia, however, if you should decide to tip your waiter, it is customary to leave between 10% and 15%. Some restaurants include a service charge, but this is unusual.

Traditional Australian Food

Australians are particularly fond of fruit and vegetables, and an Australian fruit salad is likely to surpass anything you have previously eaten. Fruit salad is the traditional dessert to accompany a barbecue, and you may be asked to bring one if you are invited as a guest. Be imaginative and include all the various fresh and exotic fruits on display in your greengrocers. Another favourite, the pavlova, is an Australian invention, also most often seen at barbecues. It was created for the ballerina, Anna Pavlova, on an Australian tour, and consists of a meringue base covered with whipped cream and seasonal fruits.

The lamington is another Australian institution, and consists of a cube of extremely light sponge which has been dipped in a special chocolate sauce and then rolled in coconut. School Parents' Associations invariably have 'Lamington Drives' as a way of fund-raising; school members take orders from students, parents, friends and relatives for at least one dozen lamingtons each, and then a battalion of parents get together to prepare this delicacy. A box of a dozen lamingtons usually sells for about $5. Everybody loves lamingtons, and there are few more effective fund-raising endeavours.

Many Australians grow passion fruit vines in their gardens, and passion fruit icing is very popular for sponge cakes. If you are lucky enough to have a passion fruit vine, make sure that you give it plenty of water and you will be rewarded with the world's most heavenly fruit right through the summer months.

The most famous Australian take-away food is the meat pie. This is traditionally eaten at Aussie Rules Football matches, and by school children (or at least by those with undeveloped taste buds) and they are always served with tomato sauce. Commercially mass-produced meat pies are pretty horrible, and you really have to be drunk or starving to eat one in these days of gastronomic variety. At a basic barbecue, perhaps one given by older Australians, expect the traditional fare of beef sausages and a big slab of steak.

Wine

Viticulture is one of Australia's leading primary industries, and wine drinking has enjoyed enormous growth over the years as wine production has become more sophisticated and eating habits have changed. Australia's climate and coastal fringe landscape is conducive to wine growing, and all states have extensive wine producing areas. The diverse climate, topography and soil types mean, however, that Australia is able to produce a wide range of wine styles, from delicate sparkling whites, to full-bodied reds, and exceptionally rich fortified wines. There are currently 44 regions of significance to the wine industry, each of which produces distinctive wine varieties. Australia has around 60 different varieties, although most wine drinkers will be familiar with around only 20 names, including Chardonnay, Semillon, Sauvignon, and Shiraz. Lesser-known types, such as Palomino and Pedro Ximenes, which do not appear on wine labels, are used for making sherry, and Pinot Meunier, is used in the production of sparkling wine. Every variety has a specific aroma and taste, known as the primary fruit characters, and many wines will use a blend of these different types. There are more than 1,300 vineyards in Australia, and 366,395 acres (148,275 ha) of land under vines. The top export markets for Australian wines are the UK and USA, and exports today total around $1.76 billion annually – and rising; wine exports exceed wine imports by ten to one. The top six wine grape varieties currently under cultivation are Shiraz, Cabernet Sauvignon, Chardonnay, Semillon, Merlot and Colombard.

Regional Varieties. Most Australian wine production is located in the more highly inhabited south-eastern provinces of New South Wales, Victoria and South Australia – the latter produces approximately 70% of Australian wine. The climate of much of South Australia is a lot like California, with a range of microclimates and a low to moderate rainfall. Inland, the weather gets hotter, and varieties of red wine can be made in almost all of the regions. Some of the best-known regional wine growing areas are described below:

Margaret River (WA). Western Australia produces about 3% of Australia's wine – but the grape harvests here account for approximately 20% to 30% of Australia's premium bottled wines. The wine industry in Western Australia was founded even before those of South Australia and Victoria, and for the next 135 years commercial viticulture was confined to the Swan Valley, around Perth. In the mid-1960s, the wine industry began to move south, with the first plantings at Margaret River and Mount Barker. Margaret River has grown to be one of Australia's finest and most vibrant wine producing regions, known for its Chardonnay, Sauvignon Blanc and Cabernet Sauvignon.

The climate of the Margaret River area is strongly maritime, more so than any other Australian wine region, and is the most Mediterranean in style. Overall, the climate is similar to that of a Pomerol or St. Emilion in a dry vintage, which accounts for the quality of its Cabernet, Sauvignon, and Merlot varieties. Margaret River's reputation was founded on its Cabernet Sauvignon, and rests on it today. Virtually every winery produces one of these blends, and the style has evolved over the last few decades. The common threads of this wine are ripe grapes, which produce a sweet core, and a slightly earthy tannin. The Chardonnay variety was pioneered by the Leeuwin Estate, and is probably Australia's greatest example of the type. It tends towards a concentrated, complex, viscous and tangy taste, which does not cloy or become heavy. Permutations of Semillon and Sauvignon Blanc are combined to produce a regional speciality known as the Classic Dry White. This wine has a pleasantly herbal or grassy flavour.

There are many fine restaurants in the Margaret River region, a number of which are attached to vineyards: the most outstanding (and expensive) is without doubt the one on the Leeuwin Estate. Important regional events include the annual Leeuwin Concert, and the Porongorup Wine Festival.

Barossa Valley (SA). Vines arrived with the first settlers to South Australia and, in the early days, suburban Adelaide was the site of extensive vineyards. The Barossa Valley (including the Eden Valley), Clare Valley, and McLaren Vale were all established in the middle of the 19th century by German immigrants, and wine growing continues to play a central role in the state's economy. In 1996, South Australia produced half of all Australia's wine. The climate of the Barossa Valley is almost identical with that of Bordeaux, and is ideal for full-bodied red wines, excellent fortified wine, and robust whites. Shiraz is the most important local variety, and the Barossa Valley is the home of Penfolds Grange, the greatest Shiraz wine made outside the Rhone Valley. Almost every Barossa winery will include a Shiraz or Shiraz blend among its offerings. The style is full bodied, rich in colour, with a touch of chocolate, and a hint of roasted flavour; the wines are long lived. Old vine Grenache and Mourvedre are currently in as much demand as old vine Shiraz, with intense competition between fortified and table wine makers for the available harvest. The Barossa Valley Reisling has a quintessentially Australian style, with strong passion fruit/tropical fruit/lime flavours, which build beautifully with bottle age. Semillon has had a renaissance in recent years, and is frequently given a toasting of American oak; it develops quickly into a robust, full-bodied wine.

Important local events include 'Barossa Under the Stars' (attracting performers such as Julio Iglesias and Rod Stewart), the Barossa Vintage Festival, and the Barossa Wine Show.

Clare Valley (SA). The Clare Valley has a continuous history of wine-making which dates back over 150 years. It is a high quality producer of long lived, intensely flavoured, and strongly structured table wines, which are all made in strictly limited quantities. The climate of the Clare Valley, in terms of its viticulture, is strongly dependent on its cool afternoon breezes which play an important role in slowing ripening on the vines. It is moderately continental, and irrigation is essential due to the winter-spring dominance of the rainfall.

Much of Australia's finest Riesling is grown in the Clare Valley; typically, it is an austere wine at first, with hints of passion fruit and lime, which quickly develops a touch of lightly browned toast. These wines are long lived and will improve in the bottle for up to 10 years. Cabernet Sauvignon is the other great wine of the region, and is always full-bodied, or even dense. Chardonnay, Semillon, Sauvignon Blanc and Grenache, either singly or in blends, contribute the other main wines of the region.

Important regional events include the Clare Valley Spring Garden Festival, and the Clare Valley Regional Wine Show.

Hunter Valley (NSW). The Hunter Valley, and particularly its upper region, was reborn in the 1960s and has become one of Australia's premier white wine areas. Typically, it produces soft, rich Chardonnays and quick maturing Semillons from its highly productive vineyards. Chardonnay is regarded as the outstanding wine of the region, with all wine-makers producing examples of real merit. Rosemount Roxburgh is considered Australia's greatest example of the style, and is rich, complex, toasty and creamy, with a strong charred oak overlay. Hunter Valley Semillons are usually fleshy, soft, and likely to be oak-influenced, although in recent years there has been a strong move towards traditional, unwooded Semillon styles. These wines peak at around two to four years of age. In February, March and April annually, the Hunter Valley hosts the Hunter Valley Harvest Festival (www.winecountry.com.au) in October, a jazz festival (www.jazzinthevines.com. au), and an opera (www.4-d.com.au).

The Australian wine industry has an excellent website at www.wineaustralia.com. au which gives general information, the location of all vineyards, and events listings for the whole country. If you plan to sip your way around Australia, this is the place to start.

Brewing

A couple of decades ago adverts for the the 'amber nectar' declared it to be Australia's favourite drink; something that many Australians would not dispute. Every state has its own local beers, which are available nationally; the best known of these are Swan and Emu from WA, Tooheys and Fosters (NSW), Victorian Bitter, or VB, from Victoria, and Castlemaine XXXX from Queensland. Australians drink 'stubbies' - 375ml bottles of beer a little shorter and fatter than the American 12 ounce beer. You will also find that most Australians also drink international lagers, and Mexican beers like Sol and Corona are particularly popular. Beer in pubs is always served ice-cold. Bitter beer or stout is not generally available on tap (draught) in pubs as Australia is an almost exclusively lager-drinking nation, and most Australians find the idea of 'warm beer' pretty disgusting. You should, however, be able to find Guinness on tap in most pubs. Ciders such as Strongbow (dry, sweet or draught) or Woodpeckers are also available. Boutique beers are now an important part of the market: Redback and Matilda Bay are major players in this field, but are expensive compared with homegrown ones. Ice-brewed beers such as Hahn Ice are also popular. There are plenty of pubs and bars all over Australia, and if you don't fancy these you can drink in wine bars, pleasant beer gardens, or with friends at home. Pubs often have a 'sundowner', or happy hour, with cheaper drinks and sometimes entertainment, usually around the hours of summer sunset. The 'Sunday Session' is a similar occasion, held on a Sunday afternoon. For older Australians, the sundowner or the Sunday session is an important part of leisure and social life.

PUBLIC HOLIDAYS

The long weekend has become an Australian institution, and is taken very seriously as an opportunity to get in some quality leisure time. On Friday afternoons at the start of a long weekend there is inevitably heavy traffic as people head out of the city to various beach and bush locations, something to be repeated on the following Monday evening as the traffic streams back. Every state legislates its own public holidays, however, there are also a number of country-wide holidays, which are usually occasions of national or religious significance.

TABLE 7   PUBLIC HOLIDAYS THROUGHOUT AUSTRALIA

New Year's Day, 1 January.

Australia Day, 26 January. This is the day on which Australia celebrates the anniversary of the landing of the first fleet at Port Philip in NSW, a date popularly considered to be Australia's birthday. All around the nation, local councils and authorities mount concerts and firework displays to help the celebrations get under way with a bang. Fireworks are considered a centrepiece of the occasion (especially as Guy Fawkes' Day is not commemorated and, after all, everyone needs an excuse to let off some rockets). In Perth, the 'Skyshow' is mounted from two barges moored in the Swan River. Hours before the show starts, the river is lined with families and friends carrying their torches (to switch on and wave about at the given signal), blankets, picnics and portable stereos. Two hours of music, lasers, fireworks and general goodwill follow, and a spirit of community dominates.

Good Friday March/April.

Easter Monday March/April.

ANZAC Day, 25 April. This national holiday commemorates the sacrifices of Australia's war heroes. Originally designed to recognise the soldiers of the Australian and New Zealand Army Corps who died at Gallipoli during WWI in a defining moment in Australian history, it now includes all Australian military personnel and commemorates their participation in campaigns in both world wars, Vietnam, and Korea. Every major city and town hosts marches by old soldiers and, these days, their descendants, wearing uniforms and medals. There are dawn ceremonies at war memorials around the country, and the day is considered to be a solemn one. Many citizens line the streets to watch the marches. These days there are also a significant number of people who believe that ANZAC day has become irrelevant to Australia's younger generation, and who resent the glorification and sentimentalising of war. *Armistice Day* (11 November) is not widely observed in Australia, and the tradition of poppy wearing is now quite rare.

Queen's Official Birthday. This is a movable holiday which always falls on the second Monday in June (except in WA where it falls on the last Monday of September).

Christmas Day 25 December.

Boxing Day 26 December.

TABLE 8	REGIONAL HOLIDAYS	
The dates of some of these holidays may be variable.		
Labour Day	7 March	(WA/TAS)
Labour Day	14 March	(VIC)
Canberra Day	21 March	(ACT)
Bank Holiday	5 April	(TAS)
Labour/May Day	2 May	(QLD/NT)
Adelaide Cup Day	16 May	(SA)
Foundation Day	6 June	(WA)
Alice Springs Show Day	1 July	(NT)
Darwin Show Day	22 July	(NT)
Bank Holiday	1 August	(NSW/ACT)
Picnic Day	1 August	(NT)
Labour Day	3 October	(NSW/ACT)
Queen's Birthday	26 September	(WA)
Labour Day	11 October	(SA)
Recreation Day	7 November	(TAS)
Melbourne Cup Day	1 November	(VIC)

TIME

Calculating the time difference between Australia and Europe or the USA can be confusing, especially in the southern hemisphere summer, when some states institute daylight saving and others don't. Queensland, the Northern Territory and Western Australia do not have daylight saving (it has been voted out in various referenda held in these states) and thus, their clocks do not move forward one hour between the last Sunday in October and the last Sunday in March. Below is a list of the time differences from Greenwich Mean Time (GMT) of the different states and territories:

Eastern Standard Time (EST) – 10 hours ahead of GMT: New South Wales, the

Australian Capital Territory, Tasmania and Queensland.
Central Standard Time (CST) – 9.5 hours ahead of GMT: South Australia and the
   Northern Territory.
Western Standard Time (WST) – 8 hours ahead of GMT: Western Australia.

The time difference between WST and CST is 1.5 hours, between WST and EST
is two hours, and between CST and EST is 30 minutes. An hour plus or minus
should be added to account for daylight saving, according to the time of year.

METRICATION

Australia fully adopted the European metric system in the late 1970s and
imperial measurements were dropped completely. Consumers were never
given conversions on packaging, for example 1lb/454g, or alternative Fahrenheit
and Celsius weather reports so people learnt new ways very quickly. If you ask
for a pound of mince at the butcher you will not be understood. All street signs
and road maps note distances in kilometres, as do speedometers; a freeway sign
which reads 'Next exit 3.5', must be interpreted as a metric distance. Weights are
calculated in grams and kilograms, and temperatures are given in degrees Celsius.
Distances and measurements are invariably expressed as a decimal rather than as
a fraction. If you have children at school, they will be expected to be conversant
with the metric system, and no instruction will be given in calculating imperial
measurement. The modern Australian child is unlikely to have any idea how many
inches there are in a foot, ounces in a pound or yards in a mile; and, in fact, this
probably applies to anyone under 40.

RETIREMENT

CHAPTER SUMMARY

- People over 60 are known as 'seniors' in Australia.

- The terms 'OAP' or 'pensioner' are considered derogatory and are not officially used.

- Generally, the Australian policy towards seniors is to keep them lively and independent for as long as possible.

- **Family Migration Programme.** Those with family living in Australia may be able to enter permanently as a retired person under this programme.

  - 1,000 Parent visas were available in 2004-2005 under the Family Migration programme.

  - Your relatives must agree to sponsor you financially for two years after your arrival.

- **Retirement Visa.** If you enter Australia on this type of visa, you will not be able to stay permanently.

  - You will have to periodically renew your Retirement visa, which has to be continually approved by the authorities.

  - The authorities are not lenient with seniors found staying illegally.

- **Retirement Villages.** All cities and large towns have purpose-built accommodation for seniors. Some are state-run and some private.

  - If you enter Australia on a Retirement visa you will not be entitled to a place in a state-run retirement village, and it will be more difficult to buy into a private one.

- **Retirement Areas.** Favourites include Queensland, especially Cairns and the Gold Coast.

- **Pensions.** Immigrant seniors are not entitled to an Australian pension until they have accrued 10 years' worth of contributions.

Introduction

Australia has traditionally been the destination of young people, and most new arrivals have generally been either backpackers travelling on Holiday Working visas or young immigrant families. Indeed, it is well known that applicants under 35 are far more likely to be granted residency in Australia, and the Points System of visa eligibility actively discriminates in favour of youth by docking points as the age of the applicant increases. In the past, the average age of the Australian population was relatively low in comparison with that of other developed countries, however, these days, in common with most industrialised nations, Australia is experiencing the 'greying' of its population. On the other hand, the elderly are perhaps not as noticeable in Australia as in Europe, as the climate allows and encourages them to remain healthy and active for much longer.

As Australia has become more accessible in terms of cost and ease of travel, there has been a marked increase in the number of older people both visiting Australia and choosing to retire there. The Australian government has introduced a visa and residence classification specifically for parents of new migrant settlers which allows any child who has gained permanent residency to sponsor their parents to enter the country on a long-term basis (see the *Residence and Entry Regulations* chapter for details). The warmer weather, cheaper housing and yearning for contact with children and grandchildren are all powerful factors influencing the decision to leave a lifetime's history behind to start a new life on the other side of the world.

Many older people moving to Australia feel that the journey itself is one of the most daunting considerations, as it is both expensive and physically gruelling. Travel agents, however, can recommend ways of breaking your journey without adding too much to the expense and enable you to recoup in stages and minimise jet lag. Alternatively, if you buy a cheap ticket, you are likely to find that it is cheap precisely because it is not a direct flight and will stop two or three times for up to four hours during the course of the journey. Many passengers take advantage of these stops to wander around the airports, helping to avoid stiffness, cramping and swollen ankles. Airlines can provide wheelchairs and support staff (who will, for example, help you collect your luggage) providing prior notice is given; you should also tell your travel agent or airline of any special medical conditions or dietary requirements at the time of booking your ticket. It is useful to know that if you order special meals for your flight, you are likely to be served first which, in a plane carrying around 300 passengers, can make a big difference to your personal comfort. In addition to practical tips and advice, this chapter provides information specifically for those wishing to retire to Australia, including the names and addresses of government support agencies.

The Decision to Emigrate

Many retired people will experience the 'empty-nest syndrome' most keenly if their offspring have moved not just away from home, but thousands of miles away to Australia. Although the warmer weather, hours of sunshine and lower cost of living are appealing factors in their own right, the deciding factor is likely to be the pull of the heart strings. The fact that many retirees who move to Australia have never previously visited the country suggests that it is the people, rather than the place, which provide the main reason. Although it takes enormous energy and motivation to move abroad when retired, it requires a significant extra input to pack up and transport yourself to the other side of the world. The images most Europeans have of Australia have been carefully packaged by marketing experts to encourage tourism, and as a consequence they are generally aimed at the young and mobile independent traveller.

> In order to make sure that Australia really is the place in which you wish to spend the rest of your days, it is highly advisable to take an extended holiday of up to six months in order to gain a more accurate impression of what life in Australia as a retiree might be like. A long stay in Australia to allow you to familiarise yourself with its people and way of life may, to a certain extent, prevent you from eventually suffering too intensely the inevitable homesickness.

There are distinct advantages to be gained by retiring to Australia. Firstly, you will not need to master a foreign language. Additionally, the weather in most inhabited parts of Australia is superb, with warm temperatures and glorious sunshine, and the coastal location of most Australian cities means that residents enjoy the benefits of fresh sea air. Senior Citizens are well looked after, and receive many special benefits and discounts for various facilities and services including public transport, holidays, utility bills, restaurants and hairdressing. Currently, the very favourable Australian dollar exchange rate, combined with the lower costs of living and property in the country, mean that moving to Australia from most European countries after retirement, particularly to join children who have already migrated, can also be very financially advantageous.

People over the age of 60 in Australia are always known as 'Seniors'. The rather derogatory terms 'old age pensioner', 'OAP', and 'pensioner' were removed from the official vocabulary years ago. Seniors are generally accorded a level of respect commensurate with their lifetime of experience.

Residence and Entry Regulations

The Residence and Entry requirements for retired people who wish to move to Australia are described in full in Chapter Two. Briefly, there are two ways in which it is possible to retire to Australia. The first method is only applicable if you do not have family already living in Australia. In this case, if you are at least 55 years of age and have no dependants other than your spouse, you may be able to enter Australia to retire providing you meet financial, health and character requirements. The Australian Government will only allow retired people who have no other connections with Australia to enter the country if they can support themselves and have the financial means to make Australian investments. In other words, you will be expected to contribute to, and not drain, Australian resources: you will need at least $870,000 capital, or a pension or income, or further capital of at least $52,000 per annum.

If you do have family in Australia, you may be eligible to enter as a retiree under the Family Stream migration programme, which enables parents to join children already living in Australia. This is by far the more common way to enter the country to retire and in the 2004-2005 Family Stream programme, 1,000 Parent visas were available. Full details of this scheme are given in the *Residence and Entry* chapter. Basically, Family Stream Migration entitles the parent of any child, who must have been a permanent resident of Australia for a minimum of two years, to be granted residency in their own right. The potentially prohibitive financial requirements applying to non-family stream retirees do not apply in this case; however, your child must guarantee to sponsor you financially for two years after your arrival in the country. Like all migrants, Family Stream applicants are assessed on an individual basis and against Australia's health and character requirements.

Obtaining a Residence Permit

If you enter Australia on a Retirement visa, you will never be granted permanent residency. You will enter the country on a six-month multiple entry visa which you then need to transfer to a four-year Retirement visa. This visa is issued on a renewable basis, so your status as resident is more tenuous, perhaps, than for other categories of residency: applications for visa renewal can be refused if your circumstances have changed significantly or if you no longer meet the financial, health or character requirements.

If you enter the country on a Family Stream Migration visa, you will automatically be granted permanent residency after you have been resident in Australia for two years.

You should note that Australia really takes a very strict line on visas and immigration, and the authorities will not hesitate to deport people who do not comply with regulations, regardless of considerations of age or compassionate circumstances. A cautionary tale is told of a British couple who, a few years ago, were deported after staying on illegally for 16 years. The couple, who had worked and paid taxes in Australia during this period, were given no leeway, and were required to leave the country immediately and permanently. They were discovered after making a pension claim.

Possible Retirement Areas

Almost every major city in Australia offers ideal retirement conditions, in terms of beautiful weather and reasonable housing costs. Darwin, Alice Springs and other cities and towns in Australia's interior or northern regions, however, often experience insufferably hot weather in summer, which many people (both old and young) find difficult to tolerate. The southern coastal regions have quite cool winters, but nowhere will conditions be as severe as a typical northern European winter. Many older people love the Mediterranean weather of Perth, Adelaide and Sydney, while others prefer the cooler temperatures of Tasmania or the unpredictable and varied Melbourne weather. A large number of Australians like to retire to Queensland, particularly favouring Cairns and the Gold coast, with its abundant tropical sunshine and cheap housing; others find the humidity oppressive and prefer a more temperate climate. In NSW, the Central Coast, particularly around Gosford, is a major retirement area, with many facilities for the elderly; and in WA, the regional towns of Safety Bay, Mandurah and Dunsborough have a special appeal for retirees.

Retirement Villages

All cities and major regional towns have special accommodation, known as retirement villages, available for seniors. The decision to enter a retirement village usually means a major financial commitment as well as a lifestyle change, and should be regarded as an investment in lifestyle rather than a financial arrangement: usually, any amount payable on refund will be considerably less than that originally contributed. By law, villages must consist of units for completely independent residents, units with assistance, including some nursing care and meals for less independent residents, and rooms with 24-hour nursing care available for the fully dependent residents. There are both government and privately owned and managed retirement villages, and many are run by church groups of different denominations.

Buying into a retirement village can be complex, and will involve a contract. Such contracts are usually lengthy and replete with legalese, and it is wise to obtain the advice of a solicitor or accountant with experience in this area. Not all legal professionals will be aware of important issues for ageing people, such as contracting incomes, and advocacy organisations such as the Council on the Ageing (addresses for each state are given below) can provide expert advice.

TABLE 9	QUESTIONS TO ASK BEFORE SIGNING A RETIREMENT VILLAGE CONTRACT

- Are there any conditions attached to changes of ownership?
- What are the annual charges?
- What are the ongoing costs? Look especially for items such as water levies, swimming pool maintenance, audit fees, and management.
- Who has decision-making powers? Are there resident panels or elected representatives?
- Are there deferred management fees?
- Is there an arbitration process available in case of disputes?

You should also note that it is not necessarily automatic that you will be moved from one tier of care to another as your circumstances change. Instead, you may be required to terminate the original agreement and buy in again. Buying a home in a retirement village is not an investment, and there is no guarantee of security: if the development has problems, there may be no protection for the money you have put in. Before you sign a contract to live in a retirement village, the retirement village administrators are required by law to provide you with the *Code of Fair Practice for Retirement Villages*. This ensures that prospective residents are given clear information about the facilities and charges, and terms and conditions of residence. The Code sets out the rights and responsibilities of both residents and the administering bodies of retirement villages. Additionally, a prospective resident is entitled to a copy of every contract required to be entered into in order to reside in the retirement village, and details of any costs associated with entering into such contracts. Using such information provided by the retirement village administrators will help you to compare villages and work out the likely costs of your preferred choice. The information should also help you decide if a village would really suit your lifestyle.

If you plan eventually to enter a retirement village, you should shop around before placing your name on a waiting list. Villages are generally modern, well equipped and are professionally managed with a high quality of care. They are often built close to shopping centres, public transport and police stations, and have contact with the community through local schools and churches. In general, the Australian attitude to seniors is to keep them active and independent as long as possible and the retirement villages, purpose-built according to strict legal guidelines, reflect this. Further information about retirement villages and other types of seniors accommodation is available from the organisations listed under *useful addresses* below.

Note that if you enter the country on the Retirement visa and you wish to buy a house in Australia, you will need to write to: The Executive Member, The Foreign Investment Review Board, Department of the Treasury, Langton Crescent, Canberra, ACT 2600; ☎02-6263 3795; fax 02-6263 2940; e-mail firb@treasury. gov.au; www.firb.gov.au. As you will never be considered a permanent resident, you will not be eligible for a place in a government retirement village, and you may also find it more difficult to find a place in a private one.

TABLE 10   RETIREMENT VILLAGE TERMINOLOGY

Accommodation Unit. The part of the retirement village in which a resident has exclusive right to reside. This can be an independent living unit, a service apartment, or a hostel bed.

Body Corporate Manager. The manager of the body corporate (legally-constituted owners' association) of a freehold retirement village. The role of the retirement village manager is usually greater than that of the body corporate manager, especially where a range of services are provided.

Deferred Management Fee. A fee paid to the operators for their part in the operation of the scheme over the time a resident stays in the village. It is usually expressed as a percentage of the price of the unit, and increases over the years as a person stays in the village.

Ingoing Contribution. The price for the right to reside in a unit in a retirement village.

Nursing Homes. Most nursing homes are regulated by the Commonwealth Government under the Aged Care Act 1997.

Sinking Fund. A fund established to provide for irregular expenditure (for example, external painting or roof maintenance). Residents usually contribute to the sinking fund through service charges.

Statutory Charge. A means of protecting residents' ingoing contributions by registering a security similar to a mortgage on the title to the retirement village land.

Types of Ownership. Generally these are either leasehold (usually 99 years), freehold or strata title. Strata title gives you ownership of the living area and a share of any property held in common.

The Pension Rights of Immigrants from the UK

In March 2001, the Australian Government terminated the social security agreement that existed between Britain and Australia. Until that time, UK citizens emigrating to Australia were able to use their UK pension contributions to help qualify for an Australian pension. Prospective migrants should be aware that now that the Agreement has terminated there will be no early access to Australia's social security system for migrants from the UK. Instead they will have to accrue 10 years qualifying residence before being eligible to claim Australian Age Pension. This means that although you are fully entitled to and will receive your British pension if you live in Australia, the level of pension payments will be frozen from the date you leave Britain, and you will not receive any cost of living increases in pension payments made after this date. In Britain, pensions are indexed to the cost of living and are adjusted annually, but when you become resident of some countries (but not others) you forfeit this adjustment. Although this may seem a nominal sum to forfeit, over the years it may become a significant amount of money and your pension may cease to be adequate. This must be weighed up against the lower cost of living in Australia and the fact that there is no council tax or VAT on electricity and gas.

The Frozen UK Pensions Issue. The frozen pension issue affects the vast majority of British pensioners who live in 48 of the 54 Commonwealth countries. In September 1994 British expatriates in five of the largest Commonwealth countries including Australia, formed an organisation, the World Alliance of British Expatriate Pensioners, as part of a continuing battle to improve the financial position of those pensioners residing in the countries where British State pensions are frozen. There are currently 205,000 pensioners in Australia; 70% qualify for an Australian pension. In those cases the Australian government pays the difference between the UK frozen rate pension and the Australian pension. Of the 932,000 British expatriate pensioners worldwide, 442,000 – mainly those residing in the European Union and the United States – *do* receive the same annual increments as pensioners in Britain.

Transferring a UK Pension to Australia. If you intend to become a permanent resident of Australia, the process of transferring your pension payments is surprisingly simple. All you need to do is go to your local social security office and inform them that you are leaving the country. They will then make arrangements on your instructions to have your pension paid to you in Australia, or into a bank account in your home country if you prefer. They can also send a cheque (in sterling) at the end of every four or 13 weeks straight to you in Australia, to your overseas bank or to someone else outside the UK chosen by you. If you are away for less than two years they can pay your benefit as a lump sum when you return to the UK. For further information, you should contact the Pensions Info-Line on ☎ 0845-731 3233 or write to the Pensions Service, Department for Works and Pensions, PO Box 60, Peterlee SR8 2WG; www.thepensionservice.gov.uk, or Centrelink International Services, PO Box 273C, Hobart, TAS 7001; ☎ 03-6222 3455; fax 03-6222 2799; www.centrelink.gov.au.

Taxation For British Immigrants

It is not often that one receives good news from the tax office, and therefore it perhaps comes as something of a pleasant surprise to learn that if you leave Britain and you are currently paid a pension, you will not have to pay any British tax on that pension when you leave the country. If you are not currently retired and therefore are not receiving a pension, it is advisable to have a Retirement Pension

Forecast made by the Benefits Agency. This is a simple process which involves going to your local social security office and picking up a BR19 form. On its completion and return, the social security will be able to give you some idea of what kind of pension you can expect to receive when you retire and whether you will be paying any tax on it. You can request a pensions forecast by contacting ☎ 0191-218 7777 and asking for the Pensions and Overseas Benefits Directorate. This kind of information may be extremely helpful to if you are considering the financial implications of moving to Australia, and may also help you with your taxation returns in Australia.

Tax on Pension Funds. Although you will not pay tax on income currently received from a state pension in the UK, British residents who settle in Australia can face taxes of up to 47% on any growth in their pension fund since leaving the UK. This developed from a ruling brought in by the Australian Taxation Office in 1994, which seeks to prevent tax avoidance through offshore funds. When British residents in Australia tap into their pension funds, any growth since the date they emigrated is now taxed as income – at the higher marginal rate of 47%. This rule, however, applies to money-purchase pensions only, and not to final salary schemes. They should also be aware that even if money is left in the UK fund, payments *will* be regarded as income by the Australian Taxation Office when it is finally drawn on and will be taxed at the pensioner's marginal tax rate.

Anyone moving or retiring to Australia who holds an existing UK pension fund should seek professional advice well before departure. Over the years, the issues of those holding such funds has passed virtually unnoticed until a Parliamentary Enquiry took place in Australia during 2002. The findings of this enquiry brought the subject to the attention of financial planners in Australia who immediately saw a new marketing opportunity. You are best placed to take specialist advice as not only has the subject now a raised profile at the Australian Taxation Office, but the tax provisions have changed. In the past, the majority of pension funds should have been transferred – now the decision is less obvious and there are strong reasons for each and every pension to be subject to an analysis which considers: leave behind in the UK, leave behind and merge into an alternative UK scheme, either these two or draw benefits in the UK, either these two but eventually transfer to Australia, or transfer as soon as possible to Australia some or all pension funds.

Today the focus has moved from the tax liability, which used to be levied on the individual, to one now paid by the scheme and at a much lower rate. A transfer of a pension fund does not take place overnight and can take several months – today's astute migrant will hedge the funds that should be transferred against falling rates of exchange. You should also be aware that UK life policies, unit trusts, personal equity plans and individual savings accounts do not necessarily carry the same tax advantages in Australia as in their country of origin, and that there may be tax implications depending on the particular product in which you have invested. Anyone in Australia in receipt of foreign source income is required by law to maintain comprehensive records of their overseas investment holdings, and penalties are in place for those failing to do so. Geraint Davies of Montfort International (Home Farm, Shere Road, Albury, Surrey GU5 9BL; ☎ 01483-202072; fax 01483-202073; email info@miplc.co.uk) is an acknowledged expert in this field, with experience of both UK and Australian tax laws, and can advise prospective emigrants of their potential tax liabilities and suggest ways of minimising them. Among many services they provide projections to see how migrants' current financial planning will be affected by a move to Australia. Migrants should be aware that your visa type will impact on your tax position. In addition, in certain circumstances costs of moves to Australia – house selling and purchase, airfares, sustenance, and removals – can be claimed against the tax man. However, in such situations careful tax planning is always a must.

Alan Collett of Collett and Co, Chartered Accountants (Enterprise House, Ocean Village, Southampton, Hampshire S014 3XB; ☎02380-488786; fax 02380-488787; info@colletandco.com; www.collettandco.com) provides tax and financial planning advice and services to people heading for Australia, and also gives free factsheets.

Destini Global Financial Services (29 Ely Place, London EC1N 6TD; ☎020-7611 4777; fax 020-7611 4701; e-mail global@destinifs.co.uk; www.destiniglobal.co.uk) specialise in transferring UK pensions to Australia and offer specialist tax and financial advice.

Australian Pensions and Health Insurance

If you meet the requirements for a Retirement visa and are granted entry into Australia, you will not be covered by Medicare (because you will not have contributed towards its costs through the Medicare levy, paid via income taxes), and you will have to make arrangements in your country of origin or take out private health insurance in Australia.

If you enter the country as a Class 103 migrant, your permanent residency entitles you to full Medicare cover once you have been in the country for two years. Your sponsor (your child) is expected to meet any medical expenses you may incur the first two years, although some of this may be refunded. It is important to check with Medicare and/or your private health insurer as to the conditions which are attached. After two years, you will be entitled to full benefits as at that point you will be granted the rights of any other permanent resident. Full details on the health care system and private medical insurance are given in the *Daily Life* Chapter.

Pensions in Australia are administered by Centrelink. Eligibility for pension is subject to a number of statutory requirements including residence requirements. Most claimants, unless covered by one of Australia's Social Security Agreements, must be resident in Australia for 10 years before being eligible for a pension. The full rate of the basic pension for a couple is currently around $20,500 per annum, with further benefits accruing to most pensioners in the form of concessions. You may also be eligible for extra pension payments if you care for dependent children or students. If you rent privately, you may also be able to claim rent assistance. Rates of payment are reviewed regularly.

The Income Test. A full pension can be paid if gross income is no more than $122 per fortnight for singles or $216 per fortnight per couple.

The Assets Test. Takes into account assets, excluding the family home. The full pension will be paid if the total net market value of your assessable assets is no more than $153,000 (for a single home-owner), or $263,500 (for a single, non home-owner), $217,500 (for a home-owner couple) and $328,000 for a non home-owning couple. If your assets exceed these limits, your rate of pension will be reduced by $3 for every $1,000 of assessable assets over the limit. If you are eligible for the pension but your spouse is ineligible, you will be paid half the combined married rate.

Tax Rebates. Pensioners receive a tax rebate of $2,230 for singles, and $1,602 for each member of a couple. The rebate reduces to nil when taxable income is over $20,000 for singles, and $16,306 for each member of a couple.

Seniors' Benefits. Most of the benefits to which pensioners are entitled in Australia are claimed by presenting various cards issued by Centrelink and other agencies. These cards give concessions to low-income earners as well as to pensioners for a number of different services. A *Pensioner Concession Card* is issued to pensioners who qualify for fringe benefits. This card entitles you to certain transport and medical services as well as other concessions provided by Government and some private organisations. Some concessions, however, do not depend on a particular Centrelink or other authorised card, but only on age, so if you are able to produce any identification documents which state your date of birth, you may also be able to claim certain concessions. It is always worth checking before you pay for anything as to whether you are eligible for a concession on the basis of age. It is estimated that seniors who take advantage of all the concessions on offer will save around $2,000 per year. The most common cards and transport, amenities and health concessions are listed below.

Seniors Card. A Seniors Card is available to permanent residents of Australia aged 60 and over who are not working full time. The cards are issued free and enable holders to get a wide range of discounts on public and commercial activities. Businesses in one state will usually recognise cards from another and such business will display a Seniors Card Welcome sticker. Seniors Card Schemes are the responsibility of each State and Territory Government, not the Commonwealth Government and the eligibility criteria and the range of benefits vary.

The Commonwealth Seniors Health Card. The Commonwealth Seniors Health Card gives older Australians access to concessions on prescription medicines through the PBS (Pharmaceutical Benefits Scheme) as well as payment of a telephone allowance. Many self-funded retirees will be eligible for the Commonwealth Seniors Health Card.

The Health Care Card. The Health Care Card gives concessions on prescription medicines. Additional concessions may be offered to Health Care Card holders including health, household, educational, recreational and some transport concessions. These additional concessions vary widely within each State and Territory.

The Pensioner Concession Card. The Pensioner Concession Card gives access to concessions on prescription medicines, hearing services and, in conjunction with a Medicare card, basic hospital and medical treatment. Another benefit for cardholders is an $18 quarterly telephone allowance. The card also entitles holders to some concessions from state and local governments (such as reduction in council rates, water and electricity bills) and from some private organisations and businesses. Concessions vary from state to state.

Transport Concessions. All states and territories offer concession travel to people over 60 years of age regardless of whether or not they are in receipt of a pension. Concessions include reduced fares on public transport, reductions on motor vehicle registration and one or more free rail journeys within the state each year. Concessions differ from state to state and though you may b able to get discounts on some products and services while travelling interstate, others may be denied you.

Amenities. Seniors are generally also able to claim a reduction (the amount varies from state to state) for council rates, as well as some other services. Enquiries should be made at your local council. A rebate on water and sewage rates is also usually offered to qualifying pensioners, and your nearest water authority office will give you further information. If you are eligible for fringe benefits, you should contact your state or territory electricity and gas authorities for any concessions that may be applicable on your electricity and gas bills. You may also be eligible to take advantage of a free mail redirecting service from your local post office if you move house within Australia. Further details are available from Centrelink offices (☎1800-050 004). The Pensioner Concession Card brochures, available from Centrelink, outline the range of pensioner concessions offered by each state or territory. The brochures include information about concession eligibility and provide a useful contact. Most local councils also offer a rebate on the registration of seniors' dogs. The *National Seniors Association* (Level 6, 243 Edward Street, Brisbane, QLD 4000; ☎07-3233 9123; fax 07-3229 0356; www.nationalseniors.com.au) offers the over-50s discounts on literally thousands of products. You can join this Association for $24 ($32 for couples), and have access to guided tours and discounts on travel and insurance, a directory of benefits and services, and a subscription to the bi-monthly *50 Something* Magazine. Under the NSA scheme, thousands of national traders offer discounts on nearly everything, from electrical products, security systems, car tyres, cinema tickets, motel accommodation, through to funeral services. Offices also in Sydney, Melbourne, Adelaide, and Perth.

Health Benefits. The Pensioner Concession Card and the Commonwealth Seniors Health Card can help with doctors' bills, cut price pharmaceuticals, and ambulance services. You will never have to pay more than $4.60 for a prescription, and if you pay more than $239.20 in a year for any drugs, all further prescriptions are free. As a pensioner, you are fully entitled to Medicare benefits, but there are many different health services which are offered at reduced rates to holders of such cards. In addition, free dental treatment is offered at some hospitals and dental clinics to holders of a Pensioner Concession Card or a Health Care Card. It is worth contacting your local hospital to obtain information on the free treatment to which you are entitled and those treatments for which you would only have to pay a concessionary rate.

Assistance may also be given for the cost of spectacles from some state government health or community service departments. You should contact your local department for details but should also be aware that this assistance is determined by a strict means test.

Government subsidised hearing aids, maintenance, repairs and batteries are also available from hearing centres of Australian Hearing if you hold a Pensioner Health Benefits Card or a Sickness Benefits Card. For assistance, you should contact your nearest Australian Hearing Centre, listed under the Commonwealth Government departments section at the front of the white pages telephone directory.

There are a number of associations which have been established to address those health problems which particularly affect older rather than younger people. These organisations offer information, advice and assistance, and have branches in every state and territory, the addresses of which can be obtained from the national bodies listed below:

Useful Addresses

Arthritis Foundation of Australia, PO Box 121, Sydney, NSW 2001; ☎02-9552 6085; e-mail info@arthritisaustralia.com.au; www.arthritisfoundation.com.au.
Australian Hearing, ☎131 797; www.hearing.com.au, has more than 70 permanent centres operating five days a week. Visit the website or phone to locate your nearest centre.
Diabetes Australia, 5th Floor, 39 London Circuit, Canberra City, ACT 2600; ☎02-6232 3800; fax 02-6230 2535; www.diabetesaustralia.com.au.
National Continence Helpline, ☎1800-330 066. Open 8am to 8pm, seven days a week.
Stroke Recovery Association, PO Box 673, Petersham, NSW 2049; ☎02-9550 0594; fax 02-9560 2306; e-mail info@strokensw.org.au; www.strokensw.org.au.

If you move to Australia as a Class 103 migrant, there is a possibility that at some time your sponsoring child will have either to care or obtain care for you as you get older. Commonwealth Carer Resource Centres are operated by Carers Association in each State and Territory in Australia. Services include providing carers with referrals to community and government services, practical written information to support carers in their caring role, emotional support, educational and training opportunities for carers and service providers, and a counselling service. In addition, respite care can be organised through the Commonwealth Carer Resource Centre (☎1800 242 636) or the Commonwealth Carer Respite Centre (☎1800 059 059). For further information, contact *Carers Australia* (PO Box 73, Deakin West, ACT 2600; ☎02-6122 9900; fax 02-6122 9999; e-mail caa@carersaustralia.com.au; www.carersaustralia.com.au).

Wills and Legal Considerations

This has been discussed in more detail in the *Setting up Home* chapter, but the clear message is that if you move to Australia, you should really make another will as there are variations in the law which may significantly and adversely affect your estate. If you wish to have a will drawn up for you in Australia, it is relatively easy to find assistance as solicitors advertise in telephone directories and also on television and the printed media. The Public Trustee Office of each state specialises in the drawing and storing of wills and it is reassuring to know that their funds are protected by an Act of Parliament. The Trustee's funds are guaranteed by the government and so the office of the Public Trustee can never die, go bankrupt or leave the state, ensuring the efficient and legal execution of the affairs of your estate. Some state Public Trustee Office's have a free will-drafting service and you should contact your state government office or website to find more details on this service. The free and independent financial information service of Centrelink (Retirement Services ☎132 300; www.centrelink.gov.au) can also advise on wills and estate planning.

If you intend to pass on substantial assets in your will, you may wish to consider establishing a Testamentary Trust. For pensioners, this means that when assets pass to the surviving spouse, those which are included in the Trust will not count against the assets test, ensuring that any pension is protected. Where child beneficiaries are involved, a testamentary trust will significantly reduce tax liability. However, since 1 January 2002, a source and control test operates for existing social security recipients and prospective recipients who have an interest in a family trust. This means that assets which in the past could be 'hidden' from assessment will now be counted if you are either the trustee or appointee of a Testamentary Trust or can influence the distribution of income or assets of the Trust. This is a highly technical area, however, and professional legal and financial planning advice is essential.

Prepaid Funerals. Although a subject most prefer not to think about, any discussion of wills and estates should include mention of funeral arrangements. Many seniors want to give their family the comfort of knowing that their funeral arrangements have already been made and paid for in advance. To serve this need, funeral directors now offer pre-paid funeral packages which involve making contributions today to offset future costs. If you enter into such an arrangement, you should ensure that the contract is covered under the Funerals (Pre-paid Money) Act, so that your contributions are paid into a trust fund. A contract should specify the amounts to be contributed, whether the amount will cover the full cost of the funeral, and any management, entry or surrender fees.

Funeral Bonds offer another alternative, and are a type of friendly society bond attracting tax and social security exemptions. The proceeds of funeral bonds must go towards the funeral expenses of the holder, but bonuses paid during the lifetime of the holder are tax-free. The capital value of any funeral bond is exempt from the Centrelink Income and Assets Tests up to $5,000.

Hobbies and Interests

Sporting Activities. In 1987 a report commissioned by the New South Wales Department of Health revealed that more than half of all physical decline in any age group aged over 65 can be attributed to boredom, inactivity and a fear that infirmity is inevitable. Since that report, there has been a widespread effort to promote continuing physical and social activities among seniors in the community. A 1999 report from the same source states that between 40% and 60% of older people live a regularly active lifestyle, and that compared to sedentary adults, those older adults who maintain an active lifestyle have a daily functioning comparable to people aged 15 years their junior.

In Australia, the favourable weather means that popular pursuits differ somewhat from those in the UK and Europe. Bingo, for example, is very much less popular in general, and many more seniors engage in outdoor activities. Bowls is especially popular, and in every suburb, seniors can be seen clad in white playing both competitive and friendly lawn bowls in the summer sun. You should contact your local shire or community centre for information on how to get involved in your local lawn bowls club. Golf and tennis are also widely played, and are not restricted to wealthy club members and most districts will have well-maintained public golf courses and tennis courts which can be used for a small daily fee. Most public swimming pools will have seniors' sessions, as well as hydrotherapy classes and seniors aquarobics. The very hardy among the senior community can also usually be seen at dawn, enjoying a communal early morning swim at their local beach; many veterans swear by this method of keeping fit, and enjoy it winter and summer. There are also a variety of associations and clubs which cater for older as well as younger members, some of which are listed below:

State Cycling Organisations. These provide organised rides as well as advice on what kind of bike to buy and maintenance.

Bicycle Federation of Australia, Suite 6, 6 Lonsdale Street, Braddon, ACT 2612; ☎02-6249 6761; fax 02-6230 6898; e-mail execdirector@bfa.asn.au; www.bfa. asn.au .

Bicycle NSW, Level 5, 822 George Street, Sydney, NSW 2000, ☎02-9281 4099; fax 02-9281 6099; e-mail info@bicyclensw.org.au; www.bicyclensw.org.au.

Bicycle Queensland Inc., PO Box 8321, Woolloongabba, QLD 4102; ☎07-3844 1144; www.bq.org.au.

Bicycle Tasmania, PO Box 1814, Hobart, TAS 7001; ☎03-6266 4582; e-mail info@biketas.org.au; www.biketas.org.au.

Bicycle Victoria, Level 10, 446 Collins Street, Melbourne, VIC 3000; ☎03-8636 8888; e-mail bicyclevic@bv.com.au; www.bv.com.au

Walking for Pleasure (6 Figtree Drive, Homebush Bay, NSW 2127; ☎131 302; fax 02-9006 3800; e-mail info@dsr.nsw.gov.au; www.dsr.nsw.gov.au) is an organisation which specialises in hiking and camping, and is a programme developed by the Department of Tourism, Sport and Recreation in New South Wales. Walks are graded Very Easy (which means it is suitable for wheelchairs and prams), Easy, Medium, Medium/Hard and Hard. The benefit of this programme is that you actually get to meet and talk to other people from every sector of society and every age group while you are exercising.

Federation of Victorian Walking Clubs, 332 Banyule Road, Viewbank, VIC 3084; ☎03-9455 1876; fax 03-9457 5438; e-mail vicwalk@vicnet.net.au.

Cultural Activities. If you prefer to be challenged cerebrally rather than physically, most universities and colleges offer part-time courses for mature age students, and you should contact the relevant institution for details. The University of the Third Age (www.u3aonline.org) runs short courses, for self-study or study in small groups, throughout Australia and its dedicated Australian site at www. u3aonline.org.au provides details covering a wide range of recreational interests. Local libraries are usually the best source of information on academic, cultural, and social activities for all age levels of the community.

Senior Citizens' Clubs and National Clubs. Senior Citizens' Clubs are very active throughout Australia and welcome new members. Most suburbs or districts will have an SCC, which will usually be affiliated with the National Seniors Association. These clubs organise a wide range of activities for their members, including talks and visits to places of interests as well as indoor activities such as regular bingo and chess afternoons, film screenings and community exchanges. Interaction between Seniors Clubs and local primary schools is especially popular, with schools in particular valuing the input from older members of the community. Seniors with special expertise or knowledge of local history may be asked to talk to junior classes during the course of their studies in relevant fields.

The Older Women's Network (OWN) was established in 1991 to counteract the marginalisation of older women, and is committed to speaking out against ageist and sexist stereotyping. This group, which has an excellent website at www. own.org.au publishes a newsletter and has its own theatre group, aboriginal studies group and health group. It also runs a consumer advocacy service. Contact details are given under *Useful Addresses* below.

If you would like to meet and socialise with other settlers from your country of origin, you should check your local telephone directory or with the Department of Immigration and Multicultural and Indigenous Affairs for information on national clubs such as the Italian Club or the Chung Wah Association. There are also Irish, Scottish, English and Welsh Clubs in most capital cities throughout Australia (check your white pages telephone directory), as well as a United Kingdom Settlers' Association in Victoria.

Religious Associations. Many churches and other religious groups also provide activities and coffee mornings during the week, as well as a welcoming service for people new to the area. Most churches advertise in their local newspaper, so you should check your local freesheet or the telephone directory for further details. In addition, members of the Anglican Church will find a very useful website at www. anglicansonline.org which has link to Anglican Dioceses and Parishes worldwide.

Seniors Travel. Many seniors like to take advantage of their increased leisure time to see something of Australia, and there are a number of travel options specially designed for this category of traveller. As mentioned above, in the section on Seniors Benefits, state governments provide subsidised coach and rail travel. Airlines frequently offer discounts, usually as part of a special promotion, and it is worth asking whether there are any new schemes or offers being launched in the near future before you book. A service called Seniors Home Exchange (www. seniorshomeexchange.com) charges US$65 for a three-year listing of your property on their listings service. As a member of the exchange scheme you will be able to take advantage of some 900 properties listed worldwide, cutting down considerably on the cost of holidays. Unfortunately a senior homestay service called 'Senior Citizens Stopovers Australia' which provides an economical accommodation option for travellers is now only available to those referred to the service by existing members. Under the scheme, seniors with a spare room in their home, or even a driveway suitable for a caravan, pay a small once-only membership fee, after which they are placed on a contact list. The list is circulated to all members, who must be available to host overnight visitors, as well as enjoying the opportunity to stay with other members on their travels.

Useful Addresses

Clubs
Australian American Association, Level 4, 401 Collins Street, Melbourne, VIC 3000; ☎03-9622 8260; fax 03-9224 5200; www.australian-american.asn.au; and PO Box 1717, Neutral Bay, NSW 2089; ☎1300 550 920; fax 1300 550 910; e-mail aaasyd@ozemail.com.au.
Australia Britain Society, National Office, PO Box 9088, Deakin, ACT 2600; ☎02-6273 2369; fax 02-6239 5954; www.aust-britsociety.org.au.
Australian Irish Society, 52 Killeaton Street, St Ives, NSW 2075; ☎02-9440 0695.

Older Women's Network, 87 Lower Fort Street, Millers Point, Sydney, NSW 2000; ☎02-9247 7046; fax 02-9247 4202; e-mail office@own.org.au; www.own.org.au.

The United Kingdom Settlers' Association, First Floor, 146 Toorak Road West, South Yarra, VIC 3141; ☎03-9787 3112; fax 03-9866 1799.

Councils on the Ageing (COTA)

The Australian Council on the Ageing is a national non-profit organisation designed to provide assistance and independent advice to seniors on issues such as accommodation, financial management or health. COTA is also a major lobby group for older Australians. It has a national branch and branches in each state, many of which have a freecall number for enquiries.

COTA National Seniors, Level 2, 3 Bowen Crescent, Melbourne, VIC 3004; ☎03-9820 2655; fax 03-9820 9886; e-mail cota@cota.org.au; www.cota.org.au.

Council on the Ageing (ACT) Inc, Hughes Community Centre, Wisdom Street, Hughes, ACT 2605; ☎02-6282 3777; fax 02-6285 3422; e-mail cotact@cota-act.org.au; www.cota-act.org.au.

Council on the Ageing (NSW) Inc, Level 4, 280 Pitt Street, Sydney, NSW 2000; ☎02-9286 3860; fax 02-9286 3872; freecall 1800 449 102; www.cotansw.com.au.

Council on the Ageing (NT) Inc, Spillett House, 65 Smith Street, Darwin, NT 0800; ☎08-8941 1004; fax 08-8941 5011; e-mail ntsenior@bigpond.net.au.

Council on the Ageing Queensland Inc, 243 Edward Street, Brisbane, QLD 4000; ☎07-3221 6822; fax 07-3221 6233; e-mail cotaq@cotaq.org.au; www.cotaq.org.au.

Council on the Ageing (SA) Inc, 45 Flinders Street, Adelaide, SA 5000; ☎08-8232 0422; fax 08-8232 0433; freecall 1800 182 324; e-mail cotasa@cotasa.org.au; www.cotasa.org.au.

Council on the Ageing (Tasmania) Inc, 2 St John's Avenue, Newtown, TAS 7008; ☎03-6228 1897; fax 03-6228 0481; www.tased.edu.au/tasonline/cotatas/.

Council on the Ageing (Victoria) Inc, Level 4, Block Arcade, 98 Elizabeth Street, Melbourne, VIC 3000; ☎03-9654 4443; fax 03-9654 4456; Seniors Info Service 1300 135 090; e-mail cotavic@cotavic.org.au; www.cotavic.org.au.

Council on the Ageing (WA) Inc., 2nd floor, Wesley Centre, 93 William Street, Perth, WA 6850; ☎08-9321 2133; fax 08-9321 2707; e-mail exec@cotawa.asn.au; www.cotawa.asn.au.

Independent Living Centres. Provide information for those with disabilities or limited mobility who live independently. They also demonstrate and develop products designed to help such people live more easily and retain their independence. Products include bathroom and toilet aids, as well as aids to help with communication, eating, drinking, walking and sitting. Transport and lifting equipment is also available. Information on where to hire such products, as well as their cost and availability, is available from these centres. The Independent Living Centres (www.ilc.asn.au) also produce a number of brochures providing information and updates. Visits to Independent Living Centres are by appointment only.

Australian Capital Territory: 24 Parkinson Street, Weston, ACT 2611; ☎02-6205 1900; fax 02-6205 1906; e-mail ilcact@act.gov.au.

New South Wales: 600 Victoria Road, Ryde, NSW 2112; ☎02-9808 2233; fax 02-9809 7132; e-mail ilcnsw@bigpond.com; www.ilcnsw.asn.au.

Queensland: Cnr Goring Street and Cavendish Road, Coorparoo, QLD 4151; ☎07-3397 1224; fax 07-3394 1013; e-mail enquiries@ilcqld.org.au; www. ilcqld.org.au.

South Australia: 11 Blacks Road, Gilles Plains, SA 5086; ☎08-8266 5260; fax 08-8266 5263; e-mail ilcsa@ilc.asn.au; www.ilc.asn.au.

Tasmania: 46 Canning Street, Launceston, TAS 7250; ☎03-6334 5899; fax 03-6334 0045; e-mail ilc@ilctas.asn.au; www.ilctas.asn.au.

Victoria: Equipment Services, Yooralla Society of Victoria, 705 Geelong Road, Brooklyn, VIC 3025; ☎03-9362 6111; fax 03-9314 9825; e-mail ilc@yooralla. com.au; http://deis.vic.gov.au.

Western Australia: 3 Lemnos Street, Shenton Park, WA 6008; ☎08-9381 0608; fax 08-9381 0611; e-mail enquiries@ilc.com.au; www.ilc.com.au.

Section II

WORKING IN AUSTRALIA

EMPLOYMENT

TEMPORARY WORK

PERMANENT WORK

DIRECTORY OF MAJOR EMPLOYERS

STARTING A BUSINESS

EMPLOYMENT

CHAPTER SUMMARY

○ One of the biggest surges of employment opportunities in Australia has been in tourism.

○ **Job Prospects.** Engineers have the highest level of employment buoyancy followed by construction and property services.

○ There are currently 39 skilled occupations which are experiencing national shortages, including nursing.

○ **Part-time Work.** A government report predicts a leap in part-time workers by 2005.

○ **Working Illegally.** From November 2000 to June 2001 155 warning notices were issued to employers who had taken on illegal workers.

  ○ Every year 50,000 people stay on after their visa has expired.

  ○ Linkage of the computers of the Immigration, Tax and Medicare (Health) departments means it is almost impossible to flout the immigration regulations indefinitely.

○ **Casual Work.** The average harvest picker can expect to earn $300-$500 for a six-day week.

○ **Pay Increases.** The average annual pay increase is estimated at 5.2%; inflation is 2.8%.

○ **Fringe Benefits.** Only the most senior positions offer benefits, which are not generally popular because of the tax implications.

○ **Private Pension Plans.** PPPs (known as Superannuation in Australia) are compulsory.

○ The most common form of incentive is the employer's contribution of up to 10% towards employees' compulsory private pension plans.

○ **Holidays.** The statutory minimum is four weeks.

  ○ Holiday leave is sweetened with a bonus of 17.5% during the holiday period.

Overview

Australia is experiencing high levels of job optimism, has a booming economy, enjoys low inflation, and currently has an unemployment rate of 5.1%. Despite an ageing workforce, the labour market experienced a solid growth of 2.1% in the 12 months to August 2004. Other employment growth drivers are international trade, new technology, labour market flexibility, and industry specific factors, such as the drought and its effect on employment prospects in the agricultural sector. The most recent figures available from the Department of Employment and Workplace Relations, show that the strongest employment growth has been in Property and Business Services in the five years to February 2004. Other buoyant and strong growth areas are in Health and Community Services, Construction, and the Retail Trade, which is the largest employing industry in Australia. While short-term trends in Hospitality have been affected by international events, growth in tourism, cafes, restaurants and catering services will underpin future job growth in this industry. Government administration, education, and finance and insurance have been the other growth areas. Although employment in manufacturing, the third largest employing industry, fell by 1% future growth is expected. The agricultural sector has shown major job losses owing to the ongoing drought situation but, across the spectrum, demand for broadband services should contribute to some growth in communication services. In the years 2010-2011, the strongest growth areas are expected to be in property and business and health and community services, followed by accommodation, cafes and restaurants, and cultural and recreational services. All States and territories experienced growth to August 2004 with Queensland (4.7%) and Victoria (2.9%) being the highest. Queensland shows the biggest rise for managers and administrators, professionals, associate professionals, tradespeople and related workers. In industry, engineers have the highest levels of employment buoyancy followed by those working in the construction and property services. Other areas where employees are increasingly being taken on are in utilities, resources, wholesale and distribution. Employment levels in the chemical and oil industry, transport and manufacturing, are all well below national expectations. Again Western Australia shows the best biggest rise in industrial industry employees. The education sector, followed by non-profit making organisations and government are most optimistic in terms of employee take up within the government and infrastructure sector. In the financial and professional services sector, the legal industry is best off, followed by service industry employees and finance and insurance service employees. Opportunities for full-time staff are better at present than for contract or temporary workers.

> **Danny Jones found Australia a good place to look for a job**
> *Work is relatively easy to find, especially for mechanical trades, and by far the best way of finding work here is to just turn up and sell yourself. It's amazing how many people will give you a job despite not having advertised a vacancy. Its rare for references to be taken, and most small employers have the 'give 'em a fair go' approach.*

State to state the financial and professional sector is the most optimistic in terms of employee take on in ACT, followed by the IT and telecoms sector, and government and social infrastructure. In New South Wales the finance and professional sector is also the most buoyant, followed by the industrial and consumer sectors. Queensland shows growth in the financial and professional sector, followed by IT, telecommunications and industry. In South Australia IT was the most buoyant sector of employment, followed by the government and social infrastructure sector, and the finance and professional sectors. Victoria showed most buoyancy in the government and social infrastructure sector, followed by the consumer, IT and telecommunications sectors. Western Australia shows the largest employee growth spread over the three sectors of industry, consumer services, and government and social infrastructure.

Current Skills Shortages. There are currently 39 skilled occupations which are experiencing labour shortages in Australia and are on the Migration Occupations in Demand List (MODL) published by the Department of Immigration and Multicultural and Indigenous Affairs. These occupations include chefs (excluding commis chefs), registered nurses and midwives, neurological nurses, registered paediatric nurses, physiotherapists, medical diagnostic radiographers, audiologists, sonographers, dentists, and secondary maths and religious education teachers. Additionally there are shortages of accountants, pharmacists, civil engineers, childcare co-ordinators and workers, and welders in regional areas. Currently, there are no national shortages of IT personnel. At least 21,000 tradespeople are needed, especially refrigeration and air conditioning mechanics, bricklayers and plumbers, hairdressers, motor mechanics, auto electricians, and metal fitters.

Skill shortages are caused by many factors, including economic and demographic change, qualified workers deciding not to work in the field in which they trained, and variations in labour demand within the states and territories of Australia. Shortages often have more to do with the lack of available tradesmen than an increased demand on the trades themselves. Vocational education has increased the number of school leavers going out into the labour market with training and specific job-related skills but in some trades skill shortages are so severe that employers have applied for special permission from the Commonwealth Government to bring in overseas-trained personnel to fill skilled jobs. Many companies are now using labour hire contractors to fill jobs that would previously have been done by apprentices.

All states show the same pattern of skill shortages, with few exceptions. New South Wales has the greatest shortage of tradespeople, from engineering and vehicle trades to construction and food, as well as dentists, and occupational therapists; and in Victoria, speech pathologists, radiation therapists, and information technology secondary teachers are in demand. In Queensland, nuclear medicine technologists, printing machinists, and cabinetmakers are needed; in South Australia, toolmakers, panelbeaters, and wood machinists; and in Western Australia, lawyers, vehicle painters, metal fabricators, sheetmetal workers, are all required, as well as chefs specialising in Asian cuisines.

The Future. The government has projected significant changes in the composition of the working population, with long-term trends towards more part-time work, a middle-ageing of the workforce, and an increased proportion of female employees. Prospects for employment vary according to industry sector and the skill level of the occupation. The largest share of new jobs is expected to come from the following occupational groups: accounting, finance and management (20%), sales assistants and storepersons (17%), health, fitness, hair and beauty (9%) and food, hospitality and tourism (8%). Although there are good prospects and career opportunities across all industries, most new jobs are expected to come form a handful of strongly growing service industries, providing more than 80% of new jobs: property and business services, retail trade, health and community services, construction, and accommodation, cafes and restaurants. To offset decline in traditional industries, the government is strongly focused on the need for vocational education, skill building, and the multi-skilling of the workforce. It is seeking to build on emerging competitive strategies to take advantage of improved technologies, innovative marketing, better management, and organisational change, and more and more mature workers now accept the need to retrain or develop their skills.

Unemployment Rates for Migrants. Unemployment rates for migrants vary depending on skill levels and proficiency in the English language. In August 2004, the unemployment rate for those born in the main English speaking countries was 4%, while the unemployment rate for those born in other countries (combined) was 6.4%. Recent arrivals generally have a higher unemployment rate than those who have lived in Australia for some time. The Department of Employment and Workplace Relations (www.dewrsb.gov.au) publishes a quarterly magazine called the *Australian Jobs Update* which is intended to give migrants an overview of the prevailing labour market conditions. DEWRSB also publishes a monthly skilled vacancy survey available at www.workplace.gov.au.

On-line Employment Sources

Australian Government Information (www.nla.gov.au/oz/gov/). Entry point to all Australian government websites.

Australian Taxation Office (www.ato.gov.au). Information on Australian tax laws.

Department of Employment and Workplace Relations (www.dewrsb.gov.au). Workplace relations in Australia, maritime transport, policy and legislation, government employment, and related sites.

Office of Small Business, Department of Industry, Tourism and Resources (www.industry.gov.au). The small business sector has accounted for 70% of jobs growth over the past decade.

Melbourne City Council (www.melbourne.vic.gov.au). Includes information on products and services of Melbourne City Council as well as details of forthcoming events, maps and guides.

NSW Department of State and Regional Development, (www.srd.nsw.gov.au). Information for potential investors and business migrants to Sydney and New South Wales.

New South Wales Government (www.nsw.gov.au). Includes information on doing business with the NSW government, rural information, reports and papers, related links.

Queensland Government Online (www qld.gov.au). Includes information on business in Queensland, and government departments and agencies.

Tasmania Online (www.tas.gov.au). Includes information on investing in Tasmania and migrating to Tasmania.

Government of Victoria (www.vic.gov.au). Includes information on state projects, arts, business, and education.

Australia White Pages (www.whitepages.com.au). Online access to eight million residential, business and government listings.

The Australian Yellow Pages Telephone Directory (www.yellowpages.com.au). National searchable database.

Residence and Work Regulations

In order to work in Australia, you must hold an appropriate temporary or permanent residency visa. The Australian immigration authorities are draconian in their treatment of illegal workers, and anyone caught working without a visa should expect to be deported immediately. A data-matching programme operated by the Department of Immigration and Multicultural and Indigenous Affairs links the computers of the Australian Taxation Office, Centrelink, and the Health Insurance Commission (Medicare), making it almost impossible to get away with flouting immigration laws. DIMIA is focusing its efforts to locate illegal workers in industries which employ large numbers of casual workers, especially in rural areas, where cash payments have traditionally made it easier to work outside the purview of the eagle eye of the tax office.

The eligibility criteria, requirements and procedures for obtaining residency in Australia, whether on a short- or long-term basis, are described in detail in the *Residence and Entry Regulations* chapter. Those visas which allow foreigners to work legally or to seek employment in Australia are described in brief below.

Working Holiday Visa. The purpose of the Working Holiday visa is to allow young people the chance to tour extensively in Australia, with the option of working for up to three months in any one area. If you are granted this visa, you will only be able to consider employment of a temporary or casual nature. Applicants for a Working Holiday Maker visa must:

- O Be a citizen of Belgium, Canada, Cyprus, Denmark, Estonia, Finland, France, Germany, Hong Kong, Ireland, Italy, Japan, the Republic of Korea, Malta, the Netherlands, Norway, Sweden, Taiwan, or the United Kingdom.
- O Be between the ages of 18 and 30.
- O Have no dependent children.
- O Have not previously entered Australia on a Working Holiday visa.
- O Meet health and character requirements.
- O Be outside Australia at the time of the visa grant.
- O Leave Australia before the expiry of the visa.
- O Be capable of finding temporary work as a means of supplementing holiday funds.
- O Have a return ticket and sufficient funds (approx. $5,000) to cover living expenses for initial stage of your holiday in Australia.
- O Have no intention of working for more than three months for any single employer.

Employer Nomination Scheme. This scheme falls under the Skilled Stream migration programme and allows employers to recruit highly skilled workers if they are unable to fill a vacancy from the Australian labour market or through their own training programmes.

The Nominee must:
- O Be under 45 years of age.
- O Have qualifications and experience that match the vacancy requirements.

- Have vocational level English.
- Be able to satisfy any mandatory licensing, registration or professional membership requirements.
- Meet mandatory health and character requirements.

The Employer must:
- Prove that they have exhausted all possible avenues to employ an Australian citizen for the position.
- Prove that the position is a full time, fixed term appointment of at least three years, with the possibility of renewal.
- Demonstrate an excellent training record and commitment to training and up-grading skills of semi-skilled Australian workers.

Business Visas. There are many different types of business visas which permit professionals to work in Australia as temporary residents on a short- or long-term basis. The conditions and requirements of these visas are detailed in *Residence and Entry Regulations*, and include not only business fields, but also educators, entertainers, and others.

- Business (Short-Stay) visa: Allows for either single or multiple entry to Australia. Holders of multiple entry visas may make a number of journeys for up to three months on each occasion. These visas are valid for five years or the life of the passport (maximum 10 years). Applicants must apply for this visa outside Australia.
- Business (Long-Stay) visa: Allows highly skilled people to work for an approved employer for up to four years. The prospective employer must apply to become a 'standard business sponsor,' which will permit them to sponsor an agreed number of overseas employees over a two-year period.

Nurses are currently in high demand in Australia and most visa applications receive priority processing. You can go to Australia independently and look for work or arrange a job with an employer before you leave. You will need to be assessed by the Australian Nursing Council to determine whether you can work there. There are a number of visa options available, for instance Skill Matching, Business (Long-Stay), Skilled, and Working Holiday.

Business Skills Migration. The Business Skills migration programme is designed to encourage successful business people to settle permanently in Australia and develop new business opportunities. Business migration benefits the Australian economy by developing its international markets, creating employment, introducing new or improved technology, and by adding to commercial activity and to competitiveness in general. Business migrants are expected to contribute to these benefits by establishing and conducting new business, by transferring capital, and by investment. Most visas are for four years initially and individuals may then apply for permanent residence after satisfactory evidence of a specialised level of business or investment activity. The Business Skills programme is divided into four categories and the following criteria apply:

Business Owners. For owners or part-owners of a business who are required to demonstrate that they have had a successful business career and have at least $200,000 net assets in a qualifying business. Business owners must also meet requirements on turnover, business and personal assets, age and vocational English ability.

Senior Executives. Senior execs must demonstrate that they have had a successful business career and that for two of the previous four years they have been employed in the top three levels of management in a major business. They must also meet requirements on turnover, business and personal assets, age and vocational English ability.

Investors. These must demonstrate a history of successful ownership and management in business and/or investment activities, as well as make a significant investment in a government approved Designated Investment for a period of four years. They must also meet requirements on assets and age.

Business Talent. This category is for high calibre business people who are owners or part owners of an overseas business and have an overall successful business career and have a commitment to participate as a principal in the management of a new or existing business. As with other categories, applicants must meet requirements on turnover, personal and business assets, age and English language ability. You will also need to show that you are sponsored by a State or Territory government.

Professional Development Visa. This visa came into operation in July 2003 and caters for government officials, groups of professionals, and managers from overseas to enhance their professional or managerial skills by undertaking professional development training in Australia. Applicants must be sponsored by an Australian organisation approved as a professional development sponsor. A centralised PDV processing centre has been established in Hobart to ensure quick sponsorship and processing times. Once a business migrant has arrived in Australia he or she must meet visa conditions and business obligations. The expectation is that he or she will establish a new business, or become an owner or part owner of an existing business and that they will take an active part in the management of that business. Having established a successful business initially as a temporary resident, a Business Skills migrant is expected to remain in Australia permanently to continue that business. The progress of business migrants is monitored after their arrival in Australia, and where no significant steps have been taking towards meeting these obligations within the first three years after arrival, the Minister for Immigration and Multicultural and Indigenous Affairs has the power to cancel the right of residence of the business immigrant and his or her family.

Permanent Residents. Migrants entering Australia on permanent residency visas are not subject to any restrictions or regulations, other than those which govern the working practices of all Australians. There may, however, be specific conditions attached to the class of visa granted, particularly if you are entering under a regionally sponsored migration scheme which may oblige you to work or settle in a remote area. The skilled stream of Australia's migration programme is designed to facilitate entry for people who have skills or outstanding abilities deemed to be valuable to Australia's economic advancement. If you have been accepted as a skilled stream migrant, you are, in effect, one step ahead in the job search process, insofar as you are likely to have been accepted on the basis that your particular experience and training are in demand. Current immigration policy addresses specific skills shortages in the Australian labour market, and this policy is applied to General Skilled migrants (sponsored by a family member already resident in the country), as well as to Independent migrants (who are *not* sponsored by a relative or employer in Australia). For detailed information on permanent residency visa criteria and requirements see *Residence and Entry Regulations*.

Skills and Qualifications

Successful applicants under the Skilled Stream migration programme are required to have a prescribed level of professional experience and qualification. As explained more fully in *Residence and Entry*, these skills are assessed during the application process by means of the 'Points Test'. Points awarded for skill levels are based on your current occupation and the level of your qualifications, which must be of a standard recognised as industry-appropriate in Australia. Your current occupation is defined as the one which you have performed over the last 12 months and which you regard as your usual occupation. Thus, if you have obtained qualifications in one field (say, a degree in modern languages) but are currently working in a field which does not *directly* utilise those qualifications, you will, in effect, be assessed as unqualified. This clause creates difficulties for many applicants who are working in areas such as information technology or office management, where in many cases skills have been acquired on-the-job or through graduate programmes. Concessions are made for workplace training, however, and each case is assessed on its individual merits. Points are awarded for length of professional experience (usually three years is required) and for membership of professional or industrial associations. The table below shows the value at the time of writing of the different qualifications under the Points Test. Trade certificates, diplomas and degrees must be recognised as 'acceptable' (equivalent to an Australian qualification) in order to score any points. DIMIA has Migration Occupation in Demand and Skilled Occupations lists.

TABLE 11	GENERAL SKILLS POINTS	
Assessed Category		**Points**
Skill		
Applicant has training specific to occupation (degree or trade certificate)		60
Applicant has a more general occupation (requiring non-specific degree level qualifications)		50
Applicant has an occupation which requires diploma or advanced diploma level qualifications		40
Age at time of application		
18-29		30
30-34		25
35-39		20
40-44		15

Language ability
Vocational English   15
Competent English   20

Work experience
Applicant has been employed in an occupation on the skilled occupation list for three
out of four years   5
Applicant's occupation scores 60 points under the skill factor, and has worked
in nominated occupation for three of four years   10

Migrant Occupation in demand
Applicant's occupation is in demand, but no job offer   15
Applicant's occupation is in demand *and* applicant has firm offer of
employment   20

Australian qualifications
Applicant has completed two academic years in full-time education at
Australian institution (post secondary degree/diploma/trade qualification)   5
Applicant has a Masters or good Honours degree from an Australian institution
after two or three years' full time study   10
Applicant has completed a doctorate at Australian institution after two
full-time academic years   15

Spouse skills
Applicant's spouse satisfies basic requirements of age, English proficiency,
qualifications, nominated occupation and work experience, and suitable skills
assessment   5

Regional/low population growth metropolitan areas
Applicant has lived and studied in one or more regional/low population growth
metropolitan areas for at least two years   5

Relationship
Applicant or spouse has a relative who is an Australian citizen or permanent
resident and is a sponsor (Skilled-Australian sponsored category within General
Skills migration programme)   15

Bonus points
Capital investment of $100,000 *or* six months work experience in Australia in
any occupation on the Skilled Occupations List *or* fluency in a
community language   5

AEI-NOOSR Bridging Courses for the Overseas Trained

Australian Education International, through the National Office of Overseas Skills Recognition (PO Box 9880, Canberra, ACT 2601; ☎1800 020 086 (freecall) or 02-6211 9334; fax 02-6123 7892; e-mail noosr@dest.gov.au; www.dest.gov. au/noosr) can provide advice on the acceptability of any qualification which you hold. They also offer bridging courses for overseas-qualified professionals whose qualifications have not yet been recognised in Australia, enabling applicants to meet the academic and professional requirements for registration or entry to regulated professions. Government-regulated professions include: dentistry, veterinary science, medicine, law, radiography, pharmacy, architecture, physiotherapy, and nursing. Accountancy, dietetics, social work, engineering and surveying are self-regulating. You will be eligible for support on a NOOSR course if you have permanent residency in Australia, have overseas professional qualifications at Bachelor's degree level or above, and you have obtained details of the training you require from the professional body which assessed your qualifications.

SOURCES OF JOBS

On-line Resources

If you are job-hunting in Australia from overseas, by far the best, quickest, and most convenient resource is now the Internet. There are dozens of Australian recruitment agencies on the Internet, all of which advertise frequently up-dated lists of positions, as well as providing registration and CV lodgement services. Two major Australian media groups, Newscorp and Fairfax, which between them publish the greater part of Australia's mainstream newspapers, also put their classified recruitment sections on-line, and these are updated daily. The websites of these two corporations together carry around 20,000 job advertisements per week. In addition, the Australian Job Network (the government job-finding organisation, details below) has an excellent site searchable by location, job type, and interactive map. In most cases, jobs listed on the AJN site will detail conditions and pay, and although it may be difficult to apply for jobs listed on this site from overseas, it will give you a good idea of the kinds of work available in almost any field.

Useful Australia-specific Recruitment Websites

Australian Job Network: www.jobsearch.gov.au.

CareerOne Services Pty Ltd: www.careerone.com.au. This Interactive site carries more than 30,000 jobs listed daily.

MyCareer: www.mycareer.com.au. This Fairfax site lists daily advertisements carried in a range of national papers. It carries around 10,000 advertisements per day, and is searchable by job type and location.

Jobnet: www.jobnet.com.au. The largest IT jobsearch website in Australia. Thousands of permanent, contract and consulting positions available for IT Professionals.

Monster.com: www.monster.com.au. Local portal for the leading global online careers network.

Willing Workers On Organic Farms Australia: www.wwoof.com.au. Willing Workers On Organic Farms (WWOOF) is a form of cultural exchange in which WWOOFers live and work as family with host farms, and learn about the skills of organic growing as well as the area they are visiting.

Individual agencies can be quickly located on the Internet by using search engines such as Google, and the search terms 'Australia' in conjunction with 'recruitment' or 'employment'.

Newspapers

UK Newspapers and Directories.

The *Directory of Jobs and Careers Abroad*: Published by Vacation Work (£12.95) has a section on Australia including contact details and other sources of employment information. Vacation Work Publications also has a very useful links page at www.vacationwork.co.uk.

TNT Group: 14-15 Child's Place, London, SW5 9RX; ☎020-7373 3377, produce a free annual 200-page guide which includes the latest information on working in Australia. The A5 guide is available from travel agents or online at www.tnt-magazine.com/anzguide. TNT have a useful website at www.tntmagazine.com to help you find your feet Down Under with thousands of jobs listed online.

Australian Newspapers. Jobs are advertised in community, local, regional and national newspapers. Most major daily newspapers carry a large recruitment section on Saturdays, and many carry advertisements for specialist professional positions on certain days (for example, tertiary education sector jobs in *The Australian* on Wednesdays). Professionals and executives are advised to consult *The Australian* in additional to their state newspapers, as most high-status jobs will be advertised in this paper, regardless of location. A list of state and national newspapers is given in Chapter Four, *Media and Communications*.

Professional Associations and Specialist Publications

Most professions in Australia have a national association or governing body, which is also likely to have state chapters. In some cases, membership of an association is compulsory for practising members, and in such instances, membership fees are tax deductible. Most professional associations publish a journal, which, in specialist fields, may be the best source of employment information. Specialist publications provide another important source, and will usually report on developments in their field, as well as advertising job vacancies. Conferences and development courses will also be advertised in such publications.

Working Holiday Assistance Schemes

BUNAC. The British Universities North America Club (16 Bowling Green Lane, London, EC1R 0BD; ☎020-7251 3472; fax 020-7251 0215; e-mail enquiries@bunac.org.uk; www.bunac.org.uk) has a 'Work Australia' programme, which is designed to help those aged 18-30 deal with all the organisational aspects of a working holiday. The service helps with obtaining flights, insurance etc, and includes comprehensive orientation sessions at home and on arrival in Australia, a group two-day stopover in Bangkok or Hong Kong en route, two free nights accommodation in Sydney. It also provides ongoing support through BUNAC's subsidiary, International Exchange Programs, including a postal service, voicemail card and the help of the Sydney resource office for general advice throughout your stay.

SWAP. Young Canadians going on a working holiday to Australia can participate in SWAP Working Holiday Programs available through the offices of Travel CUTS, Voyages Campus, the Adventure Travel Company, and Odyssey Travel.

Information on the program and contact details can be found at www.swap.ca. SWAP through its association with IEP (International Exchange Programs, PO. Box 13278, Law Courts Post Office, Melbourne, VIC 8010; ☎03-9329 3866; fax 03-9329 1592; www.iep-australia.com) provides ongoing support through IEP centres in Sydney, Melbourne, and Auckland. SWAP Working Holiday Programs is a non-profit activity of the Canadian Federation of Students (National Office, 170 Metcalfe Street, 5th Floor, Ottawa, Ontario K2P 1P3; ☎613-232 7394; fax 613-232 0276; e-mail info@cfs-fcee.ca; www.cfs-fcee.ca).

Employment Wanted Advertisements

Placing an advertisement in a local or community newspaper can be a useful way of finding casual work, but is unlikely to land you secure long-term employment. Most people using 'Situations Wanted' classifieds are looking for occasional cash jobs, such as gardening, baby-sitting, or cleaning. If you are on a working holiday, this may be one of the best ways of picking up occasional work to suit your travel schedule, and will probably pay at least $10 per hour. For graduates, short-term tutoring, particularly around exam time, can be quite remunerative, and most local papers will have a separate column for advertising services of this type.

The Australian Job Network

The Job Network is a national network of around 200 private, community and government organisations dedicated to finding jobs for unemployed people, particularly the long-term unemployed. The Department of Employment and Workplace Relations (www.dewrsb.gov.au) provides a very comprehensive website detailing available jobs, and with links to other employers at www.workplace.gov. au.

Employment Agencies

UK-based Australian Employment Agency. *Bligh Appointments* is the largest employer of working holiday-makers in both Sydney and London, and can help in the search for temporary work before you even leave home. They specialise in office support and industrial jobs, and offer good rates and an immediate start. Bligh have offices at: Level 7, Dymocks Building, 428 George Street, Sydney NSW 2000; ☎02-9235 3699; www.careerone.com.au/bligh; and 70 North End Road, London W14; ☎020-7603 6123.

Recruitment Consultancies. Recruitment consultancies generally specialise in placing staff in sales, marketing, finance, accounting, IT, engineering, office administration, and hospitality. While many employment agencies also cover these areas, recruitment consultants deal mainly with executive and upper and middle management placements. They advertise available jobs in major newspapers and usually offer a complete recruitment service. If you are seeking work of this kind, you can contact a recruitment consultancy 'on spec' to discuss your qualifications and experience, and any potentially suitable vacancies. A list of recruitment consultants and contact numbers can be found in the local Yellow Pages.

Employment Agencies. Employment agencies deal in both temporary and permanent work, usually in the secretarial, clerical, accounting and IT fields, or in hospitality or heavy industry. Most advertise in the Yellow Pages and are found in prominent locations in the Central Business Districts and other urban centres. The international firms Drake Personnel, Kelly Services, Centacom and Adecco all have agencies in Australia. In addition to the large, generalist agencies, there are many smaller, specialist firms, particularly in fields such as nursing, legal temping, banking, and IT. If you are a registered nurse or teacher looking to work in Australia, it is vital that you take proof of registration and qualifications with you. You can expect to earn around $12 an hour for clerical work, $14 for secretarial and $15 for computer work.

Useful Addresses

Adecco, Level 3, 9 Hunter Street, Sydney, NSW 2000; ☎02-9244 3400; fax 02-9223 4626; e-mail sydney@adecco.com.au; www.adecco.com.au, is the world's leading employment services company, with more than 5,000 offices in 58 countries. For office locations in other areas call 132 993.

AAA Nannies, PO Box 157, Sanctuary Cove, Brisbane, QLD 4212; tel/fax 07-5530 1123; Level 1, 789 Botany Road, Roseberry, Sydney, NSW; ☎02-9557 6644; www.nanny.net.au. Australia's leading au pair agency with offices Australia-wide.

Bayside Group, Level 17, Town Hall House, 456 Kent Street, Sydney, NSW 2000; ☎02-9261 5100; fax 02-9261 5300; www.baysidegrp.com.au. Supply executive recruitment, temporary and contract placements of legal, IT and accountancy staff.

Goldstein and Martens Recruitment Consultants, Level 4, 285 George Street, Sydney, NSW 2000; ☎02-9262 3088; fax 02-9262 3409; e-mail enquiries@goldstein martens.com.au; www.goldsteinmartens.com.au. Pays $2-$3 above the average hourly wage.

Involvement Volunteers Association, PO Box 218, Port Melbourne, VIC 3207; ☎03-9646 9392; e-mail ivworldwide@volunteering.org.au; www.volunteering. org.au.

Metro Personnel, Level 6, Thakral House, 301 George Street, Sydney, NSW 2000; ☎02-9299 5477; fax 02-9299 5941; www.metropersonnel.com.au.

Michael Page International, Level 7, 1 Margaret Street, Sydney, NSW 2000; ☎02-8292 2000; www.michaelpage.com.au. Temporary and contract work in finance and accounting, legal, sales and marketing, technology, human resources and engineering.

Select Appointments, Level 3, Select House, 109 Pitt Street, Sydney, NSW 2000; ☎02-8258 9999; fax 02-8258 9988; www.select-appointments.com.au. Specialise in placing professional, motivated travellers. They have positions for receptionists, data entry operators, secretaries, accounts clerks, medical and legal secretaries, WPOs and warehousing staff. Select also have offices in Perth, ☎08-9321 3133; Brisbane, ☎07-3243 3900; Melbourne, ☎03-8663 4700; Adelaide, ☎08-8468 8000; and Canberra, ☎02-6278 0088; www.select-appointments.com.au.

Labour Hire Contractors. Labour hire contractors specialise in placing skilled manual workers and tradespeople, labourers, storepersons, process workers and factory staff. These agencies generally do not operate high street offices and are found in industrial areas. Most advertise in the Yellow Pages, and it is usually best to visit in person, taking with you any trade or City and Guild certificates you may have. Qualified tradespeople are paid well in Australia, and in states with booming construction industries there is usually a shortage of such people. Bricklayers are particularly in demand and can expect to earn a high wage, while mine workers can earn more than $1,000 per week. Mining work is very labour-intensive and unskilled workers are often needed; modern mine sites operate equal opportunities policies, and most employ women in a wide range of capacities. There is also strong demand for skilled mechanics.

Useful Publication

A free newsletter called *Australian and New Zealand Employment Review* that provides a regular update on the employment scene is published by *Taylor & Associates (Migrant Employment Search)*, 27 Gillies Avenue, PO Box 9600, Newmarket, Auckland. New Zealand; ☎(64) 09-520 5421; fax (64) 09-520 5487; e-mail nzjobs@jobfastrack.co.nz; www.jobfastrack.co.nz. Copies are available from their UK sister company The Emigration Group Ltd, 7 Heritage Court, Chester, Cheshire CH1 1RD (☎0845-230 2526; fax 01244-342288; e-mail info@TEGltd.co.uk; www. emigration.uk.com).

Chambers of Commerce

The Australian Chamber of Commerce and affiliated state Chambers of Commerce advise and provide information on employment in Australia. They also produce detailed regional summaries of employment and economic growth, and are particularly useful as a point of contact for small businesspeople. The Australian-British Chamber of Commerce, for example, aims to promote business growth and development within Australia, and to encourage reciprocal trade between the UK and Australia.

Useful Addresses

Australian British Chamber of Commerce, Level 16, The Gateway Building, 1 Macquarie Place, Sydney, NSW 2000; ☎02-9247 6271; fax 02-9247 6671; www. britishchamber.com.

Australia and New Zealand Chamber of Commerce UK, Dudley House, 34-35 Southampton Street, London, WC2E 7HE; ☎0870-890 0720; fax 0870-890 0721; e-mail enquiries@anzcc.org.uk; www.anzcc.org.uk.

Australian Industry Group, 20 Queens Road, Melbourne, VIC 3004; ☎03-9867 0111; fax 03-9867 0199; www.aigroup.asn.au. The Australian Industry Group is an independent organisation created to help Australian industry be more competitive domestically and internationally. Aspects of industry covered include the economy and related investment issues, taxation, industrial relations policy, environmental issues, education and training.

Company Transfers and Job Exchanges

If you are currently working for a company which has offices or branches in Australia, opportunities may exist for either permanent or temporary transfer.

Outside the multinationals, it may be possible to find work in Australia under an exchange scheme. Such schemes are common in the teaching profession, and you should contact your local education authority for further information. Many exchanges provide not only a job swap, but also all the domestic necessities. You may find yourself minding your exchange colleague's pets for a year, but you'll probably also find yourself minding their pool too!

ASPECTS OF EMPLOYMENT

Salaries

Pay rates in Australia fall broadly into four bands: the lowest paid workers earn an average of $350 or less per week, mid-range salaries cluster firstly around $600 and then, in the upper-mid-range, around $850 per week, and finally, the highest paid employees can expect a weekly pay packet in excess of $1,458 per week. Rates of pay are differentiated between the public and private sector, and by gender and age. Men still tend to receive a higher weekly income than women in the same sector do (although this can be accounted for by gender divides within industry, rather than in terms of direct discrimination, which is, of course, illegal). The average weekly earnings for men is $954.10 and $805.90 for women. Younger people are likely to be paid less than their seniors. Employees earning at the top end of the salary bands are likely to fall into one of two key industries – finance and insurance, and mining – while those at the bottom end are generally found in the retail trade and in the hospitality industry. The table below illustrates the approximate full-time adult average weekly wage in Australia:.

TABLE 12	AVERAGE WEEKLY EARNINGS FOR FULL-TIME WORK ($)
Accommodation, cafes and restaurants	654
Communication services	1,000
Construction	950
Cultural and recreational services	890
Education	990
Electricity, gas and water supply	1,100
Finance and insurance	1,100
Government administration and defence	900
Health and community services	890
Mining	1,410
Manufacturing	890.00
Personal and other services	950
Property and business services	910
Retail trade	690
Transport and storage	960
Wholesale trade	800
Source: Australian Bureau of Statistics	

Earnings are related to skills obtained through education and work experience.

Work experience is related to age, especially for those in their 20s and 30s and therefore wages tend to rise with age. Unskilled workers can expect to earn between $10-$20 an hour depending on location, level of skill, and whether they are paid hourly or are on piece work rates. The traditional working holiday stand-by, fruit picking, may be easy to find but is poorly paid. Workers are often paid not by the hour but by the quantity of produce harvested. The average harvest picker can expect to earn somewhere in the region of $300-$500 for a six-day week.

> Bear in mind that a dollar goes a long way in Australia and that although earnings may seem low the same standard of living that you are used to back home can be had for less in Australia.

The Australian Bureau of Statistics estimates an annual increase of 5.2% per annum on the rates of pay. The Australian economy currently has a CPI (Consumer Price Index) of around 2.5%, an average inflation rate of 2.8%, and an unemployment rate of 5.1%. Industries with a shortage of skilled labour are expected to experience a greater increase in pay rates, while salaries in those areas where there is an oversupply of labour may see wages decline.

Award Rates – recommended minimum wages – are set by both the Federal and State governments for various trades and industries. Many, if not most, employers pay above the Award Rate, but you should find out if there is an Award in place before entering into negotiations with an employer. The appropriate union will be able to advise you on Award Rates and Conditions.

Benefits and Perks

Only the most senior positions attract additional benefits in Australia since changes in taxation laws made fringe benefits economically unattractive. Cars, health insurance plans, entertainment expenses, and even frequent flyer points are now all taxed as income, so that any benefit is offset by a commensurate loss of salary. Benefits earned under incentive schemes are also taxable. Childcare and workplace crèches, however, are not included in the fringe benefit tax, and indeed, employees using external childcare can claim a rebate on their expenses via the local Medicare office.

All employers pay superannuation (private pension contributions) for their employees at a basic rate of 9% of salary. Many employers also offer an additional percentage or two, up to around 10%, and this is now the most common form of employment incentive.

Most senior executives can still expect to receive a company car, but in general, benefits offered at any other level of employment are likely to be industry-linked. Thus, if you work for a major bank, you can expect to be eligible for subsidised borrowing, or in health insurance, for free or discounted health cover. Most Australian employees do not expect, or indeed want, any other fringe benefits which may cut into the cash in their pocket.

Superannuation

Superannuation is Australia's answer to the economic burden of state pensions in the context of an ageing population. In essence, it is a compulsory private pension planning scheme. All employees are required by law to pay a percentage of their salary into a superannuation fund designated by their employer, to which the employer also contributes an additional minimum percentage payment on the employee's behalf. If you move jobs, you are entitled to transfer your superannuation package to your new employer's chosen superannuation fund without incurring any penalty. The transfer of super from one fund to another is known as a 'roll-over'. Alternatively, if you wish to remain with your current fund, you can ask your employer to contribute to that fund instead, although they are not obliged to do so either by law or under any award. Contributions to 'super funds' are of two types: preserved and voluntary. Preserved contributions comprise the minimum compulsory contributions, described above, and these cannot be withdrawn or otherwise utilised until the age of 55. In addition, however, employees are entitled to make on-going voluntary contributions or occasional lump sum contributions to their fund, and this component is non-preserved (it can be withdrawn on leaving a job). Self-employed people are advised to take out a 'self-employed' superannuation policy available from banks and life insurance companies.

If you leave the country permanently, your superannuation will remain locked into a fund until you reach retirement age.

Working Hours, Overtime and Holidays

The Australian working week averages 35-40 hours over a five-day week, with government positions taking the middle road at precisely 37.5 hours. In most jobs, you can expect to work an eight-hour day with an hour for lunch, although some shift-work industries, such as nursing or hospitality, will usually require much greater flexibility. Flexi-time is common, and allows you to set your own working hours around a compulsory 'core time' (usually 10am to 4pm). Extra hours worked can be 'banked' against time off on full pay, which is in addition to statutory leave. Flexi-time is very popular, and is in place in almost all government jobs, tertiary education administration, and in many private companies. Minimum working pay and conditions are set by either the Commonwealth or State governments.

If you are required to work on a Sunday or a public holiday, you should be paid at twice the normal rate. At any other time, overtime is paid at 1.5 times the normal rate for the first three hours, then at double-time after that. Employees are entitled to a statutory minimum of four weeks paid leave per annum. Holiday leave is sweetened with a bonus known as 'holiday loading', which means that your salary is increased by an extra 17.5% during the period you are on leave. Many industries and professions offer increasing leave entitlements linked to length of service, and may, in some cases, offer as much as eight weeks' holiday per year. Untaken leave can usually be carried over from year to year, and many people choose to bank up holidays in order to take extended travel breaks.

After between seven and 10 years consecutive service with a single employer (10 years in government positions), an employee is entitled to 'long service leave' of up to six months on full pay or 12 months on half pay. Long service leave conditions vary considerably between employers, and in many cases additional incentives such as a travel allowance may be offered.

In addition to annual leave, all employees are granted a period of paid sick leave, the length of which will be specified in their contract. Most employers give between two weeks and three months paid sick leave. Any absence of more than 48 hours generally requires a medical certificate from a GP in order to claim payment. Many employers also offer compassionate leave of several days per year, which can be used in times of personal emergency such as bereavement. Compassionate leave and sick leave cannot be carried over from year to year.

Trade Unions

The trade union movement in Australia has become much weakened over the past decade, with fewer Australian employees joining unions than ever before. To offset loss of membership, many unions have amalgamated with others in related trades and professions, forming super-unions with increased negotiating power. The unions that have remained strongest are those representing industries in which there is continued unrest, particularly in teaching, nursing, policing, and wharfside occupations. 'Closed shops' are illegal, but the powerful BLF (Builders Labourers Federation) is occasionally known to operate union-only sites. Most workplaces have a union representative, and if you choose to join, dues can be automatically deducted from your salary. Union dues are a tax-deductible expense. The *Australian Council of Trade Unions* (ACTU, Level 2, 393 Swanston Street, Melbourne, VIC 3000; ☎ 03-9663 5266; fax 03-9663 4051; www.actu.asn.au) is the national trade union organisation and can provide advice on the union most appropriate to your circumstances and occupation.

Employment Contracts

In Australia every employee is covered either by a contract or a 'workplace agreement'. Workplace agreements are signed by both employer and employee, and stipulate the agreed conditions of employment, including hours, leave arrangements, uniform or safety-wear requirements, and notice and termination procedures. Even casual workers must be covered by one of these contracts, which is then lodged with the State Commissioner for Workplace Agreements as a legally binding document. Workplace agreements have not entirely replaced employment contracts, though they are nearly identical in purpose and effect, however, it is usually only in more senior and permanent positions that employees are covered by a contract.

A contract should specify all leave entitlements (holiday, sick, parental, and compassionate leave), overtime conditions, benefits, superannuation contribution levels, hours (including flexi-time arrangements), long-service leave, uniform regulations, and health and safety observances. It should also clearly stipulate termination procedures, which will usually follow the form of a first and second verbal warning, written warning, and formal interview (which may be attended, at your request, by a union representative). If a contract is broken by either party, the injured party is able to sue the other party for breach of contract through an industrial tribunal. Temporary workers and travellers should particularly note that if you fail to give the contractually defined period of notice of resignation, your employer is legally entitled to withhold wages equivalent to that period.

Work Practices

Different industries have different codes of practice, and you should be made aware of these by your employer at your interview or when you commence work. Most industries which expose their employees to physical safety hazards require that appropriate safety gear be worn, and this will generally be supplied by the employer. Almost all workplaces, including many restaurants, are now smoke-free, and smokers are expected to take their 'smokoes' outside the building. Health and safety regulations are rigorously upheld in the workplace, and most offices and sites will appoint a member of staff as its 'H and S' representative. This representative will make sure that regulations are not breached by any management practice and that any new legislation is promptly enforced. Australian offices are generally far less authoritarian than British ones, especially in the corporate and public sectors. The dress code is likely to be more casual, and employer and employee are expected to be on first name terms, regardless of the extent of their difference in status.

Women in Work

Discrimination on the basis of gender is illegal in Australia and equal pay for women has been an accepted basic right for decades. Nonetheless, women in Australia, like their counterparts throughout western industrialised nations are still behind in the wages stakes, and their participation at the highest levels of management and industry is still low. With girls now easily outstripping boys in educational achievement, and with the gender balance tipping in favour of women in many university courses (women now outnumber men in medicine, for example), it is likely that this situation will change in coming years. Currently, a number of incentive schemes, such as WISE (Women in Science and Engineering), are in place to encourage women into male dominated professions, and some public employers, particularly in the tertiary sector, operate positive discrimination policies to draw highly qualified women back into the workforce after childrearing. A greater proportion of female employees work part-time – 45% of females compared to 14% of men. The retail trades and health and community services are the largest employers of females, employing about 17% of the total female workforce. Women professionals outnumber men and more women than men work in intermediate clerical, sales and service work. 55% of females employed in Australia work on a full-time basis.

Women, in general, seek more flexible employment opportunities and are more likely to be found in part-time or freelance work. They are also likely to seek shorter hours, with statistics showing that single mothers work around 12 hours per week fewer than men with similar family responsibilities. In income terms, men continue to receive higher average earnings than women within the same occupation group. For example, women managers and administrators are likely to receive about 85% of a man's average weekly total earnings employed in the same profession. For tradespeople, women's earnings average out to be around 70% of men's.

Maternity Benefits, Parental Leave and Employment Rights

Maternity Benefits. Australia, along with New Zealand and the United States, is one of the few industrialised nations in which the state does not pay maternity leave benefits. Government sector employees are entitled to three months paid leave, however, few women employed in the private sector receive paid maternity leave. All women are entitled to unpaid maternity leave of not more than 52 weeks, taken either during or after their pregnancy. On the expiry of the leave, the employee is entitled to return to her previous position or an equivalent, if that position no longer exists. All new mothers who are legal residents of Australia are entitled to receive the Maternity Allowance, a one-off lump sum payment of $3,042 made by Centrelink. In cases of multiple birth, the Maternity Allowance payment is paid for each child born (including still-births). In addition, Centrelink offers an incentive payment for immunisation called the Maternity Immunisation Allowance. This allowance is designed to combat falling levels of immunisation and provides parents with a lump sum of $213.60 on presentation of proof of full immunisation in their 18-month-old child.

Paternity and Adoptive Leave. All Australian workers, and not just mothers, are entitled to parental leave, which in addition to maternity leave also comprises paternity and adoptive leave. Paternity leave may be taken in conjunction with the birth of a child to a spouse or *de facto* partner, while adoptive leave may be taken in conjunction with the adoption of a child under the age of five years. For both types of leave, 10 weeks notice of intention must be given to the employer. Any employee who has completed at least 12 months continuous service, whether full or part time (but not casual), is eligible for parental leave, however, paternity leave cannot be taken simultaneously with maternity leave for the same child. Employees are entitled to take up to 52 weeks parental leave, which must be completed before the child's first birthday (or the first anniversary of an adoption). You cannot be dismissed for taking parental leave and your application for it cannot be legally refused by your employer. On your return to work, you are entitled to your old job back or, if it no longer exists, to one at an equivalent level, and your seniority and accumulated leave must be preserved in your absence.

Employment Rights. All employees have a basic right to a fair and reasonable working environment and conditions. Reasonable working conditions include the right to personal and physical safety. If you suffer injury at work due to your employer's negligence or unsatisfactory working conditions, you have the right to claim worker's compensation for any injury, discomfort, and loss of earnings you may incur as a result of that injury. Sexual harassment is also considered to be a fundamental denial of the right to a fair and reasonable working environment, and employers have been taken to court because they have allowed offensive or pornographic posters and pictures to be displayed in common staff areas. Most public employers and many larger corporate ones will have a sexual harassment officer on their staff who will provide confidential advice and liaison in the case of complaints.

As an employee, you have the right to a fair dismissal, and each trade and industry has its own rules regarding acceptable practice. It is illegal to breach the contractually stated dismissal procedure, and if you believe that you have been treated unfairly, you can take your employer to an industrial tribunal for unfair or constructive dismissal.

Discrimination in the workplace (or, indeed, anywhere) on the grounds of ethnic origin, gender, religious or political beliefs, or nationality is against the law, and if you have reason to believe that you are experiencing discrimination of any kind, you should contact your local Department of Education, Science and Training (DEST) office for advice on how to pursue a complaint.

Useful Addresses

The Australian Council of Trade Unions (ACTU): Represents 1.9 million workers and provides information on legislated employment rights at www.actu.asn.au.
Commonwealth Department of Education, Science and Training (DEST): Have an

informative website at www.dest.gov.au.

Department of Employment and Workplace Relations www.dewrsb.gov.au. The Department of Employment and Workplace Relations aims to support an efficient and equitable labour market that links people to jobs and promotes the transition from welfare to work, and fair and flexible workplace relations at the enterprise level.

Office of Small Business: Department of Industry, Tourism and Resources, Federal Awards; ☎02-6121 6000; www.industry.gov.au.

Social Security and Unemployment Benefits

Australia has a full cradle to grave state welfare system which has, in recent years, been significantly streamlined. Social security benefits, including unemployment and family benefits, are not, however, available to temporary residents, and migrants are also ineligible to claim any kind of benefit until they have been resident in Australia for a full two years. The two-year 'no-claim' period was introduced in 1997 by the government following public concern that migrants were taking advantage of Australia's social security system; previously, new settlers could start claiming benefits within 26 weeks of arrival. The Department of Family and Community Services (faCS) and Centrelink provides detailed information on all its available benefits, including pay rates (which are regularly updated), current policy, and discussion papers, on its website at www.facs.gov.au. Within Australia, there is a Centrelink office in each capital city and in most major regional centres, where advisors will provide current information and discuss your eligibility for benefits.

Pensions

Australia is currently raising the retirement age for women to bring it in line with the male retirement age of 65 years. Currently, women can receive the pension from age 60, and this is being phased upwards in six-monthly intervals, to bring it to the point where women born after 1 January 1949 will not be eligible for the pension until age 65. The pension is paid fortnightly at a maximum rate of $470.70 per fortnight for a single person and $393.00 each per fortnight for a married couple. In addition, a pharmaceutical allowance of $5.80 per fortnight may also be payable. To be eligible for an Australian pension, you must have been resident in Australia for at least 10 years, of which five of those years must have been in a single extended period. Australian age pensions are subject to income and assets tests and various other benefits and allowances may be claimable depending on circumstance.

UK Pensions in Australia

If you currently receive a pension paid by the UK government, it will be frozen from the time you leave Britain, so that you will no longer be eligible for any pension rate increases awarded after your departure from Britain. You will, however, be entitled to full payment of your current pension once you arrive in Australia, and this can be arranged through the Department for Work and Pensions in Britain prior to your departure.

If you are a UK migrant with permanent residency and reach pensionable age in Australia, you should make arrangements with the Department for Work and Pensions in Britain in order to claim your UK pension entitlement, together with your Australian pension if you are eligible for the latter. As with retirees, your UK pension will be frozen at the rate current when you reach pensionable age and you will not receive any pension rate increases awarded in the UK.

Other retirement and pension issues are discussed more fully in the *Retirement* chapter.

SHORT-TERM EMPLOYMENT

There are many opportunities in Australia for short-term and casual employment. The Australian government has never felt it necessary to restrict drastically its working holiday-maker scheme, even in times of economic downturn, as it is clear that travellers are prepared to take on the kind of temporary jobs that locals seeking a career or job security shun. Some industries, especially in the primary sector, rely on itinerant casual workers to fill their labour needs, and the adventurous should find plenty of scope for some once-in-a-lifetime employment experiences.

Agriculture

Primary industry is the backbone of the Australian economy and there is a great variety of work available on farms and stations all year round. These opportunities are not just limited to working the land: mechanics, builders, tractor drivers, welders, domestics, cooks, and teachers are all needed. Horse riding skills or an HGV licence will improve your chances of finding work. If you have a farming background, preferably with experience in cereal crops, you will find it easy to get seasonal farm work, especially in heavy tractor soil tillage, drilling, single pass seeding, and combine harvesting. Pay varies between a flat rate of $90-$120 per day, or $9-$12 per hour before tax. You are likely to have to work between 50 and 80 hours per week, seven days a week, particularly during seeding.

Fruit farmers rely quite heavily on casual labour at harvest time and this kind of work is ideal for travellers as it is of brief duration and offers the opportunity to 'follow the crops' from region to region. The summer months, from October to April, are the prime time for harvest work around Australia. The work can be hard, but once you become proficient you can expect to earn around $300 per week after tax.

TABLE 13	HARVEST WORK OPPORTUNITIES
Month	**Crop**
Western Australia	
Feb-Mar	Grapes
Mar-May	Apples, pears
Mar-Jun	Crayfish
Mar-Jun	Oats, wheat, barley
Mar-Oct	Prawns, scallops

May-Sep	Squash, rockmelon
Apr-Nov	Melons
Jun-Dec	Peppers, tomatoes
Jul-Aug	Bananas
Jul-Dec	Wildflowers
Oct-Jan	Mangoes

Victoria

Jan-Apr	Pears, peaches, apples, tomatoes, tobacco
Feb-Mar	Grapes
Sep-Nov	Asparagus
Oct-Dec	Strawberries
Nov-Feb	Cherries, berries
Nov-Dec	Tomato weeding

New South Wales

Jan-Mar	Stone fruit, grapes, pears, prunes
Feb-Apr	Apples
Mar-Jun	Cotton picking
Sep-Dec	Asparagus
Sep-Apr	Oranges
Nov-Dec	Cherries
Nov-Apr	Oranges
Dec-Jan	Onions
Dec-Mar	Stone fruit
Dec-Apr	Blueberries

Queensland

Feb-Mar	Pears, apples
Feb-Apr	Rock melon, ginger
Mar-Dec	Wide range of vegetables
Apr-Jun	Citrus fruit
Apr-Nov	Beans
Apr-Dec	Tomatoes
May-Oct	Broccoli
May-Dec	Sugar cane
Jul-Sep	Ginger
Jul-Dec	Onions
Sep-Nov	Tobacco
Nov-Jan	Plums, cotton, peaches

South Australia

Jan-Mar	Dried fruits
Feb-Apr	Apples, pears, grapes, peaches
Feb-Aug	Brussels sprouts
Jun-Sep	Pruning
Sep-Jan	Oranges (juicing and packing)
Oct-Feb	Strawberries
Dec-Feb	Apricots

Tasmania	
Mar-May	Apples
Dec-Jan	Soft fruit
Feb-Apr	Grapes
Mar-Apr	Hops
Jan-Feb	Scallop splitting

Almost all harvest work is advertised through the Australian Job Network (AJN), and now that all Centrelink offices (under whom the Australian Job Network operates) are linked by the Internet, it is no longer necessary to go to the appropriate regional office to find out what work is available. Instead, you can visit the Centrelink office in the city or town where you are currently located and, using the computer terminal and interactive map, find out what opportunities are available throughout Australia. Alternatively you can search the online database (www.jobsearch.gov.au). Once you have found the kind of work you want, in an area that interests you, you will need to travel to that region to be interviewed by the local AJN officer, however, the online service does make co-ordinating your work and travel much easier.

If you intend to do harvest work, you will need to be fit and healthy, and capable of working long hours in hot, dry and dusty conditions. There is usually minimal accommodation available during harvest, however, most orchards have on-site camping facilities if you have your own tent or caravan. Farms can be located as much as 62 miles (100 km) from the nearest town, so this kind of work is most practical if you have your own transport. For more on this type of work consult the book *Workabout Australia* (available from www.vacationwork.co.uk).

Aquaculture

Aquaculture is a rapidly growing area of primary industry in Australia, and fishing work is available in many coastal areas. Crayfish, prawns, scallops, and abalone are all harvested according to very strict seasonal regulations, and work in these areas can be very highly paid. Many fishing trawlers, especially those with processing facilities, also take on workers. However, this kind of work often requires being at sea for extended periods and is not for the faint-hearted. The seas around Australia can be perilous.

Mining

Working in the mining industry in Australia can be both challenging and very rewarding financially. There is plenty of work available for unskilled labourers, and the best way to find such work is usually to visit the personnel offices of large mining companies at their city headquarters. If you strike lucky, you could find yourself on a plane within a few hours – finding mining work really is about being in the right place at the right time. There are mines and related mining activities all over Australia, from giant iron-ore projects in the northwest to small family-run gold and precious stone prospecting ventures in the south. Miners usually work a seven-day week, often from dawn to dusk, and sometimes for as many as six weeks straight. The pay is likely to be more than $1,400 per week, and there is very little to spend it on on-site. If you work above the 26th parallel (the Tropic of Capricorn), you are entitled to extra pay, known as the 'tropical loading' or 'remote area allowance'. Most mining companies are now prepared to employ women on-site, and indeed many prefer to do so, as women are considered to respond less aggressively to the pressure-cooker atmosphere of isolated mine sites.

Nursing

There is a huge demand for supply nurses in Australia, especially during the Australian autumn and winter months from April to December, and a shortage in every State. Specialist nurses, particularly A&E, ICU and psychiatric, are always needed and any qualified and experienced nurse is likely to have no difficulty in obtaining work from a nursing agency. The Australian government helps overseas nurses to emigrate through a new 'fast-track' migration scheme. This applies particularly to those wishing to work in rural and remote areas. Australia recognises overseas qualifications of nurses from the UK, USA, Canada, New Zealand, and Singapore but nurses from non-English-speaking countries must complete the bridging course and 80 hours practical training.

Registering with the Nurses' Registration Board. To work as a nurse in Australia, even on a temporary basis, you will need to be registered with the Nurses' Registration Board of the state in which you hope to work, and many agencies will help you with this procedure. New South Wales is the least expensive state to register in – the fee is currently $50 for one year. Before you leave home you should apply for your Authority to Practice which will prevent any delays on arrival.

Bigger agencies will provide you with a pager so that you are not tied to the telephone – an important bonus for those who have better things to do. Information on nursing in Australia is provided by the Australian Nursing and Midwifery Council (ANMC, First Floor, 20 Challis Street, Dickson, ACT 2602; Postal Address: PO Box 873, Dickson, ACT 2602; ☎02-6257 7960; fax 02-6257 7955; e-mail anmc@anmc.org.au; www.anmc.org.au). ANMC also has a list of all Nurses' Registration Boards in Australia.

Useful Addresses

Heartbeat Nurses: 12 Pitt Street, Parramatta, Sydney, NSW 2150; ☎02-9891 2255; fax 02-9806 9731; www.heartbeatnursing.com.au. Agency that supplies all leading public and private hospitals in Sydney; also jobs in country and interstate hospitals. Day or three-month contracts, Nurse Work and Travel Programmes around Australia.

Nurseworldwide: Level 3, 143 York Street, Sydney, NSW 2000; ☎02-9286 2800; fax 02-9286 2888; e-mail nww_syd@nurseworldwide.com.au; www.nurse-worldwide.com.au; and 28 South Molton Street, London W1K 5RD; ☎0845 450 0950; fax 0845 450 0951. A specialist recruitment agency established in 1986. Provides comprehensive assistance package including help with registration, visa sponsorship (if required), accommodation and 'meet and greet' at main airports.

Queensland Health: Nursing Career Advisor, GPO Box 48, Brisbane, QLD 4001; ☎07-3234 1544; fax 07-3234 0062; www.thinknursing.com. A Government department involved in all areas of health care across Queensland. For job opportunities for registered nurses please see the above website.

TEFL

Australia has a flourishing TEFL market which caters mainly to Southeast Asian students. There are large English language schools in every capital city, all of which require casual, short- and long-term teachers for their various courses. To teach English as a Foreign Language in Australia you will need a recognised TEFL qualification and some prior teaching experience, and many people on working holiday visas now choose to take an appropriate course before they leave home in order to have this remunerative option on their travel. Casual TEFL teachers can expect to earn between $15 and $25 per hour. Perth, Sydney and the Gold Coast have the largest and most active TEFL sectors.

Au Pair

Au pair work is another standby for working holiday-makers, and there is considerable work available for those with experience and good references. Once confined almost entirely to remote rural families who needed the services of a child-minder cum governess, changing work patterns have led more and more urban families to employ full- or part-time nannies or au pairs. Australian families generally will *not* expect anyone employed as a childminder to undertake household duties other than those required for the immediate well-being of their children. Extra work, such as ironing, should be specified by the employer in advance and agreed to by you, and you can negotiate extra pay for these additional duties.

Male Au Pairs: Australian anti-discrimination laws do permit employers to specify the gender of a childminder; many families prefer to employ women to care for their children, and male applicants can be legally rejected. However, some families might actually prefer a male au pair, especially if the children are boys and like playing sports. There are numerous domestic and specialist au pair agencies supplying staff in this field. References will be checked thoroughly and holding a driving licence will be an asset.

Tourism and Hospitality

Australia's tourist industry is one of the country's largest employers - more than 500,000 are employed across the nation - and there are a wide variety of jobs available. Hotels require childminders, porters and kitchenhands, in addition to more qualified and experienced employees such as chefs, waiters, and bar staff. A silver service or bar attendant qualification acquired before you leave home will equip you to find well paid work in every city.

Croupiers are required by casinos (there are one or two very large ones in most states, but no Las Vegas-style gambling mecca) and this kind of work is very highly paid; you will, however, require training and experience to be considered.

There is work available for instructor level PADI-qualified divers at the major dive spots around the coast, especially on the Great Barrier Reef and off Exmouth, in northwest WA. Divers should note that PADI is the most common certification system in Australia; BSAC-qualified divers will find it easier to find work if they convert their qualifications before travelling.

Any working holiday-makers already very experienced in the Australian outback may find work as guides in some of the national parks, particularly Kakadu, and many coach companies also take on tour leaders and coach drivers with an appropriate licence and experience. Queensland offers the greatest opportunities in terms of resort work, however, most jobs are found by word of mouth: if you hope to work, say, on the Gold Coast, the most likely way of picking up work is to go there and ask around. The Australian Job Network, once again, is the best first port of call for work in the tourism and hospitality sector.

Office Work, Telemarketing and Sales

Office temps are particularly in demand during the Australian summer months and over major holiday periods such as Christmas and Easter. Most commonly, short-term work is available in secretarial, clerical, word-processing and data entry positions, all of which require some degree of skill and previous experience. The banking, finance, and stockbroking industries always require temps, especially during peak periods such as the end of the financial year (30 June). Unskilled casual work is often also available at this time when large supermarkets and department stores do their annual stocktake. There are innumerable employment agencies supplying both general and specialist short-term staff, and these are listed in the *Yellow Pages*. The Australian Job Network is generally less fruitful as a source of this kind of work, although temporary government and public sector positions will be advertised there.

Telemarketing does not appeal to everyone, but can be financially rewarding if you are successful. Turnover is unusually high in this industry, and telemarketing firms have no hesitation in employing backpackers as it is rare for any staff, whether itinerant or not, to stay the pace for more than a few weeks. Telemarketing jobs are usually advertised in the employment classifieds of local and major city newspapers.

Job seekers are advised to avoid sales jobs offering commission-only remuneration, and especially those which advertise 'travellers welcome'. In most cases, such jobs offer one-way transport to a remote location, from which you will be required to make enough sales to fund your own way back to civilisation.

Voluntary Work

Countless charitable organisations throughout Australia rely on volunteers to help run their many aid, development and conservation programmes. Becoming involved in such enterprises offers the working holiday-maker an opportunity to experience a different side of Australian life while gaining new skills and contributing to a worthwhile cause. If you are interested in volunteering in any capacity, contact the Charities' Commission in your state (listed under Government Organisations in the White Pages) who will be able to supply you with a list of all the charities registered with them. Visitors to Australia who are interested in the country's unique landscape are often particularly attracted to conservation work, and *Conservation Volunteers Australia* (National Head Office, PO Box 423, Ballarat, VIC 3353; ☎03-5330 2600; fax 03-5330 2292; e-mail info@conservationvolun teers.com.au; www.conservationvolunteers.com.au), can help with placements in this field. Volunteers contribute $30 per day to cover accommodation, meals, and projected travel expenses.

Tax Notes for Casual Workers

Working holiday-makers pay tax on their earnings like any other Australian employee. However, as you will only be working for a short period it is likely that your earnings will fall below the tax threshold and that you will, therefore, be eligible for a tax refund at the end of your visit. Everyone who works in Australia must have a 'tax file number', and you will need to apply for one as soon as you start work or, preferably, even sooner. The tax file number can take up to six weeks to be issued, and until you receive your number and are able to pass it on to your employer, you will be taxed at the maximum rate of 49%. Application forms for a tax file number are available from all Centrelink and tax offices. Non-residents with a tax file number pay tax at a rate of 29 cents in the dollar (29% of all earnings up to $450 per week).

Before you leave Australia, you should lodge a tax return (also available from the Centrelink offices, and inside the 'Tax Pack'). Every employer for whom you have worked should have supplied you with a 'payment summary' on leaving; you will need to keep these and attach them to your tax return as proof of your total earnings. The taxation office will assess your return, usually within a couple of weeks of lodgement, and a refund cheque (if applicable) will be forwarded to your nominated address, either in Australia or overseas.

PERMANENT WORK

Agriculture and Food Processing

It is generally acknowledged that Australia got rich off the sheep's back, and today agriculture is still the backbone of the Australian economy. The traditional export products of wheat and wool, however, have long since ceded prominence to other sectors, including fisheries and viticulture, and exotic produce such as native bush meats and wildflowers.

The Australian agricultural sector is relatively stable at present, with grain and livestock farmers in a better market position than cotton and sugar producers. Wheat production is currently forecast at 21.7 million tons and live cattle exports have continued to increase. The wool industry is experiencing a rise in profitability due to the decline in sheep numbers and the increasing cost of competing fabrics. Wine is one of Australia's strongest regional export industries earning about $1.5 billion a year in domestic sales and $1.2 billion in export sales. The industry is growing rapidly with the building of new plants and expansion of existing ones. Both cotton and sugar exports remain at high levels and both industries are expected to experience steady increases in production.

The food, beverage and tobacco processing industry is Australia's largest manufacturing sector and accounts for around 20% of Australian manufacturing. It is expected to experience continued growth of around 10% per annum. It is projected that employment growth areas in this industry will shift away from factory processing and into sales, research, development and marketing. This trend reflects both a move away from convenience foods by consumers towards high quality fresh produce, as well as a competitive imported food market.

Automotive

Australia has a strong automotive industry with Ford, Holden, Mitsubishi and Toyota all producing cars in Australian factories. There are also more than 200 component, tooling, design and engineering firms. The industry is based largely in South Australia and Victoria with a small share of activity in New South Wales. In total, the automotive industry employs more than 63,000 people. Car sales are currently buoyant, reflecting the general economic situation in Australia, and sales of locally produced cars are strong as luxury taxes make imported cars expensive. All automotive manufacturers are investing heavily in robot technology, so that the employment outlook for factory floor workers is poor, while that for people skilled in computer technology is good. Exports of automotive products (the majority going to the Middle East, New Zealand, the USA, Canada, Mexico and South Korea) have grown consistently. In 2003, total automotive vehicle exports to all markets totalled about $3 billion. For automotive components, exports totalled $1,738 million. The automotive industry is experiencing a skill shortage and employment prospects in this industry are good.

Executive Employment

Executive employment prospects are generally good, particularly with smaller companies. After a period of rationalisation business has stabilised and most firms are experiencing reasonable growth. DEWR assess the employment outlook for generalist managers and administrators as average in both the short- and long-term, while those with specialist skills have above average prospects. Marketing personnel, sales reps, accountants, finance professionals and management all have good job prospects in Australia.

Finance and Property

The property and business services industry has seen a decline as both residential and non-dwelling building projects turn down sharply. Non-dwelling building has seen a downturn primarily due to the completion of a number of major projects and because of oversupply in some regions.

Finance has seen a small decrease in the number of jobs available although average weekly earnings remain very high in this sector, and are second only to mining. However, the downturn of the financial sector globally has seen a job cuts and cutbacks in banks and financial institutions. There is at present a lack of accountants in most States. Qualified graduates, with degrees in either business or finance, or with experience in a related field are most likely to succeed in finding work in this sector.

Information Technology

Information technology is a major growth sector in the Australian economy and is projected to continue to expand through 2005. Australia has a vigorous, high-tech industry, particularly in the fields of information and medical technologies. Australians are keen to maintain a leading technological edge and are continually updating their technology. Twenty international IT firms have their regional headquarters in Australia and this is in many ways due to the sophistication of the Australian IT market; as well as the fact that Australia has the second highest number of computer owners, and one of the largest number of Internet users, in the world. Job prospects are strong for well-qualified and experienced professionals, and there is a particular need for people with Powerbuilder, Linux, Unis, and SAP skills among others. The government is keen to encourage the IT sector, particularly in areas where application of new technology will enhance Australia's competitiveness in the export market.

Medical

Medical practitioners hoping to work in Australia will need to prove that there are no Australian doctors qualified to do the same job. Overseas-qualified doctors already granted permission to work in Australia are required to pass stringent registration examinations before they are permitted to practice. In 2005-2005 there were an extra 1,000 places for doctors.

Both Registered nurses and Nurse educators and researchers are in demand throughout Australia, particularly those qualified in specialist fields such as accident and emergency, intensive care, and psychiatry. You will need to have your qualifications ratified by the Nurses Registration Board in the state in which you live and then register with this Board before you are able to apply for work.

Health therapists, such as physiotherapists, occupational therapists and speech therapists, also need to have their qualifications approved by Australian authorities before practising in Australia. In some cases, further study may be necessary before your registration can be accepted. There is currently an identified shortage of dentists, physiotherapists, sonographers, midwives, radiographers and nurse managers in Australia.

Petrochemicals

There has been massive investment in oil and gas exploration, particularly in the North West Shelf Natural Gas Project off the coast of Western Australia and a record number of oil and gas discoveries were made in Australia in 2000. Engineers of all types are in demand in this industry. Almost 90% of the petroleum products consumed in Australia are produced by Australian refineries. As a result, it makes a major contribution to national welfare in terms of output, employment, exports, tax revenue and energy self-sufficiency. There are 12 major players in the oil and gas exploration and production industries in Australia: Apache, BHP Billiton, BP, ChevronTexaco, ExxonMobil, Magellan, Nexen, OMV, EnCana, Santos, Shell and Woodside.

Retailing

The retail sector employs the largest number of employees in the Australian economy at around 15%. The health of the retail industry in Australia has seasonal highs and lows; the Australian Retailers Association estimated that in the six weeks leading up to Christmas 2004 Australians spent around $34 billion, a 7% increase on the previous year. Employment prospects in both retail sales and management are good. DEWR assesses both the short- and long-term outlook for employment in retail management as sound and in retail sales as good.

Steel and Non-ferrous Metals

Australia is one of the world's largest exporters of iron ore, although its steel-processing sector is much less developed. Mining is a major employment sector, and is the highest paid industry in the country, with average weekly earning in excess of $1,000 per week. Mining continues to employ large numbers and short- and long-term employment prospects are sound in professional, skilled, and semi-skilled occupations. The Australian mining industry is one of the most highly productive in the world and is a significant investor in capital equipment. British equipment suppliers enjoy a large share of the underground black coal mining market. Australia's aluminium industry is one of the major building blocks of Australia's economy and produces nearly 40% of world bauxite, and almost 30% of world alumina, making it the world's largest producer of both. The Stanwell Magnesium Project will be the world's largest magnesium plant, with 400 jobs once the plant is running. Metal production at the Australian Magnesium Corporation plant commenced in October 2004 when the plant was commissioned. The plant will be fully operational in 2005-2006.

Australia is also rich in other natural resources including manganese, uranium, diamonds, zirconite, mineral sands, lead, zinc, copper, gold, silver, alumina and bauxite. These mining industries operate on a large scale across the country and are all significant employers of skilled and unskilled labour.

Teaching

To teach in Australia, you will be required to be four-year-qualified, that is, you must hold either a bachelor's degree plus a one year Graduate Diploma of Education (equivalent to a PGCE), or a four-year Bachelor of Education. Teachers in both the state and private education sector who are not qualified at this level are now required to upgrade their qualifications by means of external study and summer schools. Primary school teachers require a specialist degree in primary education while secondary school teachers normally teach in a subject area related to their degree major. Whereas once private schools were prepared to employ non teacher-trained graduates, this is now extremely rare and teachers arriving from overseas with experience but no qualification are unlikely to find work in either the state or private sector. Teaching, tutoring and lecturing posts in the tertiary sector are very oversubscribed and obtaining a position is highly competitive.

Education is the responsibility of the state government, and to obtain work as a teacher you will need to apply to the Ministry of Education in your state. Some states require new teachers on the permanent register to work for a period in a remote rural location before offering a choice of more convenient schools. If you are unable to do this, you may have to undertake work on a temporary or casual basis for some years before being offered permanency. Employment prospects for Primary School teachers are expected to remain low and employment has fallen slightly over the past five years. Employment of Secondary School Teachers has remained steady, while job prospects for music, dance and other extra-systemic teachers are average. Employment in this area has fallen over the last five years. Special Education teachers have good prospects of finding employment and number employed in this sector have risen in the past five years, however, job turnover for Special Education teachers remains low.

REGIONAL EMPLOYMENT GUIDE

This section summarises the employment opportunities and economic strengths of each state and territory, and should be read in conjunction with the analysis contained in the *Regional Guide* in *General Introduction*.

WESTERN AUSTRALIA

Main City: Perth (pop 1.41 million).
Other major cities/towns: Fremantle (pop 25,000), Bunbury (pop 30,786).
Regions: Coral Coast, Outback, North West, South West.
Regional Newspapers: *The West Australian, Western Australian Business News,* and *Sunday Times.*
Chamber of Commerce: Chamber of Commerce and Industry, 180 Hay Street, East Perth, WA 6004; ☎ 08-9365 7555; fax 08-9365 7550; e-mail advice@cciwa.com.au; www.cciwa.com.au.
Major Companies: Griffin Group, Western Australia Meat Exports, MG Kailis Group, Wesfarmers, and Woodside Petroleum.

Employment Prospects: Western Australia is a major exporter of a wide range of commodities worldwide and provides about 29% of Australia's exports. The state has a highly educated workforce of 850,000 and manufacturing and services are the state's fastest growing sectors of industry. The state government has identified and is promoting a group of key strategic industries in order to reduce dependence on raw materials export. These strategic industries include: building and construction, defence and aerospace, education and training services, health and medical services, information technology and telecommunications, marine industries, mining equipment and services, oil and gas equipment and services, processed foods and wine, and professional services. Asian markets play a significant role in Western Australian industry as state production is heavily export-focused. WA is also a global supplier of minerals and energy, with production totalling $27.9 billion in the period 2002-2003; in the same period oil, gas and liquefied natural gas (LNG), comprised 37.6% of output and iron ore was the state's largest mineral export at $5.2 billion. WA produces 40% of the world's diamonds; 44% of its zircon; 22% of its alumina; 13% of its iron ore and 9% of its gold, nickel and LNG.

WA has one of the world's largest and most technologically advanced mining sectors, and mineral and energy production is forecast to experience continued growth. Bulk commodity export is under some pressure, however, as a decreasing international scarcity of non-reproducible natural resources has made the market highly competitive. Reforms have been implemented within the industry to make it more competitive and these have included a decline in traditional award-type employment which has been replaced by staff-only operations. There is likely to be a sharp increase in contracting-out in the mining industry.

Western Australia has the world's largest zirconia plant. ALCOA, Worsley Alumina, and Dampier Salt are the three major investors in mineral extraction and processing, and between them employ around 4,000 people. Western Australia's goldfields are based inland around Kalgoorlie, 372 miles (600 km) east of Perth, and this area is experiencing renewed rapid growth after a period of recession. Only the diamond industry is expected to experience any decline in the short-term, with implications for the economic strength of the Kimberley region. The oil and gas industry is a major contributor to the state's economy ($9.7 billion in 2003) and is centred on the North West Shelf, which contains one of the world's largest deposits of natural gas. Oil and gas exploration is ongoing in Western Australia, and further major finds are expected. Since 1994, numerous international companies associated with the petroleum industry, including Western Geophysical, Nopec, Drillex, WS Atkins, ESD Simulators, and Global Drilling, have all established Southeast Asian regional headquarters in Perth. Engineers, metallurgists, and other mineral extraction industry professionals are in demand in Western Australia, and employment prospects in both the short and long-term are good. More than 90% of Australia's oil and gas resources are located off Western Australia. A steady increase has been forecast for the production of gas.

Western Australia has the largest marine industry in Australia. It has an international reputation for building quality ships and infrastructure for offshore oil and gas production and for providing a wide range of marine services. The state supplies about 20% of the world's lightweight high-speed ferries. A marine industry technology park is currently being developed at Lake Coogee. A State Government initiative, it aims to provide land and opportunities for marine-related high technology industries, such as ship design, maritime training and testing of naval defence systems.

Some 400 companies work in the IT and telecommunications industry manufacturing, developing and wholesaling equipment, software and services for information processing, multimedia or communications. Most of these companies are located in Perth.

There are around 3,000 different manufacturers in Western Australia. Food processing, base metal processing, wine production, and pharmaceuticals have experienced strong growth, with continued expansion forecast. The Government recognises the importance of the industry to the economy of the state and offers programs designed to assist companies in the food industry. Agriculture is increasingly focused on niche markets, such as emu, kangaroo, ostrich, deer and genetically modified animals; and on value-added crops, such as specialised noodle wheat. The raw grains market (wheat, oats, and barley) has a positive medium-term outlook. In forestry, there has been rapid expansion in eucalypt plantations in the south west of the state. The fisheries industry is experiencing rapid growth, hampered only by the restrictions of wild harvesting. Mariculture (sea-based) and aquaculture (land-based) fish production is therefore being encouraged, and these industries have a strong economic outlook. Western Australia's major success in aquaculture has been the culture of pearl oysters. Based in the Kimberleys, in the far north of the state, the industry represents Australia's largest and most successful aquaculture venture, producing quality pearls worth around $150 million a year. WA is also the world's largest exporter of live animals and a major exporter of skins and hides.

The services sector of the Western Australian economy currently accounts for more than 70% of the state's GDP. The financial sector has expanded rapidly since deregulation in the 1980s and there are now more than 20 banking groups represented in the state. WA exports consultancy services in mining, engineering, forestry, agriculture and conservation, and the state's highly regarded medical research and hospital facilities have made Perth a centre for Australia's 'medical tourism' industry. The service sector's biggest growth area is currently tourism.

In 2002-2003, Western Australia's gross state product (GSP) totalled $82.4 billion and accounted for 11% percent of the national economy, which grew by 7.5% - its strongest growth in more than a decade. Strong business investment has lifted Western Australia's economic growth above the national average for each of the past three years. Perth has become a favoured location for international companies choosing a regional base for Southeast Asia, especially in industries servicing the oil and gas sectors. Retail trade, property and business services, health and community services, manufacturing and construction employ nearly half of the workforce and employment rates in these industries continue to grow.

Temporary. Harvest work is available throughout the year, mainly in the southwest of the state. The grain harvest which takes place in the summer months in the wheatbelt and south-west regions is a traditional source of short-term country employment.Casual work in the fishing industry around Carnarvon is available between March and October. General agricultural labouring can usually be found on cattle stations, and on sheep stations, particularly at shearing time. The hospitality industry always needs short-term employees, with work available year-round in Perth and during the tourist season in other major centres (May to September in Broome, and the summer months in other areas). Unskilled mine work is relatively easy to find in the northwest and can be highly paid. In Perth, all the usual temporary employment opportunities, including office work, teaching and nursing, are readily available.

NORTHERN TERRITORY

Main City: Darwin (pop 107,000).
Other major cities/towns: Alice Springs (pop 27,640).
Regions: Top End, East Arnhem, Katherine, Barkly, and Central.
Regional Newspapers: *Northern Territory News.*
Chamber of Commerce: Chamber of Commerce and Industry, Confederation House, 1/2 Shepherd Street, Darwin, NT 0800; ☎08-8936 3100; fax 08-8981 1405; www.ntcci.com.au.
Major Companies: Bechtel.

Employment Prospects. The Northern Territory has a population of just 199,900, about 1% of the Australian total and produces 14% of the nation's exports. The Northern Territory is rich in natural resources, which are being developed by the private sector with the support of the state Government, which is undertaking a $16 million geophysical survey of the Territory. This data is being produced mainly for mineral and hydrocarbon exploration companies. Unemployment in the state is currently around 5.7%. Gross State Product (GSP) growth for 2002 to 2006 is estimated at 7%, double the national rate and the NT is set to lead the country in economic growth over the next five years by an estimated 50%.

The Northern Territory continues to experience economic growth and has benefited from an increase in private capital expenditure in mining, capital investment and tourism. Advertised job vacancies are increasing steadily in the Territory and are generally stronger in the dry season, from May to October.

The mining industry is the Northern Territory's biggest earner, and is the state's major employer. There are 14 operating mines, and minerals, including alumina, manganese, gold, bauxite and uranium, dominate the territory's overseas exports. Zinc, lead and silver are mined at Woodcutters mine, McArthur River, and uranium is mined at Alligator River. Gold mines are located in the Adelaide River/Pine Creek region, the Tanami Desert and at Tennant Creek. Oil and gas production occurs onshore at Mereenie and Palm Valley in the Amadeus Basin, and offshore on the Jabiru and Challis fields in the Timor Sea. Natural gas production for export is being developed on the Petrel and Tern gas fields in the Bonaparte Gulf. Oil and gas account for approximately 35% of the state's exports.

In the East Arnhem region of the Northern Territory, which comprises the eastern half of Arnhem Land and Groote Eylandt in the Gulf of Carpentaria, bauxite and manganese are produced in two of the world's largest mines of their type. Gove Joint Venture mines bauxite on the Gove Peninsula, exporting it as alumina and aluminium hydroxide. The mine, which is managed by Nabalco, employs more than 1,000 people, of whom 260 are independent contractors. The mine is expected to be operational until 2035. Manganese is mined by the BHP subsidiary, Groote Eylandt Mining Company (GEMCO), which produces more than 10% of the world's manganese output. Mining support businesses in the region turnover around $45 million per annum. Apart from the mining industry, the East Arnhem region supports mainly small business, in particular retail and property services.

Growth industries in the Northern Territory include building and construction, and prawn fishing. More unusually, another growing industry services the need of farming, mining, and conservation sectors to harvest the 30,000 head of wild buffalo (feral cattle), which cause massive damage as they rampage across the fragile landscape. Additionally, the Northern Territory cattle industry is also booming with exports mainly to the Philippines and Indonesia.

Traditional industries are continuing to show strong growth. The tourism industry has averaged 7% growth over the last seven years. Recent tourism-related activity suggests a positive trend and continued growth is projected. Around 1.4 million tourists visit the eco-tourism region at Uluru (Ayers Rock), as well as Kakadu National Park. The Northern Territory Government is working towards developing Darwin as a transport hub between the markets of Australia and Asia and the first stage of the construction of the $100 million East Arm Port was completed in 1999. Work is underway on the second stage of this project. The $1.3 billion, 932-mile (1,500 km) Darwin to Adelaide rail link was completed in February 2004. The railway runs from Darwin in the north of Australia to Adelaide in the south.

Oil and gas deposits in the Timor Sea has led to a shift in the focus of Australia's oil industry to the north and northwest of Australia. This has meant a continuing need for an oil and gas industry infrastructure, and services including engineering, transportation and communications continue to see growth. Timor Sea gas will be brought ashore at Darwin and this will mean the construction of about 310 miles (500 km) of sub-marine pipeline and the establishment within the new East Arm Port industrial complex of a range of service and support companies to the offshore oil and gas industries.

Temporary. Most temporary jobs are provided by the tourist industry, especially during the tourist season from May to December (all year round at Alice Springs). Remote resorts have a high staff turnover and are frequently able to offer short-term employment. There is occasional station work available to those with good horse skills.

SOUTH AUSTRALIA

Main City: Adelaide (pop 1.1 million).
Other major cities/towns: Mt Gambier (pop 22,751), Whyalla (pop 21,271), Port Augusta (pop 13,194).
Regions: Barossa Valley, Eyre Peninsula, Kangaroo Island, Mid North, Murraylands, Mount Lofty, Outback and Finders Ranges, Riverland, South East, Upper Spencer Gulf, and Yorke Peninsula.
Regional Newspapers: *The Advertiser,* and *Sunday Mail.*
Chamber of Commerce: Department of Trade and Economic Development, Level 10, Terrace Towers, 178 North Terrace, Adelaide, SA 5000; ☎08-8303 2400; fax 08-8303 2410; www.southaustralia.biz.
Major Companies: BRL Hardy Wine Company, Coopers Brewery, Orlando Wyndham, BHP Billiton, BT Financial Group, Cap Gemini, EDS Australia, Malaysia Airlines, Southcorp, and The News Corporation.

Employment Prospects: South Australia's major exports are road vehicles and automotive parts and accessories, followed by wine and wheat. The state's information technology development programme aims to make the state an internationally recognised centre in the five specialist areas of software development, multimedia, spatial information, electronic services, and education. Motorola, TechSouth, AWA Defence Industries, Telstra and Tandem have already made major investments, and SA hopes to attract more key investors. The global communications giant, Motorola, has established its Australian Software Development Centre in Adelaide and Technology Park in Adelaide is home to more than 35 technology organisations including British Aerospace Australia, Computer Science Corporation, and Celsiustech. There are a further six research centres, including the Signal Processing Research Institute, which undertakes research in mobile and defence communications. The electronics sector provides employment for nearly 10,000 scientists, engineers, technicians, production and support personnel and local industry output is currently $1.8 billion and growing at 14% per annum.

The motor vehicle sector is South Australia's largest single industry and is the state's largest employer, with Mitsubishi Motors Australia and Holden together employing more than 13,000 people. Of the 400,000 cars made in Australia in 2004, about 45% were manufactured in South Australia. The two major overseas markets for cars are the USA and Middle East. Engine components are exported to Asia. The automotive components industry in SA provides more than 20% of the national production, and directly employs a further 6,000 people.

South Australia is at the centre of Australia's defence industry and attracts around 40% of the nation's defence development budget. Defence contributes $1.08 billion to Gross State Product and employed 16,800 people in the 2002-2003 period. Facilities include the Defence Science and Technology Organisation (DSTO) complex in Adelaide, the Australian Submarine Corporation (ASC) construction and maintenance site at Osborne for conventionally powered submarines, a dedicated Defence Technology Precinct at Edinburgh Parks, the RAAF Base at

Edinburgh, and the Woomera Rocket Range test and evaluation facility. There are some 30 defence-related companies located in South Australia and breakthrough research and development is a strong attraction for multi-national companies. BAE Systems, SAAB Systems, Raytheon Systems, and Tenix Defence all have a presence in Adeliade.

The state is rich in natural resources, including coal, copper, gold, iron ore, lead, silver, uranium, crude oil, natural gas, dolomite and gypsum. The world's largest zinc smelter, owned by Pasminco and BHAS, is located at Port Pirie, and the Santos Moomba Field in Cooper Basin is Australia's largest producer of oil and gas.

South Australia is Australia's largest producer of wine, grows around 40% of the national crop, and employs about 4,000 people. There are more than 180 small to medium-sized businesses involved in wine production spread throughout the six wine growing regions. The major producers, Kingston, Orlando Wyndham, Hardy, Petaluma, Peter Lehmann, Southcorp, and Beringer-Blass, have a national and international presence. It is also a leading producer of wheat and barley. Aquaculture is also thriving and incentives are in place to encourage development in this industry. The value of the State's aquaculture harvest represents 60.5% of total seafood production. Blue fin tuna, abalone, yellowtail kingfish, mussels, and Pacific oysters are farmed and exported on a large scale. Agricultural products contribute around $3.3 billion to the South Australian economy each year.

In the minerals and energy sector, South Australia has one of the world's largest lead/zinc smelters. It also has one of the largest copper/uranium sites in the world, and its on-shore oil and gas resources are among the most significant in Australia. The state is also developing strengths in niche industries, such as water management and environmental services.

South Australia produces about $42 billion in Gross State Product, representing approximately 7% of Australia's Gross National Product (GNP). Unemployment in the state is decreasing and export figures are very healthy. New infrastructure projects such as the Adelaide to Darwin Railway and the Pelican Point Power Station are expected to improve the efficiency of South Australia's key industries and access to export markets. However, economic growth is not as healthy as it could be, mainly due to a pattern of interstate migration and a low rate of population growth, which began during the recession of the 1990s.

The South Australia government encourages new business, and the workforce is well educated and highly skilled. Government supported research and development in South Australian information industries is more than $80 million a year, accounting for one-third of all Research and Development expenditure in the state. In addition, real estate and office space is cheaper than in some of the other states. High productivity levels and low operational base costs combine to make the capital, Adelaide, more economical and responsive than other cities in Australia and significantly better than many overseas cities. Business opportunities are to be found in light and heavy industry, agriculture, IT, agribusiness, engineering (especially foundries and tool making), defence and aerospace, food and wine, aquaculture, and traded services, particularly health and tourism. SA also has well-developed links with markets in Asia, North America and Europe.

Temporary. Grape picking is available in the Barossa Valley and Adelaide Hills from February to April, as is other harvesting work throughout the rest of the year. Hospitality and office temporary work is available in Adelaide all year, particularly during the summer months.

TASMANIA

Main City: Hobart (pop 190,000).
Other major cities/towns: Launceston (pop 96,000), Devonport (pop 23,814), Burnie (pop 17,202).
Regions: North West Coast, North and North East, Tasman Peninsula, Southern Tasmania, West Coast, Central and Midlands.
Regional Newspapers: *The Mercury,* and *Western Herald.*
Chamber of Commerce: Tasmanian Chamber of Commerce & Industry, Industry House, 30 Burnett Street, North Hobart, TAS 7000; ☎03-6236 3600; fax 03-6231 1278; e-mail admin@tcci.com.au; www.tcci.com.au.
Major Companies: Classic Foods, Comalco, and Alinta.

Employment Prospects: Tasmania has been the butt of 'would the last person to leave Tasmania...' jokes for so long that it hardly needs saying that this is a state gripped by considerable economic difficulties. Many Tasmanians are optimistic, however, despite an 8.5% unemployment rate and an economy that continues behind most other Australian states. The Tasmanian Government welcomes investment, but only on Tasmania's terms. Although the state is actively pursuing economic development, Tasmanians have not abandoned their environment-friendly sentiments and all sides have made it clear that investors will have to meet various environmental and quality of life standards before their projects will be given the go ahead in the State.

Tasmania is rich in mineral resources, especially iron, copper, lead, zinc, tin, and tungsten, and a recent geological data survey has revived interest in gold mining in the region. There are seven major mining operations at Henty, Savage River, Beaconsfield, Hellyer, Mt Lyell, Pasminco Roseberry, and Renison. After a long period during which the mineral resources industry was starved of investment, the Tasmanian Government is now committed to developing the infrastructure and investment conditions necessary to encourage the growth of multiple-stage mineral processing in the state. The Government is seeking to combine innovative agricultural and manufacturing techniques with Tasmania's natural beauty and environmental cleanliness.

Tasmania has a highly diversified rural sector, of which the major components are the vegetable, dairy, sheep, and beef cattle industries. Continuing problems in the wool market have meant that the sheep industry, once the mainstay of Tasmanian agriculture, is now the poor relative of vegetable and dairy farming, and recently, beef has experienced a similar downturn. Tasmanian agriculture is strongly export-orientated, both to mainland Australia and internationally.

Dairying is considered to have the best medium- to long-term prospects and is already the state's largest agricultural industry: in addition to 747 dairy farms, Tasmania has seven fresh milk processing plants, one UHT milk processing plant, seven manufacturing plants, 10 farm cheese producers, and three cheese shredders. The industry employs 2,000 people at farm level and a further 1,600 people at factory and distribution level. Emerging rural industries include emus, poppies, lavender, and wine grapes, while apple farmers are experiencing renewed economic growth.

Sea fisheries are a rapidly growing industry; the most valuable sector of the fisheries market is Atlantic salmon, which is mainly grown in the marine farms of the state's southeast. Abalone and rock lobster account for half the total value of Tasmanian marine production, and the marine farming sector as a whole provided more than 40%. Tasmania's wild fisheries have now reached the limits of their sustainable exploitation, however, intensification and expansion is projected for in the area of cultured fisheries. Around 2,000 people are employed in marine industries in the state.

The largest sectors of Tasmania's manufacturing industry are food, beverage and tobacco, which together contribute 30%. Tasmania is also the base for Incat, one of the world's largest manufacturers of high-speed ferries. Wood and wood products, textiles, clothing and footwear, paper and paper products, chemical and petroleum products, basic metal products, fabricated metal products and transport equipment industries also contribute to the state's economic base, however, there has been a marked decline in employment in these sectors in recent years. Retailing is experiencing slow to moderate growth but there is strong growth in the tourism sector, particularly in eco-tourism.

Ongoing economic developments include the production of pyrethrum, a plant which produces a natural pesticide; the booming aquaculture industry; continued investment in the natural gas project and the Government's plan to increase its energy supply by building a gas pipeline and an electricity cable to mainland Australia. Tasmania's hydro-electric system produces 60% of Australia's renewable energy and alternative technologies such as wind power are also being explored in Tasmania. There is further expansion in the State's call centre industry, including the employment of 450 people by the Commonwealth Bank in its two call centres. Recently the Government announced a reduction in payroll tax rates so that employers with 50 employees now pay less in taxes than any other Australian State.

Temporary. Hospitality work is available in the Mount Field and Ben Lomond Ski Resorts during the ski season – from June to August. Fruit picking is available from December to April in the Huon Valley, Derwent Valley, Tasman Peninsula, and West Tamar. Scallop splitting work can be found in Bicheno in January and February.

VICTORIA

Main City: Melbourne (pop 3.5 million).
Other major cities/towns: Ballarat (pop 73,000), Mildura (pop 28,060), Warrnambool (pop 26,800).
Regions: Great Ocean Road, Grampians, Goldfields, Oasis Country, Murray River, Goulburn Murray Waters, The High Country, Lakes and Wilderness, Gippsland, Yarra Valley and Ranges, Macedon Ranges, The Islands and Bays.
Regional Newspapers: *Herald Sun, The Age, The Weekly Times,* and *The Border Mail.*
Chamber of Commerce: Department of Innovation, Industry & Regional Development, 55 Collins Street, Melbourne, VIC 3000; ☎03-9651 9999; fax 03-9651 9907; e-mail enquiries@iird.vic.gov.au; www.dsrd.vic.gov.au.
Major Companies: SAAB, Kodak, Ford, Ericsson, Mercedes Benz, BMW, Toyota, Olivetti, NEC, Oracle, Kraft, Heinz, and Simplot.

Employment Prospects: The state of Victoria accounts for 34% of the Australia's manufacturing industry and produces 26% of the country's GDP. Many international corporations have their Australian base in Victoria and the Australian headquarters of seven of the top 20 US *Fortune* 500 companies are based in Melbourne. The government of Victoria's strong commitment to encouraging international competitiveness in local business has lifted export growth, which is currently strongest in chemicals, the automotive industry, information technology, and medical and scientific equipment. Employment prospects are also strongest in these sectors. Over half of Australia's automotive industry production occurs in Victoria, with Ford, General Motors and Toyota all manufacturing in the State, together with more than 500 components producers.

Victoria's food processing industries account for around a third of the state's export earnings; agriculture and food provide more than 35% of the State's export income. 40% of the nation's aluminium production occurs at the primary aluminium smelters at Portland and Point Henry. Victoria is also the centre of Australia's textiles, clothing and footwear industries, and continued growth is expected in niche and designer sectors.

Victoria has Australia's largest industrial concentration of information technology, scientific, and medical facilities, as well as a highly skilled workforce. Almost half of Australia's $2 billion telecommunications industry is based in Victoria; around a third of the country's software development companies are based in the state.

Traded services, such as the health and education sectors, are becoming highly competitive in the export market and are actively seeking new business overseas. The education sector currently generates around $500 million in annual exports and is experiencing continued growth.

Victoria boasts a significant and prosperous history in the finance and banking sectors. Two of Australia's largest banks: the National Australia Bank and ANZ have their headquarters in Melbourne, and Melbourne stockbrokers account for more than half of all capital raisings on the Australian Stock Exchange (ASX). Melbourne is one of Australia's leading industrial centres and is Australia's leading centre for biotechnology in the Asia-Pacific region.

Melbourne has Australia's largest throughput cargo airport and its largest container seaport; the Port of Melbourne handles 40% of Australia's container trade. The two terminal operators at Swanson dock, Patrick and P&O Ports, are committed to developing their facilities to operate at international best practice performance levels and investment in the redevelopment of these terminals over the next 20 years will exceed $300 million.

Geelong is Australia's 11th largest city and plays a major role in the country's wool production and textile industries. In addition to these traditional industries, the city is now developing its economic base in high-technology industries, education and research. Geelong is home to manufacturers of textiles, clothing, footwear, petroleum and coal products, chemicals, basic metal products and transport equipment and is the centre of the Australian aerospace industry – at Avalon Airport, while major assembly and maintenance plants are operated by ASTA and Hawker de Havilland in Melbourne. Ford Motor Company, Shell Oil Company of Australia and the aluminium giant ALCOA are the largest among the many industries that have chosen to expand in the region.

As a result of the Victorian Government's approach to financial management, Victoria has very low debt levels and is in a strong economic position. Victoria as a world leader in innovation, science and technology. There has been a massive funding injection for science, technology, research, education, and skills development. The State government is committed to science, technology and innovation. The development of a biotechnology precinct in central Melbourne and the national Synchotron facility will make Victoria a global leader in biotechnology and scientific research with the aim of developing knowledge-based industries, professional services, design, advanced manufacturing and environmental management. The government has also committed funding for a high technology film and television studio facility at the Melbourne Docklands.

Victoria contains the largest concentration of research institutions in Australia and accounts for 35% of the country's total business research and development. Employment in rural and regional Victoria accounts for more than a third of the state total.

Temporary. Harvest work is available around Mildura and Shepperton from January to April, and around Echuca and Lilyfield from September through to February. The Northern Victoria Fruit-growers' Association in Shepperton, Victoria, and the Victorian Peach and Apricot Growers' Association in Cobram, Victoria, are both able to offer jobs during the harvesting season. Hospitality work is available during the ski season in the Snowy Mountains. Temporary secretarial, office and administration work, as well as hospitality work (including gaming), is widely available in Melbourne.

NEW SOUTH WALES

Main City: Sydney (pop 4.1 million).
Other major cities/towns: Gosford (pop 160,167), Parramatta (pop 145,000), Newcastle (pop 140,000), Wollongong (pop 177,000).
Regions: The North Coast, Southern Highlands, Illawarra, Southern Tablelands, Shoalhaven, Clyde Coast, Eurobodalla, Snowy Mountains, and Sapphire Coast.
Regional Newspapers: *Daily Telegraph, Sydney Morning Herald,* and *Australian Financial Review.*
Chamber of Commerce: State Chamber of Commerce, Level 12, 83 Clarence Street, Sydney, NSW 2000; ☎1300 137 153; fax 02-9350 8199; e-mail enquiries@thechamber.com.au; www.thechamber.com.au.
Major Companies: Goldman Sachs, Mastercard International, Citibank, Acer, Nokia, BAE Systems, Kellogg, Southcorp, Inghams, Windsor Farm Foods, Qantas, Boeing, and Rio Tinto.

Employment Prospects: The strength of the New South Wales' economy is due in its diverse range of industries. The state has one of the world's leading service economies, and also has a significant manufacturing and primary industry base. The state's capital, Sydney, is a sophisticated, global city, and is the base for Australia's major financial institutions – the Reserve Bank of Australia, the Australian Stock Exchange and the Sydney Futures Exchange. It is a major financial centre in the Asia-Pacific region. The majority banks, both national and international, have their headquarters in Sydney.

New South Wales is the location of the regional headquarters of a number of multinational companies in Australia and 50% of the top 500 companies in Australia are located in the state. There are a number of industry sectors present in

NSW including: information technology, telecommunications, aerospace, medical equipment, pharmaceuticals, environmental industries, industrial textiles, shipping and railways, construction and mining equipment, metal and minerals processing, processed foods, paper and pulp, banking, tourism, advertising, film, and audio products. European, US, and Japanese companies are all represented. NSW is the base for 44.8% of Australia's finance and insurance industry, 40.7% of its property and business services (including IT) industry, and 35% of its communications industry.

New South Wales is Australia's premier agribusiness state, accounting for around one third of the national primary industry output, and many leading agribusiness companies have their headquarters in Sydney. NSW agribusiness industry includes farming, processing, transport, distribution, export, and supply. The industry's strengths have traditionally been in bulk commodities and minimally processed products such as wool, grains, meat and sugar; however, recent innovation and new product development has made the sector increasingly market focused. In particular sector growth is focused on the Asian food market, with heavy demand projected for western foods over the next five years. The processed food industry employs 50,000 people and exports generate around $3 billion.

The state has a well-established chemical industry and is home to the country's largest petrochemical complex. Its mining and mineral processing industries generate an annual output of more than $12 billion, of which coal production accounts for 80%. The major minerals derived from the state's rich mineral resources are black coal, copper, gold, silver, lead, zinc, mineral sands, and gemstones. NSW is also a major minerals processing state with established steel and aluminium production, and new copper smelting capacity currently coming into operation. The government of NSW is spending $35 million to expand the geological database of the state in order to attract new mineral and petroleum exploration and development. The Lithgow Minerals Processing Park has been located in the central west of the state to encourage development in that area.

Mining is a significant industry in New South Wales generating $4.4 billion in export revenue in 2003-2004. It is a low-cost producer of metals and minerals, including coal, gold, copper, silver, lead, zinc, and gemstones. Australia currently has 95% of the world's natural opal production and NSW accounts for more than half of the national output. Coal dominates the industry with four major coalfields producing more than $5 billion of black coal annually. Coal generates 92% of the State's electricity.

The electricity sector dominates New South Wales' energy industry and employs more than 4,000 people. The government monopoly has recently been restructured to form three independent power generators, Pacific Power, Delta Electricity, and Macquarie Generation. NSW gas sector is 95% controlled by Australian Gas Limited (AGL), a publicly listed company with 2,100 employees. Environmental management is a growth industry in the state, and is currently the largest in Australia.

The state is also a leading information technology and telecommunications centre, and the base for almost half of Australia's IT industry. This sector generates $27 billion a year and employs 100,000 people, 41% of Australia's IT professionals. The state is a significant producer of digital material content for multimedia, and has a strong film and television production sector. Fox Studios in Sydney will soon become the largest film and television studios in the southern hemisphere, and will offer many opportunities in the digital post-production industry. Sydney is regarded as the contact centre capital of the Asia Pacific and continued growth in international and domestic centres is forecast.

NSW and Sydney are the major entry points to Australia, with Sydney Airport providing the bulk of airfreight and business air passenger activity. NSW is a major centre for aerospace, electronics and defence industries. These industries are among the fastest growing in the state with extremely strong investment growth expected over the next five years. The state is the base for more than 30,000 defence personnel and Sydney Harbour is an important naval base and centre for marine repair activity. Airframe and systems support, sensors, processors, and defence aerospace training systems are all under development in NSW, as is world-leading C2I technology.

Cultural industries generate an estimated $4.3 billion in turnover for NSW, and education is a growing market, with more than 50,000 international students studying at various educational institutions. Food processing comprises 8% of the state's GDP and retail trade for 15% of the economic output. Both these sectors are significant employers. The state's largest service sector is tourism, which currently injects $15 billion a year into the economy. NSW also accounts for 38.6% of national output in the 'lifestyle' industries – accommodation and food outlets, and 36.3% of cultural and recreational services.

NSW accounts for almost a third of the total Australian workforce and nearly 45% of all employees in the finance and insurance sectors. NSW also employs more than a third of the national workforce in the transport, communications, property and business services sectors.

Temporary. The full range of temporary work opportunities is available in NSW, ranging from harvest and seasonal farm work in almost every region, to hospitality and office work, particularly in Sydney.

AUSTRALIAN CAPITAL TERRITORY

Main City: Canberra (pop 322,000).
Regional Newspapers: *The Canberra Times,* and *City News.*
Chamber of Commerce: ACT and Region Chamber of Commerce, 12a Thesiger Court, Deakin, ACT 2600; ☎02-6283 5200; fax 02-6282 2436; e-mail chamber@actchamber.com.au; www.actchamber.com.au.
Major Companies: Biotron and CEA Technologies.

Employment Prospects: Employment opportunities in the ACT are concentrated in Canberra. Most permanent work available is either service-based, reflecting the city's political function, or in the extensive public service which supports the government and federal ministries. The Commonwealth Government is the territory's biggest employer.

There are more than 13,000 businesses in the ACT. Canberra's workforce is more computer-literate and highly educated than any other workforce in Australia with 51% possessing university degrees and has a relatively low unemployment of 4.1%. Several hundred national associations have their headquarters in Canberra and the city is home to a number of multinational companies including Hewlett-Packard, NEC, British Aerospace, Fujitsu, Unisys, Oracle and Intec. Companies dealing in IT & telecommunications, advanced technology manufacturing, defence related services, call centres, information and business services, light manufacturing and assembly, and agribusiness can all be found in Canberra. Small business plays an important role in the ACT and there are 20,000 companies representing 96% of all private sector businesses in the Territory. Future opportunity is in the biotechnology sector where the ACT has established capability, primarily research and development focused, in niche markets such as plant science, neuroscience, hypertension, immunology, phenomics, genetics, and medical services and devices. The space sciences industry employs 300 people and is ranked as 21st in the world for its research. Other significant industries are property and business (14% of employment and 14% of GSP), retail trade (13% and 4%), health and community services (9% and 6%), and education (9% and 5%). The ACT Government, together with other Australian Governments, has endorsed the doubling of exporters by 2007. Export markets are growth drivers in any small economy and the ACT should benefit from this national goal.

Temporary. Temporary employment in Canberra, will be available in the IT and service industries and will include clerical and hospitality work.

QUEENSLAND

Main City: Brisbane (pop 1.6 million)
Other main cities/towns: Gladstone (pop 276,000), Rockhampton (pop 59,500), Caloundra (pop 50,150), Mt Isa (pop 20,525).
Regions: Gold Coast and Hinterland, Sunshine Coast, Toowoomba and South West Queensland, Rocky and Central Queensland, Mackay and Central Coast, Townsville and North Queensland, Cairns and Far North Queensland.
Regional Newspapers: *The Courier Mail, Western Echo,* and *The Sunday Mail.*
Chamber of Commerce: Commerce Queensland, Industry House, 375 Wickham Terrace, Brisbane, QLD 4000; ☎07-3842 2244; fax 07-3832 3195; e-mail info@commerceqld.com.au; www.commerceqld.com.au.
Major Companies: QMI Solutions, Hard Metal Industries, Burley Engineering, AJM Environmental Services.

Employment prospects: Queensland is experiencing continued economic strength and recorded a Gross State Product of 3.9% in 2003-2004 which exceeded the economic growth of the rest of Australia (3.6%). Employment increased by 60,000 in this period with job improvements in construction, transport, and retail industries. The unemployment rate fell to 6.2%, a 22-year low. The state benefits greatly from rich natural resources, diversified agriculture, and a vibrant tourist industry. The state government has allocated large sums towards maintaining Queensland's favourable economic position, including a $1.6 billion Infrastructure Rejuvenation Package. A further $4.8 billion is being spent in developing the state's regional road networks, and another $690 million on Queensland Rail. Queensland has Australia's lowest state taxes and debt levels, and welcomes foreign investors. Queensland's annual employment growth is currently 1% higher than the national average.

Queensland is Australia's most decentralised state, and has the largest rail network, and more deepwater ports, than the whole of the rest of Australia combined. Infrastructure developments to which the government has made a commitment include the installation of a water management system and weir in the Atherton Tablelands, a cruise liner port in Brisbane, expansion of the Dalrymple Bay Coal Export Terminal, and a 10-year development of the Port of Mackay. The Queensland Hospital Project will upgrade all the state's hospital facilities, and gas turbine power plants will be built at Yabulu and Mt Stuart. New wharf facilities are being built at Fisherman islands to handle large container vessels.

Agriculture is the cornerstone of Queensland's economy, with grains, beef and wool dominating rural industry. Tropical and citrus fruits, dairy products, vegetables, cotton, and tobacco are also important, and the state has the world's highest yielding sugar cane industry. Queensland's fishing industry is second only to Western Australia's, with nearly 5,000 commercial fishing vessels in operation, mainly fishing prawns, crustaceans and fin fish for export to Asia, Europe and the USA. Recently established food processing plants include a high technology piggery and integrated pork processing facility (DanPork Australia), and an upgraded Golden Circle Canned Fruit and Vegetable Plant. The cattle and calf industry is the State's largest primary industry and accounts for about 30% of the State's gross value. The outlook for the sugar cane industry is favourable due to an expected increase in world sugar prices.

Mount Isa Mine is one of the world's leading producers of lead and silver, and is ranked in the world's top 10 for copper and zinc production. The state's high-grade coal and bauxite reserves are among the largest in the world, and magnesite, phosphate rock, and limestone are also mined. Queensland is the largest Australian producer and exporter of black coal. The coal industry benefited from increased industrial production in Asia, particular China, in late 2003-2004. Large resources of magnesite, oil, shale, uranium, tin, mineral sands, clay and salt remain untapped, and continued development is projected. New mines are being developed at Cannington Base Metals Deposit (BHP), Century Base Metals Project (Century Zinc), Ely Mining Project (Alcan South Pacific), Ensham Coal Mine (Bligh/Idemitsu), and Enterprise Mine (MIM Holdings), among many others. Minerals mined in these projects include lead, zinc, bauxite, copper, gold, and predominantly, coal. In addition, a number of minerals processing plants are being brought online, such as the Sun Metals Corp Zinc Refinery in Townsville, and Dupont/Ticor Sodium Cyanide Plant, and the Boyne Island Aluminium Smelter. Coal seam methane gas is being recovered from productive coal along the western flank of the Bowen Basin, and a 16-mile (27-km) gas pipeline is under construction to connect coal seam methane supplies with the PG&E gas pipeline.

Manufacturing industries in Queensland have developed to support the state's mineral processing and agricultural industries. The manufacturing sector is dominated by food, beverage, and tobacco processing, fabricated metal products, and chemicals, petroleum and coal products. The processed food industry employs around 37,000 people, and is Queensland's largest manufacturing sector. The state's service industries include the construction, wholesale and retail trades, communications, business and financial services, and tourism. New dwelling construction grew strongly in 2003-2004, rising by 22.2%.

The Environmental Management Industry is a new growth sector in Queensland and is concerned with creating sustainable development through pollution abatement and environmental protection and the monitoring, planning, management and rehabilitation of the environment. It is estimated that the global environment market is worth about $A100 billion a year with the Australian market worth at least 10% of that figure. The potential for growth and technological innovation in this sector is significant. At least 125 Queensland firms are already delivering environmental expertise and services overseas.

Queensland has Australia's most successful tourism market and this sector employs a significant proportion of the state's workforce. Four major tourist resorts have been developed at Coomera Waters, Cowan Cove, Port Hinchinbrook, and East Hill, an integrated urban/resort project, covering 605 acres (245 ha).

Japan is the major destination for Queensland merchandise exports. Major export earners for the state include coal, meat, non-ferrous metals and crude minerals. Business and investment opportunities occur in the traditional industries, and there has been recent growth in communications services, biotechnology, IT and leisure industries. The area surrounding Surfers Paradise on the Gold Coast has become Australia's third largest city, and is the fastest-growing area of Australia.

Temporary. Fruit and vegetable picking is available throughout the state, particularly at Stanthorpe, Bowen and Warwick. Employment in the hospitality sector is widely available at resorts during the tourist season, especially on the Gold Coast; and work on prawn trawlers can be found at Cairns and Karumba. Mining and cattle station work is available in the Mount Isa region.

DIRECTORY OF FASTEST GROWING COMPANIES

Major companies inevitably require staff from time to time in order to maintain their basic operations. Even though it may be more difficult to find companies that are advertising for additional staff, it is worth knowing who the big companies are so that you can approach them before they advertise. It is a good idea to approach their overseas office in your country (if applicable) before you depart.

Recent economic reports show that small to medium sized companies are now the main creators of jobs in the private sector. Many of the larger companies are reducing instead of increasing their workforce, and this is partly due to the fact that once a company has reached a threshold level, it can avoid paying payroll tax, higher superannuation benefits and/or increased training levies if it does not hire more staff. If you choose to look for employment with a smaller company, try to choose one with less than 50 staff and one which produces high-value-added, high-technology products for export to Asia as such companies have experienced growth in excess of 30% in recent years.

Australia's 100 fastest growing companies (in the three years to June 2004) are listed below (by rank). All the companies have fewer than 200 employees and include listed as well as privately owned companies. The 'Fast 100' is a list compiled with the help of researchers at RMIT University's school of marketing and is published by the *Business Review Weekly* (www.brw.com.au), Australia's leading business magazine, which also publishes league tables of Australia's top accountancy firms, the 'Australia Rich List', industry reports and the top 500 private companies. The type of industries represented will give you a good indication of those that are in demand in Australia at present and which may be worth investing in.

100 FASTEST GROWING COMPANIES

Communications

Cableman, Level 1, 1227 Glenhuntly Road, Glen Huntly, VIC 3163; ☎03-9572 8900; fax 03-9572 8911; www.cableman.com.au.

M2 Telecommunications, Level 2, 22 Horne Street, Elsternwick, VIC 3185; ☎03-9524 7555; www.m2.com.au.

People Telecom, Level 9, 76 Berry Street, North Sydney, NSW 2060; ☎02-9458 5888; fax 02-9458 5858.

SkyNetGlobal, 395 Pitt Street, Sydney, NSW 2000; ☎1-800 759 638; fax 02-8251 3809; www.skynetglobal.com.au.

Tangible Solutions, 27 Gapcreek, Kenmore Hills, QLD 4069; ☎07-3374 4188; fax 07-3374 4199.

Techex Communications, Level 5, Suite 2, 39 East Esp Manly, NSW 2095; ☎1-300 881 112; fax 1-300 882 221.

Tel.Pacific, Suite 202, 815 Pacific Highway, Chatswood, NSW 2067; ☎1-300 369 888; fax 1-300 369 222; e-mail info@telpacific.com.au; www.telpacific.com.au.

Total Cabling Solutions, 92 Havelock Street, West Perth, WA 6005; ☎08-9426 5000; www.totalcabling.com.au.

Construction

Ahrens Engineering, William Street, Sheaoak Log, SA 5371; ☎08-8524 9045; fax 08-8524 9007; e-mail ahrens@ahrens.com.au.

National Lifestyle Villages, 48 Ashley Road, Tapping, WA 6065; ☎08-9405 9393; www.lifestylevillages.com.au.

Others: *Jims Enterprises,* NSW.

Culture and Recreational Services

Imagination Entertainment, Imagination Studios, 64 North Terrace, Kent Town, SA 5067; ☎08-8366 0999; fax 08-8366 0909; www.imagination.com.au.

Jumping J-Jays Castles and Slides, 1155 Links Avenue, North Eagle Farm, QLD 4009; ☎1-800 227 853; e-mail enquiries@partycastles.com.au; www.jumpingjjays.com.au.

Magna Pacific, 61-67 Buchanan Road, Banyo, QLD 4014; ☎07-3267 9888; www.magnapacific.com.au.

Education

Amazing People, 390 The Entrance Road, Erina Heights, NSW 2260; ☎02-4367 5977.

Law & Finance, Level 4, 84 Pitt Street, Sydney, NSW 2000; ☎02-9233 1000.

Finance and Insurance

Ark Financial, Level 6, 99 York Street, Sydney, NSW 2000; ☎02-9262 3333; www.arkfinancial.com.au.

Australian Finance Group, 4 Thelma Street, West Perth, WA 6005; ☎08-9420 7888; www.afgonline.com.au.

Australian Mortgage Brokers, 390 Burke Road, Camberwell, VIC 3124; ☎03-9889 9555; fax 03-9889 9055.

Better Mortgage Management, 338 Turbot Street, Spring Hill, QLD 4000; ☎07-3831 6400; fax 07-3831 6500; e-mail brisbane@bettermm.com.au; www.bettermm.com.au.

Bluestone, Level 8, 80 Clarence Street, Sydney, NSW 2000; ☎132 583; fax 1-300 133 571; w.ww.bluestone.com.au.

Homeloans, WA; ☎133 839; www.homeloans.com.au.

MFS Group, 5 Hicks Street, Southport, QLD 4215; ☎07-5557 7700; 07-5527 0205; e-mail mfs@mfsgroup.com.au; www.mfsgroup.com.au.

Mortgage Choice, Level 7, 182-186 Blues Point Road, North Sydney, NSW 2060; ☎131 462; fax 02-9922 1258; e-mail homeloans@mortgagechoice.

com.au; www.mortgagechoice.com.
au.

Mortgagemaker Australia, Suite 117, 26-32 Pirrama Road, Pyrmont, NSW 2009; ☎02-9552 1333; e-mail info@mortgagemaker.com.au; www.mortgagemaker.com.au.

Proclaim, Level 2, 134 Flinders Street, Melbourne, VIC 3205; ☎03-9694 4494; fax 03-9694 4495; www.extremenetworks.com.

Scott Winton Insurance Brokers, 25-27 Alma Road, St Kilda, VIC 3182; ☎03-8598 9411; fax 03-8598 9311; e-mail info@scottwinton.com.au; www.scottwinton.com.au.

Terri Scheer Insurance Brokers, 102 The Parade Street, Norwood, SA 5067; ☎08-8132 3100; fax 08-8363 3811; e-mail tsibho@terrischeer.com.au; www.terrischeer.com.au.

Yes Home Loans, Suite 1, Level 1, 426 Church Street, North Parramatta, NSW 1750; ☎02-9890 1100; e-mail help@yeshomeloans.com.au; www.yeshomeloans.com.au.

Others: *Snowball Group,* NSW.

Health and Community Services

SciGen, 95 Epping Road, North Ryde, NSW 2113; ☎02-9386 9800.

Information Technology

Aconex, 31 Drummond Street, Carlton, VIC 3053; ☎03-9654 5422.

Altech Computers, Slough Business Park, Unit 37, Holker Street, Silverwater, NSW 2264; ☎02-9735 5655; fax 02-9735 5656.

Carsales.com.au, Level 2, 810 Whitehorse Road, Box Hill, VIC 3128; ☎03-8803 3000; www.carsales.com.au.

Chimo, 260 Rundle Street, Adelaide, SA 5000; ☎08-8232 9644.

Destra Corporation, Level 2, Building 10, 658 Church Street, Richmond, VIC 3121; ☎03-8415 9111.

Emailcash Marketing, Suite 1, 221 Miller Street, North Sydney, NSW 2060; ☎02-9409 8600.

Empired, 469 Murray Street, Perth, WA 6805; ☎08-9321 9401; fax 08-9321 9402; www.empired.com.

Extreme Networks, 68-72 York Street South, Melbourne, VIC 3205; ☎03-9694 4494; fax 03-9694 4495; www.extremenetworks.com.

Hostworks, 340 Findan Road, Kidman Park, SA 5025; ☎08-8461 4800; fax 08-8461 4899; e-mail hosting@hostworks.com.au; www.hostworks.com.au.

Hotshed, Level 1, 433 Upper Edward Street, Spring Hill, QLD 4000; ☎07-3839 3555; www.hotshed.com.

IFocus, Level 1, 450 St Kilda Street, Melbourne, VIC 3004; ☎03-8807 0100.

Jigsaw Services, 182 Fullarton Road, Dulwich, SA 5065; ☎08-8364 6300; fax 08-8364 6311.

Objective Corporation, Level 37, 100 Miller Street, North Sydney, NSW 2060; ☎02-9955 2288.

PageUp, Level 10, 91 William Street, Melbourne, VIC 3000; ☎03-9602 3300.

Pivod Technologies, 1st Floor, 47-49 Stirling Highway, Nedlands, WA 6009; ☎08-9318 1444; fax 08-9318 1445.

Reactive Media, Studio 2a, 108 Moor Street, Fitzroy, VIC 3065; ☎03-8415 0033; fax 03-9415 2333; www.reactive.com.

SecureTel, Level 4, 33 Erskine Street, Sydney, NSW 2000; ☎02-8235 9544; e-mail sales@securetel.com.au; www.securetel.com.au.

SitePoint, 424 Smith Street, Collingwood, VIC 3066; ☎03-9419 5200; fax 03-9419 3900; e-mail contact@sitepoint.com.au; www.sitepoint.com.au.

Supply Chain Consulting, Level 6, 122 Walker Street, North Sydney, NSW 2060; ☎02-9409 6100; fax 02-9409 6111; www.supply-chain.com.au.

Technology Warehouse Australia, 45-51 Grimwade Street, Mitchell, ACT 2911; ☎02-6242 3966; www.techwarehouse.com.au.

The Performance Technologies Group, Level 8, 35 Clarence Street, Sydney, NSW 2000; ☎02-9299 9200; fax 02-9299 9201; www.ptg-global.com.

Vivid Group, 200 Wellington Street, Perth, WA 6000; ☎1-800 010 888; e-mail info@vividgroup.com.au; www.vividgroup.com.au.

Manufacturing

Baroda Manufacturing, 78 Malcolm Road, Braeside, VIC 3195; ☎03-9587 6577.

Ecosol Waste Water Filtration Systems, PO Box 510, Modbury, SA 5092; ☎08-8395 4116; fax 08-8395 4118; e-mail info@ecosol.com.au; www.ecosol.com.au.

Parketronics, 3 Mengel Court, Salisbury South, SA 5106; ☎08-8283 1400; fax 08-8283 1411.

Redarc Electronics, 21 Heath Street, Lonsdale, SA 5160; ☎08-8186 5633; fax 08-8186 5644; e-mail power@redcar.com.au; www.redcar.com.au.

Tapex, 200 Kingsgrove Road, Kingsgrove, NSW 2208; ☎02-9554 9199.

3rdmill, 2c, 44 Oxford Street, Epping, NSW 2121; ☎02-9869 3090; fax 02-9869 4123; e-mail 3rdmill@3rdmill.com.au; www.3rdmill.com.au.

Personal and Other Services

LRS Labour Solutions, Level 1, 48 Wharf Street, Kangaroo Point, QLD 4169; ☎07-3896 4000; fax 07-3891 9922; www.l-r-s.com.au.

Property and Business Services

Assetivity, Unit 16, 11 Preston Street, Como, WA 6152; ☎08-9474 4044.

Barnson, Riverview Business Park, Unit 1, 36 Darling Street, Dubbo, NSW 2830; ☎02-6884 2944; fax 02-6884 5857; www.barnson.com.au.

Community Housing, 9 Prospect Street, Box Hill, VIC 3128; ☎03-9856 0050.

Detech Building Services, 1-20 Cliff Street, Milsons Point, NSW 2061; ☎02-8904 1580.

Derwent Howard, 75 Grafton Street, Bondi Junction, NSW 2022; ☎02-9386 4666.

Evolution Media, Suite 115, 40 Yeo Street, Neutral Bay, NSW 2089; ☎02-8969 6077; fax 02-8969 6419.

IT Matters Recruitment Services, Level 4, 36 York Street, Sydney, NSW 2000; ☎02-9279 2733; www.it-matters.com.au.

Jobwire, 1st Floor, 553 Gardeners Road, Mascot, NSW 2020; ☎02-9667 1115.

MC Labour Services, 731 High Street, Epping, VIC 3076; ☎03-9401 5000; fax 03-9401 5444; e-mail mclabour@bigpond.com; www.mclabour.com.

Maverick Marketing & Communications, Suite 7, 3 Eden Street, North Sydney, NSW 2060; ☎02-9955 5522; fax 9957 9500.

McGees Property, Level 2, 145 Eagle Street, Brisbane, QLD 4000; ☎07-3831 2711; fax 07-3831 2312; e-mail brisbane@mcgees.com.au; www.mcgees.com.au.

NetX Communications, 2 Queens Place, Balmain, NSW 2041; ☎02-9320 7200.

Property Direct, 728 Ann Street, Fortitude Valley, QLD 4006; ☎07-3620 2222; fax 07-3620 2233; e-mail enquiries@pd.com.au; www.pd.com.au.

Realestate.com.au, Suite 1, 733 Whitehorse Road, Mont Albert, VIC 3127; ☎03-9897 1121; fax 03-9897 1114; www.realestate.com.au.

Richard Luton Properties, 11 Bougainville Street, Griffith, ACT 2603; ☎02-6260 7080.

RSP Group, Level 2, 40 King Street, Sydney, NSW 2000; ☎02-9279

0324; fax 02-9279 0749; e-mail info@rspgroup.com.au; www.rspgroup.com.au.

Smart, 20 Poplar Street, Surry Hills, NSW 2010; ☎02-9285 8555; fax 02-9283 8755; e-mail sydney@smartinc.com.au; www.smartinc.com.au.

Smart Sales Marketing and Real Technologies, Level 8, 530 Little Collins Street, Melbourne, VIC 3000; ☎03-9620 7003.

Staff Australia, Clayton Staff 121b, Rayhur Street, VIC 3169; ☎03-9543 9777; fax 03-9543 9600; e-mail apply@staffaus.com.au; www.staffaus.com.au.

Whirlwind Design, Level 4, 691 Burke Road, Camberwell, VIC 3124; ☎03-9811 4444; fax 03-9882 6567.

WorkPac International, 182 Robertson Street, Fortitude Valley, QLD 4006; ☎07-3852 5050; 07-3852 5060.

Others: *Bax Property,* QLD; *FM Solutions,* QLD; *ITS People Solutions,* WA; and *M&M Real Estate,* TAS.

Retail

Australian Energy, Complex 1, 303 Burwood Highway, Burwood East, VIC 3151; ☎03-8805 6600; fax 03-8805 6699; www.powerdirect.com.au.

Boost Juice Bars, 260 Collins Street, Melbourne, VIC 3000; ☎03-9654 9220.

Ezydvd, Klemzig 29, OG Road, SA 5087; ☎08-8266 9900; fax 08-8266 9999; e-mail enquiries@ezydvd.com.au; www.ezydvd.com.au.

Liaise Marketing, Level 1, 4 Bruthen Street, Preston, VIC 3072; ☎03-9495 0700; www.liaisemarketing.com.au.

Snowdonia Airconditioning Services, 9 Brewers Street, Burpengary, QLD

4505; ☎1-300 551 460; fax 07-3888 1499.

Others: *Surfers Paradise Locksmiths,* QLD

Transport and Storage

Andrew's Airport Parking, 247 Mickelham Road, Tullamarine, VIC 3043; ☎03-9334 5777; www.andresairportpark.com.au.

Container Swinglift Services, PO Box 22, Hemmant, QLD 4174; ☎07-3906 9500; fax 07-3906 9555; e-mail css@containerswinglift.com.au; www.containerswinglift.com.au.

International Freight Consolidators, 8 Garden Dry, Tullamarine, VIC 3043; ☎03-9338 4400; fax 03-9338 4177; e-mail mail@ifc.com.au; www.ifc.com.au.

Skelton Travel, Unit 5, 182 Robertson Street, Fortitude Valley, QLD 4006; ☎07-3852 5050; fax 07-3852 5060.

Wholesale Trade

Abacus Diagnostics, Unit 5, 38 Tennyson Memorial Avenue, Yeerongpilly, QLD 4105; ☎07-3848 6898; fax 07-3848 5900.

Australia IT, Factory 14D, Centre Road, Clayton, VIC 3168; ☎03-9543 5866.

Bright Eyes Franchising, PO Box 95, Morayfield, QLD 4506; ☎07-5498 9633; fax 07-5498 3158; www.brighteyes.com.au.

Mor Cosmetics, 29 Sutherland Street, Melbourne, VIC 3000; ☎03-9600 4599; fax 03-9600 4777.

SmartSalary, Level 1, 120 Sussex Street, Sydney, NSW 2000; ☎02-9299 9111; fax 9299 4669; e-mail customerservice@smartsalary.com.au; www.smartsalary.com.au.

STARTING A BUSINESS

CHAPTER SUMMARY

- Small businesses in Australia employ 3.3 million people.

- **Business Immigration.** In 2003-2004, 5,670 Business Skills Migration visas were issued for Australia.

  - Most business immigrants come from oriental countries, South Africa and the UK.

- **Growth Areas.** Retail and construction industries are among the fastest growing sectors.

  - Between 1996-1999 the number of computer industries in Australia rose by 50%.

  - Service industries now make up 64% of the economy.

  - Buying an existing business is far less risky than starting your own.

- **Women in Business.** Women in Australia start small businesses at twice the rate that men do.

- **Company Tax.** Tax on company profits is 30% (compared with the highest rate of personal income tax 48.5%).

  - The Australian financial year ends on 30 June.

- **Courses for Entrepreneurs.** TAFE (adult education) colleges run courses in managing your tax affairs as a small business owner.

Australia used to be considered the 'Lucky Country' or the 'Land of Opportunity' and businesses of all shapes and sizes blossomed across the country. Aspiring entrepreneurs have always been a part of the Australian social landscape, and small businesses such as plumbers, caterers, painters and decorators, landscapers, hairdressers, beauticians and potters have not only found space for themselves in the Australian market, but remained solvent and generated good incomes.

With the recession of the 1980's, however, came a much more depressed business climate, and large and small businesses collapsed in dramatic profusion. Although the Australian economy has recovered well it has in general become far more difficult for new businesses to survive their first year.

Business growth is therefore now being encouraged and protected by legislation, government assistance, and an extensive network of government small business offices and advisors, to ensure that once off the ground, new enterprises stay airborne, while tax incentives are now offered in the recognition that the earlier tangle of red-tape and taxation was enough in itself to discourage new business. A recent World Bank report *Doing Business in 2004,* shows that Australia is the easiest country in which to start up a business.

The small business sector employs almost 3.3 million people and has accounted for 70% of jobs growth over the past decade and around 15% of the gross domestic product (GDP). Of the 1.2 million small businesses, 39% operate in regional Australia. Small businesses produce some of Australia's best innovations and are predominant in the property, business services, construction, and retail trade sectors.

The retail, construction and services industries are currently the most successful sectors of the market. The need to become more competitive internationally has forced small businesses to provide higher quality products and services at costs, which can challenge international businesses. Economic analysts believe that this trend is likely to continue for some time, and the government is particularly keen to encourage an export-based economy, offering many incentives to businesses to export both products and services.

The present Australian government is committed to selecting high quality business migrants, and both top-flight executives and well-heeled investors continue to head south to take advantage of the relatively stable economic conditions, highly qualified labour market, and the various incentive programmes available to help build new enterprises. Business migrants take with them to Australia a knowledge of overseas markets, business networks, cultural practices and languages other than English, as well as their specific business skills and experience. In 2003-2004, the top 10 source countries for business migrant visa grants were China, the UK, Malaysia, South Africa, Singapore, Taiwan, Zimbabwe, South Korea, Hong Kong, and Indonesia. A two-year survey of Business Skills migrants showed that 38% had settled in NSW, 20% in Western Australia, 16% in Queensland, 16% in Victoria, 1% in South Australia and less than 1% in Tasmania, Northern Territory and Australian Capital Territory. During 2003-2004, business migration was steady with 5,670 business migration visas granted to business people and their families. However, this compares with 7,364 issued in 2000-2001 and 6,260 in 1999-2000.

This chapter aims to give practical advice about starting a new business as well as suggestions as to those businesses which are likely to succeed in Australia: careful research and preparation will help prevent your business from becoming one of the failures. It also provides preliminary information regarding the taxation rules and regulations relevant to creating a new business and also the procedures for buying an existing business. The *Useful Addresses* section at the end of the chapter may be particularly helpful in providing contact names and addresses of advisors and authorities to help you get your new business venture off the ground.

ESTABLISHING A NEW BUSINESS

If you have an idea for a new venture, you will need to do some careful market research and ask yourself some searching personal questions. Do you have the right background or qualifications to set up the sort of enterprise you are considering? Are you prepared to risk almost everything to achieve your goals? You will need to be completely familiar with your product or service, and have detailed technical knowledge of it. You must also ensure that there is a market for this product and you should identify the size, geographical and socio-economic distribution of that market. Research is the key to success and you would be well advised to find out as much as possible about both your target population and your competition. This kind of information can be gained from government statistics (the Australian Bureau of Statistics, www.abs.gov.au, is particularly helpful), universities and institutes of technology, small business agencies, advertisements, and telephone directories (both the yellow pages and the business directory). In addition, you should find out whether there is a trade association that deals with the product or service you are offering as this is likely to be a good source of information, advice and assistance. The Australia and New Zealand Chamber of Commerce UK (www.anzcc.org.uk) is a primary source of information (for other contact details see Useful Addresses below) and has an invaluable database, updated daily, of more than 6,000 Australian and New Zealand businesses which provides a valuable research tool for anyone considering setting up a business in the region. This organisation also offers regular investment and business seminars, as well as a library of information on Australian and New Zealand business, taxation, and government regulations.

Intellectual Property Protection

Legally protecting your business image and the products which you have developed can be vital in maintaining your competitive advantage. Businesses built on innovation and design need to protect their intellectual property rights, which in commercial terms means your proprietary knowledge. There are several different types of intellectual property, and various methods of protecting them:

TABLE 14   INTELLECTUAL PROPERTY PROTECTION

Circuit Layout Rights. Are granted for three-dimensional configuration of electronic circuits or layout designs.

Copyrights. Are granted for original material in literary, artistic, dramatic or musical works, films, broadcasts, multimedia, and computer programmes.

Designs. Refer to the features of shape, configuration, pattern or ornamentation which can be judged by eye in finished articles. A new or original design may be registered for up to 16 years. Registration gives the owner the exclusive rights to make, use and sell articles incorporating the registered design.

Patents. Are for inventions which are recognised as new, novel, non-obvious and useful. Inventions that serve an illegal purpose or which are unrelated to manufacturing processes are not patentable. A patent lasts for up to 20 years and gives its owner exclusive rights to exploit the invention or to authorise others to exploit it.

Plant Breeder's Rights. Are also available and are granted for new varieties of plants. These are administered by the Plant Breeder's Rights Office, under the Department of Agriculture, Fisheries and Forestry-Australia (www.affa.gov.au).

Trade Marks. Are granted to protect words, symbols, pictures, sounds and smells, or a combination of these, distinguishing the goods and services of one trader from those of another. Initial registration of a trademark lasts for 10 years.

Trade Secrets. Protection covers know-how and other confidential information.

Intellectual property rights (patents, trade marks, designs, and plant breeder's rights) are administered in Australia by the Federal government agency IP Australia (Central Office, Ground Floor, Discovery House, 47 Bowes Street, Woden, ACT 2606; ☎02-6283 2999; fax 02-6283 7999; e-mail assist@ipaustralia.gov.au; www.ipaustralia.gov.au) which is division of the Department of Industry, Tourism and Resources. Formerly known as the APIO, IP Australia provides valid IP rights, monitors the Australian IP system, and partakes in the harmonisation efforts in relation to IP laws throughout the world. The agency also administers the Olympic Insignia Protection Amendment Act 2001.

The Patent Co-operation Treaty (PCT) allows companies to file an international patent application, protecting the product in all participating PCT countries. There are 77 countries participating in the PCT, including the USA, Canada, Japan, the UK, Austria, Belgium, Switzerland, Germany, Denmark, Spain, France, Greece, Ireland, Italy, the Netherlands, Norway and Sweden. There are also many other participating countries from Eastern Europe, Africa and the Asian-Pacific region. The patent application consists of several forms and a detailed set of drawings, and the cost of submitting an application is dependent upon the complexity of the drawings. A schedule of fees is available from IP Australia and applications are submitted to that office. There are Patent Offices in every PCT country.

If your product is competing with others of a similar type, it may be advantageous to register a *trademark*. A trademark can be registered with IP Australia, and once registered will be protected indefinitely provided that renewal fees are paid 10 years after the initial registration. Processing time for trademark applications is currently around six months, and this time lag should be incorporated into your business plan. On acceptance, your trademark will be published in the *Official Journal of Trade Marks*, after which objections may be filed within three months. If there is no opposition, or if opposition is unsuccessful, your trademark will be registered when you pay the registration fee (to be paid no later than six months from the date the acceptance was advertised). Your new trademark is then registered from the date you filed your application, recorded in the *Register of Trade Marks*, and you will be sent a Certificate of Registration.

New products can also be assessed by SAI Global (www.sai-global.com), formerly Standards Australia International, which is the most widely established supplier of independent conformity assessment, certification, and training services in the Asia Pacific region. If your product meets the strict standards of this organisation, you will be able to use the product certification mark and benefit from the associated product credibility.

Registering a Business

Establishing a new business means you must comply with numerous licensing laws and other regulations. You must register your business with the Australian Taxation Office and obtain a tax file number (TFN) and an Australian Business number (ABN). Depending on your business structure, you may also need to register with the Australian Securities and Investments Commission (www.asic. gov.au; info line ☎ 03-5177 3777) and obtain an Australian Company Number (ACN). Business registration with the Australian Taxation Office and with the ASIC can now be completed electronically via the Australian Government Business Entry Point website at www.business.gov.au, and this site also provides electronic links to the Business Names Registration offices in each state and territory. Before you start a business, or if you are not sure which licences, permits or approvals your business needs, you should contact your local Business Licence Information Service (www.bli.net.au, or via the Australian Government Business Entry Point website), which will provide you with all the necessary application forms.

Forming a Company

Any new company may be registered either as a proprietary company or a public company. When a company is registered under the Corporations Law it is automatically registered as an Australian company and thus may conduct business as a company throughout Australia without needing to register in each individual state or territory jurisdiction. Most companies in Australia are registered as proprietary companies under the Corporations Law. Proprietary companies are generally cheaper and easier to register than a public company. A private company only needs to have a nominal share capital to commence operating. Directors and a company secretary must be appointed and as soon as is practically possible after incorporation, a public officer has to be appointed for taxation purposes. For proprietary companies, there must be at least two directors, one of whom must be an Australian resident. Public companies must have at least three directors, two of whom must be residents of Australia. There are several steps in the process of registering a company:

Choosing a Name. First, you must select a name, which may either be one of your choice, or the companies ACN (Australian Company Number). Before you decide on a name, you should consult the alphabetical listing of company and business names available by checking the National Name Index at the ASIC Internet site. The ASIC will reject your name if it is identical or similar to any other company name. A company name must indicate the company's legal status, with a proprietary company including the word 'proprietary' or its abbreviation Pty in the name. The liability of a company's members must also be indicated, so that where liability is limited, the name must end with the word 'limited' or its abbreviation. The British form, PLC, is not used in Australia (where it is usually Pty Ltd).

Registering a Company. Next, you will need to obtain the consent of proposed directors and a company secretary, and then formally appoint them via the application process. After your application has been received and successfully processed by ASIC, a certificate of registration will be posted to the registered office of your company, and only once you have received this can the directors officially commence operating as a company. Such operations include opening bank accounts, which cannot be done prior to the completion of registration. The law requires that the company's name be clearly displayed at the registered office and at each business address, and the Australian Company Number (ACN) must appear on the common seal, every public document issued, all documents required to be lodged with ASIC under Corporations Law, and on every eligible negotiable instrument issued.

Off-the-Shelf Companies. The formation of a company from scratch takes between one to two weeks from application and will cost around $1,000, not including professional fees (which are likely to be high). If you need to establish the company very quickly, agents and solicitors can also offer ready-made 'off-the-shelf' companies, which can be purchased more cheaply, as legal expenses are then kept to a minimum. Shelf companies are incorporated with names, which in most cases will be unsuitable, and amendments will then need to be made to the company's Memorandum and Articles of Association. A change of name usually takes approximately four weeks to be processed and approved, and the ASIC must issue a *Certificate of Incorporation on Change of Name*. The additional cost of changing the name of the company and the Memorandum and Articles is around $320. If you do choose to buy a shelf company, you should consult with your advisers to consider whether the Articles of Association need to be amended. You need to consider whether the existing constitution allows for: the rights of directors to decline to register a future share transfer; the requirements if a shareholder ceases to be a director or employee or dies; the chairperson's casting vote; the shareholder/director's voting rights; and who controls the company, as different levels of shareholding confer different rights and there may also be different classes of shares conferring different rights.

When you purchase a shelf company, you should receive a complete set of first board minutes and statutory books. If you do not receive these, it would be advisable to check with the previous owners as they can often contain important information and you are expected to hold them.

Partnership/Sole Trader Legalities. If you are starting the business as a partnership or sole trader (see *Business Structures* below), there are no legal formalities involved other than the notifications required for tax purposes. In the absence of a partnership agreement, the partnership will be governed by the Partnership Act of the relevant state or territory, which will specify how a partnership should administer its affairs. Most partnerships, however, prefer to draw up a tailor-made agreement to meet their own particular needs. Partnership agreements are usually drawn up by a solicitor and should include details of the arrangements for partners' capital, banking accounts, profit sharing, salaries (if relevant), drawings, change or termination of partnership, and voting rights. This agreement is particularly important if a dispute between partners arises, but business experts claim that the more important course of action is to avoid such potential disputes by choosing the right partner/s in the first place.

If you are planning on setting up a company, please note that this information is intended only as a guide. It is *essential* that you seek professional advice in the process of forming a company, and that you are fully aware of your obligations and commitments when registering a company.

Choosing an Area

If you choose to buy an existing business your area will generally be predetermined, but if you are starting your business from scratch, the decision of where to locate your business, including the type of premises you require, can be vitally important to its future. The needs of your business should determine its location. Various factors, such as whether you expect frequent deliveries from suppliers or visits from customers and whether you need to attract passing trade, can influence your decision as to the best location. You will also need to consider the likely needs of your staff, especially in terms of public transport and parking.

Renting Business Premises

The rental rates of commercial properties vary greatly across Australia. Melbourne and Perth currently offer low rents (calculated in dollars per square metre) compared to similar properties in Sydney or Canberra. Additionally, the rates of leasing commercial property in Darwin, Adelaide and Hobart are markedly lower than that of comparable properties in the central business districts of Sydney or Brisbane.

Whether leasing or purchasing, you need to make sure that the premises have adequate facilities such as security, access, essential services (including electricity, water, waste collection, energy efficiency, sound and thermal insulation), flexibility of design should you wish to expand at a later date, and that the dimensions in terms of height and floor space are sufficient. Furthermore, you need to ask your solicitor to check that your type of business will not breach any environmental laws if you conduct that business in those particular premises. The buildings must comply with fire and safety regulations, town planning and other regulations, the Health Act and Shops and Factories Act (obtainable from the Government Printer or various technical publishers) applicable in your state or territory.

If you choose to lease premises, ensure that the lease is checked by a solicitor and, if possible, by an accountant. The terms of the lease are always negotiable, and your solicitor or accountant will advise you on the negotiation of terms and conditions. You should attempt to negotiate a rent-free period, a lower initial rental, reduced annual escalations, payment by the landlord for any improvements or refurbishments to the property, and payment by the landlord of any outgoings associated with the property. You should identify who is responsible for insurance, property taxes and maintenance, what your rights are to make alterations or renovations, and whether the lease permits sub-letting of the premises. Your negotiating power will always depend on the state of the property market at the time. At present, this tends to be favourable to lessees.

The term of the lease can be important, as a long lease may reduce flexibility. A shorter lease with the option to renew can be preferable, depending on the current economic conditions and your choice of premises. When considering a lease, it is helpful to ask for a plan which clearly states the extent of the premises being let, and make sure that the proposed use of your building does not breach any terms of the lease. Before you sign, you should also compare the rent, rates and service charges (usually given on a dollar per square metre basis), annual escalations and rent review clauses with those of other premises. You should also be aware that a verbal lease, which is binding on both parties, is recognised by law but should be avoided as such agreements are fraught with difficulties.

Your choice of premises will also have tax implications, as payments for the rent of business premises are tax deductible; but the rate of such deductions will vary according to the age of the building. Moveable furnishings and equipment within the buildings are subject to higher rates of depreciation for taxation purposes.

Raising Finance

You can have the best ideas, products and service in the world, but if you cannot manage to raise the finance to put your plans into practice, your dreams (not to mention potential profits) will remain unrealised. Before you approach any potential source of finance, you will need to be fully prepared to explain your business concept and to answer any questions about your proposal. A thorough and careful business plan is the first key to success.

The Business Plan. A completed business plan is a summary and evaluation of your business idea. It is the written result of the planning process and a blueprint for your business operations. Your ability to make it work depends on checking your progress against the plan and reviewing that plan as your business evolves. In the early stages of development, when you are seeking finance, your business plan may well be the only tangible aspect of your intentions. The business plan, which you present to a bank or other money lender should contain a fully considered financial plan, including a budget for at least the first 18 months. You should make sure that you include an allowance for unexpected and intangible expenses, in particular taxes such as provisional tax (tax paid against estimated future earnings), as one of the most common reasons for business failure is the lack of planning for such contingencies.

There are many publications available which will help in preparing your business plan, and assistance is also available from your nearest Small Business Development Corporation, industry associations, chambers of commerce, and from business advisors and accountants. The Commonwealth Bank of Australia offers a guide in its *BetterBusiness Planner* available either as a software package or in hardcopy form. The software package includes a sample business plan, financial templates which automatically calculate budgets and cash flows, and follow-up software to keep track of your business plan's progress. You can obtain the *BetterBusiness Planner* from the Commonwealth Bank's Business Line, ☎1800 657 151 (8am-8pm, weekdays) or through the business centre section of the bank's website www.commbank.com.au. There is also a very informative website covering all aspects of starting a business and supported by the Commonwealth government at www.homebusinessmanual.com. au. Australian Securities and Investments Commission offers financial tips and safety checks at www.fido.asic.gov.au.

Financing a Business

One of your first steps in drawing up a business plan is to consider the different sources of finance available to you. The Commonwealth Bank of Australia strongly recommends that business owners should look much more carefully at maximising the business's ability to generate internal funds in order to avoid relying too much on external sources for the funding of its operations. Although for the first three years a new business is hardly likely to be in the position to generate enough internal funds in order to become self-sufficient, you should think very carefully about trying to borrow as little as possible from outside sources in the long term, and incorporate self-sufficiency into your long-term business proposal. Once you have done this, you need to look very carefully at all the different financial institutions and the options available to you in order to choose one or a combination that is most appropriate to the needs and goals of your company, and your repayment capacity. Lenders will also expect a significant level of personal capital investment in your business. One of the most common reasons for finance refusal is that applicants have not allowed for sufficient personal contribution; this is seen, at best, as a demonstration of lack of commitment.

As discussed in the *Daily Life* chapter, there are many different financial institutions in Australia. Deregulation of banking has led to increased competition and, as a consequence, more innovative and sophisticated banking techniques have been introduced. In addition, opportunities to obtain loan funds have greatly increased and there are now many more options available in terms of structuring loan agreements. In an effort to encourage the growth and development of Australian industry and resources, a number of industrial banks have been established which provide development finance, equity funding and financial advisory services. Other methods of raising finance can include accessing venture capital, which may provide funding for high-risk projects, or floating a company on the stock exchange.

Types of Finance

Equity, long-term loan finance, and working capital finance are the three principal types of finance available for starting a new business in Australia. Equity is usually contributed by the owners of the business, and businesses with significant equity will find it easier to attract financial backing from other sources. If you are seeking finance for a major project, such as investment in plant and machinery for your business, long-term loan finance is likely to be the most appropriate option. In many cases the loan will be secured against the business or the equipment purchased. In addition, the financial institution will generally require personal guarantees from the business owners. There is usually a substantial difference between the amount of the loan and the value of the asset in order to allow for risk and for the costs involved should the business fail.

There are a variety of options available in obtaining long-term business finance. Firstly, it is important to calculate how much of your own personal contribution can be used as share capital and how much can be used as loan capital – this proportioning of capital can affect your taxation (see *Taxation* below for further details). Cash subscription from your family and friends can also be used as long term finance, as can cash received from any other sponsor or from venture capital. Most often, however, long-term business capital is raised through a bank or finance company loan, or through leasing or hire purchase finance. It must be noted, however that leasing or hire purchase finance generally have interest rates which are significantly higher than other sources.

In the present very competitive finance market, banks and other lenders are increasingly offering tailored loan packages, and the variety of types of finance is growing exponentially. Options are also changing almost every month, and the best advice is to start by approaching the major banks to discuss the available financing methods. Most larger bank branches now have specialist business advisors who will be only too happy to guide you – remember they are selling a product too.

Government-Backed Finance. The Australian government, at both Federal and State levels, is very keen to promote new business, and to ensure that such businesses are successful. Government agencies exist in every state to provide various kinds of assistance: technical as well as financial. Financial assistance can include direct cash grants, subsidies and tax concessions, while technical assistance will include both professional and technical advice, and research and development seminars. There are many opportunities for small business to benefit from government-backed schemes, with substantial incentives available to all kinds of enterprises. There are a number of different financial assistance schemes run by the state and federal governments, and by various industry agencies. *AusIndustry.* (☎132 846 hotline; www.ausindustry.gov.au) is the best starting point for obtaining information on these schemes. Their database contains information on all Federal, State and Territory government support programmes, as well as programmes offered by industry associations and chambers of commerce around Australia. The AusIndustry Hotline can also put you in touch with sources of information in research and development, networking, management, strategic planning, benchmarking, diagnostic reviews, environmental management, marketing, export planning and business licensing.

Rebates and subsidies are also offered to employers as an incentive to provide employment and to encourage them to provide training for their employees (or to allow employees to attend trade or development courses). Such schemes, which are usually aimed either at the youth or long-term unemployed workforce, are administered by the Australian Job Network, which can provide further information. Employment incentive schemes are a favourite vote-winner for governments and tend to be restructured with each budget and change of government.

Most states and territories also provide financial assistance in the forms of loan funds or guarantees to businesses. However, this assistance is generally only provided as a final resort. Other assistance can include transportation and freight subsidies, and advice services in such areas as effective business operations, production processes, technological development and export market opportunities. State Government assistance is generally given to encourage the establishment of new businesses or the expansion of existing industries within the state or territory, and in order to receive such assistance businesses must demonstrate that they are viable, both in the short- and long-term, and that they can provide assessable benefits to the state. The government will be likely to favour business which will create new permanent jobs, provide new skills, increase the state's technology or production capacity, tap new markets outside the state, or offer diversification of the state's industrial base or range of products. For further details about State Government assistance, you should contact your state's Small Business Development Corporation or similar body, the Australian Job Network, or AusIndustry (see *Useful Addresses* below).

Importing/Exporting

Australia has a policy of gradually and systematically removing trade tariffs on imported products. However, in those industries still subject to protection, *bounties* are sometimes offered, which are direct cash payments to Australian manufacturers (operating within Australia) in lieu of, or supplementary to, assistance provided by means of tariff or customs duty. Bounties can assist manufacturers to compete more effectively with imported products. Many imported goods will also be liable to the Goods and Services Tax. You should contact the Australian Customs Information Centre (☎1300 363 263; www.customs.gov.au) for further information.

If your business is involved in exporting goods from Australia, Austrade (The Australian Trade Commission; ☎132 878 (local); www.austrade.gov.au) will be able to provide marketing advice and assistance. Additionally, the R&D Start Program, available to non-tax-exempt Australian companies, is a merit-based program designed to assist the commercialisation of Australian industry and to undertake research and development (R&D) through a range of grants and loans. The Federal Government also offers a range of tax incentives.

Summary of Financing

Although a potential financier will want a thorough plan, they will not want a long report, so you should try to keep your proposal down to between 10 and 12 pages. You must ensure that you describe your product, the premises from which you intend to operate, relevant information about each member of the management team, your marketing strategy, your competition, past performance (if any), financial projections and assumptions relating to them, the financial resources required and what changes will be necessary if your assumptions prove to be either pessimistic or optimistic, and your assessment of the risks involved in the project. A professional-looking presentation is important, as this is the document that will 'sell' your business to lenders. It is vitally important to obtain impartial professional advice when preparing a business plan, but you must also be fully involved; when you come face to face with the bank manager, you are the one who will have to answer all the questions.

Accountants

A good accountant is essential to the success of your business. You will find that the process of creating a new business or buying an existing one is so complex and involved that you will not be able to complete it without expert assistance. Your accountant should be registered with one of the industry associations, and it is essential that you confirm this. You should also shop around and obtain quotes in respect of hourly rates and estimated annual expenses. Your accountant will act as your financial and, on many occasions, as your legal adviser, and will often undertake duties which could also be done by a solicitor. If the advice you receive is false or misguided it could mean the failure of your business and possibly even fines and legal costs. For this reason, you will want to make sure that the accountant you decide to use is reliable and reputable. Large accountancy firms are likely to be considerably more expensive, but may be more reliable and offer backup guidance. Your accountant is really another business investment you will have to make, and so you will want to reduce the element of risk. It is advisable to consult your accountant on every initial business decision you make, as a good accountant will always give you more impartial advice than you may receive from a real estate agent, bank business advisor or business broker.

Useful Addresses

AusIndustry, ☎132 846 hotline; www.ausindustry.gov.au.

Austrade, Australia House, Strand, London WC2B 4LA; ☎020-7887 5226; fax 020-7836 4250; and Atlanta Financial Center, 3353 Peachtree Road, Suite 1140, Atlanta GA 30326; ☎404-760 3400; fax 404-760 3401; www.austrade.gov. au.

Australia and New Zealand Chamber of Commerce (UK), Dudley House, 34-35 Southampton Street, London WC2E 7HE, ☎0870-890 0720; fax 0870-890 0721; e-mail enquiries@anzcc.org.uk; www.anzcc.org.uk.

Australian Copyright Council, 245 Chalmers Street, Redfern, NSW 2016; ☎02-9318 1788; fax 02-9698 3536; e-mail info@copyright.org.au; www.copyright. org.au.

Department of Industry, Tourism and Resources, 20 Allara Street, Canberra, ACT 2601; ☎06-213 6000; fax 06-213 7000; e-mail inquiries@industry.gov.au; www.industry.gov.au. ITR is based in Canberra with offices in all Australian State capitals, and representatives in North America, Europe and Asia.

Inventors' Association of Australia, Association House, Cnr Wakefield Street and Chancery Lane, Adelaide, SA 5068; www.inventors.asn.au. Has chapters in several other states.

Institute of Patent and Trade Mark Attorneys of Australia, 711 High Street, East Kew, VIC 3102; ☎03-9857 0311; fax 03-9857 0411; www.ipta.com.au.

SAI Global, 286 Sussex Street, Sydney, NSW 2001; ☎02-8206 6186; fax 02-8206 6044.

United Kingdom Patent Office, Concept House, Cardiff Road, Newport NP10 8QQ, South Wales; ☎01633-813930; fax 01633-813600; e-mail enquiries@patent. gov.uk; www.patent.gov.uk, or filings by hand may be made at Harmsworth House, 13-15 Bouverie Street, London EC4Y 8DP

Small Business Agencies

These provide advice and referral services for intending, starting and existing businesses in each state:

ACT: *ACT and Region Chamber of Commerce and Industry,* 12a Thesiger Court, Deakin, ACT 2600; ☎02-6283 5200; fax 02-6282 2436; e-mail chamber@actchamber.com.au; www.actchamber.com.au.

NSW: *NSW State and Regional Development,* Level 43, Grosvenor Place, 225 George Street, Sydney, NSW 2000; ☎1300 134 359; www.smallbiz.nsw.gov.au.

NT: *Business Services, Department of Business, Industry and Resource Development,* 2nd Floor, Development House, 76 Esplanade, Darwin, NT 0800; ☎08-8924 4280; fax 08-8924 4290; www.dbird.nt.gov.au.

QLD: *State Development and Innovation,* Albert Street, Brisbane, Queensland 4000; ☎07-3001 6359; www.sd.qld.gov.au.

SA: *Department of Trade and Economic Development,* 145 South Terrace, Adelaide, SA 5001; ☎08-8463 3800; fax 08-8463 3840; www.cibm.sa.gov.au.

TAS: *Department of Economic Development,* Business Licence Information Service, 22 Elizabeth Street, Hobart, TAS 7000; ☎03-6233 5888; fax 03-6233 5800;

www.development.tas.gov.au.

VIC: *Business in Victoria*, Level 5, 55 Collins Street, Melbourne, Vic 3000; ☎132 215 (local); fax 03-9651 9725; www.business.vic.gov.au.

WA: *Small Business Development Corporation*, 553 Hay Street, Perth, WA 6000; ☎08-9220 0222; fax 08-9325 3981; e-mail info@sbdc.com.au; www.sbdc.com.au.

Accountants

Most accountants advertise in the Yellow Pages of their state telephone directory. The Institute of Chartered Accountants, the Australian Society of Accountants in your capital city, or the National Institute of Accountants can also provide lists of professionals associated with their organisation. A brief list of other contacts is given below:

Australian Accounting Group, 56 Neridah Road, Chatswood, NSW 2067; ☎02-9411 4866.

Collett & Co, Suite 408, 370 St Kilda Road, Melbourne, VIC 3004, Australia; ☎03-9686 5580; 3/267 St George's Terrace, Perth, WA 6000; ☎08-9261 7762; and in UK at Enterprise House, Ocean Village, Southampton, Hampshire S014 3XB; ☎02380-488786; fax 02380-488787; e-mail info@collettandco.com; www.colletandco.com. Provides tax and financial planning advice to businesses and individuals heading for Australia.

Deloitte Touche Tohmatsu, 225 George Street, Sydney, NSW 1217; ☎02-9322 7000; fax 02-9322 7001; www.deloitte.com.au

Ernst & Young, 680 George Street, Sydney, NSW 2000; ☎02-9248 5555; fax 02-9248 5959; www.ey.com/au.

Institute of Chartered Accountants in Australia, Level 14, 37 York Street, Sydney, NSW 2000; ☎02-9290 1344; fax 02-9262 1512; www.icaa.org.au.

KPMG Australia, www.kpmg.com.au.

PricewaterhouseCoopers, Darling Park Tower 2, 201 Sussex Street, Sydney, NSW 1171; ☎02-8266 0000; fax 02-8266 9999; www.pwcglobal.com/au/.

Trading Banks

Australia and New Zealand Bank (ANZ), 3/287 Queen Street, Melbourne, VIC 3000; ☎1800 801 485 Small Business hotline; www.anz.com.au.

Commonwealth Bank of Australia, 48 Martin Place, Sydney, NSW 2000; ☎0061-131 998; fax 02-9378 3317; www.commbank.com.au.

National Australia Bank Ltd, 500 Bourke Street, Melbourne, VIC 3000; ☎03-9641 3500; fax 03-9641 4916; www.national.com.au.

Westpac Banking Corporation, 60 Martin Place, Sydney NSW 2000; ☎02-9226 3311; fax 02-9226 4128; www.westpac.com.au.

See also the banking section of Chapter Four, *Daily Life* for the British branches of these banks.

Merchant Banks

BNP Paribas Australia, 60 Castlereagh Street, Sydney NSW 2000; ☎02-9216 8633; fax 02-9221 3026; www.bnp.com.au. The third largest foreign bank in Australia, in terms of assets, and the 12th largest bank in Australia overall.

BT (Bankers Trust) Financial Group , PO Box 2675, Sydney, NSW 2001; ☎02-9034 4900; e-mail customer.relations@btfinancialgroup.com; www.btonline.com.au

Deautsche Bank AG, Level 20, 225 George Street, Sydney, NSW 2000; ☎02-9258 3666; fax 02-9241 2565; www.aus.deuba.com.

JPMorgan, Head Office, Level 26, Grosvenor Place, 225 George Street, Sydney, NSW 2000; ☎02-9220 1333; www.jpmorgan.com.au.

Macquarie Bank Ltd, 22 Floor, 20 Bond Street, Sydney, NSW 2000; ☎02-9237 3333; fax 02-9237 3350; www.macquarie.com.au.

Finance Companies

GE Commercial Finance (GE), 60 Carrington Street, Sydney, NSW 2000; ☎02-8234 4455; www.gecommercial.com.au.

Esanda Finance Corporation Ltd, 85 Spring Street, Melbourne, VIC 3000; ☎132 373 (local); ☎03-9666 9100 (international); www.esanda.com.au. Australia's largest asset-based finance company.

Real Estate

There are countless real estate agencies in every area of Australia. To locate those in the area of Australia to which you are moving, try searching Telstra's online database at www.telstra.com.

Useful Publications

Books and Information Packs:

Starting a Business in Australia, Vacation Work Publications (www.vacationwork. co.uk), published January 2006. Other books in Vacation Work's *Live and Work* series may be useful if you are considering setting up an export business; each book in the series contains a 'Starting a Business' section relevant to the particular country or area covered.

Australian Bureau of Statistics, Central Office, ABS House, 45 Benjamin Way, Belconnen, ACT 2617; ☎1300 135 070 (local); ☎02-9268 4909 (international); www.abs.gov.au. The Australian Bureau of Statistics has offices in every Australian state/territory and publish yearbooks containing the results of every recent survey and research project, which are useful when undertaking initial market research.

Doing Business in Australia, published by Ernst & Young as part of their *International Business* series and is available from their Australian office listed above under *Accountants* and also online from www.ey.com. Copies are also held by their international branches, and you should consult the telephone directory in your country's capital city for further information.

Periodicals

Australian Business for Sale News, PO Box 586, Darlinghurst, Sydney, NSW 1300; ☎02-9281 4599; fax 02-9212 6925; www.businessforsale.com.au. A magazine produced every three months which gives information and details about franchising, business opportunities, distributorships, and licenses, plus information on how to buy or sell a business. The periodical is available in the UK from the Subscription Department, Consyl Publishing, 3 Buckhurst Road, Bexhill-on-Sea, East Sussex, TN40 1QF; ☎01424-223111; www.consylpublishing.co.uk.

The Australian Financial Review, 201 Sussex Street, Sydney NSW 2000, ☎09-282 2833; www.afr.com.au.

Dynamic Small Business Magazine, Level 11, 80 Mount Street, North Sydney, NSW

2060; ☎02-9955 6311; fax 02-9954 7994; www.dsbmag.com.au. A bi-monthly magazine regarded as essential reading for Australian small business.

Economic Outlook, 124 Sturt Street, Adelaide, SA 5000; ☎08-8231 0941; fax 08-8231 0949; e-mail eo@econ-outlook.com.au; www.econ-outlook.com.au.

Franchising

Franchising & Own Your Own Business Magazine, is a bi-monthly which gives the latest national and international news, discussion of key industry issues, and information from the Franchising Council of Australia. The magazine also includes information on how to choose the right franchise and how to franchise your existing business. It is available from Niche Media, PO Box 2135, St Kilda, VIC 3182; ☎03-9525 5566; fax 03-9525 5678; www.franchise.net.au.

Franchisenet, is a very useful website with industry information, a links page and a franchise directory at www.franchise.net.au.

The Franchising Council of Australia, National Office, PO. Box 1498N, Melbourne, VIC 3001; ☎1300 669 030; fax 03-9509 5159; www.franchise.org.au.

RELOCATION AGENCIES AND BUSINESS SERVICES

In addition to assisting with housing, education and employment arrangements on your behalf, many of the relocation companies also specialise in finding appropriate business premises and in relocating complete companies, including plant and machinery. These services tend to be very expensive and are best suited to large, international companies. Most large relocators have offices overseas or have reciprocal arrangements with certain firms in Australia. However, many relocators in the UK are established to provide services for those relocating to the UK from other countries. If you require the services of a business relocator it may be most appropriate to engage the assistance of a specialist Australian firm, of which some are listed below.

Useful Addresses

The following relocators specialise in the relocation of executives, company personnel and their families.

Allied Pickfords, has offices Australia-wide and can be contacted at 184 Gillmore Road, Queanbeyon, Canberra, NSW 2620; ☎02-9636 6333; www.allpick. com.au, or call 132 554 to find nearest office location.

Australiawide Relocations Pty Ltd, Head Office, Abignano House, Suite 17, 19-23 Bridge Street, Pymble, NSW 2073; ☎02-9488 9444; fax 02-9488 8259; www. relocations.aust.com.

Expat International, 2/423 Bourke Street, Melbourne, VIC 3000; ☎03-9670 7555; fax 03-9670 7799; e-mail info@expat.com.au; www.expat.com.au.

Grace Removals, Executive and Commercial Relocations, Head Office, 4 Tucks Rd, Seven Hills, Sydney, NSW 2147; ☎02-9838 5600; fax 02-9838 5755; e-mail info@grace.com.au; www.grace.com.au. Grace is Australia's largest mover of business and household goods internationally, both from and to Australia.

Relocations in Melbourne, Suite 112, 620 St Kilda Road, Melbourne, VIC 3004; ☎03-9533 6831; fax 03-9525 1477; www.relocations-melb.com.au.

IDEAS FOR NEW BUSINESSES

The various state governments have all identified strategic industries in which the greatest opportunities for investment lie, and these are outlined in the Regional Employment Guide section of the preceding chapter. Most state governments can offer incentive packages to investors. In overview, Australia is currently a leading exporter of commodities such as coal, iron ore, wheat, beef and veal, petroleum and gas, and cotton. However, the export market in unprocessed foods, fuels, minerals and other primary products is declining.

Service industries now make up 64% of the economy, and Australia is becoming an information-based economy. Between 1996 and 1999 the number of computer service businesses grew by more than 50%. Australia is developing a new competitive edge in high-technology exports, such as scientific and medical equipment, telecommunications, software and aerospace products. Knowledge-based industries now contribute almost half of Australia's GDP and the information and communications technologies are Australia's fastest-growing sectors. The manufacture of components for mechanical and electronic equipment, and cars, has also recorded strong growth in the last decade. The shift from an economy based on manufacturing to services has been rapid; the growth rate of non-service industries has dropped, while service industries continue to grow. About 36.5% of Australians now work in professional, technical, managerial or administrative jobs and the service industries are Australia's biggest employers. In 1998, according to the OECD (Organisation for Economic Co-operation and Development), service industry employees accounted for almost 77% of total employment in Australia.

New businesses, which either compete directly in these sectors or which provide related services, are the most likely to succeed. Import businesses are suffering because of the relatively weak Australian dollar. Both federal and state governments are, however, strongly export-oriented, and any business which exports Australian goods and services is likely to be eligible for a variety of export subsidies and incentive schemes.

WOMEN IN BUSINESS

According to figures from Women's Network Australia (PO Box 1723, Sunnybank Hills, Queensland 4109; ☎07-3272 8222; fax 07-3272 8111; www.womensnetwork.com.au) while nine out of ten businesses in Australia are small businesses, women are opening small businesses at twice the rate of men. Currently, 32% of all small businesses across Australia are owned and operated by women and every year, 37% of women leave salaried employment to open their own small business venture. Australian women are opening businesses at nearly twice the rate of men and their businesses have a higher success rate, particularly in the first five years. Women are considered to be more successful in business because they are willing to acquire formal business skills and to develop non-formal management skills such as networking and flexibility, which may give them a competitive advantage over men.

In many states today, women-centred business networks have been developed, and these are generally viewed as valuable resources by women entrepreneuses.

A survey by *Yellow Pages Australia* found that both men and women believe that women business owners are more persuasive, more prepared to ask for advice, are better at dealing with customers, learn faster, are more hard-working, and are more pleasant to deal with. The trend in business ownership and operation by women is towards a far greater involvement in the services sector of the economy, with around 83% of businesses operating in this sector owned by women. Most states have specific programmes to encourage the development of women in business, and details of schemes can be found online at www.womensnetwork.com.au. The Australian Businesswomen's Network (4-6 Mentmore Avenue, Roseberry, NSW 2018; ☎1300 720 120; fax 1300 720 121; www.abn.org.au) is an organisation seeking to help women in business by raising their profile and providing exposure to a range of business success models.

BUYING AN EXISTING BUSINESS

One of the options you may have when starting in business is to purchase an existing operation. Getting into business in this way can be much less risky and more quickly profitable than starting your own business from scratch, but it is not entirely risk free and your success will depend heavily on how wisely you choose and evaluate the business you buy.

Buying a business will include the purchase of plant and equipment, stock in trade and, usually, a goodwill component. Goodwill is represented in part by location, existing customers and reputation, but also by other factors which can influence the profitability of the business or its income-producing capacity. The correct assessment and identification of the value of a business is crucial in the process of buying a going concern, and it is highly recommended that you obtain professional assistance in making this assessment. When you investigate a prospective business purchase you should make sure that you examine the following: financial statements, payables and receivables, employees, customers, location, facilities, competitors, registration, zoning, and image. Financial figures should be accompanied by an audit letter from a CPA (certified practising accountancy) firm, and you should make sure that business licences and other legal documents can be easily transferred and determine the costs involved in doing so. Customers are your most important asset, however, and you should make sure that they are as solid as the other tangible assets that you will be acquiring. Check if the current clientele has a special relationship with the present owner (are they long-time friends, neighbours and relatives?). How long have these accounts been with the business, and what percentage of income do they represent? Will they leave when the business passes to new hands? Make sure, too, when you are buying a business that you understand the competitive environment in which it operates. Check whether local price wars are common, or whether any competitors have gone out of business recently. You can track down this information by contacting an industry association or by reading trade publications. Finally, look at how a business is perceived locally, and in general. This 'goodwill' factor cannot necessarily be established from a balance sheet, and you will need to evaluate everything from the way a company services customers to how employees answer the phone. To learn more about a firm's reputation talk to suppliers, competitors, customers, banks and owners of other businesses in the area, and remember that it can be very difficult to change a negative perception.

Transferring Ownership

Transferring the ownership of a business from one owner to the next requires a management plan to ensure a smooth transition of the business and its assets (including goodwill and the customer base). You will need to notify the Australian Taxation Office of the transfer and, in the case of an incorporated business, the Australian Securities and Investments Commission, and supply details of new directors and the transfer of trading name. You may also have to transfer ownership of any licences which are required to operate the business, for which you should contact your local Business Licence Information Service (553 Hay Street, Perth, WA 6000; ☎08-9220 0234; fax 08-9221 3780; www.licence.sbdc.com.au).

Franchising

Australia is the most franchised nation per head of population in the world and has at least three times as many franchise systems per head of population than the United States. Because many new business owners are attracted to the ready-made brand awareness and back up available to franchisees, each year franchising contributes over $77 billion to the Australian economy. There are more than 747 different types of franchise available in Australia.

The Franchising Council of Australia (FCA) should be your first port of call if you are considering this type of business option. The FCA has a strict code of conduct which protects members from unscrupulous operators, and can also direct potential franchisees to accountants and lawyers who are members of the FCA and who understand the specialist field of franchising practice. The FCA publishes *The Franchisee's Guide: Everything you need to know as a Franchisee* for intending franchisees, available from the FCA Franchise Library for $16.50. They also have a very comprehensive website at www.franchise.org.au.

The position of the franchise in the market in which it trades should be carefully assessed. You should not only look at the particular franchised business in relation to its own activities, but also make an assessment of the prospects for the industry overall. The franchise will either be dealing in goods, products or services and you should consider whether these are new or have distinct advantages over their competitors. Check that the franchised business has been thoroughly proven in practice, or whether it is exploiting a fad or current fashion which may be transient or short-lived. If the product is strongly associated with a celebrity name, remember that a person's fame can fade as quickly as it came, and that your business, built on a name, may fade with it.

The basis of any franchise operation is the franchise agreement. This must be considered very carefully and it is advisable to consult your accountant/solicitor before signing anything. Before you enter into any franchise agreement, you need to consider whether you are technically able to deal with the product or service, as well as the extent of the competition. If the franchise involves evolving technology, you will also need to assess whether the franchiser also has the expertise and resources to be able to compete successfully in the market. If your product is manufactured overseas, or is composed of parts made elsewhere, you must identify delivery times and calculate the risk of delays and the potential for foreign currency losses. In addition, you will have to ascertain whether there are any import duties or regulations which have an impact on the price of the product. You should also be clear on how much assistance is given, and control exercised, by the franchiser, and you would be well advised to investigate the franchiser's financial credibility and stability. It can be beneficial to talk to other franchisees about the business and the franchiser's methods of operation. It is imperative that you understand what the duration of the franchise is, what costs and fees are involved, whether you have to pay a royalty to the franchiser (and if so, how much), and what the arrangements are for termination.

Franchising offers significant benefits to business owners, and can be considered as going into business with an experienced partner. A good franchiser will offer training and continuing assistance; and the franchisee will benefit from established brand recognition and a customer base. The franchisee will usually need less capital than they would if setting up business independently. Although business risk is significantly reduced because you are under the umbrella of a franchise, setting up your own business is still a risk.

Other Businesses

Most businesses for sale are advertised with real estate agents, business brokers, trading associations and in the national and local newspapers. A successful acquisition depends on a thorough study of the business or company from many different angles. Your accountant should check out the value of stock and the cash flow of the business. Profit should be calculated after the fair working salaries of proprietors or partners have been deducted. Your accountant should also advise you on the stamp duty and tax implications of the purchase of a particular business. The last three years' accounts of the company (audited if possible) should be examined, together with current management accounts and projections (if available), particularly in terms of the valuation of assets, contingent liabilities and the company's tax position. Finally, you need to ensure that you will be able to raise the finance required before committing yourself to the purchase, and this applies to the purchase of either a business or a company. Further details are given above in the section *Raising Finance*.

BUSINESS STRUCTURES

Companies

Most small businesses in Australia are embodied in some kind of legally recognised entity. Australian company law is mainly governed by the Corporations Law of individual states, which is basically the commonwealth legislation for the Australian Capital Territory with minor variations pertinent to that particular state. The Corporations Law contains the rules, procedures, accounting and reporting requirements for companies. This is administered by the Australian Securities and Investments Commission (ASIC) and detailed information regarding Corporations Law can be obtained upon request (see address below).

Public and Proprietary Companies. A company is a legal body distinct from its individual members. Generally, investors combine their capital to form a company and share its profits. Usually, this is without the risk of loss beyond their original investment or guarantee amount. Companies can buy, sell and hold property, sue and be sued, and enter into contracts. They have what is known as 'perpetual existence', which means that unless there are exceptional circumstances (such as in the case of default on payments to their creditors), they cannot be involuntarily terminated. Of the various types of companies which operate in Australia, two types of corporations have limited liability (public and proprietary/private), and there are also no-liability companies and foreign companies. Public companies can invite public subscription of their shares and be listed on the stock exchange, whereas proprietary companies cannot. A proprietary company must have at least two, but no more than 50, members. It is not allowed to invite public subscription of its shares. A no-liability company is usually only used by specific mining companies and oil and gas ventures, and a foreign company is considered to be one which originated overseas but conducts business in Australia.

THE ADVANTAGES AND DISADVANTAGES OF A LIMITED (REGISTERED) COMPANY

Advantages

- The liabilities of the company are the responsibility of the company so that shareholders are liable to lose only the share capital they subscribed although directors may be personally liable for any debts incurred when the company is unable to pay its debts.
- After tax, profits of the business can be retained within the company to provide funds for future expansion.
- In some cases greater superannuation benefits can be secured; tax on company profits is currently 30% compared to the current maximum personal tax of 48.5% (excluding the Medicare levy).
- It is easier to spread ownership of the company.
- The company has an ongoing existence and does not need to be wound up in the event of death or permanent disability of any of the directors or shareholders.

Disadvantages

- Financial and certain other information must be filed on public records (although in the case of a proprietary company accounts need not be lodged and only certain declarations and statements are required to be made).
- Loans can be made to directors of proprietary companies.
- However, in the case of other companies, the shareholders in the general meeting have to approve such loans as part of a scheme for making loans to full-time employees and disclosure of such loans must be made in the company's accounts.
- There may be tax consequences of making loans to shareholders and/or directors.
- Compliance with the extensive requirements of the Corporations Law can be time consuming and costly.
- Lenders often seek personal guarantees from directors which tends to significantly reduce the value of limited liability.
- Tax is payable when accumulated profits are withdrawn from the company as dividends or extra remuneration.
- Auditors must be appointed unless all shareholders agree that this is

> not necessary; and losses in a company are not distributable to the shareholders and therefore cannot be offset against other income of the owners.

Partnership. As an alternative to the company structure, many small businesses choose to structure themselves as a partnership. A partnership is usually formed by two or more people (individuals or companies) in order to conduct business for profit as co-owners. It is governed by the Partnership Act of the relevant state and the terms of the partnership agreement, which should be in writing. This partnership agreement means that each partner has the same rights, liabilities and powers as any other partner, unless the agreement specifically states otherwise. As a member of a partnership, each partner is jointly responsible for partnership debts. In Western Australia, Tasmania and Queensland, limited liability partnerships can be used. A limited liability partnership allows some partners who are not as involved in the management of the partnership to have a limited liability. The Australian Taxation Office requires that partnerships maintain 'appropriate' accounting records, but they are not legally required to be audited. Unlike a company, a partnership is not usually considered as a separate legal body from its partners. This means that the partnership's profits are taxable to the individual partners, regardless of the distribution of those profits. Even so, partnerships must also file an annual tax return separate from and in addition to that of each partner.

Joint Venture. Another form of business structure is the unincorporated joint venture. This occurs when an Australian entity joins with either an Australian or foreign entity to create a venture for their mutual benefit. Examples of such joint ventures are most often found in various mining and exploration projects. A contractual relationship exists between the joint venture participants and this form of business entity has recently become increasingly popular. Unincorporated joint ventures are often considered to be partnerships for tax purposes if the income is jointly derived, which means that each 'partner' is required to file partnership tax returns. It is possible, however, to set up an unincorporated joint venture so that participants share in the production rather than the income. This kind of joint venture is not considered to be a partnership by Australian law, so each venturer is required to state its share of the income and expenditure from the joint venture project in the venturer's tax return. Incorporated joint ventures are considered to be the same as ordinary companies, and are treated and taxed accordingly.

Sole Trader. It is possible to be a sole proprietor if you individually own an unincorporated business and you receive all the business profits and incur all of its liabilities. On the whole, if you are the sole proprietor, you will be actively involved in the management and conduct of the business. You can form sole proprietorship without official approval and you need not have your financial statements audited. You do, however, need to supply the tax authorities with proper accounting records.

ADVANTAGES AND DISADVANTAGES OF SOLE TRADER PARTNERSHIP

Advantages
- Confidentiality is maintained since the public has no access to financial accounts.
- PAYG (income tax) and Medicare levy contributions do not need to be paid when proprietors or partners draw cash but is paid on a partner's share of the profits.
- Losses from the business can be offset against other income.
- It is relatively easy to transfer the business to another legal structure (e.g. a limited company) at a later stage.

Disadvantages
- The owner is personally liable for the business, which means that if one partner fails to meet his share of the partnership debts, other partners will have to settle them.
- There is less flexibility in transferring ownership (for example to other family members).
- In the event of death, permanent disablement or retirement of the sole trader/partner there may be difficulties in maintaining the business structure.

Trusts

Trusts are not normally used for a sizeable partnership or joint venture with Australian residents, but more for wholly owned projects or ventures. This is largely due to the fact that a trust is not considered to be a separate legal body to the beneficiary's property, and so it may not enter into contracts in its own right. As a result, creditors and bankers will not grant credit to the trust or allow it to open and use a bank account unless personal guarantees are obtained from the trust or beneficiaries. The advantages of a trading trust are:

ADVANTAGES AND DISADVANTAGES OF A TRADING TRUST

Advantages
- Confidentiality is maintained since the public has no access to the trust's accounts, although certain information is disclosed in the trustee's accounts.
- Income is distributed to beneficiaries who pay tax on their allocation of profits at their respective personal tax rates.
- Trusts are not subject to income tax on their profits provided they are fully distributed to beneficiaries.
- A discretionary trust is usually preferred because it provides flexibility to the trustee to allocate income amongst various classes of beneficiaries under the trust.
- To some extent, limited liability can be achieved through the establishment of a trust with a company acting as a trustee.

> **Disadvantages**
> - Generally banks and financiers require assurances from solicitors that the trust has been properly constituted.
> - In the case of corporate trustees, there is a necessity for compliance with the extensive requirements of the Corporations Law.
> - Losses derived in a trust are not distributable and therefore cannot be offset against other income of a beneficiary (owner) of the trust.

There are also subsidiary businesses, branches and representative offices, but these are usually owned by existing foreign companies that wish to operate in Australia.

Duties of Directors & Company Office-Bearers

Every company, whether public or private, must appoint directors and a company secretary. These company officials have clearly defined duties under law. The directors of a company are not necessarily actively involved in the daily management of the business, but they are responsible for the actions of the management of the business. In accordance with the Corporations Law, a director must act with the utmost good faith towards the company and its members, and must not obtain any benefit for him/herself from the activities of the company, other than remuneration. A director is expected to exercise skills, which reflect his or her qualifications and experience. Although a director is responsible for the keeping of the statutory records and the books of account, this duty is usually delegated to an appropriate professional, such as an accountant. The Corporations Law clearly specifies the kinds of books and records, which must be kept and it is important that you seek professional advice in these matters. A director may accept a loan from the company providing that loan has been approved by the shareholders. It must be noted that such loans must be shown in the accounts in accordance with statutory requirements. A director has the power to appoint an alternative director who has the full powers and duties of a director. If the business becomes insolvent, the directors become personally liable for any debts contracted by the company during the period of insolvency.

Within one month of the first and every annual general meeting, companies must provide the ASIC with their directors' names, ages, addresses, company share holding and details of other public company directorships. The appointment of additional or new directors, the company secretary, and an auditor (if required) should also be made at this time. Banking arrangements and the end of the company's financial year (normally 30th June) should also be determined. Shares should be allotted and transfers of subscribers' shares should be approved. Arrangements should also be made for keeping statutory books such as the Register of Members, Register of Directors and a Minute Book, and the company's registered office must be specified. A Public Officer must also be appointed for income tax purposes.

The company secretary is responsible for statutory duties and must be a resident of Australia. Public companies must have at least five members, while proprietary companies need only have two. Wholly-owned subsidiaries, public or proprietary, have no minimum requirement. A proprietary company must have between two and 50 shareholders, whereas public companies must have a minimum of five shareholders and have no maximum limit. Shares may be sold for cash or otherwise issued, but details must be reported to the ASIC. For both public and proprietary companies, the minimum capital derived from shares is one share per subscriber. The minimum time required to establish a company is three to four days and ASIC fees must be paid during the process of registration.

RUNNING A BUSINESS

Once you have had your business plans approved, secured financial backing, established the business as a legal entity, chosen and registered its name and have obtained premises from which to operate your business, then it is time to consider the daily operations of your new livelihood. Here, the critical factors are staff and taxes. If you manage to get both of these areas right, it is likely that your business will run smoothly and be a success.

Taxation

Australian business taxation law is extremely complex and if you are starting a new business there are a certain number of things you will have to do and decisions you will have to make. Taxation issues are made even more complex if you have been employed in Australia prior to setting up your business. Furthermore, the structure you choose for your business may have significant tax consequences, so it is important to investigate taxation thoroughly when planning its structure. There is simply no avoiding the tax maze and it is vital that you get professional advice from the outset. Doing so is likely to mean considerable expense, but will save you costly mistakes in the long term.

Sole traders and partnerships are subject to very different taxes to either companies or trusts. Essentially, for a sole trader or partnership, any profit earned from the business is added to any other income that you have and you are taxed on the total. Your level of taxable income is determined by the financial statements you produce for the Tax Office, however there are some adjustments that are made to the income shown on the statements in order to arrive at a taxable income. You may, for example, be allowed to claim special deductions such as those available for research and development costs. Tax concessions and grants are available to cover research and development costs, and for businesses seeking to develop new export markets. Some of the income you receive may not be subject to tax such as the rebates paid to you under special youth employment schemes. Depreciation can be claimed on all of your plant equipment and other business fixed assets, and items valued at less than $300 or with an effective life of less than three years can be written off in the year of acquisition.

Companies are taxed differently because they are considered to be separate legal entities from their owners. A company is subject to income tax on its taxable income whereas the partners in a partnership are taxed on their share of partnership taxable income even though a tax return must be lodged for the partnership. An important difference to note is that there is no variation according to income of the tax rate for companies as there is for individuals. Both resident and non-resident companies are subject to corporate income tax of 30%.

The calculation of a company's or family trust's taxable income is roughly the same as that use to assess a partnership or sole trader, with some significant differences. Firstly, providing that it is at a reasonable level, the remuneration of the company's directors (or owners in the case of a family company) is a deductible expense in determining the company's taxable income. Secondly, there is a complicated system known as 'Dividend Imputation' which refers to the distribution of a company's dividend income. Dividend imputations distributed by Australian resident companies have a tax advantage attached to them if the dividends are paid from profits, which have been taxed in the company's hands at the company rate. Basically, this means that the system allows shareholders a tax rebate to the extent of the difference between personal and corporate income tax rates. Any excess rebate may be offset against any other income tax of the shareholder, including capital gains, and these dividends which have been relieved of tax are known as 'franked'. If the company holds on to its dividend, it will generally be subject to credit under the 'Dividend Imputation' system. Your taxation adviser will be able to explain the system of tax payment, as companies must pay instalments of tax by certain dates.

If you decide to take over an existing company, you should ask your accountant to help you draft taxation warranties and indemnities which should appear in the purchase agreement, as these will protect you from any unexpected tax liabilities that may arise as a result of the acquisition. The capital gains tax-exempt status of assets owned by a company may be lost when ownership of the company is changed.

As the owner of a business, whether new or already in existence, you will be expected to pay Goods and Services Tax, Fringe Benefits Tax and PAYG deductions. If you employ staff, you are responsible for deducting taxation instalments (PAYG) from your employees' wages and paying it to the Commissioner of Taxation. In order to do this, you must register as a group employer with the Commissioner of Taxation and each employee must submit to you their personal particulars, including a tax file number, on an income tax instalment declaration form. PAYG must be deducted from wages, overtime pay, commissions, fees, bonuses, gratuities, lump sum payments and any other allowances.

The Australian tax year ends on 30 June, and for companies that also end their financial year on this date, tax returns must be filed by the following 15 March or, in certain circumstances, 15 December of the end of the following tax year. If an alternative financial period has been adopted by the company, its tax returns must be filed at the earliest by the 15th day of the sixth month following the year-end, with a maximum extension to the earlier of the 15th day of the ninth month or 15 June following the end of the alternative financial year. Tax returns of individuals, partnerships and trusts must generally be filed by 31 October each year and an extension may be granted if the return is to be filed by a registered tax agent. It is important to note that penalties of up to 200% of tax underpayment may be imposed for filing an incorrect return, together with interest charges and penalties for the late filing of returns or payment of tax. These penalties are strictly enforced, and the sophisticated data-matching processes employed by the ATO make tax evasion nearly impossible and certainly foolish.

The Australian Taxation Office has a comprehensive website, which offers assistance to small business owners, including a wide range of electronic pamphlets to download. You can access the ATO site at www.ato.gov.au. Many TAFE colleges also now offer short courses and evening courses in managing your taxation affairs as a small business owner.

Employing Staff

Equal opportunity or anti-discrimination legislation is operative in all States and

Territories in Australia and the Human Rights and Equal Opportunity Commission investigates discrimination on the grounds of race, colour or ethnic origin, racial vilification, sex, sexual harassment, marital status, pregnancy or disability. Employers should understand their rights and responsibilities and those of their employees under the human rights and anti-discrimination law. Other legal responsibilities in relation to employees include, wages and conditions of employment, employees' awards, workplace safety and dismissal. The Government's Business Entry Point (www.business.gov.au) provides further information regarding your obligations as any employer.

Fair-Trading

Fair-trading concerns the ethical environment in which you interact with other business and customers. The Federal Government announced a fair trading reform package for small business in 1997, which strengthened the Trade Practices Act. The new package protects small businesses against unconscionable conduct, and imposes a mandatory Code of Conduct for franchisers, to protect franchisees. It also offers support for alternative dispute resolution to provide businesses with quicker, less costly, and more efficient remedies; and has extended the banking Industry Ombudsman to small businesses. The Australian Competition and Consumer Commission (ACCC), Level 7, Angel Place, 123 Pitt Street, Sydney, NSW 2000; ☎02-9230 9133; fax 02-9223 1092; www.accc.gov.au, and the Department of Employment and Workplace Relations (www.dewrsb.gov.au) can provide information on both your obligations as a trader and the laws which are designed to protect your business.

Useful Addresses

Australian British Chamber of Commerce, Level 16, The Gateway Building, 1 Macquarie Place, Sydney, NSW 2000; ☎02-9247 6271; fax 02-9247 6671; www.britishchamber.com.

Australian Bureau of Statistics, Central Office, ABS House, 45 Benjamin Way, Belconnen, ACT 2617; ☎1300 135 070 (local), ☎02-9268 4909; www.abs.gov.au.

Australian Business Economists, 251 Oxford Street, Bondi Junction, Sydney, NSW 2022; ☎02-9299 2610; www.abe.org.au.

Australian Business Research Pty Ltd, Level 10, 231 North Quay, Brisbane, QLD 4000; ☎07-3837 1333; fax 07-3236 3422; www.abr.com.au. Credit and Business Information Services.

Australian Customs Service, 3rd Floor, Tower Sydney Central Building, 477 Pitt Street, Sydney, NSW 2000; ☎1300 363 263 (local); ☎02-6275 6666; e-mail information@customs.gov.au; www.customs.gov.au.

Australian Industry Group, 20 Queens Road, Melbourne, VIC 3004; ☎03-9867 0111; fax 03-9867 0199; www.aigroup.asn.au.

Australian Securities and Investment Commission (ASIC), Level 8, City Centre Tower, 55 Market Street, Sydney NSW 2000; ☎02-9911 2500 for general enquiries, document lodgement and searches; www.asic.gov.au.

Australian Stock Exchange Ltd, Exchange Centre, 20 Bridge Street, Sydney NSW 2000; ☎02-9227 9338; www.asx.com.au.

Austrade, Level 23, Aon Tower, 201 Kent Street, Sydney, NSW 2000; ☎132 878;

e-mail info@austrade.gov.au; www.austrade.gov.au. The Australian Trade Commission has offices throughout Australia and the world. In London, Austrade can be contacted at Australia House, Strand, London WC2B 4LA; ☎020-7887 5226; fax 020-7836 4250.

Department of Employment and Workplace Relations, Garema Court, 148-180 City Walk, Canberra, ACT 2600; ☎02-6121 6000; fax 02-6121 7542; www.dewrsb.gov.au.

Department of Immigration, Multicultural and Indigenous Affairs, Benjamin Offices, Chan Street, Belconnen ACT 2617, ☎02-6264 1111; fax 02-6364 4466; www.immi.gov.au.

Department of Industry, Tourism and Resources, 20 Allara Street, Canberra, ACT 6001; ☎02-6213 6000; fax 02-6213 7000; e-mail inquiries@industry.gov.au; www.industry.gov.au.

Foreign Investment Review Board, The Executive Member, Department of the Treasury, Canberra, ACT 2600; ☎02-6263 3795; fax 02-6263 2940; www.firb.gov.au.

IP Australia (Patent, Trade Marks and Designs Office), Ground Floor, Discovery House, 47 Bowes Street, Woden, ACT 2606; ☎02-6283 2999; fax 02-6283 7999; www.ipaustralia.gov.au. Trade marks helpline, ☎02-6283 2999.

Reserve Bank of Australia, Head Office, 65 Martin Place, Sydney NSW 2000; ☎02-9551 8111; fax 02-9551 8000; www.rba.gov.au.

SAI Global, Head Office, 286 Sussex Street, Sydney, NSW 2000; ☎02-8206 6186; fax 02-8206 6044; www.sai-global.com.

Export

The Australian Institute of Export, Level 12, 83 Clarence Street, Sydney, NSW 2000; ☎02-9350 8170; fax 02-9262 3262; www.aiex.com.au

Business Brokers

Century 21 Real Estate, Level 12, 76-80 Clarence Street, Sydney, NSW 2000; ☎02-8295 0600; fax 02-8295 0601; www.century21.com.au.

Chris Couper & Associates, Business Brokerage, 93 Surf Parade, Cnr Surf Parade and Victoria Avenue, Broadbeach, QLD 4218; ☎07-5592 0687; fax 07-5531 5978; www.chriscouper.com.au.

Resort Brokers, Head Office, Level 4, 49 Station Road, Indooroopilly, QLD 4020; ☎07-3878 3999; fax 07-3878 1199; www.resortbrokers.com.au. Licensed real estate agents.

Wilsons Business Brokers Pty Ltd, 59A Stewart Avenue, Hamilton, NSW 2303; ☎02-4962 3388; fax 02-4969 5682; www.wilsons.com.au.

Taxation

Australian Investment and Taxation Services, 25 Belmore Road, Randwick NSW 2031; ☎02-9399 8333; www.aitx.com.au.

Australian Sales Tax Consultants Pty Ltd, Level 10, 1 Market Street, Sydney, NSW 2000; ☎02-9267 9344.

Australian Taxation Office, Ground Floor, Ethos House, 28-36 Ainslie Avenue, Civic Square, Canberra, ACT 2600; ☎132 861; www.ato.gov.au.

Australian Tax Planning Consultants, 122 Dutton Street, Yagoona NSW 2199; ☎02-9707 1833.

Blake, Dawson Waldron, Level 39, 101 Collins Street, Melbourne, VIC 3000;

☎ 03-9679 3000; fax 03-9679 3111; www.bdw.com.
Institute of Chartered Accountants in Australia, Level 14, 37 York Street, Sydney, NSW 2000; ☎ 02-9290 1344; fax 02-9262 1512; www.icaa.org.au.

Employment

Employers First, 313 Sussex Street, Sydney NSW 2000; ☎ 02-9264 2000; fax 02-9261 1968; www.employersfirst.org.au.
Australian Industrial Relations Commission, Principal Registry, Level 35, Nauru House, 80 Collins Street, Melbourne, VIC 3000; ☎ 03-8661 7777; fax 03-9655 0401; www.airc.gov.au.

New Zealand

Section I

LIVING IN NEW ZEALAND

GENERAL INTRODUCTION

RESIDENCE AND ENTRY REGULATIONS

SETTING UP HOME

DAILY LIFE

RETIREMENT

GENERAL INTRODUCTION

CHAPTER SUMMARY

○ Over 70% of New Zealanders live in cities with populations of 30,000 or more.

○ **The Maori.** The original Maori inhabitants have fared slightly better than the Australian aborigines.

  ○ The number of Maori descendants is increasing as a percentage (now nearly 15%) of the population.

  ○ The Maori name for New Zealand is Aotearoa.

○ **History.** Among the first Europeans to set foot in New Zealand was the explorer Abel Janzoon Tasman in 1642.

  ○ The country was named after Zeeland, a Dutch province in the North Sea.

  ○ New Zealand was able to exploit its agricultural potential fully with the development of refrigeration in the 1880s.

○ **Politics & Economy.** Britain was New Zealand's main source of income from exported goods until the UK's entry into the Common Market in 1973.

  ○ Unemployment rose to 10% by the 1990s but has since fallen to 3.8%.

  ○ Diversification of products and new trading areas have put NZ on the road to economic recovery.

  ○ The New Zealand economy is heavily influenced by events in South East Asia.

○ **Women.** New Zealand has had two women prime ministers and one is currently in office.

  ○ Women were enfranchised in New Zealand in 1893, 25 years before the UK.

DESTINATION NEW ZEALAND

New Zealand has a reputation for being an unspoiled 'clean and green' haven in the South Pacific, a diverse landscape filled with uncrowded beaches, mountains, farms and sheep. Although the economy is still largely based on the land, over the last century the proportion of people living in towns and cities has doubled, and the vast majority of people now live in urban areas. Four-fifths of New Zealanders are of European descent, mostly from Britain but also from Germany, the Netherlands, Greece and the former Yugoslavia as well as other nations. A significant and growing proportion of New Zealanders (one in seven) are descended from the original Maori inhabitants, or are Polynesian or, more recently, immigrants from Asia (the most significant numbers come from China and India).

New Zealand political traditions derive from Britain, but constitutionally it has often been several steps ahead. New Zealand gave women the vote in 1893, 25 years before they were enfranchised in the UK. New Zealand's first woman MP, Elizabeth McCombs, was elected in 1933. In 1938 New Zealand was one the first countries in the world to set up a comprehensive system of social security, from child care benefits through to old-age pensions.

Since European settlement first began in the early 1800s, links with Britain have been close. Early generations of settlers grew up regarding England as 'home'; strangely enough this attitude can sometimes still be found among older, more conservative New Zealanders, some of who have never even set foot outside New Zealand. New Zealand moved from colonial to dominion status in 1907, and in 1947 gained full independence from Britain making it an independent state within the Commonwealth. New Zealand foreign policy was basically an extension of British policy and the idea that 'where England leads, we follow', as one New Zealand Prime Minister put it, led New Zealand into a number of wars as a British ally. When Britain joined the European Community in the early 1970s, New Zealand found its own path in the world and its own identity as a Pacific country, rather than an outpost of Europe located in the Antipodes. In general, visitors and immigrants from America, Europe and Britain are warmly welcomed. New Zealanders deserve their reputation as some of the friendliest people in the world; when they invite you to come and stay, or to 'drop in any time' it is genuinely meant.

Newcomers will find that while elements of the traditional culture owe something to Europe (the national obsession with sports revolves around cricket and rugby) and New Zealand youth culture is heavily indebted to America, New Zealand is rapidly and proudly carving its own identity as a Pacific nation. The old ties with Britain have been loosened, and new relationships with neighbours around the Pacific Rim and other Asian countries are of growing importance. Maori and Pacific Island cultures are a strong and growing influence. Auckland, the biggest New Zealand city, has the largest Polynesian population in the world. There are new immigrant communities from various Asian countries and a long established Chinese community. The different groups make for an interesting cultural mix, and nearly one-third of a million New Zealanders now identify with more than one ethnic group. New immigrants will quickly find that it is important to respect the cultural traditions of various groups, most particularly the Maori as they were the first inhabitants of the islands. The Maori call themselves the *Tangata Whenua*, which means 'the people of the place'.

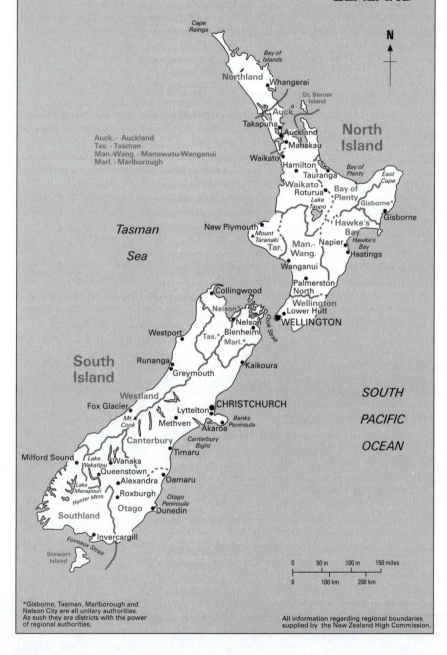

In many respects New Zealand will seem quite familiar to many immigrants. The main language is English, and the systems of government, schools and health care are similar to those in many European countries. A wide selection of arts and culture is on offer in the larger cities. If you are looking for a country with fewer social problems than Europe or the USA, where the environment is cleaner, the standard of living higher and the pace of life is more relaxed, New Zealand could be the place for you.

Pros and Cons of Moving to New Zealand

Despite having a comparatively low GDP per capita compared to other developed countries, New Zealanders enjoy a high standard of living. While it is true that income per head of the population compares unfavourably, the upside is that euros, US dollars and pounds sterling go a relatively long way in New Zealand. Other attractions for immigrants are the non-quantifiable factors that make for quality of life: clean air, clean water, miles of unspoiled and accessible beaches and native forest, and some of the most spectacular scenery in the world. If your idea of the good life is a city where 'rush hour' is nowhere near as long as an hour, and the nearest beach is no more than 30 minutes away, then you will enjoy the New Zealand lifestyle.

New Zealanders enjoy a wide range of outdoor activities in their spare time, including camping, climbing, hiking (tramping), swimming, surfing, kayaking and mountain biking. Two great attractions of the country are the parks and reserves and the sea. Even New Zealand's biggest cities are within 20 or 30 minutes of hills and forest largely free from human habitation and all the major cities, apart from Hamilton, are on the coast. With a lifestyle revolving around outdoor pursuits, the nightlife in smaller towns is not exactly lively. In the big cities the scene is more interesting. European style cafés and bars have proliferated in the last decade and there is always the traditional Kiwi pub - watering holes more noted for the cheapness of the beer than the social ambience. Licensing laws are liberal and some pubs and cafés in the big cities are open almost 24 hours.

> **Linda Kelly found moving to New Zealand something of an adventure**
> *I had no idea what to expect. It was so different to 'home'. My first impression was that it was like Noddy's Toytown – the roads and road signs, the styles and colours of the houses, and the buildings in general looked somewhat primitive and quaint. However, the scenery was breathtaking, the history enthralling, and the people relaxed, friendly, and welcoming.*

The standard working week is five days, 40 hours, although many people do put in extra hours and overtime. Many employers no longer pay extra for overtime, although you can usually expect to be given time off in lieu of hours worked if you are required to put in a significant amounts of extra time. Professionals on salaries can expect to work quite long hours, particularly at the start of their careers. Wage workers used to enjoy a high level of employment protection; national pay rates and conditions were set down in awards, legal documents which bound employers. Unions at a national level did most of the bargaining. Employment protection has been considerably weakened over the last decade and a half, and in some areas of the labour market (particularly casual work in catering, horticulture and agriculture) pay rates and conditions can be very poor. The social security system, once relatively generous, has also been trimmed back. On the other hand personal tax rates on high incomes are lower than in many European countries; there is no capital gains tax, GST (Goods and Services Tax) is 12.5% and the highest income tax rate is 39% (for incomes over $60,001 per annum). Unemployment has dropped by nearly half in the last decade, and continues to decline slowly but steadily; currently the unemployment rate is just 3.8%, which is the lowest it has been in 19 years.

Pete and Sally Plimmer found much about life in New Zealand to admire
During the 24 years that I lived in the UK I was so impoverished that my quality of life was miserable. We enjoyed a relatively, astonishingly good quality of life over the next 40 years in the USA, but I now realise that 'prosperity' and 'quality' are not necessarily related. I am now convinced that the quality of life in New Zealand exceeds that of the UK or the USA because in New Zealand there is a unique combination of components that make up the 'quality' spectrum. (1) Weather – there are no huge temperature swings, violent hurricanes or tornadoes. (2) Low crime rate. (3) Relatively clean urban areas. (4) Access to a fantastic range of year-round activities – sport, music and plays. (5) Access to the outdoors – from walking up Rangitoto to a bus tour of Abel Tasman Park, all within easy reach. (6) Access to excellent medical services. (7) A political system that is as entertaining as Gilbert and Sullivan. (8) A great suburban transportation system. (9) Great people. (10) Good value for money.

Rental accommodation is not difficult to find, although it can be expensive in Auckland and Wellington. Rental agreements may either be on a renewable basis where the tenancy continues until either side gives notice, or for a fixed term, usually twelve months. Six-month rental contracts are not as common in New Zealand as in some other parts of the world. Houses and flats are normally let unfurnished, while apartments and townhouses may be let either furnished or unfurnished. Furnished properties will almost always be more expensive.

ECONOMIC AND POLITICAL STRUCTURE

History

The original inhabitants of New Zealand were the Maori, Polynesian settlers who arrived by canoe from the central Pacific in about the 10th century. They lived a nomadic lifestyle initially dependent on hunting a large flightless bird called the moa (now extinct), but by the 12th century there were settlements scattered along the coastline. Permanent settlements were based on cultivating the kumara, a type of sweet potato, and harvesting seafood. By the time the first Europeans arrived in the 18th and 19th centuries, the Maori had settled throughout the warmer North Island. The Maori are a tribal people, with 79 traditional tribal bases throughout New Zealand. Their whanau (extended-family)-based society has always had a complex oral tradition and maintains a strong spiritual attachment to their customs and the land. The Maori were skilled craftspeople, particularly in woodcarving and weaving (which some still practise), and also in warfare. War between tribes was common at this time, as part of the competition for status and authority.

Among the first European visitors to New Zealand were members of a Dutch East Indies Company ship led by the explorer Abel Janzoon Tasman. They briefly anchored off the coast of the North Island in 1642, at a place they called Murderer's Bay because local Maori killed four of their crew there. Tasman named the country after Zeeland, a Dutch province in the North Sea. The Maori name for the country is 'Aotearoa', meaning 'the Land of the Long White Cloud'. Other explorers followed Tasman's lead. Englishman James Cook arrived in 1769 and returned again twice in the 1770s. Members of his second expedition were the first Europeans to make landfall in New Zealand and to explore the coastline thoroughly. As with Tasman's first contact with local tribes, there were misunderstandings at first, the Maori interpreting the arrival of the strangers as a hostile force. Ten of Cook's men were killed in one incident. Other meetings were more favourable for the visitors, local Maori for the most part being curious to meet the strangers and keen to trade.

Trade and commerce provided the impetus for the first semi-permanent European settlements. Whalers and sealers arrived in the 1790s. They set up bases along the coasts but generally did not make permanent homes in the new country. Next to arrive, in the early 1800s, were Christian missionaries, who established stations around the Bay of Islands, on the north east of the North Island. They began preaching their faith amongst the tribes as well as introducing European cultivation techniques, literacy and other skills. They were the first to write down the Maori language so that they could translate the scriptures into Maori. Other settlers with more worldly ambitions soon arrived. They were interested in exploiting natural resources such as timber and flax. Local Maori tribes began cultivating wheat and maize to trade with the new arrivals. New Zealand's export trade in agricultural produce began in the 1840s with the export of potatoes, wheat and pigs to Australia. Maori farmers grew the bulk of the produce. Contact between Europeans and local tribes was confined to the small areas around the settlements, the whaling bases around the coasts of the South Island and the lower North Island, the mission stations in the north and the trading settlements at various points. For most of the first half of the 19th century, the balance of power between the settlers and the tribes was still very much in favour of the Maori, as the early settlements were dependent upon the goodwill of local tribes for their survival. However this was about to change. The Maori population was declining as a result of the spread of foreign diseases (such as influenza and smallpox) against which they had no immunity, and the introduction of firearms, which had transformed the formerly ritualised inter-tribal wars into massacres.

By 1840, a balance of firepower had led to a virtual halt in inter-tribal warfare, the cost in lives being too high. The legacy of the warring period was large-scale loss of life, disruption of land tenure and social dislocation. The decline in the Maori population alarmed the missionaries. They were also concerned about the rough, lawless lifestyle of the early settlements. Accordingly, back in Britain, the Church Missionary Society put pressure on the British Government to annex New Zealand as a Crown Colony, and to establish the rule of law.

In 1840, New Zealand was made a part of the British Empire. A treaty was signed at Waitangi, a little settlement in the Bay of Islands, between the new Lieutenant Governor Captain William Hobson and representatives of local Maori tribes. Hobson then sent copies of the Treaty around the country for other tribes to agree to, but some important chiefs refused or failed to sign. The terms, significance and validity of the Treaty of Waitangi have been a source of controversy ever since. Under the English text, the tribes ceded sovereignty to the British Crown and gained the rights of British citizens. The Maori text, hastily translated by local missionary, Henry Williams, is considerably vaguer in its terms. In particular, Williams used the unfamiliar term 'kawanatanga', a transliteration of the English word 'governorship', to express the concept of sovereignty. It is doubtful that the first signatories understood that they were handing over rule of the land to the newcomers.

During the late 1830s plans for widespread colonisation were developed under the auspices of Edward Gibbon Wakefield's New Zealand Company. Wakefield intended the settlements to mimic the pre-industrial class structure of England but the actual settlements bore little resemblance to his plans. Street plans formally laid out in Britain did not necessarily take into account the geographical vagaries of the mountainous land in New Zealand.

Prospective immigrants attracted by the promise of cheap land may not have been aware that the Company and its agents did not always acquire the land legitimately from the tribes, especially as the pressure to provide more land increased. Maori land tenure is complex as land is not owned by individuals but by the tribe as a whole. Company agents were not particularly scrupulous about whose signatures they obtained on sale documents and, as the increasing numbers of new settlers demanding land put pressure on them to provide it, their methods undoubtedly became more dubious.

New Zealand was directly governed by the British Crown between 1840 and 1852. After pressure from the settlers, self-government was granted in 1852. As European settlers increased in numbers and demand for land grew, conflicts occurred with the Maori people over land tenure. The tribes disputed a number of deals undertaken by New Zealand Company agents and resistance movements to further land sales developed.

The settler government ignored its responsibilities to protect Maori rights under the Treaty. Skirmishes between the government and the tribes began in the 1860s and full-scale war developed. It took nearly fifteen years for the forces of the government, reinforced by troops from Britain, to defeat Maori opposition. Even at the end of hostilities in the 1870s, Maori tribes in the centre of North Island still held out against government control. The wars exacerbated the decimation of the Maori population and resulted in the confiscation of the land of the 'rebellious' and 'loyal' tribes alike. The loss of land and the resulting social breakdown probably contributed more than any other factor to the decline in the Maori population at the end of the 19th century.

Meanwhile European settler numbers were increasing, spurred on by the discovery of gold in the South Island in the 1870s, and the invention of refrigerated shipping in the 1880s which made the export of meat and dairy products to Europe viable. The gold deposits were soon mined out but the agrarian economy founded in the late 19th century has remained the basis of New Zealand's economic prosperity. Economic security brought on social reform, at least for the European population. First the extension of the vote to women (1893), then a new system of industrial relations, based on minimum wage rates for every industry (1894) and one of the earliest pension schemes (1898). Maori were legally equally able to vote but the property owning rule (which was based on European patterns of individual tenure, rather than an understanding of Maori communal tenure) effectively disbarred many of them until its abolition in the late 19th century.

New Zealand was involved in both World Wars as a British ally. The disastrous Great War campaign at Gallipoli in Turkey in 1915 proved to be one of the defining moments in forming a separate national identity. New Zealand lost more soldiers as proportion of its population than any other allied country; nearly one in three men between the ages of 20 and 40 were killed or wounded. The interwar years brought the election of the first Labour government, which continued the tradition of pioneering social policy programmes started by the Liberals. The 1938 Social Security Act established a national health service and a universal social security system. Public education to secondary level was free to all. World War Two saw New Zealand participating again as a British ally, but in the post-war years it began to rely less on Britain for defence and to form closer relations with Australia and the United States. Britain's entry into the Common Market in the 1970s confirmed the loosening of colonial ties. At the same time closer links were being developed with other countries in the Asia-Pacific region.

Economic restructuring resulting from the increasingly poor performance of the economy since the late 1970s and race relations have been the major policy issues over the last three decades. The prevailing belief that relations between the races were harmonious was challenged by a number of Maori political movements during the last thirty years, ranging from radical groups calling for the restoration of Maori sovereignty to tribal leaders taking a more conciliatory stance. Two common concerns unite the diverse strands of Maori protest movements: a call upon the government to honour the terms of its original treaty with the Maori people and a concern with the inequality between Maori and European living standards. Income, life expectancy, health, and education standards differ markedly between the two groups. The Treaty has become central to government policy towards the Maori and in 1985 the Waitangi Tribunal was given power to hear grievances relating to Maori land. The government's obligations towards the Maori as an equal partner under the Treaty were acknowledged. Maori became an official language in 1987 (English being the other) and knowledge of Maori culture and language is increasingly a prerequisite for employment in areas of public service departments and is stressed as equally important as cultural heritage. Tensions remain between the Maori and the Government over historical injustices, particularly the large scale acquisition of Maori land by Europeans in the 19th century through confiscation, extortion, blackmail and theft, and the Government's neglect of its duty to protect Maori rights under the Treaty.

Economy

New Zealand has a worldwide reputation as an agricultural producer with increasingly efficient and innovative methods. The country has a mixed economy that operates on free market principles and is strongly trade oriented, with exports of goods and services accounting for about 33% of total output.

Since 1984 the government has undertaken some major restructuring and transformed New Zealand from an agrarian economy largely dependent on Britain to a more industrialised and globally competitive free market economy. Technology and research have played a major part in this transformation. The temperate climate is ideal for growing grass suitable for rearing farm animals cheaply, but it took a century and a half of effort to cultivate the ten million hectares of arable land currently in production. Modern machinery and efficient soil, stock and pasture management have played an important role. Much of the land was initially unsuitable for agriculture, being heavily forested, while the mountainous terrain has provided a challenge to develop alternative cultivation techniques. Nearly two-thirds of farmland is too rugged to be fertilised and sown by tractor. Instead New Zealand farmers pioneered the use of light aircraft to spread fertiliser and seed.

New Zealand was able to exploit its agricultural potential with the development of refrigerated transportation in the 1880s. Meat and dairy products joined wool as the basis of exports to Europe. At the end of the 19th century, New Zealand was one of the richest countries in the world. As a former colony, it enjoyed close cultural and economic links with the UK. For most of the following century, three-quarters of New Zealand's exports went to the UK. Britain was also the major source of imports.

By the 1950s New Zealand was an efficient producer of wool, meat and dairy products and could compete successfully in Northern hemisphere markets. The success of the export industry allowed New Zealanders to enjoy a similar standard of living to the industrialised countries of Europe and America. The relatively high standard of living attracted a constant inflow of immigrants. In the early 1960s, as a result of a worldwide boom in commodity prices, it enjoyed amongst the highest living standards in the OECD. However, even during this relatively prosperous period, it was recognised that future economic security depended on diversifying the export base, both in terms of markets and of the range of goods being exported. New Zealand's traditional market, Britain, was not growing as fast as other countries and there was the possibility throughout the 1960s that it would eventually join the European Economic Community (now the EU).

The golden years ended in the 1970s. Several factors were influential such as the entry of Britain into the EEC in 1973 and the first oil price-shock in the same year. Britain's entry into the EEC led to the restriction of access for New Zealand exports and this coincided with the rise in the price of oil which had a severe effect on the New Zealand economy, as it was extremely dependent on importing oil to meet its energy needs. There was a sudden decline in economic performance. The cost of imports rose sharply while exports receipts dropped and the Balance of Payments deficit plummeted to 14% of GDP. Arguably however the effect of these two events only exposed the underlying weakness of New Zealand's economy rather than causing the economic decline. The government of the time decided that the best solution to the problem of New Zealand's dependency on fuel imports was to embark upon a series of major investment projects to develop domestic energy sources. Unfortunately the viability of these projects was based on the price of oil continuing to rise more than it did. Most of the so-called 'Think Big' projects turned out to be expensive white elephants.

By the early 1980s, the economy was performing badly. Inflation was high, and at the same time, unemployment was rising rapidly. Subsidies protected inefficient sectors of the economy and discouraged innovation. Years of borrowing to cover the trade deficit and the cost of the 'Think Big' experiment had increased New Zealand's foreign debt. The National government tried to control inflation by imposing a price and wage freeze in 1982. The freeze succeeded in controlling inflation, but money supply continued to grow throughout the two and half years it was in place. In 1984 a Labour government was elected. At the time of the election there was no indication that the new administration would introduce a period of radical economic reform. The Labour Party manifesto made no mention of many of the central policy changes they enacted. The programme of economic liberalisation included removal of price and wage controls, deregulation of financial markets, the floating of the dollar, the introduction of a sales tax, the reduction of agricultural and industrial subsidies, the removal of employment protection, and the weakening of the collective bargaining power of unions. This was accompanied by tight monetary policy and the selling of a number of state assets, including the railways, forests, the national airline and the telecommunications section of the post office.

During the mid-to-late 1980s the economy stagnated somewhat, entering a recession in the early 1990s. Output recovered in the mid-1990s, only to be hit by the slowdown of the economies of key Asian trading partners in 1997 and '98. The droughts of 1997/98 and 1998/99 affected large parts of the country and had an obvious impact on economic activity; in combination with an already-slowing economy, these factors contributed to a contraction of the economy in 1998.

Against the abovementioned short-term swings in government economic policy, a longer-term process of economic adjustment has also been occurring. New Zealand's export industry has diversified both in product and export markets, and the economy is still heavily dependent on overseas trade. The agriculture and manufacturing industries have been developed to suit the needs of niche markets. A free trade agreement was signed in 1982 with Australia, which is now New Zealand's main trading partner. The development of new markets in Asia has been a significant development during recent years. Japan is the third largest source of overseas merchandise export income (accounting for NZ$3,354 million) after Australia (NZ$6,050 million) and the USA (NZ$4,366 million). Europe, which in the late 1960s provided two-thirds of New Zealand's export revenue, now accounts for less than 20%. The range of exports has diversified to include horticulture and wine, and fishing and tourism have become more significant. Dairy and meat exports still make a large contribution to the economy, although wool has declined, and forestry and manufacturing exports have become increasingly important. In the 1960s, the dairy, meat and wool sectors accounted for over 80% of export revenue; they now make up less than 50%. However, although the range of products has diversified, the economy as a whole is still reliant upon exporting agricultural and horticultural commodities. This heavy dependence on trade leaves growth vulnerable to changes in economic performance, particularly in Asia, the USA and Europe. New Zealand's growth prospects are also vulnerable to climatic and environmental factors.

The adjustment process to the restructuring has been long and difficult. Unemployment rose from under 4% in 1985 to over 10% in 1990, levels not seen since the Depression years, as economic activity declined due to tight monetary policy. Farmers' gross incomes dropped by nearly half when government subsidies were removed. A large number of manufacturing industries went to the wall, unable to compete with cheap imports once tariffs were removed. The abolition of financial controls caused a brief speculative boom in the mid-1980s but the stock market crash in 1987 exposed much of the increased activity as paper wealth. The dollar rose as high interest rates attracted overseas investment, which reduced returns from exports, critical to the overall health of the economy.

Whether the social costs of economic restructuring outweigh the efficiency gains is still being debated. Some sectors of the economy have adjusted better to deregulation than others. Despite predictions that many farms would not survive the removal of agricultural price supports, there were only a few casualties. The agricultural sector has become more efficient. Manufacturing has not been as fortunate and the shedding of jobs in this sector along with the restructuring of previously inefficient government industries largely accounted for the rise in unemployment. Unemployment has now dropped to 3.8% – the lowest level for

19 years. However, the gap between high- and low-income earners has grown and poverty has emerged for the first time since the war as a visible social problem. The gap between rich and poor continues to widen and the government has been forced to introduce updated income support measures to ensure a reasonable standard of living for low-income families in work (as distinct from beneficiaries). For a country that used to pride itself on its egalitarian ethos and comprehensive social welfare system, these developments have caused much public concern.

Taxation remains a topic for disagreement and discussion. The Government is running a significant surplus, thanks largely to a bigger-than-predicted tax take; this is due in no small part to a dramatic rise in the price of fuel in recent months, among other factors. The Government maintains that these surpluses are better used by it in superannuation, while opposition parties argue that the rates of tax for both businesses and individuals should be reduced. With increasing interaction between New Zealand and Australia, it is argued by business organisations that the rates of company tax in both countries (currently 33% in NZ and 30% in Australia) should be harmonised so that New Zealand companies are able to compete on a more even playing field.

The exchange rate for the NZ dollar has strengthened in recent years, and now stands higher than it has for some time against the US dollar, the Australian dollar, and sterling. While this makes the cost of imports cheaper, it also has the effect of making exports dearer and therefore possibly less desirable in some of New Zealand's markets. Deregulation of the economy since the 1980s has meant that most protections for local and primary manufacturing industries have gone, resulting in, for example, significant sections of the clothing and footwear industries going out of business because they are unable to compete with cheaper imported goods. The small size of the New Zealand market has meant that other industries have suffered as well; motor vehicle assembly, for example, no longer exists as an industry in the country, and vehicles are these days imported fully built up from Australia, America, the UK and Asia. However, as the unemployment figures demonstrate, the economy has adapted to these downturns and employment is expanding in other, less traditional, areas.

Despite all the problems, the high growth of the past three years makes this one of the best periods in New Zealand for the last 25 years; annual average growth in the June 2004 year was 4.4%, up from the 4.1% increase in the year ending June 2003. This also makes it one of the best periods in the OECD since 2001. Domestic demand has continued to drive growth, with consumption and investment growing strongly. Exports are still recovering from their mid-2003 slump, returning to high growth, and all industries have grown recently, most by a fairly significant amount. Such strong economic growth has meant an improvement in labour market conditions, and further contributions to growth have been made by high job growth and a strong labour market, growth in labour productivity and a fall in unemployment.

For the year ended March 2004, the economy has grown 3.6%, which is down from the 4.4% increase of the previous year, ending March 2003. Economic activity in fact increased in the March 2004 quarter though, with higher consumer spending, increased investment in residential housing, increased business investment and a lift in exports all contributing. Internal demand is currently 8.3% higher than it was at the same time last year. Household spending is 7% higher than at the same time last year, and spending on durable goods is up 3.6%, with particular emphasis on products such as furniture and appliances, clothing and footwear and retail recreational goods. Investment in new housing has risen 9.8%, following a decline of just 0.8% at the end of 2003. The March 2004 year saw strong investment in new housing overall; it was up 17.7%.

Government

New Zealand is an independent parliamentary democracy within the Commonwealth. Queen Elizabeth II is the titular head of state, represented in New Zealand by the Governor-General. The current inhabitant of Government House is Dame Silvia Cartwright. The Prime Minister is the head of government, supported by a Cabinet of Ministers chosen from the elected Members of Parliament.

New Zealand has one of the most centralised systems of executive government in any western country. While levels of local government exist, they do not provide a countervailing force as their powers and responsibilities are comparatively weak. Local government bodies are funded largely by rates, and exist in the form of regional councils, community boards, special authorities and territorial authorities. Radical policy programmes can be introduced relatively quickly as was demonstrated by the fourth Labour government, which transformed the country between 1984 and 1990. The problem has been that the electorate has not universally welcomed change as was demonstrated by the electoral backlash against both the major parties in the 1993 election. Neither of the big parties gained the confidence of the electorate, and small parties got a record number of seats. The result on the night was a hung parliament, but a recount in some of the most marginal seats resulted in a narrow victory for the ruling National party.

All New Zealanders over the age of eighteen have the right to vote. Parliament is elected every three years by Mixed Member Proportional Representation (MMP); this system has now been in place for 11 years. The electorate continues to be polarised on the merits of MMP. It has the benefit, however, of allowing significant minority votes to be recognised and of providing the chance for those voters to have a seat in parliament. Three of the parties in the present parliament are represented without having won an electoral seat.

Under the MMP system, voters have two votes; the first for the political party ('party vote') that enables the you to choose which party you would like to see in Parliament, and the second, an 'electorate vote' is for the MP you want to represent your electorate. As an almost fully proportional system, MMP is a system that makes it difficult for a party to win a majority of parliamentary seats and govern in its own right. This means that coalition or minority government is the most likely form of government. Parliament is made up of 120 MPs, and the proportion of each party is dependent upon the outcome of the party vote. A total of 67 electoral representatives are chosen from the 45 general electorates in the North Island and sixteen in the South Island, as well as the six Maori electorates that cover the whole country. Voters of Maori descent may choose whether to register on the general or the Maori electoral roll. The remaining 53 MPs are called 'Party list MPs', and win their places in Parliament by making up the proportion of their party according to the 'party vote'. Party lists are the pecking order of MPs for that party. As well as pitting MPs in the same party against each other in the undignified struggle for selection, MMP makes it much easier for small parties to gain representation than was previously the case. The main party in the present government does not command a majority of seats and is reliant upon agreements with several minor parties to cobble together majorities for specific policies. The system means that, ideally, parties are required to tailor policies to reflect wider interest than simply their own. The MMP system has led to the increase in number of women MPs; about one third of MPs are now women, making New Zealand a country with an unusually high proportion of women politicians. MMP has also resulted in increased numbers of Maori and ethnic minority politicians in Parliament – the number of Maori seats increased before the last election to eight. This number will always depend on the number of electors registered on the Maori rolls and may change.

Apart from the Greens, the minor parties formed under MMP have all sprung up from the two parties that had previously dominated New Zealand politics since the 1930s – National and Labour. Two MPs in particular decided that the best way to get on the new world of MMP was leave the big parties to found a party in their own image. Former National MP Winston Peters created the New Zealand First Party, and Jim Anderton, former Labour MP, established the Alliance Party. More information concerning MMP can be obtained from The Electoral Commission (Level 6, Greenock House, 39 The Terrace, Wellington; ☎ (04) 474 0670; fax (04) 474 0674; e-mail info@elections.govt.nz; www.elections.org.nz).

Political Parties

For most of the second half of this century, the New Zealand political scene has been dominated by two major parties, National and Labour. National is a conservative party, traditionally the party of farmers and business people. It has been the dominant political party in New Zealand politics, holding office for the majority of the post-war period. The Labour Party arose out of the labour movement, but has subsequently had relative independence from the trade unions. It has often been the innovator of radical social policies, even when these have gone against its own political traditions. The fourth Labour Government, which held power from 1984 to 1990, was responsible for introducing anti-nuclear legislation that stopped American warships from entering New Zealand ports. It also deregulated the economy, ran a tight monetary policy along Thatcherite lines and sold off a number of state assets – not exactly socialist policies.

Until 1993, smaller parties were kept out of power by the First Past the Post electoral system. Parties were able to gain power holding less than a majority of votes, and small parties whose supporters were spread around the country would not even gain sufficient votes in any one electorate to elect an MP to Parliament, even though their overall share of the vote could be substantial. One of the results of MMP is that the minor party in the Government can now be quite an influence on governmental policy.

There are eight parties represented in the present Parliament: Labour, Progressives (the governing coalition), National, New Zealand First, ACT, United Future, the Greens and the Maori Party. Helen Clark is the leader of the Labour Party and has been Prime Minister since 1999. The Labour Party elected Don Brash, the former leader of the Reserve Bank, its leader in 2002. ACT changed its leader in 2004 after the resignation of Richard Prebble as leader (although he remains in Parliament) – Rodney Hide is the current leader. New Zealand First has had only one leader (Winston Peters) since it was formed. The Progressives (two members including Jim

Anderton who is the leader and a minister in the government) was formed after a split in the Alliance Party before the last election. Both the Greens and the Maori Party subscribe to a co-leader philosophy. United Future sees itself as a family-oriented party. Its leader, Peter Dunne, is a former Labour Government minister. Evangelical Christians are taking an interest in politics, with one sect (The Destiny Church) proposing to contest over 30 seats in the next election. The Church leaders have been prompted to take this stance because of what they choose to call a decline in the protection of 'family values' with the introduction of a civil unions bill and the recognition of same-sex (and de facto) relationships by the present parliament.

GEOGRAPHICAL INFORMATION

Area

Located in the southwest Pacific Ocean, midway between the equator and the South Pole, New Zealand is an island chain on the south edge of the 'Pacific Rim of Fire', an area characterised by volcanic activity and frequent earthquakes. It is approximately 1600 km east of Australia and the closest countries to the north are Fiji, Tonga and New Caledonia. Consisting of two major islands (North and South) and a number of smaller ones, New Zealand has a total land area of 270,534 sq km (103,515 sq miles). This makes it about the size of Japan, Italy, or Colorado, and slightly larger than the United Kingdom. It is nearly 1600 km long, stretching across 13 degrees latitude from 34 degrees S to 47 degrees S, only 420 km wide at its widest point. The two main islands are separated by Cook Strait, which is 32 km across at its narrowest point. Most of the country is mountainous. The snow-capped Southern Alps form the backbone of the South Island, from one end to the other, dividing the land between the rainforests of the West Coast and the dry pasture lands of the Canterbury, Marlborough and Otago. The Alps include eighteen peaks reaching higher than 3000 metres, including Mt Cook which is the tallest at 3754 metres. The Maori name for Mt Cook is *Aoraki*, meaning 'cloud piercer'. Over 360 glaciers, which carry snow and ice down from the Alps, feed the major rivers on both sides of the island. Fiordland, the south-west corner of the South Island, is almost all national park and as its name suggests consists of deep sounds or fiords carved into the bush-covered mountains. Mountains in the North Island include several volcanic cones, such as Ruapehu, Tongariro, Taranaki and Ngauruhoe. The chain of occasionally active volcanoes runs from White Island (sending up clouds of steam off the East Coast) through the central volcanic zone (where snow exists alongside hot springs and steam vents) to Mt Taranaki on the West Coast. There are active thermal areas where mud pools literally bubble and geysers send up streams of boiling water. There are many lakes throughout the country. In the South Island the major lakes originate from glaciers, while in the North Island the larger lakes lie on the central volcanic plateau. No point on either of the main islands is further than 120 km from the coast.

National Parks

Roughly 30% of New Zealand's land area is in protected conservation sites, in a network of national, maritime and forest parks. Many of these wilderness areas are untouched by human habitation, although unfortunately the effect of the animals introduced with the arrival of humans has been harder to control. The Department of Conservation (which looks after the parks) aims to preserve the flora and fauna as far as possible, while allowing people recreational access. They look after an extensive network of tracks and huts for hikers (known in New Zealand as trampers). There is usually a small fee for using the huts. The walking tracks vary in difficulty from family strolls of less than half a day to serious two or three day hikes. Most New Zealanders go tramping at some point in their lives, whether they are dragged reluctantly along on a school trip or are keen walkers every weekend.

Bear in mind, however, that although the New Zealand bush looks welcoming on a warm day, it can be a very hostile environment. The weather can change unexpectedly and, in some areas of New Zealand's national parks, you can be far away from any inhabited areas if something goes wrong. It is important to take precautions before venturing into the bush, such as bringing warm, waterproof clothing and emergency food and water supplies. It is always recommended that you inform someone of your plans, including your route and the approximate time you expect to return.

Regional Divisions and Main Towns

The following regions correspond to the territorial divisions of local government, with the exception of some of the smaller districts such as Gisborne which have been grouped with larger neighbours.

North Island: Northland, Auckland, Waikato, Bay of Plenty, Gisborne/Hawke's Bay, Taranaki, Manawatu/Wanganui, Wellington.

South Island: Nelson/Marlborough/Tasman, West Coast, Canterbury, Southland and Otago.

There are five main cities:

North Island: Auckland, Wellington and Hamilton

South Island: Christchurch and Dunedin

Population

The population of New Zealand has changed dramatically over the last century. One hundred years ago the population was just 800,000, children (under 15 years old) outnumbered older people (over 64 years old) by eight to one, and life expectancy was about 60 years. Five percent of the population was Maori, immigrants mostly came from the United Kingdom and made up one-third of population growth, and more people lived in rural areas than in the cities and towns. Now the population is 4,077,302, children outnumber older people by just two to one, and life expectancy for a newborn child is around 80 years. Maori currently make up almost 15% of the population, and, although migration still accounts for roughly a third of population growth, immigrants now come from a wider range of countries and the ethnic mix is very much richer. The vast majority of people (86%) now live in urban areas; over 70% of New Zealanders live in cities with populations of 30,000 or more.

New Zealand experienced steady population growth through the 20th century, with numbers reaching one million in 1908, two million in 1952 and three million in 1973. The highest growth was in the period 1946 to 1976. The total population is unlikely to reach five million in the next 50 years though; it is projected to grow to 4.4 million by 2021 and to reach 4.6 million by 2051, then fall back slightly to number around 4.2 million by 2101.

Maori, Pacific and Asian populations are all projected to grow at a faster rate than the New Zealand population as a whole. It is expected that the Maori population will roughly double to nearly one million by 2051, with the Pacific population almost trebling within the same timeframe to reach around 600,000. It is also predicted that the Asian population will reach 370,000 by 2016, which is about double what it was in 1996.

Infant mortality has fallen to low levels, and births still exceed deaths by 28,000 per year. Over the next century, however, it is expected that the population will reach a new stable age structure with a much higher average age. A return to higher fertility is unlikely, as the trend across all groups is towards smaller families. New Zealand's total fertility rate is similar to that of the United States, but is higher than most developed nations due largely to higher fertility amongst Maori and Pacific groups. The trend now is for the age of mothers giving birth to rise; currently the average age is 29.5 years. Women also tend to have fewer children now than in the past, and a growing number of women remain childless. Fertility is currently around replacement levels and it is predicted that it will fall further towards the levels of other industrialised countries. Growth in the proportion of older New Zealanders will quicken after 2011, as the generations born in the 1950s, '60s and '70s start to hit the 60+ age bracket.

There are concerns about an older population, most importantly the increases in old age dependency, the possibility of falling living standards for older people, and slower economic growth as output from workers will have to be shared among a larger non-working population. At the moment it seems increasingly likely that a higher retirement age may be brought into effect in the future.

Climate

New Zealand has an oceanic climate, without extremes of hot or cold except for isolated areas of the central South Island. It is temperate, but with sharp regional contrasts. Most areas enjoy ample sunshine, wind and rainfall. The seasons are not as varied as in the USA and Britain, and are the opposite of the Northern hemisphere. January and February are the warmest months, and July is the coolest. In the summer, temperatures can reach the 30s (C) in eastern and inland regions.

New Zealand's long thin shape results in considerable climatic variation between regions. The far north of the country has an almost sub-tropical climate, with mild winters and hot summers. In the south of the South Island, the country can be frozen over for three months during the winter and the summers are hot and dry. During the winter there is extensive snowfall on the Southern Alps, and the central North Island mountains. Snow does not often fall at lower levels, and when it does it is only in the southern parts of the South Island. Throughout the country, rainfall varies widely. Rainfall tends to be lowest in summer for most of the North Island and for the north of the South Island. But in inland Otago, Canterbury and Southland, and the West Coast of the South Island, rainfall seems to be lower during the winter months. The sun is strong in the Southern hemisphere, and unfortunately the ozone hole over the Antarctic has a tendency to drift north over New Zealand during December, which heightens the risk of burning even further. During the summer, a 'burn time' rating is included with television and radio weather reports to warn people of the time it takes to burn during the hottest hours of the day. This can sometimes take as few as twelve minutes. Fair-skinned people are advised to stay out of direct sun between 11am and 4pm from late October through to early April, as they will burn easily. Along with Australians, New Zealanders have one of the highest rates of skin cancer in the world.

TABLE 15	AVERAGE MAXIMUM TEMPERATURE, SUNSHINE AND RAINFALL			
City rainfall (mm)	Mean daily maximum	Jan (C/F)	Bright sunshine Jul (C/F)	Mean annual hours
Auckland	23/73	14/57	2017	1228
Wellington	20/68	11/52	2066	1250
Christchurch	22/72	11/52	2107	659
Dunedin	19/66	10/50	1604	784

Annual average since 1973.
Source: Statistics New Zealand/National Institute of Water and Atmospheric Research Ltd.

REGIONAL GUIDE

Most New Zealanders live in the North Island, one third of them in the greater Auckland region. The two major North Island cities, Auckland, the largest city, and Wellington, the capital, provide the closest New Zealand equivalent to the culture and lifestyle of big cities in the rest of the world. There is amicable rivalry between the two cities, Auckland being bigger, brasher and more commercial, Sydney for beginners according to some people. Wellington takes itself more seriously as befits a capital city. It is the headquarters of most national cultural institutions, such as the Royal New Zealand Ballet and New Zealand Symphony Orchestra, home to many thriving theatre companies, and the seat of government. The South Island is more sparsely populated but attracts more foreign visitors than the North Island because of the splendours of the scenery. Christchurch, the biggest city in the south, is very English in appearance and has a rather staid, conservative feel, perhaps because of the architecture. In the south of the South Island, the influence of Scottish settlers is very strong. About the only distinctive regional accent in New Zealand is the rolled 'rr' of the Southlander. Groups of new immigrants often used to settle in particular regions. The area just north of Auckland is full of family vineyards run by Dalmatian immigrants who arrived last century from what is now the country of Croatia. Danes settled in the Wairarapa, the area just north of Wellington.

Information Facilities

The New Zealand Tourism Board runs a network of i-SITE Visitor Information Centres throughout the country, where you can obtain maps of the area, information, public transport timetables, and answers to your questions. Information Centres can be found in most large towns. For the listing of the offices you want, go to www. newzealand.com/travel/vins and choose your destination. The address of the Head Office of the New Zealand Tourism Board is Level 16, 80 The Terrace, PO Box 95, Wellington; ☎(04) 917 5400; fax (04) 915 3817; www.tourisminfo.govt.nz. There are also offices in Christchurch and Auckland. Other useful websites for a general overview include the AA New Zealand Guide (www.aaguides.co.nz), Pure New Zealand (www.purenz.com), the New Zealand Information Network (www. newzealandnz.co.nz) and Jasons Travel Channel (www.jasons.co.nz).

Northland

Main city: Whangarei ('wh' in Maori is pronounced as 'f').

Northland stretches from north of Auckland to the very tip of the North Island, Cape Reinga, where according to Maori legend, departing souls in the form of birds pause on the tree at the very end of the land before setting off for the oceans. Northland has a semi-tropical climate, miles of diverse and stunning coastline, enormous tracts of forest (home to the ancient Kauri tree) and plentiful birdlife. The legendary Maori adventurer Kupe and his crew made their first landfall in Hokianga Harbour and the Bay of Islands on the East Coast was one of the earliest sites of European settlement. The Treaty of Waitangi, under which the British Crown gained sovereignty over New Zealand, was signed at Waitangi on one side of the Bay of Islands. On the opposite side of the bay is Russell, which was the capital of New Zealand for the first twenty years of British rule. These days one of the main areas of economic activity is tourism. Northland is also a renowned grape-growing region, producing some award-winning wines. The beautiful and distinctive scenery, wonderful beaches, historical aspects and the warm climate make Northland a popular destination for visitors from both New Zealand and overseas. Aside from the historical attractions, it is a centre for big game fishing enthusiasts, sailors and divers.

Auckland

Main city: Auckland.
Major regions: Auckland City; Franklin District; Manukau City; North Shore City; Papakura District; Rodney District; Waitakere City.

The Auckland region is dominated by the city from which it takes its name, the largest in the country with a population of 1.3 million people. The region stretches from the west coast, through the city (sometimes known as 'The City of Sails', thanks to the huge number of yachts in the harbour), to the east coast and out to the islands of the Hauraki Gulf. Two natural harbours, one on the Pacific coast, the other on the Tasman, bite deep into the land forming an isthmus, and the island consequently is narrow at this point. The city covers the width of the island between the harbours.

Auckland is the financial and manufacturing centre of the country, and the major industries represented here are technology, biotechnology, marine, film/TV production and engineering. Although Auckland has the highest population concentration in the country, it is not densely populated by the standards of other cities around the world. Most Aucklanders live in detached single storey dwellings in the suburbs, which creep further into the surrounding countryside each year. The city centre is situated beside the Waitemata Harbour and although it has a number of modestly tall high-rise buildings, it's not exactly Manhattan. In fact one of Auckland's most attractive aspects is the parks and reserves that are dotted throughout the urban area. Many of these reserves are volcanic hills, such as Mt Eden; there are in fact 48 extinct volcanic cones in the area. Another attractive feature is the beaches within walking distance of the city centre. The remainder of the country sometimes resents Auckland as it dominates New Zealand through its size and concentration of economic activity. There is also a general feeling (sometimes justified, admittedly) that Aucklanders don't think there is anything worthwhile 'south of the Bombay Hills' (the cluster of hills that marks the division between Auckland and Waikato).

Auckland has an ethnically diverse population, and Maori, Polynesian, European and Asian cultures all have a strong presence here. Different ethnic influences are evident in the thriving art and music scenes, and also through the plentiful mix of cuisines on offer. Over 70% of all New Zealand's immigrants choose to make Auckland their home, as do a large proportion of New Zealanders returning from living overseas. All in all, nearly one third of New Zealand's population lives in the greater Auckland region and this is likely to be the fastest growing area of economic activity for some time to come.

Waikato

Main city: Hamilton.

The Waikato region stretches from the Bombay Hills south of Auckland to Lake Taupo in the centre of the North Island. The lake has an area of 60,606 hectares (234 sq miles) and is the source of the river for which the region is named. The Waikato River is the longest in New Zealand. Along its 425-km (264-mile) length there are nine hydro-electric dams which provide a large part of the North Island's electricity requirements. New Zealand's dairy industry is centred in Hamilton, the largest city, and there is a strong technological-based research and development presence as well. There are several research facilities located in and around the city, including Landcare Research, AgResearch and Dairying Research Corporation. The University of Waikato and Waikato Polytechnic are also in Hamilton.

The Coromandel Peninsula, in the northeast corner of the region, is a centre for forestry production. The Coromandel is a popular holiday destination and many families own second homes there. Its rugged bush-clad mountains protect almost deserted beaches. Other attractions include the thermal regions around Wairakei, where steam is harnessed to drive turbines producing electricity, and the limestone caves at Waitomo.

The Waikato is the headquarters of the King movement, one of the Maori cultural and political movements responsible for the renaissance of Maoridom in the 20th century. The King movement is based at Turangawaewae marae (Maori meeting place and cultural centre) at Ngaruawahia, the home of the Maori king.

Bay of Plenty

Main Towns: Tauranga, Rotorua.

The Bay of Plenty is one of the main horticultural regions in the country and has a population of growing at five times the national average. Currently the economy is the fastest growing in the country, and the Port of Tauranga is New Zeland's largest port. The Bay of Plenty is located on the East Coast of the North Island above East Cape. The area around Te Puke is the kiwifruit-growing capital of the country. If you are fond of the small, furry, brown fruit, you can find them on sale at roadside stalls at ridiculously cheap prices during the season; sometimes when export cargoes are held up for any reason, growers practically give them away. The Bay of Plenty region is a good place for finding casual fruit picking work in season, although students increasingly snap up such jobs. Rotorua is famous for its geysers, mudpools, steam rising from the street drains, and distinctive sulphuric smell of the thermal activity, reminiscent of rotten eggs. New Zealand's fifth largest city, Tauranga, has a population of around 90,000, and, along with Hawke's Bay, is a popular retirement place, due to its mild and pleasant climate. People who live here will tell you that it has the highest sunshine hours and the best climate in the country. The beaches around Tauranga and Mount Maunganui are very picturesque and attract crowds (by New Zealand standards) of families and young people during the summer months.

Hawke's Bay/Gisborne

Main towns: Napier, Hastings, Gisborne.

The East Cape region is very sparsely populated, and over three-quarters of the inhabitants live in the main town of Gisborne. The Gisborne District has a population of 43,974. Dairy and sheep farming are the dominant industries, although winemaking is small but growing activity. Gisborne generally has warm summers and mild winters – temperatures as high as 38(C) have been recorded during summer months – and it is the first city in the world to see the sun each day. Gisborne has a busy city port and golden beaches with good surf. Along here the early Maori voyaging canoes made their first landings after sailing south from the islands of the central Pacific. This is also where the Captain James Cook made his first New Zealand landfall in 1769. European settlement was established in 1831. The East Cape is quite remote, Maori influences are strong and the lifestyle of local Maori is relatively unaffected by European culture. 45% of the Gisborne District population is of Maori descent.

Hawke's Bay, located south of the East Cape, is another primarily agricultural and horticultural region and has a population of 142,947. It has a mild climate with long sunshine hours and low rainfall. The area around Napier and Hastings is particularly known for its vineyards, and is maturing into one of the country's leading wine-producing regions. There is also a heavy focus on primary food processing, and other strong industrial sectors include forestry and wood processing, engineering and technologies, finance and business services, retailing, and rapidly growing tourism. Napier boasts some of the most striking architecture in New Zealand. Totally flattened by an earthquake in 1931, the city was rebuilt in the art deco style then fashionable around the world. Most of the original buildings survive undwarfed by modern tower blocks.

Taranaki

Main city: New Plymouth.

According to Maori legend, the North Island of New Zealand was originally a giant fish which the hero Maui hooked from his canoe, the South Island. If you consider the shape of the North Island as a flattish sort of fish, with a fin on each side, Taranaki occupies the western fin. The dominant feature of the Taranaki landscape is Mt Taranaki, a perfect volcanic cone, topped year round with snow.

Taranaki is dairy country and is also the centre of the petrochemical industry. Aside from these, the major industries are engineering, tourism, exports and horticulture. Sunshine hours are reportedly 2182 per year, with an annual average of 1432 mm of rain. The population of 102,858 is largely European, with about 15% Maori and a small proportion of Asian and Pacific Island peoples. Off the coast of New Plymouth are the Maui natural gas field and a number of small oil fields. The region around Mt Taranaki is a national park and there are a number of tramping paths on the mountain and surrounding area. Climbing to the summit is a popular summer activity, and the proximity of mountains to sea makes this an ideal area for outdoorsy people; you can quite literally spend the morning on the mountain and the afternoon at the beach.

Manawatu/Wanganui

Main cities/towns: Palmerston North, Wanganui, Fielding.

The Manawatu-Wanganui region stretches from Himatangi Beach, just above Wellington up to Rangiwahia in the centre of the North Island's central volcanic plateau, and the population is over 103,000. The main river in the region is the Wanganui, which is the same name as the town situated on its banks. They should both correctly be known as Whanganui, but established usage prevails. According to Maori myth, the Wanganui was first explored by the great navigator Kupe. The town was one of the earliest established by European settlers who recognised the navigable properties of the river. While other cities have expanded, Wanganui has retained the atmosphere of a quiet country town. Tourist attractions include jet boat rides on the Wanganui river. The main industry is sheep and dairy farming. Tongariro National Park, in the north of the region, has within its bounds the highest points in the North Island, the snow-capped volcanoes, Mt Ruapehu (2,797 metres), Mt Ngaruahoe (2,287 metres) and the shortest of the three, Mt Tongariro (1,967 metres). Mt Ruapehu is the main North Island skiing destination, although the eruptions that occurred inconveniently in the winters of 1995 and 1996 wrecked havoc on following ski seasons. It was feared for some time that some ski-fields would have to close, as they had lost so much income, but during recent seasons the snow and business have improved. The whole area is a popular centre for outdoor activities, from climbing and bridge swinging to jet boating and fly-fishing. In the thermal region nearby there are hot springs, and a dip in a naturally heated pool is a popular end to a day's skiing. The largest town, Palmerston North, is towards the south of the region. It has a population of 76,000, and is the home of Massey University, originally one of two specialist agricultural colleges in the country. The major industries are agriculture, science and research, education, distribution and manufacturing.

Wellington

Main cities: Wellington City, Porirua City, Lower Hutt City, Upper Hutt.

The Wellington region covers the southern tip of the North Island and has a population of 423,765. It is named for its largest city, Wellington, which is the political, financial and cultural capital of New Zealand and is home to a multicultural society of 163,824 people. The ethnic composition is roughly 80% European, 12% Maori and 8% Pacific Island. Parliament is usually housed in the distinctive circular building nicknamed 'the Beehive'. The city spreads across steep hills overlooking a harbour shaped like a natural amphitheatre. Wellington is infamous for its winds, which must easily rival those of that other windy city, Chicago. A favourite cheap thrill amongst inhabitants is watching aeroplanes battle their way into Wellington airport on a blustery day. Being a passenger on a plane trying to land at Wellington is less fun, as the landing strip is situated on a narrow strip between the harbour and the sea, and sometimes planes abort their takeoff or landing due to high winds and fly to nearby Palmerston North. The city itself is quite compact, but despite its size it is cosmopolitan, lively and energetic. There are a host of late night cafés and bars, many of which feature local bands and DJs, a thriving theatre scene, a tremendous range of excellent restaurants and several independent cinemas. As a trustee, *Lord of the Rings* director, Peter Jackson, has helped drive the $4.5million renovations of the Embassy Theatre, a grand old-style cinema on Kent Terrace, at the end of Courtenay Place. Wellington hosts a biannual arts festival, and this attracts international musicians and performing artists as well as local performers. There is also a newly completed stadium, clearly visible as you enter the city along the motorway, and this was built to host concerts as well as sporting events. Most of the other towns in the region provide commuter fodder for Wellington. There are some fascinating little towns along the edge of the harbour opposite Wellington, all with their own distinct personalities and tight communities. Most of these are scarcely more than villages as the steep hills drop almost into the sea at this point leaving only a narrow strip of land to build on. A regular ferry service takes about 25 minutes to cross the harbour to Wellington from Days Bay.

Wellington is also a thriving and creative business centre, recognised for the wide variety of innovative and unique products and services it produces. The major industries in this area include property and business services, finance and insurance, general communication services, social and political research, and manufacturing. Comprising several cities, the Wellington region offers a wide range of business, investment, employment and lifestyle opportunities.

Marlborough/Tasman

Main cities: Nelson, Blenheim.

The Marlborough and Tasman districts cover the top of the South Island and Marlborough produces a significant proportion of the country's wine exports. Other major industries here include tourism, aquaculture, forestry, traditional pastoral farming and general horticulture and fishing. The population is approximately 41,500 in Marlborough and 41,350 in the Tasman District. The climate is pleasant, hot without being as humid as northern parts, with more sunny days and less rain than Auckland. Sunshine hours are an average of 2,470 per annum with annual rainfall varying from 650mm in the east to over 2,000mm in the west. The Tasman District covers 9,786 km of mountains, lakes, parks, rivers, valleys, plains and coastline and boasts a host of special geographical features and attractions. Some of these include the Abel Tasman and Kahurangi National Parks, Farewell Spit, Lake Rotoiti and golden and white sandy beaches. The Tasman District is a popular place to retire, with many older people choosing to make their homes in the more populated areas of Richmond, Motueka, Waimea and Golden Bay. Probably the most famous person born in the Tasman District was Ernest Lord Rutherford, born in Brightwater in 1871, who is world-renowned for splitting the atom in 1917.

The area around Nelson is a centre for artisans and craftspeople, particularly potters, which may account for the slightly alternative feel to the town. It is a relaxed, laid-back place (as are most South Island towns) with a warm and welcoming community and easy access to some beautiful wilderness areas and beaches. Over the Takaka hills to the west lies the aptly named Golden Bay. There are a number of national parks in the Tasman district. The Marlborough district lies east of the city of Nelson and boasts the spectacular Marlborough Sounds, a popular yachting and holiday destination. In this area, along the water, there are many small houses accessible only by boat. Blenheim is the main town in the region.

West Coast

Main towns: Greymouth, Westport.

The West Coast is a wet and wild part of the South Island with its own distinctive breed of New Zealanders. It has the smallest population of the country, with approximately 31,000 permanent residents spread along 600km of rugged coastline. There are about 6,000 people living in Westport, about 1,000 in Reefton and 11,000 in Greymouth, and the majority of people living in these areas are of European origin. The Coast is the most isolated part of New Zealand, and there are only four passes available for road travel. These climb up the Alps in a series of hairpin bends through lush grasslands and spectacular scenery. The routes through the centre of the island are occasionally cut off by weather, which may account for the remote feeling of the Coast. Early settlers spurned the West Coast due to the lack of good farming land, and there had not even been an extensive population of Maori prior to European arrival. Maori activity in this region had been largely restricted to sourcing food and pounamu (New Zealand jade or 'greenstone') to trade on the East Coast.

However, in 1864 European explorers discovered gold and coal and the West Coast was suddenly humming with men desperate to make their fortunes. By the 1870s, the West Coast was a hub of the colony's economy, albeit briefly. The legendary rugged independence of its inhabitants may result from the area's historical legacy. In addition to mining, gum digging and possum trapping were the main industries for much of the last two centuries - all fairly solitary occupations. Consequently 'West Coasters' are renowned for their 'Man Alone' strength of character and their sincere hospitality.

There are so few cars on the road that, if driving, you end up waving to every car you pass! Popular tourist industries are as diverse as walking on the Fox and Franz Joseph Glaciers, eco-tourism and wildlife tours, to watching glass blowing and gem stone manufacture. The geography of this region is dramatic, from the 'Pancake Rocks' and blowholes on the coast in the north, to the spectacular glaciers and mountains in the south. Aoraki/Mt Cook, at 3,754 metres, is New Zealand's highest mountain, but its stature was reduced 10.5 metres in 1991 when the top of the mountain fell off in a landslide. It is a region of extremes; the rainfall is very high and the sandflies can be diabolical.

Canterbury

Main city: Christchurch.

The Canterbury region is mostly sheep farming country, miles of pastureland stretching from the foothills of the Southern Alps to the coast. The population of the whole Canterbury Province numbers around 520,000. The main city, Christchurch, is the largest in the South Island with a population of more than 343,000. Founded by an idealistic bunch of Oxford University graduates, it was named for their old college. These days it is known as the Garden City, for its botanic parks, trees and green spaces. It is set on the Avon river and is a popular destination for many tourists who like the slightly English flavour Christchurch retains. The skyline is dominated to the east by the Port Hills, and to the west by the Southern Alps. Mt Hutt, a major ski resort, is only an hour's drive from the city. East of Christchurch is Banks Peninsula, a collection of bays and hills jutting out into the Pacific. Lyttleton Harbour is the deep water port for the city of Christchurch and is connected to the city by a 1.6 km tunnel running through the Port Hills. Akaroa, the main settlement on the Peninsula, was originally founded by the French, who had ambitions to colonise New Zealand but were beaten to it by the British. These days the French influence does not extend much beyond the street names and the architecture. The Canterbury plains are prime crop-growing land. Further west on the foothills of the Alps, the land is mostly used for sheep farming. Despite the large focus on agriculture, the Canterbury is now also an important centre for electronics, telecommunications, software development, light engineering and niche-market manufacturing, and in addition boasts a number of high quality education and research facilities.

Otago

Main city: Dunedin.

The Otago region covers the southeastern part of the South Island. Land is used mostly for dairy farming and crop growing. The central Otago basin enjoys surprisingly hot, dry summers despite its latitude, and is a centre for horticulture, particularly stone-fruit orchards. The southernmost city, Dunedin, was founded by Scottish settlers and now has a population of about 122,000. As well as a vibrant restaurant and café scene, there are a number of well-connected art galleries and museums (which sometimes host international exhibitions not touring any other parts of the country), professional and amateur theatre, sports training and leisure facilities, and a rich heritage of Edwardian and Victorian architecture. Perhaps the most characteristic buildings are those of Otago University, which reflect the importance of education to the early settlers; founded in 1869, it is the oldest university in New Zealand.

The discovery of gold brought a temporary economic boom in the mid-1800s, and Dunedin grew to be one of biggest and most prosperous towns in colonial New Zealand. However, the gold largely ran out after the initial boom, and Dunedin's growth rate fell behind the northern cities. It has remained much the same size since the early days of the 20th century, and many of its historic buildings have been preserved as a result. It has also retained the somewhat austere character of its Presbyterian forefathers, although every year a new intake of students at Otago University tries to reverse this. It is the only truly 'student' town in the country, university life dominating the town during term time while the students (or 'scarfies' as they are known in this part of the country) provide much needed revenue for local businesses. The tertiary student population is roughly 25,000, and the city is noticeably emptier when the students are away! As in other places where student life dominates society, such as Oxford or Cambridge in the UK, there can be a clearly noticeable divide between 'town' and 'gown'.

Otago offers the opportunity to participate in a wide range of outdoors activities. Just by driving minutes from the Dunedin city centre you can reach miles of white sandy beaches, walking tracks, golf courses and fishing areas. Winter skiing and snowboarding, lakes and vineyards are only a few hours away and are perfect options for a day out or an exciting weekend away. Three and a half hours inland from Dunedin lies Queenstown, a major tourist area. Set on Lake Wakatipu against a spectacular mountain backdrop, it is close to ski resorts and the home of adrenaline activities. Try the 71-metre Skipper's Canyon bungy jump if you dare.

Southland

Main towns: Invercargill, Gore.

Southland, as the name suggests, is the southernmost region of the South Island and about 93,000 people call it home. It is the largest province in New Zealand, at 3.6 million hectares, and major focuses here include farming of sheep, beef and dairy animals, a variety of crops, and forestry. Off the coast, fishermen make a living from crayfish, blue cod, oysters and abalone, as well as farming salmon and abalone. Stewart Island, at the very bottom of the South Island, is the southernmost inhabited point of the country. It is off the coast of Southland, below Invercargill, the largest town in the region. At Bluff near Invercargill is the country's only aluminium smelter, powered by locally produced hydro-electricity. In the western part of the region is Fiordland National Park. It contains some truly awe-inspiring scenery, with fiords or sounds carved out by glaciers, cutting deep channels into the land. The surrounding cliffs are covered in bush and traced by waterfalls. One of the best-known parts of Fiordland is Milford Sound, the destination of the Milford Track, a popular walking trip for tourists and Kiwis alike. On the eastern coast of Southland lies the Catlins area, which features abundant wildlife (seals, sea lions, and Hector's dolphins), native forests, waterfalls and caves. The spectacular Cathedral Caves are only accessible at low tide. The people of Southland can be gruff and down to earth, note the rolled 'rr' that can be found around the city of Gore – it's the only regional variation of the New Zealand accent.

GETTING THERE

Travel Agents

Booking travel to New Zealand is a very simple affair, but if you are not confident doing this yourself it may be worthwhile considering going through an agency that specialises in long haul flights or in Australian and New Zealand destinations for your own peace of mind. Most travel agents should be up to date with any discounted or cheaper fares that may be available, although the drawback of these deals is usually that the tickets have restrictions and can be very expensive to change once booked. Some antipodean travel agencies offer other services that may be useful, for example, organising temporary accommodation, onward travel or rental vehicles for when you first arrive. However, internet travel websites increasingly offer the most economical fares and are extremely simple to use. Some will also offer you the option of including stopovers and 'multi-leg' trips, accommodation or car hire in your booking. Even if you do decide to use a 'real' travel agent, it is definitely worth researching fares and options online so that you have a more comprehensive understanding of your options and the prices you are likely to pay.

The cheapest flights from Europe are via London, so if you are travelling from another European destination it may be worth checking if it makes sense to go via Heathrow or Gatwick. From London the trip is about 18,355km, and you can either fly east or west to get to New Zealand, with a refuelling stop in Asia or the USA. From Los Angeles the flight covers 10,450km, from New York you will travel 14,180km and the journey from Vancouver is 11,310km. Tokyo is 8795km from New Zealand, Hong Kong 9125km and Singapore is 8410km away. From the West Coast of the United States, a direct flight will take you approximately twelve hours. From other places on the Pacific Rim (such as Tokyo, Hong Kong or Singapore) flights last around ten hours.

Don't forget to sign up for an 'Air-Miles' scheme with whichever airline you decide to fly; as this will be one of the longest distances you can travel, you may kick yourself later if you don't take advantage of the chance to get a good chunk of free-travel points clocked up!

BAGGAGE

Some airlines are much more generous with their baggage allowances than others. Allowances range from just 20 kg up to 64 kg, depending on which airline you fly, and whether you travel economy or business class. Air New Zealand allows two pieces of baggage per passenger (with infants permitted just one piece), and no single piece may weigh more than 32 kg. In addition, each piece should not exceed the total dimensions of 158 cm (62 in.) for length+width+height. If you are travelling through the USA, only one piece of carry-on luggage will be permitted, and this must not exceed 115 cm or weigh more than 7 kg. In addition, you may take one extra personal item (e.g. purse, briefcase, laptop, etc.). As with all air travel now, remember not to carry any sharp or pointy items in your hand luggage. Some airlines may waive fees if your luggage is just a few kilograms overweight, but the tendency is to be quite strict and airlines are liable to charge you a set fee for each additional kilogram. In practice this rarely happens, but you should be prepared for the possibility as these are the rules. If you overstep the baggage limit, there is no guarantee that any additional pieces of luggage will go on the flight with you. If you know in advance that your bags are going to be over the limit, you may be able to send them unaccompanied a week or so before you fly. This will cost around half the price of paying for additional kilograms to travel with you, and you will be able to collect the extra pieces when you arrive. All airlines seem to have different policies (and different tolerance levels!) so it is worth checking well in advance of your flight.

Sports Equipment. Many airlines offer extra weight allowances for 'sports equipment' and sometimes this can be as much as another 20 kg, but you should be sure to check with your airline well in advance to avoid any nasty surprises. Sports equipment will be classed as 'oversized baggage' and most airlines have an extra fee per piece. Air New Zealand charges $50 per item. You should also be prepared for your sports equipment to travel on a different flight to your own as this is subject to the availability of space on the aircraft; passenger luggage within the allocated weight limits takes priority and flights are often quite full.

Should you arrive at the airport and discover that you are over the limit, the best option is unaccompanied baggage. Your luggage will go on the next available flight, and usually reaches your destination a couple of days after you do. You will have to clear it through Customs at the other end and there may be storage charges as well.

Jetlag and Other Effects of Long Flights

Flying west minimises jetlag somewhat, because you are following the path of the sun so your body clock is not so disoriented. There are other ways to minimise the effects of jetlag while on the flight. Drink plenty of water, avoid alcohol, and stretch your legs, arms and shoulders every so often. This may sound like boring advice but the jetlag after a 26-hour flight across twelve time zones can be considerable and may last several days. Avoiding the free airline alcohol is not such a big price to pay for being awake and alive to enjoy your first few days in your new country. Another idea is to arrive in plenty of time for your flight so you can ask for bulkhead or exit row seats, which have extra leg-room. Many airlines now recommend that you have a check-up with your doctor before you fly, to find out about the risks of Deep Vein Thrombosis (DVT) and for information about suitable precautions such as elasticated flight socks and exercises you can do in your seat.

If you have never experienced jetlag before, it can be quite a strange and disorientating sensation, and the effects may differ from person to person. Typically, you will not feel tired when you initially arrive, as the activity of leaving the plane and the airport and the excitement of being in a new place all help to counteract the fact that you may not have slept for the previous 30 hours (worst case scenario!). It is usually not until several more hours have passed that you begin to suffer the exhaustion and 'heavy leg' feeling that some people report, or the light-headedness and sense of the ground rolling beneath your feet, as though you are on a ship at sea, that others feel. However jetlag manifests itself, it is usually best to drink a lot of water, eat light, healthy meals at the appropriate times and try to make it through as much of the day as you can until it is closer to the time you would normally go to bed – local time that is! The sooner your body clock adjusts to functioning at the right time in a new place the better; it can take from several days to as long as a week before you find that you are able to sleep properly through the night.

Useful Addresses

ABTA (The Association of British Travel Agents): 68-71 Newman Street, London W1T 3AH; ☎020-7637 2444; fax 020-76370713, e-mail information@abta. co.uk, www.abta.com.

Air New Zealand (USA): Los Angeles area ☎310 615 1111; USA including Hawaii and Alaska ☎800 262 1234; www.airnewzealand.com.

Air New Zealand (UK): Air New Zealand Travelcentre, Upper Ground Floor, New Zealand House, 80 Haymarket, London SW1Y 4TQ; ☎0800 028 4149 or (regional office) 020 8600 7600 or for the Brochure Order Line 0500 555 747; www.airnewzealand.co.uk. For information about Air New Zealand Airpoints, contact 1st Floor Building One, 26-28 Hammersmith Grove, London W6 7EN; ☎ 0800 028 4149.

Air New Zealand (Continental Europe): There are various free calling numbers and local numbers for different countries – consult the website www.euairnewzealand.com.

Air New Zealand (Canada): ☎800 663 5494; e-mail canada.reservations@airnz. co.nz; www.ca.airnewzealand.com.

ASTA (The American Society of Travel Agents): 1101 King Street, Suite 200, Alexandria, VA 22314; ☎703 739 2782; fax 703 684 8319; e-mail askasta@astahq. com; www.astanet.com.

Austravel (UK): ☎0870 055 0205 (lines are open Monday to Friday 8am to 7pm, Saturday 9am to 5pm and Sunday 10am to 4pm); www.austravel.com. London West End: 61 Conduit Street, London W1S 2GB; ☎0870 166 2120; e-mail westend@austravel.comhttp://. London Knightsbridge: 52 Brompton Road, London SW3 1HX; ☎0870 166 2140; e-mail knightsbridge@austravel.com. London City: 17 Blomfield Street, London EC2M 7AJ; ☎0870 166 2130; e-mail city@austravel.com. Birmingham: 17 The Minories, Temple Court, Birmingham B4 6AF; ☎0870 166, 2160; e-mail birmingham@austravel.com. Bournemouth: 107 Old Christchurch Road, Bournemouth BH1 1EP; ☎0870 166 2150; e-mail bournemouth@austravel.com. Bristol: 25 Trenchard Street, Bristol BS1 5AN; ☎0870 166 2110; e-mail bristol@austravel.com. Edinburgh: 33 George Street, Edinburgh EH2 2HN; ☎0870 166 2190; e-mail edinburgh@austravel.com. Leeds: 16-18 County Arcade, Victoria Quarter, Leeds LS1 6BN; ☎0870 166 2180; e-mail leeds@austravel.com. Manchester: 3 Barton Arcade, Deansgate, Manchester M3 2BB; ☎0870 166 2170; e-mail manchester@austravel.com.

Downunder Direct (USA): 6 W Lancaster Ave, Ardmore, PA 19003; ☎800 642 6224 or 800-22-79246 or 610-896-9595; fax 610-896-9592; e-mail info@downunderdirect.com; www.downunderdirect.com.

Flight Centre: Various local branches, with over 1200 stores worldwide. From the UK ☎0870 499 8436; www.flightcentre.co.uk to find your nearest branch.

Global Travel Agency: 47 Notting Hill Gate, London W11 3JS; ☎0870 011 0870; email: sales@tvl4u.com.

Golden Wings Worldwide (UK): Online Bookings Department, 55-57 High Holborn, London WC1V 6DX; ☎020 7611 1600; fax 020 7611 1690; e-mail Online@GoldenWings.co.uk; www.goldenwings.co.uk.

Korean Airlines: Frequently offer the cheapest deals to New Zealand, starting sometimes as low as just under £500; www.koreanair.com. USA and Canada: ☎800-438-5000 (see the website for listings of regional ticket offices);

Thai Airways International: Another cheap option, this time travelling through Bangkok with the option of a stopover; www.thaiair.com.

Trailfinders (UK): ☎0845 0505 891; www.trailfinder.com. London offices are in the City, Covent Garden, Kensington and Piccadilly. There are other *Trailfinder* offices in Belfast, Birmingham, Bristol, Cambridge, Dublin, Glasgow, Leeds, Manchester, Newcastle and Oxford – check the website for details.

World Connections Travel (USA): 1818 Independence Square, Suite D, Atlanta, GA 30338; ☎770-393 8892 or 800 777 8892; fax (770) 393 8882; e-mail wctravel@mindspring.com; www.mindspring.com.

Useful Websites

Cheapflights: www.cheapflights.com or www.cheapflights.co.uk. Offers a flight comparison facility, with which you can compare deals from hundreds of different companies.

Ebookers: www.ebookers.com. Has a useful and fairly comprehensive Australasia section.

Expedia: www.expedia.com or: www.expedia.co.uk.

*Jasons Travel Channel: www.*jasons.co.nz/new-zealand-motels.htm. In addition to a huge range of motel and motor-lodge listings, you will also find information about other accommodations, transport, rental vehicles, and free downloadable maps and brochures on useful topics ranging from trams and coaches, to travel agents and campgrounds.

New Zealand Information Network: www.newzealandnz.co.nz. For travel information inside New Zealand. It might be worth taking a look at before you leave, to get an idea of what you might need to arrange in terms of travel and accommodation directly from the airport. This website gives unbiased information about travel, accommodation and transportation, includes links to the immigration service and offers an information request service. There is also an automotive section for car hire, and a business economy section for information about real estate or business products and services. It incorporates an extensive links directory, options for hotel and rental car booking, and a range of constantly changing and up-to-the-minute special offers.

Opodo: www.opodo.com, www.opodo.co.uk, www.opodo.de, or www.opodo.fr. Opodo is owned by a group comprised of Aer Lingus, Air France, Alitalia, Austrian Airlines, British Airways, Finnair, Iberia, KLM, Lufthansa and Amadeus, so worth thinking about if you are already signed up for air miles with any of these airlines!

Travelselect: www.travelselect.co.uk. Part of the lastminute.com group, there are often very reasonable fares to be had if you plan carefully enough to book and pay far enough (i.e., several months) in advance.

Insurance. Working travellers and those on speculative job searches in New Zealand are advised to take out comprehensive travel insurance. You should be able to purchase travel insurance from the same source as your airline tickets; failing that, there are a number of other possibilities, including numerous online companies, general insurance providers, probably your own bank, the Post Office, and so on – even some supermarkets now sell travel insurance!

Useful Addresses

Columbus Direct Travel Insurance (UK): www.columbusdirect.com.

DirectLine: http://uk.directline.com/travelling.

DownunderDirect (USA): 6 W Lancaster Ave, Ardmore, PA 19003; ☎800 227 9246, 800 642 6224, or 610 896 9595 fax 610 896 9592; www.downunderdirect.com.

Downunder Insurance (UK): 3 Spring Street, Paddington, London W2 3RA; ☎020-7402 9211 or freephone 0800 393 908; fax 020-7402 9272; e-mail info@duinsure.com; www.downunderinsurance.co.uk or www.duinsure.co.uk.

Quote Travel Insurance: wwwquotetravelinsurance.com.

TFG Global Travel Insurance (USA and Canada): 216-2438 Marine Drive, West Vancouver, BC, V7V 1L2, Canada; ☎604-913 1150 or USA tollfree: 800 232 9415; fax 604-913 1153; e-mail info@tfgglobal.com; www.globaltravelinsurance.com.

Trailfinders (UK): 194 Kensington High Street, Kensington, London W8 7RG; ☎020-7938 3939; www.trailfinder.com. There are other *Trailfinder* offices in Belfast, Birmingham, Bristol, Cambridge, Dublin, Glasgow, Leeds, Nottingham, London (Piccadilly and Covent Garden), Oxford, Manchester and Newcastle – check the website for details.

RESIDENCE AND ENTRY REGULATIONS

The Current Position

Throughout New Zealand's history, population growth has been boosted at various points by government policies designed to attract immigrants. Britain was the main source of new arrivals for most of the first century of European settlement, and the other major source of European immigrants was the Netherlands. Sadly New Zealand missed out on achieving some of the ethnic diversity Australia enjoys by not actively encouraging immigration from other European countries in the post-Second World War period. The last major campaign to attract immigrants was during the 1950s. Those were the days when the New Zealand government paid for immigrants' passage on the condition that they stayed for at least two years. When this scheme ended, a more restrictive immigration policy was introduced, based on occupational quotas. Most potential immigrants were required to have a job waiting for them before they applied for residency.

In 1991 the Government changed the occupational quota scheme to a points-based migrant system that is similar to the Canadian and Australian schemes. Applicants for residency are ranked according to the number of points they score for attributes such as age, qualifications, work experience, family and offer of employment.

> Policy changes in 1995 caused a dramatic downturn in the number of migrants, and in the 1995-97 period these numbers were down by over 60% due to the difficulty of getting into the country. The Government has since realised that New Zealand needs migrants who will bring new ideas and skills, invest in business, create new opportunities and international contacts and who will help New Zealand compete on the global stage.

New immigration policies covering entrepreneurs, investors and those on long-term business visas (temporary residence) were introduced in 1998. In November 1999, special provisions were made for IT specialists, and in October 2001 an extra 10,000 visas a year were allocated to the General Skills and Business immigration category. The Immigration Minister of the time said that this increase reflected the 'desire to ensure that talent tops the list of residence approvals'. An entirely new category - the Talent Visa - allows highly skilled temporary residents to apply for permanent residency. This visa came into effect in April 2002 and in fact provides two options. One allows employers in New Zealand who are accredited by Immigration New Zealand to offer overseas people jobs without the people in question having to satisfy the huge raft of usual criteria. After two years of holding a work permit these people can go on to apply for residence. The other version of this visa allows particularly good sportspeople, musicians, writers, and artists, and so on, to do the same if they have a sponsoring organisation within New Zealand. There is information about both of these new types of visa in both the Self Assessment Guide and the Guide to Working (published online and in hard copy by the New Zealand Immigration Service), or by following this link: http://www.immigration.govt.nz/migrant.stream/work/worktoresidence/default. htm. For more information, contact the New Zealand Immigration Service (450 Queen Street, Private Bag, Wellesley Street, Auckland, or for National Office in Wellington documents P.O. Box 3705, Wellington; (from Auckland) ☎ (09) 914 4100, (from outside Auckland but inside NZ ☎ 0508 558 855 fax (09) 914 4119; e-mail info@immigration.govt.nz; www.immigration.govt.nz).

There are offshore branches in Apia, Beijing, Jakarta, Moscow, Suva, London, New Delhi, Shanghai, Washington, Bangkok, Hong Kong, Nuku'alofa, Singapore and Taipei. See the main website for contact details.

Applying for New Zealand Residency

If you qualify for permanent New Zealand residency you will be entitled to work in New Zealand without any restrictions. You will be issued a residence visa if you apply outside New Zealand or a residence permit if you apply from within the country. A residence permit will expire if you leave the country; if you wish to leave temporarily after taking up residence, you must apply for a returning resident's visa.

IMMIGRATION STREAMS

There are three main streams of immigration, and only a restricted number of applications in each stream will be successful. For the 2004/2005 year, Government has allocated 45,000 (up to 50,000) places for people to be granted New Zealand residence under the immigration programme. The General Skills and Business category will provide 60% of this total, this category encompassing the Skilled Migrant Category (SMC), closed General Skills category, Work to Residence, Investor, Entrepreneur, and Employees of Relocating Businesses. As a result, 27,000 (up to 30,000) people will be approved under the Skilled/Business stream as part of this year's immigration programme. Of these, 19,000 (up to 22,000) people will be under the Skilled Migrant Category (SMC), with the remaining 8,000 from the other subcategories. The Family Sponsored stream will account for 30% and includes applications under the headings of Partnership, Dependent Child, Parent, Sibling, Adult Child, Family Quota, Family-Sponsored Transitional Policy and closed Humanitarian category. 10% is made up from the International Humanitarian Stream, which includes a Refugee Quota of 750, Refugee Status, a Refugee Family Quota of 250, a Samoan Quota (1,100), Pacific Access (650), Victims of Domestic Violence, Contingency/Ministerial Direction, and International Humanitarian Transitional Policy.

Bear in mind that the New Zealand Immigration Service operates from a weighty manual that is over 1000 pages long, and acceptance criteria are complex to say the very least, so what follows in this section is no more than a rough overview. Contact the New Zealand Immigration Service for the most recent rules, categories, application forms and procedures.

Immigration Refusal Criteria

Whatever category you are applying under, there is a lot of paperwork involved. You will be required to provide medical certificates and character references. Medical certificates must be no more than three months old at the time that you lodge your application, and must be provided for your partner and all your dependent children, even if you do not have custody of the children. Forms can be downloaded from the NZ Immigration website (www.immigration.govt.nz). Chest x-rays are now required for everyone over 11 years old (except pregnant women). If you don't have an acceptable standard of health your application will be declined unless you are granted a medical waiver. NZIS will consider a medical waiver if all other requirements of your residence application are met, unless you are suffering from severe haemophilia, medical conditions requiring renal dialysis or active tuberculosis.

In accordance with the Immigration Act of 1987, you will not be accepted if you have ever been convicted of a crime and served a sentence of five years or more, or a sentence of twelve months or more in the last ten years. You will not be accepted if you are subject to a current New Zealand removal order, or if you have ever been deported from any country. And it goes without saying that you will not be accepted if it is suspected that you constitute a likely danger to New Zealand security or public order, and/or if you are believed to be associated with any group or organisation with criminal objectives. These days, because of the sensitivity of race relations and concerns over the political affiliations of the growing number of South African immigrants, you will also be required to declare that you have never been a member of a white supremacist organisation. Like the American immigration requirement to declare that you have never participated in genocide, the point is not that anyone would declare themselves to be racist but that if you make a false declaration, it is an offence under the Immigration Act and you can be deported forthwith. None of this paperwork comes cheaply. New Zealand is the pioneer of charging for the privilege of filling out official forms. See the table below for costs of the different types of visa applications.

Immigration Consultants

You may consider employing the services of an immigration consultant. The number of organisations offering advice on emigrating to New Zealand has grown substantially since the new immigration policy was introduced in 1991. Most consultants offer help with all aspects of the immigration process. They will provide general information about New Zealand to help you decide whether you want to make the move. Some consultancies will organise special tour packages to New Zealand so you can visit the country before deciding whether to emigrate. As emigration is a major life step it may be worthwhile to consider a reconnaissance trip; you can make an application for permanent residency while in New Zealand on a visitor's visa or permit if you decide you like the place.

Once you have made the decision, an immigration consultant will guide you through the daunting maze of paperwork and residency regulations. Some immigration consultants say that candidates maximise their chances of qualifying by using a reputable consultancy, but no company can guarantee that you will be successful. Some consultancies charge a fee for a preliminary assessment, which may save you wasting any further money if you are unlikely to succeed. Their final fees will vary widely depending on the services you require and the application you are making; charges may range from a few hundred to several thousand dollars. Consultancies can assist with the paperwork and will make sure you do not overlook or omit any vital pieces of information. You should be wary of any consultancy that appears to promise that they have a special relationship with the New Zealand Immigration Service. All applications are considered equally regardless of whether a consultant has been involved or not. Another useful service consultants provide is help with settling in New Zealand. Most good consultants should provide you with assistance in deciding where to live, looking for jobs, finding a house and other aspects of organising your new life. In choosing a consultant, the most important aspects to consider are the practical help they can offer. Do they have a job search branch in New Zealand? Do they have contacts that might be useful for promoting your employment chances? According to the New Zealand Immigration Service, the major consultancies they deal with regularly are all above board. If you are uncertain about whether a consultancy is bona fide, you can contact the Immigration Service to check them out. It is worth doing your research to make sure you get value for money.

Useful Addresses

The Emigration Group Ltd., 7 Heritage Court, Lower Bridge Street, Chester, Cheshire CH1 1RD; offices also in London and Manchester; ☎0845-2302526; fax 01244-342288; e-mail info@TEGltd.co.uk; www.emigration.uk.com. Provides full assistance with applications for residence and/or work visas and has a Resettlement Consultant based in New Zealand. Settlement assistance available includes removals, pet shipments, flights, bank accounts, accommodation, job search, and information about visas and residence. Sister company, *Taylor and Associates,* (see entry below) matches job seekers with employers. Together they provide an effective and total emigration service.

Taylor & Associates (Migrant Employment Search), 27 Gillies Avenue, PO Box 9600, Newmarket, Auckland. New Zealand; ☎ (64) 09-520 5421; fax (64) 09-520 5487; e-mail nzjobs@jobfastrack.co.nz; www.jobfastrack.co.nz. Taylor & Associates link migrants to the New Zealand and Australian job markets, providing the fast track way to a new job down under. Taylor & Associates also produce a free newsletter (*Australian and New Zealand Employment Review*) that provides a regular update on the employment scene; copies are available from the Emigration Group office (above).

All migration agents and consultants charge for their services.

Useful Publications

Destination New Zealand: a monthly magazine from Outbound Publishing created for 'intending emigrants'. Subscriptions within the UK are £19 for 12 months or £15 for six months, and if you live outside the UK and Europe £30 for 12 months and £19.50 for six months. Within Europe (excluding UK) 12 issues

will cost you £22 and six issues £15.50. ☎+44 (0)1323 726040; fax +44 (0) 1323 649249; e-mail info@outboundmedia.co.uk for up-to-date subscription details; www.outboundpublishing.co.uk.

The New Zealand Immigration and Relocation Report: Written by migrants for migrants, customers pay online and are given immediate access to their instantly downloadable e-book. NuKiwi also offers a range of other publications, and discount for more than one purchase as well as a money-back guarantee; www.nukiwi.com.

New Zealand News UK: published weekly, and either free or for a price of 35p, depending on where you get your copy. Contains up-to-date immigration news, and also carries information about New Zealand-focussed activities for expats and prospective migrants in the UK, mainly in London; www.nznewsuk.co.uk.

New Zealand Outlook published monthly by Consyl Publishing Ltd. (3 Buckhurst Road, Bexhill-on-Sea, East Sussex TN40 1QF; ☎01424-223111; fax 01424-224992; www.consylpublishing.co.uk). Aimed specifically at migrants, this publication is a useful way of keeping up with NZ migration policy and entry regulations. In the UK six issues cost £10.00 and twelve issues £14.75; in Europe six issues cost £12.00 and twelve issues £18.20; elsewhere six issues cost £15.00 and twelve cost £24.20. You are automatically issued a free membership discount card with a 12-month subscription, and this will give you 10% discount on any of the maps, books or magazines available within New Zealand Outlook. If you just want the latest copy, or a copy of any issue from the last 12 months, send five first class stamps per issue required to Consyl at the address above, along with a note explaining which issues you would like. A selection of articles from previous issues can be found on the website, by following the New Zealand Outlook Archive link.

Residence Categories

Skilled Migrant Category. The Skilled Migrant Category operates as a points system based around education and qualifications, work experience and age, your spouse or partner's qualifications and work experience, family and educational links to New Zealand, and access to sufficient funds to establish yourself. To be considered under this category you need to be of good health, good character, have a reasonable standard of English and be no older than 55. You will also need to meet the threshold of 100 points to register an Expression of Interest.

The points system is designed to allow Expressions of Interest to be ranked so that the New Zealand Immigration Service can extend invitations to apply for residence to those who have the most to offer New Zealand. The points are set out in Table 16 (below). Points are available for skilled employment in New Zealand, work experience, qualifications, age and family support. Bonus points are available for employment, work experience and qualifications in identified areas of growth or skill shortage. Bonus points are also available for employment outside Auckland, and for NZ qualifications gained in the country over two years, and also sometimes for your partner's employment and qualifications.

This category is designed to minimise the risk of a mismatch between the skills migrants bring and the skills New Zealand needs. The highest points will be available to qualified, skilled migrants who are already working in skilled employment in New Zealand.

Although a skilled job offer is not a prerequisite, you can see how important it is to consider ensuring that your skills are actually needed in New Zealand before you uproot your whole life to move there. Be wary of anyone who offers to guarantee you residence or sell you a job offer – this may be fraudulent practice and could result in your Expression of Interest or application being declined. Anyone attempting to bribe an NZIS officer will have their application declined and charges may be laid. If you have any doubts, check with the NZIS, and also be careful to check the official fees before handing money to an agent.

The process begins with you completing an initial self-assessment. A Skilled Migrant Quick Check is available on www.immigration.govt.nz and in the NZIS 'Self Assessment Guide for Residence'. This will help you to decide whether it is actually worth you submitting an Expression of Interest. You will then be able to complete an Expression of Interest (EOI) form and send it in. The NZIS prefer you to fill out this form online at www.immigration.govt.nz (this is the less expensive method), but you can also obtain a paper form from an NZIS office. This will provide information about your health, character, age, English language ability, and the factors that will help you to earn points. Once it is submitted, the NZIS will check it to make sure that all relevant information has been supplied.

EOIs submitted over a number of weeks will then be pooled and ranked from highest to lowest points. EOIs are prioritised in terms of points claimed and, after checking, those with the top points will be invited to lodge an application for residence. If your EOI is not selected from the pool the first time, it will remain in the pool for three months. If it is still unsuccessful, NZIS will tell you that your EOI has been withdrawn from the pool. You may lodge another if you wish to. If you have been successful, you will be sent an official invitation to apply for residence. At this stage you will need to send all the necessary documents to support the claims you made in your EOI, such as passports, qualifications and relevant certificates. The application for residence is now a much shorter form than it used to be, as you will have already supplied all the necessary information with your EOI.

Your application for residence is then assessed against government residence policy, and NZIS look closely at your ability to settle successfully and make a real contribution to New Zealand's social and economic development. Further verification of some of the information you provided with your EOI will also be undertaken at this stage. Depending on how you are able to demonstrate your ability to settle in New Zealand successfully, your application can be approved with a residence visa or permit, or a visa or permit which enables you to move from work to residence. It is then up to you to confirm your decision to move to New Zealand. A questionnaire will be sent to you after three months, as a formal follow-up and so NZIS can use your feedback to help future skilled migrants.

To give you an idea of how the points system works, see the table below.

TABLE 16	SELF-ASSESSMENT POINTS TABLE	
Factors		**Points**
1. Skilled employment	Current employment in NZ for 12 months or more (ongoing)	60
	Offer of employment in NZ or current employment in NZ for less than 12 months (but minimum of 3 months)	50
	Bonus points for offer of employment or employment in:	
	An identified future growth area	5

Identified cluster area of absolute skills shortage (amended 13 December 2004)	10
Region outside Auckland	10
Spouse/partner employment or offer of employment	10

2. Relevant Work Experience

Two years	10
Four years	15
Six years	20
Eight years	25
Ten years	30

There are additional bonus points if your work experience is in NZ:

Two years	5
Four years	10
Six years or more	15
Additional bonus points for work experience in an identified future growth area, identified cluster or area of absolute skills shortage:	10/15
Two to five years	5
Six years or more	10

3. Qualifications

Recognised basic qualification (e.g., trade qualification, diploma, bachelor's degree)	50
Recognised post-graduate qualification (e.g. Masters degree or higher)	55

Bonus points for:

Recognised NZ qualification with two years study in NZ:	10
Qualification in identified cluster	5
Qualification in area of absolute skill shortage	10
Partner qualification	10

4. Age (20-55 years)

20-29 years	30
30-39 years	25
40-44 years	20
45-49 years	10
50-55 years	5

5. Close family support in NZ   10

Remember that you must be no older than 55 and must meet the threshold of 100 points to be entitled to register an Expression of Interest.

Since 13 December 2004, applicants can gain 10 bonus points if they have a close family member who is in New Zealand and is a New Zealand resident, as long as that close family member supports the application.

POINTS TO WATCH OUT FOR

O You can only claim points for your highest qualification.

O You do not have to have a job offer although you will score more points if you do.

O Years of work experience are rounded down, so if you have nine years and eight months of work experience that will only count as eight years or four points.

O Medical assessment requirements are based on whether or not you would be a danger to public health or a burden on the New Zealand health system. Chronic manageable syndromes such as epilepsy would not disqualify you, but having a terminal disease probably would. Health requirements changed from 4 April 2005; these are outlined in the Health Requirements Leaflet from New Zealand Immigration (Form NZIS 1121).

Finding the extra points to raise you above the pass mark is an area where a good immigration consultant may be able to help. Most of them offer a job search service. You should consider visiting New Zealand and job-hunting in person, as most employers prefer to meet someone face to face before they make the offer of a job. Remember you can apply for permanent residency from within New Zealand. You will need enough money to finance your living costs while you are waiting for completion of the Immigration Service process, and this could be around six months. First hand experience of any country is still the best way to decide whether you want to live there.

Long Term Business Visa. You will need to complete an *Application for a Long Term Business Visa and Permit* (form NZIS 1058).

O You must submit all the required information when you lodge your application. If you do not supply this information, your application may be returned.

O All documents presented must be in their original form or certified copies.

O Anyone can act as your agent or representative, for example, a lawyer, consultant, or any other person (including a friend).

O All documents not presented in English must be accompanied by an official translation, certified by a recognised private or official translation service and on official letterhead which includes the name, address and signature of the translator. If you are considering applying for NZ citizenship at a later date, it may be worth having your documents translated by a provider approved by the Department of Internal Affairs. Refer to www.dia.govt.nz.

O First time applicants or those who have held a work visa and/or permit under the Long Term Business Visa/Permit category for 3 years and are applying for a further work visa and/or permit will need to pay a fee unless you are from a country listed under the fee waiver agreement. See the NZIS Guide to Fees (NZIS 1028) or www.immigration.govt.nz for details.

> O If you have held a work visa and/or permit under this category for less than 3 years and are applying for a further visa and/or permit, or are applying for consent to change your business plan, you will not need to pay a fee unless otherwise directed by the NZIS.
> O If you are in NZ, you must show that you have a current permit. Any dependents must also have current permits.
> O If you are separated or divorced and wish to bring children to NZ, you must prove that you have custody with either custody papers or a court order.

You will need to complete a business plan, covering general information, an outline of the proposed business and its viability, financial information (cash flow forecasts and financing options), your business experience, and your knowledge of the NZ market. The NZIS will assess your business plan, looking at whether you have sufficient funds, realistic financial forecasts, relevant business experience, a sound business record, sound business character, and whether you are registered (if professional or occupational registration in NZ is required for the proposed business). You must also supply information about the industry in which your proposed business sits, location of the business, maintenance funds, business status, investment capital, expectations of business achievements, proposed ownership structure, overseas links, benefit to NZ, your role, the number of employees and their skills, a marketing strategy, SWOT analysis, and a proposed timeline.

If your application is approved, you will be granted and/or issued a nine-month work permit/visa to allow you to establish and commence the operation of your proposed business. Further permits/visas may be granted or issued for the balance of the three- year period if:

O you apply within the validity period;
O you provide satisfactory evidence to demonstrate that your investment capital was transferred to NZ through the banking system; and
O you provide satisfactory evidence to demonstrate that you have taken reasonable steps to establish or invest in your proposed business.

If you wish to change your business proposal within the validity period, you must seek the consent of a business immigration specialist. Consent may be given if:

O you have genuine reasons for abandoning your original proposal; and
O you have an acceptable business plan for the proposed new business; and
O your new business proposal requires the same or a greater level of capital investment than your original business proposal; and
O you have access to sufficient capital to finance the proposed new business; and
O you have business experience relevant to the proposed new business.

Your permit may be revoked if you undertake a different business proposal without seeking consent. It is understood that a proposal may undergo some modifications or development once it is put into action, but it is best not to jeopardise your chances of staying in the country. If you are unsure whether a change you are making will require consent, you should contact the business immigration specialist who has been assigned to your case.

Further work permits and/or visas beyond the initial three years will be granted only where a business immigration consultant is satisfied on the following points:

○ Any time you spent in NZ has been spent setting up and operating your original business proposal.

○ If you made a change to your original business proposal, consent was granted for that change by a business immigration specialist.

○ You, and any family member accompanying you, have not drawn on the NZ welfare system.

○ You intend to spend the further period in NZ either implementing the original business proposed or a subsequent business proposal (which has been given consent).

○ You have, in addition to investment capital, access to sufficient funds for your own maintenance and accommodation and that of any spouse, partner, or dependent child accompanying you.

○ You meet Health and Character requirements,

In the event that your application is approved, you must agree to participate in an evaluation of the Long Term Business Visa/Permit category for a period of up to five years from the date your application is approved. You must also agree to inform the NZIS of any changes to your postal or contact addresses within five years from the date of approval of your application for the purpose of participating in the evaluation.

Business Investor Category. You will need to be under 85 years of age and have at least NZ$1 million in investment funds. Remember that if you have been in a relationship for less than 12 months you cannot include your partner's funds in your application. Your application for a visa or permit can cover your partner and unmarried children who are 19 years or younger. If they are dependent on you, your application can also cover children up to 24. To be successful you will still need to gain enough points for your age, business experience and investment funds to meet the pass mark, which is currently set at 12 points. See the points table on the NZIS website (www.immigration.govt.nz) to check whether you will qualify to apply under this category. If your application is successful you will be approved in principle and granted a visa. You will be required to keep your funds in an acceptable investment in New Zealand for a two-year period. After these two years, you will be granted a final approval for residence provided you meet all the requirements.

Entrepreneur Category. You may apply under this category if you have established and been working in your business for two years, and your business is benefiting New Zealand.

Employees of Relocating Businesses. This category covers only key employees who would not otherwise qualify for residence. The relocation of the business must be supported by New Zealand Trade & Enterprise, and the business must meet the requirements of New Zealand employment and immigration laws. This includes minimum wage rates, terms and conditions such as sick and holiday leave and requirements for health and safety of employees. If successful, NZIS will approve in principle a key employee's application for residence and grant a temporary multiple entry work visa or permit. This allows the applicant to stay in New Zealand for two years to work on the relocation of the business. During this two-year period, if the employee provides evidence that the business has relocated to New Zealand, they will then be granted residence.

Family (Partnership) Category. You are entitled to apply for residence under this category if you have a partner who is a New Zealand resident or citizen and who sponsors your application. Spouses, de facto and homosexual partners all qualify, but in the case of de facto or homosexual partners you have to go to greater lengths to convince the Immigration Service that the relationship is 'genuine and stable'. Approval is not automatic for any of these cases including spouses, and the Immigration Service will probably require an interview with both partners.

You can also qualify under family reunification if you have immediate family members who are residents/citizens and live permanently in New Zealand. You must be a dependent child, parent, brother, sister, or adult child of the person sponsoring you. Dependent children (now includes those aged up to 24 years, but they must be unmarried and childless) may qualify to be reunited with their parents if they were declared on their parents' residence application. Single adults may qualify for reunification with a New Zealand brother, sister or parent. Married and unmarried siblings, and dependent children, may now only apply for sponsorship if they have no other siblings or parents living in their own country and if they have an offer of employment in New Zealand. Under the 'centre of gravity' principle, parents may be reunited with adult children provided all their adult children live outside their country of origin, or, if they do not have dependent children, more of their adult children live in New Zealand than in any other country. If they do have dependent children, they may still apply if they have a greater or equal number of adult children living in New Zealand than in any other country. Children may sponsor parents who are alone in their home country. The definition of 'parents' has now been extended to include grandparents and legal guardians in cases where the parents are deceased.

To qualify under any of these categories you will need to provide evidence of your relationship to your family member and proof that they are New Zealand citizens or residents. The sponsor must undertake to ensure that accommodation and financial support is provided to the applicant for at least the first 24 months of residence in New Zealand. If the applicant is successful, they will be granted a Residence Visa (valid for 12 months from the date of issue), or a Residence Permit (which allows you to live in New Zealand indefinitely but expires when you leave New Zealand). You may need a Returning Resident's Visa to re-enter New Zealand. Your first Returning Resident's Visa is issued when you are granted your Residence Visa or your first Residence Permit in New Zealand, and is valid for two years from the date it is issued,

Family Quota. There is now an immigration ballot which currently allows an additional number of family members of NZ citizens and residents who are not eligible for residence under any other category. You must register your interest at a particular time each year, and if your registration is drawn from a pool (i.e., you are successful) your family will then have the opportunity to apply for a residence visa and permit. You will be notified by NZIS in the month after the draw whether your sponsorship has been successful, and, if so, you must then notify your family. Your family must then apply for a residence visa and permit within the next six months by completing an Application for Residence form (NZIS 1000). New Zealand residents/citizens may sponsor a close family member (parents, grandparents, adult children or adult brothers and sisters and their partners and children). The sponsor must be 17 years of age or over, in New Zealand and a New Zealand or Australian citizen or holder of a current residence permit. The sponsor must have been an NZ or Australian citizen (or holder of permit) for at least three years immediately before the date their registration is received by NZIS and, in each of the three 12 month periods within that three year period have spent a total of 184 days or more in New Zealand.

O The quota size is announced each year – see www.immigration.govt.nz for the latest information.
O Registration takes place every April, and winners are given six months to file their residency applications.
O Normal health, character, and relationship requirements still apply.
O Applicants must be sponsored by a family member who is a New Zealand resident or citizen living there permanently and who is aged at least seventeen years.

Humanitarian Category. Applicants under the Humanitarian category have to be suffering some kind of persecution in their home country and must have a New Zealand sponsor who is a close family member.

The Application Process

Obtain an application for visa form from a New Zealand Embassy or High Commission and complete it along with the required documentation, then return it to the High Commission. If you are applying under the Skilled Migrant Category, remember that you must submit your Expression of Interest (as outlined above) before being invited to complete an application. NZIS do prefer that you do this online.

A major cause of delay in processing applications is incorrect or insufficient documentation. Make sure, for example, that you send full birth certificates (not short birth certificates) for all family members included in an application for residency. Medical requirements include certain blood tests, and the results for these must be sent in. Once you have sent the correct documents, Immigration Service staff will check your eligibility. Processing time is often lengthy; currently applications within New Zealand are taking up to eighteen months to process, while New Zealand House in London advises that applications submitted to them are taking around six to eight months to process. However, to be on the safe side, you should begin the application process about a year and a half before your intended date of migration.

Fees must be paid by cheque (payable to 'The New Zealand Immigration Service'), building society cheque, money order or acceptable credit or debit card (Visa, Eurocard/MasterCard, Delta, Maestro), or cash payments are acceptable if you are paying in person. You must check which currency you should pay fees in with the office you will be making the payment to. Remember, irrespective of outcome, visa fees are non-refundable. Fees, like application forms, change regularly, so check you have the correct fee and current versions of the forms before submitting your application.

Fees.

These fees are for citizens from Canada, European and African countries, and, unless otherwise indicated, are shown in pounds sterling. American citizens and applicants from other countries should check the website www.immigration.govt.nz or telephone to establish the correct fee. The fees shown below are effective from 1 July 2004.

Visitor's visa	£50	Work Visa (temporary)	£80
Work Visa (Work to Residence)	£115	Working Holiday Visa	£50
Work – Long-term Business Visa	£875	Student Visa (temporary)	£80

Residence (Skilled Migrant)
NOTE: Expression of interest (EOI) fees must be paid in New Zealand in NZ$ or US$

EOI in NZ$ (manual)	NZ$465	EOI in US$ (manual)	US$305
EOI in NZ$ (online)	NZ$315	EOI in US$ (online)	US$210

Residence application   £520
Residence (Business Investor/Entrepreneur) £840   Residence (Family Migrants) £460
Residence (Family Quota) £430   Residence (Refugee Family Quota) £265
Migrant Levy (Skilled Migrant, Family and Business Categories – to be paid when the residence application is approved in principle) £115 per person up to a maximum of 4 people.

Citizens of certain countries are not charged for some visas:
Austria: No charge for Residence Visas, Returning Resident's Visas (RRV), Visitor Visas. Standard fee for Work and Student Visas.
Finland: No charge for any type of visa
Greece: No charge for Visitor Visas and RRVs. Standard fee for Residence, Work and Student Visas.
Iceland: No charge for any type of visa.
Israel: No charge for Visitor Visas and RRVs. Standard fee for Residence, Work and Student Visas.
Italy: No charge for RRVs and Visitor Visas. Standard fee for Residence, Work and Student Visas.
Japan: No charge for any type of visa.
Mexico: No charge for Visitor, Work or Student Visas. Standard fee for Residence Visas.
Philippines: No fee for Student and Visitor Visas (for visits not exceeding 59 days).
Russia: No charge for Student Visas when period of stay is less than 3 months. No charge for Visitor Visas. Standard fees for Work, RRVs and Residence Visas.
Turkey: No charge for Visitor Visas or RRVs. Standard fees for Work, Student and Residence Visas.
USA: No charge for Visitor, Work and Student Visas, Standard fee for RRVs and Residence Visas.

New Zealand Citizenship

Once you have resided legally in New Zealand for three years, you may apply for New Zealand citizenship. This will entitle you to vote and to carry a New Zealand passport. You will no longer require a returning resident's visa when you travel outside New Zealand. Children born in New Zealand to non-New Zealanders are New Zealand citizens. They can have dual nationality and are entitled to a New Zealand passport.

For citizenship inquiries you should contact the Director of Citizenship (Department of Internal Affairs, PO Box 10-526, 47 Boulcott Street, Wellington; ☎ (04) 474 8123 or 0800 22 51 51 (Freephone NZ only); fax (04) 382 3406; e-mail citizenship@dia.govt.nz; www.dia.govt.nz). Online forms are available through the website.

Entry and Work Permits

If you want to visit New Zealand and you are not a citizen or permanent resident, then you may need a visitor's visa or permit. You should apply for a visa from the New Zealand embassy in your home country before you travel. The initial period of a visa is usually three months but you can extend it by a further six months once you are in New Zealand by applying to local offices of the New Zealand Immigration Service. However, increasing numbers of travellers do not to need to obtain visas, as New Zealand has negotiated visa-free agreements with several countries. Tourists from the UK are entitled to stay for up to six months without a visa, and American, Canadian and European tourists can stay for three months without a visa. If you do not require a visa, you simply apply for a visitor's permit at the airport. You will be required to show that you have sufficient funds to support yourself while you are in New Zealand and a return or onward ticket. Like the visa, the visitor's permit is issued for three months initially and can be renewed by a further six months within New Zealand. If you have a friend or relative prepared to sponsor you, they will need to fill in a *Sponsoring a visitor* form, which they can get from New Zealand Immigration, and which must be sent to you so you can present it when required.

Australia. Australian citizens are free to travel to New Zealand without a visa and can work in New Zealand without requiring a work visa under the terms of the Closer Economic Relations agreement, which creates a free labour market across the Tasman.

Applying for a longer visa. If you know before you travel that you want to stay for longer than three months it is worth applying for a visa even if you are from a visa-waiver country. You can apply for a maximum of twelve months, and your application must be made before your current permit expires.

Studying in New Zealand. Any person wanting to travel to New Zealand for the principal reason of study or training must have a student visa before they travel. You will need to provide an acceptance letter from the New Zealand educational institution, receipt for the non-New Zealand student course fee, evidence of sufficient funds to support yourself, and an outward airline ticket. If you wish to work over the student holidays (November to February), you can apply for a

'Variation of Conditions' to your student permit. If you wish to work following the completion of your course, you can apply for a Work Permit, which will allow you to work a maximum of two years. Some tertiary students may work up to fifteen hours a week while studying. The student must be studying for a degree or diploma that would gain points under the Skilled Migrant immigration category: exchange students are not eligible. You must be studying an approved course and must have sufficient funds to cover your tuition fees and maintenance (see the *Education* section of the *Daily Life* chapter for a general idea of the cost of New Zealand courses). Dependents of a work visa holder may be eligible for a student visa without already having a place arranged at a New Zealand school. They may also be exempt from overseas tuition fees.

Working in New Zealand. If you wish to work in New Zealand for a short period and you are not a citizen or resident you will need to apply for a temporary work visa. You can apply for one before you travel if you already have a definite employment offer, or, if you find a job while visiting New Zealand, you can apply for a visa there. Your prospective employer will need to provide details of your job title, responsibilities, qualifications required, conditions and duration of employment and pay, as well as proof that they have unsuccessfully tried to recruit a New Zealander to fill the position. You can apply for a work visa for up to three years if you have a job offer before you arrive in New Zealand. However, if you apply for a work visa in New Zealand, the maximum period you will be granted is nine months. The employer will be required to provide the local Immigration Service with the information outlined above. For further information you should contact the New Zealand Immigration Service.

Working Holiday Visa. New Zealand's working holiday visa scheme allows young people from 22 partner countries to spend time in New Zealand and undertake temporary work. People between the ages of eighteen and 30 inclusive can apply for the visa, which will enable them to take casual work without requiring a separate work visa while on holiday in New Zealand. The number of places allocated overall will be increased from 31,000 in 2004/05 to 36,000 in 2005/06 and 40,000 in 2006/07. When the scheme started in 1993 only 500 visas were issued; the latest information (effective from July 2005) is that an extra 10,000 places will be divided between the schemes for Belgium, Canada, Denmark, Finland, France, Ireland, Italy, Norway and the USA, and the upper limit cap will be removed from the schemes for Germany, the Netherlands, Sweden and the UK. Work restrictions are to ease for the schemes with Belgium, the Netherlands, Sweden and the USA, and working holidaymakers from the UK will be allowed to stay for up to two years.

From July 2005, applications for all working holiday schemes will take place on the internet. This online service will be immediate, with the application being lodged, paid for and decided electronically. It has the added benefit of meaning that applicants can get their working holiday scheme visa from anywhere in the world.

From April 2005 anyone wishing to enter New Zealand and remain for more than twelve months will have to undertake a normal migration medical.

Useful address

CIEE (Council) USA: 7 Custom House Street, 3rd Floor, Portland, ME 04101; ☎tollfree: 1800 40 STUDY or 1-207-53-7600; fax 1-207-553-7699; www.ciee. org. Helps students from the USA study abroad.

New Zealand Information, Immigration and Visa Inquiries in the USA and UK

Department of Internal Affairs Office UK: 2nd Floor, New Zealand House, 80 Haymarket, London, SW1Y 4TQ; ☎020-7930 8422; fax 020-7 316 8998; Passports e-mail passports@dia.govt.nz; www.dia.govt.nz.

New Zealand Ministry of Foreign Affairs and Trade: www.mfat.govt.nz. See the website for a list of NZ consulates and embassies around the world.

New Zealand Consulate General USA: Suite 1150, 12400 Wilshire Boulevard, Los Angeles, CA 90025; ☎310-207 1605; fax 310-207 3605; e-mail nzcg.la@verizon.net.

New Zealand Embassy USA: 37 Observatory Circle NW, Washington DC 20008; ☎202-328 4800; fax 202-667 5227; e-mail nz@nzemb.org; www.nzemb.org.

The New Zealand High Commission UK: New Zealand House, 80 Haymarket, London, SW1Y 4TQ; ☎020-7930 8422; fax 020-7839 4580; e-mail info@immigration.govt.nz (visas, work permits or residency applications) or: aboutnz@newzealandhc.org.uk; www.nzembassy.com.

The New Zealand Immigration Service UK: 3rd Floor New Zealand House, 80 Haymarket, London, SW1Y 4TQ; ☎09069 100 100 (calls charged at £1.00 per minute); e-mail info@immigration.govt.nz; www.immigration.govt.nz.

NZIS Marketing Directors (USA):
Terry Murphy, Department of Labour, PO Box 146, 3527 NE 15th Street, Portland, Oregon 97212; ☎Toll free: 877-844-0697; ☎503 284 0697; fax 503 287 0621; e-mail terry.murphy@dol.govt.nz.

Don Badman, 12400 Wilshire Blvd, Suite 1150, Los Angeles, CA 90025; ☎1 310 576 9220; e-mail don.badman@dol.govt.nz.

Information for British Citizens in New Zealand

British High Commission: 44 Hill Street, Thorndon, PO Box 1812, Wellington; ☎(04) 924 2888; fax (04) 473 4982; e-mail PPA.Mailbox@fco.gov.uk; www.britain.org.nz.

Information for American Citizens in New Zealand

Consulate General of the United States of America: 3rd Floor, Citibank Building, 23 Customs Street (cnr Commerce Street), Private Bag 92022, Auckland; ☎(09) 303 2724; fax (09) 366 0870.

Embassy of the United States of America: PO Box 1190, 29 Fitzherbert Terrace, Thorndon, Wellington; ☎(04) 462 6000; fax (04) 499 0490.

SETTING UP HOME

Typical New Zealand house prices can be ascertained from the property section of some New Zealand newspapers. The main newspapers can be read online, see www.stuff.co.nz for various area options. More detailed advertisements can be found in New Zealand real estate magazines. Information may also be obtained from the Real Estate Institute of New Zealand's website (www.reinz.org.nz).

Immigration consultants may also offer advice on buying properties. The property market in New Zealand's main cities is currently quite lively as a result of low interest rates and improving economic prospects. Auckland and Wellington are the most expensive places to buy houses, but outside the main cities property prices are considerably cheaper.

Most New Zealand houses are detached, single storey houses on individual plots of land known as 'sections' (the term 'bungalow' to describe such a house is not common). The average New Zealand home consists of three bedrooms, a living room and dining room, kitchen, laundry and bathroom. Most homes near cities or towns are built of timber and stand alone. Many are insulated, but most do not have central heating or double glazing. The standard size of the New Zealand section used to be a quarter of an acre, but as urban property prices have risen in recent years, subdivisions have become more common and new houses are being built on much smaller sites. The average size of new houses is now smaller and more compact at just under 170 square metres. Although the vast majority of houses are still separate units, in recent years city apartment living has increased in popularity.

For most people, the decision about where to live is influenced first and foremost by employment prospects. New immigrants are most likely to buy houses in either Auckland or Wellington. In both cities the residential areas are mostly suburban and it is most common for people to commute by car into the city centre to work. Each suburb has its own particular character and prices can also vary considerably between areas for reasons as diverse as mere fashion or, in the case of hilly areas, related to the amount of sunshine that different parts enjoy, or the views they afford. In Auckland, for example, your property is worth more if it has a view of the harbour or Rangitoto Island. It is worth looking at the less fashionable areas, where first homeowners and young families often buy. If you are aiming at the more affordable end of the market, you will get more house for your dollar.

If you have children, your choice may be influenced by proximity to schools. The location, however, does not make a lot of difference to the standard of education on offer. Inner city schools perform as well as suburban schools on the whole. Rural schools achieve slightly lower academic results than city schools but have the advantage of smaller class sizes and better pastoral care. The best idea is to visit schools in the area and see what you think of the atmosphere. Now that school zoning has been abolished, you are free to select the school of your preference.

How Do New Zealanders Live?

New Zealand has a high level of home ownership, with nearly three-quarters of dwellings being owner-occupied. New Zealanders tend to be quite house-proud, and spend a lot of time on home improvements and gardening. The average standard of housing is high. Household services such as water, electricity and sewerage are almost universal. Over 98% of all homes have colour TVs, most have videos, and around a third have dishwashers.

Of those who are living in rented homes, a quarter live in state houses rented from Housing New Zealand, while the majority lease housing from private landlords or companies. Rental accommodation is usually provided unfurnished except for ovens, and sometimes fridges and washing machines. Local authorities do not play a major role in providing housing.

> **Kim Cullen found living in New Zealand a contrast to her life in America**
> *The majority of NZ homes do not have central heating. And winters are cold, windy and damp - at least in the lower North Island (Wellington) and South Island. It has been difficult to adjust to it being just as cold inside my house as it is outside. During the winter, there is no relief from the cold and it can affect your moods. What most Kiwis do is wear multiple sweaters and buy space heaters, electric blankets, and close bedroom doors to keep the heat in. Watch out for the utility bills during winter time; the electric and gas bills will skyrocket. The Kiwis don't complain – they just shrug and deal with it – but my American friends and I however really struggle with the winter season.*

The majority of households are made up of just one family. Amongst Maori and Pacific Island communities, where extended kinship links are important and because average incomes amongst these groups tend to be lower, households are more likely to include more than one family or extended family members. Even amongst Maori and Pacific Island homes though, one-family households are the most common. The average number of occupants per dwelling is 2.7 people.

Levels of second home ownership are also quite high. Many New Zealand families own what is known as a 'bach' (pronounced 'batch' rather than after the composer) or 'crib'. Bach is the North Island term, while the word crib is only used in the South Island. These are usually small holiday cottages near a lake or by the sea. The bach is a great New Zealand institution. These mostly unpretentious and comfortable dwellings are often furnished with various items discarded from the family home, and provide the perfect way for families to 'get away from it all' with the minimum of planning.

Buying a House in New Zealand

It is possible for a foreign national to buy a house in New Zealand, but it is important to note that this does not give the purchaser any automatic right to live permanently in New Zealand. If you are a permanent resident, there are no official restrictions on the type of property you can buy in New Zealand. If you have less than permanent residence, however, you are limited to buying a home on less than 5 hectares (12.5 acres) of land or undeveloped land up to 5 hectares, provided this land is not on, or next to, a 'sensitive area' (such as an island or a reserve).

Finding a Property

Most people begin either by approaching a local real estate agent or searching in free weekly property newspapers in their desired location. A good paper to try is the *Property Press* (PO Box 99772, Newmarket, Auckland; ☎ (09) 524 0491) which is freely available in inner city areas. Daily newspapers also carry property advertisements.

There are many types of property on offer, although the variety is not as great as in countries where architecture of many periods co-exists. European style architecture only has a short history in New Zealand and the typical period house is a wooden Victorian villa. This type is very popular with the do-it-yourself set as a renovation project. Most older houses were made of wood because of the risk of earthquake. The standard New Zealand house of the post-war period is a three bedroom, brick single-storey building on a large section. Before this, houses were generally built with a northern hemisphere model in mind and thus did not always make the most of the New Zealand climate. Modern houses are designed to capture the sun and to make the most of outdoor living during the summer, with decks and sliding doors to blur the indoor/outdoor distinction. Because of rising inner city land prices, there is a growing trend towards building town houses and apartment blocks. Town houses are compact units, often multi-level, usually built as part of group on one site. In the suburbs, where land is cheaper, you can find modern mansions with swimming pools, en suite bathrooms, separate living rooms and dining rooms, all on a huge site. Often these homes also have separate living areas and bathrooms for the children. At the other end of the budget spectrum, you will find houses advertised as 'the handyman's dream' or 'needing TLC' (tender loving care), which is real estate speak for a dwelling in dire need of repair. This type of property brings a glint to the eye of the home handyman who seems to lurk under the skin of most New Zealand males and quite a few females. If your acquaintance with nails is confined to those on your digits, then you should probably avoid this type of thing and look for something a more immediately habitable. On the other hand, inner city Victorian villas can still be picked up relatively cheaply if you are prepared to spend the money and the time on renovations and, once 'done up', they make very desirable homes.

The latest figures show that house sales move relatively quickly in New Zealand. The median number of days it takes a property to sell is 31; properties in Canterbury/Westland have been proved the quickest movers, taking a median number of just 22 days to sell, while Nelson/Marlborough property has the longest period at a median of 55 days.

Useful Addresses

As there are such a large number of real estate agents operating in New Zealand it is impossible to list them all here. All worthwhile companies are listed on the internet. To find one in your area try *Harcourts Real Estate* (www.harcourts.co.nz or e-mail enquiries@harcourts.co.nz) or *L. J. Hooker* (www.ljhooker.co.nz or e-mail enquiries@ljhooker.co.nz). Other useful websites for real estate agents include: www.harcourts.co.nz; www.harveys.co.nz; www.brafoot.co.nz; www.leaders.co.nz; www.bayleys.co.nz and www.professionals.co.nz. For general information, have a look at www.realenz.co.nz, www.propertystuff.co.nz and www.consumer.org.nz. Also try the *Real Estate Institute of New Zealand* online at www.reinz.org.

INTRODUCING THE SENSIBLE WAY TO SUCCESSFULLY RESETTLE IN NEW ZEALAND

Orientation New Zealand is a service-based company, established to assist you make a successful transition to a new way of life in New Zealand. In doing so we aim to take the stress out of emigrating.

Successful resettlement doesn't happen overnight. It takes time, planning, availability of accurate information and the right advice – which is exactly what we offer … practical help whenever and wherever you need it.

We offer a one-on-one personal service which can be tailored to your specific requirements. Our relocation consultant will provide advice and support every step of the way, starting before you depart from the UK, all the way through to after you have arrived and settled. Reassuringly we will be there for you for as long as you need us.

We offer the knowledge acquired only after living many years in New Zealand. We have the contacts, know where the best deals are to be found, know who you can trust and who to be wary of. We happily share all this knowledge with you.

Orientation New Zealand's resettlement specialists are very familiar with the British way of life. Knowing where you come from helps us know how to make things go smoothly for you when you arrive in New Zealand.

For our FREE brochure detailing the range of our services please contact us.

ORIENTATION NEW ZEALAND
Resettlement Services For United Kingdom Migrants

PO Box 58473, Greenmount, Auckland
Tel: +64 (0) 21 374500 Fax: +64 (0) 9 448 2266
Email: mandy@orientationnz.co.nz

nz. You can contact REINZ at PO Box 9284, Auckland; ☎0064 9 353 2250; fax 0064 9 353 2251; e-mail info@realenz.co.nz.

Other organisations, such as the following, may also be useful when you are doing your research. *Overseas Investment Commission*, Reserve Bank Building, PO Box 2498, Wellington, New Zealand; ☎0064 4 471 3838; fax 0064 4 471 3655; e-mail oic.govt.nz; www.oic.govt.nz. *Land Information New Zealand*, Lambton House, 160 Lambton Quay, Private Box 5501, Wellington; ☎0064 4 460 0110; fax 0064 4 472 2244; e-mail info@linz.govt.nz; www.linz.govt.nz.

Specialist companies such as *Orientation New Zealand* (address below) exist specifically to offer advice and support to those planning to move to New Zealand.

Miscellaneous Useful Addresses

Directmoving.com (USA): ☎331-4215 7500 or 331-4215 7507; fax 331-4215 7505; e-mail expat@directmoving.com; www.directmoving.com/expat.

Orientation New Zealand: PO Box 58473, Greenmount, Auckland; ☎021 374500; fax 09 448 2266; e-mail mandy@orientationnz.co.nz. Specialist advice and support for those planning to settle in New Zealand.

Relocations International: 34 Douglas Street, Auckland; ☎(09) 378 9888; fax (09) 378 8072; e-mail gspeed@reloc.co.nz; www.reloc.co.nz. Wellington office: 101-103 Molesworth Street, Wellington; ☎(04) 479 3765; fax (04) 479 3769; e-mail julia@reloc-wgtn.co.nz.

TABLE 17	MEDIAN HOUSE PRICES BY REGION
District	**House Price**
Northland	$195,000
Auckland	$337,000
Auckland City	$385,000
Metropolitan Auckland	$339,000
Hamilton City	$235,000
Tauranga	$265,000
Waikato/Bay of Plenty/Gisborne	$212,500
Hawke's Bay	$196,100
Manawatu/Wanganui	$146,000
Taranaki	$158,500
Wellington	$270,000
Wellington Central	$311,000
Nelson/Marlborough	$250,000
Canterbury/Westland	$223,250
Christchurch City	$236,500
Otago	$186,550
Dunedin	$191,000
Southland	$132,000
Median selling price	$250,000

Source: REINZ Residential Report 2004.

PURCHASING AND CONVEYANCING PROCEDURES

Buying a property is less complicated in New Zealand than in many other countries. Establishing clear title is generally straightforward because there are fewer complications like cross-leasing and leasehold properties. As a result you do not get chains of prospective buyers waiting for the next person in the chain to organise the sale of their house. Nor are there problems of establishing who actually owns the property in question.

When you wish to buy a property, you need to obtain the free copy of *Real Estate* magazine published by the combined local real estate firms. This has a photo of each property, relevant information, and details of the estate agents involved. You may attend an 'open home' (which means you turn up at that address at the time specified), or you can arrange a private visit with the estate agent. The agent is working for the seller, and receives a commission for the sale from them, but must present the property fairly to the buyer. It's possible to deal with several agents at once, as many estate agents have sharing arrangements over the commission for the sale.

It's sensible to have a solicitor check the title details when you come to sign the agreement to buy the property. A solicitor would also be useful in terms of arranging to get a Valuer's Report should you need it, or a Land Information Memorandum Report. A LIM report establishes the town planning requirements and anything that could affect the property, and is available from the local authority.

Most home-owners in New Zealand have a mortgage from a bank or financial institution. Most commercial and industrial properties are leased, as this provides an annual cost for taxation purposes. Your agreement to purchase a property can be subject to obtaining mortgage finance or the sale of your current New Zealand property. Your solicitor's charge may add around $500- $950 to your expenses, but it could save you from making a costly mistake. The market is not regulated, so you can ask around for a reasonably priced solicitor. A useful magazine published by a network of independent legal firms is *Lawlink* (PO Box 6197, Wellesley Street, Auckland; ☎ (09) 300 5470; fax (09) 309 5113) which is also online (www.lawlink. co.nz/resources).

FINANCE

Borrowing Money to Buy a Property

Mortgages are the standard method of financing house purchasing in New Zealand. The majority of properties have a mortgage on them. If you wish to apply for a mortgage, or any other finance, it will be helpful to have records from your previous bank showing repayments, pay slips, references showing your work history, evidence of any other property that you own, etc. Your solicitor will help and this should be discussed before you make an offer to purchase a property. Banks are the main lenders. Building societies used to be separate institutions from banks but since deregulation in the 1980s they have been allowed to provide the same services and most have now converted themselves to banks. The banks have responded to the competition to provide mortgages by offering more flexible repayment terms.

If you are a permanent resident of New Zealand, you will be provided with identical mortgage facilities to those provided to New Zealand citizens. This means that you should be able to borrow as much as 95% (sometimes more) of the value of the property you are buying. If you have a work permit rather than residency, banks or lenders will require more commitment from you, although their requirements will vary. Some will require that you fund at least 20% of the purchase price, but other stricter companies will require you to fund at least 50% of the purchase price. If you look thoroughly you should be able to find a loan for 80%. The maximum amount you may borrow is not always directly related to your salary but you will be expected to provide information about your monthly income as part of a hypothetical budgeting exercise and repayments would not normally be expected to be more than 30% of your income. If you are borrowing more than 60% of the purchase price, the bank may require a Valuer's Report. The amount you can borrow varies from lender to lender, but, provided you have no other significant debts, lenders will generally finance mortgages of roughly four and a half times your gross household income.

Mortgage and Associated Costs

Your lender will charge mortgage establishment/application cost of around 1% of the value of the mortgage. The Land Transfer Registration fee is $50 if you send your forms by post, although if a lawyer acts on your behalf this fee will come out of general legal disbursements. There are two types of insurance. Mortgage protection insurance is more comprehensive, and it repays the mortgage in the event of your death. Mortgage risk insurance will pay the mortgage for a fixed period if you lose your regular income. There is no government benefit to help you pay the costs of a mortgage.

Repayment Conditions

Repayments are usually made on a monthly basis, but can be fortnightly. The usual term of mortgage used to be 25 years, but it is increasingly common for people to arrange shorter term mortgages with commensurably higher monthly repayments. Most banks will not approve of a mortgage arrangement that requires you to repay more than one third of your monthly income. Interest rates can be either fixed or floating. There are three main types of mortgage: table, reducing or interest only. In a table mortgage you pay equal monthly (or fortnightly) payments of interest and capital over the whole term of the mortgage. In a reducing mortgage, monthly payments start high because you pay fixed amounts of principal, plus the amount of interest you have accrued that month. At the beginning, there will be a lot of interest to pay off, but this will decrease as the principle is repaid resulting in decreasing monthly payments. Whether you choose a table or reducing mortgage, you will also be able to choose between a variable or fixed-rate mortgage. Some borrowers take a mixture of variable and fixed-rate mortgages.

The third type is an interest-only mortgage, which is exactly what it sounds like. You pay a higher rate of interest on a monthly basis, which tends to add up to the same sum, more or less, as a repayment mortgage, but at the end of the whole term the original sum borrowed is effectively written off. The banks are quite flexible about changing the repayment conditions once you have entered into the mortgage, for example increasing or decreasing the size of monthly payments or switching to fortnightly payment intervals. You can even alter the type of mortgage or transfer it to another property.

RENTING PROPERTY

Most immigrants rent property while they look for a house. You can arrange to rent a furnished apartment before you arrive in New Zealand through an immigration consultant or through some of the newspapers for intending migrants: *New Zealand Outlook* and *Destination New Zealand*, see Chapter Two *Residence and Entry Regulations* for subscription details, or visit www.emigratenz. org online). Some travel agents will also provide assistance in finding a temporary place to stay. This type of arrangement tends to be more expensive than finding a rental house yourself, but it has the advantage of the accommodation being ready and waiting for you as soon as you step off the plane. It will certainly be cheaper than staying in a hotel while you are house hunting.

The cost of rented accommodation is quite moderate, although you can expect to pay more if you want something more than just a typical three-bedroom house. Rental properties are advertised in the daily newspapers — mostly on Saturdays, but some on Wednesdays as well. Cheaper houses can be hard to find in towns with large student populations. If you are looking for cheaper accommodation, February/March is a bad time to look as it is the start of the university year and you will be competing with students looking for flats. However, many students leave their flats in mid- to late-November, so this can be a good time to find a bargain. You can also use a Real Estate letting agency, but you may have to pay as much as the equivalent of one month's rent as a fee for them to find you a suitable flat. The majority of privately let houses are unfurnished, although they may contain the odd piece of furniture. If you require a furnished property, it is probably best to go through a real estate agent.

Tenancy Agreements

Both the landlord and the tenant must sign the tenancy agreement, and the landlord must ensure that the tenant receives a copy of the contract before the tenancy begins. Details that must be covered include the names of the parties involved, the bond, the list of chattels (inventory), start and end dates of the tenancy (if it has a fixed term) and a street address for the landlord.

There are three different types of tenancy: periodic, fixed term, and service tenancies. With a periodic agreement, the tenancy continues until either side gives notice. In standard letting contracts, the tenant must give at least 21 days written notice that they want to end the tenancy, and the landlord must give 90 days notice. The landlord is allowed to give only 42 days notice if they or their family members are moving into the house themselves, or if they have sold the house. In a fixed term tenancy the duration is fixed at the start of the letting period and cannot be changed except by agreement of both parties. In theory, this means that even if you decide to move out before the tenancy is over, you will be responsible for paying rent for the period stipulated on your tenancy agreement. A service tenancy is when an employer provides accommodation for an employee. Service tenancies are covered by the Residential Tenancies Act, but have special rules relating to rent paid in advance and notices to quit. You should ask Tenancy Services for further information if you are considering entering into a service tenancy. Most tenancy agreements are sorted out between the landlord and the tenant using the standard tenancy agreement available from Tenancy Services. It is not usually necessary to have a lawyer check the agreement. Tenancy Services are there to help in case of disputes between landlords and tenants and they will also give you information about your rights and responsibilities as tenants. The landlord is required to maintain the premises but tenants are responsible for any damage caused by misuse or abuse.

Rent and other costs

Landlords can ask for up to two weeks' rent in advance, but only one week's rent in advance if rent is to be paid weekly. You are entitled to a receipt if you pay in cash, but not if you pay by direct debit, cheque or automatic payment (in which case the transaction will be recorded by your bank). Rent increases cannot be made less than six months apart, and the landlord must provide 60 days' notice of such an increase. The amount of rent charged varies depending on demand, and there are no legal restrictions on amounts or increases. You should check local papers, real estate agents and the Tenancy Services website to make sure that the amount you will be charged seems fair in relation to other properties being offered, preferably before entering into a rental agreement. If you are convinced that your rent is well out of sync with the market, you can ask the Tenancy Tribunal for a market rent assessment. This assessment basically covers 'what a willing landlord could expect to receive, and a willing tenant to pay for the tenancy, in comparison with rent levels in similar areas'. If the Tribunal finds that the landlord is charging substantially more than this, it can make an order fixing the rent for a period of normally six months.

Landlords are entitled to ask for up to four weeks' rent as a bond or deposit, in case of damage to the property. These bonds used to be held by the landlord, but as a result of disputes between tenants and landlords over the withholding of bond money, the bond is now passed on to the Bond Centre, part of Tenancy Services. This must be done within 23 working days of the bond being paid. Bond lodgement forms are available from Tenancy Services, or can be downloaded from their website. Standard tenancy agreements (available at stationers such as Whitcoulls, or from Warehouse Stationery) usually come with a bond lodgement form attached. At the end of the tenancy, both parties sign a bond refund form and the bond is refunded to you less any agreed unpaid rent or other amounts (such as bills, repairs for damage to the property, or other disputes) owing to the landlord. If you prefer, this amount can simply be transferred to a new tenancy. In this case, you will need a bond transfer form, to be signed by you, your old landlord and your new landlord. Tenancy Services act as arbitrators between tenants and landlords in disagreements over bonds and other disputes such as rental arrears and damage to property. Enquiries regarding bonds should be directed to the Tenancy Bond Centre (☎ 0800 737 666).

Legally, landlords are also entitled to ask for real estate agent's fees and/or solicitor's fees charged for setting up the tenancy. This is fairly unusual however. A landlord may also ask for 'option money', which is basically a holding deposit of no more than one week's rent for holding a house or flat until you make up your mind. If you take the property, the amount must be refunded or put towards your rent. If you don't take the property though, the landlord may keep the money.

Aside from these costs and fees outlined above, there are no other charges that a landlord can legally request from you. In rare instances, dodgy landlords trying to take advantage of potential tenants have been known to demand 'key money', which is basically any payment for giving you the tenancy (aside from rent, bond, or agent's/solicitor's fees). Sometimes this is categorised as a deposit for the key to the house, or a deposit on the washing machine or anything else supplied with the tenancy. This is illegal, and you should refuse to pay it. Such landlords will probably back right off once they realise that you know what you are talking about and are not to be taken advantage of, but if you feel it is necessary you should contact Tenancy Services.

Useful Addresses

Tenancy Services, Advice/Mediation & Enquiries, Department of Housing and Building: ☎0800 836 262 or Bond Enquiries ☎0800 737 666; e-mail information@dhb.govt.nz; www.dhb.govt.nz/housing/tenancy/.

Citizens Advice Bureau (National Office): ☎0800 367 222 (0800 FOR CAB); www.cab.org.nz. Citizens Advice offers free confidential advice on housing, health, legal and consumer problems, employment and budgeting. There are 87 offices throughout New Zealand, from Kaitaia to Invercargill.

Community Law Centres (National Office): 281 Madras Street, PO Box 2912, Christchurch; ☎(03) 366 6870; fax (03) 366 6631; e-mail admin@comlaw-chch.org.nz. Community Law Centres provide free confidential legal advice and are staffed by solicitors and law students. There are 24 Law Centres around the country. Contact the Christchurch office for telephone contact details for your local branch if it is not listed here. Auckland: (09) 378 6085. Hastings: (06) 879 7625. Wellington: (04) 499 2928. Dunedin: (03) 477 9562. Invercargill: (03) 214 3180.

Land Information New Zealand (National Office): Lambton House, 160 Lambton Quay, Private Bag 5501, Wellington; ☎(04) 460 0110; fax (04) 472 2244; e-mail info@linz.govt.nz; www.linz.govt.nz. Government department providing land and property information. Website includes government policy, maps, valuation rates, and a searchable database.

Legal Services Agency: Level 19, BDS House, 86-90 Lambton Quay, PO Box 5333, Wellington; ☎(04) 495 5910; fax (04) 495 5911; e-mail lsa.govt.nz; www.lsa.govt.nz.

Netlaw: www.netlaw.co.nz.

Rates

Each local council in New Zealand levies a tax based on the value of your property to fund local amenities and services. Road maintenance, sewage disposal, water supply, libraries, park maintenance and street lighting are all paid for by your council rates. The value of your property and hence the amount of rates you pay is decided by Valuation New Zealand. Rates are included in the rent of rental properties.

INSURANCE AND WILLS

Wills

If at the time of your death you have a permanent place of residence in New Zealand or you are living in New Zealand for more than half the year, you are considered by New Zealand law to be a resident. This means that any property you own in New Zealand is subject to New Zealand laws if you die intestate. It makes sense therefore to make a will after you have bought a house. Property disposed under a New Zealand will is not subject to inheritance tax, provided the person is domiciled in New Zealand. If you are retaining assets in your home country, you should check with your solicitor to see that your New Zealand will is recognised there. Property in other countries is normally subject to the inheritance laws of those countries.

You do not have to use a lawyer or trustee company to draw up a will in New Zealand but it does not cost much and may save problems later. Certain procedures must be followed for a will to be valid, and the testator must sign it in the presence of two non-beneficiary witnesses. Trustee companies will draw up a will for around $85. Try the NZ Guardian Trust (☎ 0800 371 471; e-mail info@guardiantrust. co.nz; www.guardiantrust.co.nz). Offices can be found in Auckland, Whangarei, Hamilton, Rotorua, Takapuna, Tauranga, Napier, Palmerston North, Wellington, New Plymouth, Nelson, Christchurch and Dunedin.

Insurance

Taking out insurance on a new property is a sensible precaution. Most mortgage lenders will probably require you insure your new house. There are different types of cover available. Multi-risk policies (called accidental damage policies) provide blanket cover for all losses unless specifically excluded. Defined risk policies, as the name suggests, list what risks the policy provides cover for. This type of policy is less costly but accidental damage policies are probably a better option. Your house can either be insured for its indemnity value, or replacement value. The indemnity value is the depreciated or current market value of your house, excluding the value of the land. It does not replace with new, nor would it cover the cost of rebuilding, but you should be able to buy a similar house. The replacement value can be open-ended or fixed sum. The difference between this and indemnity value is that there is no deduction for depreciation. Open-ended replacement value means the insurer will pay the full cost of repairing or rebuilding as new. Fixed sum replacement value means that the insurer will pay up to the agreed sum. Typical premiums exclude the value of the land and can be reduced by increasing the excess, or installing burglar and fire alarms. Insurance for your home will cost anywhere between $300-$550, depending on where you live and the company you choose. Contents insurance varies according to what you wish to cover, but the average is around $350-$600. Premiums are cheaper outside the larger cities, and most expensive in the Auckland region.

It makes sense to take out household contents insurance with the same firm as you have your house insurance with (and maybe your car insurance as well). You should get a discount for having both types of insurance with the same company and it will save arguments over who is responsible for a claim. Again you can either get a multi-risk or a defined risk policy for either indemnity or replacement value (for a house of the same size). If you have an accidental damage policy you can sometimes buy an extension to cover your possessions outside of your house, for example, personal sports equipment.

One unique feature of buying household insurance in New Zealand is earthquake damage insurance. Because New Zealand is prone to earthquakes, a special government scheme exists to provide insurance cover against them. When you take out a household insurance policy that includes cover against fire (i.e., a total replacement policy) you also automatically gain cover in the case of earthquake, landslide, volcanic or tsunami damage. In fact, it is the New Zealand Government that underwrites the risk of earthquakes because the potential cost of a major earthquake in a big city is too great for commercial insurance companies to handle. Your insurance company will charge you a compulsory disaster insurance premium which they pass on to the Earthquake Commission's Natural Disaster Fund (Earthquake Commission, Level 10, Castrol House, 36 Customhouse Quay, PO Box 311, Wellington; ☎ (04) 499 0045; claims: ☎ 0800 652 333; fax (04) 499 0046; www.eqc.govt.nz). The Natural Disaster Fund is currently worth over $3.3billion, and the EQC has its own overseas reinsurance cover as well, in case of catastrophic earthquake. If that is not enough, the government is required to make up any shortfall. The maximum amount the Commission will pay out is $100,000 (+GST) or the amount for which you have insured your home on a replacement basis, (whichever is lower) and $20,000 (+GST) for personal belongings or the amount for which you have insured them. (Again they will pay out the lower amount). For a claim on a house, the excess is 1% of the amount of the claim, with a minimum of $200 per dwelling. For belongings, the excess is $200 and for land the excess is 10% of the amount of the claim, with a minimum of $500 per dwelling and a maximum of $5,000. The coverage is fairly basic and does not extend, for example, to motor vehicles, trailers, boats, swimming pools, jewellery, securities and documents, or works of art. Nor will the Commission pay for any indirect costs arising out of an earthquake such as, for example, the cost of having to stay in rented accommodation. Top-up cover with an insurance company will cover the items noted above which EQCover does not include, and will also cover you for the value of your house above the $100,000 covered by the government. Earthquakes large enough to cause serious damage are rare.

UTILITIES

Services such as electricity, telephones, water and sewerage are just about universal in New Zealand. The best options between electricity, reticulated natural gas and LPG cylinders depend on where you live and how much energy you use. Consumer Online investigates annual energy costs in the five main centres, using common combinations of gas and electricity in the home. You can use the survey on the Consumer website (www.consumer.org.nz) as a guide to the savings you might make by choosing the best plan for you and your household. Holiday cottages in some of the remotest areas may not be on mainline electricity and commonly will have a septic tank rather than being on mainline sewerage, but the average family home comes provided with all services. People moving into a house or flat need to arrange for the electricity or gas and telephone to be connected. An agreement for the supply is signed between the supplier and the tenant, as utilities are not the responsibility of the landlord. Credit references from your previous power, gas and telephone companies will be helpful in setting up your New Zealand accounts. Most government departments providing commercial services were turned into State Owned Enterprises (SOEs) in the late 1980s. They were set up like commercial companies, although as the name suggests they remained publicly owned, and were given commercial targets. The change in performance between the new SOEs and the old government departments was dramatic. When telecommunications were run by the Post Office, average installation time was at least six weeks. Now it seldom takes more than two days. The creation of SOEs has also brought with it some competition in the utilities marketplace. Rival telephone companies are now offering price wars on toll calls, and a freer market exists for some utilities.

Electricity

Most of New Zealand's electricity supply is generated through hydro-electric schemes on the main rivers. Hydro-energy has the advantage of being cheap, clean and renewable. Most of the power is generated in the South Island on the rivers draining the mountains of the Southern Alps. Bills come once a month, and an average monthly bill for a three-bedroom house would be roughly around $200. There is usually an initial administration charge for setting up a new account, which is around $100.

New Zealand supplies alternating current at 240 volts, 50 hertz. Equipment designed for a 110-volt system will require a transformer, but bear in mind that some specialised equipment designed for a current other than 50 hertz may not work properly even with a transformer. Any appliances you bring with you may require new plugs. It is important to also consider the fact that you may not be able to find parts or repair services for certain electrical items if they are uncommon in New Zealand. Leave behind your telephones, faxes and telecommunications equipment — it may not work with the local network, and again you may not be able to find anyone to repair it if something goes wrong. New Zealand is a high-tech nation, and the latest electronic equipment will be readily available there.

The privatisation of electrical utilities in New Zealand has caused its own problems. The city of Auckland made international news in February 1998 when the electricity supply to the inner city was cut off for several weeks. The city's power supplier, Mercury Energy, did not sufficiently maintain its cables to the city, and, during the especially hot summer, the four 110 kilovolt cables melted simultaneously. Businesses were forced to close, and residents were evacuated. Although the city retailers claimed they were losing $10 million a day from the power cuts, Mercury Energy would not take responsibility for the disaster, and blamed the collapse of the cables on a freak of nature. The rest of the country, however, seemed to enjoy Auckland's plight, and Wellington and Dunedin tourist boards advertised the 'power' and 'energy' of their cities in Auckland newspapers.

There are a number of different electricity suppliers in New Zealand, and your options will of course be limited by the area you live in. Some of the main names are Mercury Energy, Empower, Meridian Energy, Energy Online, Contact Energy, Bay of Plenty Electricity, TrustPower and Genesis Energy.

Gas

Household gas supply is not universally available. Natural gas is produced off the Taranaki coast and piped to most areas of the North Island. It is available as far north of Auckland as Whangarei, in Wellington and on the East Coast in Gisborne, Napier and Hastings. In areas which do not have a household supply, bottled gas is available. In the South Island most gas is of the bottled variety except in Dunedin and parts of Christchurch. The local supply company can be found in the front of the *Yellow Pages*. Before they will connect your property, the gas company will require you to fill in an application for the supply of gas and to pay a bond of around $100.

Water

New Zealand water is clean and quite drinkable, although it tastes better in some areas of the country than others. In Auckland and Hamilton it can have an unpleasant chlorine taste. Most people seem to put up with it, although the bottled water market is growing. People building homes and renovating kitchens now often have a water filter installed with the kitchen taps. Water shortages are not normally a problem, although Canterbury and Auckland have suffered droughts in recent summers, and water conservation is often called for in other areas such as Hawke's Bay and Canterbury depending on the weather situation. In some areas local councils charge for the water supply and your supply will be on a meter, in others the cost of water connection and supply is included in your annual rates bill.

Waste Services

Rubbish is disposed of in two ways; the local council collects everyone's rubbish bags once a week and residents can take their rubbish to the local 'tip' (dump). Most local authorities charge for weekly rubbish collection (meaning that only official rubbish bags, or bags bearing a correct sticker, will be collected) and for use of the local rubbish dump (usually depending on the size of the load you want to dispose of). In Auckland there is an inorganic rubbish collection once every month, when large unwanted household items, such as furniture, appliances and any other number of objects will be removed for your convenience. Recycling bins are available in most areas, from the council, and are normally emptied on the same day of the week as your main rubbish collection. Recycling collectors have firm rules regarding the condition of your recycling; all bottles, cans, tins, etc. must be washed and clean, and broken glass is strictly forbidden in some areas. If your green bin has been left untouched after all the others in the street have been emptied, it is likely that you have included something unacceptable and they have decided to leave the whole lot. Contact your local council for information about rubbish and recycling.

Telephone and Internet

There are at least fifteen companies offering telecommunications services in New Zealand. These include Telecom, TelstraClear (formed when TelstraSaturn and Clear Communications merged in 2001), Vodafone, Global One, WorldxChange, teamtalk, Compass, Call Plus, City Link, Zip, DigiPlus and Ihug. The main competitive services are international, national and cellular (mobile) calls. Most competitors have interconnection agreements with Telecom, and a number also have interconnection agreements with each other. Telecom, the SOE that took over running telecommunications from the Post Office, was sold off in 1990 to a consortium of two US phone companies and two local companies. The investment programme was part of the process of revamping the company prior to selling it. As a result, New Zealand's rather antiquated phone system was given a much-needed overhaul. At the same time the industry was deregulated to allow competitors into domestic supply and provision of phone units. Deregulation has led to improvements in customer service.

The downside of telecommunications privatisation is that, despite being a private company, Telecom has an effective monopoly in many areas of telecommunications services, because it owns the network. There is no industry regulator to check that the prices Telecom charges consumers are fair. Despite competition in the long distance calling market, some industry commentators argue that toll calls are still too expensive.

In most areas you are obliged to hire your phone line from Telecom as they retain a monopoly on the provision of the network, and basic residential line rental (HomeLine) costs around $43 including GST a month and includes unlimited local calling. Telecom no longer supplies rental telephones, but you can buy a telephone relatively cheaply at any number of retailers. To get your phone connected, Telecom will require personal identification (a copy of your passport) before they can set up your access. Fax 0800 42 50 00 or e-mail creditapprovals@telecom.co.nz, or fax from overseas: +64 3 374 5778.) Telecom offers a dedicated call centre for new customers (dial 123 from any touchtone phone in NZ and then choose Option 3). It takes about 48 hours to connect a new number. If an installer is required to do the connection, as opposed to a remote connection, a further visit fee is charged, and the installer will quote this on the day. You can join TelstraClear online, by filling in and submitting a simple joining form. With TelstraClear, you continue to make toll calls in exactly the same way as before, but your national and international calls automatically go through the TelstraClear network. Your telephone number won't change.

New Zealand's long distance services usually feature off-peak capped call charges, with unlimited duration. (Off-peak is evenings from 6pm to 8am the following morning, and from 6pm Friday to 8am Monday.) These deals are constantly changing, but as a general rule companies frequently have such offers as cheap capped national calls, $4 capped calls to Australia, and $6-8 capped calls to the United States, Canada, the United Kingdom and Ireland. At the time of going to print, TelstraClear was offering a deal for $9 a month for 20-minute home-to-mobile calls. Residential service competition is developing, and users should also be able to get a feature on their service plan allowing them to have capped national calls at peak times at a cost of, for example, $2.25 (up to two hours) or thereabouts. TelstraClear offers a competitive range of services and options to residential and business customers in the Wellington, Hutt Valley and Kapiti areas, as well as parts of Christchurch.

Mobile telephone services are provided by Telecom and Vodafone. The number of mobile phones (called cellular or 'cell' phones in New Zealand) has skyrocketed in recent years and 89% of households in the top quintile of annual household income ($87,600 and over) now have access to a cellphone. This is compared to 43% of households in the bottom quintile (income under $23,000). Overall, 71% of households now have access to a cellphone.

High-speed internet services are becoming common, and internet protocol telecommunications providers are increasingly available, offering competing national, international and landline to mobile calls. Telecom's Jetstream service uses ADSL technology to send high-speed voice and internet data down one telephone line at the same time, in areas where this technology has been installed. TelstraClear provides high speed internet access via cable modems connected to its co-axial cable television network. Ihug's Ultra provides high speed internet downloading via satellite dish anywhere in New Zealand, and through a microwave dish in Auckland. 62% of New Zealand households own or have access to a home computer.

Telephone books (White and Yellow pages) are supplied free by Telecom. There are several versions — each one covers a particular area or region. Most of the country is covered by both analogue and digital mobile communications networks, and almost all New Zealand homes have a telephone.

Telecom has a free call ('freephone') number for businesses with a prefix of 0800. This enables customers to call free from anywhere in New Zealand. Freephone numbers for TelstraClear start with 0508. Local calls are free for residential customers, but there is a small charge (50c) for telephoning Telecom's directory enquiries on 018. You are entitled to two enquiries per call for this charge, and can be connected to the number you requested by pressing 1 after the number is given (for a 30c charge). TelstraClear does not offer a directory enquiries service. For international directory enquiries you can dial 0170 (TelstraClear) (you will be charged for this service), dial Telecom International Directory Assistance Service on 0172 (calls cost $1.50 and you can request two numbers for this price) or see the Infobel World Telephone Directories website, which provides information and services for more than 184 countries (www.infobel.com/teldir/). Telecom's White Pages (alphabetical residents and companies listings) are on the internet at www.whitepages.co.nz, and the Yellow Pages at www.yellowpages.co.nz.

Useful Contact Details

Telecom New Zealand: PO Box 1473, Christchurch; Telecom Service Express ☎0800 000 000 (24 hours a day, seven days a week); ☎(7am to 9pm Monday to Sunday) 123 (from any touchtone phone within New Zealand); ☎0800 800 070 (Home Business) from a landline; ☎*123 from a mobile; International Roaming service ☎0800 651 000; Telecom Call Centre for new customers calling from overseas ☎+64-3-374-0253 (7am-9pm NZ time, seven days a week); e-mail there are a number of e-mail forms, for various kinds of queries (everything from sales and services questions to changing your postal address and ordering a copy of your bill), on the website; www.telecom.co.nz. Remember that while Telecom don't charge you for calls made to its service numbers, other service providers may charge you if your call originates from that service provider's network.

TelstraClear Ltd.: (except payments) Private Bag 92 143, Auckland; (payments) Private Bag 92027, Auckland; ☎0508 888 800; fax 0508 888 801; from outside NZ ☎+64 9 913 9150, fax +64 9 912 4442; cable locations information ☎0508 651 050, fax 0508 651 100; www.telstraclear.co.nz. See the website for complete contact details of all TelstraClear offices (including street and postal addresses).

REMOVALS

Packing up your possessions and getting them to the other side of the world is an expensive business. There are basically two ways of shipping your household goods to New Zealand, depending on whether the removal consists of a small or large amount. Smaller removals are usually grouped with other people's small removal lots destined for the same port, so they can be shipped in shared containers. Be aware of this when choosing a mover — if you pick a company that does not regularly handle large numbers of this type of removal, your belongings could be delayed for quite some time while they wait for other consignments to fill up the container. Larger removals are usually shipped as whole container loads, which means that they are packed up and sent off immediately on the first vessel sailing to New Zealand. Transit time can take as long as twelve weeks if you are using a shared container. For a full-container removal it will probably take around six to eight weeks.

When deciding what to bring, remember that the New Zealand electricity supply will probably be different to what you are used to. New Zealand supplies alternating current at 240 volts, 50 hertz. Having your existing appliances adapted to suit New Zealand supply may work out more costly than replacing them in the end and not worth the trouble. Your removal company should be able to advise you on these points. On the other hand, good quality household furniture, fine china and glass will generally be worth bringing with you.

Most people who are planning to move overseas for the first time make the mistake of assuming that an international move is the same as a normal domestic one. You should use a specialist international mover. Representatives who will visit you to assess your removal requirements can offer advice regarding items you may be undecided about shifting. If you know of anyone who has shifted their household, ask them about their shipping company or, if you are dealing with an immigration consultancy, find out which companies other emigrants have used successfully. You should check whether they are members of an international removals trade association and if the association offers a payment guarantee scheme if the removals company goes bust while your goods are still in transit. Two well-known ones are the Association of International Removers and the British Association of Removers.

When it comes to comparing quotes from different companies, be sure to get quotes in writing based on the same list of goods. Freighting cost quotes for a shared container will be based on the cubic volume of your goods, so it is essential to make sure the removals estimator knows exactly what you want to take as any last minute extras will cost more.

In the case of a full container quote, the price per container is standard, but you should get a quote for the costs of any excess goods in case they do not all fit in one container. Make sure you know the type of container they are quoting, as volumes differ between insulated and non-insulated containers. If the quote is based on a shared container load, make sure it includes an estimate of total volume of your goods. If you have only a small amount of effects to move, it will probably be cheaper to pack them yourself. There are few important points:

o   You should pack your possessions in stout containers, using a material such as polystyrene or paper.

O Most removals companies will provide suitable containers.
O Goods packed with straw or chaff will not pass New Zealand agricultural quarantine regulations.
O You should label baggage carefully, inside and out.

Always wait until you have received and checked a written estimate before booking your removal company. You should have written confirmation of several points, including the following:

O the list of items to be shipped;
O a cubic volume;
O special packing requirements for particular items;
O all door-to-door costs including customs and terminal charges, unloading etc.; and
O delivery instructions showing the name of your destination city or town in New Zealand.

Insurance for the Move

Insuring your possessions during the move is critical. Shipping firms will usually offer marine insurance as part of the service but you need to check the small print carefully. The cost of marine insurance may not be included in your initial estimate because this is assessed on the value of your possessions. Make sure that the policy is all risks and that it covers any storage period either in the UK or in New Zealand. If the insurance company has offices in New Zealand, any claims are likely to be settled much more quickly than if they have no New Zealand base. While rates quoted are often very similar, the level of cover can vary so make sure you obtain a copy of the terms and conditions and compare them carefully. Ask for a copy of the insurance company's proposal form well in advance so that you have plenty of time to ask any questions you may have and also to assess the values that you are planning to declare.

Useful Addresses

Abels International Moving Services: Wimbledon Avenue, Brandon, Suffolk IP27 0NZ; ☎0800 626 769 (freephone) ☎1842-816600 (Customer Management Centre); fax 01842-813613; e-mail enquiries@abels.co.uk or neilpertoldi@abels.co.uk or suebloomfield@abels.co.uk (for enquiries about storage); www.abels.co.uk.

Air New Zealand Cargo (Vancouver, BC): ☎(604) 244-2209; fax (604) 2444-2227; e-mail laxcs@airnz.com; www.ca.airnewzealand.com:80/aboutus/cargo/.

Air New Zealand Cargo (Calgary, AB): ☎(403) 717-4324; fax (403) 714-4326; e-mail laxcs@airnz.com; www.ca.airnewzealand.com:80/aboutus/cargo/.

Air New Zealand Cargo (Toronto, OT): ☎(905) 676-8928; fax (905) 676-8931; e-mail laxcs@airnz.com; www.ca.airnewzealand.com:80/aboutus/cargo/.

Air New Zealand Cargo (Montreal, QU): ☎(514) 428-4363; fax (514) 428-4365; e-mail laxcs@airnz.com; www.ca.airnewzealand.com:80/aboutus/cargo/.

Air New Zealand Cargo (LA): 5721 West Imperial Highway, Los Angeles, CA 90045; ☎310-646 9891 or 800 421 5913; fax 310-568 8620; www.us.airnz.com.

Air New Zealand Cargo (Chicago): Building 517, Suite 101, O'Hare International Airport, PO Box 661217; Chicago, IL 60666; ☎(773) 686-9837 or (800) 424-1066; fax (773) 686-9865; www.us.airnz.com.

Air New Zealand Cargo (New York): Building 87, Cargo Plaza Rm. 206, JFK International Airport, Jamaica, NY 11430; ☎718-244 1333 or (800) 400 0153; fax 718-244 1334; www.us.airnz.com.

Air New Zealand Cargo (UK): London Heathrow; ☎020-8751 5000 (hours 9am – 5.30pm, Monday to Friday); fax 020-8751 3333, www.airnewzealand.co.uk/aboutus/cargo.

Allied International: Worldwide network specialists in international removals, with over 1,000 representatives in 130 countries. Check your local phone directory for an office near you, or find one online at www.alliedintl.com. The New Zealand arm is *Allied Pickfords*: 415 Church Street, Penrose, Auckland; ☎+64 9 579 0648; fax +64 9 579 0634; e-mail ap.corporate@allpick.co.nz; www.allpick.co.nz./nz/.

Anglo Pacific International Plc, Units 1 and 2, Bush Industrial estate, Standard Road, London NW10 6DF; ☎020-8838 8434; e-mail info@anglopacific.co.uk; www.anglopacific.co.uk.

Avalon Overseas Movers (Europe): Part of the Team Relocations Group, offering advice and help with all Customs and other documentation and carrying out in excess of 30,000 relocations worldwide every year; www.teamrelocations.com. Website offers French, German and Dutch language options.

The Baggage Company (UK): 4 Hannah Close, London, NW10 0UX; ☎freephone 0500 868 500; fax 020 8324 2095; e-mail info@thebaggagecompany.co.uk; www.thebaggagecompany.co.uk.

Crystal International (USA): 1901 Camino Vida Roble Suite 206, Carlsbad, CA 92008; ☎800-307 8900 or 760-431 0266; fax 760-431-0360; e-mail info@crystalinternational.com; www.crystalinternational.com.

Excess International Movers (UK): Bases in London (including various train stations and airports), Birmingham, Edinburgh, Glasgow, Leeds, Liverpool and Manchester. Head office: 4 Hannah Close, Great Central Way, London NW10 0UX; ☎National Freephone 0800 783 1085; ☎020 8324 2066; fax 020 8324 2095; ☎International: 0044 20 8324 2000; e-mail sales@excess-baggage.com; www.excess-baggage.com.

Excess International Movers (USA): ☎Toll Free number 1 800 260 8098.

Monstermoving: Fill in the form to get an online quote; www.monstermoving.com.

PSS International Removals (UK): Head Office, 1-3 Pegasus Road, Croydon, Surrey CR9 4PS; ☎020 8686 7733; fax 020 8686 7799; e-mail sales@p-s-s.co.uk; www.pss.uk.com. You can submit a direct online enquiry form.

Unigroup Worldwide UTS (USA): One Worldwide Drive, St Louis, Missouri 63026, ☎636-305 6000 or tollfree: 1 800 325 3924; fax 636-305 6097; www.unigroupworldwide.com. You can request a door-to-door surface shipments quote online.

Customs Regulations

Information regarding the importation of household and personal effects and cars into New Zealand can be found in a series of leaflets from New Zealand Customs. New Zealand Embassies and High Commissions should have copies available, or you can obtain information on the internet (www.customs.govt.nz), or by e-mailing: feedback@customs.govt.nz. The basic principle is that if you are coming to New Zealand to take up permanent residence, you can import your household goods and car duty free. The goods must be used and not be intended for sale or commercial use. If you are a returning resident, coming back to New Zealand after an absence of more than 21 months, your household goods qualify for the duty free concession, but in the case of cars, you can only qualify for the duty free concession on the first occasion you arrive to take up residence. You are also entitled, like any visitor to New Zealand, to bring in personal effects duty free. The list of prohibited imports includes indecent articles and publications, ivory in any form, anything made from the bone of marine mammals, most weapons and some types of food. You may not bring plant material or fruit into New Zealand. The importation of firearms is strictly controlled and a Police permit is required.

Import Procedures

Provided that you qualify for the duty free exemption outlined above, importing your household goods ought to be straightforward. The complicating factor is that you and your possessions will most likely be travelling separately, you by plane and your worldly goods by sea, a process taking six weeks at minimum. You can either send off your goods well before your departure and hope that their arrival in New Zealand coincides with yours, or send them off when you leave and manage without for your first few weeks in your new country. You should make sure that your insurance policy covers any storage time, either before shipping or following delivery at the other end. If your car and possessions arrive in New Zealand before you do, you can avoid paying port storage charges by arranging for a nominee to clear them through Customs for you. The Collector of Customs at the port will require evidence of your nominee's authority to act for you and evidence that you are arriving in New Zealand for the first time to take up permanent residence. In the case of a car, additional documents proving that you have owned it for at least one year prior to departure will be required. Your nominee will be required to pay a deposit equivalent to the cost of duty on the vehicle and/or goods, which will be refunded in full once you arrive.

Whether you are picking up your goods yourself or have authorised a nominee, you need to provide Customs with an inventory of your belongings. You should be careful to thoroughly clean any garden tools or furniture, hiking boots, running shoes, or anything else that may have traces of mud or dirt on it. Your goods will be inspected by the Ministry of Agriculture and Forestry before being released to you, and they may require such items to be steam cleaned or fumigated to kill off any pests or diseases. MAF inspection charges vary depending on the consignment. If you have any queries about what types of goods you can import and the procedures contact the Collector of Customs at the port of destination (see addresses below).

New Zealand Customs: ☎Freephone within NZ: 0800 428 786; fax (09) 359 6730; e-mail feedback@customs.govt.nz; www.customs.govt.nz.
Auckland: Box 29; ☎(09) 359 6655; fax (09) 359 6732.
Auckland International Airport: Box 73003, Mangere, Auckland; ☎(09) 275 9059; fax (09) 256 8648.
Christchurch International Airport: Box 14086; ☎(03) 358 0600; fax (03) 358 0606.
Dunedin: Private Bag 1928; ☎(03) 477 9251; fax (03) 477 6773.

Invercargill: Box 840; ☎(03) 218 7329; fax (03) 218 7328.
Lyttleton: Box 40; ☎(03) 328 7259; fax (03) 328 7763.
Napier: Box 440; ☎(06) 835 5799; fax (06) 835 1298.
Nelson: Box 66; ☎(03) 548 1484; fax (03) 546 9381.
New Plymouth: Box 136; ☎(06) 758 5721; fax (06) 758 1441.
Tauranga: Box 5014, Mt Maunganui; ☎(07) 575 9699; fax (07) 575 0522.
Timaru: Box 64; ☎(03) 688 9317; fax (03) 688 4668.
Wellington: Box 2218; ☎(04) 473 6099; fax (04) 473 7370.
Whangarei: Box 4155; ☎029 250 9305; fax (09) 438 0055.

Importing Pets

Getting your pets to New Zealand is going to cost as much as getting yourself there, and require every bit as much paperwork and many more vaccinations. Requirements for importing animals into New Zealand are extremely stringent, and nearly all animals except for cats and dogs are prohibited. However, if you fulfil all the pre-flight veterinary requirements, your animals may be able to go home with you when they arrive in New Zealand without requiring a quarantine period. Pets from Hawaii and the UK do not have to be quarantined, but they do need a series of tests. From other places, the length of the quarantine period required depends on the country of origin, but it will be at least 30 days. This is likely to cost over $1000. Bear in mind that in New Zealand there are only three MAF registered quarantine facilities for domestic cats and dogs, and for importations where a post-entry quarantine period is required a Permit to Import will not be issued unless the importer has a letter from a quarantine facility confirming that a space has been booked for the animal.

There are a number of firms who specialise in the air freighting of pets (for names and addresses see below) and some international removal companies also offer this service if they are shipping your household goods for you. As this involves organising an IATA approved air travel container, which must be sealed by a vet, as well as an examination immediately prior to departure, it is probably best to hand your pets over to the professionals. If you are using the services of a professional firm, it is best to contact them a few months in advance to avoid any unforeseen documentation delays. You will need to organise some of the veterinary procedures yourself, as some vaccinations have to be given six weeks prior to departure. There are a number of compulsory tests and the results of these must travel with the animals. Most firms will suggest that you leave your pets with them for the night prior to departure.

Your pet should not be tranquilized during air travel, as this can be fatal. Most reputable firms will strongly discourage this practice, and will refuse to carry an animal that has been sedated. The firm you choose to help you may offer services to acclimatise your pet to air travel before the trip takes place, so that it is not too much of a shock for them. However, most advise that pets almost always settle down quickly and sleep for the large part of their journey. Pets are transported in the live animal cargo section of the plane; this is insulated, pressurized and temperature controlled (to the same temperature as in the passenger area of the plane). However, excessive heat or cold can prohibit airline pet transportation, and airlines place 'heat and cold embargoes' on pet transport to prevent illness or death in the height of summer or the depths of winter. Bear this in mind when arranging the time of year you want to travel. Your pet-transporting firm will be able to advise you about the best times for your pet to travel during the winter or summer. *Pet Transporter*

Worldwide advises that this is especially important in the summer months for pug-nosed dogs and snub-nosed cats, which are more susceptible to oxygen deprivation and heat stroke. Pet crates will have enough room for standing up, lying down and turning around, but not much more than this as too much space can be a hazard and cause injuries in the event of turbulence.

An Import Health Permit must be obtained prior to the importation of dogs or cats; you must apply for this permit in writing from Dr Kerry Mulqueen, National Advisor Import Management, Animal Biosecurity Group at the Ministry of Agriculture and Forestry, or it may be downloaded from the Ministry's website (see contact details below). Please note that you should apply for this permit well in advance of the scheduled date of importation.

New Zealand has quite strict laws governing the control of pets. The animals must not annoy or injure other people, and any dog found roaming freely may be impounded by the Dog Pound. There are laws to protect pets as well; the SPCA (Society for the Prevention of Cruelty to Animals) can take any person who has been cruel to an animal to court. You must also be aware that there are some areas, particularly near wildlife reserves, which have been designated cat-free zones due to the havoc that domestic cats have been wrecking on native bird populations. At present there are only a few of these areas, and the rules are enforced by general community consensus rather than the long arm of the law, but you should ensure that you do not unwittingly introduce a cat to such an area.

Useful Addresses

Airpets Oceanic: Willowslea Farm Kennels, Spout Lane North, Stanwell Moor, Staines, Middlesex, TW19 6BW; ☎01753-685571 or Freephone 0800 371554; fax 01753-681655; e-mail export@airpets.com; www.airpets.com.

Atwoods Pet Resort Travel Agency: 25103 112th St E., Buckley, WA 98321, USA; ☎253-862 9454; fax 253-862 3687; e-mail lee@petresort.com (do not e-mail reservation requests); www.petresort.com.

Import Management and Quarantine: Ministry of Agriculture and Forestry, PO Box 2526, Wellington, NZ; ☎(04) 498 9624; fax (04) 474 4312; e-mail mulqueen@maf.govt.nz; www.quarantine.govt.nz.

Independent Pet and Animal Transportation Association International (IPATA): 745 Winding Trail, Holly Lake Ranch, Texas 75775, USA; ☎(903) 769 2267; fax (903) 769 2867; e-mail ipata@aol.com; www.ipata.com. You can search online for a pet shipper by location or by business name, you can download a list of pet shippers from the website, or use the Fax-on-Demand facility; dial 1-402-951-5501, request file 176, and a complete list of pet shippers will be faxed to you immediately.

Par Air Livestock Shipping Services: Warren Lane, Stanway, Colchester, Essex CO3 0LN, UK; ☎01206-330332; fax 01206 331277; e-mail parair@btconnect.com; www.parair.co.uk.

Pet Chauffeur (New York City): ☎Toll Free 866 PETRIDE, or (718) 752 1767; e-mail info@petride.com; www.petride.com.

Pet Transporter Worldwide: Services include all flight and ground transportation, door-to-door pick-up and delivery, care in between flight connections when necessary, TSA and UDSA documentation, boarding and any other service your pet needs. See the website for a list of location-specific offices and contact numbers in the US (Arizona, California, Colorado, Connecticut, Florida, Massachusetts,

Maine, New York, New York City, North/South Carolina, Virginia and Washington), or ☎1-800-264-1287. Germany: ☎0699-7944-0025. The Netherlands: ☎020-796-5921. UK: ☎020-7071-5669; www.pettransporter.com.

Quarantine Addresses

Ministry of Agriculture and Forestry: Animal Quarantine Division, Box 2526 Wellington, NZ; ☎(04) 472 7171; general enquiries ☎+64 9 256 8547; fax (04) 474 4132; www.maf.govt.nz/quarantine/. See the 'Contacts' page of the website for telephone numbers in different areas of New Zealand.

Pussy Cat Lodge: 29 Crowther Street, Avondale, Auckland; ☎(09) 828 3410; fax (09) 828 0455. Spaces for 24 cats. (MAF Registered.)

Qualified Pet Services: 150 Airfield Road, Takanini, Auckland, NZ; ☎(09) 299 9539; fax (09) 299 9539; e-mail services@qualifiedpet.co.nz; www.qualifiedpet.co.nz. Spaces for 36 dogs and 8 cats. (MAF Registered.)

Canterbury Quarantine Services Ltd: Highfield Road, Aylesbury, PO Box 23158, Christchurch, NZ; ☎(03) 318 1279; fax (03) 318 1289; e-mail wumba@xtra.co.nz; www.canterburyquarantine.co.nz. Spaces for 30 dogs and 15 cats. (MAF Registered.)

New Zealand Quarantine Stations:

Auckland Wharf: 23 Quay Street, PO Box 39, Auckland City; ☎(09) 303 3423; fax (09) 303 3037.

Wellington: Centreport House, Waterloo Quay, Port Wellington, PO Box 3042, Wellington; ☎(04) 473 8996; fax (04) 471 2079.

Christchurch: 14 Sir William Pickering Drive, Private Bag 4765, Christchurch; ☎(03) 358 1856; fax (03) 358 1854.

Importing a Vehicle

If you are considering importing your car, you will obviously want to consider whether the original value of the car plus the cost of freight, port handling costs and insurance is lower than the replacement cost of the car in New Zealand. In general, European cars cost more to replace in New Zealand than their original value plus shipping costs, assuming the vehicle qualifies for duty free entry (see below for the conditions). Japanese and Asian cars are cheaper because of the commercial importation of second-hand vehicles from Japan, but there have been some recent problems with quality assurance so be careful if you are going this route. As a very rough guide, new cars can be purchased for anywhere between $17,000-$166,000, and second-hand cars for $5,000-$50,000. One source of information on second-hand car prices in New Zealand is the classified section of newspapers. You can order New Zealand motor trade magazines from *Destination New Zealand* and *New Zealand Outlook* or from the Automobile Association. Some car shipping companies will also provide lists of recent New Zealand prices for common models of car.

If you are emigrating to New Zealand for the first time, you can import your car into New Zealand free of duty provided you satisfy Customs that you are importing the vehicle for your own use, that you have owned it for at least a year prior to your departure, and that you are arriving in New Zealand to take up permanent residence for the first time. You will be required to sign a deed of covenant agreeing that if you sell your car or boat within two years of importing it, you will be retrospectively liable for the duty and sales tax (GST). If your car does not qualify for duty-free entry, duty is levied at 20% of purchase price for UK-made vehicles, and 30% of purchase price for other foreign cars, less depreciation. The exchange rate used in calculating the New Zealand dollar value of your car will be based on the current exchange rate at the time you clear your vehicle. The costs of shipping an average car vary depending on the size of the car and which port in New Zealand it is going to. It usually takes about six weeks. Some companies offer a cheaper option where the vehicle is not shipped in a container, but the risks of damage or theft in transit are higher. You should arrange insurance for your vehicle, whichever option you choose. Premiums are calculated on the New Zealand value of the car. Do not pack personal belongings in the car for the journey. There is a risk of pilferage, particularly if the car is not containerised during the journey, and the contents of the car will have to be declared to Customs by the shipping company or you will risk a fine.

Procedures for clearing your car through Customs in New Zealand are as follows. The vehicle will be given the once-over by the Ministry of Agriculture and Forestry (MAF) quaratine inspection and border check. A number of details about your car will be recorded and then sent on to the LTSA's Transport Registry Centre for recording on the LANDATA database as part of the vehicle's permanent record. You should allow 48 hours for information to be recorded on the LANDATA system. MAF will invoice the importer a fee to cover the cost of the border check and the quarantine inspection conducted on the wharf. If you don't want to arrange the MAF and NZ Customs Services processes yourself, you can contact a Customs broker. All used vehicles must be steam cleaned before MAF will pass them. You can have your car commercially steam cleaned before shipping but remember to keep the receipt to show to MAF in New Zealand. Some shipping companies will steam clean your car as part of the service. MAF's objective is to prevent any pests and diseases, which could endanger livestock, being brought into the country and their standards are therefore stringent. If inspectors are not satisfied that your vehicle has been thoroughly and properly cleaned, you will be required to have it done again. Your car will need to comply with New Zealand safety regulations, some of which differ from standards of other countries. Your vehicle must have front and rear seatbelts, and a high mounted rear stop light. It is a good idea to have these fitted before you leave because you will not be able to drive the car in New Zealand until it complies with local safety standards. The Vehicle Identification Number (VIN) will be issued/decoded by your Entry Certifier. The Entry Certifier verifies that the vehicle met the required standards when manufactured, carries out the vehicle inspection to confirm that it is in good condition, and decides whether the vehicle needs any repairs and/or specialist certification for compliance with legal safety requirements. They then verify entitlement to register and issue form MR2A and Warrant of Fitness. The next steps are registration and licensing, and then your vehicle can legally be driven on New Zealand roads. Check the appropriate Infosheets and Factsheets on the LTSA website for more detailed information (www. ltsa.govt.nz/importing/). Left-hand drive vehicles require special import permission. Apply to the Land Transport Safety Authority (PO Box 2840, Wellington; ☎0800 699 000 within NZ or +64 4 494 8600; fax +64 4 494 8601; e-mail info@ltsa.govt. nz; www.ltsa.govt.nz).

Next you will need to provide documentary evidence to the Collector of Customs that the car is yours and, if you are applying for a duty free entry, that you have owned it for at least one year prior to importing it. Such proof can include a dated receipt of purchase showing the date delivery was taken, registration papers, odometer details, evidence of the date on which you gave up the vehicle for shipping to New Zealand and your passport showing verification of permanent residency.

You cannot drive the car legally until it has a vehicle inspection certificate and is registered, so you will need to arrange for it to be transported from the port to the nearest vehicle inspection test centre. The VIC used to be called the Warrant of Fitness (WOF), and in some places testing centres still advertise them as Warrants. Once your car has passed, you take the certificate to a post office, along with the ownership documents and the importation documents, and obtain a registration certificate, sticker and number plates. All of this is likely to take a couple of days.

Useful Addresses

All America Auto Transport: 7514 Wisconsin Ave, Bethesda, Maryland 20814; ☎1-800-227-7447 or 1-800-CAR-SHIPPING; fax 301-215-9215; e-mail aaat@aaat.com; www.aaat.com. Will send a free information package on request.

Anglo Pacific International ☎020-8838 8000; e-mail vehicles@anglopacific.co.uk; www.anglopacific.co.uk. Offer a comprehensive car shipping service by groupage or exclusive container service.

Autoshippers UK: ☎0800 389 0784; www.autoshippers.co.uk.

Autoshipping Co. of America: www.carshipper.com (for a wide range of options).

LTSA (NZ): PO Box 2840, Wellington; ☎0800 699 000 within NZ or +64 4 494 8600; fax +64 4 494 8601; e-mail info@ltsa.govt.nz; www.ltsa.govt.nz.

MAF: www.maf.govt.nz

New Zealand Automobile Association (NZAA): ☎+64 9 966 8800; fax +64 9 966 8893; e-mail aatech@nzaa.co.nz; www.nzaa.co.nz.

New Zealand Customs Service: ☎+64 9 300 5399; fax +64 9 359 6730; e-mail feedback@customs.govt.nz; www.customs.govt.nz.

On Road New Zealand: ☎+64 9 444 6921; fax +64 9 444 1827.

PSS International Removals (UK): Head Office, 1-3 Pegasus Road, Croydon, Surrey CR9 4PS; ☎020 8686 7733; fax 020 8686 7799; e-mail sales@p-s-s.co.uk; www.pss.uk.com. You can submit a direct online enquiry form.

Seabridge International: Point Breeze Maritime Center II, 2310 Broening Highway, Suite 130, Baltimore, Maryland 21224; ☎(410) 633 0550; fax (410) 633 0556; e-mail sea@seabrdge.com; www.seabrdge.com.

TnT AutoTransport: 6352 Corte del Abeto, Suite A, Carlsbad, CA 92009; ☎800 USA TNT1 (1 800 872 8681); www.tnt-inc.com.

Transport Registry Centre: Private Bag, Palmerston North; ☎0800 108 809.

Vehicle Inspection New Zealand (VINZ): ☎+64 9 573 3055; fax +64 9 573 3059.

Vehicle Testing New Zealand (VTNZ): ☎+64 4 381 6500, fax +64 4 381 6530; e-mail technical@vtnz.co.nz; www.vtnz.co.nz.

BUYING A CAR

Having found out the cost of importing your car to New Zealand you may decide that the best option is to leave it behind. New cars are comparatively expensive but the second-hand market in Japanese and Asian cars is competitive. European cars tend to be quite pricey and parts can be difficult to obtain, as well as ridiculously expensive. Familiar models may go under slightly different names in New Zealand. There is no domestically owned brand, but most cars are locally assembled. The government is reducing tariffs resulting in fewer locally assembled cars and more new and second-hand imported vehicles. Two motor industry websites may be useful: www.autonet.co.nz and www.autovillage.co.nz.

Second Hand Cars. Buying second hand is a viable option. Cars have to be sold warranted as roadworthy. A second-hand vehicle dealer is required by law to inform the buyer honestly about the vehicle and its history, and the car must be of the model, year, and odometer mileage displayed. The Fair Trading Act operates to protect buyers, and under the Act it is not necessary to prove that a certain individual had been misled, only that a typical consumer could have been deceived. There are a number of companies offering pre-purchase vehicle checks, including the AA who will check a car without charge if you are a member. A second-hand vehicle can be repossessed if its previous owner used it as security for a loan, and the loan was not repaid. The Motor Vehicles Security Register (which now comes under the umbrella of the Personal Property Security Register) can be used to check whether there is any money owing on your car, and to determine whether a security interest is registered against a particular vehicle (☎0508 PPSR INFO/0508 777 746; www.ppsr.govt. nz.).

Car Hire. If you want to organise car hire before you arrive, your travel agency may arrange rental for you through a New Zealand firm. It is also possible to arrange your rental in advance through an international rental firm, such as Avis (www. avis.com), Hertz (www.hertz.com) or Budget (www.budget.co.nz). Hirers in New Zealand must be at least 21 years of age and will need a current international, UK or New Zealand driving licence.

Insurance

You are not legally required to get insurance in New Zealand, however it is sensible to get at least third party coverage. If you are involved in an accident and cause harm to another driver, you will not be personally liable for the injuries you cause them because of the no-faults compensation for personal injury provided by the Government through the Accident Compensation Corporation (See Chapter Four, *Daily Life*). But if you write off their car and you have no insurance then, like anywhere else in the world, you will be paying the bill. The premiums for full insurance coverage vary according to your age (under 25s pay a lot more), gender (some firms offer females a discount because they are statistically less likely to have accidents) and driving history. A no-claims record entitles you to discounted premiums. You should bring evidence of your claims record with you because a claim-free insurance record may qualify you for the bonus. As a very rough indication, insurance on a car valued at between $35,000-$50-000 will cost you somewhere in the region of $300 a year. Some firms may not be prepared to insure you until you have a New Zealand driver's licence (see *Daily Life* for requirements).

DAILY LIFE

CHAPTER SUMMARY

○ **Languages.** New Zealand has two official languages, English and Maori.

  ○ Newcomers are sometimes only able to distinguish two vowel sounds in New Zealand English; obviously New Zealanders can hear the variations!

  ○ The Maori language had no written form until the European settlers arrived.

○ **Education.** New Zealand has a shortage of secondary school teachers.

  ○ A growing number of pre-school children, not only Maoris, attend Maori language 'nests' where they learn Maori language and culture.

○ There is no television licence fee in New Zealand.

○ **Shopping.** A 'dairy' in New Zealand is a corner shop.

○ **Motoring.** Drivers in New Zealand have a reputation for being aggressive and inconsiderate.

  ○ New Zealand has one of the highest accident rates in the developed world.

○ **Getting Around.** Major population centres are many miles apart and getting between them by road and rail is time consuming.

  ○ Through a subsidiary, *Air New Zealand* runs a no frills service between Auckland, Wellington and Christchurch.

  ○ Coaches provide the most comprehensive service, but it's always going to be more convenient and less hassle to simply drive.

○ **Accident Compensation.** New Zealand has a unique system of state protection in case of personal injury or accident.

  ○ On a case-by-case basis, the government provides financial and other assistance to anyone injured in the workplace, at home or while taking part in sports.

One of the disconcerting aspects of emigrating to a country where the locals speak the same language is that there is a tendency to underestimate the cultural differences. The New Zealand accent can be difficult to understand for a start, particularly as New Zealanders are not usually particularly expressive when they speak and can be quite tight-lipped. While you will usually find the locals fairly open and welcoming in their attitudes to new arrivals, they become quickly defensive at any perceived slight towards their country. Just don't mention the sheep jokes (unless you are aiming them at Australia!) and try not to pull out the tired old line that 'New Zealand is like England was in the 1950s'. Kiwis won't thank you for that one, and even if they aren't offended by it they're likely to have heard it more than once before!

THE LANGUAGES

New Zealanders speak their own distinctive version of English. Newcomers may be forgiven for thinking that New Zealanders use only two vowel sounds, although of course Kiwis do not have trouble understanding each other! 'New Zealand' as pronounced by Kiwis may sound like 'Nu Zilind'. As well as the subtle distinctions between vowel sounds, further problems for the newcomer may arise from the rapid pace at which New Zealanders speak. Probably more of an obstacle to understanding New Zealanders than the accent is the use of uniquely Kiwi expressions. A 'dairy' is a corner store (open till late and selling most of the essentials), a 'crib' in the South Island or 'bach' in the North is a holiday home (generally on the coast or beside a lake). To 'bring a plate' to a party means you bring a plate of food along to share with others. BYO stands for 'Bring Your Own' alcohol - either to a party or to a restaurant. BYO restaurants have a licence to serve alcohol, but not to sell it. They are usually cheaper than 'licensed' restaurants, but they will generally charge a corkage fee per bottle (of about $5), or sometimes per person. To 'charge an arm and a leg' is to demand a high price for something. Some of the slang is similar to Australian, for example 'Pommy' for an English person, 'bush' for forest, 'shout' for buying a round in a pub or providing a special morning or afternoon tea for workmates (usually on birthdays or when someone is leaving). Additionally, a number of Maori expressions have become part of everyday New Zealand usage, for example *Pakeha* for a person of European descent. *The New Zealand Oxford Dictionary* (Oxford University Press), might prove useful to save you any confusion. This dictionary has been hailed as a celebration of the New Zealand language, and a revised and updated edition that includes over 10,000 words of NZ origin was launched in 2004. So if you want to find out what *gumboots, poozlers, mates' rates, wop-wops, biddy-bids, cheerios, housie, jandals, jafas, Swanndris, tinnies* and *dungers* are, the dictionary could be a good place to start. Another useful dictionary is the latest edition of the Collins English Dictionary, which includes a relatively high number of interesting and fairly obscure New Zealand words.

Maori is the other official language, although it is not widely used in everyday situations. Official signs are bilingual, as are many government documents. The number of Maori language speakers is growing and there is an active campaign to preserve this language (*Te Reo* in Maori). At least some knowledge of the language is a prerequisite for many jobs, especially those within public service. Pronunciation of Maori is not difficult to learn even if at first glance some of the place names seem impossibly long and complex. It is a good skill to master though, as correct pronunciation of Maori is a sign of courtesy and also indicates that, as a newcomer, you are prepared to integrate into the local community. The greeting *Kia Ora* which extends good health to the other person, may be repeated back with the same words. *Haere mai* means 'welcome' and Haere ra' means 'goodbye'. Generally Maori words are spelt phonetically. The language had no written form before European settlement.

TABLE 18	MAORI VOWEL SOUNDS

There are five Maori vowel sounds, each of which may be short or long:

short a:	like u in 'but'	long a:	like a in 'father'
short e:	like e in 'pet'	long e:	like ai in 'fairy'
short i:	like i in 'pit'	long i:	like ee in 'meet'
short o:	like or in 'port'	long o:	like ore in 'pore'
short u:	like u in 'put'	long u:	like oo in 'moon'

Diphthongs (double vowel sounds) retain the sound of the second vowel clearly. Consonants are as in English with the following exceptions:

wh	is pronounced f; hence 'Whangarei' is pronounced 'Fong-a-ray'
ng	is like ng in the middle of 'singer, i.e. the g is never hard
r	is slightly rolled

Word stress is rather complicated and you would do better to learn by listening to a Maori speaker. It is worth noting that many Pakeha pronounce Maori words, particularly common place names, embarrassingly badly. There is however a general trend towards more accurate pronunciation and, in recent years, the standard has risen dramatically. Incorrect pronunciation is increasingly unacceptable, as it shows a lack of respect. This change has been perhaps most noticeable among radio and TV announcers, and, in general, their pronunciation is a reasonable guide.

SCHOOLS AND EDUCATION

The New Zealand education system is dominated by the state sector, which educates the vast majority of the population. Schooling is compulsory from ages six through to sixteen, although most New Zealand children start school at the age of five and many stay until they are around eighteen. The school year has four terms, beginning in late January and running through to mid-December with holidays in April and July. Most schooling is government-funded. Each state school is given a grant for operating costs and then it is the responsibility of the board of trustees to see that it is properly maintained. However, many state schools are beginning to charge 'optional' fees to cover development and maintenance of school property, and parents are still responsible for the purchase of textbooks, stationery and uniforms if required.

There is no tradition of streaming into academic and not-so-academic schools.

Most schools have good cultural, academic and sporting facilities. Even inner city schools usually have extensive playing fields. There is a strong tradition of team sports, and not just rugby, although soccer used to be banned at some particularly strong rugby schools lest the boys be lured away from chasing the oval ball to 'inferior' versions of football. Many state schools offer outdoor activity programmes where pupils learn abseiling, canoeing, kayaking and go tramping (hiking) in national parks.

Like New Zealand society, its schools are becoming ethnically more diverse, particularly in Auckland with its significant and growing Pacific Island and Asian population. Japanese and other Asian languages are replacing foreign language instruction, which used to be predominantly in French and German. This reflects New Zealand's shift in trade focus, as Pacific Rim countries are now New Zealand's most important trading partners. The language of instruction, except in a few Maori language immersion schools, remains English.

In general, New Zealand state schools are safe and well-disciplined learning environments. Nevertheless, some parents choose alternatives to the state system for their children. Private schools are owned and run by independent boards, but they must meet certain standards. Integrated schools are those that used to be private and are now state schools. They follow state curriculum, but usually have their own individual beliefs, whether religious or ethical. They charge fees, but these are not as expensive as private schools. Like many private schools, integrated schools often offer boarding facilities. It is also possible to board at some state schools. Usually these are rural schools whose students come from a widely dispersed population so boarding is the only practical way of overcoming the problem of huge distances between home and school. However, not all state boarding schools are in the country. Nelson College and Christchurch Boys are city schools with a long tradition of providing a state boarding school education. As state schools, their boarding fees tend to be cheaper than the private sector.

At time of print, there is a fairly strong demand for overseas secondary school teachers, particularly of maths, science, technology, physical education, and information and communications technology. Demand is also growing for teachers of English and music. Secondary schools are experiencing an increase in rolls as a result of the late 1980s/early 1990s population boom. The number of students at secondary school is expected to peak around 2007, which will coincide with an increase in teacher retirements. Opportunities for early childhood teachers will continue to grow as initiatives to increase participation bring results. This sector includes a range of services; in some cases services are teacher-led, and in others parents and whanau provide care and attention. A strategy has been introduced to bring consistency in teacher-quality to this sector; by 2005 all persons responsible in licensed and chartered services, and co-ordinators in home-based services, will need to hold a qualification recognised by the NZ Teacher's Council, such as a degree or diploma in early childhood teaching. By 2012 all teachers in teacher-led early childhood services will need to be qualified and registered. Primary school rolls peaked in 2002, and are beginning to decrease in most areas as students move on to secondary schools. So demand for primary school teachers, particularly from overseas, will decrease. The exception is Auckland, where primary rolls are still growing and there will be most opportunities for primary teachers. A department has been created in the Ministry of Education for teachers wanting to come to New Zealand to work, and TeachNZ holds information seminars in England, Wales and Scotland. Contact TeachNZ for more information (TeachNZ, Ministry of

Education, PO Box 1666, Wellington; recruitment line (within NZ): ☎0800 832 246 (0800 TeachNZ); www.TeachNZ.govt.nz).

The Structure of the Education System

Early Childhood. This includes childcare centres, playgroups, playcentres (which are usually run by volunteer groups of parents and cater for children from a young age), kindergartens (usually for the over-twos), home-based care, *Kohanga Reo* (Maori language and culture immersion), Pacific Islands language groups and private crèches. Kindergartens used to be free, but now often have a small weekly charge, and there is also a small charge for playcentres. Crèches, on the other hand, can be quite expensive, although the government subsidises the running costs of all registered childcare centres with qualified staff. The majority of four-year-olds are in some kind of preschool programme. A growing number of children, not just Maori, attend *Kohanga Reo* (Maori language 'nests') where they learn *Taha Maori* (Maori language and culture).

Primary. Full primary schools cater for children aged from five to twelve years old (Year 0 to Year 8). Contributing primary schools offer education for children from Year 0 to Year 6. These children usually then move on to an intermediate school. Primary curriculum includes reading, writing, science, mathematics, and social studies. Children are usually based in one classroom and each teacher covers all areas of the curriculum. Teaching standards are high. The teaching of reading skills is particularly strong and New Zealand reading programmes are copied in British and North American schools.

Intermediate: Most children spend two years (Years 7 and 8) at intermediate school between primary and secondary (high) school. Intermediate schools were originally thought to provide a buffer zone to ease the transition between small primary schools and large secondary schools. However, some primary schools are beginning to keep their senior students for a further two years, as the interlude is now considered by some to be disruptive rather than helpful. In rural areas, state composite schools ('area' schools) have always included Years 6 and 7. At intermediate school, some pupils begin studying languages other than English (traditionally French, now increasingly Maori), and move between specialist teachers in different classrooms rather than being taught by one person for every subject.

Secondary: Secondary education covers Years 9 through to 13. In pre-recession New Zealand, when jobs were easy to come by, it was quite common for students to leave school as soon as it was legal, at age fifteen. Since then, however, retention rates have improved. The core curriculum consists of seven essential learning areas: language and languages, mathematics, science, technology, social sciences, the arts and health and physical well being. Secondary school teachers have at least one specialist teaching area. Achievement objectives are based on a national curriculum statement for each area. All students work towards a new National Certificate of Educational Achievement (NCEA). The first level takes the place of School Certificate (at the end of the third year of secondary education – Year 11), while the higher levels replace Sixth Form Certificate (Year 12) and the University Bursary exams (Year 13). Levels two and three of this certificate (for assessment during the students' final two years of secondary education) were phased in during 2002 and 2003 respectively. NCEA will include a wider range of subjects and skills than did the earlier qualifications, and students will build on their achievements over the three year levels. Candidates for NCEA can also work towards other qualifications and national certificates. For online information about NCEA see the Ministry of Education website (www.minedu.govt.nz). Foreign students at New Zealand secondary schools will probably have to pay fees of around NZ$10,000 per year. This covers enrolment, orientation, tuition, textbooks (on loan), ESOL classes and any government levies.

Further Education

Further education is divided into three main areas: universities, polytechnics and colleges of education (teacher training colleges).

Universities. University education was established in New Zealand in 1870, and the country now has eight universities, which offer degree programmes in a range of subjects. Most Bachelor degrees are three-year courses with an option of taking a four-year Honours programme. The universities are: the University of Auckland, the Auckland University of Technology, the University of Waikato (Hamilton and Tauranga), Massey University (Palmerston North, Albany and Wellington), Victoria University of Wellington, the University of Canterbury (Christchurch), Lincoln University (Christchurch) and the University of Otago (Dunedin). Standards are uniform, and each university has its own specialist subjects, such as medicine at Auckland and Otago, and veterinary science at Palmerston North. Students looking for a campus environment head to Otago or Waikato. Teaching in arts subjects is mostly done in large lecture streams with weekly tutorials of about a dozen students. Admission procedures vary depending on the institution and the specific course. Some high-demand courses, such as medicine, law and business administration, have restricted entry usually based on University Bursary results. Other courses are open to anyone who meets the general university entrance requirement. See the Universities page of www.kiwicareers.govt.nz for more information, links and contact details.

Polytechnics. There are 21 polytechnics in New Zealand, and some of these have several campuses in different locations. They offer a wide range of vocational, academic and professional courses. There is increasing crossover with universities in subject areas, although some programmes (such as business studies, marketing and accounting) can be studied either in a polytechnic (for a certificate or diploma) or in a longer degree programme at university. Many polytechnic students either study part-time while working or are on short full-time courses. See the Polytechnics page of www.kiwicareers.govt.nz for more information, links and contact details.

Colleges of Education. There are six colleges of education across the country, in Auckland, Wellington, Christchurch and Dunedin and at both Waikato and Massey universities. See the Colleges of Education page of www.kiwicareers.govt. nz for more information, links and contact details.

Student Fees. New Zealand students now contribute 25% of the cost of their tertiary education. Tuition, which used to be free, now costs New Zealand students between roughly $3,000-$23,000 for a full time year, depending on the course and the institution. Reductions are available for New Zealand students from low-income families. Fees increase every year, and many students are taking more time to complete their tertiary education as they work to support themselves. Fees for foreign students are substantially higher, undergraduate course costs will be around $18,000–$25,000 per year for tertiary study, depending on your course. Postgraduate courses cost up to NZ$40,000. This includes GST (tax), registration and enrolment, student health and counselling, language support and use of most campus facilities. You will need to pay in advance, as proof of payment is usually required for your visa or permit application. You can pay by credit card, telegraphic funds transfer, bank draft or bank cheque. If you cancel before your course starts, for instance because your visa or visa extension is not granted, or you are transferring to another institution, most or all of your tuition fee will be refunded, except for the registration and administration fees. For more information see www.mynzed.com or www.ted.govt.nz.

Student Allowances. Full time students from low-income families are eligible for means tested student maintenance grants, called student allowances. Students must be permanent residents to be eligible. For single students, the rate of allowance is dependent on age, whether the student lives at home with their parents, and taxable parental income for the last financial year (if the student is under 25). The StudyLink website offers a parental income calculator so you can work out whether you are eligible — and, if so, for what amount — quickly and easily. From January 2005, the upper parental income thresholds have been raised to $56,457 for students living at home and $62,148 for students living away from home. The lower threshold is $33,696. Students aged 25 and over are not subject to the family means test. There are different rates for those married to another student, and those with a dependent spouse and/or children. Allowances are now administered through StudyLink, and you can apply online at www.studylink.govt.nz or call 0800 88 99 00. To get Student Allowances you must apply within 60 days of your course start date or within 60 days of the day you qualify to get an allowance (if that is later).

Student Loans. Permanent resident students who do not qualify for allowances may borrow money through the government-run student loans scheme to pay for living costs, course-related costs and fees. Each year eligible students may borrow the amount of their compulsory fees payable at enrolment, plus a maximum of $1000 for course-related costs and up to $150 per week to help cover living costs. Your fees are paid directly to your education provider. The amount of loan living costs you can borrow reduces by the amount of Student Allowance you receive after tax (not counting the Accommodation Benefit or Bursary payment). For example, if you get a Student Allowance of $50 a week after tax, you will only be entitled to borrow $100 a week for living costs. Following a recent change in loan policy, students studying part-time part-year courses may now apply for a loan. The living costs component used to be accessible as a lump sum, but is now paid out in regular instalments over the course of the year. Part-time students may borrow the amount of their compulsory fees plus the proportion of the $1000 course costs (the length of their course as a proportion of a full-time course). Applications are made through the institution at which the student will be enrolling. All loans incur a $50 administration fee each year. You can pay the loan back at any stage until you earn $16,172 (before tax) per annum, at which time repayment of the loan becomes compulsory as calculated instalments deducted from wages in the same manner as taxes are paid. Interest is charged regardless of whether the borrower earns over the repayment threshold or not. However, you may be entitled to an interest write-off reduction. The repayment threshold changes on 1 April each year. The rate of interest has just been confirmed to remain at 7%. Student Loans are now administered through StudyLink, and you can apply online at www. studylink.govt.nz or call 0800 88 99 00. Repayments are made to Inland Revenue (www.ird.govt.nz/studentloans).

Foreigners at New Zealand Universities

Foreign students (that is, non-New Zealand residents) get hit even harder in the wallet than New Zealand students, as they have to pay full fees. Fees vary across courses and by university, from $14,000–$25,000 per annum for an undergraduate arts, science or humanities course, to between $18,750-$55,000 annually for medicine or dentistry. MBA courses cost roughly US$25,500 and upwards per annum in 2004. For information on studying at New Zealand universities or polytechnics as a foreign student, see the New Zealand Trade and Enterprise website (www.mynzed.com), but for specific information contact your chosen institution directly.

International Schools

There are no schools in New Zealand specifically set up for international students. However some secondary schools offer senior students preparation for the International Baccalaureate, which is an entrance qualification for most European universities. To find out more, contact New Zealand Trade and Enterprise (see above) or the Ministry of Education National Office (45-47 Pipitea Street, Thorndon, PO Box 1666, Wellington; ☎(04) 463 8000; fax (04) 463 8001; www.minedu.govt.nz).

MEDIA AND COMMUNICATIONS

Newspapers

For its size, New Zealand produces a large number of newspapers, but they will not necessarily be of the quality you are used to at home. Regional papers were established last century when provincial government was more powerful than national government and communication networks between the scattered European settlements were poor. These regional papers have all survived and as a result New Zealand has a high number of daily newspapers, but there is no truly national paper. The apparently national *New Zealand Herald* is fairly Auckland focused and not widely circulated in the South Island. In Wellington, the *Dominion Post* is published Monday to Saturday. Sunday papers, such as the *Sunday Star-Times* are more substantial, but still do not compare favourably in terms of size with their counterparts in either America or Britain. Most of the major papers are of the size and quality of a large provincial paper and betray their provincial loyalties by their selection of news stories. There is only one tabloid style newspaper, *The Truth,* which appears weekly and does not approach the shock, horror, or sheer awful appeal of tabloids in other countries.

Business news is provided by the *National Business Review*, also a weekly, which covers politics and international news as well. A growing trend is giveaway suburban and inner city newspapers, such as *City Voice* in Wellington, which includes community news and events, and extensive theatre, performance and exhibition listings and reviews.

Specialist newsagents in the main cities stock overseas newspapers, but they tend to be relatively expensive and usually arrive some days late, particularly European editions. Of course, the internet is probably the quickest and easiest way to access foreign news, with the added bonus that you don't have to wait for the papers to arrive by mail.

Main Newspapers

The New Zealand Herald: Conservative in tone and appearance, the *Herald* was founded well over 100 years ago. It is based in Auckland and the news content reflects this, despite its name. Circulation: 210,000; readership: 597,000; 46 Albert Street, PO Box 32, Auckland; ☎(09) 379 5050; fax (09) 373 6414; www.nzherald.co.nz.

The Waikato Times: Advertised as 'As Waikato As It Gets...' and is published in two editions daily. Circulation: 41,849; readership: 105,000; Foreman Road, Private Bag 3086, Te Rapa, Hamilton; ☎(07) 849 6180; fax (07) 849 9554; www.waikatotimes.co.nz.

The Dominion Post: It has a political focus, as might be expected of a newspaper based in the capital city. Published daily in the morning, the *Dominion Post* is the merger of Wellington icon paper *The Evening Post* and Central NZ daily newspaper *The Dominion*. Used to be a liberal, unpartisan scrutineer of government, but has now become something of a convert to neo-liberal economic dogma. Circulation: 99,089; readership: 272,000; The Dominion Post Building, 40 Boulcott Street, PO Box 3740, Wellington; ☎(04) 474 0222; fax (04) 474 0584; www.dompost.co.nz.

The Press: Distributed throughout Canterbury for nearly 140 years, provides the most comprehensive coverage of news and advertising in the South Island. The Press is published six days a week. Good coverage of news from the Canterbury region, less so of national and international stories. The Saturday edition is regularly 130 pages, including the pre-printed feature magazine *The Weekend*. Circulation: 91,111; readership: 239,000; 6 Cathedral Square, Private Bag 4722, Christchurch; ☎(03) 379 0940; fax (03) 364 8496; www.press.co.nz.

The Otago Daily Times: Dunedin based. Circulation: 44,546; readership: 106,000; 52 Stuart Street, PO Box 181, Dunedin; ☎(03) 477 4760; fax (03) 474 7422; www.odt.co.nz.

The Sunday Star-Times: Has the biggest circulation of any New Zealand newspaper, reaching 210,898 in 2004, with a readership of over 657,000. 155 New North Road, PO Box 1409, Auckland; ☎(09) 302 1300; fax (09) 366 4670.

The Sunday News: The national tabloid newspaper. Circulation: 108,869; readership: 535,000. 155 New North Road, PO Box 1409, Auckland; ☎(09) 302 1300; fax (09) 366 4670.

For information about other New Zealand papers, including readership and circulation statistics and contact details, have a look at the New Zealand Press

Association's website: http://nzpa-online.co.nz.

Magazines

Local political comment is provided by the *New Zealand Listener* and the *Political Review*. The *Listener* also carries TV and radio listings, as does the *TV Guide*, which has the biggest circulation of any New Zealand magazine. Other very popular magazines are *Next*, *Woman's Day* and the *New Zealand Women's Weekly*, dog-eared stacks of which can be found in nearly every doctor's surgery. *More* magazine is an upmarket women's magazine interesting and informative articles about a range of issues from health to business, and a no-nonsense practical feminist line. A number of glossy lifestyle magazines have sprung up in the last decade. Of particular note is *Metro*, the Auckland city magazine. Metro's stablemate, aimed at readers in the rest of the country, is *North and South*. Both are liberal on political issues, conservative on social welfare issues and support the economic liberalisation programme launched by the government in the 1980s. *Cuisine* is dedicated to fine food and wine. *New Zealand Geographic* is a good resource if you want to learn more about the country's history, landscapes, people, wildlife, industries and recreational pursuits. There are a surprising number of literary magazines, apparently thriving, despite small circulation. The most well established of these is the Christchurch-based *Landfall*, but the Wellington-based *New Zealand Books* also provides excellent coverage of literary happenings and boasts some pillars of the literary community amongst its regular contributors. Both magazines provide a showcase for fresh writing talent, although *New Zealand Books* is mainly a vehicle for reviews.

Magazines exist for just about every sporting pursuit, including boating, horse riding and racing, surfing and skateboarding – *NZ Rugby World*, *NZ Fishing News*, *Boating NZ*, *NZ Orienteering*, *NZ Horse & Pony* and *New Zealand Classic Car* are all popular. Also among the top 20 most popular magazines are *NZ House & Garden*, *Your Home & Garden (NZ)*, and *NZ Gardener* – see if you can spot a theme there! You can browse and order online through New Zealand Magazine Superstore – iSubscribe (www.isubscribe.co.nz) – which offers discounts off the cover price for subscriptions. Many New Zealand magazines and newspapers can be ordered through Consyl Publishing Ltd. (3 Buckhurst Road, Bexhill-on-Sea, East Sussex, TN40 1QF; ☎01424 223 111; 24 hour credit card sales ☎01424 223 161; www.consyl-publishing.co.uk). If you send a self-addressed envelope with five first-class stamps to Consyl, they will send you the latest copy of *New Zealand Outlook*, which contains a list of New Zealand publications available.

Television

Two national television channels are operated by the TVNZ Group – TV ONE and TV2. TVNZ also has several subsidiary companies, and has been redesignated as a crown-owned company under special government legislation. According to the TVNZ charter, TVNZ is required to 'inform, educate and entertain all New Zealanders, reflecting and fostering New Zealand's identity and culture'. TV ONE and TV2 broadcast to 98% of the population, and produce over 90% of the most-watched programmes. On TV ONE you can watch New Zealand and overseas drama, news, sport and information programmes. TV2 has a mix of children's and comedy, drama, movies and general entertainment, and is broadly directed at a younger audience. Imported programmes on both channels are mainly from the UK, Australia and the US.

TV3 Network Services Ltd is the country's only privately-owned free-to-air network. It is owned by CanWest Global Communications Corporation, a Canadian company, and has an emphasis on sport, news, local programming and current affairs. TV3 has exclusive agreements with FOX, Disney, and World Vision, and also sources programming from other international distributors. TV3 also runs TV4, which is aimed at the younger, urban proportion of the population and is broadcast to more than 70% of the country, 24 hours a day, seven days a week. About 2.5 million people can access the channel.

SKY Network Television is a pay company with a digital direct broadcast satellite service, which means that virtually all households in the country can receive up to 25 channels. SKY broadcasts SKY sport, SKY movies, CNN, SKY 1, Nickelodeon, Discovery and Trackside. At the last count (2004) a subscriber TV decoder was present in 37% of households, and 36% of households subscribed to subscriber TV.

Prime Television is a free-to-air broadcaster with offices in Auckland, Hamilton, Tauranga, Hastings, Wellington, Christchurch and Dunedin. In 2002, Prime began broadcasting an entertainment-based schedule, following an agreement with the Nine Network from Australia. It had initially been mainly British programming.

There are a number of small regional television services throughout the country, these local services including Family Television Network (Warkworth), Triangle Television (Auckland), Geyser Television (Rotorua), Eastland Television (Gisborne), Hawke's Bay Television and Channel 51 (Hawke's Bay), Taranaki Community Television Trust, Channel 7 (Wellington), Mainland Television (Nelson), CTV and CHTV (Christchurch) and Mercury Television (Invercargill). In addition, there is a channel called Trackside, which is owned by the TAB and broadcasts live racing, race results and programmes about racing to the whole country.

Television Licences. The national broadcasting company, New Zealand On Air, does not charge a household licence fee.

Radio

Radio New Zealand runs a network of local stations, which are funded through advertising revenue and offer a mixed diet of middle of the road popular music, talk back, news and sports. It also runs two non-commercial nationally broadcast stations, National Radio and Concert FM. National Radio's morning news show from 9am to noon, *Morning Report*, is an excellent source of news and comment on political and economic issues. The Concert Programme broadcasts classical music and information programmes. There is a large local private radio sector, including student radio, Maori language radio and community access radio. Local and national radio stations in New Zealand broadcast on 110 AM and 332 FM frequencies, so there is a great choice of radio programmes. Radio New Zealand's AM Network broadcasts all sittings of Parliament from transmitters in Auckland, Wellington, Napier, Christchurch and Dunedin. There is also a National Radio Sports Frequency. However many stations, especially FM radio, have a limited range due to the mountainous terrain of the country. An Auckland-based private radio station broadcasts the BBC World Service, with frequencies in Auckland and Wellington. Snippets from the World Service are also broadcast regularly on National Radio. For more information see www.radionz.co.nz.

Post

Postal services are handled by New Zealand Post, which has a monopoly on letter delivery up to 80 grams in weight. Parcel delivery is also provided by private courier firms. Domestic delivery is once daily, usually mid-morning. There is a network of more than 1,000 Post Offices throughout the country, the majority of which are postal agencies and provide other services as well. Many other outlets also sell stamps, including book and stationery shops, newsagents and dairies.

There are two classes of mail, FastPost, which promises next day delivery anywhere in the country, and Standard Post, which can take 2-3 days. The standard cost of a FastPost letter is 90c for a medium envelope (max 120mm x 235mm) or $1.35 for a large envelope (max 260mm x 385mm) and for a Standard Post letter 45c for a medium envelope (max 120mm x 235mm) or 90c for a large envelope (max 260mm x 385mm). There are three international services for sending items overseas – International Economy, International Air and International Express. International Express is a courier service, tracked and traced from collection in New Zealand to signature delivery overseas, and including compensation for loss or damage up to $2,000. International Air provides Track & Trace on parcels weighing over 2kg and going to Australia, the UK, the USA, and Japan for an additional fee. International Economy is cheaper, but slower and compensation for loss may be more difficult to obtain. Sending letters by International Air will cost $2 for a medium envelope to the USA or the UK, $3 for large letters and $5 for extra large letters. International Parcel rates will obviously vary depending on the weight of the item you are sending – there is an International Parcel Ratefinder calculator on the NZ Post website though, so you can work out what you will have to pay. For customer enquiries and up to date charges, call NZ Post on freephone 0800 501 501, or see the website: www.nzpost.co.nz.

Post Offices offer a *poste restante* service for letters and parcels at all locations throughout the country. Redirection service for *poste restante* within New Zealand costs $7; the price of overseas redirection will depend on the service required and the international zone the item is being sent to. There is no storage fee for letters and small packets (under 2 kg) for up to three months. There will be a small storage fee for parcels over 2 kg, which will be held for up to three months (the first seven days are free of charge). Any mail uncollected after three months will be returned to sender. Note: NZ Post is not able to redirect mail to a hotel, motel, motor-camp or boarding house.

Telephones

For information about having a telephone installed in your house, see *Setting Up Home*. New Zealand Telecom has been overhauling the phone system since 1990, introducing standard seven digit numbers throughout the country. Most of the chaos caused by the change is now over. The international code for New Zealand is 64. There are five area codes for the different regions of the country: 09 for Auckland and northwards; 07 for the Waikato and central North Island area; 06 for the southern half of the North Island; 04 for the Wellington region; and 03 for the South Island.

Telecom's toll-free phone numbers start with 0800 and TelstraClear freephone numbers start with 0508. Phone boxes are well distributed but most are now card phones, which can be irritating if you do not have a card handy. Phone cards come in $5, $10, $20, or $50 denominations and can be bought from bookshops, dairies or Post Offices. Local calls from a coin or card phone cost 50c. Very few coin phones can still be found, but you may find original model payphones, which have a button marked A on the front that you should press when the call is connected. In the cities, card and coin phones can usually be found cohabiting, and in some places, credit card phones as well.

To dial the UK from New Zealand dial 00 44 then drop the first zero from the area code. To dial the USA dial 00 1 . Fax numbers have the same prefix.

CARS AND MOTORING

It is common to see older model cars in New Zealand, this is a hangover from the days when new cars were very expensive so people drove their old car for a long time. Most of the older cars are British or American makes. Modern cars tend to be Japanese makes. Because of the absence of heavy traffic there is not much of a network of multi-lane motorways. Most state highways are single carriageways and as a general rule there are no tolls. Multi-lane motorways carry traffic into and out of the four main cities and through parts of Auckland and Wellington. Congestion on these stretches during rush hour is often a problem, but nothing compared to traffic jams in European or North American cities. To relieve problems associated with rush hour, many larger firms operate on 'glide time', which means that, within reason, employees' daily work hours start when they arrive, rather than at an exact set time.

Driving outside the main cities is usually a pleasant experience. The roads are uncluttered and the scenery superb. The weather often provides more of an obstacle to reaching your destination than other drivers do. Flooding or heavy snowfalls only occasionally block main routes, particularly the roads through the volcanic plateau in the central North Island and the cross-alpine routes in South Island. There are signs at the start of tricky stretches of road indicating which routes are open. In general the signs indicating distances and routes on the highway system are less frequent than in other countries (although to be fair there is usually only one main route to any destination). Junctions are not as well designed, and roundabouts are less common and tend to be poorly sign posted. But then, there is less traffic on the roads.

New Zealand drivers have a reputation for being fast and rather aggressive, but the advent of speed cameras and other traffic safety programmes are tending to change this attitude. It is easy to see why you might be tempted to drive well over the speed limit when there is no other traffic in sight, let alone any sign of the law. City drivers are not particularly considerate. It is rare for people to give way to allow cars from side roads to join the main stream of traffic, again perhaps because there are usually fewer congestion problems. Nor do New Zealand drivers willingly move over into the slow lane to let faster traffic past. Unfortunately driving in New Zealand is not very safe. It has one of the worst accident records per head of population in the developed world. About 500 people die on the roads each year, and the 'road toll' often appears on the national TV news. The government is trying to improve the statistics by targeting the worst-offending group, specifically young men who drink and drive, so be aware that the blood-alcohol limits are strictly enforced. Increasingly there are official random roadblocks, particularly around the festive season, in which every passing driver may be stopped and breath-tested.

According to the latest vehicle ownership statistics, households spend a weekly average of $54 on their vehicles. Expenditure on fuel was the main component, at an average of $31 a week.

Driving Regulations

The maximum speed on highways and motorways is 100 km, and in built up areas 50 km. Speed cameras are being introduced at various places in cities and on country roads. New Zealanders drive on the left-hand side of the road, and the rules of the road are similar to British driving regulations.

However, there are several important differences — at crossroads traffic turning left must give way to on-coming vehicles turning right, it is illegal to park facing the wrong way, and safety belts must be worn by the driver and all passengers. Traffic lights change straight from red to green, then amber followed by red again.

Standard international road signs are being introduced. One sign that may be unfamiliar is LSZ enclosed by a red circle, indicating a Limited Speed Zone in which the motorist should slow down to allow for children, pedestrians or other traffic. This is frequently used when state highways pass through small towns.

As noted above, drink-driving regulations are strictly enforced. The limit is 80mls per 100mls of blood — less than two pints of beer for the average adult male. Drivers under twenty years old have a lower limit: 30mls per 100mls of blood. Police officers are able to stop motorists at random and breath-test them. The maximum penalty is a $1,500 fine and six months in prison. Repeat offenders can lose their licence. Seat belts must be worn in the front of cars and in the back if they are fitted. Helmets are compulsory for motorcyclists as well as bicycle riders.

Breakdowns and Accidents

Over the last few years, the Government has made the driving test much more stringent and introduced restricted licences for the under 20s in an effort to improve road safety. If you are involved in an accident, you must contact the police. (The emergency number is 111). Unfortunately New Zealand highways are often not well provided with call boxes or emergency telephones.

Members can call the New Zealand Automobile Association (AA) at any time on freephone 0800 500 222 (or e-mail aaroadservice@aa.co.nz) to assist with mechanical difficulties or breakdowns. For membership enquiries, e-mail membership@aa.co.nz or call 0800 500 333. It costs $89 (Auckland residents only) or $77 per year to join. For more information, visit the website at www.aa.co.nz (you can apply for membership online).

Driving Licences

An International Drivers Licence is valid for a one-year period from the date of issue, and can be used in New Zealand. Alternatively, you can use your United

Kingdom Driving Licence for a period of 12 months from your original arrival date. At the end of this period, you must apply for a New Zealand Photo Driving Licence, which involves sitting a written and oral test, and then an interview with a police officer to obtain exemption from taking the practical test. Your original licence must still be valid in order to apply. Drivers under the age of twenty are eligible only for a restricted licence and are not allowed to drive after dark. If your licence is lost or stolen, you simply apply to the LTSA to have it reissued. See the Land Transport Safety Authority website (www.ltsa.govt.nz) or contact the New Zealand AA (www.aa.co.nz) for more information. If you need to prove that you are a licenced New Zealand driver, you can request a Certificate of Particulars. This sets out all the relevant details. To apply, fax or email the LTSA Transport Registry Centre (fax 0064 6 350 2347; e-mail cert@ltsa.govt.nz) with your name, date of birth and address, and the method by which you want to receive the certificate (fax, e-mail, post, etc.).

Car Registration and Insurance

Cars must be registered with the Post Office and have a current Vehicle Inspection Certificate (VIC) also known as a Warrant of Fitness (WOF). Vehicles first registered anywhere less than six years ago must have a WoF inspection every 12 months. All other vehicles must have WoF inspections every six months. Cars must also have a Vehicle Identification Number (VIN), an identification scheme to try and cut down on vehicle theft. At the time of writing, the cost of registering an ordinary motorcar was $200.10 per year. First time registration (vehicle licensing) for a new car costs approximately $340 including new number plates. Cars can be registered at any Post Office shop. Re-registration forms are sent out automatically. Most garages offer VIC testing, which takes about 25 minutes and will cost you between $40-45. The fee for registering change of ownership papers is $9.20, and this must be done within seven days of buying the vehicle. The LTSA should supply you with a 'change of ownership' card to prove that you have advised them of the change. For a $2.25 charge, you can apply to have an LTSA agent check that a vehicle isn't reported stolen, and is properly registered and licensed. Further information may be obtained from the Land Transport Safety Authority Motor Vehicle Registration Helpdesk (freephone: 0800 108 809; e-mail info@ltsa.co.nz). Of course, the price of car insurance varies depending on the value of the car, the area you live in and the age and driving record of the driver.

Useful Addresses

Land Transport Safety Authority Head Office: 4th Floor, 7-27 Waterloo Quay, Box 2840, Wellington; ☎(04) 494 8600; fax (04) 494 8601. For information on vehicle warranties and vehicle and driver licensing, call freephone 0800 699 000 or visit the website: www.ltsa.govt.nz.

The New Zealand Automobile Association: 99 Albert St, Auckland City, Auckland; ☎(09) 377 4660; www.nzaa.co.nz.

TRANSPORT

Air

As the major population centres are many miles apart, getting between cities by road or rail is fairly time consuming. It can take around ten hours to drive from Wellington to Auckland, and about four between Christchurch and Dunedin. Air travel is a popular alternative. New Zealand's national airline is the state-owned Air New Zealand. It operates out of sites in the main cities. Air New Zealand has expanded its services and now operates a 'no-frills, value-based' domestic service using subsidiary airline Freedom Air. No meals are provided, and the cost of travel documentation is reduced by ticketless travel. Freedom Air began flying the main routes between Auckland, Wellington and Christchurch in May 2001, and now flies to Dunedin, Hamilton and Palmerston North as well as several Australian destinations. Origin Pacific is a small airline offering flights from Auckland, Blenheim, Wellington, Christchurch, Dunedin, Hamilton, Palmerston North, Invercargill, Napier, Nelson and New Plymouth. It offers fares from as low as $59.

Air New Zealand offers no-frills flights, called City Savers, and special internet-only fares on the main routes. There are also special deals on late night flights or flights during off-peak hours. Holders of the International Student Identity Card (ISIC) can get a 50% discount on standby travel. On the major routes this may entail waiting around in the airport until a flight has spare seats, but it rarely involves more than a couple of hours delay unless it is a particularly busy period such as the start of the school holidays or the festive season.

Auckland International Airport handles 75% of New Zealand's international arrivals and departures. The website addresses for the three main airports are: www.auckland-airport.co.nz, www.wellington-airport.co.nz and www.christchurch-airport.co.nz.

Trains

The train network is not exactly comprehensive, and has recently been trimmed further by the closure of the Northerner service (a night train between Auckland and Wellington) in November 2004. There are only a few trains to most major destinations each day. TranzMetro (www.tranzmetro.co.nz) operates commuter-style train services in Wellington (from Johnsonville, Paraparaumu and Wairarapa into the central city). Rideline (☎(09) 366 6400; www.rideline.co.nz) operates trains in Auckland, as well as buses and ferries. Trains cost more than the equivalent journey by bus, although there are some faster services that are more expensive. Many of the routes are chiefly designed with tourists in mind; Tranz Scenic trains offer services such as the Transalpine Express from Christchurch to Greymouth across the Southern Alps, and the Overlander (from Auckland to Wellington). Other train lines are Capital Connection (a popular commuter train between Palmerston North and Wellington), and the TranzCoastal (from Picton to Christchurch). Reservations are advisable during the summer on popular tourist routes, and booking well in advance often enables you to buy tickets at reduced prices. The national reservations telephone number for Tranz Scenic is 0800 872 467 or from overseas +64 4 495 0775 or fax +64 4 472 8903. Bookings can also be made online using the website (www.tranzscenic.co.nz) or by e-mail (bookings@tranzscenic.co.nz). Bookings may be made by credit card. Students are entitled to a 50% discount off the standard adult fare (with ID). Tranz Scenic trains also have a service called Throughfares, which combines your train service with your Interislander ferry booking, so that you only have to make one reservation for your whole trip.

Coaches

Buses (usually called coaches) between major cities provide much more frequent services than the trains. There are three main companies: Newmans, Scenic, and InterCity. Newmans operates in the North Island from Auckland to Wellington, and in the South Island from Christchurch through to Queenstown and Milford Sound. Scenic is located in Auckland, Rotorua, Christchurch and Queenstown. InterCity provides the most comprehensive and economical service, running 120 services a day between 600 towns and cities across the country all the way from Kaitaia down to Invercargill. InterCity often has special limited fares available if you book in advance – at the time of print there was a $10 fare between Auckland and Wellington or between Picton and Nelson. InterCity also offers the Flexi-Pass, which is valid for most New Zealand coach transport for 12 months and works something like a pre-paid phone card – the more hours you buy the better value you get. Passes are sold in blocks of time (from 15 hours for $156.00 through to 60 hours of travel for $557.00), you can get on and off buses as you please and the pass is valid for any of InterCity's scheduled services. See the website for more detailed information: www.flexipass.co.nz.

Coach reservations can be made by telephone or over the Scenic Coachlines ☎ (09) 636 9000; e-mail mahunga@scenic.co.nz; Newmans Coachlines ☎ (09) 913 6200 fax (09) 913 6121; e-mail info@coachnet.co.nz; www.newmanscoach. co.nz; and InterCity ☎ (09) 913 6100; www.intercitycoach.co.nz. For online bookings for either InterCity or Newmans, see https://reservations.coachbookings. co.nz/ or e-mail info@intercitygroup.co.nz if you wish to book more than six months in advance.

City Transport

Public transport in most of the major cities does not provide a sufficiently comprehensive network to replace the private car as the major method of getting to work. Because urban population densities are low by world standards this does not yet produce enormous pollution and congestion problems, although it is best to avoid driving in central Auckland and Wellington during rush hour if at all possible. Inner city parking can be extremely expensive, both in metered street parks and in parking buildings, and parking wardens are vigilant. In Auckland and Wellington, commuter rail and bus networks replace the car for a small percentage of the working population.

Taxis. Taxis in New Zealand can be found at taxi stands or ordered by phone (check the Yellow Pages for local phone numbers). They do not drive around waiting to be hired, so there is no point trying to flag one down even if it looks empty. The fares are all metered so you do not need to agree a price with the driver before setting off. In many cities, mini-vans called 'airport shuttles' run a taxi service from the airport into any destination in the central city. Usually there is a flat fee per person for the ride. For an individual, this is almost always a cheaper option than a taxi, although slightly less convenient as you may not be the first person to be dropped off. If you need a shuttle to take you from the city to the airport, try to book at least one day early rather than just ten minutes before you would like to be collected. Because shuttles make more than one 'pick-up', the drivers need to plan their routes to the airport according to stops they have to make along the way. Company listings can be found in the Yellow Pages. Airport shuttles have their own stands outside terminals at most major airports.

The Inter-island Ferry

There are two types of ferry which cross Cook Strait to carry passengers between the North and South Islands: the Interislander ferry, and a fast ferry called The Lynx. Combined, these ferries offer about seven crossings in each direction daily, with a roll-on, roll-off service for cars. The trip takes about three hours on the Interislander and 135 minutes on The Lynx. All vessels carry both passengers and vehicles. The standard cost for a small family car is $215-$255, although there are specials and discounts (between 15%-50%) available for travel during the off peak season (non-holiday periods) and for non-refundable tickets booked well in advance (Ultra Saver fares). The fare for foot passengers is $55-$65 standard one way. To check what special fares are available, visit the website at www.interislander. co.nz. The North Island departure point is the Ferry Terminal on Aotea Quay in Wellington, and in the South Island the Picton Ferry Terminal. The ferries include such amenities as movie theatres, bars, smoking areas, workstations, outdoor observation decks, a nursery (with cots and changing facilities), children's play areas and cafeterias. There are also onboard shops and information centres. If the crossing is bad though, food will probably be the last thing on your mind. The Cook Strait can be a particularly rough stretch of water, and travel may be delayed or cancelled during especially bad weather. On the upside however, the scenery as you enter the Sounds is spectacular and you may see dolphins swimming alongside or in front of the ferry.

Useful Addresses

Air New Zealand: cnr Customs and Albert Streets, Private Bag 92007, Auckland; ☎(09) 366 2400; fax (09) 275 5927; www.airnz.co.nz.

Freedom Air: Level 7, 5 Short Street, PO Box 109-698, Newmarket, Auckland, 1001; ☎(09) 912 6980; fax (09) 912 6998; Reservations Freephone: 0800 600 500; www.freedomair.co.nz.

InterCity Coachlines: CPO Box 3625, Auckland; ☎0800 468 372, or (09) 639 0500; fax (09) 639 0503; www.intercitycoach.co.nz.

The Interislander and The Lynx: ☎0800 802 802 or (04) 498 3302; fax (04) 498 3090 or Freefax 0800 101 525; email: info@interislander.co.nz; www.interis-lander.co.nz.

Newmans Coachlines: PO Box 90 821, Auckland; ☎(09) 309 9738; fax (09) 302 1614; www.newmanscoach.co.nz.

Origin Pacific: PO Box 7022, Trent Drive, Nelson Airport, Nelson; ☎(03) 547 2020, Freephone: 0800 302 302; fax (03) 5477 6760; e-mail; Service@OriginPacific. co.nz; www.originpacific.co.nz.

Tranz Scenic: ☎0800 802 802; www.tranzscenic.co.nz.

BANKS AND FINANCE

New Zealand's banking system is amongst the most advanced in the world and is very convenient to use. A visit to the bank no longer need involve any paperwork as most transactions are done electronically using money cards with PINs (personal identification numbers) to access accounts. Banking hours are generally Monday to Friday, 9am to 5pm, although on Tuesdays some banks open at 9.30am because of staff training. You can use automatic tellers (cash machines) at any time to transfer money between accounts, and order statements or chequebooks. Your money card, known as an ATM (Automatic Teller Machine) card, also functions as a direct debit card for EFT-POS transactions, using your PIN. EFT-POS stands for Electronic Funds Transfer at the Point Of Sale, and is the same system as has recently been introduced to the UK as the new 'Chip and PIN' system. The amount you are charged is immediately removed from your account, meaning that if there are not sufficient funds available your transaction will be declined. Most retailers offer the EFT-POS service; this has been commonplace in New Zealand for at least fifteen years already. Cheques are still accepted by many retailers and companies, but advances in electronic banking are fast rendering them obsolete.

New Zealand banks do not issue cheque guarantee cards. The onus is on the receiver of the cheque to make sure it is not fraudulent. Retailers usually require ID for cheques in the form of a credit or EFT-POS card, and often take your name and address as well. Some retailers refuse to accept cheques, and others may be at least unwilling to take them, particularly if you do not have a local address. Credit cards are popular in New Zealand, Mastercard and Visa being the most widely used. Most bills are paid through standing orders (called automatic payment or direct credit) and your wages will probably likewise be paid into your account directly. Most banks now offer telephone banking as a standard service to their clients, for a small charge per call. Telephone banking allows you to check balances, transfer funds, make bill payments, and hear a list of recent transactions, among other options. Online banking is another popular option, as it is in most countries, and generally offers the range of services you would expect, from balance enquiries to setting up automatic payments to applying for loans or opening extra accounts. Some banks offer this service for free as part of your customer plan, while others charge a small fee. If this is an important feature for you, check the differences in fees before you choose your bank.

Banking costs. Account holders pay bank fees for their accounts. There will be a monthly account fee of anywhere between $3-$15, but exemptions may apply for students and the elderly. This fee may be waived if you maintain a certain balance in your account. There is also a fee for individual transactions on top of the monthly fee, but some banks exempt the first few entries each month. Electronic and telephone transactions usually cost between 25-50c, while manual transactions (carried out at the bank) may cost around 50c-$1. If you have an overdraft, the monthly overdraft management fee is likely to be around 12%, with a minimum charge of $2. The government charges a resident withholding tax, currently 19.5% of your interest.

Bank Accounts

The five main New Zealand banks are the Bank of New Zealand (BNZ), the Australia New Zealand Banking Group (ANZ), the National Bank of New Zealand, WestpacTrust, (an amalgamation of Westpac Banking Corporation and Trustbank, which formerly operated as local district trusts), and ASB (formerly the Auckland Savings Bank, which now operates nationwide). Branches of foreign banks also operate and some such as the Commonwealth Bank of Australia have wide experience of meeting the financial needs of immigrants.

If you wish to open a bank account in New Zealand, it is recommended that you contact the head office of the bank involved to discuss any requirements before you leave for New Zealand. Your current bank should be able to help you open a New Zealand account. There is a generally a fee for this service and a minimum deposit requirement. Some New Zealand banks now offer a new residents' service, which enables you to open your New Zealand bank account before you leave home. Details about the service offered by ASB to UK citizens may be viewed on their website (www.migrantbanking.co.uk). The National Bank of New Zealand also offers a similar service to help you set up a New Zealand account, and has a specialist New Residents Services team. See the 'Moving to New Zealand' section of the National Bank of New Zealand website (www.nationalbank.co.nz) for more information. You are able to deposit up to NZ$25,000 by International Money Transfer before you arrive. For amounts larger than this, you will need to fill in an application form. The National Bank also offers freephone numbers for 22 different countries. One advantage of opening an account before you arrive in New Zealand is that it solves the problem of transferring money; you simply arrange for a telexed transfer to your new account. The alternatives to telexing money directly to a New Zealand bank account are outlined in the section on International Money Transfers below. Opening an account once you arrive in New Zealand does not take long, but there are a few hitches for the new arrival. Some banks require proof of a regular income, such as a signed work contract, before allowing you to open a cheque account, even though you may have deposited money with them. You should be issued immediately with an ATM card, which will allow you to withdraw money from a bank or an automatic teller machine. To facilitate opening an account in New Zealand, it is a good idea to bring a letter of introduction from your bank at home.

ANZ: ☎0800 103 123, or from overseas: +64 4 472 7123; www.anz.com/nz.

ASB: ☎(09) 306 3000 or 0800 803 804; fax (09) 306 3010; www.asbbank.co.nz. If you wish to set up an account from the UK, contact Commonwealth Bank, 85 Queen Victoria Street, London EC4V 4HA; ☎020-7710 3999;fax 020-7710 3939;www.migrantbanking.co.uk.

BNZ: State Insurance Tower, 1 Willis St, PO Box 2392, Wellington; ☎0800 275 269 or from overseas: +64 4 494 9098; www.bnz.co.nz.

Commonwealth Bank of Australia, Financial & Migrant Information Service, Senator House, 85 Queen Victoria Street, London EC4V 4HA; ☎020-7710 3999; fax 020-7710 3939; www.commbank.com.au

National Bank: ☎0800 181 818 or from overseas: +64 4 382 9608; www.nationalbank.co.nz. To set up an account before you move to New Zealand, see the website for further information. Alternatively, you can call the following freephone numbers: ☎ 00 800 1255 1255 from Austria, Belgium, China, Denmark, France, Hungary, Ireland, Luxembourg, Macau, The Netherlands, Norway,

Spain, Sweden, Switzerland, Taiwan and the UK. ☎ 011 800 1255 1255 from Canada or the USA. ☎ 001 800 1255 1255 from Hong Kong or Singapore. ☎ 0061 800 1255 1255 (IDC) or 0041 800 1255 1255 (Telecom) from Japan. ☎ 09 800 1255 1255 from South Africa. There is no freephone number from other countries, but you can call +64 4 462 1615.

Westpac Trust: ☎0800 400 600 or from overseas: +64 9 912 8000; www.westpactrust.co.nz.

Banking Ombudsman

If you have a complaint about a bank in New Zealand your first step should be to contact the bank involved. If you can't resolve the problem through the bank's processes, you can contact the Banking Ombudsman. The Banking Ombudsman's Office can provide you with advice about how to make a complaint, although it will not hear the complaint until you have first approached the bank involved. The address is: Banking Ombudsman, PO Box 10573, The Terrace, Wellington; ☎(04) 471 0006 or Freephone: 0800 805 950; fax (04) 471 0548; e-mail help@bankombudsman.org.nz; www.bankombudsman.org.nz.

International Money Transfers

There are no foreign exchange controls on shifting money out of New Zealand. Getting money to New Zealand is most quickly achieved through a money wire or a telegraphic transfer. You can either do this through a specialist money-wiring company such as American Express or Western Union, through the banks, or through currency brokers. The Commonwealth Bank offers customers a superior foreign exchange service and highly competitive exchange rates. For further information contact the Commonwealth Bank 020-7710 3999 or www.migrantbanking.co.uk. The money-wiring companies cost more but the process is much faster, less than 15 minutes. Through the banks it usually takes a couple of days but the cost is about half the amount charged by wiring companies.

Making use of a specialist currency broker can help you to obtain the best rate of exchange. One such is *HIFXplc,* Morgan House, Madeira Walk, Windsor SL4 1EP; ☎01753-859170; fax 01753-859169; e-mail migration@hifx.co.uk; www.hifx.co.uk; 909 Montgomery Street, Suite 105, San Francisco, California 94133; ☎415-678 2770; fax 415-773 1822; e-mail info@hifx.com; www.hifx.com; and and PO Box 7646, Wellesley Street, Auckland, 09-306 3707; fax 09-306 3701; e-mail info@hifx.co.nz; www.hifx.co.nz.

Money

New Zealand has a decimal money system using dollars as the monetary unit, each dollar consisting of 100 cents. The abbreviation for the dollar is $ and c for cents which stand after the numbers. At the time of going to press the exchange rate was €1-$1.86, £1-$2.69 and US$1-$1.39.

Cost of Living

Living costs in New Zealand vary, as they do in every country, depending on where you live and how you spend your money. Generally, it is more expensive to live in Auckland and Wellington than the rest of the country, but then salaries are usually higher. Not surprisingly, expenditure on housing contributes the most to total household expenditure, averaging 24 cents in every dollar spent.

Kim Cullen found the cost of utilities and groceries expensive
Standard cable (no movie or sport channels) is about $60 a month. A roll of paper towels is $1.75. Ironing boards are $50. Movie tickets are $14NZ. Also, clothes and shoes are quite expensive. After living in the States where choice, customer service and convenience are everywhere, New Zealand has taken some getting used to. All stores except supermarkets close at 5 or 5:30pm. Banks are not open on Saturdays. Health care is free but a doctor's visit still costs about $50. You will only get surgery if it is necessary and/or life-threatening, and there are waiting lists for many types of surgery.

TABLE 19	AVERAGE WEEKLY LIVING COSTS PER HOUSEHOLD (ONE-FAMILY, COUPLE WITH CHILDREN ONLY)
Food (groceries, takeaways)	$143.00
Housing (rent, mortgages, rates)	$217.00
Household operations (power, furniture, appliances)	$112.00
Apparel (clothing and footwear)	$31.00
Transport (public transport and road vehicles)	$142.00
Other goods (personal, alcohol, newspapers, etc.)	$99.00
Other services (health, savings, leisure etc.)	$146.00
Total	**$888.00**

From The Household Economic Survey, *compiled by The New Zealand Institute of Economic Research (2004).*

Household Income

The latest figures show the average annual before-tax income for New Zealand households to be $60,433. This was an average weekly income of $1,159 per household, and represents a 12.3% increase on the 2000/2001 figures.

TAXATION

The taxation system was extensively reformed as part of the economic liberalisation in the 1980s. A goods and services tax was introduced, called GST (a value-added tax), and the philosophy of a 'user pays' policy resulted in a reduction in personal tax rates. GST and income tax are the main New Zealand taxes. Through the 'user pays' policy, government subsidies have been reduced for certain services like university education, and some medical costs. Some government departments have been sold off to become State Owned Enterprises, and these SOEs also charge out the cost of their services. The Inland Revenue Department (IRD) is the government agency responsible for implementing and enforcing New Zealand's tax policy, and there are IRD branches in all the cities and major towns. The income tax year runs from 1st April to 31st March of the following year. Paying income tax is now a lot simpler than it was, thanks to recent changes. If salary and wage earners ensure that they have the correct tax code, they no longer need to file tax returns.

Income Tax

TABLE 20	PERSONAL TAX RATES
Annual Income	Tax Rate
$0-$38,000	19.5 cents per dollar
$38,001-$60,000	33 cents per dollar
over $60,000	39 cents per dollar

There is a rebate system which means that low income earners may pay about 5% tax. It is then graduated up to 19.5% for $38,000 per annum. Most salary and wage earners have income tax automatically deducted from their wages under PAYE (Pay As You Earn). The employer pays the PAYE monthly to the Inland Revenue. Those who are PAYE and paying Resident Withholding Tax (on dividends or interest from a bank account) do not need to file a tax return. Self employed individuals, or those with income from a trust or rents, pay three tax instalments throughout the financial year. They receive an IR3 form at the end of the tax year, which they may complete by 7th July, but even this is not compulsory.

Banks charge a Resident Withholding Tax of 19.5% on interest and dividends, which is deducted by the financial institution before they send your payment. When you invest, you are required to provide your IRD number to the firm. You will need to apply for an IRD number before you earn money from any source. If you don't have an IRD number, your employer will deduct a higher rate of tax from your earnings. You can download an application form from the IRD website. If you have a second job, you are taxed at a higher rate (called a secondary rate or SEC). An overall adjustment will take place when you file your annual return. Because most of your income is taxed at the source, some people no longer file tax returns. It is prudent to make your calculations, though, as you may be due a refund.

The IRD will help people complete their tax return at no cost, but the individual must provide all the necessary documents. Tax accountants charge a fee, but this fee can be deducted as an expense on the following year's return. All social security and health spending is financed through general taxation. For further details contact your local Inland Revenue Office or the National Office (Inland Revenue Department, PO Box 2198, Wellington; ☎ (04) 801 9973; www.ird.govt.nz). If you have IRD queries you need answered before you arrive in New Zealand, contact the Non-Residents Centre (Inland Revenue Department, Private Bag 1932, Dunedin, New Zealand; ☎ 0064 3 467 7020; fax 0064 3 467 7083; e-mail nonres@ird.govt.nz).

Local Tax

Local authorities finance their activities by levying rates on land and property.

Some local authorities charge separately for services such as rubbish collection and water supply. Rates are levied on the value of your land plus improvements (that is, the house). Rates vary around the country and depend on the value of the land and improvements. An annual bill of between $1000-2200 would be typical for a standard family house. Valuation New Zealand revalues property every five years.

Goods and Services Tax (GST)

GST is an indirect tax on most goods and services, uniformly applied at 12.5%. It is borne by the ultimate consumer but is payable at every stage of producing goods or services. GST is almost always included in the display price. It applies to most commodities, but exemptions include rental accommodation, donated goods and services and financial services. Exports are zero rated. Businesses with a net turnover of greater than $40,000 per annum must be GST registered and must complete a GST return every six months. They can claim back the GST content of the goods and services they purchase. However, visitors cannot claim a refund on this tax.

Other Taxes

There is no capital gains tax as such, or death duties in New Zealand. However, capital gains from disposal of personal property are taxed where:

- the property is acquired for resale;
- the taxpayer's business involves dealing in such property; or
- there is an undertaking or scheme with the aim of making a profit.

Gift Duty. Gift duty is a charge on gifts worth over $27,000 made in any 12-month period which one person makes to another. However, any person making gifts with a combined total value of over $12,000 in any 12-month period must complete a Gift Statement and forward it to Inland Revenue. The Gift Statement is form IR196, and this form may be downloaded from the IRD website (www.ird.govt.nz/othertaxes/giftduty.html). The person who gives the gift is liable to pay any duty when nothing is received in return, or the value of whatever is given in return is less in value than the gift. If something of lesser value is given in return for a gift, the value of the gift, for Gift Duty purposes, is the difference between the two values. The following items would all be classified as gifts for Gift Duty purposes: transfers of any items (e.g., company shares or land); any form of payment; creation of a trust; a forgiveness or reduction of debt; and allowing a debt to remain outstanding so that it can't be collected by normal legal action. Subject to certain exemptions, duty is charged on a scale of 5% of the value of a gift worth $27,000–$36,000, $450+10% of amount over $36,000 for gifts worth $36,001–$54,000, $2,250+20% of amount over $54,000 for gifts worth $54,001–$72,000 and to $5,850 plus 25% for an amount over $72,000. Any Gift Duty must be paid within six months of the date of the gift, even if you have not received an assessment from the IRD. For a comprehensive guide to Gift Duty, download the form IR 195 from the IRD website.

HEALTH CARE, INSURANCE & HOSPITALS

Health Care

The health system is made up of public, private and voluntary sectors working together. More than three-quarters of health care is funded by general taxation; treatments are usually free or subsidised and medical treatment is generally very good. You will be entitled to publicly funded healthcare if you are a New Zealand citizen or if you are normally resident in New Zealand.

The provision of health care has been a major political issue of recent years. Major reforms have been undertaken in an attempt to streamline administration and management in the health system. Apart from charges for doctors' fees and some prescription charges, for many years health services were provided free to the user. However, the increasing cost of specialist health services coupled with the reduction in the number of tax paying workers has brought about a partial user-pays service. Health spending follows social welfare as a major item of government expenditure. The Ministry of Health, which gives the Government advice on health spending, monitors the Health Funding Authority (HFA). The HFA distributes funding for public health services, personal health and disability support. It also pays for maternity and laboratory services as well as hospital inpatient care. The general pattern of the public health system in New Zealand is that primary health care (GPs, prescriptions, out-patients' visits to hospitals) is paid for by the user, while secondary health care is provided free. Public healthcare is free for: hospital treatment, including A&E, with some exceptions such as cosmetic surgery; children's immunisations; prescription medicine for children under the age of six; and for people who need more than 20 prescriptions a year (prescriptions are free starting from the 21st prescribed item); prescriptions medicines for public hospital patients; most laboratory tests and x-rays, except at private clinics; and healthcare (including hospital stays) during pregnancy and childbirth for mother and baby. GP referrals to a public hospital for treatment are also free, as are breast-screening for women aged 50-64 and check-ups and basic dental care for schoolchildren. Healthcare that is subsidised but not free includes: prescription items; visits to GPs; visits to physiotherapists, chiropractors and osteopaths when referred by a GP; and ambulance services.

Over a third of New Zealanders have supplementary private medical insurance to cover the additional costs of private health and surgical care in the public system and to enable them to afford the costs of private hospitals. Private health insurance for a couple can cost anything from about $1450 upwards annually (that amount providing only the most basic cover for hospital and specialist treatment, not including GP visits, prescriptions, or dentists), depending of course on the company and services you choose. Some costs of health care not covered by the state, although they are subsidised.

All GPs are private practitioners and adults (unless they are receiving benefits) will pay about $45-$55 for a visit to a GP, although children between the ages of six and seventeen cost less, with a $15 subsidy, and children under six years old are entitled to a $35 subsidy. Visits at weekends or nights cost $5 or $10 more. Adults who visit the doctor frequently, or who receive social benefits, receive a $15 subsidy. Prescription charges are a maximum of $15 per item, and optometrists' (opticians') and dentists' charges are from about $70 for a checkup. If you need any work done by the dentist, expect to pay a minimum of $120 on top of your checkup charge. People on low incomes can get a Community Services Card that entitles them to cheaper primary care, but not dental care. GPs provide most basic health care. It is not necessary to register with just one doctor, although for obvious reasons most people tend to stay with the same doctor. Ambulance services are provided by non-profit, community-based services in most parts of the country. They do not operate as businesses, but make a part-charge of between about $45-$67.50 to help with running costs.

To register with a GP, you will need to take your passport and permit/visa. If you need specialist care, your GP will refer you. Specialist care is free, although there may be substantial waiting time depending on the region you are living in, urgency, and the type of treatment you require. If you opt for a private specialist, you or your medical insurance will be required to cover all fees involved. As a rough guide, the cost of private procedures in New Zealand is around $12,000 for heart surgery, $2,800 for hernia repair, $2,400 for cataracts, $5,500 for a hysterectomy, $12,000 for hip or knee replacement and $25,600 for a heart bypass.

Hospitals

New Zealand has 85 public hospitals, including some specialised facilities for the elderly and for people with disabilities. Inpatient treatments, as well as outpatient and day services, are free of charge to all New Zealanders. More services are being provided with user-charges, and waiting lists are growing. Public hospitals still provide no-charge operations but the waiting lists continue to grow and if your condition is non-emergency or life threatening, you will find there is a long wait for surgery. If your case is urgent, you will be put on an urgent waiting list. Additionally, a points system has been introduced so that people of high priority are dealt with first. Most of the bigger hospitals will have an interpreter service for patients whose first language is not English.

You are generally less likely than in many other countries to be a victim of medical misadventure at the hands of some young doctor at the end of 100-hour shift. Young doctors went on strike in the late 1980s and successfully negotiated better pay and conditions.

As a result of long waiting lists, a great number of people have taken out medical insurance and elect to go to a private hospital (there are no private beds in public hospitals). Private hospitals cater mainly for elective surgery and for those who prefer a private room and more choice of when they have their operation.

Dental Care. Dental care for adults is not subsidised by the government but is provided free for all primary school children through the school dental system. Most New Zealand primary schools will have a dental clinic on the premises. As a result of receiving free basic care, nearly half of New Zealand school children have no fillings by the time they get to high school.

Abortion. Abortion is legal under certain strictly defined conditions. If it is judged that the continuation of the pregnancy would result in serious danger to the life or mental or physical health of the woman, or that there is substantial risk that the child would be born with severe disabilities, then an abortion may be approved by two specially appointed consultants. The rate is about the same per 1000 of the population as the UK and roughly half that of the USA.

Reciprocal Agreements

New Zealand has reciprocal health care agreements with most Commonwealth countries, including the UK. Visitors from these countries are entitled to access to the New Zealand health care system on the same basis as New Zealand citizens and residents. Visitors from other countries will have to pay full price for health services. For further information see the Ministry of Health website at www.moh. govt.nz.

Private Medical Insurance

About 75% of New Zealanders have private medical insurance. The main reasons for buying private insurance seem to be to cover the additional costs of using the public system, such as doctors' fees and prescription charges, and to cover the costs of private hospital care. Getting insurance just to cover the costs of primary care is unlikely to be cost effective. The average annual costs for doctors' visits and prescriptions charges may be less than the premiums even for a budget insurance deal that only covers primary care. There are different plan types that are likely to suit people in different circumstances. Almost all plans will cover surgical hospitalisation. Many also cover costs associated with specialist visits and high-costs diagnostics. Some plans provide cover for day-to-day treatment with options for dental and optical cover. Some health insurance plans are modular, which means that you can build a plan around the type of treatment you want cover for. The main advantages of private hospital care are greater choice over the timing of an operation, and private rooms. You can get hospital-only cover, which is usually cheaper than a comprehensive policy. The public healthcare system should work for you if your condition is acute or life threatening, but for other procedures you will probably find yourself on a waiting list. Ministry of Health information in 2004 showed that more than 27,000 patients had been waiting more than six months just for their first specialist appointment through the public system.

Remember, though, that the public hospital system still provides the full range of care. The advantages of having private insurance are mostly the convenience factor. It is not yet necessary to have private medical insurance in New Zealand. Check that there is a repatriation clause in your policy if this is important to you.

For more information, contact a health insurance provider such as Southern Cross Health Insurance (www.southerncross.co.nz).

The Accident Compensation Corporation (ACC)

New Zealand has a unique system of state protection in the case of personal injury or accident, known as ACC. The government provides accident insurance cover for anyone who is injured due to accidents in the workplace, at home or on the sports field. This is a no-fault cover for residents of and visitors to New Zealand for accident, medical misadventure or certain behaviour for which criminal proceedings may be brought. Consequently, there is no right to sue for personal injury. Money for ACC comes from levies on vehicle owners, employers, the self-employed, workers and general taxes. This is another area of welfare provision that has suffered from retrenchment in recent years, and the original 1972 ACC system has been reduced. Lump-sum compensation according to a fixed scale depending on the injury has been abolished, and all assistance is made on a case-by-case basis. However assistance is available for a wide variety of costs including medical treatment, private hospital treatment, loss of earnings, loss of potential earnings, home help and child care, house modification in the case of permanent disability and training for independent living. The ACC places great emphasis on aiding people back to the workforce with rehabilitation treatment. The cost of non-work related accidents is met through the earner's premium, which is collected through the tax system, and the cost for work related accidents is collected through the employer's premium or levy. Firms are now allowed to take out accident insurance for their employees through private firms instead of ACC, if they wish.

ACC also covers visitors to New Zealand for certain personal accident injuries. Claims are started when you go to the doctor or hospital, and ACC contributes towards treatment costs, transport (getting to the treatment) costs, and rehabilitation assistance. Visitors may only get this assistance while in New Zealand.

SOCIAL WELFARE & UNEMPLOYMENT BENEFITS

Work and Income New Zealand (WINZ) is the agency which combines employment and income support roles. It has offices throughout the country, and distributed over $9billion in income support during the last year. Access to the social welfare system in New Zealand does not depend upon establishing a contribution record; benefits are available to all those who meet the residency and income criteria. Although entitlement criteria are generous, benefit rates are not: most benefits are worth considerably less than 50% of the average weekly wage. Increasingly prospective claimants face income and asset tests, for example high-income earners who become unemployed may face a stand-down period before they are entitled to an unemployment benefit and they may have to demonstrate that they have used up their own savings before qualifying for state aid. Benefits are available to those who fit the criteria and are legal residents of New Zealand, but in some cases applicants must have lived there for several years. There is a reciprocal social security agreement with the UK which entitles UK residents who move to New Zealand to qualify for New Zealand benefits under the same criteria as New Zealanders. Some UK benefits are payable in New Zealand and in some circumstances it may be advisable to keep paying British National Insurance contributions. Immigrants from other countries will have to satisfy residence criteria before they become eligible. Most benefits are taxed before payment and the net amount is paid to the beneficiary, usually directly into a bank account.

Unemployment benefit. Payments are not related to previous earnings and the weekly rate is very low. The single rate currently ranges from $164.16-$256.52 per week after tax, and for married couples, between $136.79 and $145.36 each per week, depending on whether or not you have children. Anyone under 25 years old is paid a lower rate, and people under 20 years old are paid a lower rate again. The unemployment benefit is payable to New Zealand citizens and residents only, and there are various factors that may affect entitlement, including the reason you left your last job, whether you previously earned a high income, and so on. The applicant must be actively looking and ready for work, or be involved in a training course. WINZ also helps people with finding work experience and seasonal jobs. Such work is usually in the tourist business, or in the farming, fishing, or horticulture industries.

Invalids Benefit. Available to people aged sixteen or over who are terminally ill (and not expected to live more than two years, and unable to work 15 hours or more a week), permanently blind, or unable to regularly work 15 hours or more a week because of a sickness, injury or disability which is expected to last at least two years. Generally this is not available to those who have enough money from other means to support themselves. Your partner may be included in your Invalids Benefit, but may need to enter into a Job Seeker Agreement with Work and Income, depending on your family situation. Partners who are pregnant, ill, caring for a special needs child or someone who needs fulltime care, or home schooling their child can apply for an exemption. The rates range from $166.04-$289.45 per week, depending on circumstances.

Sickness Benefit. This is available those who can't work temporarily because of sickness, injury, pregnancy or disability. In order to qualify you must be 18 or over, or 16-17 and living with a partner and children you support. You must also have a job but have had to reduce your hours and income due to sickness, injury or pregnancy, or be unemployed or working part-time but unable to look for or do full-time work. You must be a New Zealand citizen or permanent resident. You will need a medical certificate in order to apply, and then regular medical certificates from your doctor, dentist or midwife. If you are pregnant you will be eligible from your 27th week, or earlier if you have complications. Your payments can continue for up to 13 weeks after the birth if you are caring for the child. The amount you are paid in Sickness Benefit depends on your personal situation, whether you have dependents and so on, but it is likely to be between $109.43-$256.52 per week. It usually takes 2-3 weeks for payments to start. You may have to wait longer if you have been working and you got holiday pay or some other payment at the end of your job, had a high income in your last 26 weeks at work, or are getting sick pay from your employer. Payments will be made direct into your bank account.

Domestic Purposes Benefit (DPB): The DPB is available to a sole parent caring for a child (under 16). The parent must be over 18 years of age, (sixteen if legally married) and have a dependent child under eighteen who lives with them. For a single parent with one child the rate is $235.12 weekly after tax, with two or more children the rate is $256.52. If the youngest child is over six years old, the beneficiary must be actively looking for part time work. People over sixteen caring for someone sick or frail who would ordinarily need hospital care can also be eligible for the DPB. Caregivers who are also sole parents may be paid up to $289.45 weekly. The amount that someone receives depends on age and if they are married or have a partner, the number of children living with them and how much other income they have. Payments are made weekly.

Widows Benefit: This is for women whose partner has died and who have dependent children living with them, were married at least 15 years and had children, or had dependent children for at least 15 years while married or widowed or were married at least five years and widowed over the age of 50. There are various other criteria, but these can be a little complicated so you should check carefully if you think you might be eligible for this benefit. You can call Work and Income on 0800 559 009 to talk about this. If you don't have dependent children, you and your partner must have been living in New Zealand when he died and for the three years before that (or continuously for five years at another time). You can only get this benefit if you have never remarried or found a new partner. Payments are made weekly, and range from \$170.99 to \$256.52 depending on your circumstances.

Family Support. Family support is cash assistance for low income families. The IRD calculates the amount due, based on the applicant's income and the number and age of children in the family. Family Support is paid to the main caregiver of the children, and children can be counted up to the age of 18.

Child Support. Parents who are not living with their children make payments to support those children through the Child Support Agency, a division of the IRD. The amount paid in child support is based on the income of the parent paying support. The IRD passes on the payment made to the parent or caregiver with whom the children are living.

For more details on any of these benefits, or to find out about any others you may be eligible for, enquire at the local Income Support Service office or call the Head Office (freephone 0800 559 009). For residents on low and middle incomes, Income Support provides a Community Services Card, which reduces the costs of health care. Permanent legal residents can apply to the National Community Services Card Centre (PO Box 5054, Wellington; freephone 0800 999 999). Application forms can be downloaded from the Work and Income website (www. workandincome.govt.nz), and they are also available from most medical centres and Work and Income Service Centres.

CRIME AND THE POLICE

Although you should not have an unrealistically rosy picture of New Zealand society, it is generally a safe country. By world standards the police are corruption-free and for the most part are well respected in the community. The police carry out a wide range of duties; as well as enforcing criminal law, traffic patrols, carrying out investigations and search and rescue, they also perform Youth Education Services. Unfortunately the crime rate has been rising in recent years and the days when people would regularly go out without locking their front doors are over. However, violent crime is sufficiently uncommon as to be newsworthy. In general, New Zealand cities are safe places to walk around providing you use your common sense. Much of the crime in New Zealand is domestic violence. Police officers do not carry guns on normal duties, and for the most part it is illegal for ordinary citizens to carry or own hand guns or automatic weapons. Firearms are strictly controlled and gun carriers must have a special permit from the Police Arms Office. The emergency number, to access police, ambulance or fire brigade services, is 111. Cards or coins are not necessary to dial this number from a pay phone, and it will also connect from a toll-barred mobile phone.

LOCAL GOVERNMENT

Local government in New Zealand is very much subordinate to central government. Its powers and functions are set by parliament. There are two levels. Regional councils have broad responsibilities relating to the environment and land use, including control of pests and noxious plants. They also have some responsibilities over civil defence in the case of flood or earthquake. At the next level are territorial or local councils. Both are directly elected, and have the power to set rates. They mostly provide services such as rubbish collection and disposal, parks, swimming pools, cemeteries and libraries. They are responsible for a variety of regulatory measures, for example, building consent, health inspection and control of noise, pollution and parking.

Official Information

Information held by the government and its ministries, education and health institutions, State Owned Enterprises and local government is called official information. There is legislation governing the availability of this material, and members of the public can write in to the organisation concerned to find out certain facts and figures.

SOCIAL LIFE

Meeting People & Making Friends

Kiwis have similar values and a similar way of life to people in many Western countries, but there are unique features to Kiwi social values. New Zealand does not have a strong class system, or major social tensions compared to many other countries around the world. Needless formality is generally disliked and regarded as being old fashioned, a bit stuffy, or (the worst of all) a sign of 'putting on airs'; people tend to see each other as equals. It is considered quite normal to call round to see friends or neighbours without a specific invitation, and most Kiwis want you to feel comfortable visiting them in their homes. Again, excessive 'guest-and-host' formality will be frowned on and while your hosts will probably go out of their way to offer refreshments of one sort or another they will often expect you to just make yourself at home and say if there is anything you need or want. There is no English-style 'front room' rule to be adhered to and it is perfectly acceptable to request a 'grand tour' of a new friend's house when you visit. Neighbours will often drop in and introduce themselves to new people moving in, and perhaps take them some baking.

For all the immediate friendliness, New Zealanders can be quite reserved in some respects. They are not likely to tell you much about their feelings or values until you get to know them well. Kiwis can also be very politically correct, particularly in the larger cities; derogatory, patronising or sexually-motivated remarks, relating particularly to gender or race, may be deemed wholly unacceptable. Such comments are unlikely to go unchallenged and may land you in hot water. Younger generations tend to be especially passionate about egalitarian social values. However, in more rural, 'blokey' settings, or among older generations you may find the exact opposite is true! As with so many situations, it is best to look before you leap.

Social Attitudes

Perhaps as a result of their pioneering forebears, New Zealanders are an independent people. There is a great tradition of self-reliance, whether it comes to building an extension on the back of the house, or cutting off ties with the rest of the Western alliance during the Cold War period by refusing American nuclear armed ships access to New Zealand ports. Innovation is respected. Finding an ingenious, low-cost solution to a problem was obviously an asset in pioneering days. There is even a phrase for it, 'Kiwi ingenuity', which describes a pragmatic, imaginative approach to problem solving.

> **Linda Kelly admired what she found in New Zealand 26 years ago**
> *The thing that I found refreshing about New Zealand in the 1970s was the lack of the kind of class system I had experienced in England. Here, you could achieve anything with effort, ability and the desire to succeed, regardless of your background. However, a 'class system' of sorts now exists, although it is not based on the status of your birth family but rather on money and possessions, i.e., how much you have, or don't have.*

Despite approving of innovative and non-traditional approaches to problem solving, rural New Zealand remains quite conservative in outlook. Innovative or alternative lifestyles are not widely approved of. However tolerance is also a New Zealand characteristic, perhaps because the independent streak in the average New Zealander leads them to respect the rights of others to live their lives as they choose. Urban New Zealand is more liberal in outlook. Green issues receive quite a lot of support, perhaps because New Zealanders are aware they live in one of the last largely unspoilt wilderness areas in the world and they have some responsibility to hand it on to their children without ruining it. There is strong support for biculturalism and multiculturalism in theory. However Pakeha New Zealanders can sometimes be heard complaining that government treats the Maori more favourably. In fact positive discrimination programmes of the type common in the USA are more perceived than actual. There are, however, special grants for Maori business and for educational purposes. Few institutions run a formal quota system although all are required to have an equal employment policy. Maori leaders acknowledge that Maori society is increasingly dependent on welfare benefits and Maori workers are more likely to be unemployed than Pakeha.

> **Kim Cullen found New Zealand a liberal environment**
> *NZ is a fairly liberal place. The prime minister is a woman and one of the ministers is a transsexual. Marriage is not all that popular - there are many committed couples who live together and never marry. Prostitution is legal and same-sex couples generally have the same rights as heterosexual couples*

.
Like the Welsh and the Scots before them, New Zealanders feel the need to assert their own identity to prove that they are different from the English and the colonial power which shaped the early period of settlement, and hence became the original model for New Zealand culture. The need to assert themselves usually manifests itself as a fairly critical attitude towards English life, attitudes, culture and climate, on the part of those who have visited that country and even by some that have not.

This criticism is usually not intended to be rude or offensive, rather it functions as a form of commiseration for the English for having had the misfortune to have been born there rather than in New Zealand. Reciprocal ruthless honesty about the drawbacks of living in New Zealand is unlikely to be welcomed however. In fact these kinds of Kiwis tend to be defensive about New Zealand, even though they think its merits ought to be self-evident.

Smoking. Smoking is a lot less socially acceptable in New Zealand than it is in Europe. All forms of tobacco promotion, advertising and sponsorship are banned. Public buildings, including shopping malls, are smoke-free zones by law, and all workplaces are legally required to have smoke-free areas, and these areas must include shared space. The basis of government policy is that those who do not smoke should not be exposed to other people's smoke. Some employers do have smoking rooms, but these are increasingly rare. Smoking has recently been banned in bars, pubs or nightclubs, and many Kiwis are strongly in favour of this. If you are visiting a New Zealand home, it is perfectly acceptable for your host to request that you only smoke outside or in a particular place, and of course you should always ask permission before lighting up in someone else's house! Bear in mind that even a large number of Kiwi smokers don't smoke inside their own homes. Within the New Zealand population, roughly around 20% of Europeans and 50% of Maori smoke.

Entertainment and Culture

New Zealand may not be as well known overseas for its musicians and artists (pop band Crowded House and opera diva Dame Kiri Te Kanawa excepted) as it is for its sports men and women, but in fact there is a lively local cultural scene. Increasingly, performers from New Zealand are succeeding internationally. Kiri Te Kanawa is respected throughout New Zealand, not so much because every household worships opera, but because like the All Blacks she is a New Zealander succeeding internationally. She attracts huge audiences when she returns home to perform. Amongst younger generations, musicians such as Bic Runga and Scribe, and bands such as Shihad, The Black Seeds, The D4 and The Datsuns are also achieving some level of international success and are increasingly touring and being promoted overseas, mainly in the UK and the USA.

There are three fully professional orchestra companies, based in Auckland, Wellington and Christchurch, and there are a number of semi-professional and amateur regional orchestras. International soloists and chamber groups visit frequently, and every two years the Wellington Festival of the Performing Arts attracts some highly regarded orchestras and ensembles from all over the world.

Other types of performing arts thrive, particularly in Wellington where there are a number of professional theatres, the Royal New Zealand Ballet, several contemporary dance companies and the New Zealand Symphony Orchestra. The New Zealand film scene has enjoyed much success both at home and overseas. *The Piano,* made by New Zealander Jane Campion, is one of line of internationally acclaimed films which includes *Heavenly Creatures, Once Were Warriors,* and *Angel at my Table.* There is much current international interest in New Zealand film makers, as director Peter Jackson's trilogy of *The Lord of the Rings* has had tremendous international success since the first film was released in 2001. Location filming took place in New Zealand, and has significantly boosted New Zealand's profile as a holiday destination, resulting in an estimated 20% increase in tourism.

Eating Out

The traditional New Zealand European diet was mostly derived from the eating patterns of British immigrants, influenced by the relative abundance of dairy products and cheap mutton and beef. New Zealanders tend to consume too much cholesterol and saturated fat and as a result have one of the highest rates of heart disease in the western world. This is changing slowly as a result of government campaigns promoting healthier eating styles and a new interest in the diet and food of Asian countries. During the week the main meal is usually in the evening, which many New Zealanders call 'tea'.

Eating out isn't the letdown it once was, now that the country is no longer all that interested in 'traditional' British cooking. The quality of restaurants in the main cities is very high, as is the range of different international food styles on offer. Restaurants are constantly seeking to define a distinctive 'New Zealand cuisine', and come up with delicious combinations of fresh fruits, vegetables and meat.

The improvement in the domestic wine industry has helped to turn New Zealanders into more discerning gastronomes. There is a lot of interest in European food trends. Many New Zealand restaurants have what is called a BYO (BYO stands for Bring Your Own) licence. They are not allowed to sell alcoholic beverages, instead the customer brings their own wine, which the restaurant opens. They usually make a small charge called corkage for this (about $5). The advantage of BYO establishments is that you avoid the huge mark up restaurants usually put on wine and you have a much wider choice of what to drink. BYO restaurants tend to be cheaper than fully licensed places, at around $40 to $75 a head for a three-course meal, not including what was paid for the wine. A three course meal at a licensed restaurant is more likely to be in the $60 to $120 range, including the cost of wine. The cheapest and often the most interesting food can be found at fashionable cafes, which have mushroomed in the big cities. You can usually eat well in these sorts of places for less than $20.

The situation in small towns can be grim and 'greasies', such as Chinese takeaways or fish and chips, might be your best bet. You will often see 'tea rooms' in the smaller towns as you pass through, and many of these will provide a selection of solid stodge along the 'pies and toasted sandwiches' line to heavily fortify you for another leg of your journey. Of course, there are many good local restaurants in small towns but these may not be immediately obvious or easy to find, so it is worth stopping to ask someone who looks like they might know where you can get a decent meal. Vineyards open to the public sometimes include a restaurant, particularly in areas such as Marlborough, Martinborough and Hawkes Bay, but these may operate quite strict service hours so it is best to know where you are going ahead of time rather than just taking your chances. Indian restaurants are less common than in other countries, but other Asian food establishments, especially Japanese, Thai and Malaysian, are becoming more prolific. The fish and chips in takeaways are usually fresh and tasty, as instead of frying chips and other goodies in advance and letting them dry out under hot lamps, they fry your order up individually. Fish and chips still come wrapped in newspaper in most places too, with no European health regulations to interfere. No one has yet died in New Zealand of newsprint poisoning.

Tipping and Service Charges: gratuities are not necessary in New Zealand, and service charges are not added onto hotel or restaurant bills. However, a tip as recognition of extra service or consideration would be appreciated.

Sport

What can you say about a country where a former Prime Minister gets involved with the choice over the coach of the rugby team? New Zealanders are intensely nationalistic when it comes to identifying with the successes of their national teams, particularly the All Blacks rugby team. Losing a rugby match can cast a gloom over the entire nation. It is about more than just losing a game. New Zealand is such a small player in the international political and economic order, that the fact that the country's elite sports teams are capable of taking on the big guys and winning becomes a matter of national pride.

Cricket runs a close second in the interest of New Zealanders, although most New Zealanders bemoan the poor performance of their national team. However, test matches are followed closely on the television, even when broadcast from the other hemisphere in the middle of the night. In fact, television news bulletins always cover cricket and rugby — from watching New Zealand TV, you could be mistaken for thinking there are only two sports played in the country. Much less coverage is given to the Silver Ferns, the women's netball team, although they are more consistently successful on the world stage. For a brief and glorious period the soccer team (the 'All Whites') were in the limelight when they qualified for the World Cup.

New Zealanders are not just enthusiastic about watching sport. A large number of people participate in their spare time. Nearly 50% of the population belongs to some kind of sport, fitness or leisure club. The most popular activities are aquatic sports such as swimming, diving, rowing, or water polo. As well as team sports such as hockey, netball, rugby and football (usually called soccer), an increasing number of New Zealanders are involved in individual sports like surfing, snowboarding, mountain biking, rock climbing, skateboarding, tramping, triathlon competitions, or motorcross. Adrenaline sports are on the increase in the country, as thrill seekers face the challenges presented by the mountains and rivers around them. From the birthplace of bungy jumping, adventures such as black water rafting (rafting in caves) rap jumping (abseiling face-down on a building) and river sledding (going down white water rapids on a boogie board) are on offer for large sums of money. New and more terrifying sports emerge each year. But if you do not count yourself among the adrenaline junkies there are plenty of more rational and relaxing sports and outdoor activities available including scuba diving, whale watching and swimming with dolphins in the open sea.

Recreational Fishing Restrictions. Fishing is a popular sport in New Zealand, and there is an abundance of clean rivers, lakes and fish life. However, there are regulations concerning New Zealand fishing in order to protect the resource. Amateur fishermen are not allowed to take more than the daily limit, sell or trade what they caught, or catch undersized fish. There are also restrictions on the minimum size of shellfish and lobsters. Fishermen who operate commercially are required to have a fishing permit. For more information, contact the Ministry of Agriculture and Forestry Information Bureau (MAF Information Bureau – ASB Bank House, 101-103 The Terrace, PO Box 2526, Wellington; ☎ (04) 474 4100; fax (04) 474 4111; www.maf.govt.nz/mafnet (there is an online enquiries form).

MAORI CULTURE

The Maori have been in Aotearoa (New Zealand) for approximately 1000 years, a long time compared to the 150 years of Pakeha (European) settlement. Maori culture remains distinct from the rest of New Zealand culture, although each invariably influences the other.

Maori Social Customs

The Marae. The distinctive and central focus of Maori culture is the *marae* or meeting place. A *marae* consists of a *wharenui* (meeting house), a *wharekai* (eating house) and *wharepaku* (ablution block). To the Maori however, it is not the presence of the buildings that is significant, but the spiritual importance of the location, the discussions and exchanges between people and events ranging from marriages to funerals that take place on the *marae*. It is customary to welcome visitors onto the *marae* in a ceremony called a *powhiri* (welcome).

The Powhiri. Visitors (called the *manuhiri*) will gather outside the gate of the *marae*. It is considered improper to walk onto the *marae* uninvited. The visitors will be 'called on' by the host people (the *tangata whenua*). This is called the *karanga* and is usually performed by a woman from the host side. The *manuhiri* will proceed slowly onto the marae as one group. Usually the women are to the front of the group. One of these women will answer the welcoming call with a *karanga* of her own. The group will pause in silence to *tangi* (remember the dead) and then will move slowly to the seating provided. The front row of seating is reserved for those men who wish to *whaikorero* (speak). Traditionally, women do not have this right.

Whaikorero (speeches) are to welcome manuhiri, to remember those who have died, to thank *tangata whenua* and always mention the reason for the visit. Each speech is followed by a *waiata* (song), sung by the speaker's group to show their support of him. The final speaker for the *manuhiri* will lay down the *koha* (gift). Today *koha* are mostly monetary contributions towards the cost of the *hui* (gathering). The final speech is usually made by the host side.

At the conclusion of the *whaikorero* it is customary for the visitors and the hosts to *hongi* (press noses). This is usually done by shaking right hands, bracing your left hand on the other person's right arm and pressing your nose into theirs twice whilst looking them in the eye. Today some people will shake hands instead. It is best to follow the lead of the *tangata whenua*. After the formalities, hosts and guests share a meal together. It is at this point that the *manuhiri* become *tangata whenua* and the *powhiri* is concluded.

Points to Remember. The *wharenui* is for gatherings and for sleeping. You should always remove your shoes before entering the *wharenui*. Never walk on mattresses or sit on pillows. Certain places are reserved for the elders (*kaumatua*) to sit and sleep in. You should never eat in the *wharenui*.

In the *wharekai* (eating house) be careful not to put hair clips, scarves, combs, glasses or anything to do with the head on the table. This is because the head is sacred (*tapu*). Tables are also tapu, so you must never sit or put your feet on any tables. A *hangi* is a delicious feast of food that has been cooked in the ground. Rocks heated by fire are placed in a hole in the ground, and the food baskets are filled with vegetables and meat and placed on the rocks and are then covered over with earth. When serving yourself, it is polite to take small helpings (and quite acceptable to have several of them) rather than one large plateful. Before meals there will usually be grace. It is good manners to allow the *kaumatua* to eat first, and after the first meal, once you have become part of the tangata whenua, to offer to help with the dishes or preparation of the next meal.

Do not smoke in any of the buildings on the *marae* and do not use cameras or tape recorders unless given permission. Never be afraid to ask what protocol you should be following. Part of Maori culture emphasises the importance of welcoming guests and making them feel at home, so if you are prepared to be respectful of the culture and traditions, then nobody will mind explaining points of protocol to you. A useful book on Maori culture is *Te Marae-A Guide to Customs and Protocols* (Hiwi and Pat Tauroa, Heinemann Reed, 1986). If you want to find out more about Maori culture during a visit to New Zealand, the New Zealand Tourism Board publishes a leaflet called *New Zealand Maori Cultural Heritage Guide* which lists a number of tourism operators who provide visits to marae and other cultural experiences. The New Zealand Immigration Service publishes a leaflet called *The Treaty of Waitangi* which explains the relevance of the Treaty to new immigrants.

SHOPS AND SHOPPING

Most types of shops in New Zealand will be familiar to American and UK immigrants, and in some cases even the names are the same. In smaller towns, shops are open from 8.30 or 9am until 5pm or a little later, five days a week, and 8.30 or 9am until midday or later on Saturday.

> **Linda Kelly found adjusting to New Zealand shopping hours a challenge when she arrived**
> *When I arrived in New Zealand the country was naïve, unspoilt, and barely influenced by the outside world. Shops didn't open on Saturdays and Sundays, but had one late night a week. At first that seemed odd and somewhat frustrating, but it soon became appreciated in as much as the weekend provided two days of complete change from the everyday routines of working and shopping – families could spend time together.*

But things are changing. Sunday shopping began in 1989 and is now well established. Most shops also have one late night when they are open until 8 or 9pm, usually Thursday or Friday. However, with shops now opening during the weekend, late nights are no longer as important as they once were. In larger towns, many retail shops may be open the same hours on Saturdays as on weekdays, and will probably be open on Sunday as well, although perhaps not for a full day. In some larger towns suburban malls and superstores are drawing foot traffic and business out of the city centre. In some major cities, councils have made determined efforts to revive the town centres. Christchurch's Cathedral Square, Auckland's Aotea Square and Wanganui's Victoria Avenue are good examples.

Food and Drink Shopping

Most people buy their weekly groceries from supermarkets. The large supermarkets with the biggest range tend to be out-of-town, which makes access difficult for non-car owners. The major grocery chains are fairly competitive: New World, Foodtown, Pak'N Save, Countdown, Big Fresh and Woolworths (www.woolworths. co.nz). You will find the similar types of food to those you are used to, but most of the stock will be made in New Zealand as imported goods are expensive. There are definite distinctions between different types of supermarket chains in New Zealand. Some offer a cheap no-frills service with minimal overheads. These tend to be large warehouse style places where you pack your own bags and there is not a great range of goods, just all the basics sold very cheaply. Other chains are aiming at the high-income end of the market. They will offer a greater level of customer service, with a range of speciality departments in-store, including a bakery, butcher, delicatessen, seafood counter, etc. but they are comparatively expensive. Most supermarkets are open seven days a week and will usually have at least one late night when they are open until 9 or 10pm. In the larger cities, many supermarkets are open until 10pm daily. Remember that New Zealand is metric! 1kg = 2.2 pounds. 1 litre = 1.76 UK pints or 2.1 US pints.

TABLE 21	WHAT DOES FOOD COST?
Potatoes (10kg)	$4.99–$5.99
Butter (500g)	$1.79
Flour (5kg white)	$2.50
Flour (5kg wholemeal)	$4.99
Bananas (1kg)	$1–$2.70
Apples (1kg)	$2.99
Carrots (1kg)	$1.59
Cheese (500g)	$5.89
Loaf of sliced white bread	$1.75
Instant coffee (100g)	$3.99
Milk (2 litres)	$2.70
Sugar (1.5kg)	$2.19
Dried pasta (500g)	$1.85
Ice cream (3 litres)	$3.70
Lettuce	$1–$2.00
Oranges (1kg)	$1–$2.50
Soft drink (1.5 litres)	$0.99
Beer (local) (6-pack)	$6.95
Potato chips/crisps (200g)	$1.49

Local Shops. Local shops have not yet disappeared, but they are threatened by the convenience and cheaper prices of supermarket shopping. Most city neighbourhoods have a convenience store (called a dairy). Dairies stock practically everything, from ice cream to batteries, and are usually open late (until 9pm or 10pm), but because they are small they charge higher prices than supermarkets. Some neighbourhoods still have their local butcher, greengrocers and bakery but these are becoming less common.

Delicatessens. Serious foodies will probably miss the range of speciality foods available in the USA, Europe and the UK, but there is a range of excellent and unique small deli-cafes in some places. For example, try Zarbo (www.zarbo.co.nz) in Newmarket, Auckland, or Dixon Street Gourmet Deli (45 Dixon St) in central Wellington. Delicatessens stock a range of imported foods but at a price. On the other hand, most staple foods are relatively cheap and high quality fresh foods are abundant. The good news is that many New Zealand companies produce European style specialities locally. Many city bakeries now make Italian breads such as *foccacia* and *ciabatta*, and fresh pasta can be found in most towns. Olives are grown and pressed in some areas of the country, and local companies also make a variety of tempting cheeses. To keep abreast of all the delicious eating and drinking options in your new country, and to find out about what's tasty and fresh when and where (and maybe even what to do with it!), pick up a copy of Cuisine Magazine from any newsagent or supermarket (freephone NZ: 0800 424 243; e-mail subs@cuisine.co.nz; www.cuisine.co.nz)

New Zealand Specialities. New Zealand's varied climate provides suitable conditions for growing a wide range of fruit and vegetables, but you will find that what is available in the shops depends on the season, as it is mostly locally grown. Produce with a short shelf life cannot be imported to cover the off-season because the distances involved are too great. On the other hand you can buy exotic produce common to the area: Pacific Island specialities such as taro (a root vegetable), coconut and plantains are the type of imported produce that is commonly available in the bigger towns. Fresh fish and shellfish are another New Zealand speciality. Green-lipped mussels, Pacific oysters, and local salmon, smoked eel, whitebait and trout are all popular. Because export demand drives up the prices, seafood is not always cheap.

New Zealand Wines. Local wines are also generally of excellent quality. New Zealand white wines were 'discovered' by international wine writers in the late 1980s, and this had an enormous galvanising effect on the New Zealand industry. The number of vineyards multiplied, and everybody started producing Sauvignon Blanc as that was in demand. New Zealand wines are not much cheaper at home than they are overseas, but the range is greater and you will find an excellent selection of wines at the larger supermarkets for between $24 and $45 a bottle. There are over 2000 labels produced every year. You can buy not just the ubiquitous Sauvignon Blanc but also some seriously good Chardonnay, and some superb red wines — several New Zealand Pinot Noirs, Cabernet Merlots and Cabernet Sauvignons have won international acclaim. There are a number of good wineries that are worth visiting, particularly in areas like Hawkes Bay, Marlborough, and Martinborough.

Other Shopping

Most consumer goods are readily available in New Zealand. Imported goods are cheaper than they used to be as a result of tariffs being lowered in the 1980s. However it is probably not the shopping that attracts most visitors or immigrants. There is no equivalent to Regent Street or Fifth Avenue even in the big cities. Department store chains such as Farmers and K-Mart sell most of the essentials from clothing through to household goods and white goods in rather unimaginative surroundings.

Basic clothing is comparatively cheap, although design and quality standards are not particularly high in the chain stores. Independent designers flourish in the larger cities selling creative, well made and unique items of clothing, often through their own boutiques.

Hire Purchase. More expensive consumer durables are often available in New Zealand on hire purchase. Once the buyer signs a hire purchase agreement (subject to a credit check) and pays a deposit they can take the goods home to use, and pay the remainder of the price by regular instalments. If the instalment demands are not met, however, the goods can be repossessed.

TABLE 22	PUBLIC HOLIDAYS
1 January	New Year's Day
2 January	Day after New Year's Day
6 February	Waitangi Day
April	Good Friday
April	Easter Monday
25 April	ANZAC Day
June	Queen's Birthday
October	Labour Day
25 December	Christmas Day
26 December	Boxing Day

However, the only days that almost all shops are closed on are Good Friday, Easter Sunday, ANZAC Day and Christmas Day.

TIME

New Zealand is twelve hours ahead of Greenwich Mean Time. During Daylight Saving the clocks are put forward by one hour, from the first Sunday in October to the third Sunday of the following March.

METRICATION

New Zealand uses the metric measuring system for distances, weights and measures, with a few imperial hangovers. Beer, for example, is usually sold by the pint. People still talk about a pint of milk or a pound of butter, although these products are packaged in metric measurements. Road signs are all in kilometres, as are speed limits. To convert kilometres into miles, multiply by five and divide by eight. Temperatures are in degrees Celsius. As a rough guide, convert to Fahrenheit, double the degrees and add 30.

RETIREMENT

BACKGROUND INFORMATION

Around 15% of New Zealand's population is aged 65 or older, and a significant number were born in other countries. Undoubtedly for many older people, the chance to be reunited with children who have already migrated to New Zealand is a major attraction. Having adult children in New Zealand also makes it easier to get permanent residency. Otherwise migration may be difficult for people of retirement age, as New Zealand's immigration policy is aimed at attracting people into the workforce.

> New Zealand offers many advantages for those considering a change of scenery for their retirement. The standard of living is high and the exchange rate is favourable, so your savings should go a long way. British and American retirees will not have to learn a new language and will find the culture reasonably familiar. The climate in most parts of New Zealand is warmer than Northern Europe. There are the attractions of living in a less crowded country, with, in general, fewer social problems and a lower crime rate. New Zealand's population is an ageing one, so there are many clubs and services that cater for older people's interests and needs.

Although doctors' visits cost about $45 per consultation, hospital care is still Ffree for New Zealanders and immigrants from countries with reciprocal social security agreements. On the other hand, certain types of specialist medical care may be better provided in America, the UK and European countries, simply because New Zealand is too small to have the range of expertise in these areas.

The drawbacks of emigrating have to be considered as well. You will be far away from friends and family in the northern hemisphere and you may find life a little lonely at first. Many retirees mention that one of the hardest aspects of their new life is not being able to afford to return home for family events such as weddings. New Zealand is 26 hours away from London by plane, and around thirteen hours from the USA, and the trip is not cheap. Most migrants report that they find it easy to get to know New Zealanders, and although new friends are not a substitute for old, you need not fear being isolated for long in your new country.

The Decision to Leave

Making a permanent move to another country is a very different matter from just visiting it, particularly when you will be adjusting to all the lifestyle changes retirement brings as well. It may be a good idea therefore to spend a longer period in New Zealand before deciding whether to make a permanent move there. Many people make the decision to move after a visit to New Zealand to see family or friends. If you have a British passport you are entitled to visit New Zealand for up to six months without requiring a visa, and tourists from the USA, Canada and Europe are able to stay for three months without a visa. A visit may be a good opportunity to explore different parts of the country before deciding where you would most like to settle. A number of companies arrange coach and train tours with itineraries that cover most of New Zealand in a short period. One such company is Scenic Coach Tours, which arranges custom packaged vacations for senior citizens (www.sceniccoachtours.co.nz). The most popular of their tours lasts sixteen days and includes travel around both islands (coach, ferry and train tickets), accommodation, boat sailing in Milford Sound and entrance fees to various attractions. Some companies will also arrange farm and home-stay tours, which will enable you to experience the lifestyle of New Zealand families. If you wish to arrange your own homestays or farmstays throughout the country, contact New Zealand Homestay and Farmstays (88 Wairarapa Terrace, Merivale, Christchurch; ☎ (03) 355 6737; fax (03) 355 6742; e-mail info@nzhomestay. co.nz; www.nzhomestay.co.nz).

> **Linda Kelly had few reservations about having made the move**
> I have now lived in New Zealand as long as I lived in England and find it difficult to remember the things that I used to miss about my home country, such as Jaffa Cakes and Walnut Whips. It was hard leaving the family behind. I miss real English Christmases that are cold and sometimes snowy, snuggled up in front of an open fire, and I miss those great big Christmas dinners with all the trimmings, shared with the family. I don't miss the crowds and the long, cold, dark autumn/winter days, or the narrow world-view that English people seem to have. Despite the fact that the English travel regularly to package holiday destinations, they still appear to have a blinkered perception of things non-English with little enthusiasm to expand their horizons. The few that do are usually those who travel extensively, or move permanently overseas.

As has been noted elsewhere, rental accommodation is generally easy to find, so you may like to try living in your prospective retirement locality for a while. It will also give you a chance to assess the real costs of living in New Zealand. Financial considerations are an important factor when you are living on a fixed income. You can use a visit to assess the property market in order to find out what kind of housing you will be able to afford. In general, if you have sold property in the UK or USA, you should be able to afford a New Zealand house of at least an equivalent if not better standard, particularly if you choose to live outside the main cities.

Residence and Entry Regulations

Because the general migration category is not open to people aged 55 or above, the most likely route to New Zealand residency for an older person is the family reunification or business development categories. Under the family reunification category, you are entitled to apply for residency if you have an adult child or children living in New Zealand and no adult children living in your own country. Alternatively, you can apply if you have children living in your home country but you have more children living in New Zealand than any other country including your own. If you are under the age of 65 and have sufficient capital you can apply under the business investment category. The minimum amount required is NZ$1million, and you must meet the pass mark (see Chapter Two, *Residence and Entry*).

Applying for Residence

To qualify for residency under the family reunification category, you will need to provide evidence of your family relationships, and the citizenship or residency status of your New Zealand children, and of your children living in other countries. You will need to submit birth and marriage certificates and copies of residency permits. Additionally, you will have to satisfy the health and character requirements outlined in Chapter Two for general residency applications.

Possible Retirement Areas

Popular retirement areas are in the warmer regions on the East Coast of the North Island, and the north of the South Island. Many New Zealanders move to the coast when they retire, often to a beach house ('bach' or 'crib'). Some communities have a higher proportion of older people than others, which you may consider an advantage. One consideration to bear in mind is that in remoter areas you will certainly need to own a car or to live close to local services as public transport may not be convenient enough to rely on. A popular retirement option for New Zealanders is the 'ten-acre block' or 'lifestyle block', a house in the country on a large section of land. Ten acres may be the size of farm in Europe, but by the standards of New Zealand farms these are just hobby plots for city folk who want to try the rural lifestyle. Some people cultivate their land or keep animals, while others just enjoy the extra space.

Tauranga and the Bay of Plenty. On the east coast of the North Island, the Bay of Plenty has a pleasant climate and is one of the main horticultural regions as a result. In the summer time, the sun, white sandy beaches and gentle waves of the beach at Mt Manganui attract many families.

Hawke's Bay. Known for its pleasant climate and easy pace of life, Hawke's Bay is a popular retirement spot. There is a wealth of orchards and vineyards here, and Hawke's Bay is one of the premier winemaking regions in the country. Lovers of architecture will enjoy the buildings of Napier, the 'art deco capital of the world', which were built after the 1931 earthquake. A growing number of retired people live in Havelock North, a small town about twenty minutes from Napier. Hawke's Bay also boasts several beautiful beaches.

Kapiti Coast. Just north of Wellington, the west coast of the North Island is a popular retirement destination for locals. It is dotted with small towns, from Paraparaumu up to Otaki, many made up largely of holiday homes that Wellingtonians use to escape for the weekends. There are a large number of permanent residents as well, many of retirement age. Transport networks are good, there is a commuter train service into Wellington city, as well as a local bus network. The coast itself can be quite rough, but just down the coast the harbour provides more sheltered waters for boating or fishing.

Banks Peninsula. Over the Port Hills to the south of Christchurch, the peninsula was called Bank's Island on the first map of New Zealand after Captain Cook's navigator, Joseph Banks, who thought its deep inlets cut it off from the mainland. In contrast with the flat sweeping plains of Canterbury, the peninsula is all hills and valleys divided by deep harbours. Further east over the hills is Akaroa, with its echoes of the first French settlers. Streets are called 'Rues' and the building code specifies that new houses are to be built in the style of the homes of the original French settlers with steeply raked roofs. You would certainly need to be a car owner to live on the peninsula, as the bus service to Christchurch is infrequent and the remoter valleys lack local services.

Hobbies and Interests

New Zealand offers many opportunities for using your new leisure time. The country is full of keen gardeners and the climate is well suited for those who like to spend time outdoors. If you are planning an active retirement, there is a lot of beautiful countryside to be explored. There are sporting opportunities to suit just about everybody. Golf is popular, and there are public golf courses outside most towns and cities. Lawn bowls and croquet are also popular with older people. If you are interested in cultural pursuits, you should consider settling near one of the main cities. Fortunately one of the advantages of living in New Zealand is that you can combine proximity to major cities with a semi-rural lifestyle if you so desire. Banks Peninsula, for example, is only 40 minutes away from the centre of Christchurch. Every town has a senior citizens club, equally open to the recent immigrant as to the native New Zealander. These provide a chance to meet other older people as well as to make use of social facilities. Many older people use their new leisure time to return to study, either through night classes, through correspondence courses (such as those offered by the Open Polytech) or by enrolling in university part-time. Most New Zealand universities exempt mature students from formal entrance qualifications and instead will assess your ability to study and will enrol you at the appropriate level. A pre-degree certificate in liberal arts, which has less rigorous assessment procedures, may help you to get into the swing of studying. Night classes are offered in a wide variety of subjects from foreign languages through to car maintenance and self-defence at local high schools or polytechnics.

Useful Addresses

Age Concern: Level 4, West Block, Education House, 178 Willis Street, PO Box 10-688, Wellington; ☎(04) 801 9338; fax ☎(04) 801 9336; e-mail national. office@ageconcern.org.nz; www.ageconcern.org.nz. There is a local Age Concern Council in all cities and most provincial centres around the country – see the website or telephone for more specific details of your closest office.

Auckland Bowls: 1 Kimberley Road, PO Box 26 121, Epsom, Auckland 3; ☎(09) 630 5770; Infoline: (09) 630 7777; fax (09) 630 3093; e-mail ivan@aucklandbowls. co.nz or marlene@aucklandbowls.co.nz; www.aucklandbowls.co.nz.

British Pensioners Association (NZ) Inc: 6a Taikata Road, Te Atatu Peninsula, Auckland 1008; ☎(09) 834 8559; fax (09) 834 8885; e-mail britishpensionsnz@xtra.

co.nz; www.britishpensionersnz.org.nz. Provides information about rights, pensions, taxation, Community Services cards, etc., and a quarterly newsletter ('Bulldog').

Citizens Advice Bureau (National Office): PO Box 9777, Level 7, 75 Ghuznee Street, Wellington; ☎(04) 382 8759 or toll free: 0800 367 222; fax (04) 382 8647; e-mail admin@can.org.nz; www.cab.org.nz. Use the website to find a bureau near you. Citizens Advice have information about local social clubs and interest groups, and there are over 90 offices throughout New Zealand.

Grey Power: Aims to provide a voice for all older New Zealanders, and to advance, support and protect the wellbeing and welfare of older people. Provides information and advice about a wide range of issues. PO Box 200-129, Papatoetoe Central, 65 St George Street, Papatoetoe; ☎(09) 277 7854; fax (09) 277 7958; e-mail fed-office@xtra.co.nz; www.greypower.co.nz. Also produces a quarterly magazine, 'Grey Power Lifestyle Quarterly': PO Box 9711, Newmarket, Auckland; ☎(09) 307 7061; fax (09) 307 7854.

NZ Bowling Associations and Clubs: www.bowls.net.nz/NZClubs/. See the website for a list of lawn bowls associations in regions throughout the country.

NZ-American Association (Wellington): PO Box 2957, Wellington; ☎(04) 232 6053.

NZ Communities Development Trust: ☎Chris Gaelic (chairman) (09) 577 2277; e-mail chris@communities.co.nz; www.communities.co.nz. Online magazine contains information about sports, gardens to visit, hobbies and interests.

NZ Golf Association: Level 1, Xacta Tower, 94 Dixon Street, PO Box 11842, Wellington; ☎(04) 385 4330; fax (04) 385 4331; www.nzga.co.nz.

Pension Service (UK): www.thepensionservice.gov.uk.

SeniorNet: ☎toll free: 0800 SENIORNET (0800 736 467); www.seniornet.org.nz. There are 102 SeniorNet learning centres throughout the country, teaching older people about new communication and information technology. For those over the age of 55.

PENSIONS

New Zealand Pensions

Superannuation has been a fraught issue for more than 30 years, and nearly every government since 1972 has introduced change, either to the structure of the scheme or to the levels of pension. 1898 saw the first state provision of retirement income, as the old age pension was introduced, payable at 65 and subject to income and asset tests and a residence qualification. In addition, in order to qualify, a person had to be of 'good moral character and sober habits'. There were several alterations to the scheme through the years, and in 1960 universal superannuation replaced the age benefit and the state-funded retirement pension for those over 65. Income-tested age benefit remained for those aged between 60 and 65. In 1977, a compulsory contributory scheme introduced in 1975 was replaced by a national superannuation, payable at 60 without regard to income and assets and with pension rates linked to average wages. In 1989 these rates were replaced by a combined wage price indexation that saw rates move in relation to price movements. The pension was renamed 'guaranteed retirement income' and there were indications that the qualifying age would shortly be increased to the age of 65. In 1990 a higher rate was introduced for unmarried recipients living alone. In 1992 the qualifying age was increased to 65. In 1998 the minimum level for a married couple relative to the average wage was lowered from 65% to 60%. In 2000, the superannuation rate was reinstated at 65% of the net average weekly wage. The New Zealand Superannuation Act 2001 provided for funding to be set aside to finance the pension in the future, when there will be a greater number of older people.

To qualify for New Zealand Superannuation, you must be 65 years of age or over, must be a New Zealand citizen or permanent resident and have lived in New Zealand for a total of at least ten years since the age of 20, including at least five years since the age of 50. This is unless you have spent some time overseas having special medical or surgical treatment, doing special vocational training, working as a missionary, working with Volunteer Service Abroad, serving in one of the Commonwealth's armed forces or working on a New Zealand owned or registered ship trading to and from New Zealand. If you have been out of the country for any of these reasons, you must have been living in New Zealand before and after you were overseas in order to qualify. Equally, if you spent time in Australia, Britain, Jersey, Guernsey, Canada, Denmark, the Republic of Ireland, Greece or the Netherlands, that may also count as time towards your Superannuation.

National Superannuation currently pays a gross fortnightly rate of $602.66 for a single person living alone (which works out at $498.18 after tax if you have no other income) and $457.04 each a fortnight, before tax, for a married couple if both partners qualify. After tax this works out at $383.22 per person if you have no other income. If you are single, but live with other people, you will be entitled to $554.26 a fortnight before tax. If you live alone, you may also qualify for a Living Alone Payment on top of your Super. If your partner doesn't already qualify for their own Super, you can choose to 'include' them in your payments. Bear in mind though that any other income either of you earn could affect how much you receive. Contact Work and Income for more information and to see if you qualify. Your payments will usually start 1-2 weeks after you qualify, providing that you apply at least two weeks before then. Remember that it is not possible to backdate your payments. If you want your partner 'included' it may take longer to arrange. Payments will be made directly into your bank account every two weeks.

New Zealand Superannuation is taxed before it is paid to you, but you still need to pay tax on any other income. If you do have other income, talk to Income Revenue about your tax rate to avoid an unwelcome tax bill at the end of the year. Other income will affect your Superannuation if your partner is 'included' in your payments. In this situation, you can have income of up to $4160 a year before tax before your Super is affected. This works out at $80 a week. If you earn more than this, you will be deducted 70c from your payment for each dollar of income over this limit.

New Zealand currently has overseas social security arrangements with eight countries: the UK, Ireland, the Netherlands, Greece, Australia, the States of Jersey and Guernsey, Denmark and Canada. The general principal of these reciprocal arrangements is that people migrating from one country to the other are treated like citizens of their new country with regard to social security arrangements and are entitled to the same range of benefits. However, the particular arrangements differ between countries.

United Kingdom: A special banking option was introduced in April 1997 for UK pensioners living in New Zealand. People choosing this option agree to have their UK pension paid into a bank account accessible only by Work and Income. In return, these pensioners receive the full rate of New Zealand benefits or pensions. About 33,000 British pensioners live in New Zealand and roughly 23,000 of them have taken up this special banking option.

Republic of Ireland: Rates of payment vary according to the period of the person's residence in New Zealand, Irish pensions are paid to people living in New Zealand who have contributed to the Irish social security scheme. The agreement between the two countries is currently under review.

The Netherlands: Analogous Netherlands pensions are paid to people living in New Zealand who have contributed to the Netherlands pension scheme. Since July 2002 the same special banking option as was introduced for UK pensioners (see above) has been available to qualifying pensioners from the Netherlands living in New Zealand.

Greece: Greek pensions are paid to people living in New Zealand who have contributed to the Greek social security scheme.

Australia: The 1994 Social Security Agreement between New Zealand and Australia provided for Australians who have lived in New Zealand for more than 10 years to receive New Zealand's pensions and income support services, subject to certain conditions. Australia reimbursed New Zealand for pensions and income support paid for residents with less than 10 years residence in New Zealand. A revised agreement was implemented in 2002, meaning that Australia pays its entitlements directly in New Zealand.

Jersey and Guernsey: Rates of payment vary depending on the period of time that the person has been resident in New Zealand. Analogous Jersey and Guernsey pensions are paid to people living in New Zealand who have contributed to the Jersey and Guernsey social security schemes. The social security agreement between the countries is currently under review.

Denmark: Rates of payment vary depending on the period of time that the person has been resident in New Zealand. Analogous Danish pensions are paid to people living in New Zealand who have contributed to the Danish social security schemes.

Canada: Rates of payment vary depending on the period of time that the person has been resident in New Zealand. Analogous Canadian pensions are paid to people living in New Zealand who have contributed to the Canadian social security schemes.

UK citizens, if entitled to receive a British retirement pension, can continue to receive it in New Zealand. The level of the British pension is frozen from the point you leave the UK, and is not inflation adjusted. If you become eligible for the pension while in New Zealand, it will be paid at the rate that applies in the UK when you are first entitled to a pension. Under the reciprocal agreement, if you qualify for National Superannuation, the New Zealand Government supplements the British pension so that it is at the same level as National Superannuation.

Emigrants who settle in New Zealand are entitled to a pension when they reach the qualifying age of 65. The amount of the pension is dependent on the number of years in paid employment, i.e., the amount you have contributed to the social security scheme in your country of origin. The pension can be directly credited to a New Zealand bank or building society account. When you become entitled to New

Zealand Superannuation, you will receive the full New Zealand pension, made up of the pension plus the balance being paid by the New Zealand government. To apply for the UK pension, write to the Contributions Agency International Services, (Overseas Benefits Directorate, Newcastle upon Tyne, NE98 1BA, United Kingdom). Any pension you receive from an overseas government is likely to be deducted from your New Zealand Superannuation. For more details, call 0800 552 002 (within New Zealand) and ask for the International Services office.

You may also be able to apply for extra assistance with your Superannuation, depending on your income and circumstances. Options may include the Community Services Card, which reduces the costs of prescriptions and visits to the doctor, or the High Use Health Card, which you may be eligible for if you don't qualify for a Community Services Card (ask your doctor for information about this if you have to visit them regularly). If you and your family require a number of prescriptions every year, your pharmacist will be able to tell you whether you qualify for a Pharmaceutical Subsidy Card. If you are caring for dependent children, you can apply to Inland Revenue for Family Support. If you have a disability, you may be entitled to a disability allowance to help with any extra costs you have such as ongoing visits to the doctor or hospitals, medicines, extra clothes, travel, etc. There is also the possibility that you may qualify for an accommodation supplement, which contributes to the cost of renting, boarding or owning a home.

If you are not entitled to Superannuation, you may still qualify for another type of income support such as Domestic Purposes Benefit. There are also other types of income support available for widows, sole parents, people looking for work, and people who are unable to work due to sickness, injury or disability.

Useful Addresses

Age Concern NZ (Inc): Level 4, West Block, Education House, 178 Willis Street, PO Box 10-688, Wellington; ☎(04) 801 9338; fax ☎(04) 801 9336; e-mail nationaloffice@ageconcern.org.nz; www.ageconcern.org.nz. There is a local Age Concern Council in all cities and most provincial centres around the country – see the website or telephone for more specific details of your closest office. Promotes rights, quality of life and wellbeing for older people.

Citizens Advice Bureau (National Office): PO Box 9777, Level 7, 75 Ghuznee Street, Wellington; ☎(04) 382 8759 or toll free 0800 367 222; fax (04) 382 8647; e-mail admin@cab.org.nz; www.cab.org.nz.

Grey Power: PO Box 200-129, Papatoetoe Central, Auckland; ☎(09) 277 7854; fax (09) 277 7958; e-mail fed-office@xtra.co.nz; www.greypower.co.nz. A lobby group and support network for people over 50. Not aligned with any political party, Grey Power provides information about political issues and policies, superannuation, etc. See website or telephone for details of your local association.

Inland Revenue (Family Support): ☎0800 227 773.

Inland Revenue (Superannuation): ☎0800 227 774; www.ird.govt.nz. Have your IRD number handy when you call. Depending on your circumstances, you may be able to apply to Inland Revenue for a lower tax rate.

Retirement Commission: Level 3, 69-71 The Terrace, PO Box 12-148, Wellington; ☎(04) 499 7396; fax (04) 499 7397; e-mail office@retirement.org.nz; www. retirement.org.nz. This office is partly government funded, and has a range of activities aimed at raising public awareness and understanding of retirement income policies.

War Pension Unit: ☎0800 553 003. If you are a war veteran and disabled, you may be able to receive a War Disablement Pension or Veteran's Pension.

Work and Income (Ministry of Social Development): ☎0800 552 002 (call free to arrange a meeting); www.workandincome.govt.nz/get-financial-assistance/main-benefit/nz-superannuation.html. This website contains a checklist of things you will need to take to a meeting to apply for New Zealand Superannuation. Items required include: your ID and NZ residency documents (two documents for each applicant), such as passports, birth certificates or citizenship papers; name change certificates (deed poll papers or marriage certificates); evidence of bank account and IRD numbers (forms, letters, statements, etc.); a letter/statement/payslip showing any benefits or pensions paid to you from overseas, evidence of your combined income from any source for the past 52 weeks (payslips, bank statements, etc.); and evidence of any income-earning assets owned by you or your partner (bank statements, share certificates, property valuations, etc.).

Receiving Your Pension Abroad

Pension arrangements for expatriates vary. In some countries if you have established entitlement in your own country then you can continue to receive your pension in New Zealand. As noted above, some countries have reciprocal agreements with New Zealand, which entitle you to the same range of benefits as a local. You should contact your local Department of Social Security for further information. One New Zealand company that specialises in completing necessary documentation and liaising with overseas agencies is Britannia Financial Services Ltd (Building 4, 106 Bush Road, Albany, Private Box 302-369 North Harbour, Auckland; ☎0800 500 811 or (09) 414 4215; fax (09) 414 4219; e-mail britannia@xtra.co.nz; www.ukpensionstonz.com).

Taxation

Once you are a New Zealand resident, you pay New Zealand income tax on your worldwide income, including income from any overseas-based pension schemes. Residency for taxation purposes has nothing to do with your immigration status. You are deemed to be New Zealand resident for tax purposes if you have a permanent place of abode in New Zealand, regardless of whether you also have one in another country. Having a permanent abode in New Zealand is not limited to owning a dwelling, the courts will also take into account social, personal, and financial ties as evidence of where your permanent abode is. If you are in New Zealand for more than 183 days in any twelve-month period, you are regarded as a New Zealand resident for taxation purposes whether or not you have a permanent abode in New Zealand. New Zealand has double tax treaties with 24 countries including the USA, Canada, the UK, France, Germany, and the Netherlands. These treaties limit the tax liability for citizens of one country resident in the other, so that an individual does not, in theory, pay tax twice on the same income.

Useful Address

Montfort International PLC: Home Farm, Shere Road, Albury, Guildford, Surrey GU5 9BL; ☎01483-202072; fax 01483-202073; e-mail info@miple.co.uk; www.miplc.co.uk. Provides expert tax planning and financial advice to migrants to maximise on opportunities and minimise any potential tax liabilities.

New Zealand Health Care

One of the drawbacks of the New Zealand health care system for a retired person is that although hospital care is free, doctor's visits are not, and neither are prescriptions. For those pensioners on low incomes from countries with reciprocal social security arrangements, the Community Services Card is available — this reduces the costs of health care. Permanent legal residents can apply to the National Community Services Card Centre (☎ 0800 999 999). Application forms can also be obtained from any Work and Income NZ (WINZ) centre, or your doctor or local pharmacy. There is a cap on the total amount you will be charged annually for prescriptions, so if you need a lot of medication, you do not pay more than a certain amount. Private medical insurance is one option to consider, to cover the additional costs of New Zealand health care. See the Health Care section in Chapter Four, *Daily Life* for further details. Private insurance will cover the cost of treatment in private hospitals, which will give you more choice about the timing of operations. But, as is indicated in Chapter Four, the annual cost of premiums is likely to make full private insurance costly unless you are a frequent user of primary health care services.

Wills and Legal Considerations

You should draw up a will in New Zealand if you are considering buying property and settling there. Dying intestate complicates matters sufficiently for one's heirs, without doing so in a foreign country. In the event that a non-New Zealander dies intestate, the laws of their own country will apply. As it is more likely that you will be a New Zealand citizen or at least domiciled there in the eyes of the law, New Zealand intestate laws would apply. Under New Zealand intestate laws, your estate would be divided between a surviving spouse and your children, with your spouse getting the major share. This would be the case even if you had separated from but not divorced your spouse.

In New Zealand, a will does not have to be drawn up by a lawyer. However, there are obvious advantages to having your will drawn up by a lawyer or trust company. If there are any mistakes in the way the will is drawn up they can invalidate it, and the lawyer or trust company chosen to draw up your will can administer your estate. This may be a good idea, particularly if you have no close relatives in the country. In some countries, people often nominate a relative or friend(s) as executor of the will. However, it is better to have a trust company or solicitor as your executor, and this also saves problems if your nominated executor predeceases you. Many New Zealand lawyers do not charge for drawing up wills, and if you nominated the solicitor or trust company that drew up your will, you will either pay no fee or a minimal fee for the execution of the will.

A living will is separate from the will you make about your assets. It expresses your wishes about your care and welfare before your death, in the event that you are unable to express such wishes yourself at the time. It contains directives for medical decisions, including how much care you wish to receive should you develop any terminal illness, and how vigorous such care should be. There is no legal basis for living wills, but Age Concern advises that they are viewed sympathetically. For further information contact your lawyer or a Community Law Centre.

Section II

WORKING IN NEW ZEALAND

EMPLOYMENT

BUSINESS AND INDUSTRY REPORT

REGIONAL EMPLOYMENT GUIDE

STARTING A BUSINESS

EMPLOYMENT

CHAPTER SUMMARY

- **Job Opportunities:** British and Canadian people are often recruited by the health, education and legal sectors.

  - Many skilled people from India are recruited to work in IT.

- **Unemployment.** A decade ago, New Zealand unemployment was over 10%; it is now down to a 19-year record low of just 3.8%.

  - The labour force is currently 2.022million people, which means that half of the total population is in work.

- **Skills Shortage Lists.** New Zealand Immigration has Long Term and Immediate Skill Shortage Lists which are updated regularly; the latest List may be viewed online.

  - Secondary school teachers of maths, computing, technology, English and PE are needed in New Zealand.

- **Salaries.** New Zealand salaries are below those in Europe and the USA; living costs are, however, also lower in New Zealand.

- **Parental Leave.** This can last up to 12 months and can be shared between both parents.

  - If you take more than four weeks maternity leave your employer can offer your job to someone else, but is obliged to offer you a job substantially similar.

- **Unions.** Any group of employees can set up and register a trade union.

  - A trade union must have a minimum of 15 members.

- **Women.** About 65% of women over the age of 15 have jobs.

  - About a third of the female workforce works part-time.

The Employment Scene

Although New Zealand is a small country, it is a modern economy with a growing range of employment and business opportunities. With less than 0.1% of the world's population, New Zealand is never likely to compete with top international salary levels in the world's biggest businesses; however, the lifestyle attracts many skilled workers every year. Small population size and the country's relative isolation mean that it will always need migrants to fill the gaps in its economy. The Kiwi tradition of gaining overseas experience means that demand for employees often exceeds supply, and at the moment the new high-growth industries (software, wine, education services, etc.) offer a great number of employment opportunities to new migrants with the right skills. Demand for specific talent often leads employers to recruit overseas workers. British and Canadian people in particular are often recruited by the legal and health sectors, and many skilled people come from parts of Asia to work in the New Zealand IT industry every year.

In the past, the country enjoyed very low unemployment with the average level in the 1970s being less than 2%. However, throughout the 1980s unemployment increased rapidly. A large number of jobs were lost in manufacturing industries during the radical economic reforms of the 1980s. Some of the job losses can be attributed to long-term trends in the labour market and reflect the same kinds of changes that have occurred in other western countries where manufacturing industries have been unable to compete with cheaper labour costs in the newly industrialised countries of Asia. There has been a shift in New Zealand's industrial structure from manufacturing to service industries. Other job losses can be traced to the lowering of tariff barriers as a result of New Zealand's conversion to neo-liberal economic policies. Tight monetary policy aimed at squeezing inflationary pressures out of the economy also contributed to the economic downturn.

In September 1991, unemployment reached 10.9%, following a recession and the period of restructuring in the public sector. However, aside from a brief period of increase during the Asian crisis, unemployment has fallen steadily over the last ten years. At 3.8%, it is currently the lowest it has been in nineteen years. The number of unemployed is currently around 76,300, with 67% of this number actively seeking work. A recent increase in the total labour force (growth by 15,000 people) has not been as large as the growth in the working age population; this means that there are more people participating in the labour market (i.e., a rise in the participation rate). It also appears that all groups are being utilised to a greater extent than in the past. Businesses are straining to increase the labour pool, by encouraging people to return from maternity leave, and even retirement, and encouraging part-timers to work full-time and full-timers to take on even longer hours. Total hours worked over the last year have increased 3.4%, which is higher than the 2.9% annual growth rate in employment. This is consistent with the stronger growth of full-time employment relative to part-time employment over the last year. A recent analysis of labour cost inflation suggests that while the wage rate per job is increasing but not accelerating, the current low level of employment will lead to wage and salary inflation in the year ahead.

The labour market has continued to outperform expectations, and job growth (sustained by a buoyant economy) has pushed unemployment down to historic lows and attracted more people into the labour force. According to the Department of Labour, job growth is expected to ease slightly as the economy softens and labour supply growth will fall as net migration drops. However, this is not expected to lead to large rises in the unemployment rate, so skills shortages will continue to be an issue for firms and capital deepening will encourage improvements in workforce productivity. In 2004, a record number of firms (29%) reported difficulties in finding unskilled staff and lack of labour was the main constraint for 20% of firms. Overall, levels of employment have increased to an estimated 2,022,000 people, up from 1,825,000 three years ago. In 2004 there was 5.1% economic growth, and 3.1% employment growth. Employment growth for 2005 is forecast to be 2.4% and for 2006 1.5%, with the unemployment rates remaining very low.

Real GDP growth is currently 4.4%, and the median of average hourly earnings rose by 2.3% to $15.34 in the last year while the mean rose 2.1% to $18.24. The gap between male and female earnings remained steady, with female median earnings being 87.3% of what men earned (down slightly from 87.4% in 2003). Average weekly income has risen by 2.6% over the past year, to $554. Wellington has been overtaken by Auckland as the region with the highest average weekly income; in Auckland this is currently $627.

Getting a job in New Zealand may be a challenge if you have not been able to arrange work before arriving. Your chance of finding a position will be better the more skills, experience and qualifications you have to offer. But it is not unlikely for even well qualified and highly experienced migrants to take six months, or perhaps even longer, to find suitable employment. It is extremely common for highly qualified migrants to end up accepting more junior positions than they held in their countries of origin. Rather than seeing this as a blow to the ego, it is best to view it as an opportunity to get the invaluable New Zealand work experience that most employers will require, and as a chance to adjust to your new life without too much initial work stress. Such difficulties tend to diminish as time goes on and you become more settled, but it is important to ensure you are prepared for a period of adjustment, at least during your first year living and working in a new country.

> **James Pennicott found adapting to New Zealand quite straightforward**
> *I haven't had major headaches so far; the only scary thing was trying to find a job, although this is becoming far easier for new migrants as there is shortage of quality applicants in the NZ job market at present. I have been in New Zealand for ten months, and I am actually in my second job already – I started as a Credit Manager for a waste disposal firm, which was having some difficulties. I worked there for over six months and set up the credit department before securing a position with Statistics New Zealand.*

There are several useful websites containing up to date information about current trends and predictions, including those of the New Zealand Institute of Economic Research (www.nzier.org.nz), The Department of Labour (www.dol.govt.nz), Statistics New Zealand (www.stats.govt.nz), TradeNZ (www.tradenz.govt.nz) and the Immigration Service (www.business-migrants.govt.nz and www.immigration.govt.nz). An annual guide to the employment environment, employer profiles, professional education and training, and work opportunities in New Zealand, entitled *Working In New Zealand Magazine*, is available from *Working In Ltd* for $30 plus shipping costs (24 Augustus Terrace, Parnell, PO Box 3394, Shortland Street, Auckland; ☎+64 9 302 0977; fax +64 9 302 0976; www.workingin-newzealand.com).

Residence and Work Regulations

New Zealand requires that foreign nationals working in New Zealand, whether for local or foreign companies, obtain work permits for the period of employment. In most cases this may not exceed three years. Permission from the New Zealand Immigration Service must be sought prior to arrival and it must be shown that the worker has skills not readily available in New Zealand.

If you are visiting New Zealand and have found a job, you may apply for a work permit within the country, but the maximum period for which it will be granted is nine months. The same restrictions regarding skills apply. Certain groups of individuals can be subject to limitation on period of work visa/permit, ie fiancé(e)s of New Zealand citizens or residents are eligible only for a nine month work visa/permit in the first instance. For further details about work permits see *Residence and Entry* chapter.

Skills

Due to demand for specific skills in certain areas of the country, the New Zealand Immigration Service has developed Long Term and Immediate Skills Shortage Lists. These are designed to streamline the processing of work permits and approvals in principle for work permits or visas where there is a known regional labour shortage, but remember that you will still have to meet all other aspects of relevant work policy. You can download a printable PDF version from the Toolbox right-hand menu of the Immigration Service website (www.immigration.govt.nz/migrant/) or or from WorkSite (e-mail info@worksite.govt.nz; www.worksite.govt.nz).

Qualifications

In general, American and British qualifications are recognised and well regarded in New Zealand. New Zealand's university education system derives its structure from British, particularly Scottish, universities so the types of qualifications available from universities are similar in title and content to UK ones. Trade and vocational qualifications have different titles. You can apply to the *New Zealand Qualifications Authority* (the government agency that oversees the qualifications system) to have your qualifications assessed before you arrive in New Zealand. They will be assessed in comparison with current New Zealand qualifications. There is a fee for this service. For detailed information and application forms see the Qualifications Evaluation Service web page (www.nzqa.govt.nz/for-international/qual-eval/). In some cases you may be required to have your qualifications evaluated as part of your application for residency. The necessary forms can also be obtained from the New Zealand Immigration Service (www.immigration.govt.nz), or you can contact the Qualifications Authority directly (New Zealand Qualifications Authority, PO Box 160, Wellington; ☎+64 4 802 3000; fax +64 4 802 3112; e-mail helpdesk@nzqa.govt.nz; www.nzqa.govt.nz). The NZQA call centre is open for business between 8am and 5pm, Monday to Friday.

NZQA has just launched a new website called KiwiQuals. The site lists every quality-assured qualification in New Zealand of 40 credits and above, and it allows you to compare them. It is searchable in various ways, including by qualification type, subject, organisation and level of study (see www,kiwiquals.govt.nz). Qualifications on KiwiQuals are gradually being updated, and this work will be complete by August 2006.

Details of entry requirements for New Zealand universities are available from the universities themselves.

Professional Qualifications

The relevant professional bodies regulate professional employment in New Zealand. In order to work in these areas you must register with these organisations. In most cases this will involve an assessment of qualifications and experience and you may be required to take further examinations. In some professions you can arrange to sit these exams in your own country. It is important to contact the relevant professional body in good time because they usually take several months to consider applications and qualifying exams are held only once or twice a year in foreign countries. As an example of the type of procedure you have to go through, the following are the requirements for foreign lawyers intending to practice in New Zealand. Legal Practitioners seeking assessment should write to:

The Executive Director, Attn: Secretary, Admissions and Credentials Committee, New Zealand Law Society (PO Box 5041, Wellington; ☎ +64 4 472 7837; fax +64 4 915 1284; e-mail admissions@lawyers.org.nz; www.nz-lawsoc.org.nz). You will be required to include the following information:

- ○ Documentary evidence of tertiary educational standing and attainment, including original academic and admission records, showing courses completed and grades.
- ○ Documentary evidence of admission as a lawyer in your own country.
- ○ A curriculum vitae giving names, dates, and places of practice.
- ○ A copy of your law school's handbook showing the structure of the degree and the content and length of each course.
- ○ A statutory declaration verifying identity and certifying the accuracy of the above information.
- ○ Where applicable, a demonstration of proficiency in the English language.
- ○ Proof of identity (certified copy of pages from your passport).
- ○ A statutory declaration or affidavit verifying identity and certifying the accuracy and completeness of the above information.
- ○ Two bank drafts (in NZ$) in payment of application fees: one for NZ $100 payable to the New Zealand Law Society and one for NZ $885 payable to the New Zealand Council for Legal Education. If you are applying from inside New Zealand, the bank drafts must be increased by 12.5% to cover GST, so should be NZ$112.50 and NZ$995.65. Applications normally take two or three months to consider.

Not all professional bodies have such complex registration procedures. Membership of the New Zealand Society of Accountants is automatically granted to any member of the three British Associations of Chartered Accountants, that is, the Institute of Chartered Accountants of England and Wales, the Institute of Chartered Accountants of Scotland, and the Chartered Association of Certified Accountants. However, any person in New Zealand is able to call themselves 'an accountant'. It is only when they want to call themselves 'chartered' that they will need to join the New Zealand body.

Teachers have to register with the New Zealand Teachers Council after assessment of qualifications by NZQA if they wish to work in the state sector.

Addresses of Professional Bodies

New Zealand Institute of Architects: Suite 1.5, 72 Dominion Road, Mt Eden, PO Box 2516, Auckland; ☎(09) 623 6080; fax (09) 623 6081; e-mail info@nzia. co.nz; www.nzia.co.nz.

Institute of Chartered Accountants of New Zealand: Level 2, Cigna House, 40 Mercer Street, PO Box 11-342, Wellington 6034; ☎(04) 474 7840 or (04) 460 0606 (Registry Helpdesk); fax (04) 473 6303; e-mail registry@icanz.co.nz; www.icanz.co.nz.

The Dental Council of New Zealand: Level 8, 108 The Terrace, PO Box 10448, Wellington; ☎(04) 4 499 4820; fax (04) 499 1668; e-mail inquiries@dcnz.org. nz; www.dentalcouncil.org.nz.

Horticulture and Food Research Institute of NZ Ltd (HortResearch): e-mail enquiries@hortresearch.co.nz; www.hortresearch.co.nz.

Hospitality Association of New Zealand: Level 2, Radio Network House, cnr Abel Smith and Taranaki Streets, PO Box 503, Wellington; ☎(04) 385 1369; fax (04) 384 8044; e-mail nsc@hanz.org.nz; www.hanz.org.nz.

Institute of Professional Engineers NZ: 101 Molesworth Street, PO Box 12 241, Wellington; ☎(04) 473 9444; fax (04) 474 8933; e-mail ipenz@ipenz.org.nz; www.ipenz.org.nz.

The Medical Council of New Zealand: PO Box 11-649, Wellington; ☎(04) 384 7635 or free phone 0800 286 801; fax (04) 385 8902; e-mail registration@mcnz. org.nz; www.mcnz.org.nz.

New Zealand Law Society: PO Box 5041, Wellington; ☎+64 4 472 7837; fax +64 4 915 1284; e-mail admissions@lawyers.org.nz; www.nz-lawsoc.org.nz.

The Nursing Council: PO Box 9644, Wellington; ☎(04) 385 9589; fax (04) 801 8502; e-mail oseas@nursingcouncil.org.nz or nzreg@nursingcouncil.org.nz; www.nursingcouncil.org.nz.

Physiotherapy Board of New Zealand: Level 8, 108 The Terrace, PO Box 10 734, Wellington; ☎(04) 471 2610; fax (04) 471 2613; e-mail physio@physioboard. org.nz; www.physioboard.org.nz.

New Zealand Teachers' Council: Level 7, 93 The Terrace, PO Box 5326, Wellington; ☎(04) 471 0852; fax (04) 471 0870; e-mail inquiries@teacherscouncil. govt.nz; www.teacherscouncil.govt.nz.

New Zealand Veterinary Association: PO Box 11 212, Manners Street, Wellington; ☎(04) 471 0484; fax (04) 471 0494; e-mail nzva@vets.org.uk; www.vets.org. nz.

SOURCES OF JOBS

Newspapers

Many New Zealand jobs are advertised in newspapers, most of which have a daily Situations Vacant section that tends to be more extensive on Monday, Wednesday and Saturday. Job vacancies are listed in most professional journals. For further information, check the websites listed in *Addresses of Professional Bodies* (above). Executive and professional management positions are usually handled by private recruitment agencies. Most international recruitment agencies are represented in New Zealand. The Government's social security agency, *Work and Income*, provides free job-seeking services for unemployed residents.

The starting place for your job-hunt should be the major New Zealand newspapers and comprehensive employment websites such as www.seek.co.nz. A small number of jobs are specifically advertised overseas. The types of jobs that tend to be advertised directly are in areas where there is a shortage of skills locally, for example in computers and information technology, teaching, medicine or accountancy.

The major daily newspapers, and their Situations Vacant sections, can be read online, or at your local New Zealand Embassy or High Commission (remember though that these papers will be a few days out of date, due to having travelled from New Zealand, and the internet is always going to be the most complete and up-to-the-minute source). *New Zealand Herald* (www.nzherald.co.nz) mainly advertises jobs in the Auckland area, or take a look at the Stuff website (www.stuff.co.nz), which contains links to major regional papers. Consyl Publishing Ltd in the UK can obtain New Zealand newspapers as well as magazines (☎01424-223111 or 01424-223161 for 24 hour credit card sales).

Main New Zealand Newspapers
Sunday Star-Times: The biggest official circulation of any NZ newspaper at 210,898.
The Sunday News: Sunday Star-Times' sister publication. Circulation: 114,849.
The New Zealand Herald: PO Box 32, Auckland; ☎(09) 379 5050; www.nzherald.co.nz. Distributed throughout the North Island. Readership: 597,000; circulation: 210,910.
The Dominion Post: The second largest daily paper in the country. Press House, 40 Boulcott Street, PO Box 3740, Wellington; ☎(04) 474 0222; www.dompost.co.nz (through Stuff). Distributed in lower North Island. Readership: 272,000; circulation: 99,089.
The Waikato Times: Foreman Road, Te Rapa, Private Bag 3086, Hamilton; ☎(07) 849 6180; www.waikatotimes.co.nz (through Stuff). Readership: 105,000; circulation: 40,972.
The Press: Private Bag 4722, Christchurch; ☎(03) 379 0940; www.press.co.nz. Distributed in Canterbury and Nelson/Tasman region. Readership: 239,000; circulation: 91,111.
The Otago Daily Times: PO Box 517, Dunedin; ☎(03) 477 4760; e-mail circulation@alliedpress.co.nz; www.odt.co.nz. Distributed in lower South Island. Readership: 106,000; circulation: 44,546.

Specialist Publications

Some types of jobs tend to be advertised in specialist magazines. These publications are also useful sources of information about the current job scene in their particular field. It might be worthwhile placing an employment-wanted advertisement with them. Many New Zealand magazines can be purchased online from the New Zealand Magazine Shop (www.nzmagazineshop.co.nz).

Addresses – Specialist Publications
AdMedia: Profile Publishing Limited, PO Box 5544, Wellesley Street, Auckland; ☎(09) 630 8940; e-mail admedia@magazzino.co.nz; www.admedia.co.nz.

Architecture New Zealand and the annual *Directory of NZIA Practices:* PO Box 2516, Auckland; ☎(09) 623 6080; fax (09) 623 6081; e-mail info@nzia.co.nz; www.nzia.co.nz.

Commercial Horticulture Magazine: The Reference Publishing Company, PO Box 26269, Epsom, Auckland; fax (09) 358 2714; www.nursery.net.nz/products. Covers nursery industry news, views, features from NZ and around the world. You can also order *NZ Native Plants Register, NZ Nursery Register*, and back issues.

Horticulture News: order from www.nzmagazineshop.co.nz.

Hospitality Magazine: PO Box 9596, Newmarket, Auckland; ☎(09) 529 3000; fax (09) 529 3001; www.tplmedia.co.nz.

Management (The Leaders' Magazine): Profile Publishing Limited, PO Box 5544, Wellesley Street, Auckland; ☎(09) 630 8940; e-mail management@magazzino. co.nz; www.management.co.nz.

Manufacturers Federation Magazine: Published by the New Zealand Manufacturers Federation Inc., PO Box 1925, Wellington; ☎(04) 496 6555; fax (04) 496 6550; e-mail admin@businessnz.org.nz; www.businessnz.org.nz.

Marketing Magazine: Profile Publishing Limited, PO Box 5544, Wellesley Street, Auckland; ☎(09) 630 8940; e-mail marketing@magazzino.co.nz; www.marketingmag.co.nz.

Mercantile Gazette: Freepost 5003, PO Box 20 034, Bishopdale, Christchurch; ☎(03) 358 3219; fax (03) 358 4490; e-mail susan@mgpublications.co.nz; www.mgpublications.co.nz.

National Business Review: PO Box 1734, Auckland; ☎(09) 307 1629; fax (09) 307 5129; e-mail customerservices@nbr.co.nz; www.nbr.co.nz.

New Zealand Forest Industries: Profile Publishing Limited, PO Box 5544, Wellesley Street, Auckland; ☎(09) 630 8940; fax (09) 630 1046; e-mail fid@profile. co.nz; www.nzforest.com.

OnFilm: Profile Publishing Limited, PO Box 5544, Wellesley Street, Auckland; ☎(09) 630 8940; e-mail onfilm@magazzino.co.nz; www.onfilm.co.nz.

The Southern Doctor: e-mail postmaster@southerndoctor.co.nz; www.southerndoctor.co.nz.

Professional Associations

Many professional vacancies are carried in specialist magazines, which are usually published by the relevant professional associations. In some cases all vacancies appear in these publications, for example all permanent teaching jobs are advertised in the *Education Gazette*. They will also usually carry employment wanted adverts. Sometimes it is possible to subscribe just to the employment wanted pages. You can contact the professional bodies listed above for further information. Jobs in the New Zealand State sector appear on the internet at (www.jobs.govt.nz). The Association of Commonwealth Universities advertises positions at New Zealand universities on the Worldwide Vacancies section of its website (www.acu.ac.uk/adverts/jobs).

Useful Addresses

Chartered Accountants Journal of New Zealand: PO Box 11 342, Wellington 6034; ☎(04) 474 7840; fax (04) 473 6303; e-mail registry@icanz.co.nz; www.icanz. co.nz.

Education Gazette: PO Box 249, Wellington; ☎0508 300 700; e-mail accounts@apn-ed.co.nz; www.edgazette.govt.nz. You can subscribe to receive an e-mail copy for free by e-mailing: gazettedirect@edgazette.govt.nz. There is also a free vacancy alert e-mail service, to send you vacancies posted in the last 24 hours that match your search criteria. To subscribe, visit: http://www.edgazette.govt.nz/vacancies/subscribe/index.cgi.

Law Talk: New Zealand Law Society, PO Box 5041, Wellington; ☎(04) 472 7837; fax (04) 473 7909; e-mail lawtalk@nz-lawsoc.org.nz; www.nz-lawsoc.org.nz and follow the Lawtalk link.

New Zealand Engineering (e.nz magazine): ☎(04) 474 8941; e-mail scornwell@ipenz.org.nz; http://e.nz-magazine.co.nz/main.htm or www.ipenz.org.nz/ipenz/publications for the full range of publications from IPENZ.

The New Zealand Medical Journal: The New Zealand Medical Association, e-mail nzmedjnl@nzma.org.nz; www.nzma.org.nz/journal.

Trades and Skilled Craftspeople

As is the case with the professional associations, in order to work in New Zealand as a trades or craftsperson, you must join the relevant association or society. If you have qualifications and experience in your own country you will not normally be required to fulfil any additional requirements. You should contact the organisations listed below for further details. Most of these organisations publish a trade magazine, which may be a useful source of information about job prospects. The New Zealand Trades Directory provides online access to contact details for many trade associations on its website (http://nztrades.com).

In New Zealand registration is required by law in order to undertake employment as one of the following:

Architect	Medical radiation technologist
Barrister or solicitor	Nurses and midwives
Chiropractor	Occupational therapist
Clinical dental technician	Optometrist
Dental technician	Pharmacist
Dentist	Physiotherapist
Dietician	Plumber, gasfitter and drainlayer
Dispensing optician	Podiatrist
Electrician	Psychologist
Electrical service technician	Real estate agent
Enrolled nurse	Cadastral (Land Title) Surveyor
Line mechanic	Teacher
Medical laboratory technologist	Veterinarian
Medical practitioner	

Useful Addresses

Master Plumbers, Gasfitters and Drainlayers Inc: e-mail peter@masterplumbers. org.nz; www.masterplumbers.org.nz. Also publishes *NZ Plumbers Journal* (subscribe online via main website).

Plumbers, Gasfitters and Drainlayers Board: contact Colleen Singleton, 9th Floor, 70 The Terrace, PO Box 10655, Wellington; ☎(04) 494 2970; fax (04) 494 2975; e-mail colleen@pgdb.co.nz; www.pgdb.co.nz.

Registered Master Builders Federation: Level 6, 234 Wakefield Street, PO Box 1769, Wellington; ☎(04) 382 8999 or 0800 269 119; fax (04) 385 8995; e-mail MBF@masterbuilder.org.nz; www.masterbuilder.org.nz.

New Zealand Institute of Building Surveyors: Registered Office Box 1283, Dunedin; ☎0800 11 34 00; www.buildingsurveyors.org.nz.

New Zealand Institute of Quantity Surveyors: Level &, 108 The Terrace, PO Box 10 469, Wellington; ☎(04) 473 5521; fax (04) 473 2918; e-mail office@nziqs. co.nz; www.nziqs.co.nz.

Master Painters New Zealand Association Inc: 4-12 Cruickshank Street, Kilbirnie, PO Box 14 383, Kilbirnie, Wellington; tel/fax (04) 387 9755; e-mail nationalof fice@masterpainters.org.nz; www.yellow.co.nz/site/masterpainters/

New Zealand Property Institute: Westbrook House, 181 Willis Street, Level 5, PO Box 27 340, Wellington; ☎(04) 384 7094; fax (04) 384 8473; e-mail national@property.org.nz; www.property.org.nz. Also publishes the *Property Journal* (phone/fax as above; e-mail Miriam@property.org.nz) and *Property Business* (☎(09) 846 4068; e-mail subs@agm.co.nz).

International Newspapers, Directories and Websites

Only a small percentage of New Zealand jobs are advertised directly overseas, perhaps because of the obvious difficulties with labour mobility to such a remote country. By far your best option when hunting for work is to search online. In many cases, your first port of call should probably be the website www.seek.co.nz, which features a daily-updated and comprehensive range of vacancies and also allows you the option of posting your CV online where it is available for viewing by potential employers. Another excellent website is www.kiwixcareers.govt.nz; it breaks down vacancy links into various sectors, including education, IT, health, the armed forces, creative, manufacturing, engineering and industrial jobs as well as a general job vacancy section and a link to various recruitment agents. For work in the State sector, see www.jobs.govt.nz. Another useful site is EscapeArtist (www.escapeartist.com/nzjob/nzjobs.htm), which will direct you to the New Zealand segments of a number of worldwide job-search sites as well as taking you straight to some of the best and most up to date New Zealand-specific recruitment sites. For a series of vacancies grouped by category and aimed at the new migrant, see www.workingin-newzealand.com, which has a facility allowing you to submit your CV directly to featured employers online. There are two newspapers available in the UK for intending migrants to New Zealand, *Destination New Zealand* and *New Zealand Outlook*. These occasionally carry advertisements for jobs and usually carry advertisements for job-search agencies based in the UK that will help you look in New Zealand. The weekly paper for New Zealanders in London, *New Zealand News UK*, is a good source of job advertisements for positions in New Zealand. *New Zealand News UK* is distributed free in London outside central city tube stations and all three papers are available from New Zealand House in

London, or can be obtained on subscription from the addresses below.

Useful Addresses

Destination New Zealand: a monthly magazine from Outbound Publishing created for 'intending emigrants'. Subscriptions within the UK are £19 for 12 months or £15 for six months, and if you live outside the UK and Europe £30 for 12 months and £19.50 for six months. Within Europe (excluding UK) 12 issues will cost you £22 and six issues £15.50. ☎+44 (0)1323 726040; fax +44 (0) 1323 649249; e-mail info@outboundmedia.co.uk for up-to-date subscription details. www.outboundpublishing.com.

New Zealand News UK: published weekly, and either free or for a price of 35p, depending on where you get your copy. Contains up-to-date immigration news, and also carries information about New Zealand-focussed activities for expats and prospective migrants in the UK, mainly in London. www.nznewsuk.co.uk

New Zealand Outlook: Consyl Publishing Ltd, 3 Buckhurst Road, Bexhill-on-Sea, Sussex TN40 1QF; ☎01424-223111; e-mail consylpublishing@btconnect.com; www.consylpublishing.co.uk. Published monthly.

TNT Magazine: 14-15 Child's Place, Earls Court, London SW5 9RX; ☎0207 373 3377; fax 0207 341 6600; e-mail enquiries@tntmag.co.uk; www.tntmagazine.com. Another free weekly distributed throughout London; contains some NZ information, but probably of more use to people interested in Australia.

Approaching Employers Direct

Advertising and screening applicants is lengthy and expensive. A well-written CV which lands on the personnel manager's desk at the right time could save them time and money, and find you the type of job you want. It is estimated that around 70% of jobs in New Zealand are filled without actually being advertised, so it is worth researching companies and contacting employers that interest you, whether or not they are currently advertising vacancies. It is also worthwhile asking friends, people in the community and also in job centres if they know of any jobs in your field. English language skills are obviously very important, and the biggest hindrance for immigrants in New Zealand trying to find employment, so the fact that you speak English is a good start. You can begin your research by finding contact details for New Zealand companies working in your area of expertise. One place to start is the Yellow Pages, which you can consult at the New Zealand Embassies and High Commissions, or over the internet (www.yellowpages.co.nz). The Information Office on the Second Floor of New Zealand House in London has business directories but is not a job search service. You can obtain a copy of *Working In New Zealand* from New Zealand high commissions or from the internet (www.workingin.com). There is a list of major New Zealand employers at the end of this chapter.

Chambers of Commerce & Professional Institutes

Chambers of Commerce operate to promote the interests of their members, local businesses, not as job search agencies, but they are usually prepared to help with information. Local chambers of commerce should provide you with a list of their members for a small fee. A list of Chambers of Commerce in the main cities can be found in the *Regional Employment Guide* below. Other organisations that will have details of member companies are the professional institutes. Also listed below are the Australia-NZ-UK Chamber of Commerce and the American Chamber of Commerce, which publish directories of British and American companies respectively with branches, affiliates or subsidiaries in New Zealand.

Useful Addresses

Chambers of Commerce

American Chamber of Commerce in New Zealand: PO Box 106 002, Auckland; ☎(09) 309 9140; fax (09) 309 1090; e-mail amcham@amcham.co.nz; www.amcham.co.nz.

New Zealand Chambers of Commerce and Industry: Level 9, 109 Featherston Street, Wellington; ☎(04) 914 6500; fax (04) 914 6524; e-mail info@wgtn-chamber.co.nz; www.chamber.co.nz or www.nzchamber.co.nz.

Australia New Zealand American Chambers of Commerce (ANZACC) Washington DC: c/- Embassy of Australia, 1601 Massachusetts Avenue, N.W., Washington, D.C. 20036; (202) 797 3028; fax (202) 797 3457; e-mail info@anzacc-national.org; www.austemb.org/chambers.htm

Australia & New Zealand Chamber of Commerce UK: 34-35 Southampton Street, London WC2E 7HE; ☎08708 900 720; fax 08708 900 721; e-mail Kelly.ryan@anzcc.org.uk; www.anzcc.org.uk.

Professional Institutes and Registration Bodies:

Architects Education and Registration Board: PO Box 11106, Wellington; ☎(04) 801 8972; fax (04) 801 7010; e-mail registrar@aerb.org.nz; www.aerb.org.nz.

Australia and New Zealand Institute of Insurance and Finance: Level 1, 143 Nelson Street, PO Box 344, Auckland; ☎0800 103 675 or (09) 379 7128; fax (09) 367 0639; e-mail emenzies@theinstitute.com.au; www.theinstitute.com.au.

Electrical Contractors Association of New Zealand: Metro Thorndon Building, 220 Thorndon Quay, PO Box 12 434, Wellington; ☎(04) 494 1540; fax (04) 494 1549; www.ecanz.org.nz.

Engineers Registration Board: Molesworth House, 101 Molesworth St, PO Box 12241, Wellington; ☎(04) 473 9444; fax (04) 474 8933; e-mail ipenz@ipenz.org.nz; www.ipenz.org.nz.

Medical Council of New Zealand: Level 13; Mid City Tower, 139-143 Willis St, PO Box 11-649, Wellington; ☎(04) 384 7635 or free phone within NZ 0800 286 801; fax (04) 385 8902; e-mail info@mcnz.org.nz; www.mcnz.org.nz.

New Zealand Bankers Association: Level 12, Grand Arcade Building, 16 Willis St, PO Box 3043, Wellington; ☎(04) 472 8838; fax (04) 473 1698; e-mail nzba@nxba.org.nz; www.nzba.org.nz.

New Zealand Institute of Management: Level 7 Microsoft House, 3-11 Hunter St, PO Box 67, Wellington; ☎(04) 495 8303; fax (04) 495 8302; e-mail national_office@nzim.co.nz; www.nzim.co.nz. See the website for your local office, or to complete an online enquiry form.

New Zealand Teachers Council: 93 The Terrace, PO Box 5326, Wellington; ☎(04) 471 0852; fax (04) 471 0870; e-mail inquiries@teacherscouncil.govt.nz; www.teacherscouncil.govt.nz.

Nursing Council of New Zealand: PO Box 9644, Wellington; ☎(04) 385 9589; fax (04) 801 8502; e-mail oseas@nursingcouncil.org.nz or nzreg@nursingcouncil.org.nz or admin@nursingcouncil.org.nz; www.nursingcouncil.org.nz.

Pharmaceutical Society of New Zealand: 124 Dixon Street, PO Box 11640, Wellington; ☎(04) 802 0030; fax (04) 382 9297; e-mail p.society@psnz.org.nz or enquiries@pharmacycouncil.org.nz; www.psnz.org.nz.

Plumbers, Gasfitters and Drainlayers Board: PO Box 30229, Lower Hutt; ☎(04) 589 5310; fax (04) 589 5390; e-mail enquiries@pgdb.co.nz; www.pgdb.co.nz (www.pgdb.co.nz/files/Migrants_appn.doc to download the Migrant's Application form).

Real Estate Agents Licensing Board: 29 Gillies Avenue, Epsom, Auckland; ☎(09) 520 6949.

Real Estate Institute of New Zealand: PO Box 5663, Auckland, ☎(09) 356 1755; fax (09) 379 8471; e-mail reinz@reinz.co.nz; www.reinz.org.nz. *Veterinary Council of New Zealand:* PO Box 10 563, Wellington; ☎(04) 473 9600; fax (04) 473 8869; e-mail registration@vetcouncil.org.nz; www.vetcouncil.org.nz.

Placing Employment Wanted Adverts

Another approach is placing an employment wanted advert with the newspapers and specialist publications listed above. You can contact the newspaper and magazine publishers directly for current advertising rates.

EMPLOYMENT AGENCIES

International Organisations

There are a number of organisations that can help you find a job in New Zealand. *Taylor & Associates* specialise in finding jobs for intending migrants, others recruit on behalf of employers and sometimes have New Zealand assignments. The latter type operate on behalf of employers and do not search on behalf of prospective workers, however they will fill some vacancies from people they have on their books so it may be worthwhile sending them a CV and a speculative application. As has been mentioned elsewhere, help with job seeking is one of the services immigration consultancies usually provide.

Recruitment and Job Search Agencies:

Adecco: Level 9, Qantas House, 191 Queen Street, Auckland; ☎(09) 309 7572; fax (09) 309 4197; e-mail auckland@adecco.co.nz; www.adecco.co.nz.

Geneva Health International: 40-42 Parker Street, London WC2B 5PQ; ☎020-7600 0859; fax 020-7600 0944; e-mail janec@genevahealth.co.uk; www.genevahealth.com. NZ: PO Box 106 339, Auckland; ☎(09) 916 0200; fax (09) 916 0201; e-mail info@genevahealth.com.

Global Career Link: International recruitment specialists in finance, accounting, banking, IT, law, HR and sales and marketing. ☎Toll free in NZ: 0800 499 325 or Wellington: +64 4 499 3250, Auckland: +64 9 370 1180; e-mail info@globalcareerlink.co.nz; www.itfutures.co.nz.

JobCafé International: www.jobcafe.co.nz/.

NewJobz: www.newjobz.co.nz.. Attend the *Emigrate* and *Opportunities NZ* Expos in London.

Parker Bridge Recruitment Ltd: UK Offices in London, Edinburgh and Reading; www.parkerbridge.co.uk. London: ☎020-7464 1550; fax 020-7464 1999;

e-mail info@parkerbridge.co.uk. Edinburgh: ☎0131 718 6002; fax 011 718
6125; e-mail Edinburgh@parkerbridge.co.uk. Reading: ☎ 0870 351 7170; fax
0870 351 7171; e-mail reading@parkerbridge.co.uk. NZ offices in Auckland
(☎(09) 377 3727; fax (09) 303 1496) and Wellington (☎(04) 472 4380; fax
(04) 472 4379); www.parkerbridge.co.nz or see the Parker Bridge listings on
www.seek.co.nz. Financial sector.
Prime Recruitment Contracts: 37 Locks Heath Centre, Locks Heath, Southampton,
SO31 6DX; ☎01489-559 090; fax 01489-559995; e-mail contracts@prime-
recruitment.co.uk; www.prime-recruitment.co.uk.
Psych Recruitment: e-mail enquiry@psych-recruitment.com; www.psych-recruit-
ment.com. Psychologists recruitment agency.
Taylor & Associates: PO Box 1401, Chester CH1 1FF; e-mail nzjobs@jobfastrack.
co.nz; www.jobfastrack.co.nz. Initial enquiries are best addressed to the UK
representative office; ☎0845 230 2526; e-mail info@TEGltd.co.uk.
TMP Worldwide Inc: Visit the website to complete an online 'Contact' form;
www.tmp.com. Advertising and communications, and directional marketing.
The website has pages specifically for those from the USA, Australia, Belgium,
France, Germany, Hong Kong, Ireland, Italy, Malaysia, the Netherlands, New
Zealand, Singapore, Spain and the United Kingdom.

Other Useful Websites. For job listings try: www.job.co.nz, http://joblist.co.uk,
www.nzjobs.co.nz, www.kiwicareers.govt.nz; www.monster.com, www.netcheck.
co.nz, www.seek.co.nz and www.workingin-newzealand.com. Bear in mind
though that these do not necessarily represent the entire job market, particularly
towards the senior executive end. For the latest information about the employment
scene, see: www.nzherald.co.nz/employment/.

WorkSite: the New Zealand Employment Service

The Department of Labour in New Zealand provides job-search assistance through
WorkSite, a national network of offices advertising local vacancies. They carry a
wide range of vacancies for casual, skilled and unskilled work, and offer advice and
information on training for job seekers. It also provides a service specifically for
linking the skills of new migrants with the needs of New Zealand employers (e-
mail newkiwis@chamber.co.nz; www.newkiwis.co.nz), which allows you to enter
your details and CV on a database to be searched by potential employers. There is
no fee to use WorkSite or NewKiwis, but you have to be a New Zealand resident or
citizen. Contact WorkSite (e-mail info@worksite.govt.nz) for an office near you.
The New Zealand Department of Labour website may also prove useful (www.
dol.govt.nz).

Employment Agencies in New Zealand

Increasingly, the global talent shortage means that employers rely on agency
databases to supplement responses to their vacancy advertisements. There are a
large number of private employment agencies in New Zealand, and they tend to be
generalist rather than specialist by nature. Most cover all sectors of the economy,
both public and private. Within the consultancies, however, there are often
specialists who focus on specific areas. These agencies charge the employer when
they make a successful placement and are usually free for the job seeker, although

they will offer other services such as career assessment and advice on preparation of CVs for which there may be a charge.

Useful Addresses

Computing/Information Technology

Candle IT&T Recruitment: Level 10, 3-11 Hunter Street, Wellington; ☎(04) 473 9149; fax (04) 460 8676; e-mail equiry.wgtn@candle.co.nz; Level 16, 1 Queen Street, HSBC Building, Auckland; ☎(09) 309 6534; fax (09) 309 3525; e-mail enquiry@candle.co.nz; www.candle.co.nz.

Enterprise Staff Consultants Ltd: 3rd Floor, Ferry Building, 99 Quay Street, Auckland, PO Box 1799, Auckland; ☎(09) 306 2160; fax (09) 307 1285; e-mail auckland@enterprise.co.nz; www.enterprise.co.nz.

Icon: Level 9, Qantas House, 1 Queen Street, PO Box 5151, Wellesley Street, Auckland; ☎(09) 377 3848; fax (09) 377 8685; Level 3 Johnston St, Wellington ☎(04) 472 1566; fax (04) 472 1562; www.iconrec.co.nz.

Information Technology Recruitment (ITEC): PO Box 6798, Wellesley Street, Auckland; ☎(09) 302 5304; fax (09) 373 2968; e-mail Suzan@itec.co.nz (permanent) or Richard@itec.co.nz (contracting); www.itec.co.nz.

IT Futures: PO Box 3246, Wellington: ☎ (04) 499 3250 or 0800 499 325; fax (04) 499 3208; Auckland: ☎(09) 379 1180 or 0800 499 325; fax (09) 379 8114; e-mail info@globalcareerlink.com; www.itfutures.co.nz.

Mercury Consulting Group: Level 3, Optimation House, 1 Grey Street, PO Box 10-605, Wellington; ☎(04) 499 2624; fax (04) 499 6880; e-mail MercuryRegister@mercuryrecruit.co.nz; www.mercuryrecruit.co.nz.

QidR Limited: PO Box 99-319, Newmarket, Auckland; e-mail info@qidr.co.nz; www.qidr.co.nz

Qube Associates Ltd: 5 Reeves Road, Pakuranga, Auckland; ☎(09) 576 7415; fax (09) 576 2894; e-mail info@qube.co.nz; www.qube.co.nz.

Engineering

Career Engineer: PO Box 331 330, Takapuna, Auckland; ☎(09) 489 0820 or 021 666 821; e-mail enquiry@careerengineer.co.nz; www.careerengineer.co.nz.
Engineering and Technical Personnel: www.engineerjobs.co.nz.

Match 2 Recruit: PO Box 30-442, Lower Hutt; ☎(04) 570 0179; fax (04) 570 0122; e-mail cv@match2.co.nz;.www.match2.co.nz

Rob Law Consulting Group: PO Box 10080, Wellington; ☎(04) 499 8800; fax (04) 499 0955. PO Box 8934 Eden Terrace, Auckland; ☎(09) 309 9555; fax (09) 309 0008, e-mail alans@roblaw.co.nz; www.roblaw.co.nz.

TAD Technical Careers and Contracts: Level 9, Qantas House, 191 Queen Street, PO Box 105-199, Wellesley Street, Auckland; ☎(09) 309 9316; fax (09) 309 0212; e-mail auckland@tad.co.nz; www.tad.co.nz.

Technical Recruitment Solutions Ltd: www.trs.co.nz. Offices in Auckland, Wellington and Christchurch.

Farming

Agfirst Consultants NZ Ltd: PO Box 1261, Hastings; ☎(06) 876 9200; fax (06) 876 9225; www.agfirst.co.nz. More than 20 consultants in 12 locations throughout New Zealand: Bay of Plenty (admin@agfirstbop.co.nz), Central Otago (agfirst@ibbotsoncooney.co.nz), Gisborne (gisborne@agfirst.

co.nz), Hawkes Bay (hawkesbay@agfirst.co.nz), Lincoln (alan.street@agfirst. co.nz), Motueka (motueka@agfirst.co.nz), Nelson (bealing@agfirst.co.nz), Rotorua (centralr@agfirst.co.nz), Waikato (john_hall@clear.net.nz and jamesallen@clear,net.nz), Wairoa (ag1@xtra.co.nz) and Whakatane (mark. mac@agrist.co.nz).

Fegan&Co: PO Box 428, Cambridge; ☎(07) 823 0105; fax (07) 823 0107; e-mail enquiries@fegan.co.nz; www.fegan.co.nz.

Fencepost: www.fencepost.com.

Marvin Farm Services: 95 Awara Street, PO Box 248, Matamata, Waikato; ☎(07) 888 6025; fax (07) 888 6023; e-mail info@marvinfarms.co.nz; www.marvin-farms.co.nz.

Nederburg Consultancy: Job & Doortje Huizinga Bruins; 455 Puketutu Road, Matamata; ☎(07) 888 1712; fax (07) 888 1715; e-mail enquiries@nederburg. co.nz; www.nederburg.co.nz.

Finance, Accounting and Banking

Chandler Macleod Group (Recruitment Solutions): Ground Floor, Huddart Parker Building, 1 Post Office Square, Wellington; ☎(04) 473 7693; fax (04) 498 8969; Level 5, HSBC Building, 290 Queen St, Auckland; ☎(09) 379 8771; fax (09) 379 8772; www.recruitmentsolutions.co.nz.

Clayton Ford Recruitment: PO Box 10 083, Wellington; ☎(04) 473 6223; fax (04) 471 2100; e-mail wnweb@claytonford.co.nz; PO Box 7697, Auckland; ☎(09) 379 9924; fax (09) 379 7785; e-mail support.akl@claytonford.co.nz; www.claytonford.co.nz.

DG&A Recruitment Consultants: PO Box 4006, Auckland; ☎(09) 358 0888; fax (09) 303 0254; e-mail debbie.graham@dgal.co.nz; www.debbiegraham.co.nz.

Food Technology

McFoodies Ltd: PO Box 272 1297, Papakura, Auckland; ☎(09) 294 8088 or 021 293 2190; e-mail cathy@mcfoodies.co.nz; www.mcfoodies.co.nz.

Hotel/Catering

Bravo Hospitality Recruitment: PO Box 68-809 Newton, Auckland 1032; ☎(09) 360 9333; fax (09) 360 9330; e-mail 4info@bravogroup.co.nz; www.bravo-group.co.nz. Member of the Restaurant Association of New Zealand.

HHES Hospitality Recruitment: PO Box 90198 AMSC, Level 2/139, Wellesley Street West, Auckland; ☎(09) 379 7532; fax (09) 379 4966; e-mail wayne@hhes. co.nz; www.hhes.co.nz.

Spectrum International Hospitality Services: PO Box 91 083, Auckland Mail Centre; ☎(09) 357 6442; fax (09) 358 0474; e-mail info@spectrum-international.co.nz; www.spectrum-international.com.

Medical/Health

Auckland Medical Bureau: PO Box 37 753, Parnell, Auckland; ☎(09) 377 5903; fax (09) 377 5902; e-mail doctors-amb.nz@xtra.co.nz; www.doctorjobs.co.nz.

Eden Health Recruitment: Free phone from within NZ: 0800 445 999, or from the UK: 0800 0322 107. PO Box 3843, Wellington; ☎(04) 471 4876; fax (04) 471 2100. PO Box 7697, Auckland; ☎(09) 300 4315; fax (09) 918 2031. E-mail general@edenhealth.co.nz; www.edenhealth.co.nz

eNZed Paramedical: 65 MacDonald Road, Glenview, Hamilton 2001; ☎(07) 843 0080; fax (07) 843 0081; e-mail enzedpa@wave.co.nz; www.enzedparamedical.

co.nz.

Health.career.co.nz: http://health.career.co.nz. Adcorp New Zealand, Level 1, 21 Allen Street, Wellington; ☎0800 523 267; e-mail health.career@adcorp.co.nz.

Health Recruitment International: PO Box 205, Wellington; ☎(04) 499 1885 or 0800 188 688; fax (04) 499 1600; e-mail health@recruitment.com; www. healthrecruitment.com.

Medical Staffing International: 35 Kesteven Avenue, Glendowie, PO Box 25-172, St Heliers, Auckland; ☎(09) 575 4258; fax (09) 575 4259; e-mail info@medicalstaffing.co.nz; www.medicalstaffing.co.nz.

Medlink International Recruitment Centre Ltd: Recruit specialist physicians. PO Box 337, Wanganui; ☎(06) 348 7664; fax (06) 348 7665; e-mail info@medlink. co.nz; www.medlink.co.nz.

Professional/Managerial/General

Aacorn International Management Systems: PO Box 101-890, North Shore Mail Centre, Auckland; ☎(09) 357 5090; e-mail aacorn@aacorn.co.nz; www. aacorn.co.nz.

Advanced Personnel: 829 Colombo Street, Christchurch; ☎0800 365 4322; fax (03) 365 7356; Auckland ☎(09) 263 4322; www.advancedpersonnel.co.nz. Also has branches in Invercargill and Nelson.

Drake International: www.drake.co.nz.

IDPE Consulting Group: Level 13, St John House, 114 The Terrace, PO Box 5288, Wellington; ☎(04) 472 2212; fax (04) 472 2211; e-mail info@idpe-consulting. co.nz; www.idpe-consulting.co.nz.

Wheeler Campbell: PO Box 205, Wellington; ☎(04) 499 1500; fax (04) 499 1600; Box 191, Shortland Street, Auckland; ☎(09) 303 4500; fax (09) 303 4501; www.wheelercampbell.co.nz.

Company or Organisation Transfers

One alternative to finding work straight away in New Zealand is to find work with a company with prospects of being transferred to New Zealand. Unfortunately few companies recruit staff with the promise of being posted to a particular country, however if you choose a New Zealand company to work for, your chances are obviously greater. Still this process is likely to be a long-term route into the country. The British/New Zealand Trade Council (Private Bag 92014, Auckland; ☎ (09) 303 2973; fax (09)303 1868; www.brittrade.org.nz) publishes a trade directory of member companies, which might be useful if you are looking for New Zealand companies in the UK. The American Chamber of Commerce in New Zealand publishes a directory of American companies operating in New Zealand (see the address above). The big multinationals also have subsidiaries in New Zealand, sometimes under different names.

JOB APPLICATION

A typical job application will comprise of a letter of application or covering letter and a curriculum vita (CV). Companies short-list on the basis of CVs and interview the selected candidates before making a decision. Depending on the level of job you are applying for, and the company, you may be asked to attend more than one interview.

Application Letters and CVs.

If you are sending off speculative letters it is worth taking the time to ring up the company and find out who the personnel or relevant department manager is. A personally addressed letter is much more effective than one which is clearly a copy of one sent to a dozen other companies.

- O Letters, whether applying for a specific vacancy or inquiring about possible future vacancies, should be formal in tone, brief (one side of an A4 sheet), and should outline why you are particularly qualified to work for the company.
- O Your Curriculum Vitae should provide a concise summary of your contact details, residence status (i.e., permanent residence, work visa, etc.) education, qualifications and computer skills, professional/trade skills, work experience and achievements, professional goals and referees. In New Zealand CVs list jobs and qualifications in reverse chronological order, i.e., the most recent job first and the earliest last.
- O Try to keep your CV brief – somewhere between two and four pages is best – and make sure it is clearly laid out. This is particularly important if you are faxing applications to New Zealand as fax machines blur copy slightly and, if the typeface on your CV is too small, some important details may be lost.
- O These days, most companies prefer you to e-mail your CV to them if you are applying from overseas, so make the effort to ensure that any files you send are well-formatted, clearly laid out, and can be opened in standard programs with a minimum of fuss.
- O It is worthwhile getting some professional advice on the preparation of your CV; services that assist with CVs can be found under Employment Agencies in the Yellow Pages. Do not send original documents with applications.

Your Skills and Qualifications

Some employers require you to have professional registration even if this is not a legal requirement. This means that the status of your professional training and qualifications is extremely important. Although you may be professionally qualified in you home country and even have a number of years experience, this does not mean your experience and qualifications will automatically be recognised in New Zealand. The *New Zealand Qualifications Authority* (NZQA) evaluates professional and academic qualifications. This is done as a comparison with similar qualifications obtainable in New Zealand, and is designed to determine whether or not qualifications from overseas meet the same standards as are applied in New Zealand. If your qualifications do not meet New Zealand standards, you may have to undertake retraining or extra study to secure the kind of job you want. Bear in mind that, although NZQA evaluations are official assessments, they are not binding on employers, professional bodies or educational institutions.

It is a good idea to contact the NZQA before you set out for New Zealand. You should ensure that you bring original or certified copies of all certificates, diplomas, degrees and professional qualifications with you when you move, as prospective employers may well need to sight these for themselves.

References

Unlike in the UK, in New Zealand it is customary to have several written references from previous employers, which you offer to provide when applying for a position. Some advertisements will ask that you send a covering letter, CV and references. This does not usually mean a list of people for prospective employers to contact, although your usual list of verbal references should still accompany your application. In New Zealand it is customary for each employer you work for to provide you with a reference (you still need to request this though) when you leave a job. Bearing this in mind, it is worthwhile at least asking your most recent employer for a written reference before you leave home. If references and academic/professional certificates are not requested with the application itself, they will be requested later for review during the job selection process. Make sure that you either deliver these personally or by courier, and that they are returned to you once the job selection is completed.

Interview Procedure

If you are applying for a job in New Zealand from overseas, and a company wishes to interview you, in most cases they will not be prepared to pay your travel costs. Some companies will arrange interviews by video link or telephone. Another option to consider is arranging a number of job interviews to coincide with a visit to New Zealand, or your arrival if your residency has been approved. There are international job search companies that specialise in lining up job interviews before you set off for New Zealand. If you are using an agency to assist you with your residency application, they may have an employment-search facility or should at least be able to point you in the right direction by recommending recruitment agencies in your field.

Job interviews in New Zealand tend to be quite formal and you should dress appropriately for a work situation. If you are concerned about brushing up your job search and interview skills, most bookshops stock 'how to' guides for finding work.

It is illegal for employers to discriminate on the basis of gender, race, colour, marital status or sexual orientation. Firms will usually have an Equal Employment Opportunity (EEO) policy in their Mission Statement and will have a quota set of the proportion of their workers who are from minority groups.

ASPECTS OF EMPLOYMENT

Salaries

You should not expect a New Zealand salary to be the same as a salary in your home country once the exchange rate is taken into account. Salaries in New Zealand are lower than those for equivalent positions in the USA, the UK and Europe. In some areas, living costs are lower as well, although many new migrants report surprise at the costs involved in living in Auckland and Wellington, in particular.

> **Kim Cullen found salaries low compared to North America**
> *Because of the high cost of living we are not planning on staying down here permanently. Once I finish school, we will be moving back up to the Northern Hemisphere - the States, Canada. . . . wherever I can get a good job for my skills. I would advise not moving here if you have any large US debt - credit card, student loan, etc. Several Americans I know have left NZ because they could not afford to live here at the same time as saving a little money and attempting to pay off their US debt. Unfortunately, New Zealand salaries have not kept up with the high cost of living. Travelling around NZ for several months and obtaining a short-term work visa might be the way to go if money is an issue for you.*

It is difficult to make a direct comparison of living standards because so many factors are difficult to compare. For example, going overseas for an annual holiday becomes very expensive when the nearest country is three hours away, and that is only Australia. On the other hand, you have easy access to great beaches and can enjoy much better climate than northern Europeans, year round. As a generalisation, it would be fair to say that living standards are equivalent for most middle income earners.

It is a good time to look at working in New Zealand, providing you accept that working life there may be quite different to working in your home country. There have been dramatic changes in employment trends in many industries over the last ten to fifteen years, and the changes are ongoing. Similar changes are occurring in most developed (OECD) nations. As the workforce is growing older and there has been a big drop in the birth rate, there aren't so many young people to replace those who retire. An increasing number of people from other countries are working in New Zealand, so the workforce is becoming more multi-ethnic. Another change is the types of jobs that people are working in — more jobs are part-time as people become less willing to sacrifice their lifestyle and family life for their work. That's not to say that they aren't still looking for a good salary though!

As you might expect for a relatively lightly populated country, typical New Zealand businesses are small compared to those in other countries. However, many large multinational businesses have offices in New Zealand, and there is a strong government sector, particularly in Wellington. The job market varies widely from one region to another, and obviously most of the government jobs and positions within large organisations are based in the bigger cities. Depending on your chosen occupation though, there may well be exciting opportunities in regional centres as well.

The minimum legal wage is $7.20 per hour for workers aged 16-17 and $9.00 an hour for those over 18 years old. Despite New Zealand's egalitarian attitudes and equal employment policies, there is still some pay disparity between men and women. The Statistics New Zealand lists average ordinary time hourly earnings as $21.17 for males and $18.21 for females.

TABLE 22	AVERAGE HOURLY EARNINGS 2004
Average:	$19.81
Private sector:	$18.53
Public sector:	$24.77
Accommodation/cafes/restaurants:	$13.16
Retail:	$13.97
Construction:	$17.62
Personal Services:	$18.68
Transport, storage and communications:	$19.17
Manufacturing:	$19.06
Health and community services:	$20.12
Wholesale trade:	$20.63
Cultural and recreational activities:	$20.88
Forestry and mining:	$21.13
Property and business services:	$22.68
Education:	$24.89
Government administration and defence:	$25.22
Electricity, gas and water:	$27.04
Finance and insurance:	$27.79
(based on the Statistics New Zealand Employment Survey 2004).	

Working Conditions

Standard conditions of employment are still generally 40-hour weeks, 8.30am-5pm, five days a week. However, with flexible working arrangements under the industrial relations legislation, variations on this theme, such as glide time, have become increasingly common. For example Fisher & Paykel, New Zealand's largest manufacturer of kitchen and laundry appliances has shifted to ten hour shifts, four days a week, in some of their divisions. Rates for overtime are another area changing due to the impact of new legislation. In most industries, overtime was one and half times the standard rates, but in many sectors now, particularly for casual workers and in the service sector, overtime rates are being cut back or disappearing entirely. You are more likely now to be awarded a day or hours off in lieu of extra hours worked, rather than actually being paid for them. In areas such as retail you may be paid overtime if you are required to work a public holiday. Longer working hours are also becoming a feature of many industries. Holiday provision is still protected by law under the Holidays Act. After twelve months' continuous employment, the employee is entitled to three weeks paid leave. In addition, there are eleven paid public holidays annually. Employees do not have to work on public holidays unless they agree or their contract provides for this. Remember that these will only be paid holidays if they actually fall on a day on which you would normally work. There is no compulsory retirement age anymore, although entitlement to National Superannuation is assessed from the age of 65.

Parental Leave

The minimum legislative rights to Parental Leave are laid out in the Parental Leave and Employment Protection Act 1987. Employees adopting a child under six years old are also entitled to parental leave. It is not automatic, you must apply for it. The period of leave is the same for adoptive parents, but there are differences in the advanced notice you are required to give. There are different entitlements for leave, depending on whether the employee has worked for the same employer for an average of at least 10 hours per week for either the immediately preceding six months or the immediately preceding 12 months before the expected due date or adoption of a child. To be eligible, you must have worked at least an average of 10 hours each week, including at least one hour a week or 40 hours per month, for the same employer for 12 months before the expected due date or adoption. The types of leave are as follows:

Special Leave. Up to ten days during pregnancy for women to have ante-natal appointments or classes.

Maternity Leave. Up to fourteen continuous weeks for the mother, which can start up to six weeks before the expected date of birth or adoption. Maternity leave may be commenced up to six weeks before the date of birth or adoption.

Partner's/Paternity Leave: Up to two continuous weeks for the father around the expected date of birth or adoption. The mother may transfer the entitlement to parental leave payments to her partner, in which case the period of the partner's/paternity leave is extended to match the length of time the payment is received by the partner.

Extended Leave. Up to 52 continuous weeks, excluding any maternity leave taken in the twelve months after the birth. Extended leave may be shared by both parents but may not exceed 52 weeks in total.

All leave must be taken in the first year after the birth or adoption. You will not be eligible for another period of parental leave unless the expected date of delivery or adoption of subsequent children is at least 12 months after your return to work from a previous parental leave. Each partner must take any period of extended leave in a continuous period. The leave can be taken at the same time or separately, to suit the needs of the parents and the child. You are required to give three weeks notice of your intention to either return or not return to work. In the case of miscarriage, stillbirth, death or adoption, you may return to work early, but are still required to give 21 days notice.

Job Protection. If you take less than four weeks parental leave, your job must be kept open. If you take more than four weeks, the employer may decide that the job cannot be kept open, but you have a right to challenge that decision. If you accept this decision then you are entitled to a preference period of six months when the employer must offer you a job substantially similar to the one you have left. In the small number of cases where an employer does not have to keep the job open, the employee is still entitled to 13 weeks paid leave. You may not be dismissed for becoming pregnant or for applying for parental leave. Your employment contract may contain special provisions. For further information, contact the Employment Relations Service (☎ 0800 800 863; www.ers.dol.govt.nz).

Trade Unions

Prior to the Employment Contracts Act of 1991, New Zealand unions enjoyed a monopoly over workplace representation and union membership in many industries was compulsory. The resulting system of wage determination was highly centralised and inflexible. If unions and employers negotiating in each industry at a national level could not agree, the dispute would be settled through compulsory arbitration by a tribunal made up of members from both sides. As a result of this system, employment conditions were guaranteed at some minimum level in just about all industries, and the disparity between the high paid and the low paid was not very great.

The Employment Contracts Act of 1991 removed union monopolies over bargaining in the workplace, abolished compulsory membership, and the Arbitration Tribunals. Wage fixing is now in theory completely decentralised, although some of the bigger unions still negotiate at national level. Employers and employees negotiate employment contracts, which may be either collective or individual. Employees may nominate someone to act as their bargaining agent. Employers are obliged to recognise whomever an employee nominates as their bargaining agent, although this does not mean they must negotiate or settle with that agent. Trade unions no longer have a protected legal status, and total membership fell from approximately 683,000 in 1985 to approximately 339,000 in 1996, and has grown from less than 200,000 three years ago to almost 300,000 today. The number of employees on collective agreements has also fallen sharply; the majority of the workforce is now employed on individual contracts. Flexibility has brought benefits to some employees and industries but has weakened the position of others. Part time workers, those in workplaces with only a few employees and the service sector generally all have less job security, fewer employment protections and in some cases have seen a real reduction in pay.

The Employment Relations Act (2000) inserts into all collective agreements a requirement to deduct union fees where the employee consents. Unions and employers may vary these arrangements in a collective agreement. Employers must allow union representatives to come into the workplace and union officials must exercise their access rights in a reasonable way. Union members are entitled to attend two union meetings (of up to two hours each) each year. Employers must pay union members who attend these meetings during their normal working hours. Under this Act, any group of employees can set up and register as a union, provided they first become an incorporated society (under the Incorporated Societies Act, 1908) and then register as a union under the 2000 Act. Such groups must have a minimum of fifteen members, be independent of employers, and have a set of union rules.

Most New Zealand unions belong to the national body: The New Zealand Council of Trade Unions (PO Box 6645, Wellington; ☎ (04) 385 1334; fax (04) 385 6051; www.union.org.nz or www.ctu.org.nz). The NZCTU publishes a comprehensive directory of all trade unions in the country. The Employment Relations Service can also provide information (☎ 0800 800 863; www.ers.dol.govt.nz).

Employment Contracts

At the beginning of your employment you will negotiate an employment contract with your employer. You can be covered under an existing collective contract if it provides for new workers to join and if your employer agrees. Otherwise you will negotiate an individual contract. Individual contracts can be either written or oral but it is desirable to have a written contract. If you wish to have a bargaining agent represent you, you have a choice between joining a union or employing a private bargaining agent. Remember that though your employer must recognise your bargaining agent they are not obliged to settle with them. An employment contract must by law have certain provisions. There must be an effective personal grievance procedure and disputes procedure. The minimum conditions outlined above — wages and holiday provision and the parental leave provisions — cannot be overridden, although they can be improved upon. A good checklist for individual employment contracts can be obtained from the magazine published by a network of independent legal firms called *Lawlink* (PO Box 6197, Wellesley Street, Auckland; ☎ (09) 300 5470; fax (09) 309 5113), or found on their website (www.lawlink.co.nz).

Employment Tribunal & Employment Court

Two institutions for resolving disputes were set up under the Act — the Tribunal, which mostly mediates in disputes, either personal disputes or grievances arising from breach of employment contracts, and the Employment Court which deals with matters referred on by the Tribunal, and more serious issues such as disputes involving strikes and lockouts. There is no right to strike while an employment contract is still current.

Women in Work

Around 60% of New Zealand women (over the age of 15) work in either full- or part-time jobs. This figure has been steadily increasing since the 1960s, although it seems to have reached a plateau in recent years after it dropped off slightly in the late 1980s, which may reflect the effects of the economic downturn. The participation rates for women are considerably lower than the corresponding figures for men across all age groups, and particularly in the 25-34 age group, reflecting the fact that women are still the primary care givers for children.

Despite still bearing more family responsibilities than men, New Zealand women are moving into previously male dominated areas, particularly the professions. Female students outnumber men in areas such as medicine and law, although this is a recent development and men still dominate at senior levels in these professions.

Equal pay for the same work was established under the Equal Pay Act of 1972, and other forms of discrimination in the workplace based on gender, race or any other non-relevant factor is illegal under the Human Rights Commission Act of 1972. If you believe you have been discriminated against unlawfully, you can either use the personal grievance procedures in your employment contract or you can make a complaint to the Human Rights Commission. Between 1987 and 2003 there was a substantial reduction in the gender pay gap; the average hourly earnings of women rose during that time from 79% to 88% of men's average hourly earnings. However, there is still a significant difference in income levels between men and women. Women are still concentrated in a narrower range of occupations, which, in general, pay less well. Equal pay claims are also harder to establish in the new environment of individual contracts. Discrimination in individual cases is much harder to prove than in a situation where everyone receives the same rate of pay for a job. However, the attitude towards women in employment in New Zealand is generally positive. Childcare is becoming more affordable now that the government subsidises pre-school care centres. Some of these advances have been achieved through the efforts of women politicians. Women have a high profile in New Zealand public life. A third of the members of parliament are women and Helen Clark is New Zealand's second female Prime Minister.

For more information about women in New Zealand contact the Ministry of Women's Affairs (PO Box 10 049, Wellington; ☎(04) 915 7112; fax (04) 916 1604; e-mail mwa@mwa.govt.nz; www.mwa.govt.nz) or the National Advisory Council on the Employment of Women (NACEW, c/- Department of Labour, PO Box 3705, Wellington; (04) 915 4260; fax (04) 915 4040; e-mail NACEW@dol. govt.nz; www.nacew@dol.govt.nz).

PERMANENT WORK

Executive Employment Prospects

Prospects are good for executive employment as the local labour market is unable to provide enough suitably skilled applicants for the growing demand. However, the executive vacancies are for people with a high level of technical and interpersonal skills.

Information Technology

There is always a demand for skilled programmers, particularly those with university level qualifications. New Zealanders qualified in these areas tend to be attracted overseas by the comparatively higher salaries, for a time at least. As a result, 'IT Specialists' is a constantly recurring entry on the Long Term and Immediate Shortage Lists (Long Term Skill Shortage List) (occupations listed on the Priority Occupations List are considered to be in shortage in all regions). There are a few rules of course – you will need a Bachelor of Science, with majors in computer science or information science, and you must be qualified, which, in this case, means a minimum of three years full-time work experience with at least 12 months work experience in the past 18 months in at least one of the specifications on the Information Technology Skills List.

TABLE 24 INFORMATION TECHNOLOGY SKILLS LIST	
Type	Specialisations
Application Development	C
	Delphi
	Visual Basic.net
	C#
	C#.net
	Embedded C
Networking Technologies	Cisco
Databases (DBMS)	Oracle
	Data –
	Warehousing
ERP (Enterprise Resource Planning)	SAP
	People Soft
	Navision
Other	Citrix
	.net

Medical

Doctors. The numbers of foreign doctors registering with the Medical Council has increased in recent years and there is some concern that this may lead to an oversupply of medical personnel. The increase in numbers seems to be the result of an increase in numbers of skilled immigrants, particularly from South Africa, which has resulted in a reverse 'brain-drain'. The situation in New Zealand has usually been the opposite with trained New Zealanders going abroad leaving opportunities for qualified migrants. You should contact the Medical Council for an accurate assessment of employment opportunities. As has been noted already, you must register with the Medical Council in order to practice as a doctor in New Zealand. Doctors from Australia, Britain, Ireland and South Africa, who have been registered in their own country, are usually accepted for registration without requiring further qualifications. Doctors from other countries will usually have to sit registration exams.

Nurses. Nurses must apply to be registered with the Nursing Council of New Zealand. There is a current demand for general nurses, and especially for experienced nurses and midwives with specialist skills.

Teaching

There are excellent work opportunities within the New Zealand education system. At the time of print, there is a particular demand for early childhood teachers and secondary school teachers of English, mathematics, physics, chemistry, ICT, technology, computing and physical education. Teachers of children with special needs are also needed in early childhood services, and primary and secondary schools. Qualified, experienced teachers of children with learning or behavioural issues, those working with children with physical disabilities and teachers of English to speakers of other languages are sought after at present. The majority of overseas-trained teachers appointed to New Zealand schools come from The UK, Ireland,

Australia, Canada and South Africa. Across the board, there is such demand that registered teachers originally from New Zealand who have gone overseas to work are being offered a $5000 incentive to return home to work. Contact TeachNZ for more information (TeachNZ, Ministry of Education, PO Box 1666, Wellington; www.teachnz.govt.nz).

As noted earlier in this section, immigrants intending to teach must have their qualifications verified and checked for comparability with New Zealand qualifications by the New Zealand Qualifications Authority. Teacher registration is compulsory for all teachers in the state sector in New Zealand. The TeachNZ website has details and you can electronically request the relevant forms. The *Education Gazette* is published fortnightly and advertises all permanent teaching positions in state and independent schools. You can read the *Gazette* online, where it is constantly updated (www.edgazette.govt.nz), or by subscribing directly to PO Box 249, Wellington (☎ (04) 917 3990; fax (04) 917 3991). Teaching positions in universities and polytechnics are usually advertised on the institutions' own websites.

SHORT-TERM EMPLOYMENT

Short-term employment prospects are improving as the economy continues to grow. However, as already noted in *Residence and Entry* unless you are a New Zealander or have residency you will have to get a work visa to work while in New Zealand, even for a short period. One of the conditions of these visas is that you are doing jobs for which there are no appropriately qualified New Zealanders. Given that the types of jobs most people obtain while travelling are unskilled labouring jobs, your chances of working legitimately are not great. There is a lot of paperwork for your employer to get through (see Chapter Two) just to hire a fruit picker.

Alternatively, if you are a British, Dutch, French, German or Irish citizen aged between 18 and 30 you can apply for a working holiday visa before you leave for New Zealand (see the *Residence and Entry* chapter for details). If you do not have a work permit, some farmers may not be too concerned if they have short term jobs, particularly seasonal jobs in rural areas, and cannot find locals interested in doing them. Under these circumstances you may find that employers are more interested in whether you are hard working than legal. But be careful, because in recent years the Immigration Service has been doing sweeps of picking gangs in remote areas to check whether they have work permits. You may endanger your chances of staying in New Zealand if you try to bend the rules on working.

Horticulture and Agriculture

There are many opportunities for keen workers in orchards, even if you have little or no experience. However, since the work is unskilled you will find that pay rates are far from high. Fruit picking tends to be paid at what is called piece rates (rates per kilo or bin filled). Obviously as you get better at the work your pay rates will improve, but it can be discouraging at first, as well as backbreaking depending on the crop; asparagus picking is reputed to be the worst. It is possible to follow the different harvests around the country as each type of produce comes into season and to find work virtually year round. In the main horticultural areas during the harvest, work will not be hard to find. Farmers advertise locally, sometimes contacting local youth hostels or backpackers' accommodation, or simply putting a sign up at the gate. There is occasionally accommodation available, albeit of a rather basic kind, and you may be provided with some food, such as fresh fruit and vegetables or dairy products. Generally the remoter the area, the more difficulty the farmers have in attracting local labour, so the better your chances. However this is no guarantee that they will be able to pay more, they are just more likely to provide non-wage perks such as accommodation or food in order to get the workers. For details of the timing and locations of various harvests see *Work Your Way Around the World* available from Vacation Work Publications (9 Park End Street, Oxford OX1 1HJ; ☎01865-241978; fax 01865-790885; www.vacationwork.co.uk). Alternatively, see the website www.seasonalwork.co.nz for different kinds of jobs all around the country, or e-mail Janine@seasonalwork.co.nz.

Unlike fruit picking, working on farms usually requires some experience. For example, you will see almost daily advertisements in the Waikato papers for milkers, but they require people who are already skilled. Some unskilled work is available in shearing sheds, for example the job of rousie (the person who picks up the shorn fleeces), which does not require much beyond a strong pair of arms. If you have some practical farming experience under your belt and want work on a New Zealand farm, you can look for vacancies on the Farm News website (www.farmnews. co.nz) or advertise your skills on the Agrijobs website (www.agrisupportonline. com). Another useful contact might be FRENZ International, which specialises in permanent and temporary placement for dairy farm workers. You can use an online application form to apply. (PO Box 7582, Wellesley Street, Auckland; ☎+64 (0)9 361 2658; fax +64 (0)9 361 2683; e-mail mail@frenz.co.nz; www.frenz.co.nz.

Wine production is one of New Zealand's fastest growing industries. Innovative sustainable and environmentally friendly vineyard and industry practices are ensuring that New Zealand meets the international demand for wine produced in a 'clean, green' environment. Further expansion is expected as the number of vineyards continues to increase. Often there is casual work available on vineyards tying up the vines, and also during the grape harvest, particularly in the Marlborough and Hawke's Bay regions. The Wine Industry jobsite might be a useful place to start looking (www.wineindustryjobs.com.au). For general information about seasonal work see the WINZ website (www.winz.govt.nz).

Au Pair/Nannying

There is some demand for nannies and au pairs in New Zealand — the generic term child-carer is more usual. With the growing number of training courses available in New Zealand, you probably stand a better chance at these jobs if you actually have a child-care qualification. Posts are advertised in the daily papers or on community notice boards. There are several specialist agencies that can be found in the Yellow Pages or on the internet. Wages are quite low, but such jobs sometimes involve 'living in', so you may avoid food and accommodation expenses.

Useful Addresses
NZ Nanny Support Service: (for preschoolers) ☎0800 462 669; www.nanny.

co.nz.

PORSE Nanny Childcare Network: Offices in Auckland, Rotorua, Johnsonville/ Tawa and Upper Hutt, Lower Hutt, Hastings, Wellington, Howick, Napier, Hamilton, Tauranga, Papamoa, New Plymouth, Palmerston North, Christ-church; see the website for location-specific contact details: www.porsenz.com.

Teaching English

New Zealand is a popular destination for Asian students wanting to learn English, because of its reputation as a safe and friendly country. As an employment prospect you will almost certainly need the appropriate TEFL or ESL qualifications or experience in order to get a work permit, because as has already been noted above, the Immigration Service has to be satisfied that you have skills not possessed by New Zealand job seekers. Speaking English as your first language is not enough to qualify you. There are many public and private English-language schools, mainly based in Auckland, Wellington and Christchurch.

Useful Addresses

Aspect ILA New Zealand: Head Office, 116 Worcester St, PO Box 25170, Christ-church; ☎(03) 379 5452; fax (03) 379 5373; e-mail ilachch@ila.co.nz; www. ila.co.nz.

Capital Language Academy: 119-125 Ghuznee Street, Post Box 1100, Wellington; ☎(04) 801 6010; fax (04) 385 6655; e-mail enquiries@cla.co.nz; www.cla. co.nz.

Dominion English Schools: 67 Customs St, Auckland, PO Box 4217, Auckland; ☎(09) 377 3280; fax (09) 377 3473; e-mail english@dominion.co.nz; www. dominion.school.nz.

Dominion English Schools: 4th Floor, 116 Worcester Street, PO Box 3908, Christchurch; ☎(03) 365 3370; fax (03) 365 5215; e-mail study@dominion.school.nz; www.dominion.school.nz.

Garden City English School: Level 2 Vero House, Hereford Street, PO Box 2851, Christchurch; ☎(03)3770091;fax(03)3771251;e-mailinfo@EnglishLanguage. school.nz; www.EnglishLanguage.school.nz .

Languages International: PO Box 5293, Auckland 1036; ☎(09) 309 0615; fax (09) 377 2806; e-mail info@languages.ac.nz; www.langsint.co.nz.

Seafield School of English: 71 Beresford St, PO Box 18516, New Brighton, Christ-church; ☎(03) 388 3850; www.seafield.co.nz.

Southern English Schools: 69 Worcester Bvd, PO Box 1300, Christchurch; ☎(03) 365 6022; fax (03) 365 6133; e-mail info@ses.co.nz; www.ses.ac.nz.

Tourism/Hospitality

There are a lot of opportunities for casual workers in the tourist regions. Tourist destinations are a good place to start looking for hotel, bar and catering staff positions. It is usually easy to find café work in the main cities, and knowing your way around an espresso machine gives you a definite advantage. Kitchen hand and table waiting jobs are often advertised in local newspapers by the restaurants of large hotels. Working hours are long and the pay relatively low, but on the other hand, the location may make up for the working conditions and it's a good way to make some new friends. Tourists tip better than locals do, as New Zealanders traditionally do not tip serving staff. If you can ski and have the relevant qualification, there are many opportunities on New Zealand ski fields for ski instructors or ski patrol personnel. Other types of skills that may help you find employment include aquatic sports skills such as scuba diving, water skiing, or life-saving skills. New Zealand beaches are patrolled mostly by volunteer surf life savers who are well trained and experienced in rescuing people from the often turbulent and dangerous waters, so you are more likely to find employment looking after hotel or private pools. Qualified aerobics instructors and personal trainers should find opportunities at the many private gyms around the country. Word-of-mouth or being in the right place at the right time is often key to securing these kinds of positions, so don't be shy about walking in and enquiring as to whether there are any vacancies, or leave your CV, and let the people you meet locally know what you are looking for as well. Sometimes it's not what you know, it's who you know!

Voluntary Work

If you want to avoid work permit hassles and still be legal, there are voluntary schemes whereby you can work in exchange for food and lodgings. The most well known scheme goes under the name of WWOOF, which stands for Willing Workers On Organic Farms. There are many organic farms in New Zealand so there is the possibility that you could see quite a lot of the country without actually paying for your own keep. Usually you do about half a day's work in exchange for board. The work can be quite varied and you will usually be supplied with strictly vegetarian rations. You should contact Jane and Andrew Strange directly in New Zealand (PO Box 1172, Nelson; tel/fax (03) 544 9890; e-mail support@wwoof. co.nz) to join for a fee of US$30/CAD$38/£16/24 Euro. See the WWOOF websites for further information (www.wwoof.co.nz and www.organicvolunteers. com).

Some members of the BioDynamic Farming and Gardening Association (NZ) Inc offer food and board in exchange for work at certain times of the year. For further information and a list of members, see the website (www.organicpathways. co.nz).

The NZ Trust for Conservation Volunteers is another organisation that offers volunteer work. Projects include such activities as beach clean-ups and planting native forest. Lists of upcoming projects, and contact details for organisers, can be found on the website (www.conservationvolunteers.org.nz). Project lengths vary, and so does the provision of accommodation and food depending on where, when and for how long you will be going.

BUSINESS AND INDUSTRY REPORT

From late 2005, net exports are forecast to start making a positive contribution to growth for the first time since late in 2001, according to the Treasury and Statistics New Zealand. This turnaround is due to ongoing growth in the world economy and the delayed effects of exchange rate depreciation. While there has been rapid growth in import volumes recently, this is set to calm down and remain relatively subdued while export volume growth accelerates significantly. Economic growth begins to rebound in late 2005 and early 2006, with annual GDP growth steadily increasing to around 3.4% at the end of 2006 and beginning of 2007. Increase in export volumes contributes to strong growth in export earnings and nominal export earnings are forecast to grow by 9.4% in the 2007 March year. Gross national expenditure also begins to pick up, although in a more modest manner, increasing from 2% to 3% during 2006 and signalling gentle domestic growth demand. Annual wage growth is anticipated to drop below 4% in early 2006, but will remain above 3.5%. Businesses should look to seek improvements in labour productivity rather than suddenly and dramatically increasing employment levels. It looks as though employment will increase annually by about 1.5% from the end of 2006 onwards, and this will combine with lower population growth to lower the unemployment rate further. By 2007/08 real GDP growth of 3.0% is forecast, and domestic demand will grow at approximately the same rate as GDP. Nominal GDP is forecast to rise at a rate of about 5% a year.

Agriculture and Forestry

The agriculture and forestry sector is one of the largest in the New Zealand economy, and together with its processing and support components regularly contributes more than $21 billion a year (about 20%) to the GDP. Major exports from this sector include meat, dairy products, wool, wood products and horticultural products, as well as a number of specialised products for international niche markets. New Zealand meat processors annually produce 660,000 tonnes of beef and veal, 430,000 tonnes of lamb and 110,000 tonnes of mutton. The dairy sector exports more than 370,000 of butter, 29,000 tonnes of cheese and 140,000 tonnes of casein products. The forestry industry produces the equivalent of 23million cubic metres of wood and exports the roundwood equivalent of 16million cubic metres (9 million of this is unprocessed logs and chips).

From horticulture, exports include about 65million trays of kiwifruit and 17million cartons of apples each year. Export earnings are predicted to rise to $2.3billion in 2005, and to reach $3.5billion in 2010. The one area where decline is expected is pipfruit; as increasing competition will come from southern hemisphere suppliers, especially Chile, and rising production in some northern hemisphere countries. This is expected to stabilise, however. As well as fruit, the industry also includes vegetables, nurseries, and horticultural property services such as landscape gardening and arboriculture. The main areas of production are Northland, Greater Auckland, Bay of Plenty, Gisborne, Hawkes Bay, Nelson, Marlborough, Canterbury and Otago. In these areas, horticulture is one of the key employers and economic contributors, providing direct returns to producers, marketers and processors, and contributing to the local infrastructure. It is estimated that over 44,000 people are employed in this industry throughout the country, with thousands of additional workers employed seasonally by orchardists and flower and vegetable farmers to assist with harvesting and packaging produce. The size of the horticulture industry is estimated to exceed $3.7 billion, and the main export markets are Asia (including Japan, the EU, the UK, the USA and Australia, but produce is sent to over 100 countries around the world. Sales in the domestic market also generate around $2million.

New Zealand's is one of the most efficient agricultural sectors in the world and farmers receive no government subsidy. The removal of supplementary minimum payments in 1984 was predicted by many in the farming sector to be a disaster.

Instead, although some farmers were forced to sell up, the sector responded by becoming more efficient and although farmland prices have not yet recovered to their pre-SMP prices, farm profitability is once again favourable. Farmers are now vulnerable to world prices in agricultural commodities and as a result many have diversified in order to spread their risk. Reliance upon traditional production areas has declined: sheep numbers dropped in response to low wool prices, but New Zealand is still the second largest wool exporter in the world. Despite the uncertainty of trading at world prices, the removal of subsidies seems to have done the industry good. The diversity of output has helped the country expand its export markets.

Agriculture is a major employer and at the time of the last census there were 114,000 people employed in agricultural production (7% of total employment in the country). Out of this number, 26,900 were employed in horticulture and fruit growing, 36,600 were in grain, sheep and beef cattle farming, 35,000 were in dairy cattle farming and 15,500 worked in poultry and other livestock farming. Forestry and first-stage wood processing accounted for 22,500 (at the time, 1.3% of the workforce).

The impact of the 1995 GATT agreement improved market access for New Zealand's agricultural exports. The European Union has lifted the restrictive quotas, which prevented access for New Zealand butter and lamb into European markets. The most important export markets are the USA, Japan, Australia, Korea and the UK. The industry is good at reacting to world market demand by changing land use to suit demand, moving to more profitable areas, and specialising and developing products for niche market areas, as it has done with manuka honey and fine merino wool. It is expected that increasing world demand for organic products will be positive for New Zealand, as its isolation, strict organic-growing regulations and 'clean and green' image put it in an excellent position to take advantage of the fact that demand is exceeding supply in many other countries. Organic growers currently contribute approximately $500million to export earnings.

The wine industry has expanded rapidly over the last decade, due to increased demand from overseas consumers, and exports account for over $230 million. It is anticipated that wine exports will double over the next five years. Major wine markets are the UK, the US and Australia. Over 50% of the area planted with grapes is in the South Island – the Nelson/Marlborough region being the largest wine-growing region.

For further information, see www.maf.govt.nz, www.fedfarm.org.nz, www. organicsnewzealand.org.nz, and www.nzwine.com.

Agritech and Life Sciences

These sectors are adding significant value and high tech innovation to New Zealand's oldest foundation industries. The agritech sector has revenues in excess of $3billion, and as such is a major contributor to New Zealand's economic wealth. New Zealand agritech companies are world leaders in their field, and have grown their annual exports to over $650million as they have adapted to international markets. This sector is diverse, but covers all pre-harvest inputs for agriculture including fertilisers and grass seeds, breeding genetics and animal remedies, equipment, and also agricultural tourism. The equine industry is another land-based sector that has thrived in New Zealand, achieving exports of around $150million and a world-class success record. The natural products sector is a new but fast-growing export industry for New Zealand, and includes 'nutraceuticals', health products and health foods. Currently (and conservatively) exports are calculated to be around $100million annually. Biotechnology is another important facet of the life sciences sector and will be discussed further below. Suffice it to say that the Government has recently highlighted this area as one integral to the long-term future economic growth of New Zealand. During the next three to five years, New Zealand Trade and Enterprise (NZTE) has a plan in place to focus activities in these areas on increasing the number of markets and finding niche markets for New Zealand products within other farming methods worldwide. International business development is also a priority, with particular emphasis on high-growth markets in North America, Europe and North Asia.

Biotechnology

Along with ICT and the creative sectors, the biotechnology has been identified as a key potential contributor in terms of economic growth in the Government's Growth for Innovation (GIF) Framework. With over 300 support organisations involved, as well as the scientific community and research institutes, this industry sustains at least 3,900 jobs. Current export earnings for this sector are estimated at about $250million annually. It is a growing industry; almost 50% of the 42 core biotechnology companies were created in the last three years.

Finance and Insurance

Finance includes activities such as banking, accounting, sharebroking, financial planning, and business administration. Finance contributes around 4% to GDP and, combined with the insurance industry and services, has recently seen annual profits of nearly $8 billion. In 2001 there were just over 73,000 people employed in the combined finance and insurance industries, and this is expected to increase to nearly 80,500 by 2006. Statistics New Zealand figures show that, in 2003, 7,320 people were employed in the insurance industry. Most of the large companies and banks in New Zealand are internationally owned companies operating globally, and competition for market share has resulted in many mergers and takeovers as well as regular reshuffling over the last few years. There are 17 registered banks in the country; of these only the Taranaki Savings Bank (TSB) and Kiwibank are New Zealand-owned. As a result of the dominance of multinational companies, smaller businesses have to diversify and offer extra services in order to attract clients. In recent years, some of the foreign owned large companies have shut their doors in New Zealand and now base their Australasian operations in Australia. Most insurance companies operating in New Zealand are also part of large multinational firms. Although there are 313 insurance companies registered in New Zealand, the most dominant companies in the general insurance field are State and NZI. For life insurance, some of the largest companies are AMP, AXA and Sovereign. The main area of growth in insurance work has been in customer service and call centre roles. The increase in call centre work is linked to the centralisation mentioned above, as call centres allow nationwide queries to be handled in one location.

Businesses have become more accountable to their shareholders, and to government authorities, which means that insurance companies have more constraints placed on them through general laws (such as the Privacy Act and the Consumer Guarantees Act), and, because of this increased accountability, businesses are taking out more liability insurance, so demand is growing in that area. Most finance and insurance companies are now centralised (although at one time many of these companies would have had branches nationwide), and Auckland and Wellington provide the largest number of employees to this sector.

The fast growth in employment in this sector between 1986 and 1991 was, in part, due to deregulation of the financial sector as part of the programme of economic reform instituted by the Labour government in the 1980s. As a result of deregulation there was a rapid growth in money market activity, particularly in the areas of foreign exchange, where all restrictions over transfers were lifted. New Zealand's relatively undeveloped financial industry enjoyed a boom. A range of new financial instruments was introduced such as forward contracts, options and exchange rate futures and secondary markets such as in government securities grew. The share market soared due to the increase in money supply resulting from deregulation. The boom was short-lived however and the inevitable collapse came in October 1987 when the main share price index, the Barclays share index, dropped to below its 1984 level. It has not recovered to pre-crash levels.

The second stage of deregulation in the financial sector occurred in the late 1980s. The regulations governing the supervision and registration of banks was relaxed under the Reserve Bank of New Zealand Act of 1986, and as result most building societies registered as banks and a number of foreign banks established New Zealand subsidiaries. Two further acts in 1987 and 1988 further removed distinctions between trading banks, trustee banks and building societies. The increase in the number of financial institutions and the range of activities they were involved in resulted in a rapid growth of employment in this area. More recently, technology such as e-commerce and Internet communication has had a major impact on the way that many financial institutes and business service providers operate. It has also meant an increase in demand for insurance cover against electronic risks, most particularly related to e-commerce. Over the next few years slow growth is expected in this sector, but it is likely that the merging of companies will continue and more procedures could be coming from overseas.

For more information, see www.icnz.org.nz, www.icanz.co.nz, www.nzier.org.nz and www.nzse.co.nz.

Construction

After a downturn over the past few years, confidence in this area of industry is now lifting. Construction currently employs 115,000 people, 7% of the employed workforce. Indirectly, it also employs thousands of other people in support jobs related to manufacturing, material supplies and transport services. The highest proportion of building construction enterprises is in Auckland, Wellington and Christchurch. There are three main parts to the industry — residential (homes), non-residential (offices, etc.) and civil construction (bridges, roads, hospitals, etc.). Economic factors, including low interest rates and a rise in the numbers of migrants arriving in New Zealand, have led to increased demand for residential housing. In hotel building, retail and factory building, further growth will be influenced by factors such as the state of the tourism and manufacturing industries (which are currently buoyant) and also by government spending. One of the key issues for this sector at present is the shortage of skilled workers, which may hinder growth. Although the apprenticeship system has recently been revived, there are skill shortages in a range of trades as well as at managerial levels.

Energy, Coal and Petrochemicals

Coal is New Zealand's largest energy resource, and just under three million tons of coal are produced annually, mainly sub-bitumous coal from North Island fields. The West Coast of the South Island is the biggest source of bitumous coal, most of which is exported to Japan, India and China. The quality of New Zealand coal makes it ideal for use in the chemical and steel industries. Industrial usage consumes nearly three-quarters of the remaining production. Coal is no longer a feed stock for thermal power stations as gas is becoming more competitive. In the future dual process stations such as the power station at Huntly, north of Hamilton, which can use either gas or coal, may go back to using coal as domestic gas supplies decline. The petrochemical industry is concentrated around the natural gas and oil fields off the coast of Taranaki. Six fields produce crude oil, condensate and natural gas, which provide about 50% of New Zealand's energy needs. Gas from the Maui and Kapuni offshore fields provides 95% of total gas production. Maui is expected to last until 2006 and Kapuni until 2014. Around a third of the natural gas produced is used to make synthetic petrol at a processing plant near Motonui. Natural gas is the single largest source of primary energy in New Zealand and accounts for 16% of the total North Island energy market. Major companies in this area are the Natural Gas Corporation, Fletcher Challenge Energy, Shell Petroleum, the Todd Corporation and Enerco. Almost all organisations operating in the gas industry are privately owned. Electricity generation has a major influence on the demand for natural gas, as electricity generation companies are the largest gas consumers.

Hydroelectric generators on major rivers, mostly in the South Island, produce 75% of New Zealand's electricity supply. The generating authority until 1999 was the Electricity Corporation of New Zealand (ECNZ), a state owned enterprise. It has now been split and its operating assets transferred to three new generation SOEs - Mighty River Power (MRP), Meridian Energy and Genesis Power. ECNZ is managing down its remaining activities with an eventual view to winding up completely. The main assets of Genesis are New Zealand's largest power station, at Huntly, and the Tongariro and Waikaremoana power schemes. Meridian's core assets are the South Island hydroelectric generators at Manapouri and Waitaki river, which have an average annual generation capacity of 12,500 gigawatt hours (GWh), 26% of New Zealand's total electricity generation. Meridian also has three-quarters of New Zealand's total hydro-storage capacity. MRP generates electricity primarily from the Waikato River hydro power station, and from Mokai and Rotokawa geothermal. Between them, Meridian Energy, Genesis Power and MRP generate approximately 89% of the country's electricity. Private companies operating stand-alone electricity and/or electricity cogeneration plants produce the rest.

Electricity is distributed through power stations, which are connected to a national grid that runs the length of the country. Network companies (also called distribution or lines companies) own the power lines in local areas that are connected to the national grid. Electricity retailers (power companies) sell electricity to business and residential users, and, as a result of New Zealand's electricity reforms, customers can now buy power from any electricity retailer. Electricity can either be traded privately or bought and sold on the New Zealand Electricity Market (NZEM); on the NZEM the price fluctuates every 30 minutes, depending on supply and demand.

Major Companies: Transpower Limited, MRP, Meridian Energy, Genesis Power, BP New Zealand, Fletcher Challenge, Dominion Oil Refining, Mobil Oil New Zealand, Caltex NZ.

Fishing and Aquaculture

New Zealand's clean waters provide fish of exceptional quality. Seafood is the country's fifth largest primary industry, contributing $1.4billion towards GDP, and is the fourth largest export earner. About 90% of the annual seafood harvest is exported. Major export markets are Japan, the USA and Europe, as well as Australia and Hong Kong. More than 26,000 people are employed in the industry and in supporting jobs, and almost a third of the total seafood workforce is employed in the aquaculture sector. New Zealand's exclusive economic zone (EEZ), wherein the Ministry of Agriculture and Fisheries controls all fishing, extends for 200 nautical miles from the coastline and is the fourth largest in the world, covering a total of 2.2million square miles. MAF runs a system of transferable quotas which has been in place since 1986, and more recent legislation has further tightened the procedures operated by the 'Quota Management System' (QMS). Quotas cover most major commercial species. Assessments are made about the size of the fishstock and the sustainable commercial catch for each species is estimated. The total catch is allocated between fishing companies through individual quotas, which companies can buy or sell. There are over 2000 quota holders, but the majority of quotas are held by seven leading fishing companies (listed below). 20% of quotas for new species are allocated to the Maori under a deal between the tribes and the government settled in 1992, and Maori stakeholders control one-third of the total quota through ownership of 50% of the largest fishing company, the Sealord Group. An organisation called Te Ohu Kai Moana focuses on furthering the interests of Maori in the fishing industry.

There is a small but growing crustacea and shellfish farming industry, which includes rock lobsters, scallops, oysters, clams, cockles and crabs. The main export products are Pacific oysters and green-lipped mussels. Increased diversity is expected in the next decade. Paua (a large New Zealand shellfish) farms and seaweed trial projects have already been established. This industry, like much of New Zealand's agricultural and horticultural output, is vulnerable to disease which can wipe out an entire season's crop, as happened in the summer of 1992/93 when toxic algae bloom resulted in shellfish harvesting being suspended. The other major threat to the seafood industry comes from trade barriers. About 85% of industry revenues come from exports, but most of the markets New Zealand trades with have volume restrictions (quotas) on imports. New Zealand currently has less than 2% of world seafood trade and could expand this if the quotas were increased.

The main commercial fishing areas are in the South Island and are run through Nelson, Lyttleton and Timaru ports. 80% of aquaculture exports come from the Marlborough Sounds. Other significant areas include Stewart Island, the Coromandel and Northland. Aquaculture now accounts for 20% of the total seafood industry income.

Major Companies: Sealord Group, Sanford Group, Treaty of Waitangi Fisheries Commission, Amaltal Fishing Corporation, Vela Limited, Moana Pacific Fisheries, and Talley's Fisheries.

Manufacturing

At the end of 2004, manufacturing activity levels continued to expand. The ANZ Business NZ Performance of Manufacturing Index (PMI) value for October was 56.7, which was lower than the PMI in October of 2003 and 2002 (a reading above 50 points indicates expansion and below 50 indicates decline). The highest levels of expansion were seen in the areas of new orders and production, while deliveries, finished stocks and employment have declined slightly. The rate of expansion within manufacturing conditions has slowed over recent months, hampered somewhat by labour shortages and the high New Zealand dollar.

Metal Products, Machinery and Equipment. This includes assembling motor vehicles, electrical goods, electronic goods, machinery and metal goods. In 1989 New Zealand's import licences were removed and tariffs on imported vehicles were reduced, leading to a decline in the country's vehicle assembly industry and a quick increase in the number of imported Japanese cars. 67% of cars on the road have been imported from overseas. New Zealand motor assembling plants have developed successful production of vehicle componentry totalling $400million, of which roughly $150million comes from exports.
Major Companies. Ford NZ, General Motors NZ, Toyota NZ.

Textiles, Clothing, Footwear and Leather Goods. This section of the industry is highly dependent on export markets, which provide a majority of the earnings. Although profitability is increasing, there are still a number of businesses in this area that are only marginally profitable and remain vulnerable to pressures such as further tariff reductions, which make imported goods cheaper. Growth is dependent on the ability of businesses to create new opportunities and develop new products. There is now less emphasis on sending raw products, such as wool, overseas and much of the industry is made up of small, owner-operated companies creating high-quality products for small niche export markets. Some businesses are collaborating with scientists to improve the quality of raw materials, such as creating textiles from a combination of merino and possum fur, or smart textiles with electricity-conducting properties. Increased production of higher-value items aimed at niche markets is projected to grow employment 6%, so that it reaches around 21,300 by 2006. Currently, although there is increased international interest in New Zealand's fashion designers, many clothing companies are small-scale and are losing orders because they are unable to meet demand. There is a shortage of people with production, pattern-making and machining skills. Increased on-the-job training and newly introduced cadetship programmes should help to redress this issue.

Steel and Non-ferrous Metals. Steel and aluminium are the only metals produced in any quantity in New Zealand. The ironsands on the west coast of the North Island are the largest reserves of iron ore in the country, and were noted as far back as 1769, by Captain James Cook. The New Zealand steel works at Glenbrook produces steel from these sands by a unique direct reduction process. BHP New Zealand Steel remains the world's only producer of steel from ironsand, with a total production of around 700,000 tonnes. Unwrought aluminium from the Comalco smelter near Bluff is a major export earner using raw bauxite imported from Australia. Employment opportunities in this sector have decreased because of capital upgrades by firms to increase efficiency, and decreased demand from Asian countries cut export prices.
Major Companies: BHP New Zealand Steel, Pacific Steel, Comalco-CHH Aluminium, Steel and Tube Holdings Limited, Superior Industries Ltd.

Electronics. Electronics is one of the success stories of the restructured New Zealand economy. Under the old regime of protected domestic industries the sector was predominantly involved in the manufacture of consumer electronics. Now most of these goods (TVs, videos, etc.) are imported from Asia where costs are cheaper. The major exception is the domestic whiteware industry (the local term for fridges, dishwashers, ovens, etc.) where New Zealanders show a strong preference for long established local brands such as Fisher and Paykel. The electronics industry, instead of declining with the reduction in tariffs, has diversified and found niche markets in high tech commercial and industrial products. For example, one Christchurch based company, Dynamic Controls, is the world's leading supplier of mobility control systems for power wheelchairs and scooters. Software is another area where New Zealand firms have developed specialist markets. Big international firms such as Ericsson and IBM have introduced technological advancements and teamed up with companies like Synergy to develop cell phone and mobile internet software in New Zealand. Job prospects for skilled workers in the industry are good. There is currently a skills shortage from assembly workers through to engineers and software designers. The size of the New Zealand industry has limited the numbers being trained so that it has been unable to keep up with the current leap in demand for its products.

Major Companies: AWA New Zealand, Dynamic Controls, Ericsson, Fisher and Paykel Electronics, IBM New Zealand.

Food and Beverages. This is a major industry, contributing to 5% of GDP and producing almost half the country's exports. The largest sectors are dairy products (accounting for 19% of NZ's total export earnings and 31% of the world trade in dairy products) and meat products (13% of export earnings and 55% of the world's trade in sheep meat). More than 60 varieties of cheese are produced (around 30,000 tonnes), and roughly 90% of this is exported. Beverages for the domestic and export market include wine, soft drinks, fruit juice, spirits and beer, teas, fruit wines and water. The wine industry is an area of major growth – since 1990 exports increased from a value of $18.4million to $231million in 2002, and are expected to reach $736million by 2006. It is estimated that New Zealand has more than 2000 specialty food manufacturers, producing such things as honey, pastries, confectionery, beverages and gourmet foods, and employing over 33,000 people. There is an increased and continuing need for multi-skilled process operators with science and engineering knowledge. There is also concern that the current shortage of food technologists will hinder the country's success in turning agricultural products into the more diverse and value-added products required to keep up with consumer demand and appeal to new markets.

Major Companies: Bluebird Foods, DB Group, Cerebos Gregg, Goodman Fielder, Kraft General Foods, Nestle New Zealand, Lion Nathan, Abels, Montana Wines, Villa Maria Wines.

Tourism and Hospitality

Tourism is one of the largest New Zealand industries, and the latest figures show that it employs 104,070 people and accounts for 9.1% of GDP as well as 14.7% of export earnings. There are anywhere up to 18,000 small to medium-sized businesses in this area, and around 80% of these employ less than five people. The largest numbers of visitors come to New Zealand from Australia (33%), the

UK (12%), the USA (10%) and Japan (7%). There are also a number of visitors from China and South Korea. 88% of international tourists say that they will visit New Zealand again in the future, and the Tourism Research Council predicts that by 2008 international visitor numbers will reach 2.86million arrivals. The most visited areas are Auckland, Christchurch, Rotorua, Queenstown, Wellington and Dunedin, and the highest proportion of hospitality enterprises are in the Auckland, Wellington, Canterbury and Waikato regions. The profile and visibility of New Zealand overseas has been enhanced by the use of the landscape in various productions such as the *Lord of the Rings* trilogy, *Vertical Limit* and *The Last Samurai*. Other contributors have included The America's Cup, Discovery Channel programmes, Billy Connolly's recent series and the Tourism NZ advertising campaign '100% Pure New Zealand'. Domestic tourism is also important, and accounts for 60% of the tourism industry. The main attractions for most are the clean environment and beautiful scenery, but a growing number of tourists are after more active holidays, skiing trips, jet-boat rides, white water rafting, black water rafting, even bungy jumping. This has lead to the growth of a new type of tourism, called 'adventure tourism'. Another area that is beginning to take off is 'green tourism' or 'eco-tourism'. Often thought to be a contradiction in terms because the impact of visitors upon the environment is usually harmful, green tourism aims to combine sharing the environment with tourists and protecting it. Activities such as whale watching off the Kaikoura coast above Christchurch, and visiting bird sanctuary islands already attract many tourists and Kiwis alike.

International tourism has been dramatically affected by world events such as the war in Iraq, the outbreak of SARS and the terrorist attacks on the USA, but the rate of cancellations of travel to New Zealand has not been particularly high. The country is still considered a highly desirable and safe destination, and once long-haul travel confidence returns the tourism industry is expected to recover any losses. The number of international travellers has a key role in determining demand for hotels and motels, but the majority of people making use of such places are domestic travellers. Annual expenditure on food, beverages, hospitality and related tourism in New Zealand currently exceeds $13million, and in the last year international travellers spent $6.1million while visiting. The hospitality industry is experiencing strong growth as the number of restaurants and cafes has increased. Employment and career opportunities are good, and the number of people entering the industry is expected to remain high.

There have been significant changes in New Zealand's travel industry over the last few years; an unsustainable oversupply of agencies resulted in a number of mergers and redundancies, and travellers are increasingly using the Internet rather than agencies to make their own travel arrangements and bookings. In addition, the financial pressures many airlines have found themselves under have led to them reducing commission fees paid to agencies and enlarging call centres to increase direct sales.

For more information see wwww.hanz.org.nz, www.his.co.nz and www. tourisminfo.govt.nz.

Transport

As a small exporting economy at great distances from many of its markets, New Zealand is highly dependent on maintaining its external transportation links. Internal transportation networks are also important as its small population is spread over two islands nearly 2,000 kilometres in combined length. Early transport developments were largely the result of government investment. The rail network, harbours, and road building were all extensively developed under a programme of major public works during the 1870s. State ownership and investment was the pattern for transportation development over the next century. The government owned and ran the railways, a shipping line, and eventually the national airline. State ownership of transportation links diminished under the programme of state asset sales begun by the Labour government in the 1980s. Now private sector investment is behind most new transport projects, with the exception of road building, which remains the responsibility of Transit New Zealand, a government authority. Road transportation was deregulated during the 1980s as was public transport in most cities. New Zealand Rail was sold to a consortium made up of a Canadian, an American and a New Zealand company in 1993. Port authorities were set up as companies, largely owned by local authorities, with two partly privately owned.

Transport is very dependent on other areas of the economy, such as agriculture. Recent growth in logging, tourism and dairy, as well as production industry centralisation, means that there is currently increased demand for transport services and this is likely to continue. Bulk freight, such as steel, coal, and cargo including dairy products, is mainly transported by rail. The highest proportions of rail transport enterprises are in Wellington, Canterbury and Manawatu-Wanganui regions. International trade relies heavily on water transport, as almost 99% of all exports are carried by sea. The main ports are at Auckland, Wellington, Tauranga and Lyttleton. There are three main international airports — at Auckland, Wellington and Christchurch. There are two New Zealand airlines operating international flights; Air New Zealand and its subsidiary Freedom Air. Qantas Australia plans to enter the market, as does Virgin Blue. Such expansion would create many more employment opportunities.

REGIONAL EMPLOYMENT GUIDE

THE UPPER NORTH ISLAND

Northland and Auckland

Major Cities: Auckland (pop. 379,600), Manukau (pop. 344, 400), North Shore (pop.193,000), Waitakere (pop. 141,000), Whangarei (pop. 47,600).
Newspapers: *The New Zealand Herald* (www.nzhearld.co.nz), *Northern Advocate.*
Chambers of Commerce: Auckland Regional Chamber of Commerce and Industry: 100 Mayoral Drive, PO Box 47, Auckland; ☎(09) 309 6100; fax (09) 309 0081; e-mail akl@chamber.co.nz; www.chamber.co.nz. Northland Chamber of Commerce: 3-5 Hunt St, PO Box 1703, Whangarei; ☎(09) 438 4771; fax (09) 438 4770; e-mail info@northchamber.co.nz; www.northchamber.co.nz.
Industry/Other Comments. The Auckland region is the main business and

industrial centre and employs nearly one third of the total workforce. Around half are employed in the services sector, comprising wholesale, retail, community, social and personal services and also including tourism, film, television and sport. The Auckland region provides a wide range of job opportunities in manufacturing and distribution, boat building, construction, and business and financial services. Auckland has a container port and an international airport. Employment prospects in the area are good and continue to improve. The region is predicted to remain the leader in economic growth over the next few years and this is reflected in the number of businesses looking to expand their workforce. Numbers of job advertisements continue to increase, and growth industries in the future are likely to be construction and information technology and telecommunications. In Northland, job prospects are likely to be associated with the growth of tourism and the expected improvement in agricultural export volumes, dairy farming and fruit growing, and ceramic clay and cement mining. There are also opportunities to work in areas such as boat building, tourism, forestry (exotic forest) and aquaculture for coastal shellfish farming. New Zealand's only crude oil refinery is located at Marsden Point, near Whangarei, on the East Coast. South of Auckland, at Glenbrook, is the BHP New Zealand Steel factory that uses a unique production process based on the reduction of local ironsand. West Coast beaches in New Zealand are characterised by the high proportion of iron ore in the sand, which results in black coloration.

THE CENTRAL NORTH ISLAND

Waikato, Bay of Plenty, Gisborne and Hawke's Bay

Major Cities: Hamilton (pop. 138,800), Tauranga (pop. 103,200), Rotorua (pop. 53,000) New Plymouth (pop. 47,800), Gisborne (pop. 31,400), Hastings (pop. 59,600), Napier (pop. 54,800).

Newspapers: *The Waikato Times* (www.stuff.co.nz/stuff/waikatotimes), *Bay of Plenty Times* www.stuff.co.nz/bayofplenty), *Hawke's Bay Today* (www.hbtoday. co.nz).

Chambers of Commerce: Waikato Chamber of Commerce: 190 Collingwood Street, PO Box 1122, Hamilton; ☎(07) 839 5895; fax (07) 839 4581; e-mail admin@waikatochamber.co.nz; www.waikatochamber.co.nz. Chamber of Commerce Tauranga Region: 306 Cameron Road, PO Box 414, Tauranga, ☎(07) 577 9823; fax (07) 577 0364; e-mail chamber@tauranga.org.nz; www.tauranga. org.nz. Hawke's Bay Chamber of Commerce: 2 Market St South, Hastings; ☎(06) 876 5938; fax (06) 876 3748; e-mail admin@hawkesbaychamber.co.nz; www.hawkesbaychamber.co.nz.

Industry/Other Comments. The Waikato is one of the main dairy farming regions in the country. Horticulture, particularly citrus fruit and kiwifruit, is the predominant industry in the Bay of Plenty on the East Coast. There are also opportunities for expansion within the tourism, forestry and food processing industries. Hawkes Bay is a premium wine-making district, and has some of the oldest established wineries in the country; the Mission Vineyard, run by Catholic monks, first began producing wine last century. It is also a significant farming and fruit-growing region and there are many job and investment opportunities in agriculture, food processing and tourism. Hamilton is home to a number of manufacturing enterprises, a university, and a large wholesale and retail sector. Most industry in the Waikato region is based on the processing of agricultural and forestry raw products, as well as dairy, technology, bloodstock, and education and research. The central region of the North Island is the main centre for the pulp and paper-making industry. Large plantation forests of radiata pine provide the raw materials for the production of newsprint, wood pulp, paper and paperboard. The Waikato is the largest coal-producing region in the country, with seventeen mainly open cast mines producing over half the total annual sub-bitumous coal output of the country. Main industries on the East Coast and in Gisborne are tourism, wine making and forestry (there are large exotic forests with opportunities for further expansion). Gas is main product of the petro-chemical industry based on the Taranaki coast near New Plymouth. The Taranaki region supports many energy related industries, including specialised engineering, and is a major dairy area with value-added food processing opportunities. The region is also a tourist destination. Major attractions include the thermal region around Rotorua and the network of limestone caves near Waitomo. Economic prospects in the region are favourable particularly for horticulture and forestry, and associated industries.

THE LOWER NORTH ISLAND

Taranaki, Manawatu-Wanganui and Wellington

Major Cities: Wellington (pop. 167,700), Palmerston North (pop. 72,400), Wanganui (pop. 38,900).

Newspapers: *The Dominion* (www.stuff.co.nz/stuff/dominionpost), *Manawatu Standard* (www.manawatustandard.co.nz) *Wanganui Chronicle* (www. wanganuichronicle.co.nz).

Chambers of Commerce: Wellington Chamber of Commerce: Level 9, 109 Featherston St, Wellington; ☎(04) 914 6500; fax (04) 914 6524; e-mail info@wgtn-chamber.co.nz; www.wgtn-chamber.co.nz. Wanganui Chamber of Commerce: Enterprise House, 187 Victoria Ave, PO Box 88, Wanganui; ☎(06) 345 0080; fax (06) 348 8210; e-mail info@wanganuichamber.co.nz; www. wanganuichamber.co.nz. Taranaki Chamber of Commerce: 15 Young St, PO Box 2, New Plymouth; ☎(06) 759 9080; fax (06) 759 9145; e-mail taranaki. chamber@xtra.co.nz.

Industry/Other Comments. The capital city Wellington is the headquarters of central government. Most major law firms, accountants and management firms have their base in Wellington as well, although some firms prefer to have their head office in Auckland, reflecting that city's commercial dominance. Wellington is the centre of the performing arts, as the national orchestra and ballet are based there, and there is an abundance of dance companies, opera groups and professional theatres in the city. Wellington also hosts a biannual International Festival of the Performing Arts. Business, government and retail enterprises dominate the main urban area. Manufacturing industry is concentrated in the outlying suburbs and on the Petone seafront at the northern end of the Wellington harbour. Growth industries in the Wellington region are information, communications, education and film. There are secondary processing opportunities in forestry, agriculture, horticulture and wine making. Outside the urban area, to the north, the Wairarapa district is dairy and sheep farming country. The main industries in the Manawatu-Wanganui area are forestry, dairy, food processing, specialised engineering, intensive horticultural activities, education and agriculture technology, and research based on tertiary institutions and the area's strong farming base. Martinborough, north of Wellington, is one of the major players in wine production.

THE UPPER SOUTH ISLAND

Nelson-Marlborough, West Coast and Canterbury

Major Cities: Christchurch (pop. 343,800), Nelson (pop. 56,200).
Newspapers: *The Christchurch Press* (www.thepress.co.nz), *The Nelson Mail* (www.nelsonmail.co.nz).
Chambers of Commerce: Canterbury Employers' Chamber of Commerce: 57 Kilmore St, PO Box 359, Christchurch; ☎(03) 366 5096; fax (03) 379 5454; e-mail info@cecc.org.nz; www.cecc.org.nz. Nelson Chamber of Commerce, PO Box 1121, Nelson; ☎(03) 548 1363; fax (03) 546 8373; e-mail info@commerce. org.nz; www.commerce.org.nz.
Industry/Other Comments. Marlborough is the largest wine-making region in New Zealand, and opportunities for expansion include wine making, tourism, forestry and food processing. The Canterbury region is the largest sheep-farming region in the country. It has a container port nearby at Lyttleton and the second busiest international airport in the country. As well as agricultural industry, Christchurch is the largest region for manufacturing employment after Auckland. Canterbury has a number of high-tech electronic manufacturing and software firms, as well as wine making, horticulture, floriculture, food processing businesses. Tourism is a major source of economic activity in the region, thanks to the scenery and the skiing. Christchurch is only an hour away from the ski fields of Mt Hutt. Other important services here include education and research. The country's first legal casino opened in the former Christchurch railway station in 1994. Nelson is an important deep-sea fishing base and seafood processing location. West Coast industry is traditionally based on resource extraction - gold mining, coal mining and timber. This area is benefiting from its new deep water port, and the development of three new coal mines, which are expected to boost its already healthy coal exports. The strongest opportunities for expansion on the West Coast lie in tourism.

THE LOWER SOUTH ISLAND

Southland and Otago

Major Cities: Dunedin (pop. 107,000), Invercargill (pop. 45,400).
Newspapers: *The Otago Daily Times* (www.odt.co.nz) *The Southland Times* (www. southlandtimes.co.nz).
Chambers of Commerce: Otago Chamber of Commerce and Industry

Incorporated: Level 7, 106 George Street, Dunedin; ☎(03) 479 0181; fax (03) 477 0341; e-mail office@otagochamber.co.nz. Chamber of Commerce Southland Inc.: PO Box 856, Invercargill; ☎(03) 218 7188; fax (03) 218 7927 e-mail office@commercesouth.com.

Industry/Other Comments. The strong agricultural base of the rural economy in Otago and Southland is mainly concentrated on sheep farming with smaller numbers of dairy and beef farms. Other important activities include food processing and tourism, as well as horticulture, particularly stonefruit. Vineyards are relatively new to the region. Until recently the climate was thought to be too cold for grape growing, but several local wineries have established an enviable reputation. Main industries in Dunedin are education, tourism, food processing and niche manufacturing. Apart from Dunedin, manufacturing in the region is concentrated around Invercargill with the exception of the Comalco Aluminium smelter, which is located at Tiwai point near Bluff. Bluff is also known for its production of oysters.

DIRECTORY OF MAJOR EMPLOYERS

Accommodation and Hospitality
CDL Hotels NZ Ltd: Level 13, 280 Centre, 280 Queen St, Auckland; ☎(09) 309 4411; fax (09) 377 0764; e-mail sales.marketing@mckhotels. co.nz; www.cdlhotels.co.nz.
Restaurant Brands NZ Ltd: www.restaurantbrands.co.nz.

Accountancy
Gosling Chapman Chartered Accountants: Human Resources Manager, PO Box 158, Auckland; ☎(09) 303 4586; fax (09) 309 1198; e-mail mail@goslingchapman.com; www.gosling.co.nz.

Agriculture and Forestry
Landcorp Farming Ltd: Lumley House, 3-11 Hunter Street, PO Box 5349, Wellington; ☎(04) 471 0400; fax (04) 473 4966; e-mail enquiries@landcorp.co.nz; www.landcorp.co.nz.
Sanford Ltd: 22 Jellicoe St, Freemans Bay, Auckland; ☎(09) 379 4720; fax (09) 309 1190; e-mail info@Sanford.co.nz; www.sanford.co.nz.

Banking, Insurance and Financial Services
AMP Financial Services: www.amp.co.nz.
ASB Group Career Centre: www.asb-bank.co.nz.
Bank of New Zealand: www.bnz.co.nz also see http://nationalgroup.hire.com.
Deutsche Bank: Human Resources Manager, PO Box 6900, Wellesley Street, Auckland; ☎(09) 351 1000; fax (09) 351 1001; www.deutsche-bank.co.nz.
KPMG: National Human Resources Manager, KPMG Centre, 18 Viaduct Harbour Avenue, Auckland; ☎(09) 367 5800; fax (09) 367 5875; www.kpmg.co.nz.
Meritec: HR Development Manager, PO Box 4142, Auckland; ☎(09)336 5376; fax (09) 379 1220; www.meritec.org.
Reserve Bank of New Zealand: HR Administrator, PO Box 2498, Wellington; ☎(04) 471 3974; fax (04) 472 3759; e-mail recruitment@rbnz.govt.nz; www.rbnz.govt.nz.
Tower Limited: PO Box 590, Wellington; ☎(04) 472 6059; fax (04) 473

2669; www.tower.co.nz.

The Treasury: HR Advisor, PO Box 3724, Wellington; e-mail human. resources@treasury.govt.nz; www. treasury.govt.nz.

Business and Management Services

AMP: www.ampnz.co.nz.

Ernst & Young: Recruitment and Retention Manager, PO Box 2146, Auckland; ☎ (09) 377 4790; fax (09) 309 8137; www.cy.com.

Construction and Engineering

Beca Carter Hollings & Ferner Ltd: HR Advisor, PO Box 6345, Auckland; ☎ (09) 300 9000; fax (09) 300 9300; e-mail humanresources@beca. co.nz; www.beca.co.nz.

Delta: Contract Services Manager, PO Box 1404, Dunedin; ☎ (03) 479 6693; fax (03) 479 6694; www.4delta. co.nz.

Fulton Hogan Limited: General Manager Southern, PO Box 39185, Christchurch; ☎ (03) 357 1400; fax (03) 357 1450; www.fhcareers.co.nz.

Meritec: HR Development Manager, PO Box 4142, Auckland; ☎ (09336 5376; fax (09) 379 1220; www.meritec.org.

MWH Worldwide: www.bfound.net.

Opus: Recruitment, PO Box 12343, Wellington; ☎ (04) 471 7243; fax (04) 473 3017; e-mail cheryl. dudfield@opus.co.nz; www.opus. co.nz.

Cultural and Recreational Services

NZ Lotteries Commission: 54-56 Cambridge Terrace, PO Box 3145, Wellington; ☎ (04) 802 7000; fax (04) 385 2787; e-mail info@nzlc.co.nz; www.nzlotteries.co.nz.

NZ Totaliser Agency Board: 106-110 Jackson St, Petone, PO Box 38 899 Wellington Mail Centre; ☎ (04) 576 6999; fax (04) 576 6942; www.tab. co.nz.

Sky City Recruitment Centre: Level 6 Federal House, 86 Federal St, Auckland; ☎ (09) 363 6044; www.skycity.co.nz.

Sky Network Television Limited: 10 Panorama Rd, Mt Wellington, PO Box 9059, Newmarket, Auckland; ☎ (09) 579 9999; fax (09) 579 0910; www.skytelevision.co.nz.

Television New Zealand Limited: http:// corporate.tvnz.co.nz and http://jobs. haineslink.co.nz/tvnz/.

Education

Open Polytechnic: www.topnz.ac.nz.

SES (Specialist Education Services): www. ses.org.nz.

TeachNZ: www.TeachNZ.govt.nz.

Health

Auckland District Health Board: ☎ (09) 630 9900 or 0800 733 968; fax (09) 630 9927; e-mail jackieb@ahsl. co.nz; www.adhb.govt.nz or www. aucklandhealthcareers.co.nz.

MidCentral District Health Board: e-mail vacancy@midcentral.co.nz; www.MidCentral.co.nz.

Southern Cross Healthcare: Private Bag 999 34, Newmarket, Auckland; www.southerncross.co.nz.

South Auckland Health: HR, Middlemore Hospital, PO Box 93311, Otahuhu, Auckland; e-mail recruitment@middlemore.co.nz; www.jobpulse.co.nz/cmdhb/.

Taranaki District Health Board: HR Advisor, Private Bag 2016, New Plymouth; ☎ (06) 753 6139; fax (06) 753 7770; e-mail hr@tdhb.org. nz; www.thcl.co.nz.

Waitemata District Health Board: ☎ 0800 472 284 or (09) 441 8953; fax (09) 489 0533; e-mail recruit@waitematadhb.govt.nz; www.waitematadhb.govt.nz.

Waikato District Health Board: PO Box 934, Hamilton; e-mail Smiths@waikatodhb.govt.nz; www. waikatodhb.govt.nz.

West Coast District Health Board:

Recruitment Co-ordinator, PO Box 387, Greymouth; ☎(03) 768 0499; fax (03) 768 2791; e-mail amartin@westcoastdhb.org.nz;www.westcoastdhb.org.nz.

Information Technology and Telecommunications

Ernst & Young: Recruitment and Retention Manager, PO Box 2146, Auckland; ☎(09) 377 4790; fax (09) 309 8137; www.ey.com.

Commsoft Group Ltd: www.commsoftnz.com.

Computerland: ☎(04) 460 6000; fax (04) 460 6001; www.computerland.co.nz.

Deltec Telesystems International Ltd: www.deltec-telesystems.com.

Ericsson: www.ericsson.co.nz.

Inland Revenue (IT Dept): PO Box 2198, Wellington; ☎(04) 382 7007; fax (04) 382 7054; e-mail hr.it@ird.govt.nz; www.ird.govt.nz.

JADE: Staff Development Manager, PO Box 20 152, Christchurch; ☎(03) 365 2500; fax (03) 358 6050; e-mail js@jadeworld.com; www.jadeworld.com.

Meritec: HR Development Manager, PO Box 4142, Auckland; ☎(09336 5376; fax (09) 379 1220; www.meritec.org.

Microsoft NZ: www.microsoft.com/nz/.

Oracle: HR, Oracle Tower, 56 Wakefield Street, Auckland; ☎(09) 359 3300; fax (09) 377 8847; e-mail jobs_nz@oracle.com; www.oracle.com/global/nz or http://jobs.oracle.com.

Orion NZ Ltd: ☎(09) 638 0608; e-mail jobs@orionhealth.com; www.orion.co.nz.

SolNet Solutions Ltd: e-mail employment@solnetsolutions.co.nz; www.solnet.co.nz.

Sungard Treasury Systems: HR Manager, 15b Leslie Hills Drive, Christchurch; ☎(03) 343 7350; fax (03) 343 7349;

www.sungardtreasury.com.

Synergy International Limited: ☎(04) 499 3000; fax (04) 460 5703; www.synergy.co.nz.

Telecom New Zealand: www.telecom.co.nz and www.telecom.co.nz/tcnzcareers.

TelstraClear: www.telstraclear.co.nz.

Vodafone: www.vodafone.co.nz.

Wireless Data: Recruitment Manager, PO Box 37-866, Parnell, Auckland; ☎(09) 379 4710; fax (09) 379 7360; e-mail jobs@wirelessdatanz.com.

Law Firms

*Chapmann Tripp:*www.chapmanntripp.co.nz.

Lane Neave: Meryll Waters, PO Box 13 149, Christchurch; ☎(03) 379 3720; e-mail meryll.waters@laneneave.co.nz; www.laneneave.co.nz;

Morrison Kent: Level 5, 55-65 Shortland Street, Auckland; ☎(09) 303 2164; Morrison Kent House, 105 The Terrace, Wellington; ☎(04) 472 0020; www.morrisonkent.co.nz.

Russell McVeagh: National HR Manager, PO Box 8, Auckland; ☎(09) 367 8000; fax (09) 367 8163; www.russellmcveagh.com.

Simpson Grierson: 92-96 Albert Street, Private Bag 92518, Wellesley Street, Auckland; ☎(09) 977 5000; fax (09) 977 5038; e-mail enquiries@simpsongrierson.com; www.simpsongrierson.com.

Manufacturing and Marketing

Allied Domecq (NZ) Ltd: 171 Pilkington Road, Auckland 1130; ☎(09) 570 8400; e-mail employment@adwnz.com or information@adwnz.com; www.adwnz.com.

Alliance Group Ltd: 51 Don St, PO Box 845, Invercargill; ☎(03) 214 2700; fax (03) 214 2708; www.alliance.co.nz.

Bendon Group Ltd: 33 Birmingham Road, East Tamaki, Auckland; ☎(09) 274 4244; fax (09) 274 5904;

e-mail info@bendon.co.nz; www. bendon.co.nz.

Carter Holt Harvey Ltd: 640 Great South Road, Manukau City, Private Bag 92106, Auckland; ☎(09) 262 6000; fax (09) 262 6099; e-mail chhcontact@chh.com; www.chh. co.nz.

Cavalier Bremworth Limited: 7 Grayson Avenue, Papatoetoe, PO Box 97-040, Auckland 1730; ☎(09) 277 6000; fax (09) 278 7417; www.cavcorp. co.nz.

DB Group Ltd: www.db.co.nz and www.jobs.db.co.nz.

Dynamic Controls: www.dynamic-controls.co.nz.

Fairfax New Zealand Ltd: Level 3, 40 Boulcott Street, PO Box 2595, Wellington; ☎ (04) 496 9800; fax (04) 496 9841; www.fairfaxnz.co.nz.

Fisher & Paykel Healthcare Ltd: PO Box 14-348, Panmure, Auckland; ☎(09) 574 0100; fax (09) 574 0136; e-mail recruit@fphcare.co.nz; www.fphcare. com/careers.

Frucor Beverages Group Ltd: PO Box 76-202, Manukau City 1730; ☎(09) 250 0100; fax (09) 250 0150; www. frucor.com.

Goodman Fielder NZ: www.goodmanfielder.com.au.

Methanex NZ Ltd: HR Advisor, Private Bag 2011, New Plymouth; ☎(06) 754 97821; fax (06) 754 9701; e-mail nzmarketing@methanex.com; www. methanex.com.

NZ Refining Company Ltd: Marsden Point Road, Ruakaka; ☎(09) 432 8311; fax (09) 432 8035; e-mail corporate@nzrc.co.nz; www.nzrc. co.nz.

Nuplex Industries Ltd: PO Box 12841, Penrose, Auckland; ☎(09) 579 2029; e-mail nuplex@nuplex.co.nz; www.nuplex.co.nz.

PDL Holdings Ltd (Schneider Electric): 14 Charann Place, Avondale, Auckland; ☎(09) 829 0490; fax (09) 829 0491; Head Office: PO Box 15-355,

New Lynn, Auckland; 14 Hazeldean Road, Addington, PO Box 1367, Christchurch; ☎(03) 338 9059; fax (03) 338 9842; www.pdl.co.nz.

Powerware New Zealand: 39 Princess Street, PO Box 111-88, Christchurch; ☎(03) 343 3314; e-mail dc.info@powerware.com; www.powerware.com.

Pulse Data International Ltd: HR Manager, 1 Expo Place, PO Box 3044, Christchurch; ☎(03) 384 4555; fax (03) 384 4933; e-mail enquiries@pulsedata.com; www. pulsedata.com.

Steel and Tube Holdings Ltd: 15-17 Kings Crescent, PO Box 30 543, Lower Hutt, Hutt City 6315; ☎(04) 570 5000; fax (04) 569 9622; www. steelandtube.co.nz.

Tait Radio Communications: Technical Recruitment Officer, 540 Wairakei Road, PO Box 1185, Christchurch; ☎0800 662 453; fax (03) 358 2029; www.taitworld.com.

ZESPRI International Limited: 400 Maunganui Road, Mt Maunganui 3002, PO Box 4043, Mt Maunganui South 3030; ☎(07) 575 8864; fax (07) 575 1646; www.zespri.com or www.zespri.careers.co.nz.

Mining

Newmont (Martha Mine): www.marthamine.co.nz

Solid Energy NZ Ltd: 2 Show Place, PO Box 1303, Christchurch; ☎(03) 345 6000; fax (03) 345 6016; www.solidenergy.co.nz.

Science, Research and Development

ESR (Institute of Environmental Science and Research Limited): www.esr.cri. nz.

Hortresearch: www.hortresearch.co.nz and www.hortresearch.co.nz/careers/ vacancies.

Industrial Research Limited: Gracefield Research Centre, Gracefield Road, PO Box 31-310, Lower Hutt, Wellington; ☎(04) 931 3000; fax (04) 566 6004; www.irl.cri.nz.

Transport
Air New Zealand: ☎(09) 336 3668 or 0800 747 500; e-mail recruitment1@airnz.co.nz; www. airnz.co.nz.

Mainfreight: 12-14 Southdown Lane, Penrose, PO Box 14 038, Auckland; ☎(09) 526 0950; www.mainfreight. com.

Transit New Zealand: Logical House, Level 8, 186-190 Willis Street, PO Box 27 477, Wellington; ☎(04) 891 2580 fax (04) 801 2599; www.transit.govt.nz.

Utilities
Contact Energy Ltd: Level 1, Harbour City Tower, 29 Brandon St, PO Box 10742, Wellington; ☎(04) 499 4001; fax (04) 499 4003; www. mycontact.co.nz.

Energy Online: Level 11, Newcall Tower, PO Box 8288, Symonds St, Auckland; ☎(09) 361 2154; fax (09) 361 2159; www.energyonline.co.nz.

Genesis Energy: HR Advisor, Greenlane Office, Auckland; www.genesisenergy.co.nz.

Mercury Energy: Private Bag 92008, Auckland; www.mercury.co.nz.

LineLogix: e-mail info@linelogix.co.nz; www.linelogix.co.nz

Meridian Energy Ltd: www.meridianenergy.co.nz.

Mighty River Power Limited: Level 19, 1 Queen St, PO Box 90399, Auckland; ☎(09) 308 8200; fax (09) 308 8209; e-mail enquiries@mightyriver. co.nz; www.mightyriverpower.com.

Natural Gas Corporation Holdings Ltd: Level 8, The NGC Building, 44 The Terrace, Private Bag 39980, Wellington Mail Centre, Wellington; ☎(04) 462 8700; fax (04) 462 8600; e-mail information@ngc.co.nz; www.ngc. co.nz.

Pure Energy: PO Box 99882, Auckland; e-mail info@pureenergy.co.nz; www. pureenergy.co.nz.

Transpower NZ Ltd: Level 7, Transpower House, 96 The Terrace, PO Box 1021, Wellington; ☎(04) 495 7000; fax (04) 495 7100; www.transpower. co.nz.

Trustpower Ltd: Private Bag 12023, Tauranga 3001; www.trustpower. co.nz.

United Networks Limited: 101 Carlton Gore Road, Newmarket, PO Box 99882, Auckland; fax (09) 978 7799; www.unitednetworks.co.nz.

Vector Networks: ☎ (09) 978 7788; fax (09) 978 7799; www.vectornetworks. co.nz.

STARTING A BUSINESS

New Zealand is a very straightforward place to do business. It has an efficient market-oriented economy, stable and reasonably secure business environment and is relatively free from corruption. The workforce is, for the most part, highly educated and skilled, and the labour market is flexible and deregulated. The business scene is strong and flourishing. With one of the lowest tariff rates in the world, New Zealand companies are naturally competitive exporters. Comparative costs also make it a feasible place to set up a business — in cost-critical industries like call centres and back office business staffing costs will be up to 30% less than in Australia and up to 50% less than the USA. This is because there is no payroll tax, no social services tax and no superannuation tax. There is just a small levy for accident compensation. Property and energy costs are relatively low.

In principle, it is quite feasible for foreigners to set up a business or to buy part or all of an existing business in New Zealand. The prevailing attitude towards business ventures, whether started by New Zealanders or immigrants, is positive and helpful. To make a success of the venture requires, of course, the same blend of careful planning, energy and luck that you need in any country. More than anything, you need to research your chosen potential market or markets to ensure that the products or services you offer are geared to meet a real demand at an appropriate price. Much of your groundwork can be done in advance, but there is no substitute for visiting and seeing for yourself the environment in which you wish to try the venture. It may well be worth considering spending a reasonable amount of time living and working in New Zealand before making a final commitment to a particular enterprise.

In most cases, therefore, it is likely that you will have obtained New Zealand residency before setting up a business on your own. Most New Zealand investment does not require approval. Only proposals involving international investment equity of a company of 25% or more, which have a value of NZ$50million or more, or are related to fishing quota or particular land purchases require the permission of the Overseas Investment Commission (*OIC:* Level 9, 2 The Terrace, PO Box 2498, Wellington; ☎ (04) 471 3838; fax (04) 471 3655; e-mail oic@oic.govt.nz; www. oic.govt.nz). Permission is dependent on the extent to which the projected business will contribute to the economy. However these restrictions will not affect most immigrants considering setting up a small business in New Zealand.

If you are organising your application for New Zealand residency with the intention of setting up a business there, you should note that a special scheme exists to attract business investors. (See the *Residence and Entry* Chapter). The sums required to qualify for the Business Investment category are substantial. If you do not have the necessary capital to qualify under this category, then you will need to apply under the Skilled Migrant or Family categories.

In recent years, regulations governing setting up business in New Zealand have been relaxed. The Companies Act was substantially amended in 1994 to make the process of incorporating a company simpler. There are an increasing number of government agencies set up to help small businesses and the attitude towards entrepreneurs is positive. As part of encouraging individual initiative and competitive economic environment, the government is trying to cut down on the amount of red tape involved in doing business, and to encourage small businesses to set up and survive. The result is that it is a good time to be starting up a new business in New Zealand. This chapter will look at what is involved in buying a business in New Zealand or in starting your own.

PREPARATION

Choosing a Business

Since in broad terms, New Zealanders engage in similar business, cultural and social activities to Europeans, there are similar potential markets for anyone contemplating setting up a new enterprise. The differences need to be borne in mind, however, not the least of which is that the comparatively small total population and its distribution will have a significant effect on the structure of potential markets. For example if you are considering setting up in the hospitality industry you will find that in the larger cities restaurants, cafés and wine bars abound; the market is pretty well saturated and thus very competitive. Such businesses are stretched to find some new competitive advantage and that is often manifested as gimmickry, which of course has a short-lived novelty appeal. In the rural areas, there are fewer restaurants and wine-bars, however there is less population to support them as New Zealand is not particularly densely populated. This may provide an opportunity, yes, but maybe one that requires a lot of 'up front' investment in marketing and publicity. Given that moving to a new country is going to be pretty challenging in itself, it may be wise to opt for a safer bet such as selecting an enterprise for which there is a known or an established market, or one in which you have particular skills and experience. Obviously there is an advantage in buying an already established business in this respect, however before you buy you should research the track record of your chosen enterprise. Remember that the majority of businesses succeed not on the uniqueness of the concept but on the application of sound and careful management techniques.

Researching Your Business

New Zealand business is characterised by the prevalence of small firms; the country has a high rate of entrepreneurship. 85% of firms employ five or fewer people. Research shows that most small firms either stay small or expire — few grow to significant sizes, so it is important to find a solid starting point for your business.

Whether it is your intention to buy a business or to set up from scratch, researching the potential market for your business is essential. The specific information that you need to determine whether there is a viable market will depend greatly upon the type of business, the services or the products you have in mind. There are companies specialising in market research in the major cities in New Zealand, which would be able to provide data on most aspects of the market or would offer to conduct specific enquiries, for a fee, in areas of the market which were less well researched. This type of service is usually beyond the budget of those setting up a small business. There are some companies offering research services specifically tailored for small businesses and you can do some of the research work yourself.

One of the first places to start looking for information is the local public library. Most public libraries run an information service for local businesses and for those intending to set up a business. They will have information on market trends, local suppliers, possible competitors, planning and development strategies. Some libraries offer a contract research service and will do a lot of the legwork by investigating the feasibility of a project for you. This may be a cost-effective option simply because they will be familiar with the sources of information and will be able to find out quickly what you need to know. Information on businesses and commerce in specific regions can be obtained from the local Chamber of Commerce. Chambers of Commerce in the main cities are listed below. Statistics New Zealand (www. stats.govt.nz) runs a professional consultancy service for data on imports, prices, population, etc. They publish the *Quarterly Economic Survey* of various sectors of the economy. Predominantly this is income and expenditure data, although they also collect investment data. Each year this is gathered into the more detailed *Annual Enterprise Survey*. More general data on the New Zealand economy is published in the monthly *Key Statistics*. They also publish the *New Zealand Yearbook*, and have a detailed business and economy information menu on their website as well as several useful links (see below). If your business is involved in the export market, the Ministry of Foreign Affairs and Trade can help with economic and political information about your target markets. The New Zealand Immigration Service has established a section of its website to provide information for people coming to New Zealand to set up businesses (www.immigration.govt.nz – follow the 'Invest' link to the 'Starting a Business' page).

Researching market opportunities in New Zealand from overseas is naturally more difficult than doing the groundwork once you arrive. There are companies that offer an information gathering service specifically for intending immigrants, in areas ranging from business opportunities to education prospects (see 'Business and Market Research Organisations' listed below). Another source of information is the *New Zealand Yearbook*, which provides a highly detailed picture of social, demographic, and economic trends in New Zealand. It is a useful introduction to the structure of the economy and the main business sectors. The disadvantage of the *Yearbook* is that the information is based on five-yearly census data, so while it is very detailed, it is not always up to date. The last census was at the end of 2001. Copies of the *Yearbook* can be found in some libraries or from Statistics New Zealand, or bought at the Kiwifruits New Zealand Shop, which specialises in New Zealand products (7 Royal Opera Arcade, London SW1Y 4UY; ☎0207 930 4587; e-mail theteam@kiwifruitsnzshop.com; www.kiwifruitsnzshop.com). New Zealand High Commissions and Embassies also have copies of the *Yearbook* as well as individual chapters on specific topics. Another excellent source of information is the New Zealand Institute of Economic Research (☎(04) 472 1880; e-mail econ@nzier.org.nz; www.nzier.org.nz), which is a primary source of information about economics in New Zealand and provides independent consulting services to the public sector, industry and businesses. It also publishes the *Quarterly Survey of Business Opinion*, which surveys private sector enterprises with at least six employees in the manufacturing, building, distribution and services industries.

Employment patterns are changing as New Zealand business develops; many new industries, such as biotechnology and wine-making, are based on agriculture, but there are a number of new and fast growing industries in other sectors. These include ICT, tourism and education services. In addition, there is a growing international appetite for creative industries, such as film and television, yacht design, fashion and art. The fact that the economy is growing and diversifying means that business legislation is being revised constantly, so you will need to keep an eye on the latest legal aspects as you are researching your business ideas.

Useful Addresses

Chambers of Commerce

New Zealand Chambers of Commerce: www.nzchamber.co.nz.

Northland Chamber of Commerce: 3-5 Hunt St, PO Box 1703, Whangarei; ☎(09) 438 4771; fax (09) 438 4770; e-mail info@northchamber.co.nz; www.northchamber.co.nz.

Auckland Regional Chamber of Commerce and Industry: 100 Mayoral Drive, PO Box 47, Auckland; ☎(09) 309 6100; fax (09) 309 0081; e-mail akl@chamber.co.nz; www.chamber.co.nz.

Waikato Chamber of Commerce: 190 Collingwood Street, PO Box 1122, Hamilton; ☎(07) 839 5895; fax (07) 839 4581; e-mail admin@waikatochamber.co.nz; www.waikatochamber.co.nz.

Chamber of Commerce Tauranga Region: 306 Cameron Road, PO Box 414, Tauranga, ☎(07) 577 9823; fax (07) 577 0364; e-mail chamber@tauranga.org.nz; www.tauranga.org.nz.

Hawke's Bay Chamber of Commerce: 2 Market St South, Hastings; ☎(06) 876 5938; fax (06) 876 3748; e-mail admin@hawkesbaychamber.co.nz; www.hawkesbaychamber.co.nz.

Wanganui Chamber of Commerce: Enterprise House, 187 Victoria Ave, PO Box 88, Wanganui; ☎(06) 345 0080; fax (06) 348 8210; e-mail info@wanganuichamber.co.nz; www.wanganuichamber.co.nz.

Taranaki Chamber of Commerce: 15 Young St, PO Box 2, New Plymouth; ☎(06) 759 9080; fax (06) 759 9145; e-mail taranaki.chamber@xtra.co.nz.

Wellington Chamber of Commerce: Level 9, 109 Featherston St, Wellington; ☎(04) 914 6500; fax (04) 914 6524; e-mail info@wgtn-chamber.co.nz; www.wgtn-chamber.co.nz.

Nelson Chamber of Commerce: PO Box 1121, Nelson; ☎(03) 548 1363; fax (03) 546 8373; e-mail info@commerce.org.nz; www.commerce.org.nz.

Canterbury Employers' Chamber of Commerce: 57 Kilmore St, PO Box 359, Christchurch; ☎(03) 366 5096; fax (03) 379 5454; e-mail info@cecc.org.nz; www.cecc.org.nz.

Otago Chamber of Commerce and Industry Incorporated: Level 7, 106 George Street, Dunedin; ☎(03) 479 0181; fax (03) 477 0341; e-mail office@otagochamber.co.nz.

Chamber of Commerce Southland Inc.: PO Box 856, Invercargill; ☎(03) 218 7188; fax (03) 218 7927 e-mail office@commercesouth.com.

Business and Market Research Organisations

BERL (Business and Economic Research Ltd): Level 5, 108 The Terrace, PO Box 10277, Wellington; ☎(04) 931 9200; fax (04) 931 9202; e-mail info@berl.

co.nz; www.berl.co.nz.

Business Research Centre (BRC): Level 7, Forsyth Barr House, 45 Johnson Street, PO Box 10617, Wellington; ☎(04) 499 3088; fax (04) 499 3414; e-mail info@brc.co.nz; www.brc.co.nz.

Business Information Service: Auckland City Library; ☎(09) 307 7790; e-mail bis@aucklandcity.govt.nz. Fee-based information service, annual membership subscription costs $180 excluding GST.

New Zealand Institute of Economic Research: 8 Halswell Street, Thorndon, PO Box 3479, Wellington; ☎(04) 472 1880; fax (04) 472 1211; e-mail econ@nzier.org. nz.

Government Departments

NZ Ministry of Foreign Affairs and Trade: 195 Lambton Quay, Private Bag 18 901, Wellington; ☎(04) 439 8000; fax (04) 472 9596; e-mail enquiries@mfat.govt. nz; www.mft.govt.nz.

Statistics New Zealand (Head Office): Aorangi House, 85 Molesworth Street, PO Box 2922, Wellington; ☎(04) 931 4600 or 0508 525 525 for the Information Centre; fax (04) 931 4610; e-mail info@stats.govt.nz, library@stats.govt.nz or publications@stats.govt.nz; www.stats.govt.nz.

Statistics New Zealand: Information Consultancy Groups:
Auckland: UniServices House, 70 Symonds Street, Private Bag, 920003, Auckland; ☎(09) 920 9100; fax (09) 920 9198.
Christchurch: Dollan House, 401 Madras Street, Private Bag 4741, Christchurch; ☎(03) 964 8700; fax (03) 964 8964.

Choosing an Area

Having decided on your line of business, the next logical step is to decide where to locate it. Obviously the type of business will determine this in many cases; for example choosing where to site a horticultural enterprise will largely be determined by climate. The tourism industry was once concentrated in the geothermal area around Rotorua, and the South Island more generally, with most visitors staying in Christchurch or Queenstown. Auckland and areas to the north, such as the Bay of Islands, are attracting visitors for longer stays and are growing tourism areas. Another growing sector is adventure tourism, with the south of the Waikato region around Waitomo caves, Nelson and the West Coast likely to benefit. Export manufacturing is strongest in Auckland and Christchurch. Forestry, another export sector predicted to grow is likely to benefit the region around the central North Island. Overall Auckland is likely to continue to enjoy the highest economic growth over the next few years, but the outlook is also positive for Canterbury and the Bay of Plenty.

USEFUL BOOKS & PERIODICALS

New Zealand Books is a company that sells New Zealand-published books over the internet and ships them worldwide (www.newzealandbooks. co.nz). You should also be able to order any titles you want through most bookshops.
8 Secrets of Investment Success: M. Hawes, Penguin.

Accounting for Small Business: Sari Hodgson, Tandem Press, 2000.
Basic Marketing (6th edition): Marketing in the Third Millenium: Paul Rose, Dunmore Press, 2004.
Business and New Zealand Society: Longman Paul, 1994.
Foundations for Growth: A New Zealand Guide to Business Improvement: New Zealand Trade and Enterprise, September 2004.
Growing Tall Poppies: Michele Cox.
New Zealand: Business Law Handbook: International Business Publications USA, 2002.
New Zealand Dictionary of Business Terms: Martin Lawrence and Kay Switzer, Dunmore Press.
New Zealand: Investment and Business Guide: International Business Publications USA, 2002.
Penguin New Zealand Small Business Guide (3rd ed.): Higham and Williams, Penguin, 1999.
Planning for Success: NZ Trade & Enterprise; ☎0800 555 888; www.nzte.govt.nz. Updated January 2004.
Property Investment in NZ: A strategy for wealth: M. Hawes, 2001.
Small and Medium Sized Enterprises: a New Zealand perspective: Alan Cameron and Claire Massey, Pearson Education NZ Ltd, 1999.
Small Business Survival Tactics: Glen Senior and Ian McBride, Enterprise Pub., 2000.
The Small Business Book: Leith Oliver and John English, Bridget Williams Books, 2002.
Winning Legal Strategies: Doing Business In New Zealand: An In-Depth Analysis of Regulations, Corporate Climate & Other Critical Issues Every Company Needs to Know About: David Quigg, John Horner and Michael Quigg, Aspatore Books, 2004.
Your Successful Small Business: A New Zealand Guide to Starting Out and Staying In Business: Judith Ashton, Viking Pacific, 1992.

Periodicals
Bright: New Zealand Trade & Enterprise (replaces Industry New Zeaiand's *Venture* magazine and Trade New Zealand's *Trademark*). Articles are available in pdf format from the NZ Trade & Enterprise website: (www.nzte.govt.nz). ☎0800 555 888; e-mail bright@nzte.govt.nz.
The National Business Review: Level 31, Vero Centre, 48 Shortland Street, PO Box 1734, Auckland; ☎(09) 307 1629; fax (09) 307 5129; e-mail customerservices@nbr.co.nz; www.nbr.co.nz.
NZ Investment Journal: 9th Floor, Willbank Court, 57 Willis Street, PO Box 5398, Wellington; ☎(04) 499 3592; fax (04) 499 3590; e-mail invest@nzij.co.nz.

Small and Medium Enterprises

New Zealand is an economy of small businesses, and 86% of registered New Zealand businesses employ fewer than five people. There are a number of community-based enterprise and employment centres involved with developing new employment and small business initiatives; contact your regional council for details. The Small Business Company also provides information, education and resources to owner-operators and managers, also offers online training and a free newsletter (Level 6, 138 Victoria Street, PO Box 25 159, Christchurch; ☎(03) 365 4242; fax (03) 365 4243; e-mail info@tsbc.co.nz; www.tsbc.co.nz). If you employ fewer than 25 people and your business is less than six months old, you are eligible for a business mentor with the Business in the Community Mentoring Programme. The mentors are experienced and successful businesspeople who are willing to share their expertise to help you grow your business. You can apply online for a Business Mentor to assist you in developing your business (at www.businessmentor.org.nz), or contact the National Office of Business in the Community (PO Box 12397, James Fletcher House, Level 4, 581 Great South Road, Penrose, Auckland 1135; ☎0800 103 400 or 0508 103 400; fax (09) 525 0482; e-mail bitc@bitc.co.nz; www.businessmentor.org.nz). The Policy Advice Division of the Inland Revenue Department runs a small business advisory service, which provides help with working out your tax obligations. It can be contacted through your local IRD offices, or see the website (www.taxpolicy.ird.govt.nz/publications/files/html/makingtaxeasier/). The Business Information Zone (biz) is a specialist business information service for individuals and small and medium enterprises; it will help you identify organisations, people, training programmes and resources to help develop your business (☎0800 424 946; fax (04) 499 8654; e-mail info@biz.org.nz; www.bizinfo.org.nz). Biz produces a number of useful publications, based around the general themes of 'Considering Starting a Business', 'Starting a Business' and 'Growing a Business'. The website provides important regulatory information, including help with taxes, ACC, workplace safety and employing staff, information on training and a number of other useful resources. It also gives details about Business Incubators, which are facilities designed to assist businesses becoming established and profitable during start-up. The incubation period is normally one to three years, and provides business with advice and services, networking, mentoring, managers and shared premises. US statistics have shown that Business Incubators increase the success rate of start-ups from 20% to 87%. The New Zealand Trade and Enterprise website provides information about Business Clusters, or groups of companies that collaborate to grow business using a collaborative team approach. NZTE provides tools, advice, facilitation and funding to businesses, regions, and groups of organisations (www.nzte.govt.nz).

There are 52 Small Business Enterprise Centres (sbec) throughout New Zealand; these community-based organisations specialise in helping small businesses. They offer: practical business facilitation; referral to other help agencies; introductions to government departments, local businesses and consultants; business courses, seminars and workshops; and ongoing support and networks. They provide independent, confidential, competent and practical assistance to encourage economic enterprise and employment development. Some of these centres also provide specialist services for new migrants who want to start a business. See the website (www.sbecnz.org.nz) for more information about membership, products and services, links, resources and free information. For general enquiries, contact Sarah Anderson (Small Business Specialist: PO Box 5157, Palmerston North; ☎(06) 354 6900; fax (06) 350 1814).

Buying a Business v Setting up from Scratch

The decision between buying a business or setting up your own is basically about the degree of risk you are prepared to take and what kind of capital you can raise. Buying a business requires much more money, but on the other hand, you will be buying a going concern that will provide an immediate source of income. Setting up from scratch can be done on a shoestring, but if you underestimate your financial needs at the beginning, your enterprise may not last long. Your first years in business may be difficult in terms of cash flow and unanticipated expenses, so it is important not to miscalculate the size of the budget you can realistically manage on. You may also find that the stress of changing your country of abode is enough to cope with during your first years in New Zealand, and the move to set up your own operation may be easier after you have acclimatised to New Zealand in other ways. If you do decide to go ahead and buy an existing business, the place to start looking is the daily newspapers classified sections. Specialist business estate agencies can be found in your local *Yellow Pages*, or see www.nzbizbuysell.co.nz where you can view lists of NZ businesses currently for sale.

RAISING FINANCE

Banks & Business Plans

There are various sources of loans available for small businesses, the most common being the banks. However, any lender or giver of grants will expect some reassurance of serious commitment from the person or persons asking for help. This means, in most cases, evidence that they are committing a significant amount of their own capital to the venture. As was noted above, the major reason for small business failure is bad financial planning so, in order to convince a bank that you are a worthwhile investment you need to produce a business plan. Some organisations, such as Biz, New Zealand Trade and Enterprise (NZTE), and The Small Business Company, may be able to offer you some assistance (see contact details above). Without going into too much detail here, your business plan should include:

- A summary containing a broad outline of your vision of the business.
- A brief CV of each person involved in the business, highlighting skills, experience and expertise relevant to the scheme.
- A description of the main services or products that you intend to offer.
- Evidence that a viable market exists for your services or products.
- An outline of your marketing communication strategy (how you intend to contact your potential customers).

It should also include financial information:

Expenditure
- Start-up costs
- Cash flow projections
- Salaries
- Running (operating) costs including materials, production, utilities, premises (rent), etc.

O Other expenses (remember to make a generous allowance for contingencies).
O **Projected income** – income from sales.

Remember that you are trying to present a positive case to your audience; the more professional and credible the plan, the more chance you have of success. Clarity and a realistic, rather than optimistic, view will enhance your proposal. If the realistic approach suggests that the idea is not sound, then you must review it or even come up with another idea.

A final comment on business plans: there are people who can offer advice on how to write your plan, and you should listen to that advice. There are also people who will write it for you, but if you prepare it yourself, then you will be that much closer to an understanding of your projected business.

Investment Incentives

There are several investment incentive schemes available directly from central government. New Zealand Trade and Enterprise Development Grants are aimed at assisting companies to gain additional business skills and obtain external expertise and assistance in developing business projects – both start-ups and established businesses can apply. In addition, Enterprise Network Grants are available to assist groups of businesses; contact NZTE to check whether you are eligible (☎0800 555 888; www.nzte.org.nz). Application forms should be e-mailed to edg@nzte. govt.nz. NZTE also manages the Cluster Development Programme Fund, which is to facilitate clusters with significant growth potential. Biz provides free access to information about assistance available to businesses, including courses (☎0800 424 946; www.biz.org.nz). If your idea involves practical environmental initiatives, the Ministry for the Environment Sustainable Management Fund may be a possible source of funding. SMF will consider funding projects that fit under one of its four main topic areas: Freshwater Management Initiatives; 'Adopt A' Schemes; Urban Sustainability; and Community-level Climate Change. Contact the SMF for further details (PO Box 10362, Wellington; ☎(04) 917 7400; fax (04) 917 7523; e-mail smf@mfe.govt.nz; www.smf.govt.nz).

Technology NZ is a government-funded agency that provides a range of programmes to assist businesses with technology-based development projects. Guidelines and application forms on the TechNZ website provide a clear outline of the requirements for proposals, and you should use the Project Assessment Guide to focus your proposals. TechNZ Investment Managers will assist applicant companies to prepare a good proposal. Further assistance may be obtained from independent consultants, private sector research companies, Crown Research Institutes (CRI) and University business managers as well as accountants. (Level 11, Clear Centre, 15-17 Murphy Street, PO Box 12-240, Wellington; ☎(04) 917 7800; fax (04) 917 7850; www.frst.govt.nz). If your business concept has an arts focus, Creative NZ is a worthwhile place to ask about funding possibilities (National Office, Old Public Trust Building, 131-135 Lambton Quay, PO Box 3806, Wellington; ☎(04) 473 0880; fax (04) 471 2865; e-mail info@creativenz.govt.nz; www.creativenz. govt.nz). Creative New Zealand offers a range of contestable funding programmes, grants to one-off arts projects and support to professional arts organisations on an annual or three-year basis. For businesses with a community or social service focus, the NZ Lotteries Commission's Lottery Community Committees make grants for developmental or preventative projects, welfare and support services, and projects that help improve the well-being of people in the community. You can download a pamphlet entitled *Applying for Grants Online* in pdf format from www.dia.govt.nz. For more information, e-mail grantsonline@dia.govt.nz, call ☎0800 824 824, and see the *Community Development Grants Online* homepage: www.cdgo.govt.nz.

Addresses of NZ Trade & Enterprise Offices

Auckland: Level 11, ANZ Centre, 23-29 Albert St (cnr Albert, Federal and Swanson Streets), PO Box 8680, Symonds Street, Auckland; ☎(09) 366 4768; fax (09) 366 4767.

Hamilton: 29 Liverpool Street; PO Box 9515, Hamilton; ☎(07) 838 2880; fax (07) 838 2885.

Tauranga: 306 Cameron Road, PO Box 568, Tauranga; ☎(07) 577 6199; fax (07) 577 6010.

Gisborne: 79 Childers Road, c/- PO Box 238, Gisborne; ☎(06) 867 8905; fax (06) 686 7524.

Napier: 40 Niven Street, PO Box 3344, Onekawa, Napier; ☎(06) 843 7726; fax (06) 843 8099.

Wanganui: 187 Victoria Street, c/- Enterprise Wanganui, PO Box 781, Wanganui; ☎(06) 348 0333; fax (06) 348 8210.

Palmerston North: 164 Broadway Avenue, PO Box 12065, Palmerston North; ☎(06) 354 1812; fax (06) 350 1804.

Wellington: Level 9, 22 The Terrace, PO Box 2878, Wellington; ☎(04) 910 4300; fax (04) 910 4309.

Nelson: 54 Montgomery Square, PO Box 840, Nelson; ☎(03) 546 8084; fax (03) 546 7253.

Christchurch: Level 8, Price Waterhouse Centre, 119 Armagh Street, PO Box 468, Christchurch; ☎(03) 962 3838; fax (03) 365 2555.

Dunedin: WestpacTrust Building, Level 2, 106 George Street, PO Box 5642, Dunedin; ☎(03) 955 3016; fax (03) 477 0983.

BUSINESS STRUCTURES AND REGISTRATION

Businesses in New Zealand can take various forms: Company, Partnership, Non-Profit or Sole Trader. The three most common forms for small businesses are sole trader, partnership or company. The form of your business determines who benefits from it but also who is liable should something go wrong. It is not uncommon for businesses to start up in one form then change into another as they expand so you don't have to make a once-and-for-all decision before you start.

Sole Trader. In this structure, you are the sole owner, controller and manager of your business, are personally entitled to all the profits and will be personally liable for all business taxes and debts. This is the simplest form of business structure to start up: you simply tell the IRD you are becoming self-employed and there are no formal or legal processes that must be followed. You may employ other people to help run the business. If your business has an annual turnover greater than $40,000 (excluding GST) you will also need to register for Goods and Services Tax (GST), but these are the only legal formalities required. GST registration is optional if your annual turnover is less than $40,000. The disadvantage of the simple structure is that as a sole trader your personal assets can be taken as payment for any debts incurred by your business.

Partnership. Partnerships are formed by private agreement between two or more people. Partnerships are quite flexible, dependent upon the terms of that agreement. Each partner shares the responsibility for running the business, shares in any profit or loss equally, unless the partnership agreement states otherwise, and is liable for any debt within the partnership. It is a good idea, although not legally necessary, to have a lawyer draw up or check your formal partnership agreement. Juliet Ashton, in her book *Your Successful Small Business*, suggests that the agreement should cover the following:

- the name of the partnership and the business;
- the date of the agreement;
- an indication of how long the partnership is intended to last;
- the amount of capital invested by each partner in the firm and the interest on it;
- how the profits will be split;
- who is responsible for management and control of the business;
- arrangements about holidays, illness, division of responsibilities; and
- what will happen if one of the partners dies.

There is a tendency to assume you will work things out as you go along, particularly if you are going into business with a friend. However, there are many potential pitfalls in this approach, and although it may seem legalistic it is a better idea to have written clearly who is responsible for what aspect of the business rather than put your partnership under strain by not having a clear understanding from the beginning. You should in any case think twice before going into business with a friend. You need to assess objectively their strengths and weaknesses as a potential businessperson, as well as how you will get along with them under pressure. As with a sole trader structure you are personally responsible for any debts incurred by your business, even if your partner made the decisions that led the business into difficulties. The partnership itself does not pay income tax; instead it distributes the partnership income to the partners and the partners then pay tax on their own share. In some cases, some partnership profits or losses are distributed to a relative or associated person. However, if IRD consider this distribution to be excessive or unreasonable, it may be reallocated.

Limited Companies. As distinct from partnerships and sole-trading operations, if you own a company you are not personally responsible for its debts. The company has a separate formal and legal existence and your liability is limited to the extent of your share ownership. However it is worth noting that if you have to borrow money to set up your company, banks will commonly require personal guarantees from the directors, so you will not be protected by the company's legal status. You can either buy a company off the shelf from one of the businesses that specialise in selling shelf companies (advertised in the *Yellow Pages*) or you can set one up yourself. Company incorporation in New Zealand was simplified under the *Companies Act* of 1993. There is now only one type of company and there is no longer any minimum or maximum number of directors or shareholders required.

To set up a company you require the following:

- a name;
- at least one shareholder;
- at least one director;
- at least one share;
- a registered office; and
- an address.

The director and shareholder can be one and the same so in fact it only needs one person to set up a company. You begin by registering the name you have chosen with the Registrar of Companies. Obviously you have to pick a name that no-one else has used already. Once the name has been approved you can apply to have your company registered. Along with your application (which must state the company's name, registered office and address) you must include consents from all directors to act as such and certificates stating that they are not disqualified from acting, consents by shareholders to take the stated number of shares, notice from the Registrar reserving the company's name, and the constitution of the company if there is one. Providing certain conditions are met, directors and shareholders can elect that their company becomes a qualifying and/or loss attributing qualifying company, by completing an election form (IR436). Benefits can include the ability to make tax free capital distributions and offset company losses to shareholders.

It is now possible to incorporate a company over the internet, by lodging incorporation documentation with the Companies Office (www.companies.govt. nz), which is a Business Unit in the Ministry of Economic Development (www. med.govt.nz). This process has made registering a company significantly cheaper and easier, as, theoretically, it can be done in a matter of minutes. The first step is to reserve your company's name online, which costs $10. The second step is registering the company, which costs $50. You will receive an electronic response from the Registrar of Companies and a certificate of incorporation, which you can print out.

IDEAS FOR NEW BUSINESSES

Most new immigrants will need a chance to look around once they arrive in New Zealand before deciding what line of business to take up. There are a lot of established avenues for the first time businessperson, as you will see when looking at the 'Businesses For Sale' section in the papers. Should you want to consider trying something different, the following suggestions may give you some ideas.

Accommodation. As long as the tourist boom continues, providing accommodation is likely to be a reasonably safe bet. B&Bs are not as common in New Zealand as they are in the UK, although the idea is beginning to catch on as an inexpensive accommodation option. However, you will need to research the potential market carefully. Many tourists arrive on package deals with accommodation organised through the large hotel chains. Another relatively undeveloped type of accommodation in New Zealand is the country house hotel. While there are a number of luxury country lodges at top prices, the market is by no means oversupplied at the high end.

Flower growers and exporters. Big increases are being expected for New Zealand's richly coloured exotic flowers. There has been a recent surge of interest in Europe and the USA, with Japan the most significant market. There are other markets that look promising, including France, Germany, Switzerland and East Asia. Exports of cut flowers and bulbs are currently worth about $60million annually, but demand is growing steadily.

Investing in property. Buying residential property or holiday homes to rent out is one investment opportunity. Other options include investing in vineyards, orchards or farms. The best bargains these days are probably to be found in the South Island, but you should take your time and have a careful look around.

Farm-sharing. This is a new theme in New Zealand farming, and is gaining in popularity. Basically it involves clubbing together with other like-minded buyers. Owners may have differing degrees of ownership and responsibility for running the farm, or may have their farm/s run by professionals, while they carry on their primary homes and employment elsewhere. Lifestyle blocks are another solution, offering a similar chance to enjoy some of the space that New Zealand has to offer.

IT Personnel. The current expansion of the New Zealand IT&T industry means that many businesses are crying out for qualified and/or experienced IT staff. Although there are several large specialist recruitment agencies in the IT area, there is still room for expansion, particularly if you target your business towards providing an avenue for employers to access a selection of IT specialists looking to emigrate to New Zealand.

Gourmet foodstuffs. With such a wide variety of produce available, it's no wonder that special New Zealand-made gourmet products are proving hugely popular. Olive oil is one of the country's newest and fastest-growing gourmet food industries, and the premium quality oil is gaining international attention. Excellent olives are produced in the Marlborough and Hawke's Bay regions. Some businesses are also beginning to manufacture avocado oil. Export markets present the greatest long-term growth opportunities. Fruit pastes and pates, to complement cheeses, and fruit vinegars, are another innovative manufacturing and export line that is reaping rewards. There are many opportunities to trade on New Zealand's 'clean and green' image by coming up with unique ideas in organic food and beverage manufacturing.

RUNNING A BUSINESS

Employing Staff

You must register as an employer before you actually employ anyone. To register, you must fill in an IRD form, which you can do online (www.ird.govt.nz). You will need an IRD number to do this (see below).

As an employer you may negotiate individual contracts of employment with your staff, or a collective contract with some or all of your employees. Employees can either nominate a bargaining agent in the negotiations or represent themselves directly. While there is a lot of flexibility over negotiating terms and conditions relevant to your workplace, certain statutory protections remain for workers.

- There is a legal minimum hourly wage of $9.00 ($72.00 for an 8-hour day, $360.00 for a 40-hour week) for a person over the age of 18. A youth rate of $7.20 an hour applies to those aged 16-17 years.
- There are eleven paid public holidays. All employees are entitled to a paid day off on a public holiday if it would otherwise be a working day for them. These public holidays are separate from and additional to annual holidays. If the Christmas and New Year holidays fall on a weekend, and your employee doesn't normally work on the weekend, the holiday is transferred to the following Monday or Tuesday so that the employee still gets a paid day off if they normally work those days. Other public holidays are celebrated on the days on which they fall. In years where Waitangi Day or Anzac Day fall at the weekend, employees who do not normally work on the weekend have no entitlement to payment for the day.
- Under the Holidays Act 2003, all employees are entitled to a minimum of three weeks paid annual holidays. On 1 April 2007 this will change, and employees will be entitled to four weeks annual holidays.
- Annual leave accrues after one year of service and two weeks leave should be made available within the next six months.
- Annual leave is paid at the rate of average weekly earnings or not less than the ordinary rate of pay when leave began, whichever is greater.
- Anyone employed on a part-time basis may agree with the employer that holiday pay will be included in the hourly rate, although it must be shown as a separate amount.
- Untaken annual leave and lieu days must be paid out when employment terminates.
- There are provisions for special leave in the case of bereavement, sickness (of partners, children or dependent parents) and parental leave (both maternity and paternity, although new dads get less time off than new mums).

When you register as an employer, IRD will send you an information pack containing all the books and forms you need to get started, See *Working Conditions* in the *Employment* chapter for further details. For more information, contact Business NZ (Level 6, Lumley House, 3-11 Hunter Street, PO Box 1925, Wellington; ☎(04) 496 6555; fax (04) 496 6550; e-mail admin@businessnz.org. nz; www.businessnz.org.nz). Or see the Employment Relations Service website (www.ers.govt.nz), or call the ERS Infoline ☎0800 800 863.

Contracts. Employment contracts must contain a section on dispute settlement, and there are standard procedures for dealing with personal grievance cases against employers for unjustified dismissal.

Wages & Time Record. You are required to keep a wages and time record for each employee. Wages must be paid in cash unless there is an agreement to payment by cheque or direct credit. All deductions must be agreed, unless required by law. Employees or their representatives are entitled to see their own wage and time record and to claim back any arrears or wrongly-made deductions.

Taxes. Your other legal obligations as an employer concern taxation. You are required to deduct payroll taxes (known as PAYE) from your employees' wages and make returns of the same to the Inland Revenue Department. Legally required taxes include: PAYE (including ACC earner premiums); levies; child support payments; and student loan repayments. Other tax deductions may include withholding tax (from payments to people who work for you on a contract-for-service basis), superannuation scheme contributions, etc. If you provide any perks for staff as part of their employment package, then you have to pay fringe benefit taxes on them. (See *Taxation* below for more details.) For more information about your tax obligations as an employer, contact the IRD (☎0800 377 772; www.ird.govt.nz/employers/).

Accountants

As has been noted, the major reason for small business failure is poor management, usually poor financial control. You would be well advised to consult an accountant who specialises in dealing with small businesses to help you look after this important area. You can find a list of local accountants through biz (www.biz. org.nz), through your local Small Business Enterprise Centre (www.sbecnz.org. nz), or through your local Chamber of Commerce. In the case of companies, there are certain statutory requirements you must fulfil with regard to financial reporting. Every company is required to keep a full, true and complete record of its affairs and transactions, including providing a Profit and Loss Account and a Balance Sheet. Accounting practice is regulated by the Institute of Chartered Accountants of New Zealand (Level 2, Cigna House, 40 Mercer Street, PO Box 11-342, Wellington; ☎(04) 474 7840; fax (04) 473 6303; www.icanz.co.nz) which provides mandatory standards for company financial reporting called Statements of Standard Accounting Practice (SSAPs). Any material departure from these has to be disclosed in financial statements. The standards are intended for use by other types of business, though not compulsory.

Taxation

The Inland Revenue Department publishes a guide for small businesses on their tax obligations. You can obtain copies from any IRD office or see the website (www. ird.govt.nz). They also run the Small Business Advisory Service which advises beginning business people on taxes they need to know about, what records to keep, how to complete tax returns and when to file returns and make payments. To get in touch with the service, you simply indicate when you register for GST or as a new employer that you would like an advisory consultation. You can either go into an IRD office for an appointment or an advisor will come and visit your office. Information about business income tax, getting an IRD number, provisional tax, depreciation, claiming expenses, records and tax on interest and dividends is also available from biz (www.biz.org.nz)

Applying for an IRD number. One of the first requirements of any type of business operation is an Inland Revenue Department (IRD) number. Your business must have its own IRD number if it is a partnership, company, non-profit organisation or trust/estate. Each person in a partnership must also have their own personal IRD number. If you are a sole trader, you may use your personal IRD number rather than obtaining a different one for your business. You will need a passport or birth certificate as identification for a personal IRD number. In the case of a partnership, you must provide the IRD numbers of the partners, and for a company IRD, a copy of the certificate of incorporation. If you are an individual in business you will need to fill in an IR595 form, or an IR596 if you are a partnership, trust, company or other organisation. Both types of forms can be downloaded as pdfs from the IRD website (www.ird.govt.nz/business-info/starting/irdnumber.html), or you can telephone the Business Income Tax and General Enquiries Line on 0800 377 774 (+64 4 801 9973 from overseas).

Types of Taxes. There are four major types of taxes which you will have to deal with when doing business in New Zealand; income tax and company tax, Goods and Services Tax (GST), Accident Compensation Levies and Fringe Benefit Tax.

Income Tax and Company Tax: Income tax is payable by all persons or business entities. Individuals are taxed on a progressive rate system whereby 19.5% is payable on earnings up to $38,000, 33% over $38,001 and 39% over $60,001. Resident companies are taxed at a flat rate of 33% on income earned, whereas non-resident companies are taxed at 38%. If your gross annual PAYE deductions are less than $100,000 then you are classed as a small employer. PAYE deductions must be paid to the IRD monthly, by the 20th of the month following the payment they were deducted from.

Income tax is payable on the net profit from your business, which is all income that comes into your business, minus allowable business expenses. Business income is income earned from goods and services you sell (including invoices you've issued but have yet to receive payment for). If you have not been making tax payments during your first year in business, your tax will need to be paid by 7 February in the following year if you have a 31 March balance date (or by 7 April if you have an agent). If you want a balance date other than 31 March, you must apply in writing stating your reasons. After your first year in business you may be required to pay income tax in three instalments throughout the year. This is called provisional tax.

Goods and Services Tax (GST): All businesses with an anticipated turnover greater than $40,000 per annum are required to register for GST. GST is not a tax on your own business, it is a tax on sales to your customers (called 'taxable supplies') which you collect on behalf of the IRD. You must charge and account for GST of 12.5% on these supplies. Under the $40,000 threshold you can choose whether or not to register. If you deal with other registered businesses it may be worthwhile because they will be charging you GST which you will not be able to claim back. You should be aware, however, of the extra accounting processes and time that will be required. You pay GST on all your business inputs, supplies, etc. You then add GST to all the sales you make. You make GST returns every six months. For more GST information contact the IRD (☎ 0800 377 776) or obtain the IR365 booklet (as a pdf from the website) and complete the attached IR360 registration form.

Fringe Benefit Tax and Accident Compensation: If you provide any extra benefits to your employees, such as a company car, then you must pay fringe benefit tax. This includes benefits provided through someone other than an employer. Even if you do not provide any perks, you must send in a yearly return. For an FBT guide, see www.ird.govt.nz/fringebenefittax/. ACC is a fixed levy on each member of your workforce, however, from June 1998, there is a provision for workplace accident insurance to be arranged through private insurance firms. ACC earner premiums are included in PAYE deductions.

Tax Returns. Different returns will be required depending on whether you are a sole trader, a company or a partnership. The tax year runs from 1st April to 31 March, and although businesses can use different year-end dates for reporting purposes, the balance date will be related to the nearest 31st March for tax purposes. Sole traders, partnerships and companies must all complete different returns. Each company shareholder must also file an individual return. Included with each return must be a copy of the accounts. It is now possible to file monthly payroll details to the IRD online, using the ir-File Service. Large employers are obliged to do this, but small employers are encouraged to do so as well. For an interactive demonstration and registration instructions see the website (http://ir-file.ird.govt.nz) or telephone 0800 473 829. For more information about any aspect of taxation, contact your local Inland Revenue Office, see the website (www.ird.govt.nz) or phone the IRD General Inquiries line (0800 377 774).

Appendices

PERSONAL CASE HISTORIES

AUSTRALIA

NEW ZEALAND

APPENDIX I: PERSONAL CASE HISTORIES

AUSTRALIA

NIGEL WORSLEY

In search of an improved lifestyle, Nigel and his wife moved to Western Australia where they find the cost and standard of living achievable - even though food prices are generally higher than in Britain. Having worked for the national press in the UK, Nigel is now with the West Australian newspaper in Australia while his wife is a registered general nurse (RGN) working part-time for the Maine Health Group in Joondalup.

Although they found the country 10 to 15 years behind the rest of the world, they acclimatised quickly to a life less stressful. They enjoy the weather conditions, the cheap petrol, and have met friends through work who are in a similar situation to themselves. However, red tape and the health system has caused them one or two problems but they have no regrets about leaving the UK and have every intention of staying Down Under.

TONY MULLEN

Fed up with the UK, Tony relocated to Perth in Australia and after working as a TV engineer for a couple of years – his trade in the UK – is now a property developer.

Why did you decide to move to Australia?
Lifestyle, climate, and a better life for my children.

Did you have any problems with red tape?
I came over on a business visa (457) so everything was quite straightforward.

What were your fist impressions of Australia?
Spotlessly clean compared to the UK.

Was it difficult to find accommodation?
It was extremely hard to find furnished accommodation for the first few weeks.
We bought our own house within six weeks of arrival because all the unfurnished
rental properties we looked at were of a very low standard.

How did you go about finding work?
Placed an advert in the paper and waited for the phone to ring – which it did!

How do you find working in Oz compared to back home?
More 'laid-back' and comfortable.

Did it take long to acclimatise?
Two years at least.

**How does the quality of life compare to other countries you have lived in? Do
you find it expensive?**
The quality of life in Perth is wonderful and I do not find it expensive at all.

What is the social life like?
It's easy to make friends if you put yourself out in order to meet people. Our social
life is 10 times better than it was in the UK.

What do you like best and least about Australia?
Cleanliness, weather, fun but the worst thing are the flies.

Do you have any regrets about leaving Britain?
One – I wish I had left 10 years earlier.

**What advice would you give someone thinking of living and working in
Australia?**
Homework – do your homework.

NATHAN MALES

Nathan's parents taught Gypsy children for a number of years from a mobile
school parked by the side of the road. As a result, Nathan's earliest memories
are of falling off the backs of donkeys and of knocking about in hedgerows
and scrap yards with assorted tangle-haired kids. This early nomadic, outdoor
experience of life led to the wanderlust that eventually took Nathan to Australia. It
also laid the foundations for his interest in the environment – Nathan now works
for Bush Heritage, an Australian national organisation dedicated to protecting
bio-diversity through protecting the bush and the creation of reserves on private
land.

Of his life – pre-Australia – Nathan remembers: 'When I was still young we
settled down in the north of England and it all seems lush, green and idyllic now
after all this time living in Tasmania. At the time it was wellies and raincoats, rope
swings, cuts and bruises. My parents were teaching and renovating houses so our

holidays were short and close to hand, largely spent on the midge-infested West Coast of Scotland. After school and university, I chose to train as a teacher, and later, discovering it to be one of the least romantic jobs there is, I fell in love, in a bookshop, with an Australian traveller. She chose to stay a few days, then "just a little while longer" which turned out to be a long hot summer and more. Then in 1997, a few days after my final exams, I found myself on a plane to Australia.'

What were your first impressions of Australia?
I flew directly to Tasmania, to Hobart, a small city nestled between the banks of a big river and the slopes of a big mountain; an outpost of the world overlooked by development. I loved it instantly. Having no plans, I wandered for a day or two, and checked out the boats in the harbour. It wasn't long before one of the owners came along and by the next day I was employed sanding woodwork, scraping off old paint and varnishing decks. I was in a heaven full of wooden yachts. I was quickly to learn that Australians are opportunists, quick to judge, laugh and take advantage of a brand new pom for less than the minimum wage. I didn't mind; I was enjoying myself. Work was easy to find; when it dried up at the boat yard I became a waiter and then made coffee in a bar. By the end of my first year, I was living with the girl from the bookshop and I had to make a serious choice. On the one hand I had an offer to join the crew of a tall ship and sail to America; on the other a job offer in an Art's Centre. It was 'a real job' and would mean staying in Hobart. I chose to stay.

What is your visa status? Is it easy to change the status once you are in the country?
I had arrived with a year's Working Holiday visa allowing me to work for each employer for three months. The department of immigration has a reputation for being very strict about not letting people extend their stay as a tourist. Many friends with similar visas have had to go to New Zealand to apply for a new tourist visa so they could return. I was lucky as the only visa (to my knowledge) that lets people stay during the application process is one for couples where one party is Australian. I applied, was granted a bridging visa, and stayed and waited.

The department didn't seem to regard my application as being a priority, which I suppose it wasn't, and the process dragged on for almost 18 months. During this time, we were interviewed by the department and had our relationship examined with a fine-tooth comb, to the extent of having to submit exchanged letters (none of them written with the expectation that a third party in a suit would ever read them). We both survived the embarrassment and the visa arrived. I was a permanent resident.

What is Australian bureaucracy like? How does it compare with Britain?
Australian bureaucracy seems much the same as bureaucracy everywhere, everything goes along fine until you upset someone or want something that is outside of procedure and then it all gets complicated. My experience is that it is generally fair and I have never experienced anything dishonest. The police are armed, but friendly and fair.

What sort of place do you live in?
We live in a rented weather-board house on the outskirts of Hobart. As Hobart is small, getting from the edge to the city centre for work takes only ten minutes

by bike. The toilet and laundry are separate, and you have to go outside to access them. There are trees all around us and a creek that runs past the end of the garden. It costs $130 a fortnight, which is about £45.

We are also building a weekend house on a little island south of Hobart. Its waterfront position looks out onto a sheltered bay – very scenic. I am always amazed that with our salaries, we can afford two houses. Land and houses are relatively cheap in Tasmania, as there is no population growth and, consequently a low demand.

Did it take long to acclimatise?

I acclimatised to Hobart instantly. The climate is something like the best of English weather most of the time. I imagine it would be different if I had moved to tropical or arid Australia. Australia has a whole range of climatic conditions and it is impossible to generalise. Hobart's architecture is distinctly Australian with many buildings dating from the settlement and convict era in the 1800s. They are based on English styles and I felt at home with them quickly.

The one thing that took me a long time to appreciate was the bushland. Most forest and woodland here is eucalyptus trees. They are dry-looking scraggy things with long ribbons of loose bark hanging down and a dusty, grey appearance. For a few years I would look at it and think, 'what a mess'. I remember the day when I first looked at a bit of bush and thought, 'that is beautiful'. Now I love it.

What's the social life like?

The Australian social life is fantastic. There is a great outdoor culture and a great tradition of a couple of cold beers after work. A regular social event in Hobart is an outdoor band that plays Latin jazz in a courtyard every Friday after work. People pour out of their offices and come along. There is a total cross section of society ranging from suits to scruffy-types, all drinking and dancing together. There is much less snobbery here. It still exists but it doesn't pervade society.

Another great favourite is coffee at the markets. Sitting at the outdoor tables of the cafés with the craft and vegetable markets going on all around, you always run into friends and a quick coffee becomes a whole morning affair, a feast. The coffee is excellent.

How does the standard of living compare with Britain?

I can put my hand on my heart and say that the standard of living you can achieve for the same money is far, far higher in Hobart than in England. Rent and housing is inexpensive, cars and fuel are cheaper. Life is outdoors and the best things are free.

There is something about the values system and attitudes here that make life simpler and rather more enjoyable. It is acceptable to drive a shabby car, nearly everyone does, and the dirt roads make new cars into shabby ones quickly anyway. The sense of sprinting to keep up with the Joneses just isn't so strong here and it gives you time to relax, go to barbecues and play cricket with the lads in the paddock.

The combination of the relaxed lifestyle, fresh seafood, which you can buy at the wharf, lots of vineyards producing superb local wine, clean air, clean water and thousands of acres of world heritage wilderness only an hour's drive away are a potent lifestyle combination. Cultural life is also strong; Hobart is alive with music and theatre. There is a symphony orchestra. Summers are busy with music festivals, arts festivals, food and wine festivals, outdoor cinema, and many events are free.

One could live a full and interesting life in Hobart on a shoestring. I know lots of people who do.

What do you like best about Australia?
For me, the exciting thing about Australia is the sense of extremes. Rural and outback Australia has a heady sense of frontier. The land is harsh, dry and hot and there is a sense of being out there, humans against the elements. In the outback people wear big hats and drive pick-ups. I've seen men on horseback driving huge herds of cattle along wide dusty roads, a cloud of red dust kicked up by the hooves. In stark contrast, the big cities, especially Sydney, are ultra-modern.

What do you like least about Australia?
If I think of anything I'll let you know.

Do you think you will stay in Australia?
I haven't decided whether to stay yet, that's not to say I've decided to go either. We both have jobs that would benefit from our moving either to mainland Australia or overseas. Tasmania and Hobart are microcosms of Australia. The population is small and as a result specialist work is scarce. As you move through a career and get more specialised, you end up forced to move away or to do something different. It's a tough decision which we are postponing as long as possible.

Do you have any regrets about leaving Britain?
My main regret about leaving Britain is leaving friends behind. I keep in touch with a handful of close friends, but e-mail and telephone doesn't replace being there to help repaint the lounge room or defrost the fridge. Most of my friends and family have visited, but it's too far to see each other often. I miss the mundane things – they are irreplaceable in relationships.

What advice would you give someone thinking of coming to live and work in Australia?
Australia isn't a place for wimps or whingers. It's a bold, brash culture in a bold, harsh climate. You have to give as good as you get in order to fit in. If you love life and, if you are prepared to grab it with both hands, Australia isn't bad.

DANNY JONES

Danny trained as a mechanical technician in the UK and worked for various companies before eventually ending up in London employed by a fuel injection development company. Several of his workmates were Australian which, he believes, was responsible for rekindling 'an interest I'd had in Australia since my early childhood. I am fairly sure that Skippy the Kangaroo sparked off my initial interest in Australia.'

Danny visited Australia on a Working Holiday visa, travelled around as much as possible and remembers that, 'my first impression of Australia was how difficult it was to appreciate the sheer size of it.' He returned to the UK determined to migrate and is now an Australian citizen, having entered the country as a permanent resident under the witness protection act and taken the Oath after the minimum two years. He now lives in a fairly large house on a quarter acre block of land in one of Melbourne's older suburbs.

Accommodation in the major cities can be difficult to find he says, 'especially when you're from overseas, as it's not so easy for agents to check your history. Leases are normally for one year so choosing the right area is important. However, the standard of living is higher than in the UK, and you get paid more while being taxed less. And houses, fuel and food are all far cheaper – although the gap does seem to be narrowing.

'It takes a lot longer to acclimatise than you think, and even after five years here we still don't quite fit in. Work is relatively easy to find, especially for mechanical trades, and by far the best way of finding work here is to just turn up and sell yourself. It's amazing how many people will give you a job despite not having advertised a vacancy. Its rare for references to be taken, and most small employers have the 'give 'em a fair go' approach.

'By far the best thing about Australia is the open space and wildlife. You never forget the first time you see a large 'roo in the wild, or a snake.' Danny's greatest dislike of Australia is its obsession with sport and the hero worship of sporting people and he gets the impression that education doesn't seem to be valued as it is in the UK. As for the famed Australian stereotypical view of the Brits, 'believe me, Australians can out whinge the British ten to one. Not that I'm whinging about it, its just an observation!'

Danny has few regrets about relocating to Australia but says, 'you miss people. And whilst they're only ever a phone call away it's difficult to talk to somebody who's sitting by the phone on a cold winter's morning when you're in your best evening mood on a hot summer night on the other side of the world. I think there's a certain amount of truth in the aboriginal belief that you belong *to* the land, not it to you, and so you will always miss the country that you were born in.'

As for the advantages of moving to Australia, 'It is the age-old scheme of life that if you work hard here you will eventually get somewhere good. My only advice to any one coming to live and work in Australia is don't fall into the trap of comparing it to home. It's not better, it's not worse, but it is certainly different!'

SALLY STARLING

Sally is a part of history, as she went to Australia in 1971 as a 'ten pound pom' – one of the thousands of UK immigrants lured down-under by promises of sunshine and prosperity. 'In those days,' Sally remembers, 'they paid you to go. I was living in London at the time, and was fed up with the cold and endless minor winter illnesses. When I saw a poster in the tube advertising the £10 scheme, I made up my mind to go on the spot, and within weeks I was on my way.' Sally arrived in Melbourne and soon moved to Sydney where she quickly found work as a secretary. She remembers that the difference in her health and general wellbeing improved very rapidly after she arrived, and her overwhelming impression was one of good fortune.

Sally lived in Sydney for four years, during which time she saved money to travel abroad. Unfortunately, whilst living in Canada, she let her immigrant status lapse, and when she decided it was time to go back to Australia she found herself having to apply anew to emigrate. 'Luckily, it was still relatively easy at that time to move to Australia, and I was absolutely convinced, after spending a few years travelling, that Australia was the country where I wanted to spend the rest of my life. To me, it had become home.' Her application was accepted and she returned to Perth where she has since made a permanent home.

When asked to describe any difficulties in adjusting to her new environment, Sally mentioned the language barrier! 'When I first arrived I just couldn't understand what people were saying,' she said. 'I found it quite intimidating when I was out in a group of people, and it took me a while to feel comfortable socially.'

Sally now owns her own highly successful business which she established, and enjoys a relaxed and prosperous lifestyle. She and her husband have recently successfully sponsored her mother-in-law's application to migrate as a retiree, and they have also attempted to sponsor Sally's brother, although this application was turned down on age grounds under the points system. Sally maintains strong links with the UK and returns for holidays and family visits regularly.

APPENDIX II: PERSONAL CASE HISTORIES

NEW ZEALAND

KIM CULLEN

Kim met her husband, Peter, when they were both living in Lexington, Kentucky. He had left NZ ten years prior for his Overseas Experience and had lived in London for while but also wanted to experience the US. Peter was working as a contractor and had been living in Kentucky for about seven years when they met, and the couple were together and then married for a total of two years before deciding to move to NZ. Peter had been previously married and had gone through the Green Card process with his first wife. Interestingly, and something to seriously consider before moving abroad according to the American Consulate in Auckland, as a result of moving to NZ Peter has lost his Green Card privileges for the US and if they move back to the States, they have to reapply and go through the whole process again.

Kim and Peter decided to move because they wanted something different — they were tired of Lexington but didn't know where to go. It seemed natural to move to NZ and for Peter to go home for a while and be near his ageing mother. Kim had no problems obtaining residency because she was married to a Kiwi. She did have to show proof of marriage (notarized copy of marriage license) and provide wedding photographs, which were promptly returned in the mail. She now has all the same benefits as a Kiwi – even paying domestic university tuition fees instead of international – and she doesn't have to worry about applying for work visas every six months.

The immigration paperwork was a bit overwhelming and Kim had to read everything very carefully several times. She did everything herself simply because there was no need to worry about the points system. Applying for residency was costly – Kim estimates she had to spend a total of about US$2500. There were chest x-rays to pay for, doctor appointments to complete the comprehensive physical and then application itself and residency papers fees. The New Zealand Embassy in Washington DC was very helpful and efficient. Kim and Peter have now been living in Wellington for 18 months.

Neither had jobs waiting in NZ when they first arrived; they had just saved money so that there would be something to live on while job-hunting. They lived with Peter's mother for the first two weeks until they found an apartment. Fortunately, she only lives an hour away from Wellington so while transportation was a bit of a nightmare, at least there was no need to spend any money on hotels.

Back in the States, Kim worked as a researcher and part-time lecturer at a university. She was unable to secure anything along the same lines in NZ because her background is social work, which is very country- and policy-specific. There were two university social research jobs that she applied and interviewed for, but did not get because of a lack of familiarity with NZ law or policy despite having the required research and analytical skills required for the positions. Once she had arrived in the country, it took Kim seven weeks to find her job. Although she knows this isn't a long time to wait, she recalls that it was agonizing waiting for work in a new country where she didn't know a soul.

'I found my job through the newspaper, which is apparently rare. A lot of Wellingtonians network to get new jobs, which makes it tricky to try to get your foot in the door for a newcomer. I work as a Project Manager for a government agency. When converting my NZ salary into US dollars, I make less despite a fluctuating NZ dollar. Plus, I make over $15,000 more than the average mean salary for a Kiwi!

New Zealand is a very expensive place to live. Homes around Wellington and Auckland are outrageous – $300,000 for a two-bedroom with one bathroom! The cost of living in Wellington is much higher than where I am from in the States. American friends of mine argue whether it is more expensive living in New Zealand than New York City or Los Angeles. Homes are cheaper an hour away from the cities in New Zealand so if long commutes, small communities, and a rural lifestyle is what you want, then perhaps the high cost of living down here won't be an issue for you.

Utilities and groceries are expensive also. Standard cable (no movie or sport channels) is about $60 a month. A roll of paper towels is $1.75. Ironing boards are $50. Movie tickets are $14. Also, clothes and shoes are quite expensive. After living in the States where choice, customer service and convenience are everywhere, New Zealand has taken some getting used to. All stores except supermarkets close at 5 or 5:30pm. Banks are not open on Saturdays. Health care is free but a doctor's visit still costs about $50. You will only get surgery if it is necessary and/or life-threatening, and there are waiting lists for many types of surgery.

The majority of NZ homes do not have central heating. And winters are cold, windy and damp – at least in the lower North Island (Wellington) and South Island. It has been difficult to adjust to it being just as cold inside my house as it is outside. During the winter, there is no relief from the cold and it can affect your moods. What most Kiwis do is wear multiple sweaters and buy space heaters, electric blankets, and close bedroom doors to keep the heat in. Watch out for the utility bills during winter time; the electric and gas bills will skyrocket. The Kiwis don't complain – they just shrug and deal with it. My American friends and I however really struggle with the winter season… and the mould in the houses that results from the wet and cold.

Because of the high cost of living we are not planning on staying down here permanently. Once I finish school, we will be moving back up to the Northern Hemisphere – the States, Canada… wherever I can get a good job for my skills. I would advise not moving here if you have any large US debt – credit card, student loan, etc. Several Americans I know have left NZ because they could not afford to live here at the same time as saving a little money and attempting to pay off their

US debt. Unfortunately, New Zealand salaries have not kept up with the high cost of living. Travelling around NZ for several months and obtaining a short-term work visa might be the way to go if money is an issue for you.

On a positive note, NZ is a gorgeous country and the pubs, cafes and restaurants stay open late. Wellington is a lovely city with vitality and a lot to offer especially in arts and culture. The architecture is different and the shopping, while expensive, is plentiful. It is also nice to be near the water. My husband is sailing again and I find hiking in the hills surrounding the city to be great exercise. It is lovely drinking wine after work on the wharf with friends. It is interesting and refreshing to live in another culture and see how that society runs. The Maori, the indigenous people of NZ, are an empowered and politically savvy group. They still rank poorly in income, education, and health issues but there seems to be more of a collective effort in NZ to help those less fortunate.

NZ is a fairly liberal place. The prime minister is a woman and one of the ministers is a transsexual. Marriage is not all that popular – there are many committed couples who live together and never marry. Prostitution is legal and same-sex couples generally have the same rights as heterosexual couples. The typical Kiwi is a pleasant, if somewhat reserved, individual with a lot of interests. No Kiwi that I met just sits at home – they tend to be adventurous sorts who go out a lot.

In conclusion, while I have enjoyed living in another country, New Zealand is expensive and living here has actually set my husband and I further back regarding savings and retirement. We are paying more for food, rent, utilities, gas, car, and everyday expenses while earning less than we earned in the States. I do not have any regrets because I have learned so much about myself and about living abroad. I do however look forward to moving in a few years and earning what I am worth in a country where the cost of living is affordable.'

JAMES PENNICOTT

I am originally from Chatham in Kent although before moving to NZ I lived for two years in Amsterdam. I moved to NZ because I met a Kiwi girl when she was on her OE in London. We were together for three years and she decided she wanted to go home. So I decided that it was time to settle down and followed her home. I have been in NZ for 10 months. We live in the suburb of Spreydon (Christchurch) and my wife chose the house whilst I was still in Amsterdam. She chose the place as it was close to town, which was ideal as I didn't drive when I first arrived in NZ (although I have passed my test now!).

My wife told me that she wanted to live on the 'Mainland', and most of her family and friends are from the South Island. I had also spent more time in the South Island myself and enjoyed the relaxed lifestyle. I did not want to go to another large city again so Auckland was a no-no.

I am actually in my second job already – I started as a Credit Manager for a waste disposal firm, which was having some difficulties. I worked there for over six months and set up the credit department before securing a position with Statistics New Zealand. I am a permanent resident, and planning to stay permanently, but I don't have plans to become a Kiwi at this stage.

The major difference between here and the UK is that there seems to be more time here for living your life, although this sounds crazy as you have the same amount of time in the UK. People just work to live here and not live to work – it's a cliché, but one I have definitely bought into. Also, people are certainly friendly here; at first that can be disconcerting for Pom who is used to not acknowledging anyone that they don't know. But it is more appealing and makes life more enjoyable if you can chat with anyone you meet without feeling that they have ulterior motives. The climate is not too dissimilar to the UK, although no one would ever admit it. I think my career prospects are good in New Zealand, although not as good as they were in the UK/Europe. The lifestyle here is much more focussed on spending time with friends and family at home, having barbecues and parties and so on, and less about going out to bars and restaurants. I miss being able to travel cheaply and quickly to European cities, so the remoteness of NZ can be a little daunting in that respect.

I haven't had major headaches so far; the only scary thing was trying to find a job, although this is becoming far easier for new migrants as there is shortage of quality applicants in the NZ job market at present. The only other difficulty I have had is getting used to having left loved ones behind, although calls are cheap and we live in the world of e-mail and cheap air travel so no major dramas anymore.

LINDA KELLY

My reasons for moving to New Zealand were purely romantic; I had met a New Zealander in 1977 who was 'doing his big OE', working as a butler in a local manor house, and I was a checkout operator at the supermarket where he shopped for the manor's groceries. I fell in love with his accent and his relaxed and friendly manner, which was so refreshingly different from the stiff and stuffy people who surrounded me in England. When he returned to New Zealand a year later I was invited to join him and the great adventure began.

New Zealand House in London was unable to help with residency or a work visa, and advised me to travel on a six-month holiday visa and apply for a work visa on arrival in New Zealand. That wasn't as easy as it sounded – regular trips to the Immigration Office in Auckland, waiting in massive queues to reach the immigration officer were all to no avail. I didn't qualify for a work visa! To cut a long story short, some supportive letters from our MP (Rob Muldoon, no less – the Prime Minister at the time) resulted in a temporary work permit with the proviso that after the expiration of that period, I must marry the man who brought me to New Zealand, or return home. We married 12 months later and residency followed. However, I did not apply for citizenship, as is the right of the spouse of a New Zealand male, but earned it in my own right five years later.

Moving to New Zealand was a bit of an adventure. I had no idea what to expect. It was so different to 'home'. My first impression was that it was like Noddy's Toytown – the roads and road signs, the styles and colours of the houses, and the buildings in general looked somewhat primitive and quaint. However, the scenery was breathtaking, the history enthralling, and the people relaxed, friendly, and welcoming.

I lived in Auckland for the first four years, which was a bit daunting for a girl straight out of a small English village who had never been outside of the UK. It was so spread out and it took ages to travel from one point to another. Shopping in the city centre was disappointing; there were no High Street stores such as Marks and Spencer, Dorothy Perkins, Debenhams, Boots, W.H. Smith, etc. Choices were limited, and prices high. I missed Mars Bars and locals told me that there were chocolate bars called 'Moro' which were the same as Mars Bars – yeah right!

Finding work was not difficult in Auckland once I had a valid work permit. I worked for the Bank of New Zealand for the first three years. The Bank had some very old-fashioned policies at that time. At my six-monthly reviews I was always asked if I was intending to start a family in the near future – promotion was dependent upon the answer!

The other thing that shocked and embarrassed me was that the male members of staff wore walk shorts and socks to work rather than suits. I can still remember the sight of the Accountant standing next to my desk – a tall ginger-haired man with long hairy legs... One of the tellers used to come to work wearing a boob tube, and when she stood behind the counter she looked as if she was naked! The dress code was very different to the one that I had been accustomed to in the bank where I worked before I left England. I was rather pleased when I had the opportunity to move into legal work where there was a more enlightened view of a woman's role in the workplace, not to mention a stricter dress code.

I spent four years in Auckland before my husband's employment took us to Wellington. The legal network enabled me to find employment before the move. At first I thought that moving to Wellington was the biggest mistake I had ever made; the weather was wet and windy much of the time, and the streets were narrow and winding, unlike the warm, sunny, roomy Auckland that I had become used to.

I grew to love Wellington and achieved a lot there; I completed my Legal Executive Certificate and gained valuable knowledge and experience in a large supportive legal firm, then went to university and earned a BA – something I would not have had the opportunity to do in England. Growing up as a working class girl in England in the 1950s and '60s meant that opportunities were limited. There was little encouragement or expectation to continued in education past age 15, and certainly very little opportunity to go to university.

In 1990 another employment move for my husband took us to Hastings in Hawkes Bay. The weather was great, and again, the people very welcoming. Employment was harder to find but I was able to put my legal skills to good use, finding temporary work for various legal firms until I was offered a permanent position. Despite the great climate, I was never enamoured with Hawkes Bay. I was disappointed at the lack of employment opportunities and there was an air of superiority amongst the people who had lived there most of their lives. To get on in Hawkes Bay it seemed to be a case of 'who you knew' rather than 'what you knew'.

After 26 years in New Zealand the novelty is wearing off. New Zealand society and its values have changed so much in that time. When I arrived in New Zealand the country was naïve, unspoilt, and barely influenced by the outside world. Shops didn't open on Saturdays and Sundays, but had one late night a week. At first that seemed odd and somewhat frustrating, but it soon became appreciated in as much as the weekend provided two days of complete change from the everyday routines of working and shopping – families could spend time together.

Over the last 15 years the overseas influences have been glaring obvious with the appearance of the café lifestyle in cities and small towns alike, shops open seven days a week and offering a vast array of products at competitive prices, modern upmarket bars rather than the pubs that 'ladies' wouldn't be seen dead in. In addition, the former emphasis on achievement has been replaced with an emphasis on money and possessions. The very thing that I found refreshing about New Zealand in the

1970s was the lack of the kind of class system I had experienced in England. Here, you could achieve anything with effort, ability and the desire to succeed, regardless of your background. However, a 'class system' of sorts now exists, although it is not based on the status of your birth family but rather on money and possessions, i.e., how much you have, or don't have.

I have now lived in New Zealand as long as I lived in England and find it difficult to remember the things that I used to miss about my home country, such as Jaffa Cakes and Walnut Whips. It was hard leaving the family behind – mum and dad, two sisters, two brothers and umpteen nieces, nephews, great-nieces and great-nephews. Telephone calls were few and far between because the cost was prohibitive; birthdays and Christmas were the only times I heard their voices. I have been back to the UK several times since leaving in 1978. I love to catch up with family, friends, and neighbours, to walk through the village where I used to live (which has houses and history dating back to the 12th century), to visit the many historical places nearby and throughout the country, and I enjoying the shopping. I miss real English Christmases that are cold and sometimes snowy, snuggled up in front of an open fire, and I miss those great big Christmas dinners with all the trimmings, shared with the family. I don't miss the crowds and the long, cold, dark autumn/winter days, or the narrow world-view that English people seem to have. Despite the fact that the English travel regularly to package holiday destinations, they still appear to have a blinkered perception of things non-English with little enthusiasm to expand their horizons. The few that do are usually those who travel extensively, or move permanently overseas.

Complete guides to life abroad from Vacation Work

Live & Work Abroad

Live & Work in Australia & New Zealand £12.95
Live & Work in Belgium, The Netherlands & Luxembourg £10.99
Live & Work in China £11.95
Live & Work in France.. £11.95
Live & Work in Germany £10.99
Live & Work in Ireland £10.99
Live & Work in Italy £11.95
Live & Work in Japan £10.99
Live & Work in Portugal £11.95
Live & Work in Russia & Eastern Europe £10.99
Live & Work in Saudi & the Gulf £10.99
Live & Work in Scandinavia.. £10.99
Live & Work in Scotland £11.95
Live & Work in Spain £12.95
Live & Work in Spain & Portugal £10.99
Live & Work in the USA & Canada... £12.95

Buying a House Abroad

Buying a House in France £11.95
Buying a House in Italy.. £11.95
Buying a House in Portugal.. £11.95
Buying a House in Scotland £11.95
Buying a House in Spain.. £11.95
Buying a House on the Mediterranean £13.95

Starting a Business Abroad

Starting a Business in Australia.. £12.95
Starting a Business in France £12.95
Starting a Business in Spain... £12.95

**Available from good bookshops or direct from the publishers
Vacation Work, 9 Park End Street, Oxford OX1 1HJ
Tel 01865-241978 * Fax 01865-790885 * www.vacationwork.co.uk**

**In the US: available at bookstores everywhere
or from The Globe Pequot Press (www.GlobePequot.com)**